THE HAGIOGRAPHER AND THE AVATAR

SUNY series in Religious Studies

Harold Coward, editor

THE HAGIOGRAPHER AND THE AVATAR

The Life and Works of Narayan Kasturi

ANTONIO RIGOPOULOS

SUNY
PRESS

Cover: Dattatreya, by Raja Ravi Varma (1848–1906). Printed circa 1910 at Ravi Varma Press, Malavli, near Lonavala, Maharashtra.

Published by State University of New York Press, Albany

Printed in the United States of America

For information, contact State University of New York Press, Albany, NY
www.sunypress.edu

Library of Congress Cataloging-in-Publication Data

Name: Rigopoulos, Antonio, 1962– author.
Title: The hagiographer and the avatar : the life and works of Narayan Kasturi / Antonio Rigopoulos.
Description: Albany : State University of New York Press, [2021] | Series: SUNY series in religious studies | Includes bibliographical references and index.
Identifiers: LCCN 2020056891 (print) | LCCN 2020056892 (ebook) | ISBN 9781438482293 (hardcover : alk. paper) | ISBN 9781438482286 (pbk. : alk. paper) | ISBN 9781438482309 (ebook)
Subjects: LCSH: Sathya Sai Baba, 1926–2011—Friends and associates. | Kastūri, Nā., 1897–1987. | Hagiographers—India—Biography. | Hagiography—History and criticism.
Classification: LCC BP605.S14 R54 2021 (print) | LCC BP605.S14 (ebook) | DDC 294.5092 [B]—dc23
LC record available at https://lccn.loc.gov/2020056891
LC ebook record available at https://lccn.loc.gov/2020056892

10 9 8 7 6 5 4 3 2 1

To Giovanni

I firmly believe there is none kinder than You,
to shower Grace on me.
Tell me, is this not the reason why
I am at Your Lotus Feet?
I firmly believe You will respond quick
When I do pray and plead.
Tell me, is this not the reason why
I am crying aloud for you?
I firmly believe You are ever beside me
to guide my steps aright.
Tell me, is this not the reason why
I am yours thro' day and night?
I firmly believe You can never say 'No'
Whatever I ask from You.
Tell me, is this not the reason why
I long for a glance from You?
What have you designed for me this time?
Why this dire delay to offer boons?
However long you make me wait and wail
I will not leave, I'll be standing still
Until Your loving eyes do turn on me.

Post Script

Kasturi, begin the New Year with the above prayer.

Endowed with long life and sound health, surrounded by children, grandchildren and friends, keep on imbibing joy through *bhakti* and *jñāna*. I bless that your days be spent in the service of Sarveśvara, the Lord of All; spend your life in abundant peace and happiness.

Baba
January 1, 1960

[N. Kasturi, *Loving God: Eighty-Five Years Under the Watchful Eye of the Lord* (Prasanthi Nilayam: Sri Sathya Sai Books & Publications, 1982), 82–83]

Contents

List of Illustrations xi

Preface xv

Acknowledgments xxiii

Introduction: Narayan Kasturi's Hagiographical Enterprise 1

1 Narayan Kasturi's First Life: Investigating the Hagiographer's Roots 13

2 Narayan Kasturi's Magnum Opus: *Sathyam Sivam Sundaram*, Parts 1 & 2 39

3 Narayan Kasturi's Magnum Opus: *Sathyam Sivam Sundaram*, Parts 3 & 4 91

4 The Hagiographer's Multiple Roles within the Sathya Sai Baba Movement 143

5 A Conversation with Professor Kasturi 177

6 Understanding Sathya Sai Baba in the Light of Dattātreya 217

7 Narayan Kasturi's Last Years 263

8 Epilogue: Narayan Kasturi's Legacy Lives On 287

Illustrations

1.1	Narayan Kasturi as a young College lecturer	20
1.2	Sathya Sai Baba in Bangalore in 1948.	28
1.3	The inner shrine of the Old Mandir in Puttaparthi in 1949.	32
1.4	Janakamma, N. Kasturi's mother, with the marriage party on the way to Puttaparthi.	34
1.5	Padma and Balachandran (center) on the day of their wedding in Puttaparthi's Old Mandir. They are surrounded by Balachandran's parents (left) and Padma's parents, i.e., Rajamma and N. Kasturi (right).	34
1.6	Sathya Sai Baba with, from left to right, Kasturi's son M. V. N. Murthy, N. Kasturi, M. V. N. Murthy's two children, Kasturi's mother Janakamma, and Kasturi's wife Rajamma.	36
2.1	One of the earliest purported materializations of Sathya Sai Baba: a picture of Shirdi Sai Baba surrounded by Kṛṣṇa, Rāma, Śiva, and Hanumān.	44
2.2	The anointment ceremony of Sathya Sai Baba by his father and mother on the day of his birthday inside the *mandir*. Kasturi (right) assists them.	52
2.3	N. Kasturi with Sathya Sai Baba on the Kashmir hills.	54
2.4	The first photograph of young Sathya taken after his declaration of being Shirdi Sai Baba.	58

2.5 The anointment ceremony of Sathya Sai Baba by N. Kasturi and his wife Rajamma on the day of the guru's birthday inside the *mandir*. 82

3.1 Prof. Narayan Kasturi. 104

3.2 N. Kasturi holding the ceremonial umbrella (*chattrā*) over Sathya Sai Baba. 128

4.1 Sathya Sai Baba correcting N. Kasturi's English translation during one of his speeches. 147

4.2 Padma, Kasturi's daughter, in her small apartment. Prasanthi Nilayam, February 11, 2016. 156

4.3 N. Kasturi delivering a lecture at Sathya Sai Baba's presence. 164

4.4 Kasturi's son M. V. N. Murthy (left) together with his father performing the recital and commentary of the *Sai Bhagavatham*. 165

5.1 Prof. N. Kasturi leaving the lecture hall after his morning talk. Prasanthi Nilayam, November 1985. 179

5.2 The Polaroid photo of Dattātreya showing Sathya Sai Baba's countenance as his central face. 201

6.1 The three-headed god Dattātreya. 222

6.2 Sathya Sai Baba's production of *vibhūti* over a silver statue of Shirdi Sai Baba. N. Kasturi holds the supposedly empty urn. 240

6.3 Sathya Sai Baba at the inauguration of the Dattātreya temple in Puttaparthi in January 1986. 243

6.4 Left: Dattātreya's icon in Puttaparthi's temple. The deity's posture recalls Shirdi Sai Baba's typical posture (center), which young Sathya Sai Baba consciously mirrored (right). 244

6.5 Sculpture of Dattātreya in the Sri Sathya Sai Sanjeevani hospital recently built in Naya Raipur, Chhattisgarh. 258

7.1 Kasturi and Sathya Sai Baba on Christmas day of 1982, the hagiographer's birthday. On this day Kasturi's autobiography *Loving God* was released. 265

7.2 Kasturi's wife Rajamma, together with her husband, offering a garland to her lord. 268

8.1 Sathya Sai Baba and Kasturi on the day of the guru's birthday. 300

Preface

This book explores the seminal roles played by a hagiographer in the making of a charismatic religious movement: the post-sectarian, cosmopolitan community of the Indian guru Sathya Sai Baba (1926–2011), the center of which is the ashram of Prasanthi Nilayam in Puttaparthi, in the Anantapur district of the southern state of Andhra Pradesh. The case study's protagonist is Narayan Kasturi (1897–1987), a distinguished litterateur and the holy man's official biographer, who first met Sathya Sai Baba in 1948 and who lived at his hermitage more or less continuously from 1954 up until his death.

My contention is that in order to deepen our understanding of this pan-Indian hero and his movement, attention must especially be focused upon Kasturi's background, worldview, deeds, and overall aims and expectations. This is all the more necessary given the almost complete lack of research on this figure. Despite the influence exercised by the four volumes of his hagiography titled *Sathyam Sivam Sundaram*—venerated as a sacred text by all devotees and covering Sathya Sai Baba's life from his birth in 1926 up to 1979—little scholarly notice has been paid to this truly remarkable intellectual. My study is therefore intended as a biography of Narayan Kasturi, sharing heretofore unknown or little-known information. There being no English-language academic studies on Kasturi and his significance in the construction of the Sathya Sai Baba organization, I hope that the wealth of data on him will be appreciated by both scholars and general readers.

Kasturi's life and writings are inextricably intertwined with the development, growth, and public expressions of Sathya Sai Baba's movement. The texts written by the hagiographer played and still play a major role in the expansion of the guru's fame and an in-depth analysis of them is indispensable for an appreciation of the distinctive features of the guru's cosmopolitan community. True to his neo-Hindu upbringing and conviction, Kasturi originally wrote all his books and articles on Sathya Sai Baba in English, not in Telugu or Kannada. From the time he moved to the holy man's ashram, he consistently utilized the medium of English precisely in order to reach out to the ever-increasing constituency of his beloved master.

Given the normative status of the hagiographic genre, the enterprise of the hagiographer stands out as a crucial factor in the establishment and transmission of the defining characteristics of sainthood. Although Sathya Sai Baba exercised thorough control over the representation and communication of his identity and charisma—most effectively through the astounding variety of his alleged miracles—it is hard to overestimate Kasturi's importance given his association with the guru of Puttaparthi for more than thirty years. Practically all accounts on Sathya Sai Baba as the preeminent divine incarnation (*avatāra*) of this wicked Kali age—embodying all names and forms of god—depend upon his foundational narrative.

I must point out that my approach to the figures of both Kasturi and Sathya Sai Baba is sympathetic. As a researcher, I have cultivated an empathic attitude throughout my studies on these and related subjects since my first fieldwork in Puttaparthi and the ashram of Prasanthi Nilayam in the early 1980s. Unlike other writings on gurus and their movements, which are located in the hermeneutics of suspicion, in my analysis of Kasturi's life and works I have strived to be sympathetic and balanced at one and the same time, honoring the hagiographer's centrality.

The book is divided into eight chapters, following a chronological and logical order. Chapter 1 examines Kasturi's early life and brilliant course as a student, teacher, and litterateur up until he met the young guru of Puttaparthi and became his staunch devotee. Indeed, Kasturi's life can be divided into two halves: prior to his meeting with Sathya Sai Baba and after his meeting with him, the year 1948 marking as it were a divide in his biography. Special attention is devoted to his involvement in the Ramakrishna Mission in a variety of service and educational activities in favor of the so-called Harijans or untouchables; to his university career as an esteemed lecturer in history at the Maharaja's College of Arts affiliated to Mysore University, up to his being appointed principal of the Intermediate College of Davangere; and to his noticeable literary achievements in Kannada, which gave him fame as one of the leading South Indian novelists and humorists.

Chapters 2 and 3 present a careful overview of the contents of each of the four volumes of *Sathyam Sivam Sundaram*, Kasturi's magnum opus, followed by a critical evaluation of each of its parts in order to appreciate the discursive strategies and thoughtful design of his storytelling. The purpose is to uncover the underlining fabric of *Sathyam Sivam Sundaram*, the relations of dependence that constitute it, and to highlight its main goals, which were definitely affected by the context in which the hagiographer and his intended audiences were situated. It will be seen how Kasturi's socioreligious background, education, and literary skills made him an ideal promoter of Sathya Sai Baba's figure and universalist/inclusivist organization, wholly consistent with the Vivekanandian outlook which they both shared.

Chapter 4 offers a description and an evaluation of the multiple tasks and leading functions played by Kasturi within the Sathya Sai Baba movement: unofficial secretary of the guru; editor of the monthly newsletter *Sanatahana Sarathi* since its inception; translator from Telugu into English of the saint's speeches; translator and compiler of the first eleven volumes of the *Sathya Sai Speaks* series, that is, the guru's public discourses, and of fifteen *Vahinis*, a series on various spiritual topics written by his master; president of the Sathya Sai Baba Organization of the State of Karnataka; lecturer to overseas devotees; emissary of his Swami all over India. A gifted writer, the hagiographer penned several important books and articles on Sathya Sai Baba as well as his own autobiography titled *Loving God*. Kasturi was always very close to the guru, spending many hours with him every day and accompanying him in most of his travels. So intimate he was with him that even Easwaramma (1890–1972), the holy man's mother, looked at the hagiographer as the mediator and intercessor between herself and her son.

In chapter 5 I give as it were the floor to the hagiographer. On November 8, 1985, less than two years before his demise, I had the opportunity to meet Kasturi and have quite a long conversation with him. What I present is the full content of this interview, which was recorded at his small apartment within the precincts of Puttaparthi's ashram. It happened to be one of the hagiographer's last assessments concerning his beloved guru-god and it bears the solemnity of a final disclosure. In this primary document, Kasturi offers a detailed presentation of Sathya Sai Baba as the god Dattātreya, that is to say, as the embodiment of the *trimūrti* of Brahmā, Viṣṇu, and Śiva which Dattātreya is believed to incorporate, linking the saint to his purported previous "incarnation" as Shirdi Sai

Baba (d. October 15, 1918) and to his future one as Prema Sai Baba (to be born in the Mandya district of Karnataka, as per Sathya Sai Baba's prediction). Altogether, the three Sai Babas are interpreted as one avatāric descent, thus, as Dattātreya in his triune character: this is the hagiographer's distinctive argument. Theologically, his portrayal of the guru as Dattātreya is most revealing since it had never before been argued in such a systematic, thorough way. The deity's integrative paradigm stands at the root of the holy man's syncretistic ability of spanning through the dichotomies. Mirroring Dattātreya, Sathya Sai Baba was perceived by devotees as the fountainhead of all possible meanings, allowing them to reflectively choose from his manifold identities and teachings the ones that appeared to be best suited for their spiritual uplift.

As a follow-up to the interview, I briefly discuss what I consider to be the most relevant issues that emerge from the hagiographer's testimony: Shirdi Sai Baba's place of birth, early years, and guru; the relation between Shirdi Sai Baba and Kabīr, the popular fifteenth-century poet and mystic of Benares; Sathya Sai Baba's foundational claim of being the reincarnation of Shirdi Sai Baba; the guru's "materialization" of a picture of Dattātreya and the special characteristics of this deity, which agree with Sathya Sai Baba's persona; on Dattātreya and Kabīr as being associated figures; on Sathya Sai Baba's "materialization" of gems and rings; on the contemporaries of Shirdi Sai Baba who were revered as *avatāras* of Dattātreya; on the Parsi holy man Merwan Sheriar Irani (1894–1969), better known as Meher Baba; and last but not least on an interview that Sathya Sai Baba granted in 1976 to journalist R. K. Karanjia, founder and owner editor of the Bombay weekly *Blitz*, which Kasturi considered of utmost importance.

In chapter 6, I present an overview of Dattātreya's icon from its inception up to its modern development with the emergence of the *Dattasampradāya* in the Marāṭhī cultural area in the sixteenth century, and focus upon the various ways through which the god has been appropriated by both Shirdi Sai Baba and Sathya Sai Baba. The identification with this originally minor Purāṇic deity serves important purposes within the guru's movement, legitimizing and strengthening the saint's claim of being the highest of the high. In his extensible persona, Sathya Sai Baba was able to embrace and bridge Hinduism and Islām (via the appropriation of Shirdi Sai Baba), the *trimūrti* and the Trinity, that is, Hinduism and Christianity, this-worldliness and other-worldliness, the domains of Brahminical purity and Tantric impurity, caste hierarchy and equality, traditionalism and cosmopolitanism, and even the male and female genders through his purported androgynous nature. Herein, I especially concentrate upon the Trinitarian import of the triad of *Sathyam Sivam Sundaram* and illustrate how it resonates with other Vedāntic triads such as *sat cit ānanda* and *karman bhakti jñāna*, which all concur to the definition of the triune Sai Baba as the *trimūrti*/Trinity. Via the "Dattātreya tool" the guru of Puttaparthi could claim to be not only Brahmā, Viṣṇu, and Śiva but also the Father, Son, and Holy Spirit, expanding his universalism to embrace the "religion of the West" and promoting himself as the quintessential truth (*satya*) of all creeds, the ultimate divine principle (*Brahman*), which is none other than man's innermost reality (*ātman*). All of Kasturi's books and his line of argumentation in the interview he granted me confirm his competence as a theologian, also hinting at the future developments of the Sathya Sai Baba movement, which, after the hagiographer's death, was destined to become a more and more mass-mediated phenomenon.

In chapter 7, I offer an overview of Kasturi's last years up to his passing away on August 14, 1987, and the solemn funeral rites which the guru commanded to be held in his honor so as to emphasize the spiritual stature of his foremost devotee. In the last period of his life the hagiographer had to face the deaths of his son Murthy and of his wife Rajamma, along with the inexorable deterioration of his health. Apparently, he bore these physical and psychological hardships with composure and, over time, grew more and more indifferent to worldly ties. On July 11, 1987, day of *Gurupūrṇimā*, he announced to his grandson Ramesh and his daughter Padma, much to their astonishment, that Kasturi had "died" and that he was *ātman*, that is, that he had attained self-realization. From then onward he stopped talking, ate less and less, and, given the worsening of his physical conditions, was taken to Puttaparthi's hospital as per the guru's command. He breathed his last a month later, on August 14, after one last visit by his Swami who blessed him and "materialized" ash (*vibhūti*) for him, applying it to his forehead and throat. The guru repeatedly assured his daughter and relatives that he had "attained his feet." The whole narrative of Kasturi's last days and of his funeral ceremony is clearly meant to sanctify him. Not only Sathya Sai Baba but also the priest who performed the hagiographer's last rites, Sri Karunyananda, told his daughter that he was a superlatively great man and that he had attained *kapālamokṣa,* the kind of release that is believed to occur when the soul "floats away" from the body breaking the center of the skull.

Chapter 8 attempts an overall assessment of the hagiographer's enduring legacy within the guru's movement. If over the years Sathya Sai Baba ascended more and more to international fame, being regarded as the "trademark" of India's spirituality, this success is to a nonnegligible extent due to Kasturi's tireless work and devoted service. In particular, I focus attention on three topics, which are tightly linked to one another: (1) the guru's radical type of universalism, in which all religions and names and forms of the divine are not merely incorporated but transcended. Sathya Sai Baba's movement is a planetary movement, above and beyond particularized faiths. The assumption is that the fulfillment of the Hindu *sanātanadharma* requires that it finally be exceeded, since pure love (*preman*) knows no rituals, no rules and regulations, thus, "no reason and no season" as the master liked to say. Kasturi's claim is that Sathya Sai Baba qua Dattātreya incarnates the freedom of the supreme renunciant (*avadhūta*) taken to its maximal extension, beyond the cultural boundaries/limits of India and Hinduism: this is the utopian theological conviction that the hagiographer and the guru mutually upheld. What they have taken pains to articulate is a most flexible canon, capable of adapting itself to the different needs and expectations of the movement's cosmopolitan constituency, in India and throughout the world; (2) the experience of *darśan,* that is, of seeing the guru and being seen by him, and the utilization of old and new media in conveying such visual interaction. One of the hagiographer's main objectives was to span the dichotomy between visibility and invisibility, seeing and non-seeing, which he accomplished by articulating Sathya Sai Baba's omnipresence through his powerful narratives of the guru's miracles and magic. Kasturi put his plural competences at work by thoroughly utilizing the media that were available to him, first and foremost the written word. But he also made the best use of his experience as an actor and a journalist, having worked for several newspapers and most importantly for the *All India Radio*. Kasturi even acted as consultant and screenwriter for the first films that were produced on the guru and through the telling of the *Sai Bhagavatha* poem—which he himself wrote—he played a role akin to that of a traditional song-sermon performer (*kīrtankār*). Though he did not live to see the emergence of computer technology, he certainly would have not missed the opportunity to put the World Wide Web to use in order to spread the good news of his lord, as the official Sathya Sai Organization has effectively done through its websites. The competent devotees who are in charge of what their guru-god defined as being the new "tricknologies"—an ironic neologism, given Sathya Sai Baba's fame as a trickster—are walking in Kasturi's steps and are to be regarded as the hagiographer's natural heirs, the dangers and ambiguities of the internet's "open government" notwithstanding; (3) education and service to society, which are understood to be the most significant features of Sathya Sai Baba's avatāric mission. To Kasturi, who via the Ramakrishna Mission had enthusiastically dedicated himself to a variety of pedagogic activities from his early years, it came only natural to full-heartedly embrace his lord's *sevā* projects. He knew all too well that his vocation was to devote himself to *karman,* that is, "love in action," since he was not made for a life of passive contemplation. Under the guru's supervision, over the decades the Sathya Sai Organization has undertaken a variety of projects in the fields of education and social service—in India as well as overseas—primarily through its schools and hospitals, and this continues to be its distinguishing mark even today. Life is understood as an oblation to god and one's fellow beings: the secret of existence, its raison d'être, resides in donating it, in "giving and forgiving," as the guru used to say. The etymological understanding of Datta/Dattātreya as "the given one" encourages an *imitatio* of the deity, favoring an understanding of one's existence in terms of self-sacrifice, which is regarded as the royal path for achieving divine communion. As a professor and educator, Kasturi put his professional skills at the service of his lord, who untiringly reminded students and devotees alike that "the end of education is character." All pupils of Sathya Sai Baba's schools regarded the hagiographer as being second only to their master in authority and wisdom, and indeed through his oratorical competence Kasturi was able to hold his young listeners spellbound for hours on end. As per his guru's order, throughout the decades he instructed a multitude of social servers, Indians as well as Westerners.

Kasturi and the god-man, through their painstaking endeavors, were successful in promoting the Sathya Sai Organization as a transnational movement active in a variety of overlapping fields such as education, social assistance, and medicine. For both of them, the Ramakrishna Mission and neo-Hindu gurus of the colonial period such as Sivananda (1887–1963) were inspirational models. Ultimately, the hagiographer was acknowledged as Sathya Sai Baba's exemplary *bhakta,* he being a householder (*gṛhastha*) who was capable of achieving liberating knowledge (*jñāna*) by means of selfless service rather than through the elitist path of asceticism and renunciation (*saṃnyāsa*).

Theoretically, this study focuses upon a set of issues that are deemed to be relevant to both South Asianists and historians of religion: (1) the contextualization of the hagiographer's figure through an investigation of his socioreligious milieu and the characteristics of his narrative and intended audiences; (2) the variety of functions that the hagiographer, acting as mediator between the saint and his followers, plays within a given religious movement; (3) the peculiar relation that binds together the holy man and the hagiographer, in which the fortune of the former is inextricably tied to the rhetorical skills of the latter; (4) the significance of the hagiographer as a theologian in his own right, whose work is not second to the saint's own definition of himself; (5) the many ways in which the discourses of the hagiographer and the holy man reciprocally influence and reinforce one another, resulting in the construction of a unified canon.

Acknowledgments

My special thanks go to the teachers who first kindled my interest in religious studies and in the religions and philosophies of India, Prof. Franco Michelini Tocci of the University of Venice and Prof. Mario Piantelli of the University of Turin, whose inspiration and scholarship were decisive in directing my research on the life and teachings of Shirdi Sai Baba, starting in the early 1980s. I also wish to express my debt of gratitude to Prof. Gerald James Larson, under whose masterful guidance I studied Sanskrit and earned my PhD in 1994 at the University of California, Santa Barbara, with a comprehensive study on the god Dattātreya.

It gives me great pleasure to thank all those who assisted me during my sojourns and field research in Puttaparthi from the early 1980s up to my latest trip in the winter of 2016, and in general to all Sathya Sai Baba devotees who taught me about the *līlā*s and teachings of their guru. In particular, I wish to thank the Agrawal family for offering me such generous hospitality in their homes in Mumbai and Khamgaon and providing me with transportation and all necessities. In Prasanthi Nilayam, all the members of the Sathya Sai Organization proved extremely helpful and supportive. I especially wish to thank the library personnel for their kind assistance in retrieving many books and Smt. Padma Kasturi, daughter of Narayan Kasturi, for welcoming me into her home and sharing her precious memories of her father and of Sathya Sai Baba.

In India, I also wish to thank Mr. Robin Agarwal of New Delhi for constantly providing me with firsthand information and bibliography on Shirdi Sai Baba and the *Dattasampradāya*, and Dr. M. V. Krishnayya, retired professor of philosophy and religious studies of Andhra University, Visakhapatnam, for teaching me about Dattātreya sites, temples, and lineages in Andhra Pradesh.

In Italy, I must acknowledge the many suggestions received from a host of scholars: Giuliano Boccali of the University of Milan, Alberto Pelissero and Gianni Pellegrini of the University of Turin, Raffaele Torella of the University of Rome, and Francesco Sferra of the University of Naples. I also wish to thank my dear colleagues and friends at the Ca' Foscari University of Venice, with whom I have been in constant conversation: Stefano Beggiora, Thomas Dähnhardt, Andrea Drocco, Gian Giuseppe Filippi, Shyama Medhekar, Sara Mondini, Stefano Pellò, Massimo Raveri, Federico Squarcini, and Luigi Vero Tarca. In particular, Federico Squarcini and my doctoral student Marco Guagni pointed out to me many useful texts on the study of Indian hagiographies and hagiographers: the many hours spent with them discussing these matters were most rewarding.

Along the years and especially during my undergraduate and graduate courses on the guru institute and the hagiographic traditions of South Asia, several students at the University of Venice proved helpful and supportive, stimulating my own thinking with their questions, comments, and writings. In particular, I wish to mention Nicola Biondi, Alberico Crafa, Antonio Fadda, Margherita Fracchia, Monica Guidolin, Claudia Romano, Francesco Stermotich Cappellari, and Eloisa Stuparich.

The discussion that followed a seminar I taught at the Institut für Südasien-, Tibet- und Buddhismuskunde at the University of Vienna in June 2015, titled "The Construction of a Cultic Center Through Narrative: The Founding Myth of the Village of Puttaparthi and Sathya Sai Baba," helped me to deepen my understanding of the guru's roots via his own retelling and appropriation of the founding tale of his birthplace, centered upon termite mounds (*puṭṭa*s).

A seminar that took place at Giorgio Cini Foundation and Ca' Foscari University in June 2018 titled "Fountainheads of Toleration: Forms of Pluralism in Empires, Republics, Democracies," organized by Reset-Dialogues on Civilizations in partnership with the Giorgio Cini Foundation, Nomis Foundation, Ca' Foscari University of Venice and its International Center for the Humanities and Social Change, gave me the opportunity for an in-depth focus on Vivekananda's neo-Hinduism and his notion of tolerance, that is, his inclusivism.

My gratitude extends to the personnel of the Library of the Ca' Foscari University for their assistance in acquiring numerous texts and articles, and to Ms. Carla Bonò, secretary of the *Centro studi di civiltà e spiritualità comparate* of the Giorgio Cini Foundation of Venice, for her constant encouragement.

Finally, heartfelt thanks go to my beloved wife Emanuela Botta, who always inspired me along the way, and to our dear children Sofia and Giovanni, who must have wondered precisely what it was that kept me busy in my studio for so many hours every day for the last four years.

A. R.
Venice, Italy

Introduction

Narayan Kasturi's Hagiographical Enterprise

Whereas a biography is understood to be based upon the sheer objectivity of the reality of history, a hagiography is aimed at revealing the truth of history, its ultimate meaning. Yet, despite their programmatic differences there is always an intriguing relation between biography and hagiography, the writing of a life and the writing of saintliness, given that within any hagiography there is an inextricable interweaving of myth and history.[1] As sacred biography, a hagiography is the recording of the holy life of an exceptional individual who is thought to have lived on both a human and transhuman plane at one and the same time, typically performing a great number of miracles.[2] Its goal is to afford direction toward the sacred, of being inspirational as a means for salvation.

In Hinduism there are three main genres of hagiographical writing—usually a male enterprise[3]—which are all characterized by the sentiment of *bhakti,* devotion, implying the reciprocity between the human and the divine: these are the *Purāṇa*s ("Legends"), the *Carita*s ("Biographies"), and the *Kathā*s ("Stories"), though such classification is never rigid or mutually exclusive but rather fluid.[4] Whereas the *Purāṇa*s of post-Vedic Hinduism are a huge body of scriptural texts, mostly in Sanskrit verse, which deal with the ancient past and relate the mythologies of the major gods (Brahmā, Viṣṇu, Śiva, and the Goddess), also incorporating extensive genealogies and royal dynasties,[5] the *Kathā*s are narratives of a didactic content, both secular and religious, which are intended to be read or recited aloud in a conversational style more like folk tales.[6] In turn, the *Carita*s (also spelled *Caritras*) tend to differ from both *Purāṇa*s and *Kathā*s, since they are concerned with the deeds of a specific individual. Their aim is to extol their hero by recounting his or her exemplary life. *Caritas* have been written and continue to be written in all Indian languages, in Sanskrit as well as in vernacular idioms, and their characteristic is of being well-crafted, literary works, either in verse or prose.[7] A *Carita* may also narrate the life of an ordinary human being, since its purpose may be secular. A famous example of a secular *Carita* is the *Harṣacarita* or "The Deeds of Harṣa," written by Bāṇa in the seventh century CE as an account of the exploits of the North Indian emperor Harṣavardhana (c. 590–647).

Narayan Kasturi's magnum opus *Sathyam Sivam Sundaram* is by all standards an example of a modern *Carita* (lit. "deeds"). Departing from tradition, he decided to write it in English. His choice of English for this and all his other books on Sathya Sai Baba (later to be translated into Telugu, Kannada, Hindi, etc.) was motivated by his willingness to reach out to the whole world, starting with the urban middle and upper classes/castes of India to whom he himself belonged and which he envisioned as his first, intended audience. From the very beginning of his interaction with the god-man of the village of Puttaparthi,[8] Kasturi realized that the gospel of the *avatāra* of the age was not to be limited to India but was required to be spread to the entire world.

Sathyam Sivam Sundaram is a work of careful literary composition aimed at the glorification of its hero. Every action of the guru is represented as being pure and perfect, with none of the false turnings that characterize human existence. In fact, Kasturi's work is the mirror image of a hagiography in its being the record of the public life of Sathya Sai Baba—the fullest incarnation of the divine (*pūrṇāvatāra*) in this degenerate Kali age (*yuga*)—in his interaction with ordinary men, not the life account of a human being who gradually achieved saintliness and a transcendent state.[9] In Sanskrit literature, its prototype is represented by the tenth book of the *Bhāgavata Purāṇa* (ninth or early tenth century CE), which tells the story of the various deeds of the *avatāra* Kṛṣṇa.[10] A paradigmatic example of a divine *Carita* is the *Rāmcaritmānas*, or "The Lake of the Deeds of Rām," written in Avadhi by Tulsīdās (1532–1623), undoubtedly the most popular scripture in the Hindi-speaking region of North India.

As all *Caritas*, Kasturi's opus is to be understood as an exercise in cognitive governance: its presentation of the god-man's exemplary life calls for the implementation of the set-up objectives, at an individual level as well as at a social level. The values and virtues embodied by Sathya Sai Baba[11]—one of whose favorite sayings was "My life is my message"—

require imitation, and Kasturi was fully conscious of the practical, disciplinarian function of his work, the exaltation of the guru-god and his teachings serving the purpose of orienting the minds and lifestyle of his readers, so as to inspire them to become part of the "Sai family" and eventually become members of the Sathya Sai Organization.

One must also bear in mind that any hagiography stands in an inevitable competition with the hagiographies written on other god-men, and indeed Kasturi had to put all his literary and theological talents to use in order to convince his audience that Sathya Sai Baba was above and beyond all other gurus and Swamis of his times. As Françoise Mallison observes: "Hagiographies are weapons for earning followers, securing an idol, defending a doctrinal point, etc."[12]

There are various factors that need to be taken into consideration in the production of any hagiography. In particular, three of these are of utmost significance: the person or institution, if any, that commissioned the work; the hagiographer's cultural background and his characteristics as a writer; the destination of the work, namely, its target audience. In the case of *Sathyam Sivam Sundaram*, it will be seen how it was the young god-man himself who asked Kasturi to write his *Carita* on their very first meeting. Kasturi was stunned at hearing the guru's words, since he had never dreamt of writing his life and such an assignment was to worry him a lot over the years of its preparation. Thus, it was not any other individual or institution that took the initiative of commissioning the work nor was it Kasturi's plan: it was the guru who selected him as his chosen instrument, also giving instruction on how he should proceed in his research and referring him to the people he should interview so as to acquire firsthand information. He told him: "I shall tell you whom to consult for details—parents, brothers, kinsmen, neighbors, teachers, etc. I shall also help."[13]

The fact of Kasturi being a contemporary of Sathya Sai Baba who daily interacted with him is also noteworthy given that the hagiographer is frequently someone who appears on the scene at a later date and who may have never known the saint in person. A hagiographer's aim is to present the deeds of the god-man either according to the wishes and ideological concerns of the individual or institution who commissioned the work to him/her or according to the agenda and vested interests of the community/caste to which he/she belongs. Thus, what needs to be understood is the underlying politics of any religious biography.[14] Furthermore the hagiographer, who is often an anonymous figure, does not usually stand in isolation but is part of a literary group and of a hagiographical tradition, since he/she produces his/her opus by taking into account the discourses of the hagiographers that preceded him/her, imitating them in terms of style and literary conventions.[15] Of course, there can be disagreements among hagiographers and the same saint can be viewed differently by different writers, given the competing visions of the communities/castes to which they belong, be they contemporaries or belonging to different times and contexts.[16]

Kasturi was not the heir of any particular hagiographical tradition and wrote his opus following his own ideas and narrative style, though always under the guru's supervision, he being in the company of Sathya Sai Baba almost every day starting in 1948. If he was no doubt affected by the guru's will (*saṃkalpa*) and mentality, still it should be stressed that the god-man and the hagiographer both shared the same religiosity, to such an extent that they successfully complemented each other by never ever having any kind of theological disagreement.

While the leading force behind the construction of a saint's renown is either a hagiographer or a group of hagiographers, in Sathya Sai Baba's case Kasturi acted more as a collaborator with the guru, given that the latter exercised full control over the presentation and dissemination of his own charisma, also deciding when it would be the right moment to publish Kasturi's opus. For instance, whereas Robin Rinehart has pointed out the decisive role of hagiographers in the making of Swami Ram Tirtha (1873–1906) as a modern holy man—"and so . . . the man who resisted all attempts to found an institution in his name, the man who fled to a lonely mountain cave to escape the adulation of his admirers, sending away even his closest disciples, is now an avatar and supersaint whose memory lives on in ways he could not possibly have imagined"[17]—Kasturi's role was in fact subsidiary to that of his master. Here we witness a reversal of the more common situation, since it was Sathya Sai Baba who selected and "moulded" the hagiographer, and the hagiographer, in turn, acted as his assistant in the enterprise of spreading his fame as the ultimate godhead.

Having said this, Kasturi's crucial function as disseminator of his guru's renown through *Sathyam Sivam Sundaram* and through all his remarkable talents cannot be underestimated. It is my contention that his contribution was outstanding, particularly in his role as a creative theologian in his own right. Indeed, he was second only to the guru's own promotion of himself, which he fostered primarily through the "visiting cards" of his innumerable, purported miracles. Kasturi's presentation of Sathya Sai Baba's life and teachings has been an inspirational model for all the numerous books that have been published on the guru of Puttaparthi. Perhaps inevitably, most authors—devotees as well as non-devotees—have followed in Kasturi's steps.[18] This is precisely what happens in the case of the most successful *Carita*s, which become *exempla* for all future hagiographers/biographers to follow.

Given his cultural background, Kasturi was especially suited for the task of writing Sathya Sai Baba's biography. Professionally, he was both a university professor of history as well as a litterateur and a poet. He was familiar with the practice of historical research, of collecting and organizing data, and at the same time he was a fine writer with noticeable rhetorical skills. Religiously, he had been a follower of Ramakrishna and Vivekananda since his early days and had imbibed the Vivekanandian neo-Hindu outlook. Thus, he asserted universalism while advocating the supremacy of Advaita Vedānta: he emphasized devotionalism (*bhakti*) and the practice of service (*sevā*) to one's fellow men and the society at large, a form of *karmayoga* understood as a "practical Vedānta," that is to say, a socially applied nondualism. These characteristics, coupled with his fluency in English, made him an ideal promoter of Sathya Sai Baba's image among the Indian bourgeoisie as well as among Westerners. The young guru immediately recognized the professor's qualities, and this is the reason why he decided to appoint him as his future biographer as early as July 1948.

Vivekananda's spirituality was a key factor, which influenced Kasturi both consciously as well as unconsciously. In those days his neo-Hindu mentality was shared by the majority of the urban, English-speaking, politically moderate middle and upper classes/castes, which Kasturi viewed as the chief audience of his *Sathyam Sivam Sundaram*. He knew what these people were looking for and what they needed: the outlining of a loving, charismatic guru endowed with the fullness of an *avatāra*'s powers in whom they could recognize their compassionate father and lord, be it Viṣṇu, Śiva, or the Goddess; not a revolutionary or a fundamentalist, but a moderate capable of accommodating within his all-encompassing persona both traditionalism and modernity, who would be suited for the modern times while being rooted in his own village of Puttaparthi and the traditions of rural Hinduism; a god-man who would deliver a Vedānta teaching that all might be able to understand and practice: a lay spirituality based on the love of god and the brotherhood of man, on service rather than on renunciation (*saṃnyāsa*) and the performance of esoteric rituals. And all this, undeniably, was what Kasturi had ultimately found at the feet of Sathya Sai Baba.

In his presentation of his lord's life he could not but document on almost every page what the guru's most striking characteristic was that attracted the masses toward him: that of being a miracle worker who would perform all sorts of "materializations" and wonders.[19] Thus, Kasturi presents the god-man's purported powers in detail, especially the ones he judges to be crucial for the unfolding of his narrative, although he cautions his readers by repeatedly pointing out that the miraculous should not be given too much weight, it being negligible in the *avatāra*'s mission of restoring *dharma*. To counter the criticisms of those who denounced such display of powers as nothing but magical tricks and the objections of those who viewed them as an inappropriate exhibition of *siddhi*s (albeit conceding their genuineness), Kasturi emphasizes the authenticity of the guru's faculties by insisting that they were not acquired through any yogic practice or Tantric *sādhana*, being rather an inborn characteristic of his full *avatāra*hood, a charisma he was endowed with from birth.[20]

Along with the defense of the guru's powers, another major task of Kasturi's hagiography is to convince his audience that the god-man of Puttaparthi is none other than Sai Baba, the popular *faqīr* from the village of Shirdi in Maharashtra who had "left the body" on October 15, 1918, and of whom Ratnākaram Sathyanārāyaṇa Rāju alias Sathya Sai Baba, officially born on November 23, 1926, claimed to be the reincarnation. The latter's appropriation of Sai Baba's icon, paradigm of an integrative spirituality, was a most powerful way to legitimate himself throughout India. By doing so he was able to elude his humble origins and the absence of any authoritative *guruparamparā*, positing himself at an altogether higher level, creatively combining his *avatāra*ness with his Sai Babaness.

Despite all of Sathya Sai Baba's and Kasturi's efforts, along the years only a minority of Shirdi Sai Baba devotees came to acknowledge the god-man of Andhra Pradesh as being the same as their lord. But this in no way diminished the attractiveness of the guru of Puttaparthi, since his presentation from his early years as Sai Baba and *stricto sensu* a full (*pūrṇa*) *avatāra* proved extremely successful. Moreover, his claim that the Sai Baba *avatāra* will be characterized by a triple incarnation, so that some years after his death he will reappear as Prema Sai Baba—upholding the religion of universal love and bringing his mission to completion—proves his ability to bypass the thorny issue of succession by assuring that he himself will come back in another body to fulfill his task: a *longue durée* spanning more than two centuries, having begun with Shirdi Sai Baba's birth sometime around the midpoint of the nineteenth century.

It should be noted that like Sathya Sai Baba even Shirdi Sai Baba had given similar methodological advice on how to write his *Carita* to his hagiographer Govind Raghunath Dabholkar, alias Hemadpant (1859–1929),[21] also saying that he would be his chosen instrument.[22] Here, however, it was Dabholkar who took the initiative and asked him for the permission and blessings to write his biography in Marāṭhī. The outcome was the *Śrī Sāī Saccarita*, a work subdivided into fifty-three chapters and comprising 9,308 verses, the veritable "Bible" for all Shirdi Sai Baba's devotees. The holy man is reported to have said: "Make a collection of all the authentic stories, experiences, conversations and talks, etc. It is better to keep a record. He [Dabholkar] has my full support. He is but the instrument; I myself will write my own story."[23] Significantly, Kasturi liked to compare himself to Dabholkar viewing himself as nothing but an instrument in the guru's hands. He must certainly have read the *Śrī Sāī Saccarita* or an abridged version of it in English, Telugu, or Kannada translation, deriving inspiration from it.

Although both the hagiographers' works are replete with the miracles and astounding feats (*līlā*s) performed by their respective heroes, stylistically they are very different, reflecting their own times and intended audiences. Dabholkar's versified Marāṭhī opus is said to follow the traditional style of the renowned *Eknāthī Bhāgavata* of the Maharashtrian poet-saint Eknāth (1533–1599),[24] narrating the saint's wondrous deeds with little care for chronological accuracy. The literary model of the *Śrī Sāī Saccarita* is believed to be the *Gurucaritra*, the founding text of the *Dattasampradāya* (lit. "the tradition of the Datta/Dattātreya [followers]") composed around the middle of the sixteenth century by Sarasvatī Gaṅgādhar, which tells the deeds of the Brahmin gurus Śrīpād Śrīvallabh (c. 1323–1353) and Nṛsiṃha Sarasvatī (c. 1378–1458) venerated as the first "historical" *avatāra*s of the god Dattātreya. On the other hand, Kasturi's is a modern work in plain English prose which takes pains to articulate a careful chronological order of the god-man's life along the lines of a neo-Hindu discourse. Whereas the *Śrī Sāī Saccarita* was intended for a local, Maharashtrian audience, and consciously aimed at being identified as part and parcel of its time-honored hagiographic tradition, *Sathyam Sivam Sundaram* is an autonomous text with no apparent link to any local tradition of hagiographical writing, its aim being that of reaching out to the middle and upper classes/castes of India and to the entire world.

When Kasturi first reached Puttaparthi there already existed a short Telugu poem presenting Sathya Sai Baba as the reincarnation of Shirdi Sai Baba and offering information on Shirdi Sai Baba's birth and early years in a distinct Purāṇic fashion: the *Sri Sayeeshuni Charitra*, published in Dharmavaram in 1944 by V. C. Kondappa, who had been a school teacher of the young guru at the Bukkapatnam Higher Elementary School.[25] In his Preface, Kondappa says that it was Sathya Sai Baba himself who one night called him and revealed "Sai's story" to him.[26] It is reported that the young guru took keen interest in the preparation of the text and that, after it was released, asked one M. L. Leela to read it in his presence at the nearby Chitravathi riverbed, on which occasion he would have granted a vision of himself as Shirdi Sai Baba.[27] This was the first work ever composed on him, and naturally Kasturi took careful notice of its contents in the preparation of his "official biography," though he consciously departed from its traditional style of hagiographical writing. The *Sri Sayeeshuni Charitra* also took the form of a *śataka,* a devotional composition in a hundred verses known as the *Sri Sai Sathakamu*, which is frequently memorized and chanted by *bhaktas*.[28]

If a "divine" *Carita* bears the characteristics of its own genre and does not need to justify the documentary sources upon which it may—or may not—depend given that ultimately its value lies in its "theological truth" and intrinsic literary quality, in the case of *Sathyam Sivam Sundaram* this is only partially true, given that Kasturi repeatedly underlines the factual, historical foundation upon which his opus is grounded, it being a biography based upon many years of dedicated research and the interviewing of dozens of witnesses. His aim is to present the public life of Sathya Sai Baba as accurately as possible, chronologically documenting the breaking in of the metahistorical dimension of the guru-god within the world. In other words, his objective is to offer a vivid, eyewitness report of the presence of the divine, literally accounting for the historical "descent" (*avatāra*) of a god into the world of men.

Even the vast repertoire of divine personalities and astounding deeds to which Sathya Sai Baba's life is assimilated—such as Kṛṣṇa and his many *līlā*s, as told in the *Bhāgavata Purāṇa*—are never thought of as purely mythological but as thoroughly historical, as Sathya Sai Baba's own prodigies are believed to be. Thus, the wondrous *līlās* of the *avatāra* of this Kali age stand out as an implicit confirmation of the historical reality of Kṛṣṇa's *līlās* in the preceding Dvāpara age. And this notwithstanding their incredibility: in fact, it was the guru himself who in the early days told Kasturi to wait before publishing his biography on the grounds that the time was not yet ripe and that people would judge it a fairy-tale!

Kasturi's opus strikes the reader as a thoroughly modern *Carita,* concerned with facts and chronology while at the same time accounting for Sathya Sai Baba's deeds in terms of both a historical and a transhistorical reality. If, as Richard Barz observes, all of the episodes of the classic *Buddhacarita* ("The Deeds of the Buddha") by the great poet Aśvaghoṣa (first century CE, one of the first hagiographical works in Indian literature) are meant to instill Buddhist doctrine and "the manner and order in which the events actually occurred or the question of whether they happened at all are not issues of importance"[29]—which is precisely what makes of Aśvaghoṣa "a typical hagiographer"[30]—Kasturi's *Carita* is remarkably different, being based on the available documentation of Sathya Sai Baba's public life and teachings following a chronological sequence. The relationship of a hagiographer to historiography, which is generally thin and highly problematic,[31] in our case is incontrovertibly strengthened by the fact that the hagiographer was a university professor of history, a brilliant intellectual who cultivated a critical mind and was professionally accustomed to verifying his sources by sifting through the evidence.

By the same token, true to the *Carita* genre Kasturi's opus was never intended as a scholarly presentation—he does not furnish us with a bibliography or details on the sources of his narrative—but as a devotional account inextricably mixing together the chronicling of the guru's deeds with the vast reservoirs of Vaiṣṇavism and Śaivism treasured in the Epics and in the *Purāṇas*, wishing to reveal their hidden links so as to convince his audience that the guru's advent is to be understood as the fulfillment of the truths enshrined in those ancient texts. Ultimately, Kasturi aims at illuminating the god-man's biographical data through his own theological understanding of the import of his incarnation. *Sathyam Sivam Sundaram* is therefore neither a "scientific" treatise nor by any means a decontextualized, purely mythical account. It endeavors to demonstrate the purpose of god's descent on earth by chronicling his advent and the unfolding of the various phases of his biography or, better said, stages in his avatāric career. These stages are thought to have a decisive impact on the world's future and humanity's destiny, given their eschatological relevance within the scheme of the threefold Sai Baba incarnation.

As with all hagiographies, *Sathyam Sivam Sundaram* is in itself a precious source of information on the social and religious concerns of the author who wrote it and of the people who read it. It is revelatory of the historical context in which it was conceived and produced, being a testimony of its own times. As in a game of mirrors, Kasturi's opus, notwithstanding the guru's supervision, reflects none other than Kasturi himself given that he inevitably displays his own Sathya Sai Baba, which is in all respects similar to him. The hagiographer highlights the expectations and needs of the community to which he himself belongs and to which his work is addressed. As Jean-Yves Tilliette has noted: "The society, to use a formula which has by now become classic, produces the saints it needs."[32]

Thus, *Sathyam Sivam Sundaram* is replete with the spirit of tolerance and hierarchical inclusivism, as per Swami Vivekananda's lesson, positing nondual Vedānta, that is, its contemporary incarnation as Sathya Sai Baba, as the highest of the high. Its stress on the service of man and education in human values, its call to reform the school system and the entire society on the basis of *satya* (truth), *dharma* (righteousness), *śānti* (peace), *preman* (love), and *ahiṃsā* (nonviolence), while being motivated by religious concerns—the guru's and Kasturi's commitment toward the implementation of a "practical Vedānta"—was also the expression of a nationalistic pride, of a patriotic élan, which galvanized the youth and large sectors of Indian society in the postindependence period, especially the urban, educated middle and upper classes/castes, in an effort to contribute to the resurgence of "Mother India" as a nation. Even Kasturi's choice of writing *Sathyam Sivam Sundaram* in English was intended as a way to prove to his countrymen the worldwide significance of his hero: he enthusiastically portrays Sathya Sai Baba as India's gift to the world so as to make Hindus proud of their immemorial culture. His narrative is wholly consistent with the rhetoric of India's religious superiority from the time of the *Vedas*, Hinduism being extolled as the "Mother" of all world religions and Advaita Vedānta as personified in Sathya Sai Baba being magnified as the acme of truth and the ultimate revelation to mankind, thus, as the fulfillment of all religions.

For both the hagiographer and his primary audience, Sathya Sai Baba was the guru they had been waiting for, even without their being aware of it, since he filled their nostalgia for a pure, idyllic past represented by village Hinduism. It functioned as a modern surrogate, which soothed their hearts and minds, meaning their often traumatic experience of uprootedness, many of them having been forced to leave their native locales in order to seek fortune in urban contexts. Such a rupture with their past inevitably determined a sense of loss, which devotion to the guru of Puttaparthi and belonging to the "new family" of his devotees—"the company of the good," *satsaṅga*—promised to alleviate and compensate, reestablishing a connection with their often only imagined cultural roots.

Since 1961, *Sathyam Sivam Sundaram* has not only been silently read or proclaimed aloud by generations of *bhakta*s for devotional purposes—what is known as the individual or collective practice of *pothīpārāyaṇa*—but it has functioned as an object of veneration, being *the* authoritative repository of Sathya Sai Baba's life. From its very appearance and through its many editions Kasturi's opus has been recognized as the "Bible" by all of the guru's *bhakta*s, on analogy with Dabholkar's *Śrī Sāī Saccarita.*

A useful survey, which however exceeds the limits of the present monograph, would be to evaluate the history of *Sathyam Sivam Sundaram*'s reception, the different interpretations and emphases to which in the course of the past half-century it has been subject to in culturally specific contexts, both in India and in the West. Though hagiographies are never scrutinized as if they were *sūtra*s, that is, works that require detailed explanatory commentaries (*bhāṣya*), a tentative history of both its "exegesis" and performative usage could tell us a lot about the life the text has enjoyed and continues to enjoy among the communities of the guru's devotees.[33]

Finally, it must be underlined how Kasturi was the guru's righthand man for more than thirty years, being involved in a variety of strategic roles: as his personal secretary, as editor and English translator of the god-man's public talks and writings, as editor of the monthly newsletter *Sanathana Sarathi*, as public speaker to both Indian and overseas devotees, and as the author of many other books on Sathya Sai Baba. He also accompanied the guru in most of his travels throughout India as well as in East Africa in 1968 and played a pivotal role in the rise and development of the Sathya Sai Organization.

All in all, Kasturi was definitely the most influential figure within the ashram of Prasanthi Nilayam, second only to his Swami. This is noteworthy since it proves the trust and esteem in which he was held by Sathya Sai

Baba: he knew he could always count on Kasturi and Kasturi, in turn, was totally devoted to him and to the promotion of his avatāric mission. Indeed, there was such a profound intimacy and complicity between the two that for Kasturi it was hard to bear the physical separation from his beloved, even for just a few days.

Kasturi's life shows us how the weight of being an "official biographer" may in fact exceed his function as writer of a *Carita*. Being Sathya Sai Baba's lieutenant, all devotees revered him as a unique mediator and often asked him to intercede with the guru on their behalf. If there was someone who could claim to be close to the god-man and to be able to understand him this was Kasturi, given that he alone had the privilege of spending several hours with him every day. This book is intended as a case study of the various functions a hagiographer may come to perform within a religious organization and of his capacity to influence its direction and overall goals, playing the role of a protagonist in its expansion. To be sure, an in-depth investigation of Kasturi's life and works is a mandatory task in order to try to come to terms with his unpredictable, elusive master.

But it is now time to immerse ourselves into Narayan Kasturi's biography, starting from his very birth and first life, before he knew anything about Sathya Sai Baba, so as to reconstruct his social and cultural roots and learn about his personality and notable achievements.

1

Narayan Kasturi's First Life

Investigating the Hagiographer's Roots

Early Years and Education

Narayan Kasturi Ranganatha Sharma,[1] who was later to shorten his name to Narayan Kasturi, was born on Christmas Day 1897 in the town of Thrippunithura in Cochin State, nowadays Kerala, as the only child of a Brahmin *vaiṣṇava* couple that hailed from Tamil Nadu.[2] Regarding the meaning of his name, he himself explained:

> *Kasturi* means musk, the fragrant stuff used to put a dot on God's forehead. Krishna had "*kasturi tilakam*" on His forehead. It is not only black, but also fragrant. There is a temple in South India, where the God is known as Kasturi Ranganatha, the Director of the Divine play, wearing a musk dot. I am named after that God.[3]

At birth he was regarded as an exceptional soul having six fingers on each palm and six toes on each foot, which astrologers viewed as an auspicious sign.[4] His mother Janakamma (b. 1882) spoke Tamil and thus from birth he was fluent in both Tamil and Malayalam, the language of Kerala.[5] His father, who was a stamp-vendor and a stamp-writer in Cochin High Court, died in 1902 of smallpox, so that from when he was five years old he was brought up by his mother.

Coming from a poor family, his grandfather[6] wanted to hand him over to a free residential Sanskrit school for Brahmins (*pāṭhaśālā*), but his mother insisted that he should attend English schools and receive an English education, not the traditional Brahminical instruction. She was so determined that she proceeded to sell her gold ornaments to pay his school fees. Kasturi's daughter recalls:

> She had no money to educate him. She struggled a lot. With the help of her brother, somehow she managed to give her son education in an English medium school. He was very bright, studied well, got scholarships and graduated from the College with a degree. It is due to her determination that her Kasturi was able to study English.[7]

Also, thanks to the economic support of his maternal uncle, from 1903 to 1914 young Narayan did his schooling in Thrippunithura and went through high school under the guidance of his beloved headmaster Gopal Krishna Iyer,[8] who first kindled his devotion for Swami Vivekananda[9] (1863–1902) and Shri Ramakrishna[10] (1836–1886). Kasturi writes:

> Passages from Swami Vivekananda's *Thunder-bolt* address at Madras . . . were prescribed for the Elocution Contest for students of my High School . . . in 1912, by my Headmaster; I won the first prize and in appreciation I was given the full speech to read and assimilate. It thrilled me to the very marrow of my bone. I browsed in the same field, over wider areas, until I came to the speech given by Swami Vivekananda in the Unites States on *My Master*. When I read it, Guru Dev [Ramakrishna] entered my heart and mastered my impulses, inclinations and intentions.[11]

During his schooldays, he had to walk four miles twice a day to have his free meals at the nearest feeding house established "for Brahmins only" by the Maharaja of Cochin. But despite all hardships, he emerged as a brilliant pupil, and during the three years of high school earned a merit scholarship of five rupees a month. In 1911, at age fourteen, he was married to Rajamma who was just nine years old and came from a small village near Kaladi.[12]

At the School Leaving Certificate Examination held in Ernakulam, Narayan stood out first for the entire State of Cochin in the subjects of history and Malayalam language and literature. Having become eligible for a monthly scholarship of ten rupees for two years, between 1914 and 1916 he did his pre-university studies at the Maharaja's College of Ernakulam, passing his intermediate examinations with first class marks. He then enrolled in an Honors course at the Faculty of History of the University College of Trivandrum, where he earned the Grigg Memorial Fellowship valued at twelve rupees a month for three years. At that time, he was a free boarder at the Maharaja's temple at Trivandrum. Under the guidance of Prof. K. V. Rangaswamy Iyengar,[13] he specialized in Indian history and at age twenty-one obtained an Honors degree in history, ranking second in the entire Madras Presidency.

In Trivandrum, young Kasturi actively collaborated with the Ramakrishna Mission,[14] taking part in its activities and collecting donations for the local Ramakrishna temple. He eagerly imbibed the Advaita Vedānta teachings and the life stories of Ramakrishna and Vivekananda, and was determined to follow their example and consecrate his existence to their ideals. In order to maintain himself and his household—comprising his mother and mother-in-law—in 1919 he accepted a job as teacher in a private high school of Trivandrum on forty rupees a month and simultaneously attended evening classes at the local College of Law, where he obtained a Bachelor of Laws degree.[15]

Around 1921, Kasturi and his family transferred to Mysore where he secured a better position as lecturer in history at the Dharmaprakash Banumaiah Collegiate High School, with a monthly salary of one hundred rupees. He loved his pupils and greatly enjoyed his work as a teacher. He did not like the mannerisms of the school's founder, however, and soon started searching for a new job. For some time, in order to prop up his financial situation, he even considered becoming a lawyer, though he was never attracted to the legal profession. "But—as he states in his autobiography—Bhagavan Ramakrishna Paramahamsa[16] pulled me back from the brink."[17]

Secretary of the Ramakrishna Ashram and University Professor: His Service Activities

In December 1922, Gopal Marar, who had been his best classmate and friend at Thrippunithura's high school, came to search for him in Mysore.

He was the son of one of the senior princes of the royal family of Cochin and had continued his studies in Madras (nowadays called Chennai) at the Christian College. More importantly, he had become a monk of the Ramakrishna Order and his new monastic name was Swami Siddheshwarananda (1897–1957).[18] He had been instructed to take charge of the newly opened Ramakrishna Center in Mysore and, knowing that his boyhood chum was in the area, came looking for Kasturi to propose to him to join in the adventure.

When they met, Kasturi's joy knew no bounds and, without hesitation, he accepted the invitation to become the secretary of the Mysore branch of the Ramakrishna ashram, of which Swami Siddheshwarananda was to be the president: he was to untiringly serve the Ramakrishna Mission for a full seventeen years. Here is the testimony of Kasturi's first son, M. Venkata Narayana Murthy:

> My childhood was spent on the loving laps of the monks of the Ramakrishna Ashram at Mysore. Certainly freedom from caste consciousness and the desire to share in Seva activities were planted in me. The Ashram was my Nursery School, a boon not enjoyed by many children. . . . The sadhus of the Ramakrishna Ashram poured their love and affection on me during those tender years.[19]

This new role gave Kasturi the opportunity to move out from behind the school walls and come in contact with eminent religious figures, both within and without the Ramakrishna Mission, such as Swami Nikhilananda (1895–1973)[20] and the guru and mystic Ramana Maharshi (1879–1950) of Tiruvannamalai.[21]

At the Ramakrishna ashram, Kasturi lectured extensively in English and in Kannada,[22] which he quickly learned and to which he came to be increasingly attracted. Within a Vedāntic framework, he lectured to hundreds on the lives and teachings of the saints and sages of India, past and present, and particularly on the lives and teachings of his "Gurudev" Ramakrishna and Vivekananda, both in Mysore and in nearby towns and villages, especially among illiterates.[23] Moreover, he led the way in undertaking many projects of social service (*sevā*), which was the task he enjoyed the most. In order to recruit the youths to serve under the Ramakrishna flag, at the ashram he started offering free "coaching classes" for the rehabilitation of those students who had failed the University Entrance Examination.

He was creative, enrolling as a trainee at a camp for Rovers (Senior Boy Scouts), which he renamed Vivekananda Rovers, as well as writing and staging popular plays, of which all entrance fees were donated to the ashram. The scout movement, the stage, and the training for backward students were used to foster the principles of the Ramakrishna Mission.

In 1927, he received his formal initiation (*dīkṣā*) within the order and was given the Shri Ramakrishna *mantra—Jay Guru Dev*—by the famous Swami Shivananda (Tarak Nath Ghosal, 1854–1934), popularly known as Mahapurush or "Great Soul," a direct disciple of Ramakrishna who happened to pass by Bangalore on his tour of Southern India. Kasturi recalls:

> Luckily, I had a very great guru of Ramakrishna Mission, one of the closest disciples of Ramakrishna himself. A person who had moved along with Vivekananda, who did a great deal of *tapas* in the same place where Buddha had sat under the "Bodhi Tree" in Gaya. He was called "Mahapurushji," a great personality. I got the mantra from him, and I repeated it regularly.[24]

Kasturi's forte, however, was not yoga, prayer, or meditation, which he viewed as individualistic and ultimately barren practices. His daughter Padma writes: "My father never liked these *japam*, *dhyanam* (chanting, meditation, etc.). . . . My father liked [social services and feeding the poor] because in the Ramakrishna Ashram too they did these *Daridra Narayana Seva* [service to god Nārāyaṇa, i.e., Viṣṇu, as manifested in the poor]."[25] His path was that of worshipping god in man, that is, *karmayoga,* along the lines of a Vivekanandian interpretation of the *Bhagavadgītā*. Kasturi's active approach to religion was in consonance with the spirit of the time. As Richard H. Davis states:

> Through Vivekananda's direction (no doubt influenced by the organizational practices of the Christian missionaries he otherwise disdained), the *Gita*'s this-worldly orientation took institutional form in India in the Ramakrishna Mission. The monastic followers of Ramakrishna would devote themselves not to meditation or devotional worship but instead to alleviating

> poverty and suffering by establishing hospitals and schools as well as organizing relief during famines and natural disasters.[26]

As Kasturi often repeated, he was addicted solely to service, that is, to the ethical application of the Upaniṣadic doctrine of the identity of *ātman* and *Brahman*.[27] He espoused Vivekananda's "practical Vedānta"[28] with all his heart and involved himself in a variety of *sevā* activities, especially in the suburbs and in the villages surrounding the Mysore area, to the point that he came to be considered a "ruromaniac."[29] He offered instruction on issues of health and hygiene, and actively denounced village "superstitions" and factionalism, caste discrimination, and the exploitation and isolation of Harijans,[30] the untouchables. Kasturi remembers:

> When I was a professor in a college at Mysore, under the influence of Ramakrishna Paramahamsa and Vivekananda, I used to lead the college boys for social service right into the *Harijan* colony. There were about 2,000 houses of *Harijans* in the outskirts of Mysore. Whenever I entered their colony with students, they would protest, "Sorry, you are a *Brahmin*, don't come inside, there will be some calamity for us!" We have made their mind so hard and mechanical in thinking, that when an idealist starts sympathizing with them and begins to improve their lot, they think of the calamity that may befall on them, because he is breaking the rule. But, I am glad that in spite of it we were able to do some useful work.[31]

True to Swami Vivekananda's gospel, he believed that god resides in everyone and that it was imperative to go beyond the differentiations of caste and creed. His social consciousness led him to reach out to all people, since he never wanted to waste his talents within restricted intellectual circles and the upper castes.[32] Kasturi even took his family along with him[33] and convinced several of his colleagues and especially his students to join him. He had the University Union rent a house in the center of a cluster of more than 1,500 untouchable houses—Adikarnatakapuram—and led students to fraternize with the villagers through literacy classes, *bhajans*, news readings, games, and caring for the sick.

Young Kasturi communicated the message of individual and social uplift also through plays and *harikathās*, one-man shows reciting the stories of Hindu mythology, embellished with music and theatrics.[34] He was an accomplished actor and it is remarkable that several young men who would later become famous actors received guidance in stagecraft from him.[35] He writes:

> As organizer of the Village Service activities of the Union, I led a batch of students, men and women, every Saturday for more than two years for a whole-day camp to Corgahalli, a village ten miles to the west of Mysore. Reaching the place by bus, we gathered the children, taught them games and told them stories. In twos and threes we entered their homes and conversed casually on problems which were presented by them or which interested them. We had doctors with us who examined, diagnosed and prescribed remedies. We enacted plays and read out spiritual books on lives of great men and women. . . . We were welcomed as brothers and sisters and we soon became close friends and trusted guides.[36]

It was under the leadership of B. M. Srikantayah (1884–1946), father-figure of Kannada literature, that Kasturi and his associates conducted literacy classes for adults in many villages around Mysore city. Even at the Ramakrishna ashram, he liked to surround himself with Kannada litterateurs and poets. In the early 1920s, he sheltered for full twelve years K. V. Puttappa (1904–1994) who was to become a great poet and novelist popularly known as Kuvempu.[37] Until he completed high school and college education and became himself a teacher, Puttappa lived at the ashram nursed by the love and affection of its president and secretary, absorbing the moral values of the Ramakrishna Mission. Kasturi points out: "We . . . learnt from Puttappa the richness of Kannada Classics, wherein Jain, Saivite and Vaishnavite bards extol the spiritual victories won by themselves and the saints of this land."[38]

In June 1928, he finally succeeded in leaving the Dharmaprakash Banumaiah Collegiate High School by securing a position at the Intermediate College of Mysore. Soon after, he was transferred to the adjacent Maharaja's College of Arts, affiliated to Mysore University, which he joined as a lecturer for 150 rupees per month. Here he taught graduate and postgraduate courses, and had "unlimited facilities for browsing in the University Library, and developing constructive companionships with students

Figure 1.1. Narayan Kasturi as a young College lecturer.

through dramas, debates and service camps in rural areas."[39] "Lecturer" was his official designation,[40] and during his many years at the Maharaja's College Kasturi mainly taught Indian History and Social Anthropology. H. K. Ranganath (b. 1923), one of Kasturi's closest students who was to become a radio broadcaster and a scholar of Karnataka theatre, remembers:

> He was easily approachable yet he commanded great respect and we, in fact, feared him. He inspired hundreds of students. . . . His fraternity of friends and family was very large. To belong to the "Kasturi clan" was a matter of pride.[41] The community as a whole held him in high regard. . . . In the class, Kasturi's lectures were like fairy tales. He cast a spell on the students. . . . I place Kasturi on the top of the list. His teaching style was inimitable. Lecturing on Greek history and mythology, he would depict Atalanta's running, using his fingers, and she would be stamped in your memory forever. . . . Because

> of him Henry the Eighth, Napoleon, Bismarck, Disraeli, Gladstone and our own Ashoka, Pulikeshi, Harsha and Tippu have become etched in my mind. . . . We admired him, adored him and worshipped him. The path he took became holy trail for us. Where he stayed became a shrine. What he said became scripture![42]

Literary Achievements in Kannada: His Fame as a Humorist

Kasturi's love of Karnataka and of its language and literature became so intense that together with other colleagues he translated into Kannada Percy Bysshe Shelley's essay *Defense of Poetry*, Thomas Carlyle's *On History*, and Bertrand Russell's *A Free Man's Worship*. He was an advocate of Kannada literary and cultural renaissance, and the doyens of Kannada literature fondled him as if fate had restored him to Karnataka after having been kidnapped into Kerala.[43] Despite his protestations, he was paraded like a circus animal and was a victim of mass adulation, a situation that was similar to that of the protagonist of his novel *Gaaligopuram*. He points out:

> "*Kannadam Katthuri Althe?*" "Is not Kannada Kasturi?" asked Kannada a poet of the seventeenth century. He referred of course to the language and extolled its pervasive perfume, for Kasturi means musk. I discovered the fragrance and was fascinated by it. For 33 years I offered homage to the language and to the people who foster it. I was warmly welcomed by literary and cultural groups throughout Karnataka.[44]

As the distinguished litterateur L. S. Seshagiri Rao observes, "He learnt Kannada after he came to Mysore, and mastered it so superbly that he would critically read old Kannada classics, and write with genuine humor."[45] Moreover, M. N. Rao remarks how "the years he spent at the University gave ample scope for his mercurial personality and he glittered in the public eye. He had ample scope for his gifts of a quick-witted gab and a fertile brain."[46]

To be sure, the university milieu was a productive ground for his literary talents to flourish, primarily in Kannada but also in English. It might be said that he was a history professor[47] that gradually transformed himself into a man of literature. While he strengthened his academic position by writing a book on marriage customs (*Maduve*, 1940) and a monograph on the Maurya emperor Aśoka (r. c. 272–231 BCE),[48] he manifested his true nature as a humorist and satirist and, between 1923 and 1948, published more than twenty works in Kannada.[49] Indeed, he became famous as a humor writer and had a large reading public. His sarcasm was lighthearted and without sting, never vulgar or offensive, and his satire was mainly focused upon social and political evils.[50] He was soon recognized as an avant-garde in Kannada humor literature and came to be ranked among the stalwarts of the innovative *Navodaya* School.

He started his literary activity by writing parodies and puns in the University Union Magazine and these were so successful that a collection of them was published as a book with the title *Yadwa-tadwa*, "As is, so is." He then gave free rein to his literary vein by writing poems (*Anaku minaku*, 1947), satirical essays (*Allola, Donku bala, Kallola, Navaratri-kempa maisurige hodaddu, Upāya-vedānta*), innovative impromptu plays[51] (*Bank divali, Citra-vicitra, Ekacakra, Gaggayyana gadibidi, Ramakrishnaiahna darbaru, Tapatraya tappitu, Vara pareekshe*), and popular novels (*Chakradristi, Chenguli cheluva, Gaaligopuram, Grihadaaranyaka, Ranganayaki, Shankha vadya*).[52] The novels stand out for their literary quality and show Kasturi's serious side, amid a language full of humor. The reader can identify himself/herself with the various characters and with their lives of many struggles and compromises. For instance, *Chenguli cheluva* (1953) is the autobiography of an illiterate coolie, *Gaaligopuram* or "Castle in the Air" (1940) is the description—largely autobiographical—of the travails of a victim of mass adulation, and in *Chakradristi* (1944) the protagonist is a clerk who never appears and ten different characters speak about him, in the process revealing themselves as absurd, delightful caricatures of people we see around us all the time.[53] Kasturi's novels exhibit an undercurrent of pain and compassion and are laced with subtle humor, exposing the muddled and mediocre adventures of the ordinary mind. In his own words: "Every page raising the dilemma, 'Should we laugh or must we weep?' at the absurdity, the obscurity, the incongruity, the quixoticity, the pomposity or the obscenity."[54]

He also published a dictionary, or better a fictionary/frictionary, as he called it, the *Anarthakosha* (lit. "senseless dictionary"), in which he coined new terms, twisted proverbs, invented new meanings for old words and offered deliberately absurd and perverse definitions. As L. S. Seshagiri Rao writes, Kasturi was "a genius in coining new words on the analogy of existing words and twisting the meaning of words to suggest new angles and create humor."[55] The *Anarthakosha* is truly a gem of his humoristic cleverness and a one of its kind book in Kannada, of which new editions continue to be published.[56]

Also noteworthy was Kasturi's activity as a translator into Kannada, which he cultivated up to the early 1960s, even after becoming a devotee of Sathya Sai Baba. He translated Western classics such as Charles Lutwidge Dodgson's alias Lewis Carroll's *Alice in Wonderland* (*Pataladalli papacci*, 1935) and Victor Hugo's *Les Misérables* (*Nonda jivi*, 1956), as well as the *Memoirs of Babur* (*Dilliswarana dinachari*, 1930). In the early twentieth century, the nationalist movement inspired many writers to translate Western classics into Indian languages. Kasturi's translation or, better, adaptation of *Alice in Wonderland* for Kannada children was especially innovative. He domesticated and abridged the story by utilizing local names and Hindu myths, "Kannadizing" it with a Brahmin touch.[57] Among his other translations are a play by the famous humorist Sir Pelham Grenville Wodehouse (*Kadane*) and a popular book such as *Elephant Bill* (*Gajendra loka*, 1958), written by James Howard Williams in 1950. He even translated short stories from China and Japan (*China Japan kathegalu*, 1962) and the Malayalam novel *Chemmeen* [*Prawns*] (*Kempu meenu*) written by Thakazhi Sivasankara Pillai (1912–1999) in 1956.[58]

When Dr. M. Shivaram (1905–1984), the doyen of Kannada humor literature, popularly known by his pen name Rashi, launched the Kannada monthly *Koravanji* in March 1942, Kasturi was right by his side. Inspired by the British satirical magazine *Punch*, the name *Koravanji* refers to the fortunetelling tribal women of rural India.[59] For more than ten years, Kasturi contributed to it with pages of brilliant humorous skits, parodies, quips and quixotic essays, limericks, and lighthearted poems under various pseudonyms, such as Rudramma and Srimathi Kesari. Rashi especially appreciated Kasturi's subtle sense of humor, which could hit without hurting and which was never obscene.

It was Kasturi who brought to *Koravanji* a few gifted students from Maharaja's College such as S. K. Nadig (1928–2008) and R. K. Laxman (1921–2015), who was later to become India's top cartoonist.[60] He had noticed the latter's drawings in the college magazine and immediately recognized his talent. It was Laxman who created the *Koravanji Mascot*, which appeared on the cover of the very first issue of the magazine and, from 1942 to 1946, he worked side by side with Kasturi authoring more than one hundred illustrations. For more than seven years, Kasturi even contributed to *Shankar's Weekly*, the humorist Delhi magazine created by K. Shankar Pillai (1902–1989), the father of Indian political cartooning, better known as Shankar. Kasturi wrote in English and had a column of his own, *Mere Prattle*, and to be sure he "prattled, on the lower half of page number three, right under the Cartoon for the Week by the redoubtable Shankar himself."[61]

Sometime around 1941 Prof. M. V. Gopalaswamy, a colleague of Kasturi's who taught in the psychology department, involved him in broadcasting educational programs for rural folk, children, and women. Soon the range of the broadcasting station in Mysore became wider and the programs more varied, to the point that Gopalaswamy asked Kasturi to join him as full-time assistant director: it happened to be the first private radio station in the country. Thanks to his creativity and entertaining style of conversation, Kasturi did a wonderful job, and raised the radio to historic heights by weaving a host of programs: plays, sketches, interviews, topical discussions, music, *kathās*, etc.[62] He enjoyed his work a lot and experimented with new and better methods of communication. He even started publishing a monthly broadcast journal titled *Tharanga Ranga*, with the detailed list of all programs.[63] H. K. Ranganath, who in those years collaborated with him at the broadcasting station, states: "It might appear as an exaggeration but the Kasturi era of Kannada broadcasting was indeed, its golden era."[64] Apparently, it was Kasturi who invented the name Akash Vani (lit. "sky-voice") for the station, a designation that was wholeheartedly approved by its director, M. V. Gopalaswamy, and later officially adopted by *All India Radio* in 1956. The term *Akash Vani,* truly an appropriate metaphor, has stuck to this day.[65]

Despite these brilliant achievements, due to some friction with Gopalaswamy who wanted him to cancel a program that he thought might hurt the sensibility of some VIPs—which Kasturi refused to cancel—in 1944 he was abruptly fired and his place was taken by Prof. A. N. Moorthy Rao, a colleague at Maharaja's College. As a further punishment, from 1944 to 1946 he was sent to an Intermediate College in Shimoga, then a malaria-infested highland region, where notwithstanding all difficulties he continued to actively promote projects of rural uplift.

In 1946, he was finally posted to the Intermediate College in Bangalore where he taught history and also lectured on the constitutional and social history of Britain to the students of the Central College. S. Ramaswamy, former professor of English at Bangalore University, recalls: "Na. Kasturi was my Professor of History in the Intermediate College, Bangalore, in 1948–49 and I can never forget his enthralling Greek and Roman History classes, so full of facts but at the same time periodically punctuated with his humor. I never knew that history—ancient history at that—could be so alive and contemporary."[66]

Even before he reached the age of fifty Kasturi had become a celebrity in the cities of Mysore and Bangalore, having attained considerable fame throughout Karnataka. For more than a decade, he toured the region extensively in the company of well-known artists, scholars, and students, participating in music and dramas.[67] He was a versatile figure who held many pens in his pocket: that of a history professor, a dedicated social worker affiliated to the respected Ramakrishna Mission, an esteemed litterateur and novelist, a popular humorist, an actor, and even a successful journalist and radio programmer. H. K. Ranganath writes that he "catered humor to Kannadigas on a regular basis for over a half century. One of the great fortunes of my life was my association with him."[68] In 1981, Kasturi was the recipient of the State Sahitya Academy Award for his contributions to Kannada literature, being reputed to be among the best humorists of the State of Karnataka.[69]

From Despair to Fulfillment, from Ramakrishna to Sathya Sai Baba

In August 1947, just a few days after India had attained independence, a heartrending tragedy hit Kasturi and his family. Due to an attack of typhoid fever he lost his younger son Venkatadri (1929–1947),[70] the darling of his heart and a brilliant student who was in his third year at the Engineering College in Bangalore. Kasturi, his wife Rajamma and his mother Janakamma proved inconsolable.[71] Whereas their house used to overflow with "spiritual vibrations" in the worship of Shri Ramakrishna and the god Veṅkaṭeśvara of Tirupati[72]—their family deity (*kuladevatā*)—they now decided to give away all the pictures enshrined in their *pūjā* room. They felt that since god had given them up by taking away their dear son, he had no more place in their hearts and home.

Kasturi first heard about Sathyanārāyaṇa Rāju, alias Sathya Sai Baba (1926–2011; Telugu: Satya Sāyibābā), the young guru of the village of

Puttaparthi (Telugu: Puṭṭaparti) in the Anantapur District of Andhra Pradesh, by one Gopi who was a friend of his son Venkatadri and a devotee of the saint. A few days after learning of his friend's death, Gopi had rushed to Puttaparthi and told Sathya Sai Baba about it.

In those days Puttaparthi was a tiny hamlet. If, today, by car it can be reached from Bangalore in approximately three hours, back in the 1940s the village was not easily accessible. From Bangalore one could go by train only as far as Penukonda. From there, an occasional bus took passengers to Bukkapatnam. From Bukkapatnam via Karnatanagapalli, one had to take a bullock cart and cross the Chitravathi River[73] in order to reach Puttaparthi. The journey of about one hundred miles from Bangalore took an entire day, and even up to three days in the rainy season.[74]

Sathya Sai Baba gave Gopi a few packets of sacred ash (*vibhūti*)[75] for the distressed parents, and Gopi immediately brought the *vibhūti* to Kasturi. But the latter reacted negatively, refused to take the ash and instead gave it to a neighbor who he knew kept an image of Sai Baba[76]—the saint of Shirdi (d. 1918) of whom Sathya Sai Baba was believed to be the "reincarnation"—in his shrine. Reminiscing about those tragic days, many years later Kasturi recalled his thoughts: "Who is this Baba? Which Baba can help me now? My tragedy cannot be saved by any Baba or any vibhuti now. I don't use the vibhuti."[77]

Soon afterward, one Mr. Iyer, an aged kinsman of Kasturi who along with his family was a staunch devotee of the young Baba, assured him that the saint's *vibhūti* was efficacious and could quench their grief and bring them solace. The wife of Kasturi's first son, M. Venkata Narayana Murthy (1923–1983), was the daughter of Iyer's cousin, and thus Iyer—whom Sathya Sai Baba nicknamed "Potti," that is, the dwarf—had free entry into his home.

But Kasturi was not moved by Potti Iyer's narratives of the guru's alleged powers. All the miraculous stories of materializations, healings, mindreading, etc. aroused in him only pity at Potti Iyer's gullibility, and he considered him a fanatic. As per Ramakrishna's teachings, he was suspicious of anyone who claimed to "perform" miracles (*camatkārs*, lit. "astonishments").[78] Following the rationalist inclination of the Ramakrishna Mission and Vivekananda's disregard for miracles—which the latter regarded as the greatest stumbling blocks in the way of truth—Kasturi criticized this display of powers as a devious demonstration which had nothing to do with authentic saintliness. This criticism will constantly be moved against the guru of Puttaparthi, whose miracles were his "visiting cards."[79] Moreover, in an impertinent twist of humor Kasturi noticed that the term *Sai* itself was quite inappropriate: "I told the old man that 'Saayee' conveyed a curse in the Kannada region: the imprecation, 'Get thee gone and die.' "[80] In later years, Kasturi remarked:

> My sense of humor was so stupid and sharp that I even ridiculed Him. In Kannada, the language of Karnataka where I was, "Sai" was an ominous word meaning death. I was saying, "How can anybody call out a person whose name is death? So long as Kannada is spoken in this area, He has no entrance! It is out of bounds for Him!"[81]

A more persuasive advocate of the young Baba, however, turned out to be Potti Iyer's grandson, T. P. Balachandran. A brilliant graduate of St. Joseph's College, he studied Indian history and the British Constitution under Kasturi's guidance in order to prepare himself for admission into the Indian Administrative Services. His intellectual qualities coupled with his mild temperament and soft-spoken nature endeared him to both Kasturi and his wife, who started thinking about the possibility of him marrying their daughter Padma (b. 1934) and becoming their son-in-law. The professor did not lose time, and more than once suggested to Potti Iyer that his grandson should wed Padma.[82] Meanwhile, listening to Balachandran's enthusiastic accounts of Sathya Sai Baba's deeds kindled Kasturi's curiosity and he finally agreed to take a look at the Baba the young man was fascinated by.

It so happened that in June or early July 1948 Balachandran convinced Kasturi and his family to accompany him and Potti Iyer's party to see Sathya Sai Baba. At the time, the guru was in Bangalore visiting the house of one Thiruvenkatam Setty, located on Bull Temple Road.[83] At this first *darśan*,[84] which lasted no more than ten minutes, Kasturi was not particularly impressed. Sathya Sai Baba sat on a sofa, silent, and due to the crowd that surrounded him he could only see from a distance his huge bluff of kinky hair. On the way back home, having witnessed the astounding loyalty of Potty Iyer's party to the young guru, he confided to his wife Rajamma: "These people consider this silent Sai as their Master. If he says a word, these people will agree to receive Padma into their home."[85]

Figure 1.2. Sathya Sai Baba in Bangalore in 1948.

By this time, Kasturi had realized that the Iyers were not at all interested in his daughter. Only their guru could have them change their minds, though he knew too well that this was mere wishful thinking. Indeed, T. P. Balachandran's parents had other plans and hoped to find a more prosperous match for their son. Kasturi recalls:

> They feared that my bank passbook was too thin to provide the dowry that their son could earn. In truth, the father had, on his own initiative, volunteered, in a friendly way, to explore for a son-in-law for me! I took this promise as a soft soothing device.[86]

Though the professor and his family led a comfortable life they were certainly not rich.[87] Kasturi was therefore stunned when, a few weeks later, he was told by Parameshwara Iyer—Balachandran's father—that a few nights before he had had a dream in which the guru summoned him to go and meet him in Bangalore the very next day, to whose "order" he had unhesitatingly obeyed. He explained to the bewildered professor that the moment Sathya Sai Baba saw him he reprimanded him severely, saying that he should have not turned aside Kasturi's proposal. The guru stated: "She [Padma] is a very good girl and you must go and get him [Balachandran] married with that family. Her father is a Professor and their house is near Wilson Garden. . . . This is my *agya* (command)!"[88] Parameshwara Iyer solemnly concluded: "He wanted me to ask your pardon and to tell you that your daughter shall wed my son."[89] Kasturi could scarcely believe his ears. He was overjoyed to hear the news and yet wondered at how the guru of Puttaparthi could possibly know his name and heartfelt wish. He asked Parameshwara Iyer: " 'Did he mention my name?' . . . 'Yes,' he replied. 'Your name and your daughter's name!' "[90]

In July 1948, when Sathya Sai Baba was again in Bangalore at the house of Sri Purnaiya,[91] chief commercial manager of the South Indian Railways, Potti Iyer offered to take Kasturi to see him. The professor earnestly wished to thank the guru for interceding, unasked, on his behalf. This time he had a personal contact with Sathya Sai Baba, who immediately smiled at him and called him in for a private interview. Kasturi writes that the day was a Friday, so it could have been either July 2, 9, 16, 23, or 30 (one of the last three dates being more probable). Initially, he was suspicious of the young guru. He recalls:

> I desired to know whether he could recognize the Kasturi whom he pretended to know so well. So, I sat amidst some young men from the Indian Institute of Science, full fifteen yards away from where I made Iyer sit. Baba was in the inner room where Bhajans were being sung. . . . We heard the Arathi bell which announced the close of the Bhajan. My neighbors told me that Baba will be coming along the line of seated devotees, with the camphor flame on a silver plate. Everyone can then "warm his hands"; He would halt before each person. While passing, he might say, "Go into the hall," to a few. And, later, he grants interviews to those thus chosen. My temperature rose

> as he approached me. Will he? Will he not? Oh! How tender those feet! What a sparkle in those eyes! He smiled . . . the smile of recognition, of welcome! He spoke! "Go in," in Tamil. We were about six persons in the hall. One by one, he called us into an inner room, I was the fourth. He closed the door himself and we were together. He gave me an affectionate pat, as if I was a long lost friend![92]

Here follows Kasturi's record of the guru's momentous words to him and of his reaction:

> "You are glad I fixed that boy? You wished that I intercede with Potti Iyer and make them agree. You lost a son, poor fellow! This boy will be a son-in-law and a son to you. Do not worry. I know you have not got from the University the status that you deserve. Very soon, you will receive that too. Your old mother will be happy now . . ." He placed his hand on my shoulder. He stood facing me . . . "Have the wedding at Puttaparthi. Come and tell me whatever you need. And . . . after retiring from the University, come and stay with me. You can write my *Jiva charithra*, Biography," He said. "Me?" I ejaculated. "Yes. I shall tell you whom to consult for details—parents, brothers, kinsmen, neighbors, teachers, etc. I shall also help." . . . Was this a reprimand, a dig at my decrying him, a clarification, a joke at my conceit as a writer, a warning that I should not merely prattle in Weeklies, a call to come to grips with my destiny?[93]

Kasturi was mesmerized and stunned into silence at this torrential disclosure. The young guru had read him like an open book, immediately recognizing him and blessing him. As he says:

> It was too good to be true, too sweet to swallow, too sudden to sink in, too light to keep in mind! O! the gifts He showered! The wedding of my daughter, the acceptance of my request, the gracious offer to advance my official status, the chance to write a book on His childhood, boyhood and youth! Yes, it was no dream, no projection of my wish, no hallucination called forth by a muddled subconscious. "It was real God-send" said Iyer.[94]

When he came out of the interview room he was a changed person, cleansed of all his previous prejudices and cynicism. Sathya Sai Baba had conquered his heart and from this moment he would consecrate the second half of his life to his new master. He was a mature man of fifty and his guru a youth of twenty-one.[95] Kasturi synthesizes his condition at the time when the guru of Puttaparthi called him with these telling words:

> [H]e broke open my heart's door, so that He could get in. I was a devotee of Ramakrishna Paramahamsa and Vivekananda, a good man not capable of harming anybody, a teacher in a college, being the wisest in the class room putting something in children's head, doing my spiritual practices, proud of my intellectual abilities. I was also a writer of humorous essays, teasing everyone, rudely pointing out people's bad deeds.[96]

Looking back critically at himself, he writes:

> The sense of humour that had earned for me a mini-niche in the Hall of Fame at Delhi and Bangalore had easily trespassed into the forbidden field of ridicule and lampoon. . . . My involvement in the teaching profession for 34 years had planted and promoted in me the occupational diseases of dogmatism, authoritarianism, morbid uppishness and, to coin a word, philoflatterism. I suffered like all teachers from the incurable book-worm disease; and also from the inevitable slovenliness and "absence of mind."[97] . . .
>
> [W]hen I fell at the Feet of Swami [Sathya Sai Baba], I fell, because I was heavy with pride. My heart was sour. My habits were slovenly. My smile was a mask. My looks were tinged with malice and misogyny. My steps were unsure and my goal was kaleidoscopic and hazy. The only *sadhana* I knew was *Seva* but perhaps I adopted it because it inflated my ego. I laughed at the idiosyncrasies and pomposities of others not realizing that I spotted these because I myself had them.[98]

In particular, the totally unexpected assignment of writing the guru's biography was a shock to him, like the dropping of a bombshell, and worried him a lot. Meanwhile, he and his wife recovered a picture they had hidden of the Swami, dusted it and framed it, and installed it at the center of their home altar, which for long had been empty. It marked the beginning of their new lives as devotees of Sathya Sai Baba.

Kasturi began visiting the guru at the so-called Old Mandir of Puttaparthi, and on the occasion of his first stay he witnessed one of his "materializations": in the evening, on the sands of the Chitravathi River, the young Swami created a rosary (*japamālā*) for a lady devotee. It was not a "new creation," however, but purportedly the very same *japamālā* that her dying mother had given to her years ago and that she had lost four years back in Bangalore![99] According to Mrs. Vijayakumari—an early devotee who first met Sathya Sai Baba in 1945—though at the Chitravathi the guru let Kasturi decide where he should sit and allowed him to ask

Figure 1.3. The inner shrine of the Old Mandir in Puttaparthi in 1949.

for whatever item he desired, the various "materializations" he witnessed did not dispel his doubts. She relates that on different occasions Kasturi asked the guru for an out-of-season fruit, for rain, and for a rainbow, and always got what he asked for.[100]

According to Padma, her father became fully convinced of the guru's powers when, once, the latter, having come out of a trance, told him of having been to far-off Dehradun—the capital city of the State of Uttarakhand in northern India—to give *darśan* to a dying devotee, the mother of one Dr. Krishnamurthi. A few days later, he discovered that all details given to him by Sathya Sai Baba were true, being confirmed in a letter written by Dr. Krishnamurthi himself. Kasturi got so excited that he ran home from the Mandir shouting "*Ānandam, ānandam*! We have got Bhagavan," that is, god, and for some time he refused to take any food.[101] The guru's trances and purported "extracorporeal journeys" were frequent in the early days.[102]

Undeniably, Kasturi's conversion was determined by the holy man's initiative. Nonetheless, the events which prepared it, namely, the tragedy of his son's death and the thorny issue of his daughter's marriage—a pivotal rite of passage[103]—were powerful (re)activators of religious experience and guru seeking.[104] It is precisely in times of mourning and existential crisis that the search for authoritative guidance and ultimate meaning surfaces, so as to psychologically relieve oneself of the painful stress and find comforting answers to one's misfortunes. If Kasturi felt unjustly abandoned by god when faced with the tragedy of Venkatadri's demise, and as a forsaken lover decided to turn his back on him, his rejection of religion and gurus was in fact only temporary. As deeply religious a person as he was, his existential turmoil marked the transition from his old allegiance to Ramakrishna—a guru to whom he could not turn but in his thoughts and prayers—to his new, enthusiastic consecration to the young Sathya Sai Baba: a living guru, indeed a *bolte calte dev*, "a speaking and walking god," to whom he could effectively relate.

The wedding of Padma and Balachandran, whom everyone called Chandran, was joyously celebrated in Puttaparthi on October 11, 1948,[105] day of Dasara,[106] and the bridegroom's parents, in their loyal acceptance of the guru's command, did not demand any dowry from Kasturi.[107] Meanwhile, Sathya Sai Baba's promise of higher status and salary in Kasturi's career came true and he was nominated Principal of the Intermediate D.R.M.[108] College of Davangere, a city located in the very center

Figure 1.4. Janakamma, N. Kasturi's mother, with the marriage party on the way to Puttaparthi.

Figure 1.5. Padma and Balachandran (center) on the day of their wedding in Puttaparthi's Old Mandir. They are surrounded by Balachandran's parents (left) and Padma's parents, Rajamma and N. Kasturi (right).

of Karnataka, where he continued to successfully implement his educational programs, service activities in favor of the Harijan community, and *kathās*.[109] His daughter Padma remembers:

> His heart always went out to the deprived and desolate. He would create *Harikathas* . . . on noble people and perform them in the prisons, and such would be the impact of his inspired presentations that the stone-hearted would soon start sobbing and repenting, even prostrating in front of him. And he liked the *Harijans* . . . the most. He would take his enthusiastic and energetic band of boys and entertain those in misery, bringing on their faces forgotten smiles.[110]

Kasturi worked in Davangere for approximately five years, from 1949 to April 1954, after which he retired at age fifty-seven, after more than thirty years of teaching, on a monthly pension of 180 rupees.[111] During this time, Kasturi visited his beloved Swami in Puttaparthi as often as he could.

On December 16, 1951, per Sathya Sai Baba's request, he gave in the guru's presence his first speech in English, on the occasion of the inauguration of the Sri Sathya Sai Baba District Board High School in Bukkapatnam, a town a few kilometers away from Puttaparthi: it was the holy man's first venture in promoting spiritual values in education. At the time, Kasturi could neither read nor write in Telugu and Sathya Sai Baba would correspond with him in Kannada. With the help of a Telugu teacher, he had written down in Malayalam script the Telugu version of his Kannada speech: but the young guru dismissed his text telling him that the speech should be "heartificial," not artificial. He was thus allowed to speak in English.

On the occasion, the guru referred to Kasturi as a PhD. When the embarrassed professor told him that he did not hold a doctoral degree—he correctly presented himself as an MA, BL—Sathya Sai Baba much to his amazement said that he was a PhD of Puttaparthi University.[112] From then onward, Kasturi's determination to master his lord's language became so strong that in subsequent years he quickly learned to speak and write in Telugu.

Soon after Kasturi's retirement, the guru advised him to go on a pilgrimage to North India together with his mother and wife. After he returned, he and his family—as per their wish—were allowed to reside in a small apartment close to the Prasanthi Nilayam Mandir, thus becoming inmates of Puttaparthi's ashram from 1954.[113]

Figure 1.6. Sathya Sai Baba with, from left to right, Kasturi's son M. V. N. Murthy, N. Kasturi, M. V. N. Murthy's two children, Kasturi's mother Janakamma, and Kasturi's wife Rajamma.

With the exception of a fifteen months' stay in Bangalore,[114] from then on Kasturi would permanently reside in Prasanthi Nilayam as the closest disciple and collaborator of Sathya Sai Baba, dedicating all his energies to propagating the guru's gospel. When he settled down at the ashram, he didn't bring a single copy of his earlier works with him but gave them away to various libraries. He used to say: "It all belonged to my previous life (Poorva Ashram). Why should I carry them here?"[115] In his autobiography, he writes:

> I must cast overboard the tawdry academic acquisitions that weighed me down. They did not help me at all to rise in Baba's estimation—the University Degrees, the pedagogic self-esteem, the metropolitan veneer of hollow etiquette. . . . I strove to make myself fit to be in the Divine presence by eschewing my ancient and deep-rooted *Koravanji* tendency to seek out the

> failings and faults of others. I attempted to divert my sense of humor towards discovery, within the layers of rough rocks, the precious veins of goodness and godliness.[116]

Though he continued cultivating his studies of Kannada literature,[117] deep down in his heart he knew that Prasanthi Nilayam "was indeed the consummation and crown of human aspiration for the Supreme Peace."[118] When Kasturi's colleagues and friends learned of his new loyalty they generally reacted negatively, receiving him with derisive smiles of contempt and sighs of pity.[119] They wondered how one whose prodigious irony was long used to puncture the reputation of fakes and fakirs, tricksters and quacks, could fall a prey to a Baba half his age. They were utterly dismayed at having lost such a brilliant personality and they did not care to inquire.[120] About them, Kasturi says:

> I have very great sympathy for such, for I too demurred, doubted and disbelieved with all the sarcasm and satire found in the Kannada novels, dramas, and essays which I wrote and published, from 1923 to 1948. For many years, I too in my stupid pride did not make any effort to meet Him.[121]

Some of his acquaintances, however, came to Puttaparthi out of curiosity. In his devotional enthusiasm, he wished to introduce them to his Swami, hoping that his charisma and the "wave of his hand," that is, his miracles, would transform them and dispel their prejudices. But only a few were attracted to the young guru. Among them was Kasturi's student G. P. Rajarathnam (1909–1979), who was to become a distinguished Kannada poet and writer, especially popular for his children's poems: when Kasturi definitely moved from Karnataka to Andhra Pradesh, he characterized it as a movement from a lake to the ocean.[122]

In the beginning, Kasturi had problems in reconciling his old faith in Ramakrishna and Vivekananda[123] with his new devotion for Sathya Sai Baba, and inevitably felt guilty. Although Swami Siddheshwarananda had complimented him on securing the young Swami as his master,[124] most of the monks and fellow devotees at the Ramakrishna Mission saw him as a defector and did not approve of his new spiritual allegiance to a "miracle-worker." In the early days, Sathya Sai Baba once told Kasturi's wife:

> Poor fellow, he does not know that it was Ramakrishna who brought him to me. Ramakrishna rewarded him for his long loyalty. He led him up to Kottacheruvu (He said this with a chuckle; Kottacheruvu is a village about 9 km. from Puttaparthi). He guided him to this place and left, for the Guru has nothing more to do once his pupil has come face to face with Himself.[125]

In a similar vein, Shirdi Sai Baba likened his devotees to birds with strings tied to their legs:

> I bring my men to me from long distances under many pleas. I seek them and bring them to me. They do not come (of their own accord). . . . However distant—even thousands of miles away—my people might be, I draw them to myself, just as we pull birds to us with a string tied to their foot.[126]

Through this analogy the saint of Shirdi highlighted the invisible tie that binds a disciple to his guru. This connection is believed to span many lifetimes and to transcend the constraints of space and time. Along these lines, Sathya Sai Baba once told Kasturi that he knew him even before his latest birth in Kerala.[127] Ultimately, the retired professor was fully convinced of the truth of his guru's words[128] and came to recognize him as *both* Ramakrishna and Vivekananda, "for He had in Him the love and power, the innocence and the wisdom, the mergence and the resurgence, the calmness and the courage that they embodied."[129]

The fundamental difference he envisioned between Ramakrishna and Sathya Sai Baba was that whereas the former had seen god, the latter *was* god. He used to say that the guru Ramakrishna acted as a nurse, taking him to "Mother Sai."[130] Moreover, he came to realize that there was no contrast in their teachings since in essence they taught the same, perennial truths.[131] If the monks of the Ramakrishna Mission advocated sobriety and a more rational, intellectual approach to religion, Kasturi was quick to respond that the powers of the Swami of Puttaparthi were not acquired but rather inborn, being the natural characteristic of a full, divine incarnation, that is to say, a *pūrṇāvatāra*.[132] From the early 1950s, the future hagiographer would take pains to articulate Sathya Sai Baba's uniqueness with respect to all other gurus and Babas.[133]

2

Narayan Kasturi's Magnum Opus

Sathyam Sivam Sundaram, Parts 1 & 2

The Hagiographer's Task

The importance of Kasturi's opus derives from Sathya Sai Baba's having explicitly appointed him to the task, acknowledging his work as *the* authoritative text on his life.[1] He, significantly, wrote it in English and it became such a success that along the years it has been reedited many times—Part 1, issued in November 1961, had reached its eighth edition by 1980—and widely translated in many languages, in India and throughout the world, selling hundreds of thousands of copies. Kasturi himself felt the urge to write the Kannada version of it, whereas the Telugu translation of Part 1 was undertaken by Brahmasri Doopaati Thirumalachar and published in February 1963.[2] The readers that Kasturi had in mind were Hindus of the urban middle and upper classes/castes, from which all leading representatives of the guru's constituency came, as well as a general Western audience. To his Indian and Western readers, the hagiographer took pains to present Sathya Sai Baba as the incarnation of all the values that Hinduism stood for and simultaneously as the universal savior that mankind was waiting for.

Kasturi's seminal work became a bestseller, being recognized as a sacred scripture by millions of devotees in India and abroad: to this day, practically all accounts on Sathya Sai Baba's life and deeds—to date, more than 340[3]—depend upon it.[4] Kasturi compared himself to Govind Raghunath Dabholkar alias Hemadpant (1859–1929), the author of Shirdi Sai

Baba's *Śrī Sāī Saccarita*, who had obtained the blessings of the saint to write his Marāṭhī opus.[5] He envisioned a correspondence between the miraculous events that were at the origin of the *Śrī Sāī Saccarita*—Shirdi Sai Baba warding off a cholera epidemic by grinding wheat and having it distributed all around the village boundaries so as to establish an unsurpassable magic circle—and his own work:

> When Kesava told us how cholera was kept out of Puttaparthi by the Pandari Bhajan Group, I felt that the "Sathya Sai Sathcharitha" which He had assigned to me was being inaugurated with an identical Leela, for, this Baba was that Baba come again.[6]

Devotees regarded and still regard Kasturi as a contemporary Vālmīki (the anthill sage to whom the composition of the *Rāmāyaṇa* is ascribed) and Vyāsa (the mythical compiler of the *Veda*s and author of the *Mahābhārata* and *Purāṇas*). In November 1958, Sathya Sai Baba himself addressed him as Nannaya Bhaṭṭa, the first and foremost poet (*ādikavi*) of Andhra Pradesh who flourished in the eleventh century.[7] Kasturi's characteristics made him an ideal instrument for promoting Sathya Sai Baba's life and mission, he being a Brahmin with a full-fledged Vivekanandian outlook, who rather than Sanskrit—of which he only had a basic knowledge—had a full command of English and who understood religion in terms of devotion to god and service to man. Like many middle- and upper-class Indians of his times and the Anglophone gurus of the colonial era, Kasturi regarded English as the language of religious propaganda.[8] Moreover, he was a popular writer and a respected intellectual, a university professor of history with remarkable literary skills.[9]

For him, writing the normative biography of Sathya Sai Baba was an act of embodied devotion toward his beloved guru.[10] The opus, which was to be instrumental in attracting myriads of people to the saint of Puttaparthi, was under preparation for a long time. He began collecting data on Sathya Sai Baba's childhood and early life already in 1948, much before his retirement, and meticulously carried on his research for several years, interviewing the guru's family members, teachers, classmates, as well as various villagers and early devotees. In particular, he transcribed many hours of conversation with Sathya Sai Baba's mother Easwaramma (1890–1972), his father Pedda Veṅkama Rāju (1885–1963) and his brother Seshama Rāju (1911–1985) about his early years.[11]

If in the late 1960s the American playwright Arnold Schulman (b. 1925), who was the first Westerner to write an informative and well-researched book on the guru of Puttaparthi, observed that "Baba has forbidden his family and devotees to talk about his childhood,"[12] nonetheless his conclusion was that "it wasn't Baba's intention to suppress information he was afraid might be revealed," but rather that his intimation "was the simplest way to keep Baba's well-meaning devotees from distorting the truth. A slight exaggeration here, an embellishment there could ultimately contaminate his entire reservoir of credibility."[13] Moreover, Schulman noted that "for every story of Baba's childhood there are any number of conflicting stories and . . . it is no longer possible to sift out the facts from the legend."[14]

And yet to argue that "all records of his early life have been effectively erased, so the hagiography is his biography," as Tulasi Srinivas does,[15] is an oversimplification: what we have is, rather, an inextricable fusion, a mixture (*miśra*) of biographical testimonies, primary sources,[16] and hagiographical superimpositions. Kasturi's work is clearly not a scientific, scholarly biography but a *Carita,* a devotional account. Nonetheless, it must be clear that his aim was to offer a factual, historical testimony. The faith of the devotee and the intellectual acumen of the history professor are fused in his narrative. The result is neither a purely mythical story nor a scientific treatise. The purpose of his narrative—which ties together immanence and transcendence—is constitutively twofold: to offer a chronological presentation of the main facts of his hero's public life and, most importantly, to illumine these data through a theological interpretation of who "he really is," delving into the significance of his advent. That Kasturi did not offer a bibliography and a detailed list of the sources upon which his opus is based does not automatically imply an absence of factuality nor, as Bill Aitken writes, that "the demands of objectivity . . . are invariably ignored."[17]

Kasturi proposed to publish the first part of his *Carita* in 1954, but Sathya Sai Baba demurred, saying: "Readers will not accept the book as authentic. . . . They will treat it as a fairy tale. . . . Wait. . . . Now, people will doubt your sanity; later they will blame you for under-estimating Me."[18] Actually, it is not so much the case that Kasturi, caught in a hagiographical furor, exaggerated his guru's claims. It is, rather, the other way round, namely, that Sathya Sai Baba's claims were so "in-credible" and mind-blowing that the exaggeration, if any, rested with them and with the guru of Puttaparthi himself. It was only in 1959 that Sathya Sai Baba decided that the time was ripe and told Kasturi that he could proceed to write and publish his official biography:[19] up until then no books were available on him.[20] The first of the four English volumes was released on November 23, 1961, on the occasion of the guru's birthday.[21] Sathya Sai Baba's attentive supervision deserves notice: the canonization of his charisma is something he accurately programmed and directed. The guru was an active participant in the realization of his official biography, given that he himself on various occasions told his own story—both in public discourses as well as in private conversations—and Kasturi took notice of all of his autobiographical/"autohagiographical"[22] anecdotes, integrating his text accordingly.

The professor's opus is a work of careful literary composition which follows the criteria of the *Carita* genre and is therefore uninterested in offering details on the sociopolitical context of the village of Puttaparthi and surrounding areas.[23] Its aim is to glorify Sathya Sai Baba through the presentation of his deeds, which have none of the wrong decisions that characterize an ordinary existence. And yet, on occasions the guru admitted making mistakes. Thus, he admitted his error when, as a boy at the village fair of Pushpagiri, he gambled and—thanks to his omniscience—collected twelve *annas*[24] from a man who sat on the roadside with cards spread on a cloth. He remarked: "In My heart, I felt that I should not have resorted to this type of gambling. We are all aware how much Yudhishtira had to suffer by playing the game of dice."[25] But in his biography, when referring to this episode Kasturi simply comments: "He could have secured more, but he sympathized with the poor fellow whose earnings were not much."[26] Overall, what we have is a presentation of the saint's exemplary life aimed at inspiring devotion so as to map the way to salvation (*mokṣa*). In and of itself, the *Carita* is revealing of the author's own mentality and major concerns.

In order to assess the hagiographer's strategy and uncover his depiction of the holy man's charisma, focus must be placed on the text's narrative structure, its style and contents. Its programmatic title *Sathyam Sivam Sundaram* [*Truth Goodness Beauty*], is itself revealing, bearing a distinct Upaniṣadic touch and at the same time recalling the "transcendentals" of Christian Scholasticism, that is, the triad of *verum* (the domain of theology), *bonum* (the domain of ethics), and *pulchrum* (the domain of esthetics), as per the famous dictum *Ens et unum, verum, bonum, pulchrum convertuntur*, "Being and one, the true, the good, the beautiful are interchangeable." The hagiographer informs us that, after struggling long to find a title worthy of his lord, he first thought of it "one night while waiting for a train on the platform at far-off Davangere,"[27] and the guru immediately approved of it. Kasturi believed that this holy triad, which recapitulates the reality of *Brahman*—possibly adumbrated in *Bhagavadgītā* 17.15b, wherein that speech which is true (*satya*), pleasing, and beneficial (*priya-hita*) is praised as the austerity of speech—was inspired to him by Ramakrishna via Vivekananda, and that it was ultimately due to Sathya Sai Baba's grace. Kasturi was convinced that the title was transmitted to him by Guru Maharaj (Ramakrishna) through Vivekananda, given that the words *Satyam Shivam Sundaram*, in this order, are found in a talk on *bhaktiyoga* which the latter delivered in America, while speaking of the arrival of the Avatar of the "Lord of Truth," which the hagiographer identified with Sathya Sai Baba. It should be noted that in a *kīrtan* sung by young Vivekananda in October 1882 and August 1883 in Ramakrishna's presence we already find these words, albeit not in the same order: "Oh, when will dawn for me that day of blessedness/When He who is all Good [*Sivam*], all Beauty [*Sundaram*], and all Truth [*Sathyam*],/Will light the inmost shrine of my heart?"[28] In the end, Kasturi came to the conclusion that it was none other than his beloved Swami that had revealed to him this most appropriate title.[29] The guru of Puttaparthi will often utilize this triad in his public discourses. For instance, we read: "You resent being called 'liars' for your true nature is 'Truth'; you resent being described as 'ugly,' for your true nature is 'Beauty'; you resent being damned as 'evil' for your true nature is 'Goodness.' " And Kasturi comments: "Thus, He inspires us to worship the Universal source of all Truth, Beauty and Goodness, from which we have been individualized and separated,"[30] namely, Sathya Sai Baba qua *Brahman*. Last but not least, Kasturi must have thought it most appropriate that the initial word in the title of his work be *Sathyam* since it honored his hero's name and the primacy of truth as per the teaching of M. K. Gandhi (1869–1948) that "truth is God."[31] Along the decades the triad of *Satyam Shivam Sundaram* has become most popular and is nowadays the official motto of Doordarshan, the Indian government television. Already in 1977, *Satyam Shivam Sundaram* was the title of a film by Raj Kapoor (1924–1988). There is no doubt that the renown of Kasturi's opus played a pivotal role in its diffusion.

The English prose of *Sathyam Sivam Sundaram* is fluent and captivating. Nowadays, as back in the 1960s, it is widely appreciated by devotees all over the world.[32] Despite repetitions across the four volumes—a characteristic feature of the *Carita* genre—the narrative proceeds smoothly throughout, interspersed with a touch of humor. Deborah Swallow's characterization of Kasturi's opus as "simplistic, unsophisticated, and intellectually undemanding," strikes me as unfair. Moreover, when she qualifies it as "dramatic" and "exaggerated," she clearly fails to appreciate its literary genre.[33] At times, the hagiographer expresses himself in a stereotyped coded parlance that is reminiscent of Victorian English: a rhetorical trait which is typical of many Hindu movements of the period.

Following a chronological order from Sathya Sai Baba's birth onward, the *Carita* is characterized by a succession of miraculous happenings of the saint's public appearances, which are constitutive of his persona (purported "materializations," out-of-body experiences, healings, etc.).[34] As Lawrence

Figure 2.1. One of the earliest purported "materializations" of Sathya Sai Baba: a picture of Shirdi Sai Baba surrounded by Kṛṣṇa, Rāma, Śiva, and Hanumān.

A. Babb noticed, it is impossible to write about the private life of Sathya Sai Baba: "All that is available are his public surfaces, his self as formally presented as an object of devotional attitudes of his followers."[35] Despite the sometimes hectic interspersing of events, anecdotes, and memories that build up the narrative—another typical characteristic of the *Carita* genre—a clear sequence is discernible.

Given the frequency of the miraculous in Sathya Sai Baba's daily interaction with people, Kasturi's narrative strives to chronicle what he envisages as actual facts, that is to say, he does not at all think of his account as a fiction or fairy tale[36] but as a series of real, documented events, even though people reading it might question his sanity.[37] Even a more objective follower such as Robert Priddy, who in subsequent years dismissed Sathya Sai Baba as a fraud, defines Kasturi's biography as "a highly-reliable sourcebook for the major events in Baba's life through about 1980."[38] By the same token, Kasturi's portrayal of the saint's life endeavors to link/identify Sathya Sai Baba with all the major gods of the Hindu pantheon such as Kṛṣṇa, Viṣṇu, Śiva, and Rāma. As is typical of all hagiographies, the narrative is interspersed with references to the *Vedas*, the *Rāmāyaṇa* and *Mahābhārata* epics, the *Bhagavadgītā,* and the *Purāṇas*.

From his childhood, the guru of Puttaparthi is presented as a veritable "miracle machine,"[39] everything being suffused in the miraculous. Kasturi supports his interpretations by presenting episodes in the saint's public life that he actually witnessed, as well as by quoting Sathya Sai Baba's own utterances. When he needs to rely on others' testimonies the hagiographer bases himself on firsthand accounts, including many from the earliest years. Even the holy man's teachings (*upadeśa*), which are definitely what Kasturi values most and endeavors to articulate in full detail for his readers, are inevitably enmeshed in a vast array of *signa* and *portenta*: with their power of attraction, the miracles are the pathway to the teachings, since they acquire "heaviness" (*gurutva*) through them. Here is how the guru himself explained the raison d'être of his miracles:

> The purpose of the *chamatkaras* is to lead you to the ultimate reality. The four steps are: *chamatkara* (miracles), *samskara* (development and evolution of character/nature), *paropakara* (selfless service) and *sakshatkara* (self-realization). Therefore, these *chamatkaras* are not an exhibition, but a divine manifestation with a divine purpose and they cause no harm to the world.[40]

Sathyam Sivam Sundaram, Part 1: An Overview

Part 1 of *Sathyam Sivam Sundaram*, comprising fifteen chapters plus a short epilogue (*For You and Me*), extends for more than 290 pages in its 1980 edition and covers the first thirty-four years of Sathya Sai Baba's life, from his birth in 1926 up to 1960. As is customary of a *Carita,* the guru's biographical events are transfigured as stages of a predestined triumphant tour, a *vijaya* (lit. "victory"). Kasturi underlines how Sathya Sai Baba himself said that in his life the first sixteen years would be marked mainly by *līlā*s or divine pranks, the next sixteen by *mahimā*s or miracles, and the subsequent years by *upadeśa* or teaching.[41] At the same time, in order to stress his hero's divinity the hagiographer presents Sathya Sai Baba as a timeless character, avoiding having to treat his story in developmental terms. His extraordinary nature is constantly underlined: throughout his opus he is simply the best, superior to all, and everything about him is perfect. From the outset, Kasturi highlights his universalism by saying that he encompass all names and forms of god: Rāma, Kṛṣṇa, Buddha, Jesus, Allāh, etc. As he notes:

> I was struck by the universality of His Mission and Message, for, He said, during His discourse, "I am the Servant of every one"; "You can call Me by any Name, I will respond; for all names are Mine. Or, rather, I have no particular Name at all"; "Even if I am discarded by you, I shall be behind you"; "In My view there are no Nastikas [atheists] at all; all are existing by and for the Lord; denying the Sun does not make Him disappear."[42]

Universalism appears to have been a characteristic of the guru of Puttaparthi from the very beginning. Recalling his schooldays, he once observed:

> I used to sing the following prayer song daily in the school assembly:
> Moment to moment, Thy clarion call resounds.
> Hearing Thy magnanimous words,
> The Hindus, Buddhists, Jains, Parsees, Muslims and Christians,

> Come to Thy throne, from East and West,
> Making the garland of love.
> Hail to Thee who unites all humanity!
> Hail to Thee who controls the destiny of Bharat!
> Hail to Thee! Hail to Thee!
> Thus, I taught the unity of all religions in the world even in those days.[43]

In V. C. Kondappa's Telugu poem *Sri Sayeeshuni Charitra*, dated 1944, the earliest record of Sathya Sai Baba's prophetic words when he was just eighteen, we read:

> Sai devotees have no caste or religion. Anyone can become his devotee to realize the goal of life. Sai will enter *samadhi*[44] after uniting disparate religions and giving happiness to the country. He will enter *samadhi* and take birth again after some years and give devotees the path of *jnana* (knowledge).[45]

Kasturi emphasizes his lord's compassion as well as his "democracy"/equality and poverty, so as to counter the early, frequent accusation directed at him of being partial to the rich and the aristocratic.[46] He tends to minimize or show the inconsistency of all criticisms moved to Sathya Sai Baba, underlining how the guru succeeded in overcoming all doubts, obstacles, and falsities.[47]

It must be noted that in the early days Sathya Sai Baba had to face various oppositions, in Puttaparthi as well as in his family.[48] Many people in the village and surrounding areas were hostile to him and tried to degrade him.[49] Even the village Karnam,[50] perhaps jealous of his wife's devotion to him, opposed him.[51] It is reported that locals poisoned him,[52] set fire to his hut,[53] and that young Sathya was even forced to move out from the village and live for some time in caves.[54] Even Kasturi's daughter recalls how in 1950 many people who lived in and near Puttaparthi did not believe in the young guru and openly criticized him.[55]

In this regard, mention should be made of Seshama Rāju's doubts and fears, which he expressed as early as 1947 in a letter to young Sathya in which he cautioned his simple village-grown brother about the outcome of his activities and bade him to discontinue them.[56] He had witnessed his many wondrous acts and had seen his constituency grow, and yet

> he had also noticed how Baba's devotees came only from distant places like Bangalore, Mysore, Madras and Kuppam and very few from their own neighborhood. In fact, he felt scared and concerned when those from nearby places scorned Baba for His acts. He was further troubled by the derogatory comments being written about Baba from time to time.[57] The brother in him could not take these insults lying down because he believed the meteoric rise of Baba would soon have a crashing fall.[58]

The young guru of Puttaparthi responded to his queries in a famous letter dated May 25, 1947. Here are some excerpts taken from it:

> It is not good for us to go by the words of ignorant people. Sathya will always be victorious, untruth will never succeed. . . . You might also have read the life stories of great legendary characters and incarnations of God and known of the great trials they have faced. It is quite natural for Mahatmas to be criticized in this manner. Why do you worry of such things? . . . Self-reliance and beneficial activity—the great ones tread upon these paths. As long as we are engaged in promoting the welfare of devotees and allotting them the fruits of their actions, why at all should we worry? . . . I have a "Task:" to foster all mankind and ensure for all of them lives full of Ananda [Bliss]. I have a "Vow:" To lead all who stray away from the straight path, again into goodness and save them. I am attached to a "Work" that I love: To remove the sufferings of the poor and grant them what they lack . . . I will never give up those who attach themselves to me. When I am thus engaged in my beneficial task, how can my name be ever tarnished, as you apprehend? . . . But I will not let go of my hold, my assurance and my nature. The work, for which I have come, concerns me. Fame or ill fame, good or bad does not concern me. All are alike to me. . . . Nobody can do me any harm. Do not think even in your dreams that I will be spoilt. . . . You will witness my full glory in the coming years.[59]

The first five chapters of Kasturi's opus—titled *In Human Form*, *Balagopala*, *Natanamanohara*, *Gana-Lola*, and *The Serpent Hill*—present the divine hero's extraordinary conception,[60] birth, and infancy up to his school years, culminating in the startling disclosure of his being none other than Sai Baba, belonging to the Āpastamba Sūtra[61] and Bharadvāja *gotra*,[62] which then triggers the beginning of his mission in October 1940.[63] Few in Puttaparthi and surrounding villages had ever before heard the name Sai Baba. Yet, there are testimonies that the holy man was known and worshipped by local people, even in Sathyanārāyaṇa's family. It is reported that his second cousins, Veṅkaṭarāma Rāju and Veṅkaṭasubba Rāju, were *bhakta*s of Sai Baba long before he made his announcement. Moreover, "Venkatasubba Raju often read aloud the biography of Sai Baba. Whenever he erred while reading, Raju [Sathyanārāyaṇa] would point out the mistake and explain where the mistake was, including page number, stanza or line."[64]

Ratnākaram Sathyanārāyaṇa Rāju, alias Sathya Sai Baba (Telugu: Satya Sāyibābā), was the fourth of the five sons[65] of Pedda Veṅkama Rāju and Meesaraganda Easwaramma, who were cross first cousins (the related parents of each cousin being brother and sister).[66] The hagiographer points out that the Ratnākaram[67] family was a poor family of vaiṣṇava peasants. Kasturi's account follows his guru's words and states that Sathya Sai Baba's family was very poor, to the extent that as a child he did not even own a pin to keep a torn shirt held together.[68] In his reminiscences, the guru of Puttaparthi recalls how in the old days he could not afford to eat rice like his other school friends, but had to content himself with some semi-solid *ragi sankati* (gruel made of *ragi* cereals).[69] Apparently, his mother Easwaramma also belonged to a poor family.[70] This notwithstanding, there has been debate as to whether Sathya Sai Baba's family was actually so destitute. The caste to which he belonged, the house in which he lived, and the good level of education of several of his family members point to the fact that young Sathya was not so underprivileged. Anyway, his family was certainly not rich, the only wealthy family of Puttaparthi being that of the Brahmin Lakshmīnārāyaṇa Rao, the village Karnam.

The Rāju or Bhatrāju caste is a Kṣatriya subcaste of bards and genealogists, most of whom are Viṣṇu worshippers. In Andhra Pradesh, the Bhatrājus are generally occupied as teachers or speaking minstrels, popularizing sacred literature through songs and poetry. The Rājus are said to be a "scholarly race" in Kondappa's earliest account of Sathya Sai Baba's life.[71] The only non-Brahmin caste that performs the duties of a religious teacher, they are described as touring around villages making ex tempore verses in praise of householders and being rewarded by gifts of old clothes, grain, and money. It is said that some Bhatrājus "have *shotriems* and *ināms*," where *shotriem* is land given as a gift for proficiency in the *Vedas* or learning, and *inām* is land given free of rent.[72]

The miraculous is the characteristic of the saint's early days. For example, we are told that as the newborn baby lay in a bed of piled clothes, the parents noticed that it was being raised and lowered by something underneath; when they investigated, they discovered a cobra beneath the clothes. Such a story is aimed at equating young Sathyanārāyaṇa with Viṣṇu, and the cobra with the divine serpent Śeṣa/Ananta. Sathyanārāyaṇa's grandfather, the pious Ratnākaram Kondama Rāju, is said to have been the first to realize his grandson's divine nature.[73] This man had musical and dramatic talent and was quite respected in the village, knowing by heart many Epic and Purāṇic myths culled from Sanskrit and Telugu sources.

Sathyanārāyaṇa would frequently fall into states of trance, and was especially fond of writing and singing devotional hymns (*bhajan*) and enacting epic and mythological plays. By the time he was sixteen he had written hundreds of *bhajans*, which he taught to his friends: their chanting will always characterize the daily routine at Puttaparthi's ashram.[74] From the early years, Sathyanārāyaṇa used to identify himself with Viṣṇu-Kṛṣṇa, Rāma, Śiva, and practically all deities of the Hindu pantheon.

Kasturi's account is replete with *mirabilia,* first and foremost a bewildering variety of "materializations." Besides *vibhūti* or ashes—his most characteristic miracle, which he would give out as a token of his grace—he is credited with the production of various types of food, fruits, candies, oil, rings, stones, rosaries, pictures, statues of deities, watches,[75] etc. For instance, it is reported that he would bless the food or touch it and say *akṣaya*, "unending," and the vessels containing the food would never become empty.[76] Moreover, the hagiographer emphasizes his acts of healing all sorts of diseases as well as his ability to grant visions. Indeed, the saint's infancy and childhood is saturated with the miraculous and is reminiscent of Kṛṣṇa's youth, who is the veritable paradigm of Kasturi's portrayal.[77] Emblematic of Sathya Sai Baba's wonders in his early years is the so-called *kalpavṛkṣa* or wish-fulfilling tree, a particular tamarind tree to which he took his friends and devotees and from which he playfully extracted all kinds of different fruits, in and out of season.[78] A major characteristic of the guru was his unpredictability, which Kasturi presents as part and parcel of his divinity, that is, of his *līlā,* his play as a trickster.

Accordingly, Sathya Sai Baba would often instruct his devotees to "love his uncertainty."[79]

Chapter 6, *Bala Sai*, focuses on young Sathya striving for legitimacy and succeeding in affirming his divine status: first in Puttaparthi—with the establishment of his first temple and headquarters (Old Mandir) in 1945—then in Bangalore[80] and other southern areas through his visits to towns and major pilgrimage places such as Tirupati, the celebrated abode of lord Veṅkaṭeśvara, which he first visited in January 1946.[81] Fifteen years later, in 1961, Sathya Sai Baba publicly declared that his native village of Puttaparthi would become another Tirupati.[82] Significantly, the guru's devotees highlight the similarity of the areas of Puttaparthi and Tirupati: of its towered gateways (*gopurams*), shops, blocks of flats, and general appearance.[83] In fact, already in 1943 young Sathya prophesized to *pūjārī* Lakshmaiah the future glory of the village which, as per its myth, he described as "a very holy place, but under a curse. Sai will save it. . . . The Sai *Pravesh* (advent) will make it the *Prasanthi Pradesh* (region of peace)."[84]

Chapter 7, *Prasanthi Nilayam*, lit. "Abode of Highest Peace," is devoted to Sathya Sai Baba's Prayer Hall (*mandir*)—intended for meditation (*dhyāna*) and the practice of the remembrance of the divine name (*japa*)—which was inaugurated on the occasion of his birthday on November 23, 1950: it took two years to build.[85] Within this new *mandir*, two lifesize oil paintings of Shirdi Sai Baba and Sathya Sai Baba dominate the scene,[86] with a silver figure of the saint of Shirdi at the center, while portraits of various gurus and god-men decorate the walls, among whom are Ramakrishna and Vivekananda.[87] Kasturi recalls: "I was commissioned by Baba to bring from Bangalore large-sized portraits of Zoroaster, Buddha, Mahavir, Jesus, Shankara, Ramanuja, Madhwa, Nanak, Meera, Surdas and Basava."[88] In order to reinforce the Prayer Hall's universalism, the hagiographer remarks: "Except *bhajans* twice a day . . . there is no regular worship, as is generally done in places where an idol is installed and consecrated. There are no fixed rites . . . nor are there any scheduled prayers or *pujas* . . . the Hall is a prayer Hall, no more, no less."[89] He further notes how the *bhajans* that are sung therein are not all in praise of Sathya Sai Baba or Shirdi Sai Baba but "cover the widest possible range . . . through all the *avatars* of Vishnu, Shiva, Ganesha, Vitthala, Venkatesha and other forms of godhead, and they are sung in Telugu, Tamil, Kannada, Hindi and Sanskrit."[90] Verse 6 of the "waking up" song (*suprabhāta*) daily chanted by devotees at dawn in honor of their guru—a ceremony that appears to have started in the 1950s—already hinted at the cosmopolitanism of the Sathya Sai Baba movement, while reaffirming the primacy of the *Vedas*: "Saintly people who have arrived from different countries with great desire to see your divine form are rejoicing by chanting sacred Vedic hymns. O Lord Satya Sai, may the morning be auspicious!"[91]

At the very beginning of chapter 7, Kasturi writes that on June 29, 1959, Sathya Sai Baba inaugurated his ascetic grove (*tapovana*) by placing a thick copper plate with mystic markings (*sasana*) underneath a *vaṭa* tree, declaring that "Yogis who have reached a certain stage of Tapas will automatically come to know of this tree and this Sasana and they will be drawn by a mysterious force towards the Tapovana."[92] In his universalist élan, Kasturi observes that the tree "may be said to symbolize Sanathana Dharma [the "eternal religion"], for its branches reach out in all directions and draw sustenance from every type of faith and every spiritual striving."[93]The hagiographer also offers a description of three festivals celebrated at Prasanthi Nilayam, namely Dasara, Mahāśivarātri (with *liṅ-*

Figure 2.2. The anointment ceremony of Sathya Sai Baba by his father and mother on the day of his birthday inside the *mandir*. Kasturi (right) assists them.

gas—the aniconic, ellipsoidal stones symbolic of Śiva—"materializing" in the guru's body and emanating through his mouth)[94] and Sathya Sai Baba's birthday, and notes how all who come to Puttaparthi have the privilege of earning an interview with Baba in his private room, before departure.

Chapter 8, *From Cape to Kilanmarg*, presents Sathya Sai Baba as presiding over the 9th All-India Conference of the *Divine Life Society* (DLS),[95] held in June 1957 in Venkatagiri, a town of cultural distinction situated near Kalahasti and not far from Tirupati: this was a most important event in the young Swami's promotion of himself and was sponsored by the *rāja* of Venkatagiri, an early *bhakta* of his.[96] As Kasturi notes, when Swami Satchidananda of the DLS, who was then in Tiruvannamalai, came to know that Sathya Sai Baba would preside the Conference "he was taken aback, for on inquiry there, he learnt that He was versed only in Magic (!) and that he was a poor speaker, at best. 'But,' said Swami Satchidananda, 'I discovered soon that my informant was profoundly ignorant.' "[97] Along these lines, Kasturi quotes the testimony of a pundit present at the conference, who began his discourse by saying: "I came to Venkatagiri . . . primarily to meet Sri Sathya Sai Baba, for I had heard all kinds of versions of his greatness and I jumped eagerly at the chance to test those versions. In short I came to defy! And I am going back, deified! I am happy to confess this before you and I apologize to Baba for my error."[98]The pundit especially appreciated the guru's speech and his poetic depiction of the flute (*muralī*) on Kṛṣṇa's lips:

> "What would you like to be in the hands of the Lord?" He asked and He Himself suggested the answer. "The Flute." He wanted everyone to be straight without any crookedness, hollow without any pride or individuality or will or idea or self, to inhale only the breath of God, to transmute that breath into melodious music that confers on every fleeting moment the Joy of Eternity.[99]

Kasturi then mentions Sathya Sai Baba's tour of various places in the South (Kodaikanal, Cape Comorin, Kanyakumari, Madurai, etc.), characterized by his "materializations" and miraculous deeds, and ends the chapter by presenting his first trip to North India in July 1957,[100] his guru having been invited to Rishikesh by the DLS president himself, Swami Sivananda[101] (1887–1963), for whom Sathya Sai Baba "materialized" a large quantity of

Figure 2.3. N. Kasturi with Sathya Sai Baba on the Kashmir hills.

sacred ash (*vibhūti*), especially meant for improving his health, and a magnificent *rudrākṣa* garland of 108 beads.[102] The young guru stayed at Swami Sivananda's hermitage for a week, and this is the only ashram of another saint he is known to have visited. Near Rishikesh, Sathya Sai Baba paid a visit to Swami Purushottamananda, a disciple of Swami Brahmananda of the Ramakrishna Order who lived as a recluse in a cave (*Vasishtha guha*) for thirty years, and blessed him with an effulgent vision of himself as Viṣṇu Padmanābha.[103] Then via Delhi he went to Mathura and Brindavan, and later left for Srinagar and visited the Kashmir Valley. He was back in Puttaparthi by mid-August.

Chapter 9, *The Wave of the Hand*, as well as chapter 13, "*I am Here*," are dedicated to the guru's miracles, especially the "materializations" of *vibhūti* and of a plethora of other items through the waving of his hand,[104] and his trances and extracorporeal journeys, which are described as a common feature of his early days and a tangible proof of his omnipresence.[105] Kasturi constantly counters the depiction of Sathya Sai Baba as a magician and underlines how the performance of miracles is only natural to a divine incarnation: they are intended as a sign of his love and grace (*kṛpā*), and are not meant to impress people.[106] Once, the guru himself explained his "materializations" to John S. Hislop:

> Some objects, Swami creates in just the same way that he created the material universe. Other objects, such as watches, are brought from existing supplies. There are no invisible beings helping Swami to bring things. His sankalpa, his divine will, brings the object in a moment. Swami is everywhere. His creations belong to the natural unlimited power of God and are in no sense the product of yogic powers as with yogis or of magic as with magicians. The creative power is in no way contrived or developed, but is natural only.[107]

Moreover, Kasturi notes that the guru does not attribute much importance to these "materializations," miracles being compared to a mosquito on an elephant, and insists on the insignificance of these feats, viewing even his astonishing cures as incidental and secondary.[108]

On the other hand, it should be noted that to scholar and amateur magician Lee Siegel—for whom Sathya Sai Baba is "the modern version of the court magician who, in traditional India, was consulted by the king"—one Prof. Bhagyanath told: "Sai Baba's uncle was a street magician. Young Sai Baba . . . began by doing little magic tricks, but since he wasn't very good, it wasn't likely that he would have much success on the stage. That's why he became a god-man. It's easier to be a god-man than a stage magician. And certainly the income is better."[109] In the available sources, however, I was unable to find any confirmation to the claim that an uncle of the *guru* was a street magician.

Kasturi's tenth chapter, *The Same Baba*, is the longest—forty-two pages—and entirely dedicated to proving Sathya Sai Baba's claim of being none other than Shirdi Sai Baba, the latter portrayed as the paradigm of the holy man. The guru of Puttaparthi emphasized his oneness with Shirdi Sai Baba especially in his early years. In a discourse he held in Prasanthi Nilayam in October 23, 1961, we read:

> When this *Mahashakti* [Great Power] decided to leave the previous body in 1918, Kaka Saheb Dikshit was told that in 8 years' time this will take birth again. Abdul Baba was also

> informed that in 7 years this will appear in Madras State. Three months after the *samadhi* (burial), appearing before a house at Kirkee, the declaration was made in answer to a query that the body had passed away, "The body has gone, but I will appear again." It was said 6 months after the *samadhi* when there was an appearance at *Dwarakamayi* [the Shirdi mosque] with the familiar tin can. Word was sent to Das Ganu and Mhalsapathi. The statement made to Kaka Saheb was that the Manifestation will take place after 8 years, not "as an eight-year-old-body." It was recorded so because Kaka Saheb relied on his memory and wrote it down only much later. The figure 7 came true; for this body incarnated in 1926 after spending ten months in the womb. So even the statement of 8 years made to Kaka Saheb is true.[110]

The hagiographer will reiterate the sameness of the two Sai Babas in all his works.[111] Through this peculiar claim, the guru of Puttaparthi legitimated his charisma, with no need to refer himself to any *guruparamparā* or genealogy of spiritual descent. Kasturi emphasizes their similarities—such as their habit of handing out sacred ash (*vibhūti*, *udī*) to their devotees—and stresses the identity of their mission, Sathya Sai Baba having come to expand the Hindu-Islamic brotherhood of his predecessor so as to include in his universalist message all the major world religions.[112] He reports testimonies from devotees of Shirdi and lists several parallel miracles and episodes, which are found in the *Śrī Sāī Saccarita* of G. R. Dabholkar. Though stressing the religious universalism of both Babas, Kasturi significantly tends to Hinduize the Shirdi *faqīr*. Following his guru, who presented Shirdi Sai Baba as a Brahmin,[113] he also regards him as such, minimizing his Sufi identity.[114] In fact, the composite personality of the Shirdi saint was the result of a complex, nondual process of identity development, part and parcel of the pluralistic, integrative religious landscape of the Deccan, freely combining Sufi and Hindu elements.

Chapters 11 (*The Rain Cloud*), 12 (*Sai Sadguru*), and 14 (*The Sarathi*) are dedicated to a presentation of the guru's teachings (*upadeśa*) and of his mission as *avatāra*. Within a nondual (*advaita*) framework, primary importance is given to devotion (*bhakti*), the practice of meditation (*dhyāna*), and the constant remembrance of the guru's name (*nāmasmaraṇa*). Emphasis is placed on adherence to the human values of *satya* (truth), *dharma* (righteousness), *śānti* (peace), *preman* (love), and *ahiṃsā* (nonviolence) and on the practice of *sevā* in the realization that everyone is a "walking temple," meaning that god is present in all beings.[115] In Sathya Sai Baba's organization, *sevā* will primarily take the form of village aid especially through the creation of schools for the education of the young based on the teaching of human values, as well as through sanitary assistance, that is, the establishment of dispensaries and hospitals.[116] The assumption is that selfless service to humanity is the royal path leading to the realization of divinity. In order to explain the spirit of unconditional love, which should animate true *sevā,* the guru said: "When a thorn pricks the foot, the hand automatically goes to remove it without creating an obligation for the foot to thank the hand. That is how service must be rendered."[117]

Kasturi reiterates throughout his opus that Sathya Sai Baba's message is universal and coincides with the "eternal religion" of *sanātanadharma.*[118] In particular, chapter 14 presents the monthly magazine *Sanathana Sarathi*, devoted to the moral and spiritual uplift of humanity through *Sathya, Dharma, Santhi*, and *Prema*, which Sathya Sai Baba inaugurated on February 16, 1958, day of Mahāśivarātri. The creation of *Sanathana Sarathi* was the guru's idea, and Kasturi was not the "apparent originator of the project" as Tulasi Srinivas suggests.[119] As the magazine's editor, Kasturi had the responsibility of publishing the guru's speeches and writings, translating them from Telugu into English.[120] The series of articles on particular subjects, called *vāhinī*s (lit. "river," "stream"), were later published as separate booklets (such as *Prema Vahini, Dhyana Vahini, Prasanthi Vahini, Jnana Vahini*, etc.).[121] It should be noted that the guru of Puttaparthi delivered his first public speech in Karur, Tamil Nadu, in October 1947.[122] However, it was only starting in 1953 on the auspicious occasion of Vijayādaśamī that Sathya Sai Baba began to deliver public speeches on a more or less regular basis. Here is the *incipit* of his first discourse, as edited and translated into English by Kasturi:

> When I was at Uravakonda, studying in the high school, you know I came away one day, threw off My books, and declared that I have My work waiting for Me. The Telugu pundit described the incident of that evening to you all, in his speech. Well, that day, when I came out publicly as Sai Baba, that first song I taught the gathering in the garden, to which I went from the

Telugu pundit's house, was: *Manasa bhajare guru charanam, dustara bhava sagara taranam*. I called on all those suffering in the endless round of birth and death to worship the feet of the guru, the guru that was announcing Himself, who had come again for taking upon Himself the burden of those who find refuge in Him. That was the very first message of Mine to humanity. *Manasa bhajare*. "Worship in the mind!" I do not need your flower garlands and fruits, things that you get for an *anna* or two; they are not genuinely yours. Give me something that is yours, something which is clean and fragrant with the perfume of virtue and innocence and washed in the tears of repentance![123]

Figure 2.4. The first photograph of young Sathya taken after his declaration of being Shirdi Sai Baba.

The first eleven volumes of his discourses, titled *Sathya Sai Speaks*, cover almost twenty years (from 1953 to 1972) and were all compiled by Kasturi from notes he took on the spot.[124] With few exceptions, the guru would address his audiences in Telugu.

The final, fifteenth, chapter, titled *The Mission Begun*, presents Sathya Sai Baba's installation of a marble image (*mūrti*) of Shirdi Sai Baba in the Naga Sai temple of Coimbatore, on February 26, 1961. As Kasturi notes, this was the first time he formally installed for daily worship an image of his "previous manifestation" outside of Puttaparthi. This solemn act was part of his wide strategy to legitimize himself as none other than the Shirdi saint, which especially in the early years was a major concern of his. It is noticeable that he never visited Shirdi, though he claimed to have been there on several occasions in his "subtle form," through his "extra-corporeal" journeys. The closest he came to Shirdi was when he visited the ashram of the female guru Sati Godavari Mata (1914–1990) located in Sakori, a few miles away from Sai Baba's locale.[125] In presenting the installation of the Shirdi Sai Baba image in the Coimbatore temple, Kasturi quotes his guru's words, which he interprets as an epoch-making declaration:

> It is really amusing, is it not, that I should install this idol of Myself. I am doing so for a very valid reason. This day deserves to be inscribed in letters of gold, for this function is the beginning of a new era, the Sathya Sai era, when Saayi will become the Hrudayasthayi, the Inner Motive Force of all. The only other instance of a similar kind, of an Avatar installing an idol of the Lord, is that of Rama installing the Iswaralinga at Rameswaram. That was done as a preliminary to the destruction of Ravana and the Rakshasas, to the Divine task of Dushtanigraha. Now, I am doing this as a preliminary to the other task of all Avatars, Dharmasthapana, the Establishment of Dharma in the World.[126]

After a short stay in Madras, around the end of March 1961 the guru embarked on a second tour of North India in order to visit the holy sites of Ayodhya and Benares. Besides Kasturi, who as usual was part of his entourage, in his visit he was accompanied by another prominent devotee, the governor of Uttar Pradesh, B. Ramakrishna Rao,[127] an indicator of the guru's growing status and prestige.[128] At the famous Viśvanātha temple in Benares he applied sandal paste and *vibhūti* to the sacred *liṅga,* which he "materialized" on the spot, and by the wave of his hand he also "produced" a wonderful jewel, symbolic of the primeval sound *om,* with which he garlanded the *liṅga.* He then visited Allahabad and returned to Puttaparthi on April 8, halting one day at Tirupati on his way back.

In the month of June, the guru decided to embark on another tour of the Himalayas and to visit Badrinath. Both Kasturi and his wife joined the Swami on his *yātrā.* Even on this occasion, the governor of Uttar Pradesh accompanied him and met him in Haridwar. In the temple of Badrinath, he "materialized" a four-armed statue of Viṣṇu Nārāyaṇa, a golden lotus, and a *netraliṅga,* said to have been one of the five *liṅga*s originally brought there from Mount Kailāsa by the famous Śankara (eighth century CE), the founder of nondual (*advaita*) Vedānta.[129] Kasturi writes that "[the *netraliṅga*] had been charged with immense potency and the Temple was consecrated anew by the Manifested form Himself."[130] On that occasion the guru scolded the professor for his poor knowledge of Sanskrit *mantra*s. Kasturi's daughter recalls:

> Those present [at the Badrinath temple] were asked to recite the *rudram, namakam,* and *chamakam* [the *Śatarudrīya* hymn of the one hundred names of Rudra-Śiva]. Swami turned to my father and said, "What Kasturi? Don't you know all these? *Papam* [Shame], all your life has been spent in ABCD—how could you learn all these?" After returning from Badri my father learnt these *mantra*s and recited them in Swami's room, while Swami was taking bath. My father used to offer leaves of "*bilva*" and "*tulsi*" at His Lotus Feet every day after Swami's bath. What a chance—offering *puja* to the *Sakshat Shiva*![131]

The Badrinath Temple Committee accorded welcome to Baba at a special meeting in the temple premises, and the governor of Uttar Pradesh translated his discourse into Hindi. After this visit he proceeded to Nainital via Rishikesh and Haridwar, and finally came back to Puttaparthi on July 4.

A Critical Evaluation of Part 1

From a critical reading of Kasturi's text a few significant points emerge. In the first place, though he tries to minimize it, it is clear that the young charismatic was seen with diffidence and even hostility by other competing movements, such as the Ramakrishna Mission and the Divine Life Society, who placed emphasis on a thorough knowledge of Vedānta and Yoga philosophy rather than simple devotion.[132] Moreover, Sathya Sai Baba was generally ignored and even regarded with contempt by the bastions of Hindu traditionalism, such as the Śaṅkarācāryas. When a disciple of a famous Śaṅkarācārya wanted to come to Puttaparthi, the latter refused to give him permission, saying, "No, no going and doing *namaskaram* to a person who is not even a Brahmin! He is a Kshatriya, the other caste!"[133] Though he was not a Śūdra—as even recently David M. Knipe has erroneously written—he was nonetheless considered "a lowly rank to the high-born Vaidikas and presumably one not to be touched."[134] Sathya Sai Baba's mother Easwaramma, who was worried that her son might be caught in rivalries with other monastic orders, had pleaded with Kasturi to act as his defensor![135]

The reasons why the guru of Puttaparthi was perceived negatively by other religious institutions, modern as well as traditional, had to do with his originality and "difference," and were basically three: (1) His not being linked to any established tradition (*paramparā*), he being a charismatic "freelance" who, besides not being a Brahmin, also claimed to be the reincarnation of a "Muslim" saint and miracle worker; (2) His emphasis on powers (*siddhi*) and the miraculous, which was seen with suspicion and even embarrassment by the religious elites; (3) His presumed ignorance, since he came from a remote village and had not received any formal education and training as a renunciant. Although an anti-erudite tendency is a characteristic of many neo-Hindu gurus, the saint of Puttaparthi was met with prejudice by most religious leaders and groups—be they the Ramakrishna Mission, the Divine Life Society, or other organizations—and disparagingly viewed as naive and uneducated. In 1972, Kasturi himself, evidencing the "human side" of his lord, told American devotee Howard Levin that "he's only from a village" and could not know "the difference between a photostat and a forgery."[136]

Acutely aware of his own marginality,[137] young Sathya Sai Baba had to look elsewhere for social recognition and economic support in promoting his avatāric career. His first sponsors were the Brahmin wives of the village chieftain and, later, some wealthy families of the urban middle and upper classes/castes—mainly in Bangalore—as well as a few rich rulers of ex-princely states such as the *rāja* of Venkatagiri, the Chincholi royal family, the *mahārāja* of Sandur and the *mahārāja* and *mahārāṇī* of Mysore.[138]

Indeed, it was thanks to the sponsorship of *bhaktas* such as the pious Subbamma[139] and Kamalamma, wives of the Brahmin Lakshminarayana Rao, the local Karnam, that his worship was launched with the building of the *Sri Sai Baba Bhajan Temple,* inaugurated on December 14, 1945.[140]

The seminal invitation to the Divine Life Society's meeting of 1957 did not come from the DLS monks—who were rather prejudiced against him—but from the *rāja* of Venkatagiri, Velugoti Sarvagna Kumar Krishna Yachendra Bahadur (d. 1971), who was a staunch devotee of his. Young Sathya Sai Baba had given a vision of himself as god Rāma to the faithful *rāja*—Rāma being his "chosen deity" (*iṣṭa-devatā*)[141]—and, as his eldest son and heir V. V. Rajagopal Yachendra (b. 1924) remarked, "if our family is one of the few holding on to the older traditions, it is entirely because of Swami, because he wants these traditions to go on. He is the custodian of Dharma. He is Rama Himself."[142] In Kasturi's autobiography *Loving God*, the DLS monks' initial displeasure with him is not softened as in his hagiography but spelled out in open terms:

> For them [the DLS Swamis] he was only a protégé of the Raja and nothing more. In order to please the Raja who hosted the Conference, they were obliged to accept Sri Sathya Sai Baba, though as far as they knew, He had no academic distinction or Acharya status.[143]

In an effort to legitimate him, the 1983 Reprint of Part 1 of Kasturi's work encloses a smiling photo of Sathya Sai Baba with Swami Sivananda which was taken when the former visited him at his ashram in Rishikesh. Both of them are seated side by side, with the young guru of Puttaparthi in the foreground. Sivananda, however, sits on a higher seat with his arms resting on the armchair, in a dominating position. While Sivananda wears a flower garland, Sathya Sai Baba holds one in his hands.[144] This is the only picture that I know of in the various editions of *Sathyam Sivam Sundaram* in which the saint of Puttaparthi figures side by side with a famous master who was indeed "the pioneer among modern gurus."[145] As Bill Aitken rightly argues, his visit to Swami Sivananda was "a pilgrimage that marked his entry into mainstream Hindu culture,"[146] since it lent credibility to his claims to divinity. Throughout his opus, Kasturi is careful to articulate the purported superiority of his beloved Swami with respect to Sivananda and all other teachers, as when he notes that "while Sivananda greeted Baba with folded hands, as is his wont, Baba acknowledged the greeting with the Abhayahashta [the gesture of fearlessness], that has conferred Santhi on thousands of troubled souls."[147]

In order to affirm himself and counter all objections and criticisms, the guru's traditionalist strategy—which is Kasturi's strategy throughout *Sathyam Sivam Sundaram*—was to present himself as *stricto sensu* an *avatāra*,[148] god incarnate. This purported transcendence has always been the basis of his authority. Grounded in his *avatāra*hood, he was able to bypass the mediation and agency of established religious institutions and neo-Vedānta movements. This was a most significant move, given that prior to him the explicit claim to *avatāra* status by a guru had never been articulated in such an emphatic way. From the early years, Sathya Sai Baba's persona and sayings reflect his self-awareness of being a divine descent whose charisma and teachings—grounded in devotion, *bhakti*, and nondual (*advaita*) Vedānta—are traditional through and through.[149]

In so doing, he posited himself as the pristine source and ultimate goal of Hinduism, of both modern neo-Hindu movements[150] as well as time-honored *sampradāya*s and *paramparā*s.[151] Moreover, in a universalist fashion he presented his advent as being the fulfillment of all world religions. His tactics were twofold: to constantly stress his divinity and, at the same time, to tolerantly encompass all religions *as if they were his own,* that is, as if they emanated from him—the "Grandfather" of them all—and to him were destined to return. In his persona he aimed at recapitulating religious pluralism and the ultimate truth of Advaita Vedānta. He argued:

> Let the different faiths exist, let them flourish, let the Glory of God be sung in all the languages and in a variety of tunes; that should be the ideal. Respect the differences between the faiths and recognize them as valid as far as they do not extinguish the flame of unity.[152]

He fully subscribed to a Vivekanandian universalism, or, better, hierarchical inclusivism,[153] given that he viewed all religions as being ultimately included in Vedāntic Hinduism, which is not thought of as a religion among others but rather as Religion itself. Thus, he exalted the *sanātana-dharma* of Hinduism as the comprehensive context for all other faiths, being understood as their source and final destiny. In Swami Vivekananda's words:

> Ours is the universal religion. It is inclusive enough, it is broad enough to include all the ideals. All the ideals of religion that already exist in the world can be immediately included, and we can patiently wait for all the ideals that are to come in the future to be taken in the same fashion, embraced in the infinite arms of the religion of the Vedanta.[154]

In Swami Vivekananda's footsteps, the guru of Puttaparthi declared: "Chronologically and logically, Vedic Dharma is the grandfather, Buddhism the father, Christianity the son, and Islam the grandson."[155] On the other hand, Sathya Sai Baba's innovation was precisely to posit *himself* as the final destination of all beings and religions, substituting his "name and form" (*nāmarūpa*) for the abstract notion of Hinduism/Vedānta. Thus, he successfully conjugated in his avatāric persona divine immanence and transcendence, proposing himself as *both* the way and the goal (as in *bhakti* theology, in which love/devotion is at the same time the way and the goal, making *bhaktiyoga* superior to all other spiritual paths).[156]

Kasturi effectively portrays the difference between his lord and other Indian saints of modern times such as Ramakrishna or Ramana Maharshi by stressing how Sathya Sai Baba never prayed or meditated, never practiced any *tapas* or spiritual training (*sādhanā*). With him, he argues, there is no question of attainments, of yogic *samādhi*s or enlightenment, since he descended into this world armed with the fullness of divinity. In *Sathyam Sivam Sundaram*, Kasturi quotes an explicit declaration of his:

> I engage in no Tapas, I have no Dhyana at all; I do not study; I am no Yogi or Siddha or Sadhaka; I have come to guide and bless all Sadhakas. . . . I did not come uninvited to this world; sadhus, saints, sages, good men of all creeds and climes called out and entreated; so, I have come. You may be seeing Me today for the first time, but, you are all old acquaintances for Me; I know you, through and through.[157]

He is thus recognized as "the form of all gods," *sarvadevatāsvarūpa*,[158] incorporating all deities and divine incarnations even outside Hinduism. The universalistic claim is that he belongs to all times and places and that he has come to strengthen the roots of all religions, to establish the validity of all paths to god. As Kasturi writes: "He is the eternal and the universal (Desa Kala Aparischinna) not limited to one country or one age."[159] Through him, all people may have direct access to divinity.

In the hagiographer's presentation of his strategic trips to the traditional *sancta sanctorum* of Hinduism—the glorious sites of Benares, Badrinath, Ayodhya, Brindavan, etc.—we witness a radical reinterpretation of the legitimizing tour upon which countless sages and saints of India have embarked along the centuries. In fact, Sathya Sai Baba does not visit these sacred sites as a devout pilgrim, but as a superior living/"movable god" who goes to meet other gods who are clearly inferior to him. Positing himself as the supreme godhead, he recognizes none other than himself in the "mirror" of the immovable *mūrti*s and *liṅga*s, which he sanctifies by his mere presence. Indeed, Kasturi writes that the underlying aim of his trips is the recharging of the gods' "old batteries": through his visits and awesome "materializations" he is said to revitalize them and restore their potency (*śakti*) to the full, he being the very reservoir of holiness.[160] Thus, the hagiographer insists on saying that he is not to be mistaken as an ordinary Baba or guru.[161] Although centered in Puttaparthi, which is elevated to the status of a modern Tirupati, his inclusive godliness radiates in all directions.[162] In Kasturi's account, Sathya Sai Baba's auspicious *parikrama* (lit. "curcumambulation")—a conventional feature of Hindu hagiography, during which the saint's confrontation with rival figures often takes place—is taken to a wholly different, superior level, since his hero meets the other gods "face to face," as it were, and deliberately avoids any kind of confrontation with religious actors, who are merely human.

The idea is that Sathya Sai Baba, being an *avatāra,* does not teach any new revelation, special *sādhanā,* or yogic technique. Rather, his message is said to coincide with the ancient, eternal *sanātanadharma* which was proclaimed by all past incarnations. As per his avatāric role, his mission is to preserve and (re)establish *dharma* (*dharmasthāpana*), and this is precisely the reason why he is not any innovator but rather a traditionalist and a conservative on fundamentals.

On gender issues, he was no feminist, and reiterated the traditional Hindu position of woman as the bulwark of spiritual culture, whose ideal should be that of a loving mother and faithful wife, subordinate to her husband, willing to sacrifice herself for her family. But he also insisted on the complementarity of male and female and, paraphrasing one of Vivekananda's sayings, pointed out that "it is not possible for a bird to fly on only one wing." Hugh B. Urban remarks: "By no means a liberal or progressive in the realm of women's rights, he warns his devotees against the evils of Western-style sexual freedom."[163]

The guru's fundamental aim, argues Kasturi, is to reawaken the consciousness of all humans to their ātmic, divine nature, and this can be accomplished solely through the power of pure love (*preman*) of which Sathya Sai Baba is said to be the perfect embodiment. Love and liberating knowledge (*jñāna*) are viewed as the two sides of the same coin, and the hagiographer skillfully links the guru's purported miraculous powers to his omniscience, thus proclaiming his innate wisdom. In this way, he can simultaneously extol Sathya Sai Baba as the embodiment of supreme love *and* knowledge: the knowledge of the *Veda*s and of all Hindu authoritative texts (*śāstra*s) but also of all world scriptures.

Sathya Sai Baba and his organization must be understood as an offshoot of the Hindu reform movements of the nineteenth and twentieth centuries. His teaching is homogeneous with a Vivekanandian universalist/inclusivist perspective, both theologically as well as ethically, and symptomatically it privileges a lay spirituality. That was the guru's shared worldview and this is the reason that our hagiographer—who was molded in that same cultural and religious climate—could find no substantial differences between the teachings of Vivekananda and Sathya Sai Baba. On occasions, the guru of Puttaparthi would explicitly quote Vivekananda as an authority. We read:

> All our scriptures assert that God is present in every one. According to Vivekananda, "God is present in all." The only thing that is manifest and common to the whole world and, in fact, governs and directs the entire universe, is Divinity. Nothing else really exists except Divinity.[164]

Sathya Sai Baba's *upadeśa* is straightforward, being grounded in Vedānta and *bhakti*. To his followers, he recommended the constant remembrance of their chosen deity (*iṣṭadevatā*) through *nāmasmaraṇa* and the implementation of human values through the practice of a variety of service activities (*sevā, karmayoga*). But ultimately the center and goal of his teachings is he himself, his irresistible charisma: all *bhakta*s were and are convinced that their final destination is to merge in him. As Lawrence A. Babb noticed, devotees care less about what Sathya Sai Baba has to say than that *he* is the one saying it: "His devotees long to see him, to hear him, to be near him, to have private audiences with him, to touch him (especially his feet), and to receive and consume, or use in other ways, substances and objects that have been touched by him or that originate from him."[165]

Although Kasturi writes that the guru of Puttaparthi does not want to be narrowly confined to a cult figure and that one can and should call him by any name,[166] the fact remains that everyone and everything are made to converge upon him, he being understood as the *alpha* and *omega*. While Sathya Sai Baba would repeatedly state that he has not come to set afoot a new cult and that he does not speak about himself in his discourses or mention the name Sai in the *bhajans* he sings, he also stressed that no distinctions should be made between the various names of god, for ultimately they are all *his* names.[167] His dictum that "there is only one religion, the religion of love, there is only one God, He is omnipresent,"[168] if on one hand underlines the universality of his message and the oneness of humanity, on the other invariably refers back to his own persona since such universality is believed to find its crowning in none other than he. As per his saying, "My life is my message,"[169] the essence of his teachings ultimately coincides with him. If it is true that he spoke against conversion from one religion to another[170] and argued that one did not at all need to become a devotee of his—since many are the ways to god and one should strive to live up to the sublime principles of his/her own religion—he invariably proposed himself to each and all, calling everyone to take refuge at his feet. Again, Sathya Sai Baba's position was attuned to that of Vivekananda: the latter saw no need for conversion since he understood Hinduism to be the mother of all religions encompassing them all, and the guru of Puttaparthi taught that each and all religions ultimately found their sustenance and fulfillment in himself.

Significantly, Kasturi's portrayal endeavors to keep together what are perceived as the traditional values of Hinduism and the democratic stances of modernity. Thus, Sathya Sai Baba is an upholder of the caste system (the *varṇāśramadharma*) and yet in his behavior and discourses he exhibits an egalitarian trait, as when he partakes food together with all people irrespective of their caste, and emphatically proclaims that the world is one family, that is, that there is only one caste, the caste of humanity (or two "castes," male and female).[171] Apparently, this was the guru's teaching and practice from the 1930s, when he was still a boy: thus, it is reported that he accepted the invitation of an untouchable and had lunch at his house.[172] In the early *Sri Sai Sathakamu*, we read: "Parama Kalyana! Sri Puttaparthi Sai! You destroy the difference of caste and religion and treat all as equal and feed them in a single row."[173] Bill Aitken observes: "An equally egalitarian outlook which remains aloof from any priestly involvement is the hallmark of both Shirdi Baba's and Sai Baba's philosophy."[174]

As Lawrence A. Babb has argued, his ideal social order is based on a noncompetitive complementation.[175] While pointing out the innate, irreducible differences among humans,[176] the guru of Puttaparthi looked at the *varṇa* and *jāti* ideology in flexible and certainly nonontological terms, that is, mainly from an ethical perspective, consistent with the way Vivekananda and M. K. Gandhi reinterpreted caste.[177] Kasturi even argues that "Swami has revolutionized [the caste system] by bringing changes in the old practices, that are restrictive and limiting."[178] Thus, the guru told to journalist Rustom Khurshedji Karanjia that in order to achieve cooperative brotherhood, "what we need today are one single caste of humanity, one common religion of love and one universal language of the heart."[179]

Sathya Sai Baba's ambivalence is constitutive of his charismatic persona, of his capacity of spanning the dichotomies—of divinity and humanity, male and female, traditionalism and modernity, etc.—and of embracing both poles. As Purushottama Bilimoria noticed: "Encountering the teacher and some of his activities, can be quite confusing, as he appears on the one hand to be the most traditionalist of traditionalists, and on the other, the most modern among moderns."[180] Several scholars have unilaterally stressed the limits of Sathya Sai Baba's syncretism/universalism, especially with regard to his conservatism over caste and gender, failing to appreciate his ability to encompass the dichotomies.[181] Such assimilative ability is part and parcel of his Vivekanandian universalist/inclusivist élan, pointing toward a postsectarian spirituality that is nonetheless solidly rooted in Hinduism.[182] In Sathya Sai Baba's own understanding of himself and his mission we witness the interplay and crossings between a reformist and a traditionalist perspective, and it is important to realize that reform as a component of religious and cultural nationalism was and is inseparable from revivalism.

Moreover, it would be wrong to view Vivekananda's—and Sathya Sai Baba's—neo-Hinduism as a misrepresentation of a supposedly "pure," traditional Hinduism or as the mere native restatement of ideas originating in the West. His work stands out as a most powerful interpretation of the supposed nature of Hinduism, since the main ingredients of his ideology were not alien but part and parcel of Indian religiosity, a defensive and at the same time proactive reaction against the onslaught of Westernization and Christian missionizing. Vivekananda's Advaita Vedānta was largely based upon its medieval and early modern developments rather than along the lines of Śaṅkara's thought, it being a dynamic and diversified philosophical school.[183] The clear-cut opposition between a "pure," static *smārta* traditionalism and a "corrupt," Westernized neo-Hinduism, which is often theorized, is simplistic and ultimately untenable given that the very idea of an ahistorical "Tradition" is an ideological fabrication. In fact, Vivekananda's neo-Hinduism is much more Indic and "traditional" than it is thought to be: it must be appreciated as an intellectually sophisticated reappropriation and reshaping of one's vast, plural heritage. In his colonial-inflected vision, Vivekananda had no alternative but to reduce India's complex, pluralistic civilization to an "essential" Hinduism that needed to be presented as nothing less than a world religion in order to meet the challenges of a Westernized world. This was inevitable, given that the rules of the game were dictated and determined by the Eurocentric context.

Reflecting Vivekananda's outlook, the very openness of Sathya Sai Baba's inclusivism was a form of self-assertion. Remembering the old days when he was just a child, the guru of Puttaparthi pointed out that even then his teaching was one and the same:

> There were a sizeable number of Muslims in Puttaparthi. They used to celebrate the festivals of Muslim Fakirs, in which the Hindus also used to participate. In that context, I used to teach the children, "It is not the religion that is important. Morality is important. In fact, morality is the life-breath of a person. Hence, cast off all your differences of religion and caste and be friendly with everyone. You also participate in the festivals of Fakirs." While I was teaching thus, one boy got up and told Me, "Raju! My parents will not agree to my participation in a Muslim festival. We are Brahmins." Then I explained, "My dear, first and foremost, you are a human being. Your religion is love and your caste is the caste of humanity. Therefore, you always keep that principle of unity as your goal."[184]

Politically, Kasturi's hero mirrored his own self and was clearly a moderate, being adverse to both the fundamentalist, right wing theorists of *hindutva* as well as the atheistic ideology of communism.[185] The guru repeatedly voiced his objection to *hindutva* and the Hindu Right.[186] When in 1999 in relation to the so-called Ayodhya dispute (culminating in the destruction of the Babri mosque by Hindu extremists during a political riot on December 6, 1992, on the assumption that the mosque had been sacrilegiously built on the site of Rāma's birthplace) Ashok Singhal, general secretary of the *Vishwa Hindu Parishad* (VHP), begged him to reveal the exact birthplace of Rāma so that Hindus could erect a temple there, Sathya Sai Baba replied that the true birthplace of Rāma, like the one of all mortals, was none other than the womb of his mother Kausalyā.[187] The guru advocated what R. K. Karanjia defined as "spiritual socialism."[188] Despite Sathya Sai Baba's proximity to contemporary Hindu nationalist leaders such as Atal Bihari Vajpayee (b. 1924), his self-representation and teachings are incompatible with the ideology of the *Bharatiya Janata Party* (BJP) or the *Vishwa Hindu Parishad.*

His ideals of a universal religion coinciding with universal ethics, of social service, and of education in human values, are an expression of a global, inclusivistic worldview, which is Vivekanandian through and through.[189] As Joanne Punzo Waghorne remarks: "[Vivekananda's] ontology was so thoroughly universalistic—and yes, literally *inclusive*—that his nationalism never merged into an exclusive ethnicity."[190] I think this same conclusion applies to a cosmopolitan guru such as Sathya Sai Baba. It is precisely in this neo-Vedāntic light that one must understand his statements of nationalistic pride, India being viewed as the leading country in the spiritual revolution destined to unite all the nations of the world. As he repeatedly stated, it is only in India that *avatāra*s take birth, given the country's spiritual eminence from Vedic times.[191] In order to stress his point, he would even quote the words of authoritative Western orientalists such as Friedrich Max Müller (1823–1900): "India is the only Heaven; what is not in India is nowhere."[192] Sophie Hawkins's assertion that "Sai's universalist agenda neatly disguises a Hindu nationalism in much the same way that the rhetorical appropriation of a democratic equality obscures a fiercely gendered and classist ideology," is way off the mark.[193]

Sathyam Sivam Sundaram, Part 2: An Overview

Part 2 of *Sathyam Sivam Sundaram* was released on March 29, 1968, on the occasion of the Hindu new year's day. Comprising fourteen chapters, the last one being but a short epilogue (*The Call—The Response*), it extends for 266 pages in its 1981 edition and covers seven years of Sathya Sai Baba's public life, from 1961 to 1967. Chapter 1, titled *Resume (1926–1961)*, is, as the name indicates, a brief summary of Part 1. In it, Kasturi gives ample space to the letter young Sathya wrote on May 25, 1947, to his elder brother Seshama Raju in answer to his fears, which the hagiographer presents as a manifesto of the guru's mission (he specifies that the letter is in his possession). Kasturi underlines that his Swami's primal role as an *avatāra* is that of teaching, of being a spiritual guide.

Chapter 2, titled *The Sugar and the Ants*, carries on the narrative from Sathya Sai Baba's return to Puttaparthi from Badrinath on July 3, 1961. On Dasara of that same year, he proclaimed himself the fullest of all *avatāras*: "Rama was the embodiment of Sathya and Dharma; Krishna, of Santhi and Prema. Now, when skill is skipping faster than self-control, when science laughs at *sadhana,* when hate and fear have darkened the heart of man, I have come, embodying all the four."[194] Kasturi insists on his guru's being all the gods and at the same time transcending them, being beyond (*atīta*) religion itself. He then gives details of Sathya Sai Baba's installation of *mūrti*s of Shirdi Sai Baba in various temples in the South, also recalling how, back in 1949, for the Shirdi Sai Baba temple in Guindy near Madras, the twenty-two-year-old guru had miraculously left the indelible impression not of his own, slender feet but of Shirdi Sai Baba's long and heavy feet.[195] The hagiographer emphasizes the importance of his guru's words when he says that Sai is not to be conceived as a temple dweller since he resides in the hearts of all, being immanent in every creature.

Kasturi reports that after celebrating the festival of Mahāśivarātri in Puttaparthi in March 1962, Sathya Sai Baba proceeded once again to Tirupati. For the hagiographer it is essential to offer detailed information of all of the guru's movements as testimony of his ever-expanding fame, his trips and tours being of utmost significance for assessing his meticulous strategy of self-promotion.

On September 29, 1962, during Dasara, Sathya Sai Baba solemnly announced his determination to protect and preserve the *Veda*s (*vedasaṃrakṣaṇa*) and foster Vedic scholarship (*vidvatpoṣaṇa*), these objectives being at the very basis of his avatāric mission as upholder of *dharma*. In November 1962, on the occasion of his birthday, he referred to the Chinese attack on India's borders and announced that the day would not be marred by any dispiriting news and that *sanātanadharma* would suffer no harm. To be sure, Kasturi and all devotees interpreted the retreat of the Chinese army as due to the guru's miraculous intervention: "He announced that the Chinese hordes will not advance and mar the joy of His Birthday Celebrations . . . and they mysteriously started withdrawing on the night of Nov. 22: the unexpected retreat was by an advancing army (!) for no known reason."[196]

Chapter 3, *The Task*, is the longest—forty pages—and almost entirely dedicated to illustrate the various actions that Sathya Sai Baba carried out to promote the *Vedas*. Initially, Kasturi narrates how between 1963 and 1965 the guru visited various temples in the South as well as in Maharashtra and "recharged their batteries," multiplying their potency (among them, the Mallikārjuna temple of Srisailam and the Viṭṭhal temple of Pandharpur, where he "materialized" a marriage thread (*maṅgalasūtra*) and tied it around the neck of goddess Rukmiṇī, Viṭṭhal's bride).[197] The hagiographer then proceeds to describe a major Vedic sacrifice that was performed at Prasanthi Nilayam and which lasted seven days: the *Vedapuruṣasaptāhajñānayajña*.[198] It was held in October 1965, during Dasara,[199] in the presence of about a hundred Vedic pundits who convened from all over India. The first *Vedapuruṣasaptāhajñānayajña* had been held in Prasanthi Nilayam three years earlier, during Dasara of 1962. It was divided in two parts: the morning sacrificial sessions of Ati-Rudra-homa (understood to be the highest form of Śiva worship),[200] with all its complementary rites, and the evening sessions of Jñāna Yajña where the pundits explained the meaning and significance of the rituals. Kasturi highlights that the guru of Puttaparthi defined the *Vedapuruṣasaptāhajñānayajña* of 1965 as no ordinary sacrifice but as a revolution, a veritable turning point whose efficacy was aimed at promoting the welfare and peace of the whole world, not solely of India. Sri Ganapati Sastri, president of the Jñāna Yajña section of the sacrifice, is reported to have described it as the best perfect *yajña*.

In order to stress the continuity between the two Sai Babas, Kasturi writes that "the Kamandalu or Water-vessel of Shirdi Sai Baba which miraculously found its way into Prasanthi Nilayam was placed on the Yagamantapa to hold the ceremonial water used for most of the mystic rites."[201] He thus established a most improbable link between the practice of orthodox Vedic *yajñas* and the spirituality of an eclectic Sufi *faqīr*: indeed a noticeable hagiographical accomplishment!

Kasturi recognizes that Sri Ganapati Sastri and most of the Vedic scholars and pundits that had come to Puttaparthi for the sacrifice were originally "infected with the prejudice that Baba was only an adept in magic."[202] In the end, however, they came to realize that he was a veritable incarnation of god, or Kṛṣṇa come again. To support such "revelation," Kasturi quotes the authoritative testimonies of both Sri Ganapati Sastri and Vidvatkavi Vemparala Suryanarayana Sastri.[203] He devotes several pages to argue how Sri Ganapati Sastri and all other ritualists highly praised Sathya Sai Baba's scholarship, being "struck with wonder at the depth and width of His knowledge."[204] To reinforce this point, he quotes their words of recognition. Here is an example:

> In all His speeches there was not the slightest deviation from the Sastras nor the faintest whisper contrary to the trend of their teachings. And, the subjects He handled! They were indeed the most profound! The methodology of exposition was in strict conformity with the canons laid down in the scriptures. There was no repetition of argument, no irrelevant digression, no jeering criticism, no jarring adulation, no over-emphasis. . . . The nectar of His Love filled every word of His parables and explanations. It was overpowering Grace that made Him pity the poor understanding of the listeners and search for tiny tasty stories that could clarify the profundities He was unraveling, the Goals He desired to picture.[205]

In the excerpts of Sathya Sai Baba's discourses, which Kasturi abundantly quotes, the Swami presents himself as the upholder of Brahmin's superiority in the social hierarchy, a superiority that is justified because of their ritual knowledge and sacrificial practices. Vedic culture is extolled by him as the only culture that can save mankind, since only India, namely, he himself, can and must guide the world with the lamp of *sanātanadharma*. Along these lines, on the occasion of his birthday in November 1964 he inaugurated at Prasanthi Nilayam the Sathya Sai Veda Shastra Pathasala, a school of Vedic recitation, in the presence of the highly esteemed Sri Ganapati Sastri. "My Prema towards the Vedas," he proclaimed, "is matched only by My Prema towards humanity."[206] As the decline in private and public morals is explained in terms of the neglect of Vedic rites and *mantras*—exemplified by the initiation (*upanayana*) rite and the *gāyatrī mantra*—the establishment of this school in the very home of the *avatāra* is explained as the foundational and propulsive center whose "pure vibrations" will successfully counter the present state of disorder (*adharma*).

Thus, Kasturi reports how the affluence of the school and the performance of the *upanayana* ritual and *gāyatrī mantra* for the youth increased year by year: 35 *upanayana*s were performed in 1963, 300 in 1964, 450 in 1965. The Veda Pathasala started with thirty boys and in a few years it grew to more than a hundred students. It was not meant only for Brahmins, however, since boys from other castes also joined. Along with the *Veda*s they were taught Sanskrit, Telugu, and English. Kasturi's grandson Ramesh (b. 1951), the first son of his daughter Padma, stood out as the most brilliant pupil of the Veda Pathasala and Sri Kamavadhani, the Vedic teacher, was especially fond of him.[207]

The guru of Puttaparthi declared that the practice of Vedic rituals was in total harmony with Advaita Vedānta, and to be sure Śaṅkara was the authority to whom he most often referred.[208] A year later, in October 1965 on the occasion of Dasara, he established in Prasanthi Nilayam the Prasanthi Vidwan Mahasabha, that is, the All-India Academy of Vedic scholars, of which B. Ramakrishna Rao, ex-chief minister of Andhra Pradesh and governor of Kerala and Uttar Pradesh, was nominated president. Here is how Kasturi celebrates its fundamental functions:

> Baba is the Guru who shows us the path of attaining right knowledge. His Prasanthi Vidwanmahasabha which is spreading its activities all over India is intended (1) to show humanity the road to right knowledge, leading to self-realization; (2) to clear that road of overgrowth which is making passage difficult; and (3) to train the traditional exponents of Sujnana as found in the Vedas, to communicate their experience to the people.[209]

While stressing his guru's mission as restorer of the *Veda*s, Kasturi even quotes the imperious answer that Sathya Sai Baba gave to a Sanskrit scholar from the Sorbonne, who pleaded with him to foster Vedic scholarship, fast declining in India: "I have come for that very purpose, for Vedic revival. It shall be done. I will do it. Wherever you are, you will know of it. The world will share that joy, that light."[210] The inaugural meeting was held at the royal palace of the *rāja* of Venkatagiri, the foremost early sponsor of Sathya Sai Baba's avatāric career. To aptly emphasize the importance of Venkatagiri and its royal family, Kasturi quotes his Swami's words:

> Venkatagiri has been for centuries the seat of a Royal Family dedicated to the support and protection and promotion of

> Dharma. Consider how many temples were built or renovated and maintained by its munificence! Take count of the Pundits it has patronized so far and the number of religious books its donations have helped to reach the masses. See the interest the family takes even now, for the upkeep of temples and mutts although their State and status have been overwhelmed by the storms of political change.[211]

Kasturi further documents the inauguration of other All-India Academies of Vedic scholars in Mysore, Maharashtra, and other states of India. While referring to Maharashtra, he narrates a few incidents meant to confirm the identity between the two Sai Babas. He ends the chapter by emphasizing how Sathya Sai Baba is Vedamātā, "the mother of the *Veda*s," and that his actions of fostering the *Veda*s and *Śāstra*s represent the dawn of the golden era for the liberation of humanity.

In chapter 4, titled *The Call*, the hagiographer focuses upon the guru's invitation—to be dated around 1961–62—to direct each and every person to Puttaparthi as the place where the Lord can be found, *bhaktarakṣaṇa* or the protection of devotees being one of his prime tasks. Nonetheless, Sathya Sai Baba remarked: "[N]o one can come to Puttaparthi, however accidental it might seem, without my calling him. I bring only those people here who are ready to see me, and nobody else, nobody, can find his way here. When I say 'ready' there are different levels of readiness." [212] And in 1960 Kasturi told Daniel Roumanoff that one should never leave the ashram without having secured the guru's permission.[213]

Kasturi recalls the wondrous "materialization" of *liṅga*s that form themselves within Sathya Sai Baba's body, which has been taking place since 1940. He ends the chapter by stating once again that the guru's mission is the propagation of Vedic *dharma* throughout India and the world, and that his teaching of nondual Vedānta in accordance with the Upaniṣadic revelation is the pinnacle of wisdom, the experience of which leads to freedom from rebirth and final liberation.

Chapter 5, titled *This Siva-Sakthi*, is of utmost importance in the unfolding of Kasturi's glorious saga. The hagiographer offers a detailed report of the repeated strokes and the paralysis of the left side that affected his Swami on the evening of July 6, 1963, which he compares to the 1886 episode narrated in the *Śrī Sāī Saccarita* of Shirdi Sai Baba's "leaving the body" for full three days, which also would have marked a turning point in the latter's life.[214] Sathya Sai Baba's paralysis lasted eight days, at the end of which period the guru spectacularly cured himself in a trice on the day of Gurupūrṇimā,[215] in front of an ecstatic mass of about five thousand devotees who had assembled in Puttaparthi to have his *darśan* and listen to his speech. Kasturi describes this event as the miracle of miracles. Having regained his normal status, Sathya Sai Baba began his speech in a triumphant way. He explained his strokes and paralysis[216] as the taking upon himself of a devotee's illness, as he often did in Shirdi.[217] He said he had been keeping back from devotees a secret about himself, which he would disclose on this sacred day. He then narrated a fascinating story, bearing a Purāṇic flavor, linking the Sai Baba avatāric lineage to Śiva's mythology, namely, to a boon Śiva and Śakti would have granted *in illo tempore* to the seer (*ṛṣi*) Bharadvāja due to the latter's piousness in the preparation of a sacrifice taught to him by Indra.[218] He revealed that he was the second in a triune avatāric descent: Shirdi Sai Baba had been an *avatāra* of Śakti, he, as Sathya Sai Baba, was Śiva-Śakti, and a third Prema Sai Baba[219]—to be born in the Mandya district of Karnataka—would finally incarnate as Śiva.[220] Moreover, he remarked that the indifference shown to Bharadvāja by Śakti was the karmic reason why he had to suffer a weeklong paralysis of his left side (Śakti).[221]

Chapter 6, *The Constant Presence*, details a case of Sathya Sai Baba's bilocation[222] and his habit of appearing in people's dreams, in an effort to highlight his ubiquitous reality, while chapter 7, titled *With Wounded Wings*, focuses on the Swami's compassion and service to the lowly. Kasturi presents the exchange of letters between his guru and some prisoners in jail, showing how Sathya Sai Baba was able to transform them into good people and ardent devotees. In order to counter the criticism of his guru being partial to the rich, Kasturi throughout his narrative is careful to note that Sathya Sai Baba has equal attention for the poor and "materializes" objects for them also as a token of his grace.[223] In Part 4, he will state how the poor are the guru's primary concern and will quote his words: "I give Myself first to the needy and the poor."[224] The hagiographer's point is that his lord abides in the hearts of all (*hṛdayavāsin*) and has no preferences whatsoever.

In chapter 8, *Incredible–Still*, Kasturi again takes pains to articulate the sameness of the two Sai Babas adducing various testimonies such as that of M. S. Dixit, nephew of Hari Sitaram (Kakasaheb) Dixit, who was a close devotee of the Shirdi saint. He even reports an episode that endeavors to establish the identity between Sathya Sai Baba and an old *faqīr* follower of Kabīr, whom a devotee met in Darjeeling: this *faqīr* is understood to be none other than Shirdi Sai Baba.[225] In hagiographical sources, the saint of Shirdi is often linked to the celebrated poet and mystic Kabīr (d. 1518), the Muslim weaver (*julāhā*) of Benares. Apparently, Shirdi Sai Baba himself said that he was Kabīr in one of his past lives and once declared that his religion was Kabīr.[226] In passing, the hagiographer notes that the guru of Puttaparthi announced that Vivekananda had been reborn: "[H]e is growing up in Ceylon; he will come to me and join in my task,"[227] which is again indicative of his appropriation of his figure and teachings.[228]

In chapter 9, titled *Holy Joy*, Kasturi recalls his thirty years of carping criticism of the antics of social and religious leaders and his original dislike of miracles, due to contact with the Ramakrishna Mission. But again he highlights Sathya Sai Baba's difference from all other gurus and Babas: he being an *avatāra,* miracles are only natural to him. He underlines his Śiva nature and affirms that his main task is the reestablishment of Vedānta and of the Vedāntic way of life in India and the world. The hagiographer describes the importance of Sathya Sai Baba's visits to villages, which the guru—true to his conservatism—praises as the repository of traditional values as opposed to towns, which, being prone to Westernization, are criticized as harbingers of vice.[229] Kasturi reiterates the "democracy" of his beloved Swami: in the light of his grace, all differences due to caste affiliation and economic status are said to simply disappear.[230] The chapter is brought to a close by presenting the inauguration in 1965 of the Sanatana Bhagavata Bhakta Samaj (under the wings of the Prasanthi Vidwan Mahasabha) and the performance of the Saptāhā Yajña (the seven-day Vedic sacrifice, yearly held in Puttaparthi during Dasara) in the presence of the governor of Andhra Pradesh. Kasturi extols the pundits of the Vedic *Śāstra*s who attended the celebrations in Prasanthi Nilayam, and again stresses the prime importance of training the youth in the traditional values and in the practice of service.

Chapter 10, *Gifts of Grace*, documents the "materialization" of *vibhūti* as well as of oil, nectar (*amṛta*), red powder (*kuṃkum*), turmeric (*haldi*), honey, sandal powder, etc. oozing out from the pictures of Shirdi Sai Baba and Sathya Sai Baba (as well as from the pictures of Jesus and other gods and holy men) held in the home shrines of various devotees.[231] In chapter 11, *Cities Aflame*, Kasturi insists on Sathya Sai Baba's identity with Śiva (as "proven" by the emergence of *liṅga*s from his mouth yearly since

1940) and highlights the importance of Bombay (now renamed Mumbai) as the center of *dharma* revival. Although the guru of Puttaparthi is said to be above all countries and labels, the entire mankind being his family, the capital of Maharashtra is regarded as crucial to the expansion of his avatāric mission. In 1966, Sathya Sai Baba visited it for the third time and the hagiographer approvingly quotes the words of P. K. Savant, the Maharashtrian minister of agriculture, who delved upon the identity of the Shirdi and Puttaparthi Sai Babas.

Kasturi again mentions the main criticisms that are directed at his hero, namely, that he is a magician and lives luxuriously,[232] which he counters by saying that miracles are but the spontaneous expression of his divinity and that "Baba eats the food of the poorest of this land. . . . He sits and sleeps on the same mattress . . . and uses dilapidated cars or taxis in cities, lest the masses recognize Him and follow Him, for the coveted darshan!"[233] In 1964, in Venkatagiri, Sathya Sai Baba had even cited Ramakrishna on the issue of miracles:

> These miracles, as you call them, are but means towards the establishment of Dharma, which is My task. Some people remark that Ramakrishna Paramahamsa has said that miracles produced by the faculties earned by Sadhana are obstructions in the path of the Sadhaka and they should be avoided by those who want to reach the goal of Self-realization. Ramakrishna said that the Sadhaka will be tempted to overdo the demonstration and so inflate the ego. This is correct advice, so far as Sadhakas are concerned. But, the absurdity lies in equating Me with the Sadhaka whom Ramakrishna warned.[234]

Moreover, the hagiographer argues that the saint of Puttaparthi wants no publicity, as proved by the fact that he has always been against the building of temples dedicated to him. To the slander of his critics, he invariably opposes Sathya Sai Baba's compassion and discipline. Kasturi notes that in Prasanthi Nilayam everything is under his personal supervision, in all circumstances, nothing being done without his permission, his sole objective being that of promoting *sanātanadharma*. The hagiographer further notes that on August 4, 1966, Prasanthi Nilayam was declared separate from the village of Puttaparthi, thus, an independent administrative unit: a tangible sign of the ashram's expansion, of its material and economic growth.[235]

The chapter ends with the chronicling of the guru's visit to Tiruchirappalli in Tamil Nadu, where devotees had arranged a three-day session of the Prasanthi Vidwan Mahasabha, and to various other sites in Kerala.

Chapter 12, *Signs and Wonders*, is dedicated to Sathya Sai Baba's miracles, especially his acts of phenomenal healing,[236] and the final chapter 13, *Facets of Truth*, concentrates upon the guru's declaration that *sanātana-dharma* belongs to the whole world. Kasturi remarks how the Swami—being Śiva and all the gods—is Sarva-mata-sammathaya, the one to whom all religions are equally acceptable. In 1967, on the occasion of Mahāśivarātri, the *sarvadharma* emblem, symbol of Sathya Sai Baba universalism, was officially inaugurated. It consists of a lotus flower with five petals and five small leaves. In each petal is the symbol of one of the major religions found in India: starting at the top and moving clockwise we find the *om* of Hinduism, the wheel of Buddhism, the fire of Zoroastrianism, the crescent and the star of Islām, and the cross of Christianity.[237] The symbol of Hinduism is regarded as supreme and placed in the highest position, the upper petal. Within the center of the lotus is a pillar that represents the spinal cord channelizing the fire of Yoga, with a number of rings to indicate the stages of yogic practice: yogic enlightenment, which coincides with the recognition of one's identity with *Brahman*, leads to the unfolding of the lotus of the heart, whose petals are borne on top of the pillar.[238] The underlying idea is that all religions are but different facets of the one ultimate truth and that Hinduism is the first and foremost of them.

On April 20–21, 1967, the All-India Conference of the Office Bearers of the Sathya Sai Baba Organizations was held in Madras, in the Swami's presence. Kasturi defines it as a historic event for the uplifting of *dharma*, which saw the participation of more than one thousand delegates from all over India as well as from overseas countries (he mentions Norway, Ceylon, Hong Kong, and East Africa). On April 22–24, the Prasanthi Vidwan Mahasabha sessions were held in the same town in the presence of its president, the influential B. Ramakrishna Rao. Alongside Sathya Sai Baba's discourse, Kasturi offers details of the speeches held by two other illustrious figures of devotees: V. K. Gokak, one of the major Kannada writers of the Navodaya literary movement, and S. Bhagavantham,[239] an internationally renowned physicist and scientific advisor to the Ministry of Defense of the government of India. The emphasis is placed upon the guru's universal message, he being a world redeemer, a savior whose mercy beckons every son of earth to god.

Kasturi then narrates how a few weeks later Sathya Sai Baba moved up to the Horsley Hills, a charming hill resort of Andhra Pradesh. He mentions the presence along with the Swami of the Australian Howard Murphet (1906–2004), an adept of the Theosophical Society[240] who was one of the earliest Western devotees of Sathya Sai Baba.[241] The hagiographer approvingly quotes Murphet when he says that "we must not lose sight of the greatest miracle of all! This is the miracle of his Prema—his Divine Love. While universal (going out to all men) it is at the same time individual. You feel it beamed directly and blissfully on you."[242] Murphet, while noticing the correspondence of some basic theosophical teachings with Sathya Sai Baba's message (universalism, brotherhood of man), underlined what he considered to be the major difference, namely, the lack of the devotional element in theosophy vis-à-vis the fundamental importance of it in the guru's teaching. He therefore viewed Sathya Sai Baba's message of love as a correction/expansion of the Theosophical Society's perceived intellectualism.[243] Overall, the guru of Puttaparthi did not share the Theosophical Society's esotericism.

In an effort to emphasize his guru's stature, Kasturi states that even Maharishi Mahesh Yogi (1917–2008), the popular guru of the Beatles and proponent of Transcendental Meditation, "wanted that Baba should *bless* the 'leaders of the youth of the world who are training themselves at Sankaracharya Nagar, Hrishikesh, to become the guides of Youth!' "[244] The guru of Puttaparthi, however, had a negative opinion of "Mahesh Yogi," whom he considered to be "lower than the lowest student," having done "serious harm in America" and constantly searching for publicity "on television with the singers," that is, the Beatles.[245]

On September 14, 1967, B. Ramakrishna Rao died and Kasturi notes that the Swami drove four hundred miles by car to be at his bedside in Hyderabad: a clear indication of the strong tie that existed between them, this influential figure having been a precious ally in Sathya Sai Baba's emergence as a god-man. The hagiographer next mentions a few Westerners who were among the first devotees of the guru of Puttaparthi. Among them, the Australian-American Charles Penn (d. 1993)[246] and the Russian-born American Indra Devi (Eugenie V. Peterson, 1899–2002), a renowned Yoga teacher[247] who first learned about Sathya Sai Baba from Howard Murphet and his wife, whom she met at the Theosophical Society in Madras.[248]

In October 1967, the *Vedapuruṣasaptāhajñānayajña* annual festival of Vedic revival was held in Prasanthi Nilayam, together with the fourth anniversary celebrations of the Prasanthi Vidwan Mahasabha. Kasturi brings Part 2 to a close by mentioning the consecration—on November 2, 1967—of the spot upon which was to be erected the Dharmakshetra building in Bombay at Andheri, on the then-outskirts of the city. It was to become the headquarters of the Sathya Sai Baba Seva Organization for the Bombay area as well as the guru's Bombay residence. While in Bombay, the Swami inaugurated the Sathya Sai Seva Dal, "an organization of young Sadhakas who strengthen and supplement their Sadhana by efficient and earnest service rendered to the weak, the disabled and the distressed."[249] On November 23, during his birthday celebrations at Puttaparthi, the guru solemnly announced that a World Conference of Sevaks and Sadhaks of the Sathya Sai units would be held at Dharmakshetra, Bombay, in May 1968. Kasturi ends Part 2 with these words: "The World Conference of Sevaks and Sadhaks of the Sathya Sai Organizations and Groups will inaugurate that Golden Era of Universal Love."[250]

A Critical Evaluation of Part 2

The years 1961–67 were seminal in launching Sathya Sai Baba's organization throughout India, especially in the Southern States and in Maharashtra, setting the stage for its future world expansion. While chronicling the main events of this period, Kasturi skillfully highlights the two fundamental axes along which the guru affirmed and legitimated his avatāric role: Vedic revivalism and the universal character of the mission. Though these might strike us as contradictory objectives they are here understood as coterminous, constituting a harmonious whole. The hagiographer's narrative ably ties them together in order to prove that they mutually sustain each other, representing them as the veritable *grund* of the golden age that the *avatāra* has come to inaugurate.

As Smriti Srinivas has pointed out, the aim was to foster a discourse of "rooted universalism," that is to say, of a universal sacred persona and message that are solidly grounded in what is understood to be traditional Hinduism.[251] Kasturi's audience, constituted in the main by urban middle- and upper-class Hindus, was very sensitive to these themes. For these people, resorting to Sathya Sai Baba's fabulous charisma while paying tribute to the "eternal religion" of their fathers via the performance of Vedic rituals was a way of reappropriating one's tradition and family roots, of psychologically reconciling oneself with the guilt of having abandoned time-honored values and customs, paradigmatically represented by the guru institute and the socio-ritual dimension of village Hinduism. In other words, it was a way of healing and recomposing one's torn, disrupted identity.[252]

The guru's strategy, which was the hagiographer's strategy, was crowned with success. Presenting himself as the advocate and (re)establisher of the immemorial *dharma* was the first, fundamental move one would expect an *avatāra* to make, and Sathya Sai Baba played it well. The Vedic ritualists, which he annually brought together in Puttaparthi for the spectacular performance of sacred *yajñas*, were instrumental in the promotion of his divinity: in fact, the Vedic godhead to whom all sacrifices were directed was none other than the guru himself! Sathya Sai Baba's promotion of Vedic rituals in such grand style was an exhibition of his richness—given their high expense[253]—and an indicator of his growing fame and success. It reinforced his adherence to tradition envisaged in its purest form, Vedic *yajñas* being axiomatically revered as the fountainhead of wisdom.

Significantly, Kasturi remarks that the ritual performers explicitly recognized the truth of the guru's self-proclamation as Vedapuruṣa and

Figure 2.5. The anointment ceremony of Sathya Sai Baba by N. Kasturi and his wife Rajamma on the day of the guru's birthday inside the *mandir*.

Yajñapuruṣa: he is the supreme personification of the *Vedas* and of sacrifice, who benignly accepts/receives the sacrificial offerings and grants their rewards to humanity.[254] To be sure, the guru's physical presence as "presiding deity" was regarded as indispensable for the correct performance of the rituals. Therefore, Kasturi is careful to pinpoint that he is not to be mistaken as the promoter of the sacrifice, much less as the performer of it. Rather, all gods are said to pray to him to save the *Śāstras* from decline.

The hagiographer's insistence on the guru of Puttaparthi as being the veritable Vedapuruṣa is meant to legitimate his claim to divinity at the highest possible level of Hindu orthodoxy. Sathya Sai Baba's revival of Vedic *yajñas* and his promotion of a "Vedic renaissance" at this crucial stage must be understood as part and parcel of his effort to present himself as the ultimate *avatāra.* As the *Vedas* are the root of *dharma,* so is he the root of the *Vedas* and actually their embodiment! If the appropriation of the rhetoric of the supreme wisdom of Vedic revelation (*śruti*) is a common characteristic of neo-Hindu movements, past and present, what is peculiar in the guru of Puttaparthi's strategy is precisely his presenting himself as none other than the incomparable Vedapuruṣa.

Following along these lines, all boys who attended Sathya Sai Baba's schools had to learn how to chant the *Vedas* properly. Here is the testimony of a visitor in Prasanthi Nilayam, dated February 1967:

> We attended the *Veda Parayana* when about 50 boys, all clad beautifully in yellow uniform chanted the Veda. We were deeply impressed by the manner in which the Veda was recited and the deep interest the saint evinced in the proper recitation of the Veda. It was a very happy and memorable day in our lives indeed.[255]

The *Vedas* and their rituals are regarded as the essence of Hinduism and at the same time the fountainhead of all religions. Following his master, Kasturi is keen in presenting the *Vedas* as a universal *śruti,* a revelation that is intended for all mankind. In this way, he is able to simultaneously establish the primacy of India and of Hinduism, that is, of Sathya Sai Baba, and to extol the Vedic revelation—coinciding with the guru's message of love and service—as the means for the emancipation of all men and women, irrespective of their caste, race, and creed. Thus, the *sanātanadharma,* which the guru incarnates, is rationalized as the highest spiritual goal of humanity as a whole, beyond the barriers of institutionalized religions.

A turning point in the guru's career was his spectacular declaration of being the *avatāra* of Śiva-Śakti. If in Part 1 Kasturi emphasizes the kṛṣṇaite/vaiṣṇava, more immanent, characterization of his lord, in Part 2 he invariably emphasizes his śaiva, transcendent characterization while all along insisting on his identity with Shirdi Sai Baba. He is not only Śiva, however, but also Śakti, which is to say, he is both male and female, Prakṛti and Puruṣa. The guru of Puttaparthi presented himself as the fullest of all *avatāras*, recapitulating in himself god's female counterpart (Devī), thus revealing his androgynous character as Ardhanārīśvara,[256] "the lord who is half female."[257] In his transcendental inclusiveness, he characterized himself as both the divine mother and father, and this is precisely the meaning he assigned to his name, Sai Baba being interpreted to mean divine/good (*sa*) mother (*āi*) and father (*bābā*).[258] As he once told Arnold Schulman: "I'm not a man, I'm not a woman. I'm not old. I'm not young. I'm all of these."[259] Already in the early days, young Sathya is reported transforming himself into a woman wearing a sari and appearing as the goddesses Rādhā and Pārvatī.[260] During his school days in Uravakonda, he even played the part of a famous female dancer, Rishyendramani.[261] Diana Baskin (d. 2014),[262] an early devotee since 1969, noticed: "His beauty Divine, is almost liquid in its ability to change from the delicately feminine to the strongest masculine appearance."[263]

Moreover, by announcing the coming of a third Sai Baba to be born in the Mandya district of Karnataka who would bring the avatāric mission to completion,[264] the guru potently projected his charismatic influence into the future and anticipated that there would be no ordinary mechanism of succession or *guruparamparā*. To be sure, Kasturi must have been thrilled at the idea that his master's third and final avatāric descent would take place in Karnataka: he would thus ultimately speak in Kannada, the hagiographer's beloved language, after having expressed himself through the mediums of Marathi/Deccani Urdu (in Shirdi) and Telugu (in Puttaparthi). Quoting Sathya Sai Baba's words, Shakuntala Balu states that the future birthplace of Prema Sai Baba will be the village of Gunapalli or Gunaparthi.[265] On the other hand, ex-devotee Robert Priddy writes that in a lecture for foreigners in January 1985 at Prasanthi Nilayam, which he attended, Kasturi said that once while driving with Sathya Sai Baba past a small village called Chandrapatna in Karnataka State—circa 38 km.

southwest of Bangalore—the guru said that he would "take rebirth" there and that the hagiographer would be his mother.[266]

In his autobiography, Kasturi writes that Sathya Sai Baba would have revealed himself to him as Śiva-Śakti years before his public declaration.[267] Padma, the professor's daughter, recalls: "[T]he merciful Lord blessed him with a vision of Shiva-Shakthi too, but he would never reveal much about it saying it is 'Daiva-rahasya' meaning, 'Divine mystery' and 'I do not want to talk about it.' "[268] Kasturi, however, disclosed details about this vision to Samuel H. Sandweiss:

> Professor Kasturi told me that he personally reveres Baba as *Shiva* and that he has had marvelous experiences with him that have deepened his reverence. Once when they were alone and talking about his *Shiva/Shakti* (*Shiva*'s consort) aspect, Baba said, "Kasturi, look at me." Kasturi relates that as he looked up, what he saw was startling and deeply moving. Instead of Baba's familiar appearance he saw *Nandi* the bull (*Shiva*'s vehicle), upon which sat *Shiva* on one side and *Shakti* on the other in a characteristic pose. The vision remained before his eyes for a few seconds and then melted back into the Baba that we all recognize. "*Now do you understand, Kasturi?*" Baba gently asked.[269]

Going beyond the Śiva-Śakti paradigm, the hagiographer was keen to underline Sathya Sai Baba's universal character, beyond Hinduism, by remarking that he has come to feed the roots of all creeds and races. As the Swami used to say:

> I have come to repair the ancient highway to God. . . . I have not come on behalf of any sect or creed or religion. I have come to light the Lamp of Love in the hearts of all humanity.[270]

Thus, the guru claimed to be Śiva-Śakti but also Viṣṇu, Kṛṣṇa, and all gods, Indian as well as non-Indian. Sathya Sai Baba exemplifies a dynamic charisma, expanding itself over time. And indeed it is just a step forward to expand one's comprehensive Hinduness to a global universalism, encompassing all world religions. The series of the guru's expansive self-definitions—constant throughout his career—document Sathya Sai Baba's ascendancy from village guru to international guru. As Tulasi Srinivas has written in her excellent monograph on the guru's movement: "The operational core of the guru-sant-avatar-future fourfold narrative is the modality of strategic ambiguity . . . the various plastic forms [of his divine identity] cover the various possibilities. This modality of strategic ambiguity located in temporal stretching enables Sathya Sai Baba to transform himself from local guru to global godman."[271]

Symbolically, his postsectarian universalism is powerfully represented by the *sarvadharma* emblem, which incontrovertibly mirrors a Vivekanandian ideology, tying together the superiority of Hinduism and the essential goodness of all faiths, which are included in the symbol as different paths leading to the same, ultimate goal.[272] These latter ones are incorporated as subsidiary petals, aspects of the one supreme lotus flower, the blossoming of which coincides with Sathya Sai Baba's boundless religion of universal love. The guru of Puttaparthi would often declare the superiority of India and Hinduism in unambiguous terms. For instance, in one of his public speeches he remarked: "Every religion has disciplines to suppress ego, but the oldest, most effective, and most successfully practiced are the Vedas and moral codes of India."[273] The hagiographer emphasizes that India's culture is truly international and that its role is to lead mankind to the goal of self-realization. India's role is Sathya Sai Baba's role, and he observes that he "does the task of Dharma-sthapana through many channels: direct teaching, writing, discoursing, exhorting, explaining, strengthening the props of Dharma (like temples, holy places and pundits) cleansing the ancient texts which have been tarnished by the slush of time and by the touch of slimy pens."[274]

The guru noted how *avatāras* are born only in India. In one of his speeches, he stated that "India is the region where Divine Incarnations re-establish Dharma."[275] Along the same lines, he argued that "America is Arjuna; Russia is Bhima; both must bow before India, who is Dharmaraja and upholds right against might."[276] On various occasions, he put forward statements such as the following: "India is entitled to be the Guru of the world"; "India is the Spiritual Academy of Humanity"; "In the spiritual dominion, India is the sovereign nation"; "The Mine of spiritual wisdom and treasure is India."[277]

In order to counter the evils of modern society, the guru of Puttaparthi warned his devotees not to indulge in Western fads and attractions, such as the ones conveyed through the movies, which he openly denounced as propagators of violence and moral corruption.[278] Kasturi echoes his master by saying that "discipline starts with . . . giving up sensual entertainments like the cinema and the reading of degrading literature."[279] Among other things, the guru pronounced himself strongly against family planning via contraceptives and artificial methods, implying that this would cause a fall in public morality. He remarked: "It is only rigorous self-control through Sadhana [spiritual practice] that can ensure the acceptance of parental responsibility; country-wide movements to spread artificial aids will bring about the fall of moral standards."[280]

From the early days, Sathya Sai Baba plainly declared that the "decline of Indian religion and culture is due to the influence of the West."[281] He sadly noticed that "India is the most ancient center of civilization that survives with its heritage intact, but it is being ignored and replaced by Western ideas and ideals," and that "Vedas and Sastras are the eyes of India, but blind imitation of Western cultures and blind carping on the native culture have dimmed them."[282] In this regard, Tulasi Srinivas has rightly pointed out that the guru has been voicing "one of the few religiously based, indigenous, and embedded postcolonial critiques of the West."[283]

The guru's "universal love" was and is practically defined in two ways: (1) love of god, that is, of Sathya Sai Baba or of any of his innumerable forms (since all names and forms are his) through various devotional practices (remembrance of the holy name, *bhajan*s, meditation, etc.); and (2) educational and service activities—a typical implementation of the neo-Hindu commitment to social reform—to become more and more important in the definition of his organization and overall mission mainly through the establishment of schools and the education in human values, the building of hospitals, the uplift of villages, the feeding of the poor (*nārāyaṇasevā*), the bringing of drinkable water to remote areas, etc. The guru's social welfare projects evidence his egalitarian or "democratic" ideal, based on the conviction that instruction, medical care, food, and water are people's right, irrespective of caste, gender, and creed. Even future achievements such as the Super Specialty Hospitals in Puttaparthi (1991) and Whitefield (2001) will be meant as exemplary models, so as to instill in devotees and especially in students—who the guru said were his only true "property"—the spirit and joy of service.

In the first chapter of Part 3 of *Sathyam Sivam Sundaram*, the hagiographer lucidly summarizes the two fundamental guiding principles upon which his writing of Part 2 is built. Thus, he points out that it is only through the *Vedas*' authority and through universalism, that is, the acknowledgment of the religious experience of the saints of all lands—implicitly understood to be one and the same—that the "seeds" his master planted through his travels across the country can effectively grow and bring fruit:

> He himself moved over the land like a raincloud, showering courage and conviction on hearts parched by the cruel rays of doubt, disappointment, disputation and dilemma. This was the Sowing of the Seeds—*Sathya*, *Dharma*, *Shanthi* and *Prema*—seeds reinforced with the authority of ageless Vedas and the indisputable experience of the sages and seers of all lands.[284]

In these years of intense activity during which the guru of Puttaparthi succeeded in promoting himself and his mission, we see the constituency of his devotees—in the South as well as throughout India—grow at an extraordinary speed. If the Vedic pundits played a key role in legitimating his claims to divinity, another key role was played by "big-men" of the political establishment such as B. Ramakrishna Rao who, as the governor of Uttar Pradesh and Kerala, actively collaborated in the expansion of Sathya Sai Baba's name and fame. Alongside the crucial role played by influential political figures and decayed royal families (Venkatagiri), an increasing number of wealthy exponents of the Hindu middle and upper classes/castes contributed in a decisive way to the economic growth of the guru's movement—both through the expansion of the ashram of Prasanthi Nilayam as well as through the establishment of residences of the Swami and centers of the organization in key, strategic places such as Bangalore/Whitefield, Madras, Bombay, etc.[285] If the domains of religion, politics, and economy are inextricably co-implicated in the guru enterprise, it is out of question that Sathya Sai Baba proved himself to be a most skillful domain crosser.[286]

The mid-1960s were the time when prominent figures of intellectuals came to strengthen the guru's constituency. Among these, a few words must be said of Vinayak Krishna Gokak (1909–1992), who first met Sathya Sai Baba in 1966. Besides having been a distinguished English professor and the principal of several colleges, he was one of the most eminent Kannada writers and poets—deeply influenced by D. R. Bendre (1896–1981)—having received many prestigious awards (among them, the

Padmashree in 1961). His Kannada epic *Bharatha Sindhurashmi,* for which he received the Jñānpīṭh Award in 1990, is the longest epic (35,000 lines) ever written in any language in the twentieth century, and his Kannada novel *Samarasave Jeevana* is one of the most characteristic works of the *Navodaya* literary movement.[287] There are noticeable similarities between him and Kasturi, since Gokak breathed the same cultural and religious atmosphere, fully embracing its active call for reform and service to society. As S. Minajagi writes:

> Both Aurobindo and [Sai] Baba were great attractions for him. Of all the elderly writers in Kannada, Gokak like prof. N. Kasturi and G. P. Rajarathnam was increasingly drawn towards Baba's socio-cultural zeal to reform the society.[288]

In 1971, Gokak gave up his vice-chancellorship of Bangalore University to go live at Sathya Sai Baba's residence in Whitefield for five years. Like Kasturi, he was close to his guru and worked for him as an interpreter and also as an organizer of the Summer Schools in Prasanthi Nilayam, which began in 1972. In 1974, Sathya Sai Baba sent him to the United States to spread his renown and help set up the Sathya Sai Baba Organization of America. Later, between 1981 and 1985, he served as vice-chancellor of the Sri Sathya Sai Institute of Higher Learning. The most important book he wrote on the guru of Puttaparthi is *Bhagavan Sri Sathya Sai Baba: The Man and the Avatar (An Interpretation)* (New Delhi: Abhinav Publications, 1975).[289] Interestingly, Anil Kumar Kamaraju writes that the Shirdi Sai Baba Sansthan had invited Gokak to accept the post of Shirdi Sai Sansthan Trust president, but that Sathya Sai Baba "stated that one cannot sail in two boats nor do justice to both. In this regard, Swami stated that even though all are one, each has one's own speciality or image."[290]

With few exceptions, it was from around the mid-1960s that Westerners found their way to Puttaparthi. The Frenchman Daniel Roumanoff (1936–2015), who paid a visit to Sathya Sai Baba in February 1960, was one of the first Westerners to find his way to the ashram.[291] Erlendur Haraldsson (b. 1931), a psychology professor at the University of Iceland who conducted researches on Sathya Sai Baba's alleged miracles for decades, notes that even though he lived and traveled throughout India for one whole year from the fall of 1962, staying longer in Madras than in any other place, "the name Sri Sathya Sai Baba never came to my ears (how

I wish it had); nor did I ever see a photo of him as far as I can recall. What a change had taken place when I visited India last year [in 1979]. His name had become a household word."[292]

Foreigners were always welcome at Prasanthi Nilayam, though they were requested to adapt themselves to the strict rules of the ashram concerning bodily practices, especially with regard to sex and food via the enforcement of gender separation and the adherence to a pure (*sāttvika*), vegetarian diet.[293] Among the first Westerners, the theosophist Howard Murphet was to become a significant figure in the guru's movement. In particular, he was the author of four widely read books on the saint of Puttaparthi of which the first—*Sai Baba: Man of Miracles* (London: Muller, 1971)—was instrumental in drawing the attention of many more Westerners to Sathya Sai Baba from the early 1970s. Along with Kasturi's biography, this book became a classic of Sai Baba literature, being translated into many languages.[294]

3

Narayan Kasturi's Magnum Opus

Sathyam Sivam Sundaram, Parts 3 & 4

Sathyam Sivam Sundaram, Part 3: An Overview

The third part of Kasturi's opus was released on March 16, 1972, on the occasion of the Hindu new year's day. Comprising eighteen chapters of which the first is but a short prologue (*The Ascending Sun*) and the last an equally short epilogue (*One Word More*), it is 227 pages long in its 1981 edition and it covers approximately four years of Sathya Sai Baba's public life, from 1968 to 1971.

Chapter 2, titled *Attention: World at Prayer*, is dedicated to the inauguration of the Dharmakshetra building in Bombay on May 12, 1968, and to the presentation of the First World Conference (and Second All India Conference) of the Sri Sathya Sai Seva Organization, which began on May 16 and was held at the *Bharatiya Vidya Bhavan*'s Campus in Bombay at the presence of Sri Morarji Desai (1896–1995), a prominent political figure who had been a lieutenant of M. K. Gandhi and who was to become the fourth prime minister of India (1977–79). Kasturi writes that the founder and president of the *Bharatiya Vidya Bhavan*, Dr. K. M. Munshi (1887–1971)—whose guests they were—had reservations about Sathya Sai Baba but was soon conquered by him. Apparently, the guru cured him of his Parkinson's disease, also "materializing" a beautiful ring for him.[1]

As the call for a world conference indicates, by 1968 Westerners had begun to be increasingly attracted to the ashram of the guru of Puttaparthi.

For the first time, the Sathya Sai Organization welcomed foreign delegates from all over the world—Ceylon,[2] Singapore, the Philippines, Kuwait, Dubai, Casablanca, Mombasa, Nairobi, Kampala, Hong Kong, Fiji, Tehran, Tokyo, the West Indies, Peru, Brazil, and the United States[3]—and Kasturi remarks that among them were Indra Devi and Charles Penn, who was to be the editor of the American edition of *Sathyam Sivam Sundaram*.[4] He also mentions the presence of Lucia Osborne (1904–1987), the Polish-born wife of Arthur Osborne[5] (1906–1970) who in 1957 authored a biography of the saint of Shirdi titled *The Incredible Sai Baba*, which for the first time made him accessible to the Western public.

The hagiographer writes that at the conference, Sathya Sai Baba underlined the universalism of both his persona and his mission, which now was to expand its focus to the whole of humanity. The guru emphatically argued that the tracks (religions) are many but the summit (god) is one, and that the Sai form is verily the embodiment of all the names of god: "This Human Form is one in which every Divine entity, every Divine principle, that is to say, all the Names and Forms ascribed by man to God, are manifest."[6] Moreover, he observed that

> this was the first time in the history of this world that a World Conference of the devotees of an Avatar was being held, in the immediate physical presence and under the direct supervision and observation of the Avatar himself![7]

Attuned to his guru's aims, Kasturi remarks how all countries should pay homage to India, it being the birthplace of *avatāra*s and the veritable guru of humanity.

In chapter 3, *The Awakening Continent*, the hagiographer presents Sathya Sai Baba's visit to Kenya and Uganda as an indicator of the expansion of his mission, which would rapidly transform the whole world, ushering it into a new era.[8] As the guru told John S. Hislop in December 1968:

> Countries are like carriages. The engine is God. The first carriage is India. The other carriages will follow. According to the astrology of ancient times, the change in world conditions to be brought about by Swami's influence will come in about 15 years. This was predicted 5,600 years ago in the Upanishads. The coming of Baba, the Sai Avathar, which includes the three

> incarnations, is all forecast quite clearly. People born in this present generation, may consider themselves quite fortunate.[9]

And Kasturi echoed his guru's words when he noted that "each country is a room in His mansion, each nation an actor in His drama."[10] Already in July 1963, after his declaration of being the *avatāra* of Śiva-Śakti, the guru had stated: "I have to go to lands beyond the seas also, for, there are people in distress there too, people who are good and virtuous and immersed in love of God clamoring for a Vision."[11]

In fact, the visit to East Africa was to be his only trip outside India[12] and his decision not to travel abroad anymore—despite the insistence of Western devotees that he should visit their countries and the guru's own assurances that he soon would[13]—is to be seen as one more sign of his traditionalism, given that according to orthodox Hinduism India alone is the *karmabhūmi* (lit. "realm of action"), the pure land where action bears results.

Sathya Sai Baba and his small entourage, comprising Kasturi and the American Bob Raymer (1921–2008) who was a devotee of Paramahamsa Yogananda[14] (1893–1952), landed in Nairobi on June 30, 1968. By car, the guru and his party proceeded straightaway to Kampala, Uganda, where Dr. Chotabhai G. Patel, the organizer of his visit, expected them. During his sojourn, Sathya Sai Baba met the devotees of the Indian communities living there: the thirty or so Sathya Sai Baba Centers present at the time in East Africa were established by the numerous Indian diaspora.[15] Through Dr. Patel, he also met the local representatives and some political and military authorities. Among others, he met with General Idi Amin Dada the then-chief of staff of the Ugandan army: three years later, in 1971, he was to seize power through a military coup, inaugurating his brutal regime, which lasted until 1979. According to Dr. Patel and Dr. D. J. Ghadia, the guru foretold that Indians would be asked to abandon Uganda in four years' time, and advised them to leave the country.[16]

The hagiographer reports that in his African speeches the guru emphasized his universal message of the fatherhood of god and brotherhood of man, that is, the religion of love (*preman*) based upon service and the implementation of human values. On July 12, 1968, while they were touring the country, Kasturi had a car accident, in which he was slightly injured, and was confined to bed for a couple of days. He narrates how his guru poured upon him his motherly love, caring for him as though he was a child: the attention he received from his Swami was so overwhelming that he wished he were sick like that forever.

Sathya Sai Baba and his party flew back to Bombay on July 15, where the guru addressed a huge gathering at Dharmakshetra presided over by K. M. Munshi.[17] In his speech, the Swami remarked that the African people told him that the vision of the Indian sages alone could save them and give them peace. He consequently announced his avatāric task of exporting India's culture and spirituality to the whole world: "The splendor of the genuine culture of India will spread in this manner from continent to continent, from country to country, from community to community in the days to come. That is My Task. That is My Will."[18]

Chapter 4, *Example and Precept*, is dedicated to the guru's role as educator, which is said to be a crucial aspect of his *dharmasthāpana* mission, in India and throughout the world. As Kasturi remarked in his commentary to the Swami's 108 names: "Baba endows vigour and vitality to Dharma and to centres of Dharma, like monasteries and seminaries, temples and places of Divine worship which keep Dharma and the Dharmic way of life, constantly before the conscience of man, in all lands."[19]

On July 22, 1968, Sathya Sai Baba established the first Sri Sathya Sai Arts and Science College for women at Anantapur, making it the first college in the Sai University network of campuses. In the same year, the guru founded the Women's Wing of the Sathya Sai Baba Organization, the Mahila Vibhag. The separation of men and women was always a cornerstone of the guru's discipline: in all schools and service activities, as well as during ritual and devotional activities at the Puttaparthi ashram, men and women were and are separated. On June 9, 1969, he established the Sri Sathya Sai Arts and Science College for men at Brindavan, Whitefield (inaugurated by the chief minister of Mysore State, Sri Virendra Patil).

Kasturi underlines how the primal role of the *avatāra* is that of educating the young in *satya*, *dharma*, *śānti*, and *prema*,[20] avoiding the contaminating Western influence, which is rampant in the cities.[21] The hagiographer points out that the guru's plan is to establish one or two Sathya Sai colleges in every state of India, "all to be knit together later into a University as an instrument forged for his Task."[22] Education in action is said to take the form of selfless service. Thus, Kasturi presents the chain of education, which, from childhood to manhood/womanhood, is epitomized by the organization's service groups: the Bal Vikas, the Junior Seva Dals, the Seva Dals (at age eighteen), and the Seva Samithis or Service

Centers. In his autobiography, he notes that the guru's concern for the youth and social service was a salient characteristic from the early days:

> The Children's Day celebrated since 1945 has blossomed into Bal Vikas classes all over the world and the "Education of Children in Human Values" that is now being increasingly adopted in most States of India. The Social Service Day has since expanded into the formation of the Seva Dal.[23]

Kasturi then focuses on the books written by his guru, the series of the *Vahinis* (lit. "streams"), which were first published in the monthly magazine *Sanathana Sarathi* and translated from Telugu into English by Kasturi himself. The hagiographer points out that Sathya Sai Baba also "edited" the *Bhāgavata Purāṇa* and the *Rāmāyaṇa* epic by giving his own version of them in the *Bhagavatha Vahini* and the *Ramakatha Rasa Vahini*. The aim of the guru is said to be that of awakening everybody to the truth of their ātmic core, and this is the reason why he addresses all gatherings with the opening words *divyātma svarūpulara*, "incarnations of the divine *ātman*."

Chapter 5, *Sign and Signature*, is devoted to the remembrance of the holy name (*nāmasmaraṇa*) and to the importance of having faith in its efficacy. This is the reason why at Prasanthi Nilayam the day starts at 4:00 a.m. with the Nagar Sankirtans, the choral chanting of the names of god by distinct groups of men and women walking in procession all around the village. Kasturi underlines how this *avatāra* has come to coordinate the apparently differing paths leading to god, such as the Vedāntic schools of Madhva (dualism), Rāmānuja (qualified nondualism) and Śaṅkara (nondualism). Just like Kṛṣṇa in the *Bhagavadgītā*, Sathya Sai Baba is said to operate a sublime synthesis, an integration of the paths of action (*karman*), knowledge (*jñāna*), and devotion (*bhakti*).

In chapter 6, *The Festival of Lights*, the hagiographer chronicles the guru's tour of Karnataka, Goa, and other southern locales, celebrating him as the awakener of the divine light. He points out that Sathya Sai Baba held his first discourse in Kannada in October 1968, at Dharwar University. In chapter 7, *White Man's Burden*, Kasturi concentrates on the first Westerners who came in contact with the Swami, those foreigners whom the guru used to call "for-nears" since they came for someone they could clasp as near and dear. Besides Charles Penn, Indra Devi, Howard Murphet, and Bob Raymer, Kasturi offers details on Elsie and Walter

Cowan,[24] John S. Hislop[25] (1904–1995), Hilda Charlton[26] (1906–1988), and Arnold Schulman[27] (b. 1925), narrating how they were first attracted to Sathya Sai Baba and describing their experiences with him. As the hagiographer puts it:

> Thus they come, from all quarters. Many like Hislop have to their credit long years of *sadhana*, guided by adepts in their own countries—in Japan (Zen teachers), in Burma (Buddhist monasteries), in Nepal (Saivite Gurus), in Ceylon (Viharas), and in India (Yoga adepts). In many cases, their appetite for spiritual achievement had been whetted through contacts with the Ramakrishna Mission, the Self-Realization Fellowship, The Hare-Krishna Movement, the Kriya-Yoga Conference, and various other inducements for self-examination, self-mastery, and self-realization. Others who feel the thirst for Light come to Baba, mauled and maimed by quacks and crooks who promise quick results against tidy rewards. And some others come desperate and sick of catering to pride and greed and the hardy brood of impulses, in search of a way out, in search of peace.[28]

In particular, Kasturi emphasizes that several of these Westerners came to identify Sathya Sai Baba with Jesus and quotes their thoughts and conclusions. At the same time, he underlines how the guru encouraged faith in the oneness of Sai and Jesus, both through his speeches as well as through his "materialization" of the cross or of Jesus's image.[29] Indeed, Kasturi does not miss any opportunity to highlight the similarities between Jesus and Sathya Sai Baba since this was of crucial importance for promoting the guru's universal appeal. He argues that "truth" (*satya*) is their common name, that they share a motherly love for all their children, that they both take upon themselves the sins of others, and that they have descended to earth in order to rescue all men and save the lost sheep. Thus, the guru's persona is likened to Christ and his message to Christian theological concepts.

As many Hindus revere Sathya Sai Baba as Kalkin (lit. "[having] a white horse"), the tenth, eschatological *avatāra* of Viṣṇu who will put an end to this Kali age—the most degenerate of the four world ages (*yugas*)—and usher humanity into the golden age,[30] Kasturi invites Westerners to look upon him as none other than Jesus. In the inclusivistic logic that governs his whole project, the hagiographer reiterates that "Baba is the multi-faceted *Avatar*—Rama, Krishna, Christ, Buddha, Allāh, Sankara, Gauranga, Ramakrishna, Zarathustra—all in one."[31]

In chapter 8, *The Shirdi Feet*, Kasturi again delves into the universalist significance and symbolism of the Dharmakshetra building and counters criticisms of the Swami's powers, arguing that he does not break any law of nature since he, rather, transcends these laws. Once more, Sathya Sai Baba's powers are said to be inherent to him and not the result of any yogic accomplishment. Kasturi quotes the words of his master: "Mine is not mesmerism, miracle or magic. Mine is genuine Divine Power. . . . My body, like all other bodies, is a temporary habitation but My Power is eternal, all pervasive, ever-dominant. . . . It is just like sport—My natural behavior. It is a sign which helps you to develop faith, devotion, inquiry and realization of your own atman. As the Intention or the Will arises in the mind, the thing is made!"[32] Repeating what he had stated in a speech held in Venkatagiri back in 1964, the guru declared:

> Some of you remark that Ramakrishna Paramahamsa has said that the siddhis or yogic powers are obstructions in the path of the sadhana. Yes, siddhis may lead the sadhaka or the spiritual aspirant astray. Without being involved in them he has to keep straight on or his ego will bring him down to the evil—the temptation of demonstrating his yogic powers. This is a correct advice which every aspirant should heed. But mistake lies in equating Me with the sadhaka like the one whom Ramakrishna wanted to help, guide and warn. These siddhis or yogic powers are just in the nature of the avatar.[33]

All "materializations" are said to be acts of creation, which depend upon the guru's power of concentration.[34] Kasturi argues that ultimately they are impossible to comprehend and should not be confused with so-called "apports," items already in existence that are brought/transferred from one place to another. The hagiographer notes that the guru may "materialize" more than a pound of *vibhūti* per day, and that its characteristics are varied: "It is also of many grades of smoothness, of many colors from white to dark brown, of many tastes—sucrose to bitter—and of many smells from rose to camphor to iodine!"[35]

Kasturi then chronicles Sathya Sai Baba's inauguration of the boys' Arts and Science College affiliated to the Bangalore University (on June 9,

1969), and his master's visit to the Shirdi Sai Baba temple in Guindy, near Madras, where back in 1949 he had "energized" the *mūrti* with his *śakti* and had left the impression of Shirdi Sai Baba's feet in lieu of his own.[36] The hagiographer observes how on July 29, 1969, day of Gurupūrṇimā, the guru warned his devotees against institutionalizing religion and compartmentalizing society, since "it is good to be born in a church, but it is not good to die in it."[37] He brings the chapter to an end by presenting the celebration in Prasanthi Nilayam of Kṛṣṇa's festival, detailing his master's teachings on the god's nature and declaring that the Kṛṣṇa principle is now embodied in Sathya Sai Baba.

In chapter 9, *Delta of Delight*, Kasturi presents the main events that characterized the guru's forty-third birthday in November 1968, during which the Swami spoke about the four varieties of children (*nyāsaputra*s, *ṛṇaputra*s, *suputra*s, and *upekṣāputra*s).[38] Of these four, he extolled the *upekṣāputra*s who, like himself, have no attachment whatsoever and are destined to become *avatāra*s. The hagiographer insists on the fact that *avatāra*s are born in India alone and that even Aurobindo Ghose (1872–1950) prophesized Sathya Sai Baba's advent: "24th November, 1926, was the Descent of Krishna into the physical. . . . A power infallible shall lead the thought, in earthly hearts kindle the Immortal's Fire, even the multitude shall hear the Voice!"[39]

Kasturi next describes the guru's tour of the Godavari Districts of Andhra Pradesh in January 1969. He focuses attention on his visit to the Konasima area, the delta of the Godavari River, which is magnified as Vedasima, the region of Vedic knowledge, being the home of pundits such as the *ahitagni*s who have established the ritual fires in their homes.[40] Kasturi underlines Sathya Sai Baba's love of the *Veda*s and his avatāric function as upholder of Vedic revelation. He then proceeds to describe the Śivarātri festival held in Prasanthi Nilayam and the "miracle" of the emergence of the ellipsoidal *liṅga* (*liṅgodbhava*) from the Swami's body, which he defines as "that in which all things merge and out of which all things emerge."[41] The guru's identification with Śiva and Śakti is once again magnified. Among the wonders that the hagiographer documents in almost every page, mention should be made of a motionless trance of the Swami, during which he would have "left his body" on a transcorporeal journey that lasted about one hour, allegedly going on a "mental roaming" (*mānasasaṃcāra*) around the world in order to offer tangible signs of his love and omnipresence to his *bhakta*s on holy Śivarātri.

In chapter 10, *The All in All*, Kasturi chronicles the Dasara festival of 1969—during which the customary *Vedapuruṣayajña* was held—as well as the Śivarātri festival of February 1970. On the latter occasion, the guru solemnly restated his identity as Śiva-Śakti, while once again operating the miracle of the *liṅgodbhava*. The hagiographer does not fail to mention the third All India Conference of Bhagavan Sri Sathya Sai Seva Organizations, which was inaugurated in Prasanthi Nilayam on November 20, 1969. In chapter 11, *Unearthing the Light*, after underlining the importance of the remembrance of god's names through chanting, that is, the daily practice of Nagar Sankirtans, Kasturi insists on the Swami's call for a new educational system, from elementary schools up to colleges and universities, to be based upon the human values of truth, righteousness, peace, love and nonviolence that each and every teacher must effectively embody and transmit.

Kasturi then proceeds to offer details of his guru's stay in Bombay at Dharmakshetra and of his trips to various locales in Gujarat, including Jamnagar, Dwarka, and Somnath. The hagiographer, who was part of the guru's retinue during this tour of May 1970, narrates how Sathya Sai Baba alias Śiva-Śakti "recharged" the "*liṅga* of light" (*jyotirliṅga*) of the Somnath Temple and how he "materialized" the original Someśvaraliṅga, which manifested in his palm as an oval of brilliant light. On his way back to Puttaparthi, which he reached on June 5, the Swami stopped in Bangalore, where he was invited to give a speech at the local center of the *Bharatiya Vidya Bhavan*. Here, he was welcomed by Sri R. R. Diwakar as "the greatest and the most effective moral force in the world today."[42] On his part, Sathya Sai Baba remarked that

> it is the responsibility of the Bharatiya Vidya Bhavan and other such institutions to uphold the validity of *Bharatiya vidya* or *Atmavidya*. . . . Churn the sacred scriptures and the text books on Yoga and other paths for self-realization, and after collecting the nutritious butter, use it for the sustenance of mankind which is starving in the midst of pseudo-prosperity. Every worker at the Bhavan must shape himself into a perfect picture of the munificence of *Bharatiya vidya*; that is to say, he must be tolerant of all faiths, patient in the face of all odds, reverent towards the old, the sacred and the historic, and humble in spite of the insidious urge to demonstrate and display.[43]

Kasturi dedicates chapter 12, *Filling the Emptiness*, to a presentation of his guru's many miracles and to the therapeutic efficacy of his *vibhūti,* understood as the Swami's love concretized. Several stories are told of the sacred ash as well as of other substances mysteriously appearing on the holy man's pictures. Here is an example:

> "This day, two devotees of Lord Venkateswara joined us for the *bhajan*. When *Arti*[44] was performed, something fell from the picture of Baba. It was found to be *Sripadarenu*,[45] given to devotees at Thirupathi, after worship offered to Lord Venkateswara," writes Sri Muralidharan, the Station Director of All India Radio, Kohima.[46]

The hagiographer points out that the miracles of Sathya Sai Baba must be regarded as lessons in spiritual discipline, as *signa* which are aimed at promoting discrimination and spiritual inquiry, turning one's life away from sin and worldly pursuits and redirecting it toward god. After detailing several other miracles, Kasturi comes to the conclusion that the guru of Puttaparthi is the incarnation of the Trinity, of the one universal god.

In chapter 13, *So Kind! So Kind!*, the hagiographer presents the Seva Dal Conference, which was held in Prasanthi Nilayam on the occasion of the Dasara festival, in October 1970. He also offers details of the fourth All India Conference of Bhagavan Sri Sathya Sai Seva Organizations, which was held on November 20, 1970. He is keen to emphasize what he regards as the prime teaching of his guru, namely, that service to man is the best *sādhanā* or spiritual exercise, being a "discipline of love" (*premayoga*), and that society must not be viewed as a trap but rather as the privileged locus where one must learn service and compassion and sanctify his/her life. Among the recommended acts of *sevā* he lists the following: blood donations, literacy classes, slum clearings, *bhajans* in jails, classes in remand homes, cleaning of temples, visiting patients in hospitals, first aid, and firefighting.

Kasturi underlines that one must learn to see the guru in all forms and thus love all and serve all, since god is love: this is the truth that Sathya Sai Baba has come to reveal, since *preman* is his distinctive mark. He quotes his master's words on the need to realize how everyone is but a spark of the triadic divine principle and is in fact "three-eyed" (*tryambaka*), that is, a manifestation of the triads of Will-Work-Wisdom,

Doer-Duty-Deed, and Strength-Sweetness-Light. In commenting upon the Absolute *Brahman* as the triad of being (*sat*), consciousness (*cit*) and bliss (*ānanda*), the guru remarked:

> There are three desires or urges which every "I" has to fulfill: (i) I must live. This is the call from the core of Immortality (*Sath*). (ii) I must know. This is a reminiscence of the Omniscient, of which the "I" is but a spark. (iii) I must be happy. This is evidence of the *Ananda* which is innate in the individual.[47]

The Swami directed the office bearers of the Sathya Sai Seva Organizations to assist devotees to efficiently organize Bal Vikas, Seva Dals, Mahila Vibhags, study circles, *bhajan* groups, and Nagar Sankirtans. He stated:

> This organization has spread far and wide. About 3,000 persons participated in the conference, although only the Presidents and the Secretaries were invited, and no proxy attendance was permitted. . . . The Sathya Sai Organization is established to translate the principles of Love and Non-violence into daily practice. . . . The Sai Organization has to work with persons of all faiths. If you have love in you, you will be welcomed by all men everywhere. I have come to ensure *lokasangraha* (the welfare and happiness of the world);[48] so when you live in concord with all around you, your activity will certainly please Me.[49]

Kasturi brings the chapter to a close by quoting the guru's words on *sādhanā,* which in order to be effective must be conceived as a harmonious whole, combining the inner and outer disciplines of *japa, dhyāna, bhajans,* and *sevā.*

In chapter 14, *The Miraculous Appendix*, the hagiographer chronicles the Swami's trip to Goa in December 1970, where he suffered from an acute appendicitis attack which he later explained as due to his taking up the illness of a devotee who otherwise would have not survived: apparently, he cured himself while at the residence of Sri Nakul Sen, the lieutenant governor of Goa at the Raj Bhavan.[50] On this occasion, doctors had insisted that he should be immediately operated on, but he refused. It is reported that his illness was so bad that it was mistakenly announced on the radio that the guru had died. In particular, Kasturi writes that on December 10, 1970, while talking of Dattātreya, the three-headed god who represents the *trimūrti*, Sathya Sai Baba waved his hand—even as he announced that he was, indeed, Dattātreya—and "materialized" a picture of the god. Wonder of wonders, the picture showed the same head thrice, on the right, center, and left, and it was the head of the Swami himself as Brahmā, Viṣṇu, and Śiva. The hagiographer writes: "It was a picture which we were privileged to see for the first time in our lives."[51] It should be noted that an image showing three identical Sathya Sai Babas in a row and which bears the caption "Datta-Thraya" figures in the 1983 Reprint of Part 1 of Kasturi's work,[52] in the chapter *I am Here*, where the guru is extolled as an *avatāra* of Dattātreya.

In chapter 15, *Live in Love*, the hagiographer portrays his guru as the incarnation of compassion, whose *preman* extends to all creatures, comprising animals such as dogs and buffalos. He points out that Sathya Sai Baba has always loved to surround himself with pets: in particular dogs but also rabbits, peacocks, and the elephant Sai Gita.[53] The hagiographer underlines that god lives in all things and that devotees should come to realize their ātmic identity by practicing meditation (*dhyāna*). The method recommended by the guru was meditation upon light (*jyotis*), which he said was the easiest and safest: "Imagine the flame in the middle of the brow, and the light entering the cave of the heart to illumine. Let this light destroy hate, greed and selfishness, and let it flood your entire being. Let its ever-widening circle embrace all mankind."[54] The contemplative path is said to be characterized by three stages: (1) I am in the light; (2) The light is in me; (3) I am the light.

In chapter 16, *Beacon of Bliss*, Kasturi quotes his master's teachings on a variety of subjects. In particular, he remarks that Sathya Sai Baba emphasizes the importance of work and discipline and of always being conscious of one's obligations: "Duty is God and Work is Worship."[55] His emphasis on duty calls to mind Gandhi's thought that duties come before rights, since the very right to live accrues to us only when we do the duty of citizenship of the world.[56] If the goal is to live in god's presence, the path the guru prospects is set out in three stages: work, worship, and wisdom. Kasturi observes that whenever embarking upon an action, one should always ask oneself: Will the guru approve of this? The hagiographer then presents his master's sayings on the *neti neti* ("not this, not this") theology of the *Upaniṣads*, the significance of the *liṅga*, and the meaning of the popular invocatory verse on the guru, "The guru is Brahmā, the guru is Viṣṇu, the guru is Śiva Maheśvara," taken from the hymn of the *Gurugītā*.

Kasturi writes that the Maharashtra, Gujarat, and Mysore state conferences of the organization were held in May 1971, and that the Anantapur College for Women was formally inaugurated on July 8, 1971, day of Gurupūrṇimā, at the presence of a galaxy of personalities comprising the president of India, Sri V. V. Giri and his wife, as well as several ministers and state governors. With reference to the Anantapur College he quotes the words of S. Bhagavantham, who emphatically observed how "the College at Anantapur is a concrete manifestation of something superhuman. At an enormous cost of rupees four million, within a record time of ten months, Baba has reared a structure which is good enough for a University,"[57] and of V. K. Gokak, who stated that "this college, and the others that Baba has planned to establish in every State of India, will inculcate Indian culture in its essence and purity."[58]

Chapter 17, *The Names We Know*, brings Part 3 to a close and herein Kasturi focuses attention on the Swami's names and *avatāra*hood, elaborating upon the meaning of the terms *Sai* and *Bhagavan*. He observes that power is a special characteristic of god or Bhagavan and this is what precisely distinguishes an *avatāra* from a saint. He then reaffirms his thesis that Sathya Sai Baba is the quintessential divine principle known and worshipped in different forms all over the world and that he is one with past and future incarnations. As always, he corroborates such assertion by quoting the words of his master: "I am all deities in one. You may endeavor your best for thousands of years and have all mankind with you in your search, but you cannot understand My Reality."[59] The hagiographer notes that the *avatāra* has seven unique characteristics: the power to create (*sṛṣṭi*), the power to foster, guide, and protect (*sthiti*), the power to destroy (*laya*), the power to make things disappear (*tirodhāna*), the power of grace (*anugraha*)—which is twofold, namely, grace for the deserving ones, and grace conferred regardless of the recipient deserving it or not—and the power of being present wherever his name is uttered and his form is recognized. Finally, Kasturi extols his Swami as the teacher of the truth of Vedānta, he being the dispenser of pure love and the restorer of the essence of spirituality to mankind.

A Critical Evaluation of Part 3

Part 3 of Kasturi's work documents how the years from 1968 to 1971 were of prime importance in the expansion of the guru's movement, both in India and in the West. The Dharmakshetra building in Bombay and the first world conference of the Sathya Sai Seva Organization in May 1968 marked the beginning of Sathya Sai Baba's global, cosmopolitan appeal.

Sathya Sai Baba's connection to the *Bharatiya Vidya Bhavan* academy and a big-man such as K. M. Munshi, whom Kasturi defines as a "veteran Gandhian, scholarly statesman, patriotic writer, practical administrator and devoted student of Bharathiya Culture,"[60] deserve attention. Kanaiyalal Maneklal Munshi, a Gujarati Brahmin who had trained under Aurobindo Ghose at Baroda College, was a Hindu traditionalist and a prolific writer in both Gujarati[61] and English, who joined the Congress Party shortly after 1928 and proclaimed himself a Gandhian. More to the point, he was a Hindu nationalist ideologue and, as Manu Bhagavan has argued, "through K. M. Munshi, Hindu nationalism was reconfig-

Figure 3.1. Prof. Narayan Kasturi.

ured, made acceptable to mainstream nationalists in the Congress party. Munshi and other allies . . . utilized the power of this key organization [the *Bharatiya Vidya Bhavan*] to press forward an agenda in synch with the wishes of the religious right."[62] As a Congress politician, Munshi was embraced by the Hindu Mahasabha members because of his anti-Muslim attitudes. For him, Indian culture was equivalent to Brahmanical Hinduism and the *Bharatiya Vidya Bhavan*, which he founded in 1938, was a venue for Hinduism's systematization, modernization, and nationalization.

Nonetheless, if Sathya Sai Baba found in Munshi and the *Bharatiya Vidya Bhavan* an important source of legitimization, it must be stressed that he refused to get himself involved in politics or be associated with any politico-religious movement, always distancing himself from chauvinist parties and organizations. Indeed, the guru and his movement were explicitly apolitical, just like the Ramakrishna Mission and other neo-Hindu movements.[63] In later years, the Rāma Janmabhumi agitation in Ayodhya, which culminated in the destruction of the Babri Masjid by Hindu extremists, found no favor with him.[64]

Under the leadership of Indulal H. Shah (d. 2019),[65] a prominent *bhakta* and a tireless worker for the guru's cause, an effective corporate structure of the Sathya Sai Seva Organization took shape. At the end of the 1970s, I. H. Shah could proudly remark:

> There are over 3,600 main centres and over 10,000 sub-centres spread in every district of India and over 36 countries in the world. The activities of these centres are divided into three groups—spiritual, educational and service to humanity—which are conducted by the three wings of the Organization, namely Samithis or Centres, Mahila Vibhag or Women's Wing and Seva Dal or Service Wing. . . . Today there are over 10,000 *public* Sai bhajan centres spread all over the world.[66]

The organization was strengthened through the promotion of All-India conferences and, later, of international conferences. Foreign interest in the guru of Puttaparthi grew rapidly, especially during the period 1965–1975. Through their testimony and books, a few select Westerners, primarily from the United States, came to be co-helpers in Kasturi's endeavor of expanding the guru's fame, paving the way to the ever-growing "Western invasion" of Prasanthi Nilayam that would characterize the 1970s and even more so the 1980s. By the end of the 1960s, the first Sathya Sai Baba centers were established outside India, primarily in America but also in Europe and other parts of the world, and the year 1971 saw the publication of the first books about Sathya Sai Baba, written by Arnold Schulman[67] and Howard Murphet. The 1970s witnessed a general growth in the number of foreign devotees and the Americans were no doubt the driving force of the guru's movement.[68] The American branch of the Sathya Sai Organization was founded in 1975, with John S. Hislop as chairman.

Despite the daily performance of Vedic chants and the occasional celebration of Vedic *yajñas*,[69] the ritual element in the Sathya Sai Baba movement—as in most neo-Hindu groups—did not and does not play a major role. Wishing to present himself as a global divine actor capable of attracting people from all quarters, ritual practices were never his primary concern. Actually, along the decades Hindu rituals have even come to be perceived as a potential hindrance to his self-promotion, given that the center of attraction is he alone, the guru-god. Because of the global appeal of his charisma, Sathya Sai Baba often advised Western devotees to sing their devotional hymns in English instead of the standard Hindi or Sanskrit.[70] With regard to the recitation of the guru's 108 names, Kasturi writes: "He does not even say that they should be in Sanskrit. . . . He answers to any Name, whether it is lisped or mispronounced, or crude or meaningless, provided the call comes from a yearning heart."[71]

To date, the performance of *yajñas* and Vedic rituals coexists with the guru's international constituency, though they are limited to select, solemn circumstances. Rituals are resorted to *cum grano salis,* as a powerful tool for affirming the holy man's self-identification with an immemorial, transcendent revelation interpreted as the pristine *depositum fidei* of India and of mankind as a whole. A major instance of the guru's fostering of Vedic sacrifices has been the Ati Rudra Maha Yajna, an eleven-day ritual fire-sacrifice which was held in the Sai Kulwant Hall in Prasanthi Nilayam in August 2006. Devotees claim that this sacrifice involved the greatest number of Vedic priests ever assembled. The Ati Rudra Maha Yajna was reenacted a few months later in Chennai in January 2007, always with the guru's attendance as presiding deity.

All in all, the utilization of Vedic ritual served and still serves the purpose of reinforcing the discourse on India as the cradle of spirituality and wisdom, since an exotic, orientalist rhetoric was and is highly appealing both to a Western audience and to Westernized Hindu middle and upper classes/castes.[72]

With the steady increase of Westerners, the hagiographer will more and more emphasize Sathya Sai Baba's oneness with Jesus. Thus, when commenting with some Western devotees on the Goa episode, that is, the guru's spectacular recovery from a painful appendicitis attack, Kasturi observed: "Just think of it, here in Christian Goa, in a building that was once a monastery, Baba has shown the people His identity with Christ. There's even a cross towering up from the roof. What a perfect symbol! He looked more beautiful tonight than ever."[73] Moreover: "The Goa episode was for me another amazing adventure into the mystery of Swami. Rarely does a person secure the chance of witnessing and watching the Redeemer on the cross and of covering oneself with delight when the cross disintegrates, revealing the resurgent Lord on the Heavenly Throne."[74]

From around 1969, references to Shirdi Sai Baba faded out in Sathya Sai Baba's speeches. Instead, from Christmas Day 1970 the Swami started speaking more and more about Jesus. The growing importance of Jesus in Sathya Sai Baba's and Kasturi's discourses coincides with the internationalization of the Swami's movement and parallels the progressive minimization of the foundational claim of the guru of Puttaparthi, his identification with Shirdi Sai Baba.[75] Sophie Hawkins observes: "[T]he earlier posters always include Shirdi Sai Baba whereas in the more recent images the latter has been gradually phased out by a (political) preference for Jesus."[76] Given the overall success in the establishment of himself as the reincarnation of the saint of Shirdi, which marked his early years, with the opening of this new phase and the globalization of his charisma Sathya Sai Baba needed to intensify the rhetoric of his oneness with all divine incarnations and in particular with Jesus—also referred to as Isa/Issa, which is the name for Jesus used by Muslims[77]—so as to be recognized by Western devotees as none other than the lord of their own religious tradition, the cosmic Christ.[78]

In order to expand his popularity toward the West, the guru's strategy was to assimilate Christianity, the "Western religion," although his containment of Jesus was not always successful and free of controversy. As Tulasi Srinivas aptly notes, some deities are more difficult to enfold than others and this determines occasional "translation failures."[79] For instance, the guru did not like his devotees to think of themselves as sinners and warned that man should never be identified with his/her mistakes. He argued: "Do not condemn yourselves as weak, sinful, conceited, etc.; when doing that, you condemn Me, your inner self."[80] Moreover: "I have stopped people from reciting sayings that proclaim man is sinful, born in sin, etc."; "There is no sin as such; there are only errors due to ignorance, greed, envy, or hatred."[81] Kasturi voiced the same argument and pointed out: "He [Baba] says there is no sin, what is so called is the effect, the false self of ignorance, ignorance of one's high heritage, destiny, equipment and excellence. Baba does not encourage self-condemnation, especially the sloka repeated by many during worship 'Paapoham Paapajanmanaam etc.' in which the individual calls Himself a sinner born in sin, rolling in sin. How can you condemn yourselves so, when you have as your core, Sai Himself, He asks."[82] The guru's position may have been influenced by Vivekananda, who was strongly opposed to the Christian doctrine that man is sinful by nature: "The Vedanta recognizes no sin, it only recognizes error. And the greatest error, says the Vedanta, is to say that you are weak, that you are a sinner, a miserable creature, and that you have no power and you cannot do this and that."[83] Vivekananda argued that the Christian doctrine of original sin is "a standing libel upon human nature" and stressed that men are not sinners but "heirs of immortal bliss."[84]

In pictures purportedly "materialized" by the guru of Puttaparthi, his future incarnation as Prema Sai Baba bears a Christ-like countenance,[85] and the Swami himself presented the mission of the third and final *avatāra* as the ultimate gospel: "Finally, Prema Sai, the third Avatar, will promote the evangel news that not only does God reside in everybody, but everybody is God. That will be the final wisdom which will enable every man and woman to go to God."[86]

In a speech he delivered on Christmas 1971, the guru announced that Jesus had come to realize his identity in three ascending stages: at the beginning, he thought of himself as messenger of god (the *dvaita* or dualistic stage); subsequently, he envisioned himself as son of god (the *viśiṣṭādvaita* or qualified nondual stage); and ultimately, he realized his oneness with the Father (the supreme *advaita,* nondual stage). He added that "there is a stage beyond the above three which is known as *turyavastha,* and that is akin to the Holy Ghost in Christianity."[87] Here again, the guru followed in Ramakrishna's and Vivekananda's steps who had classified the schools of Vedānta and all creeds according to the hierarchical scheme of nondualism (Advaita, the highest form), qualified nondualism (Viśiṣṭādvaita, a lower form), and dualism (Dvaita, the lowest form), thus providing a universal typology of religion.[88] Advaita Vedānta, Viśiṣṭādvaita Vedānta, and Dvaita Vedānta were understood as the three levels of spiritual growth in man, whatever one's conviction, which Vivekananda argued could be detected even in Jesus's sayings in the New Testament:

> To the masses who could not conceive of anything higher than a Personal God, he said, "Pray to your Father in heaven" (*Matthew* 6.9). To others who could grasp a higher idea, he said, "I am the vine, ye are the branches" (*John* 15.5), but to his disciples to whom he revealed himself more fully, he proclaimed the highest truth, "I and my Father are One" (*John* 10.30).[89]

Sathya Sai Baba stated that Jesus had traveled to India, had spent years in the Himalayan monasteries of Kashmir and Tibet practicing meditation, and that he had become fully aware of his oneness with god while in India.[90] This belief was first popularized in 1887 by the Russian war correspondent Nicolas Notovitch (1858–1916) through his purported discovery of the manuscript of the *Life of Saint Issa* in the Buddhist monastery of Hemis in Ladakh.[91] In a conversation with John S. Hislop, the guru gave the following details: "Jesus realized that he was Christ in his 25th year. For eight years following his 16th birthday, he travelled in India, Tibet, Iran, and Russia. He was variously regarded as a beggar or as a sannyasi. Jesus had no money. His parents were very poor and practically abandoned him at an early age."[92] On the other hand, contemporary Christian scholarship rejects the hypothesis of Jesus having been to India, Tibet, or surrounding areas, it being without historical basis.

From the early 1970s, the effort of both the guru and his hagiographer has been to highlight that Sathya Sai Baba and Jesus are fundamentally one and the same, the essence of their message—the love of god and brotherhood of men—being equivalent. Throughout his opus Kasturi cultivated such ecumenical spirit. Beginning in 1972, the Christmas celebrations in Prasanthi Nilayam—depicted by the hagiographer as a "New Jerusalem"[93]—complete with carol singing concerts and children's dramatic reenactments of Jesus's life, became a major feature and thousands of foreign devotees came to the ashram to celebrate Christmas at the presence of "Sai-Isa." During his discourse of Christmas 1972, the guru claimed not only that Jesus had predicted his advent but that he was the Father of Jesus:

> The statement of Christ is simple, "He who sent me among you will come again!" and He pointed to a Lamb. The Lamb is merely a symbol, a sign. It stands for the Voice: Ba Ba; the announcement was the advent of Baba. "His Name will be Truth," Christ declared. Sathya means Truth. "He will wear a robe of red, a blood red robe." (Here Baba pointed to the robe He was wearing). "He will be short, with a crown (of hair)" . . . Christ did not declare that He will come again. He said, "He who made me will come again." That Ba-Ba is this Baba and Sai, the short, curly-hair-crowned red-robed Baba, has come. He is not only in this Form, but, He is in every one of you, as the dweller in the Heart. He is there; short, with a robe of the color of the blood that fills it.[94]

Speaking to a Christian audience, the Swami thus portrayed himself as the ultimate godhead, the Father, who in his eschatological role will save humanity once and for all. Providing authority to his *pūrṇāvatāra* claim through Jesus's purported words, he simultaneously reinforced his nondualistic universalism.

By the same token, in his narrative Kasturi insists on glorifying his master as Śiva-Śakti, which amounts to recognizing the fullness of his divinity from a Hindu perspective. In an effort to show that Sathya Sai Baba is the inner core/truth of all religions, throughout his work the hagiographer provides his readers with a fusion of theological horizons in which Jesus, the Father, Śiva-Śakti, Rāma, the Buddha, Kṛṣṇa, Veṅkaṭeśvara, etc. are interchangeable with Sathya Sai Baba and amount to the same reality.[95] Along these lines, in commenting upon the ninety-fifth of the guru's 108 names—*Oṃ Śrī Sarvamata Sammatāya Namaḥ*—Kasturi extols him as the one who accepts all religions, stressing the universality of his teaching and mission:

> So Baba is here glorified as He who accepts all religions. This is in recognition of the universal teaching of Baba. Baba has come to fuse, not confuse. He revives Sanathana Dharma,

> the eternal universal faith which speaks of "Ekam" the one of which "Vipraah" (the wise) "Bahudha Vadanthi" (speak, as many).[96] . . . Just as He declared the world to be His mansion and each country a room in that mansion, every human being is Himself. . . . "All names are mine. I am also the nameless one," Baba has announced. So, by whatever name He is called He responds. He declares, "there is no atheist at all, for even those who deny God, do love something or someone, do seek peace and joy. That love is God, that peace is God, that joy is God." . . . He is in every mind as its motive-force, whether the man labels himself as Sanathani, Arya Samajist, Adwaithin, Visishtadwaithin, Dwaithin, Jain, Sikh, Buddhist, Christian, Moslem, Rationalist, Agnostic or even Atheist![97]

As noted, the approach of the hagiographer and his master to all world religions was Vivekanandian through and through. It insisted on their purported common ethical and spiritual ideals minimizing their differences, subsuming all faiths under the umbrella of Vedānta metaphysics.[98]

In particular, the identification of the Swami with the god Dattātreya, as will be argued more thoroughly in chapters 5 and 6, is instrumental in highlighting his oneness with the Hindu *trimūrti* of Brahmā, Viṣṇu, and Śiva *and* the Christian Trinity of the Father, Son, and Holy Ghost. On various occasions, the hagiographer utilizes the triadic pattern as a theological *passepartout,* a most powerful tool for representing at one and the same time the unsurpassable fullness (*pūrṇatva*) and universality of godhead, simultaneously speaking to a Hindu and a Christian audience.

Overall, what emerges as the dominating theme in Kasturi's narrative is the guru's educational mission through the building of schools and colleges and the implementation of his program in human values meant to foster discipline, duty, and devotion in the hearts and minds of the youth. The idea is that the guru's implementation of colleges and schools marks an epochal turn. If the keystone of Sathya Sai Baba's plan is the transformation of man, the hagiographer underlines that this can be achieved only through a renovated educational program, namely, a purportedly nonsectarian spiritual education, from primary schools up to university level, which is to be implemented via the establishment of Sathya Sai institutes and colleges in each and every state of India. As the guru told some Western devotees around 1970: "I want to build two colleges in every state in India."[99] The guru emphasized the need to promote human values in public schools. He argued: "Religious schools would appeal only to the religious, whereas Baba's task is to raise the general public into devotion and spiritual life. One aspect of Baba's task is to reform education, and if that were impossible He would not have come."[100] The conviction of both Sathya Sai Baba and his hagiographer was that proper education could be achieved only by reforming the school programs. If, in the guru's words, "India is being forged into a *bhogabhoomi*,"[101] that is, a land that is prey to lust, characterized by the imitation of alien cultures, the aim of the *avatāra* was to counter this state of affairs and restore on solid bases the land's values and perennial *dharma* through a revolution in its educational system.

This theme is inextricably linked to that of service to society, to the Bal Vikas and Seva Dal programs. Though the Bal Vikas programs were deemed to be nonsectarian, Lawrence A. Babb has rightly pointed out that "the symbolism deployed in the classes is distinctly Hindu."[102] Sathya Sai Baba's mission based upon education and service to all—irrespective of caste and creed—coincided with Kasturi's heartfelt conviction and practice, from the time when he was a young teacher and the secretary of the Ramakrishna Mission in Mysore. Even prior to meeting the guru of Puttaparthi, the hagiographer believed that a morals-based education and selfless service to one's fellow men were the two pillars of religious life, much more important than silent sitting and meditation: indeed, there was perfect consonance between Kasturi's *karmayoga* orientation and Sathya Sai Baba's teaching and action. The relevance of education and service was grounded in Vivekanandian ideology, which influenced both of them profoundly, consciously as well as unconsciously, as it characterized many other religious movements of the period. To be sure, Kasturi and his guru shared this common understanding, which was part and parcel of the reformist spirit of their times.

Sathyam Sivam Sundaram, Part 4: An Overview

Part 4 of *Sathyam Sivam Sundaram* was first issued on July 27, 1980, day of Gurupūrṇimā, and comprises two brief prologues (*Between You and Me* and *The Song He Sings*)[103] and a total of eight chapters, of which the last, titled *Tomorrow*, is but an epilogue. Endowed with a glossary, it extends for 183 pages in its 1981 edition and covers approximately eight years of Sathya Sai Baba's public life, from September 1971 to November 1979. In fact, only the second chapter is dedicated to a chronological presentation of the guru's life, whereas the subsequent five concern select topics dealing with aspects of Sathya Sai Baba's life and teachings.

Chapter 1, *In Confidence*, is a résumé of the guru's early days up to his announcement of being Sai Baba. Kasturi emphasizes young Sathya's poverty[104] and remembers the latter's habit of writing poetry and dramas. The hagiographer could not but rejoice in noticing the literary and artistic vein of his master, energized by the force of his ethical end educational message:

> Swami said that even as a boy He had been intent on correcting the vagaries, vices, defects and deficiencies of society, by means of ridicule and satire expressed in drama and poetry. "*Cheppinattu Chesthara*?" which means, "Are your deeds in accordance with your words?" is a fine example of His educative experiments. It exposed the hypocrisy of parents and teachers—an evil which children and pupils spontaneously absorb. So also today, Baba exhorts us to coordinate thought, word and deed. . . . He composed long lampoons in folk meters, on the evils of drink, the absence of literacy and the irresponsible accumulation of debt by the villagers. These songs were quickly learnt by the children who were taught by Baba, and were recited by them in groups in front of every house. Some householders were angered at this onslaught on their shortcomings and fixations, but many encouraged the boys to continue their reformatory task.[105]

With respect to the guru's miracles, Kasturi cites a book by Nagamani Purnaiya, who first met the Swami in 1945. Titled *The Divine Leelas of Sri Satya Sai Baba* (Bangalore: House of Seva, 1976; originally published in Telugu), it presents more than 140 early miracles of the saint, of which the author says that "more than 115 were witnessed by me with abundant joy."[106]

In chapter 2, *Love on the March*, Kasturi summarizes in a little more than fifty pages the main events of Sathya Sai Baba's public life up to November 1979. It is inevitably less chronologically detailed than the preceding chapters of Parts 1, 2 and 3, focusing on what the hagiographer deems to be most relevant. At the outset, he explicitly links the title of his work to Vivekananda's "prophetic declaration," when in his discourses on *bhaktiyoga* he announced the coming of a divine teacher, a "Lord of Truth" who would reveal "the most wonderful things regarding truth, goodness and beauty."[107] The hagiographer humbly notes: "I had no inkling of this truth. Vivekananda himself must have led me to the teacher, the Lord of Truth."[108] He again voices his conviction that it was Vivekananda along with his master Ramakrishna who guided his steps and took him to Sathya Sai Baba. Kasturi even quotes the guru's exegesis of *Sathyam Sivam Sundaram*: "Sathyam is the feet, Sivam is the trunk and Sundaram the head. On *Sathyam* we stand, on *Sivam* we act and on *Sundaram* we think. In Truth we are born, in Goodness we live, and into Beauty we merge."[109]

The hagiographer then presents the All India Conference of the Sri Sathya Sai Seva Organisations, which was held in Madras during the last week of December 1971. Devotees were particularly excited since the Indo-Pakistani war that led to the creation of Bangladesh had ended on December 17, as per the guru's prediction that it would not interfere with the conference (apparently, he had assured his *bhakta*s that it would be over by that time and so it was). Sathya Sai Baba's paternalistic comments immediately after the India-Pakistan conflict, duly reported by Kasturi, are meant to highlight the guru's patriotism:

> The civil war in Pakistan, between its western and eastern halves, forced millions of terror-stricken people to take refuge in India. They prayed in their agony that we should help them. True to our culture and tradition we sacrificed a great deal, gave them food and shelter and sent them back to their homes after ensuring that they could be safe and live there in peace. We do not wish to expand or dominate or injure anyone.[110]

In passing, Kasturi mentions the purported resurrection of the American devotee Walter Cowan on Christmas Day 1971, quoting the testimony of his wife Elsie and the words of Walter Cowan himself. He notes that six years later, on April 28, 1977, the Cowan Block of the hostel at the Brindavan Campus was inaugurated by the president of India, Sri B. D. Jatti, himself an ardent devotee of Sathya Sai Baba.[111]

The year 1972 was an important year, with the establishment of the Sri Sathya Sai Central Trust with the guru of Puttaparthi as its chairman and sole trustee. In time, it came to absorb other Shri Sathya Sai trusts such as the Medical Trust and the High Learning Trust.[112] After writing about the foundation stone of the Sathya Sai Brindavan College for boys which the guru laid on March 16, 1972, near Whitefield,[113] Kasturi proceeds to offer details of Sathya Sai Baba's nine-day stay in Delhi, from March 25 to April 2. The hagiographer quotes the positive reports of the Delhi newspapers and the words of the U.S. ambassador, Prof. Keating, for whom Sathya Sai Baba "materialized" a ring and who was impressed by the reverence shown toward the guru by the Delhi crowds. In particular, Kasturi writes that the Swami advised all renunciants to keep away from politics and quotes his master's words: "I warned the *sanyasis* (ascetics) of the corrupting influence of institutionalism and hierarchism. I told them to keep away from the contamination of political involvements."[114] This statement mirrors the guru's position of never wanting to be linked to any political movement and party. He rather aimed at presenting himself as a good patriot,[115] as when in January 1973, while in Bangalore, he blessed the members of the Indian armed forces in their function as defenders of the country.[116]

At various points, Sathya Sai Baba's conservatism, accommodating traditionalism, and universalism emerge from the hagiographer's account. The love he is said to have for all "untouchables" (Harijans) does not prevent him from upholding the caste system, the sacredness of which is affirmed in the *Vedas*. Kasturi narrates how the guru celebrated free mass weddings with no caste distinctions[117]—emphatically declaring that "there is only one caste, the caste of humanity; there is only one religion, the religion of love; there is only one language, the language of the heart; there is only one God and He is omnipresent"[118]—while simultaneously advocating the sanctity of the *varṇāśramadharma*. Following Vivekananda's and Gandhi's lesson, the Swami argued that the duties pertaining to castes (*varṇa*) and stages of life (*āśrama*) needed to be rightly interpreted, that is to say, understood in ethical rather than ontological terms.

The hagiographer next turns to the presentation of the first Summer Course on Indian Culture and Spirituality, willed by the guru as another means of reorienting Indian education, which was held at his ashram in Whitefield, outside Bangalore, from May 1 to May 31, 1972.[119] The monthly Summer Course was offered to select senior students—fifteen students from each state of India—and was held under the guidance of educationist V. K. Gokak. The Summer Course, which in the 1970s saw the participation of an increasing number of students as well as of devotees and guests from all over the world, was regularly held from 1972 to 1979—with the exception of 1975—and later lost its continuity (in the 1980s it was never held; in the 1990s it was held five times: in 1990, 1991, 1993, 1995 and 1996; in the 2000s it was held twice: in 2000 and 2002).[120]

Kasturi relates that on May 6, 1972, the guru's mother Easwaramma died at Whitefield, and underlines Sathya Sai Baba's equanimity on this sad occasion.[121] He then proceeds to chronicle the Conference of Seva Dals held in Prasanthi Nilayam in the fall of 1972 and, following this, he delves into some prodigious "materializations" of his guru: a *liṅga,* various Hindu *mūrtis,* and a crucifix with Jesus on it, one inch high, for the American devotee John S. Hislop. This latter "materialization" was especially significant for Western followers, given that the Swami claimed that it showed Christ as he really was at the time of his death, also adding that the wood of which the cross was made was taken from the actual cross on which he was crucified. This purported prodigy reinforced the guru's intimate link to Jesus and convinced his Western followers that he was indeed one with Christ and no less than the Father who sent him. Here is how Kasturi explained the inner meaning of crucifixion to overseas devotees: "The crucifixion is a process by which you are able to enter the realm of the Father, and be by His side or merge in Him. That is the inner meaning of crucifixion. Swami reveals to us the inner meaning of symbols, of parables and stories found in scriptures."[122]

From his early discourses the guru taught that the "I," when crossed out, becomes the symbol of the cross: what is crucified is the ego.[123] Here is Hislop's own testimony as to what happened when the guru broke off two twigs in a bush and made a cross. It was the evening of Mahāśivarātri of 1973:[124]

> Baba . . . closed his fingers over the twigs and directed three somewhat slow breaths into his fist, between thumb and forefinger. Then he opened his hand to reveal a Christ figure crucified on a cross, and he gave it to me. He said: "This shows Christ as he really was at the time he left his body, not

> as artists have imagined him or as historians have told about him. His stomach is pulled in and his ribs are all showing. He had no food for eight days. . . . The cross is wood from the actual cross on which Christ was crucified. To find some of the wood after 2,000 years took a little time. The image is of Christ after he died. It is a dead face."[125]

In his hagiography Kasturi writes:

> Later, he [John S. Hislop] got the wood examined, and was informed that it was at least twenty centuries old. He had the little silver icon photographed and the photographs enlarged. He was surprised to note that there were marks of sweat on the brow and signs of froth at the corners of the mouth. It had all signs of pain heroically borne.[126]

In order to offer a "scientific" proof of Sathya Sai Baba's powers, Kasturi even dedicates a paragraph to the uniqueness of the guru's aura, supposedly detected by Dr. Frank G. Baranowski (d. 2002) of Arizona University when he visited the holy man in Bangalore in July 1977.[127]

As always, the hagiographer covers in some detail the guru's travels, and in particular his extensive trip to the North and West of India—from March 14 to April 4, 1973—when he visited the States of Punjab, Haryana, and Himachal Pradesh and the cities of Delhi, Jaipur, Bombay, Pune, Rajkot, and Hyderabad. Kasturi emphasizes his guru's words that service (*sevā*) should be conducted in all villages, as per his instruction that every unit of the Sathya Sai Organisation should "adopt" a village. By the same token, he points out that the holy man advocates the need to serve nature, to protect and revere the natural environment along with one's fellow men. He further describes the prodigy of the "emergence of the *liṅga*" (*liṅgodbhāva*) from Sathya Sai Baba's body during the festival of Mahāśivarātri of 1974,[128] also noting how the last *liṅgodbhāva* took place on Mahāśivarātri of 1977.

In an effort to prove his hero's detachment (*vairāgya*), Kasturi observes how the guru spoke against asking and giving money during his birthday celebrations of November 1974. He emphasizes that the Swami leads a simple life, with no luxuries, and how the offerings he receives are spent for promoting education, health, and the general uplift of villages, that is, integrated rural development. The hagiographer remarks that Sathya Sai Baba had the ancient temples of Puttaparthi renovated—among them the Veṇugopālasvāmin temple[129]—and its *mūrti*s replaced with new silver ones. In the acknowledgment that all religions lead to the same goal, he even had a new mosque built for the local Muslim community.[130] In November 1979, a Śiva temple was erected at the guru's birthplace, which was meant to confirm his divine status.

As a further sign of the global expansion of the organization, the hagiographer notes that, starting in 1976, special programs of *akhaṇḍabhajan*s were held in all Sathya Sai Baba centers throughout the world, comprising twenty-four hours of uninterrupted chanting of devotional hymns. While in Prasanthi Nilayam Vedic *mantra*s and *yajña*s continued to be performed, typically in October during the Dasara festival, non-Indian devotees were allowed and even encouraged to sing the guru's praise in their own languages, avoiding the Sanskrit/Hindi medium, which they could hardly understand, thus accelerating the inevitable *miśra* ("mixture") or hybridization of a more and more cosmopolitan movement.[131]

Throughout chapter 2, Kasturi reiterates the priority of the educational mission of his guru—from Bal Vikas to university level—through the establishment of schools, colleges, auditoriums, libraries, etc. He stresses how the ideal of "Sai education" is based on the triad of duty, devotion, and discipline, which alone can bring about the integration of mankind, and quotes Sathya Sai Baba's words: "Students are My hope, the source of My delight. They are what I live by."[132] The idea is that true power is character and character can only be built through education, which alone will allow India to preserve its traditional, immortal values. Following his master, Kasturi refers his readers to Kṛṣṇa's solemn words in *Bhagavadgītā* 12.13–20, which is a passage frequently quoted by Hindu gurus when asked for a universal teaching that might be appreciated even by non-Hindus. The hagiographer highlights how the Swami dedicated the last Summer Course of the 1970s precisely to a study of "India's Gospel," the *Bhagavadgītā*, a significant choice symptomatic of the educative function attributed to this glorious text.[133] The hagiographer illustrates the guru's universalist teaching through the example offered by the students of his schools:

> During the Dasara celebrations in 1979, students of different religions from the Sri Sathya Sai college in Puttaparthi, presented

> themselves in their ceremonial customs and described, to the great delight of the vast gathering, the main principles of each religion. A Sikh from New Delhi, a Zoroastrian from Bombay, a Christian from Hawaii, a Muslim from Libya, a Buddhist from Sikkim and a Hindu from Kabul were the participating students. When Baba stood in the centre of the group as they finished, all were pleasantly surprised that Sai, the sum of all religions and the goal of all *sadhana*, had condescended thus to teach them the unity of faith. The students of Sai colleges have mastered the art of coordinated labor. They have presented orchestras and plays on Sri Ramakrishna, Sankaracharya and Jesus, besides having set the Ramayana and the Sai stories to music. Bhagavan is, of course, the invisible and also, almost always, the visible source of all their achievements.[134]

In chapter 3, *The Call and the Echo*, Kasturi recalls the prophecy of the magnificent future of Puttaparthi that the guru back in the early years had made to *pujārī* Lakshmiah: not only the village but the entire region surrounding it would be transmuted into a Prashanti Pradesh, a land of supreme peace. He observes that such a prophecy, which appeared utterly impossible, has come true, and again extols his Swami as he who unites all men and religions through the irresistible call of his love.

With reference to the guru's powers, the hagiographer dedicates several pages to his habit of appearing in dreams and calling people to him through such means. He observes that the guru is in full control of the natural elements, and endorses the genuineness of his "materializations" through several testimonies. For the first time in his hagiography, he recognizes the fact that many people have set out to expose Sathya Sai Baba as a fraud, a juggler and a trickster, being quick to add that they "failed to tarnish even the hem of His robe."[135] Elsewhere, Kasturi quotes these telling words of the guru: "Praise of Me is rising up like a mountain on one side and defamation like another mountain on the other side. I stand in the middle blessing both."[136] Moreover:

> Love . . . Love . . . Love first . . . Love, as long as life lasts. For Myself, I can say, I shower more blessings on those who decry or defame Me than those who worship and adore Me! For, those who spread falsehoods about Me derive joy therefrom;

> I am happy that I am the cause for their exultation and joy. You too must accept this line of argument and be very happy when someone derives joy by defaming you. Do not respond by defaming that person; then the chain of hatred will bind both and drag both down. Life will become a tragedy. Conquer anger by means of fortitude; conquer hatred by love. Do not feed anger with retaliation; do not feed hatred with fury.[137]

Kasturi reminds his readers that back in 1948—when he was famous throughout Karnataka as a humor writer—he also shared the Ramakrishna Mission prejudice on miracles and miracle-men and hoped that the guru of Puttaparthi could be exposed. His final conclusion, after having had many years of interaction with the Swami, is that the latter's miracles and powers are genuine, and he further notes how he has transformed even skeptics into devotees.[138]

Chapter 4, *Words with Wings*, is quite long and entirely dedicated to Sathya Sai Baba's writings, that is, to his Vedāntic teachings. Kasturi praises him as the "teacher of truth" (*satyabodhaka*) and gives ample space to his message since he very well realizes that it tends to be overshadowed by the astounding miracles that are attributed to him.[139] The hagiographer's aim is to highlight the importance of the holy man's teaching activity, since this was truly a primal concern of Sathya Sai Baba, who exercised his intense pedagogic action through public discourses, private interviews, articles/books, and letters. With reference to the Swami's public discourses, he calls attention to the significance of his proems, the extempore verses and poems that he sang before beginning his speeches, which *in nuce* are said to contain the *rasa,* the sap or essence of his intended instruction.

The guru's writings found their collocation in the monthly *Sanathana Sarathi*—the newsletter devoted to the moral and spiritual uplift of humanity through *satya, dharma, śānti,* and *preman*—which was inaugurated on February 16, 1958, on the auspicious day of Mahāśivarātri.[140] Kasturi, who was the editor of *Sanathana Sarathi* from its inception, notes how the holy man wrote in simple, elegant Telugu and sometimes directly in English. What later came to regarded as the guru's books, the *Vahini*s, were originally a series of articles, which the hagiographer painstakingly translated from Telugu into English. Kasturi presents in some detail each *Vahini* in chronological order, saying that the first to appear was *Prema Vahini* on pure love (in which the guru shows how the three paths of *jñāna*, *karman*, and *bhakti* constitute one indivisible whole). It was followed by fourteen other *Vahinis*: *Sandeha Nivarini* (lit. "clearance of doubts," in the form of a dialogue between a *bhakta* and the guru),[141] *Dharma Vahini*, *Prasanthi Vahini* (comprising the guru's commentary on the eightfold path of Yoga), *Dhyana Vahini*, *Jnana Vahini*, *Upanishad Vahini* (a brief commentary to the ten principal *Upaniṣads* as well as to the *Brahmānubhava Upaniṣad*), *Geetha Vahini* (a commentary to the *Bhagavadgītā*), *Sathya Sai Vahini*, *Prasnothara Vahini* (comprising the guru's answers to a variety of spiritual questions), *Leela Kaivalya Vahini* (on god's cosmic play), *Sutra Vahini* (a series of aphorisms on the supreme *Brahman*), *Vidya Vahini* (on spiritual education), *Bhagavatha Vahini* (a synthetic retelling and commentary of the *Bhāgavata Purāṇa*), and the *Ram Katha Rasavahini*, Part 1 & 2 (a synthetic retelling and commentary of the *Rāmāyaṇa* epic).[142] Kasturi praises Sathya Sai Baba's writings as invaluable guides for aspirants to liberation, treasures that shed light on intricate problems of spiritual discipline.[143]

The hagiographer devotes several pages and the final part of the chapter to an appraisal of the many letters written by the *avatāra* "to persons anguished by doubt or defeated by disaster."[144] As an example, here is an excerpt of a letter that the guru addressed to his students on Janmāṣṭamī, the birthday of lord Kṛṣṇa, which falls in the lunar month of *śrāvaṇa* (July–August). It is centered on the true self, and nicely ties together his nondual teaching with the call to lead a life of detachment and service:

> What is the Self? It is the Self that says "not I," for if it says "I," then it is the unreal self. The real Self is selfless, and has no thought either of or for itself. It is the Self that has now forgotten itself, because somehow, it can visualize itself only in others. It is the Self that loves selflessly, because pure love is but selfless affection. It is the Self that seeks the truth with selfless determination, because truth is selfless wisdom. It is the Self that is quiet, because in silence lies cessation from all worldliness. It is the Self in wordless meditation, because wordless meditation is the conquest of the mind through union with the Divine. It is the Self that does not judge, but evaluates. It does not compare, seek security, or even see itself. It is the Self that has completely absorbed itself and yet, in a strange and mystical fashion, it is more itself, more complete and more real than it has ever been. This is the real Self.

> God is love, and love is selflessness. Selflessness is the abolition of all sense of the ego and separativeness, of all spurious identification with the isolationist life of that counterfeit thing called "self"; self is separativeness, and separativeness is the denial of wholeness, holiness, God.[145]

Chapter 5, *Moves in His Game*, narrates various episodes of the guru granting *darśan* at the moment of a devotee's death, as a token of grace and liberation. In presenting the last moments of *bhakta*s who were blessed by Sathya Sai Baba's presence, the hagiographer also recalls an episode that saw Ramakrishna protagonist, once again in an effort to highlight their similarity. In chapter 6, *Closer and Closer*, Kasturi focuses attention on the significance of being granted an interview with the guru. Daily, the Swami used to call devotees in for personal interviews. When in Puttaparthi he would select a group of people twice a day, during morning and afternoon *darśan,* and meet them soon afterward in a small room on the ground floor of the Prasanthi Nilayam *mandir*. The hagiographer presents John S. Hislop's first encounter with the guru in 1968 and delves on the transformative power of the master's love in the course of these interviews.

To be called by Sathya Sai Baba and have an interview with him was what all *bhakta*s craved for, it being the crowning of one's pilgrimage to Puttaparthi. On these occasions, the guru would offer instruction, answer personal problems, cure the ill, and "materialize" many things such as *vibhūti*, rings, rosaries, oil, etc. Here is how Howard Levin describes his exit from a private interview with the guru on Christmas Day 1971: "I bent down to the floor and kissed his feet. He helped me up and gently but swiftly led me to the outer room where the others were waiting. It's hard to describe how I felt. It was as if I had been opened up and filled with love from head to toe."[146] The hagiographer notes how to a devotee clamoring for an interview the guru once said that he was giving him interviews everyday through his inner voice but that he was not "receptive" to it: he himself placed a barrier and prevented the "enter-in-view," the fruitful spiritual intimacy with his master.

The Swami, just like Kasturi, loved playing with words. Here are a few examples: "Put apart the I" for Puttaparthi; "heartificial" for artificial; "proper ties" for properties; "die mind" for diamond; "god is now here" for god is nowhere; "inner view" for interview.[147] He would offer new meanings to Sanskrit words and compounds: Kṛṣṇa's epithet Madhu-sūdana or

"Destroyer of [the demon] Madhu" in the *Bhagavadgītā* became "Destroyer of sensual pleasures" (*madhu* also meaning "honey"), and Arjuna's epithet Kuru-nandana or "Son of the Kuru [clan]" became "he who finds joy (*nandana*) in action" (*kuru* also meaning "do!," being the imperative, second person singular, of verbal root *kṛ*, "to do").[148] As Lawrence A. Babb notes: "One of his most characteristic rhetorical devices is the ad hoc (and often false) etymology. For example, he has stated that *Hindu* means 'one who is nonviolent' by the combination of *hinsā* (violence) and *dūr* (distant)."[149]

In order to support the claim of his master's divinity—not to be regarded as a mere particle of *Brahman* but as the full (*pūrṇa*) manifestation of it—Kasturi quotes the words of Swami Abhedananda, a disciple of Ramana Maharshi who in 1962 had an interview with Sathya Sai Baba in Prasanthi Nilayam. Here is his testimony, which proves the importance of the hagiographer's work in spreading the guru's fame and indirectly confirms how even in the old days the miracle-worker of Puttaparthi was not seen with favor by other monks and renouncers:

> To be frank, I must admit that I have been hearing of Sri Sathya Sai Babaji and about his *mahimas* for a long time. But hearsay does not convey a good opinion about Him. Recently . . . I got your book, *Sathyam Sivam Sundaram*, . . . It is very interesting and illuminating, and is driving me to have a *darsan* of the Divinity. . . . I must thank you for being instrumental in exposing me to Baba's grace, which helped clear all my doubts. I was really astonished to find my old-age infirmities disappear and my weakened limbs regain strength merely by His touch. His clear exposition, with analysis and analogies, not only put an end to my long-harbored doubts, but made me see Truth face to face. . . . His transformation at the time of my leave-taking into *Muralidhara Krishna* (Krishna with the flute) in dazzling splendor, is a sight I shall never forget. The *darsan* of *Saguna Brahman* (the Universal Absolute incarnated as a "limited" being), was a blessing bestowed on this poor soul to reveal the oneness of *saguna* and *nirguna*. . . . I was still a believer only in *Nirguna Brahman*, and considered everything that was visible to be *mithya* [false]. This gracious transformation of His changed me, and made me see everything—visible and imagined—to be *Sathya*, a part of that same Absolute Principle. . . . I am not

> quite convinced with the popular view attributing avatarhood to Baba. He seems to me to be the perfect *Poorna Brahman,* personified to end the unsettled state of the world by making man realize his own real nature, which is Bliss.[150]

Kasturi's seventh and final chapter of his magnum opus, *Dabbling and Diving*, stands out as a passionate defense of his beloved master against all those who in various ways accused him of being a fraud. Indeed, if in the 1970s the international renown of Sathya Sai Baba expanded more and more—the movement having spread to Japan as well as to South America already by 1974—the charismatic guru also attracted many criticisms, being especially charged with sleight of hand.[151] The hagiographer responds by noticing that this is nothing new, since it had happened since his first declaration of being "Sai Baba" in 1940. He argues that to attract criticism and denigration is the destiny of all prophets and divine personalities: only the tree that bears fruit becomes the people's target, and young Sathya had attracted a campaign of vilification since he was fourteen.[152] Even his parents thought he was mad or possessed by an evil spirit and that he needed to be exorcised.[153] Kasturi observes that he came under the attack of many different people, especially journalists and scientists/rationalists, who wanted to investigate him by means of a series of invasive tests to which the guru refused to submit himself. Kasturi quotes his guru's words:

> How can science, which is bound by physical laws, investigate transcendental phenomena, for these lie far beyond its scope and comprehension. . . . I have repeatedly declared that those who want to understand Me are welcome here. It is the spirit of investigation that is important. Foreign parapsychologists have come here and examined Me in a positive and constructive spirit. They do not write slanderous letters or make public demands. But the very approach of these people (the "investigators") was wrong. That is why I refused them. I want people to come, see, hear, observe and experience Me. Only then will they understand and appreciate the Avatar.[154]

To be sure, at the time several derogatory articles had appeared in yellow journals, periodicals, and newspapers. Even the guru's universalist teaching came under attack and was slandered. But in Sathya Sai Baba, the hagiographer points out, there is nothing exotic or esoteric. Whereas small minds dabble—he argues—those who really want to understand must dive into the saint's mystery with an open mind.[155] Following his guru's observations, he gives the positive example of Dr. Karlis Osis,[156] director of the American Society for Psychical Research, and of his colleague Dr. Erlendur Haraldsson, who are said to have scientifically investigated Sathya Sai Baba in a proper and thorough way beginning in 1972.[157] In order to strengthen his thesis of the guru's divinity, Kasturi quotes Dr. Osis's words:

> The abundance of the phenomena encountered and the magnitude of the miraculous effect, were a complete surprise to seasoned parapsychologists like us. . . . I have been an active researcher for twenty-five years and have travelled widely, but nowhere have I found phenomena which point as clearly and forcibly to spiritual reality as the daily miracles of Baba.[158]

Relying on the authoritativeness of Western scientists who are pro-Sathya Sai Baba, he cites the case of the American psychiatrist Samuel H. Sandweiss, who first visited the master in June 1972 and was to become a prominent devotee and the author of two important books.[159] Kasturi also details the case of the Marxist journalist Rustom Khurshedji Karanjia, editor of *Blitz*—a popular newsmagazine from Bombay—who in September 1976 came to Puttaparthi to interview and "unmask" the god-man but was in the end conquered by his words and charisma, coming to the conclusion that he was in fact divine and that "campaigns of calumny indulged in by a few misled people can hardly touch him."[160] After all, even Dr. Sandweiss had "journeyed to Prasanthi Nilayam and 'dived' with the intention to prove its barrenness, but to his own amazement, his efforts yielded pearls aplenty. His apprehensions about mass hypnotism, group hysteria and uncanny influences, were quickly laid low."[161]

Once again, Kasturi's rhetorical strategy is to underline how the saint's powers are only natural to him, inherent to his avatāric status. His whole *Carita*—verily a *camatkāramālā*, a "string of miracles"—is aimed at demonstrating the Swami's divine spontaneity. Kasturi is aware that his claim is hardly acceptable to the modern man and his/her rational mind, and remembers how in 1954, when he proposed the publication of Part 1 of *Sathyam Sivam Sundaram* to the guru, the latter asked him to wait, saying that readers would treat it as a fairy tale and doubt his sanity. At the end of his opus, the hagiographer wishes to stress one more time that Sathya Sai Baba's array of prodigies must not be understood as acquired *siddhis*, or worse, as tricks or sleight of hand, but as a characteristic of his inborn divinity. Thus, he argues that the guru does not perform miracles since he is no "performer" at all: miracles, as people call them, are "only a concretization of His love."[162] He observes that what is extra-ordinary and in-credible to man is simply ordinary and natural to god, and that his narrative is to be understood as an eyewitness testimony to such radical overturning. With respect to his guru's detractors, he points out that "as simply and naturally as Christ's plea from the cross, for forgiveness for those 'who know not what they do,' Baba blesses the calumniators."[163]

Finally, wishing to counter the long-standing accusation of the guru of Puttaparthi favoring the rich,[164] the hagiographer quotes the latter's words and writes that "to those who feel hurt by His treating the rich as lovingly as the poor, the reply is, 'They bring to Me their troubled hearts and sick minds. I cure them by asking them to divert their wealth and power to spiritual ends like *seva*.'"[165] Sathya Sai Baba's answer was patterned along the lines of the 'Jesus model' as found in the Gospels: "It is not the healthy that need a doctor, but the sick; I did not come to invite virtuous people, but sinners" (*Mark* 2.17).

A Critical Evaluation of Part 4

All in all, the aim of Kasturi's storytelling in Part 4 is to show that the Sathya Sai Baba Organization and its leader's renown constantly grew over the 1970s. This is achieved by on the one hand highlighting the consolidation of the Organization in India itself and on the other by signaling the ever-growing expansion of the guru's fame in the West, with the establishment of Sathya Sai Baba centers throughout the world. Besides S. H. Sandweiss, other prominent American devotees that reached Puttaparthi during this decade were Phyllis Krystal,[166] Al Drucker,[167] Isaac Tigrett,[168] Robert A. Bozzani,[169] and the filmmakers Richard and Janet Bock.[170] Mention must also be made of writers Peggy Mason and Ron Laing from the United Kingdom, who first came to Sathya Sai Baba in 1980.[171]

While chronicling his guru's public activities in chapter 2, the hagiographer especially insists on the crucial importance of education and service. But these inextricably linked themes cannot be appreciated if one fails to take into account the guru's own teachings, and no one more than Kasturi was aware of this. This is the reason why he dedicates chapter 4 to a thorough appreciation of his Swami as *stricto sensu* a teacher. For Kasturi, this is of fundamental importance since he is even too conscious that Sathya Sai Baba's purported powers inevitably tend to overshadow his *upadeśa*. In terms of structure and content, this chapter is to be regarded as the center of Part 4, which intends to ennoble the guru's figure by proving the excellence of his Vedāntic teaching, steeped in the *Veda*s and in the ancient scriptures of India. Throughout his life, teaching was Sathya Sai Baba's primary concern, in the first place through nonverbal, heart-to-heart communication, as happened twice a day during the silent *darśan*s, as well as through his writings, letters, speeches, and conversations. He started delivering regular public speeches in 1953 and continued to do so up to his last years. His collected discourses, the *Sathya Sai Speaks* series, comprise more than forty volumes.

The hagiographer's valorization of his Swami's theological excellence is meant to prove his worth to the intellectually inclined, and thus to shun the idea of any inferiority complex of his guru with respect to other traditional emblems of holiness such as the time-honored Śaṅkarācāryas. Certainly, this was a need that he himself, as a Vivekananda and Ramakrishna adept, keenly felt. Kasturi's praise of the holy man's commentaries to the *Upaniṣad*s, *Bhagavadgītā*, *Bhāgavata Purāṇa*, *Rāmāyaṇa*, etc. serves the purpose of placing him on a par with the great *ācārya*s of the past and of the present, and of highlighting his erudition. The hagiographer's aim is to underline Sathya Sai Baba's stature as a scriptural exegete thoroughly conversant which the ancient texts and their commentarial tradition: the claim, once again, is that he did not acquire such wisdom through any formal training since it is, rather, ingrained in him.

Ultimately the guru's teachings coincide with his life: as he often proclaimed, "My life is My message." Therefore, he himself sets the example that devotees must imitate. The theological truths he preaches and which have manifested in his avatāric persona must be implemented in one's everyday's conduct. The hagiographer reiterates the utmost relevance of ethics and service, and it is here that his own penchant toward action (*karmayoga*) rather than contemplation reveals itself. Kasturi is keen to stress how the essence of Sathya Sai Baba's teaching *and* life can be summarized

Figure 3.2. N. Kasturi holding the ceremonial umbrella (*chattrā*) over Sathya Sai Baba.

in one word: *preman,* pure love, since this is his own-being (*svabhāva*). As the guru pointed out to John S. Hislop:

> The most subtle aspect of Swami's teaching is love. The circle around that subtle point, in order to realize it, is the spiritual practices such as meditation, repetition of the name of the Lord, talking with good people, directing the mind away from harmful thought and so on. In themselves these spiritual practices are of no value. The only thing of real value is love itself. In dealing with people, Swami looks to the good and ignores the bad so as to intensify the good.[172]

Kasturi underlines that the guru's nature is the same as that of all creatures, since he is everyone's innermost core. Therefore, there can be no question of "reaching" him, since there is no ontological difference between Sathya Sai Baba and his/her devotee. What the latter lacks is the awareness of his/her own divinity, and this is precisely the ignorance (*ajñāna*) that the guru has come to remove once and for all. Along these lines, the hagiographer reports that when a doyen of Hindu metaphysics asked the Swami by what path could one reach him soonest, the guru replied: "I am too near to you to prescribe a path for you. You cannot reach Me. If you need Me, I am yours."[173]

An inbuilt circularity characterizes Kasturi's endeavor, since the guru's teaching inevitably refers back to his charismatic persona, that is, they are one and the same. Just like Jesus, Sathya Sai Baba would claim: "I am the way; I am the truth and I am life" (*John* 14.6). And yet, given the overwhelming weight of the miraculous in the guru's public life the professor needs to revert to this issue in his last chapter so as to pronounce the final defense of his lord. In his discussion of the genuineness of the saint's powers, Sathya Sai Baba is depicted as an *alter Christus* who is inevitably a "sign of contradiction" (*Luke* 2.34) to his contemporaries: he faces similar accusations and, in his mercy, forgives those who oppose and deny him since "they do not know what they are doing" (*Luke* 23.34). The criticisms of fraud/sleight of hand and partiality to the rich—linked to the increasing wealth of the guru's organization—were the main ones from which Kasturi had to defend his Swami from the early days,[174] since other allegations against Sathya Sai Baba such as his purported sexual abuses and financial mishandlings were to be voiced against him starting in the 1990s, when Kasturi was no more.[175]

The hagiographer simultaneously defends Sathya Sai Baba and his opus *Sathyam Sivam Sundaram* by arguing that the guru's life and miracles constitute an indivisible whole and cannot be separated. Just as miracles are constitutive of Jesus's life as it is narrated in the Gospels—and one would be left with quite a slim and hardly comprehensible portrayal of the rabbi of Nazareth if they were eliminated[176]—in the same way the Swami's public life and his *camatkāra*s are inextricably intertwined. Moreover, Kasturi aims at convincing his readers that Sathya Sai Baba is even higher than Christ, that he is Christ's father and the holy ghost, the supreme trinity, which he is quick to homologize to the Hindu *trimūrti* of Brahmā, Viṣṇu, and Śiva.

In the 1970s and 1980s, the guru's purported "materializations" were rejected by a number of rationalists and skeptics, first and foremost Basava Premanand (1930–2009).[177] On the other hand, Kasturi could count on the testimony of an accomplished amateur magician such as doctor Eruch B. Fanibunda, a Parsi who first met Sathya Sai Baba in 1970 and who was convinced of the genuineness of the guru's "materializations." Erlendur Haraldsson reports: "He told us in an interview that he had numerous opportunities to observe Baba when producing objects, that he has travelled with him and filmed him extensively, but that he has found no evidence of fraud."[178] The matter was inevitably controversial throughout the guru's life. Doug Henning (1947–2000), the world-famous Canadian magician, argued that if Sathya Sai Baba could produce objects on demand, then he was performing feats that no magician could duplicate.[179]

The hagiographer's line of defense with regard to the guru's wealth was to argue that the latter always lived the life of a renunciant (*saṃnyāsin*), relinquishing all possessions in his youth and never owning any personal property ever since. The money and all the many resources which over time were offered to him and his organization are claimed to be under his management as a trustee, not as an owner, to be used for charitable purposes only. Around the end of the 1960s, the guru pointed out to Arnold Schulman: "I have no land, no property of my own where I can grow my own food. Everything is registered in the name of someone else."[180] The Swami would often say that his only property were his devotees.[181]

When R. K. Karanjia asked the guru what was his solution to the escalating conflict between wealth and power on the one side and poverty and weakness on the other, his response was the following:

> The transformation of both into a single cooperative brotherhood on terms of equality without competition or conflict. This can result only from truth and love. The main issue is to fuse the two classes into one single class. The problem, however, is one of bringing them together on a common base or platform. Wealthy people live isolated in a certain state or condition. The poor also are similarly isolated in another state or condition. How do we bring them together? I do so in many subtle ways by breaking the barriers of wealth and poverty and creating a feeling of equality and oneness between the poor and the rich. In this ashram . . . you find them living and working together,

> even performing menial labor on terms of complete equality. Here there are no distinctions whatever, nor any special facilities for the rich. They live, eat, work, worship and sleep like the poor. All live like a community of workers to share the common austerities of the ashram.[182]

Over the years, the criticism of the guru's alleged partiality to the rich was extended to the organization's wealth, since it is indisputable that Sathya Sai Baba succeeded in establishing a fabulously rich "kingdom." At his death in 2011, his Trust was reported to be worth at least $8.9 billion.

In conclusion, it is crucial to emphasize the sacredness of *Sathyam Sivam Sundaram*, which was due to the guru having explicitly appointed Kasturi for the task. The official character of his biography has always been underlined by both Sathya Sai Baba and the organization, and the hagiographer himself reinforced it by extensively quoting the guru's words throughout his opus. By building on his guru's utterances, Kasturi was able to articulate a persuasive narrative, which has been read by millions of people in India and all around the world, offering a fundamental contribution to the definition and canonization of Sathya Sai Baba's sanctity.

Among other things, the hagiography documents the transformation of the small hamlet of Puttaparthi into one of India's main pilgrimage centers. With the globalization of the guru's fame and mission,[183] the formerly unknown and mud-hut village was turned into an ideal polis of sorts. Poignantly, Smriti Srinivas has referred to Prasanthi Nilayam as an example of architecture as rhetoric, meaning that the place's huge buildings represent values that are important in the movement.[184] Along the years the ashram has been expanded with the construction of fine roads and edifices, an auditorium, schools, a university, a planetarium, the museum of religions, and the huge Vidyāgiri stadium. The transformation of Prasanthi Nilayam and its surrounding area has been ongoing: in 1991, just a few years after Kasturi's death, the famed Super Specialty Hospital was inaugurated at the presence of the then-prime minister Narasimha Rao and in subsequent years the Sri Sathya Sai Airport was brought to completion.

The normative force of the hagiographic discourse lies in its performativity since what it says calls for action, text and practice being inextricably linked. As per the intended aim of all hagiographies, *Sathyam Sivam Sundaram* stands out in its persuasiveness, offering to its audiences tools through which to interpret the world and through which readers can positively intervene in it. In other words, it generates a worldview and ethical perspectives that call for the transformation of one's ordinary, deluded self and of society as a whole. Throughout his storytelling, Kasturi cogently presents his objectives, which are meant to determine collective responses. These can be summarized into four basic points:

1. The "good news" of Sathya Sai Baba's advent, the *pūrṇāvatāra,* cannot be limited to India but must be understood as the ultimate divine revelation to mankind, ushering into a new golden age. The spreading of the "good news" is inextricably tied to the global affirmation of his organization and of the guru as the "lord of the universe," given that all names and forms are his. Significantly, at Puttaparthi's Chaitanya Jyoti Museum he is represented as straddling the globe, balancing the universe on one finger. The museum also displays a satellite photograph of the village and surrounding areas, which is believed to miraculously reveal Sathya Sai Baba's profile and "imprint" on earth;[185]

2. The guru has come to embark upon a mission—which was begun before him by Shirdi Sai Baba and will be concluded after him by Prema Sai Baba—aimed at the reestablishment of *sanātanadharma,* the "eternal religion," and the restoration of the universal human values of truth (*satya*), righteousness (*dharma*), love (*preman*), peace (*śānti*), and nonviolence (*ahiṃsā*), and will infallibly succeed;

3. Devotees, both as individuals and as a community, are expected to actively participate in such mission of *dharmasthāpana*, involving themselves as "collaborators" of the Avatar, preferably, though not exclusively, through their adherence to the Sathya Sai Organization. They must imbibe the values taught by the master and transmit them within their own societies. These "spiritual seeds" must be nurtured within Sathya Sai Baba centers through dedicated study circles[186] and disseminated through education in human values (EHV) programs implemented at all levels, from elementary schools up to universities, and through charitable actions of service to one's fellow men. Phyllis Krystal writes: "[Sathya Sai Baba] intends to revive and teach the old values as expounded in the Vedas and other ancient writing. . . . His goal is a revolution in the entire education system with more stress on human values and moral and spiritual concepts in addition to the regular academic curriculum."[187] Moreover:

> This programme . . . is based on very broad multi-religious principles, anchoring itself on the respective religions of children.

> It teaches them religious tolerance and values such as respect for parents and elders, hard work, sincerity, charity, devotion to duty, discipline and to adhere to values such as Truth, Right Conduct, Peace, Love and Non-violence.[188]

The assumption is that the values of *satya, dharma, śānti, preman,* and *ahiṃsā* are shared by all human beings, though they require to be adapted to the context and historical conditions of each society. When applying them, teachers need not refer to their original inspirer or even to Hinduism, since this might undermine their purported universalism;

4. Sathya Sai Baba's teachings are aimed at guiding each and every individual to the awareness of his/her ātmic nature. Therefore, they don't recognize any separateness based on religion, caste, color, or creed. In 1980–81, at the Third World Conference[189] of the Sai Organizations and Ninth All-India Conference, a permanent charter was granted by the guru which briefly spelled out his essential *upadeśa* along these lines. The exhibits held at the Spiritual Museum—Praganan Pradarshan—located at the Sri Sathya Sai Art Science and Commerce College in Whitefield, are a paradigmatic example of the Organization's educational system aimed at the realization of the "divinity within."[190]

In line with his self-awareness as the ultimate *avatāra*, Sathya Sai Baba viewed his teachings as being traditional through and through, the quintessence of the perennial Hindu *dharma* and of religion per se. Implicitly as well as explicitly, both he and his hagiographer shared a Vivekanandian worldview, which they did not perceive as representing a recent manifestation of the encounter between India and the West—what has been termed neo-Hinduism, with its program of an ethically and socially applied Advaita Vedānta—but rather thought to be thoroughly in keeping with one's immemorial tradition, encapsulating the essence of the *sanātana-dharma*, understood to be constitutively inclusivistic. Symptomatically, the guru presented Vivekananda's ideas as his own. A telling example, which I gather from M. J. Spurr's PhD dissertation *Sathya Sai Baba as Avatar*, is found in his *Sathya Sai Vahini*, where in a chapter titled "The Avatar as Guru" he paraphrases one of Vivekananda's writings. I quote Sathya Sai Baba's text first, followed by Vivekananda's:

> Though Gurus of the common type have increased in numbers, there is available for man, a Guru far more supreme and far

more compassionate than any or all of them. He is no other than the Avatar of the Lord. He can, by the mere expression of His Will confer on man the highest consummation of spiritual life. He can gift it and get man to accept it. Even the meanest of the mean can acquire the highest wisdom, in a trice. He is the Guru of all Gurus. He is the fullest embodiment of God as man. Men can cognize God only in the human form. The Bharathiya Spiritual Stream has been declaring, over and over again, that adoring God in the human form is the highest duty of man. Unless God incarnates as man, man can never hope to see God or listen to His Voice. Of course, man may picture God in various other forms, but he can never approximate to the genuine form of God. However much one may try, man cannot picture God in any form except the human. People can pour out wonderful discourses and talks on God and the nature and composition of all that exists in the Universe. They may satisfy themselves, asserting that all accounts of God descending in human form are meaningless myths. That is what the poor ordinary eye can discern. This strange inference is not based on Jnana [wisdom]. As a matter of fact, Jnana is absent in these assertions and declarations. What we can notice in them is only the froth floating on ego waves.[191]

Such great teachers of spiritual truth are indeed very few in number in this world, but the world is never altogether without them. . . . Higher and nobler than all ordinary ones are another set of teachers, the Avatāras of Ishvara [the Lord], in the world. They can transmit spirituality with a touch, even with a mere wish. The lowest and the most degraded characters become in one second saints at their command. They are the Teachers of all teachers, the highest manifestations of God through man. We cannot see God except through them. We cannot help worshipping them; and indeed they are the only ones whom we are bound to worship. No man can really see God except through these human manifestations. If we try to see God otherwise, we make for ourselves a hideous caricature of Him and believe the caricature to be no worse than the

> original. . . . Talk as you may, try as you may, you cannot think of God except as a man. You may deliver great intellectual discourses on God and on all things under the sun, become great rationalists and prove to your satisfaction that all these accounts of the Avatāras of God as man are nonsense. But let us come for a moment to practical common sense. What is there behind this kind of remarkable intellect? Zero, nothing, simply so much froth.[192]

Following in Vivekananda's footsteps, the Swami promoted himself as the fulfiller of tradition, viewing the cosmopolitan expansion of his mission as the accomplishment of Hindu *dharma* and of all world faiths.

Kasturi's hagiography portrays his guru as the incarnation of love, that is, of the one, supreme principle (*Brahman*, *gurutattva*) toward which all religions tend and in which all beings find their fulfillment. In this universalist perspective, it is claimed that true devotion to him makes a Christian a better Christian, a Muslim a better Muslim, a Buddhist a better Buddhist, etc., since the faith of each and every one finds its consummation in Sathya Sai Baba. To be sure, in *Sathyam Sivam Sundaram* the master's deification and his message go hand and hand and are, in fact, inseparable. The hagiographer's belief is that the more devotees will be able to expand—via the guru's grace—his "kingdom," the sooner the "golden age" of truth, righteousness, peace, love, and nonviolence will be established throughout the planet.

It would be a mistake, however, to view Kasturi's authorship in purely individualistic terms. We must be aware that any given text—and *Sathyam Sivam Sundaram* is no exception—is in fact a concatenation of (sub)texts, that is to say, an intricate mixture of diachronic and synchronic layers. The hagiographer was inevitably a man of his times, molded by the religious and cultural context in which he was brought up and by the intellectual milieu in which he was educated and of which he became an authoritative exponent as university professor and litterateur. Therefore, Kasturi's work must be understood as the exemplary reflection and expression of a precise historical and hermeneutical situation. Besides being a docile instrument in Sathya Sai Baba's hands, he was a receptacle of Vivekanandian ideology and part and parcel of a textual network, in both an active and passive sense: as much driven by implicit/unconscious ideological presuppositions as by his explicit will to write a comprehensive, well-designed biography.

Kasturi's endeavor is but a segment in a long and many-branched genealogical line of modern Hindu texts. Herein, Vivekananda—the leading figure of modern Hindu self-awareness—stands out as the primal source of inspiration, along with other eminent figures such as M. K. Gandhi, Aurobindo Ghose, and Sarvepalli Radhakrishnan (1888–1975).[193] *Sathyam Sivam Sundaram* presents the guru of Puttaparthi as the apex and consummation of an inclusivist/universalist theological agenda. And just as Vivekananda regarded Ramakrishna as the inner fulfillment of the Hindu tradition,[194] Kasturi presented Sathya Sai Baba as the ultimate *avatāra,* the fulfillment of all world religions ushering humanity into a golden age. Wilhelm Halbfass's words with respect to Vivekananda's ideology and overall project would have been subscribed by our hagiographer, for whom the guru of Puttaparthi was the realization of all of Vivekananda's highest dreams:

> The spread of the supposedly Vedāntic ideas of spirituality, tolerance, and harmony amounts to a conquest of the world by Hinduism. The Indians are repeatedly called upon to "conquer" the world, and in particular the West, with their spirituality. Western colonialism and imperialism is thus up against a kind of spiritual expansionism and "imperialism." . . . More important is his conviction that Hinduism does not require any conversions at all, that the remaining religions are all in truth encompassed by Hinduism from their very inception and, moreover, that Hinduism in principle already anticipates all future developments within itself.[195]

Kasturi's fluent English prose proved to be extremely effective in the dissemination of Sathya Sai Baba's gospel. The unprecedented success of *Sathyam Sivam Sundaram* was in no small part due to its literary quality, to the narrative and rhetorical skills of its author. Although Kasturi wrote that "with each successive edition of this Book . . . a depressing sense of utter inadequacy arises in me,"[196] nowadays, as back in the 1960s, the text is alive and well, since Indian and Western devotees alike consider it a must read. As Ms. Rajeshwari Patel, faculty member in the Anantapur Campus of Sathya Sai University puts it: "Professor Kasturi's style was inimitable and unmatched. He brought to life for millions of Bhagavan's devotees the thrilling, exhilarating accounts of those early golden years. One feels as if one is present on the occasion when one reads Swami's biography. . . . He had a special Kasturi-touch—literally."[197] His biography is regarded as a classic and a Bible of sorts by all *bhaktas*, second in importance only to Sathya Sai Baba's own discourses. Moreover, the variety of *Sathyam Sivam Sundaram*'s uses and performances is noteworthy: some devotees read it aloud as a meritorious act and as part of their *sādhanā*, and Sathya Sai Baba Centers throughout the world organize public readings of its chapters and conduct study circles centered on its contents. As Tulasi Srinivas remarks: "This 'biography' is the central text that devotees discuss repeatedly and use to construct an image of Shri Sathya Sai Baba."[198] Kasturi himself used to quote from his opus during his public lectures at Prasanthi Nilayam, offering his own commentaries to it.

Sathyam Sivam Sundaram's Subsequent Volumes by B. N. Narasimha Murthy

Kasturi planned to continue writing the life of his guru and envisaged that other authors would continue his work after him. As he wrote in his preface to the 1982 edition of *Sathyam Sivam Sundaram*, Part 1: "Part 5 will deal with the subsequent years. Other parts are bound to follow."[199] But Kasturi was already quite old and debilitated in the first half of the 1980s and never attempted the writing of Part 5. It was only in 2005, a quarter of a century after the release of Part 4, that the fifth volume was issued. That such a long time elapsed before resuming the task of writing Sathya Sai Baba's biography is indicative of Kasturi's authoritativeness and of the sacredness attributed to his opus: nobody thought himself/herself worthy of taking the place of the venerable hagiographer who in the ashram was and is revered as a holy figure, second in importance only to the guru.

In 2003 an advisory committee, prompted by Sathya Sai Baba, was formed to help in producing the subsequent parts, consisting of four veteran devotees: G. Venkatraman, Jayalakshmi Gopinath, Smt. Sitalakshmi, and B. N. Narasimha Murthy. The committee entrusted B. N. Narasimha Murthy (b. 1945) with the task of preparing the volumes' texts, with assistance from its members and V. N. Prahlad. He thus became the new biographer and Part 5, divided up in twelve chapters covering the years from 1980 to 1985, was released in 2005.[200] In rapid succession, Narasimha Murthy brought to completion two more volumes of the guru's biography:

Part 6, in twelve chapters, chronicles the major events of his public life from 1986 to 1993, while Part 7, in sixteen chapters, covers the years from 1994 to 2001.[201] These three texts follow a meticulous chronological sequence, each containing a useful appendix detailing a year-by-year synthesis of the main events. What will presumably be the last volume in the series is under preparation and will cover the last decade in the *avatāra*'s life.

Narasimha Murthy first met Sathya Sai Baba in Puttaparthi in 1964, when Murthy was nineteen years old, and devotedly served him ever since. On that occasion, he also met Kasturi, who was tirelessly typing away on his typewriter, oblivious to the clutter and confusion around. Here is his testimony on our hagiographer:

> But anybody could go and interrupt him; he was so simple, gentle and welcoming. . . . He knew no strangers; he will not even ask the person's name and willingly share Swami's glory. And if anybody came to him with any ailment—mental, physical or emotional, he would empathize immediately. In fact, he would even go to the extent of interceding on a devotee's behalf with Swami, though this can often be dangerous for people living in His close proximity.
>
> I remember one such incident. . . . It was in 1981 and we had organized a spiritual retreat in the Muddenahalli Sai School Campus, where I was warden then. On that occasion, along with Prof. Kasturi were Prof. K. V. Ramakrishna Rao and Jagadanandaji Maharaj. The latter, who was a monk from the Ramakrishna Mission, gave a wonderful discourse, and after his talk asked Mr. Kasturi if he could accompany him to Puttaparthi to see Swami. And Prof. Kasturi agreed to this readily. So, all of us came to Prasanthi Nilayam, but by that time the *bhajans* had concluded and Swami had gone upstairs. We all waited down, while Mr. Kasturi went up and informed Swami about our arrival. And in the next few minutes, the Kind Lord granted all of us an interview! And it was an interesting session. Jagadanandaji had a chronic health problem and Swami, graciously, materialized *vibhuti* and gave him. Then he told Swami, "I have this ailment for many years now." The reply that Bhagavan gave him that day was revealing, "Develop

> more faith and devotion in Guru Maharaj. You will be cured," He said. Swami was referring to his master, Sri Ramakrishna Paramahamsa.
>
> That is how Mr. Kasturi helped a spiritual aspirant secure the Grace of Sai, but on occasions Swami severely censured him too for such "Gatekeeper to God" endeavors to ensure that his ego was never inflated.[202]

Narasimha Murthy's formative years were spent in the *Loka Seva Vrinda*, an order of committed youngsters founded by Madiyal Narayana Bhatt (1927–1977), an eminent Karnataka educationist. The *Loka Seva Vrinda* established two schools, one in Alike (in 1963) and one in Muddenahalli (in 1973), both of which came under the governance of the guru of Puttaparthi in 1978, after M. N. Bhatt's premature death in a car accident. Narasimha Murthy was chosen to serve as the warden of the Sathya Sai Hostel within the Brindavan Campus of the Sri Sathya Sai Institute of Higher Learning at Whitefield, and later was appointed warden of the Muddenahalli Campus. In his four-decades' service, he has molded many thousands of students. More recently, he has served as the chief mentor of the Sri Sathya Sai Loka Seva Institutions.

Narasimha Murthy also authored a book titled *Sri Sathya Sai Divya Kripashraya* (Prasanthi Nilayam: Sri Sathya Sai Sadhana Trust, 2010), an autobiographical account of the first eighteen years of his association with Sathya Sai Baba, from 1965 to 1983, and of the development of the Sri Sathya Sai Loka Seva institutions. Following his guru's instructions, he wrote a sequel to it titled *Sathya Sai Divya Sannidhi* (Prasanthi Nilayam: Sri Sathya Sai Sadhana Trust, 2011), dwelling on his personal experiences with Sathya Sai Baba from 1983 up to the latter's death in 2011.

It is significant that, after Kasturi, the guru appointed as his biographer a professional educationist who, basing himself upon his life-long experience, could detail the Swami's achievements in the dissemination of Sathya Sai schools and charitable services. Education and service being the most relevant assets of the Sathya Sai Baba Organization, Narasimha Murthy was best equipped to authoritatively describe them and explain their underlying "philosophy."

Currently, Narasimha Murthy is one of the leaders of a separate movement of Sathya Sai Baba devotees that has distanced itself from the official organization based in Prasanthi Nilayam. It so happened that soon after Sathya Sai Baba's demise in April 2011, Narasimha Murthy became convinced through dreams and other "revelations" that the *avatāra* is still active in his subtle body (*sūkṣmaśarīra*) with the aim of completing his mission.[203] He claims that the guru inspired him to write a book on what the *avatāra* is now accomplishing in his subtle body. This text, titled *Sathya Sai Divya Anandam* (Muddenahalli: Sri Sathya Sai Premamruta Prakashana, 2013), is conceived as the sequel to *Sathya Sai Divya Sannidhi*.

Based in the Sathya Sai Grama in Muddenahalli,[204] he and other devotees—among them prominent figures such as Isaac Tigrett and the late Indulal H. Shah—believe that Sathya Sai Baba has chosen Madhusudhan Rao Naidu, an alumnus of the Sri Sathya Sai Institute of Higher Learning, as his temporary medium/communicator and, most recently, they have come to revere him as none other than the guru himself, that is, as "Madhusudhan Sai."[205] Not only does the latter give public discourses as well as answers to individual queries but he also travels throughout India and the world with his entourage giving *darśan,* taking devotees' letters, blessing people, and offering *prasād* and *vibhūti*, effectively mimicking what used to be Sathya Sai Baba's style and behavior.[206]

In October 2018, Madhusudhan Rao Naidu announced that Prema Sai Baba will arrive at the Sathya Sai Grama of Muddenahalli as a boy of twelve around 2020 and will manifest his *avatāra*hood at the age of nineteen. On March 30, 2019, he further announced that this would be the last phase in his mission: characterized by many miracles, it will last up until 2021 (Sathya Sai Baba's ninety-sixth birthday), after which six years of silence will follow. In this time period (2021–27), the future Prema Sai will be educated in Muddenahalli from his thirteenth to his nineteenth year. More recently, Narasimha Murthy has offered a slightly modified chronology: he has declared that Prema Sai will begin his avatāric career starting in 2030, given that "Madhusudhan Sai"'s own mission will last up until 2022, after which there will be an interval of eight years before Prema Sai's actual manifestation.

In July 2019, on the occasion of Gurupūrṇimā, Narasimha Murthy solemnly articulated the three phases of Madhusudhan Rao Naidu's unique experience:

> Today Sri Madhusudhan has become a Sadguru[207] because he manifested the courage to take up the burden of the cross of Bhagavan Sri Sathya Sai Baba. . . . There was a time when

> Baba was using Madhusudhan as his communicator, just communicating His messages . . . it was the first phase of Sankarshana . . . attracting men, women and children. . . . This was over after the first three years of subtle form. Then came the phase when Madhusudhan emptied himself of himself . . . this was the next phase of Sandarshana, for three years he was a vehicle, Swami worked through him. And today has started the third phase of Sankramana and Swami is manifesting Himself in the body called Madhusudhan so that you and I and the whole world understand that there are not two; Madhusudhan and Bhagavan Sri Sathya Sai Baba are one.[208]

Thrice, I had the occasion to witness Madhusudhan Rao Naidu's behavior when, during his tours around the world, he came to Padua, Italy, along with Narasimha Murthy and his entourage in April 2015, 2016, and 2017. Through his slow movements and gestures he clearly imitates Sathya Sai Baba. His speeches, both in style and content, resemble those of the guru. In 2017, he started "materializing" *vibhūti,* rings, and other items, just as the guru of Puttaparthi used to do. Apparently, Prime Minister Narendra Modi (b. 1950) has supported his claims. At the inauguration in New Delhi of a second Super Speciality Paediatric Surgical and Research Centre, he stated: "Sai Baba is now in the Sookshma Shareera Form and is continuing His mission of service, building free hospitals, schools and social service projects for the poor."[209]

These happenings have determined an inevitable schism within the movement. The official Sathya Sai Organization condemns them as devious and deplorable, a sacrilege, on the grounds that the guru never utilized any intermediaries between himself and his *bhakta*s and never possessed anybody.[210] In 2017, the Shri Sathya Sai Central Trust has filed a lawsuit against Narasimha Murthy and the Muddenahalli-based faction, accusing them of fraud.[211]

Only time will tell whether this schismatic group will be successful in supporting its claims, and in which ways it will evolve vis-à-vis the guru's official representatives based in Prasanthi Nilayam. Narasimha Murthy holds that it is only thanks to the inspiration and will of Sathya Sai Baba in his *sūkṣmaśarīra* that six new educational institutions bearing his name were established in Karnataka between 2012 and 2015. Two hospitals specializing in pediatric cardiology, the Sri Sathya Sai Sanjeevani, have also been recently built in Naya Raipur, Chhattisgarh, and Baghola, Haryana. Other hospitals, schools, and spiritual centers are said to be in the making in various parts of India and all around the world: "Miraculously, in three short years, Sai Baba has initiated construction of thirty Educational Institutions, five Super Speciality Hospitals and twenty-one Multi-Faith Spiritual Centres on five Continents, to be completed before His Mission ends."[212]

Future developments are inextricably tied to the time when Prema Sai Baba will actually appear on the scene, and to how efficacious he will be in promoting himself as the third, final *avatāra* prophesized by Sathya Sai Baba.[213] The first image of Prema Sai Baba was disclosed to John S. Hislop in the late 1970s, when the guru "materialized" a ring for him bearing his countenance. Hislop writes:

> It was a brownish stone, highly glazed, sculptured in profile, the bridge and length of the nose visible and a suggestion of the arch of the left eye, a noble head with shoulder-length hair, mustache and beard, the head resting on or emerging from a lotus flower. His countenance was tranquil, peaceful, majestic.[214]

4

The Hagiographer's Multiple Roles within the Sathya Sai Baba Movement

This chapter explores the multiple roles played by Kasturi in the promotion of his guru's organization, the efficacious and creative ways in which he painstakingly contributed to expand its constituency and spread Sathya Sai Baba's renown in India and throughout the world. Indeed, his activity was not restricted to the writing of the four volumes of *Sathyam Sivam Sundaram*. His influential hagiography was part of a wider, comprehensive project aimed at consolidating the guru's eminence, which absorbed him completely up to his last breath.

He himself in his autobiography notes how ashramites and devotees honored him with epithets such as poet, linguist, philosopher, official biographer, private secretary, first disciple, foremost devotee, Vyāsa, anthill sage, Vālmīki, etc.[1] Though he refused to be acknowledged as such saying that these titles only disfigured him, it is a fact that from the late 1940s Kasturi held key roles within the Prasanthi Nilayam ashram and the Sathya Sai Baba Organization, being the guru's right-hand man. No other person was ever as close to Sathya Sai Baba as he was, interacting with him for many hours every day, for decades.

If Kasturi is keen to point out that he was a mere *chaprasi*, a peon who promptly obeyed the *avatāra*'s orders, and that Prasanthi Nilayam must not be mistaken for an ordinary ashram in which there is "a male or female disciple who runs the show, who picks and chooses, who knows the cards and who can often manipulate the Master,"[2] still it is out of question that he played plural and crucial roles within the guru's movement, and that Sathya Sai Baba successfully utilized him in a vast array of enterprises in which he was able to manifest his talents.

Kasturi and his family led a simple and austere life at Prasanthi Nilayam, with no privileges or material comforts whatsoever. As per his guru's instruction, the hagiographer would travel only by bus; unless the guru gave him permission, he would not get inside a car. Till the end of his life, he lived in his tiny apartment following the ashram's routine, sustaining himself on his meager pension and incessantly working for his Swami, day and night.[3] His sober, almost ascetic lifestyle set an example for all followers.

Kasturi as Editor and Translator into English of the Guru's Discourses

From the time of Sathya Sai Baba's public speech of October 17, 1953, day of Vijayadaśamī, Kasturi became the editor and English translator of his discourses. For twenty years this was to be his first occupation, though it all began quite casually. It was not the guru who asked him to transcribe his Telugu speech, since he acted out of his own initiative, wishing to preserve his words of wisdom: "Fortunately, I had my pen in my pocket and someone lent me sheets of paper. I could secure His words and put them together."[4] With no tape recorder available, the hagiographer had to rely on his ability to memorize and write down his guru's words as fast as possible, and this was even more difficult given the speed of the latter's "Ganga," his torrential speech.[5] To be sure, the master spoke very fast and also extempore, never resorting to a prepared speech. As Kasturi states: "Imagine my struggle to scribble on the pages of my notebook the series of adjectival or adverbial clauses that hurry one behind the other from His lips and the nouns and the verbs encasing ideas, personalities and principles."[6]

Robert Priddy, who interviewed Kasturi in January 1987, observes:

> Now, anyone who has been present during a Baba discourse and heard the amazing speed and fluency with which the interpreter must work . . . will realize the nature of the feat Sri Kasturi performed during the decades. . . . [A]s Kasturi pointed out, he never had time to transcribe more than a note or reminder while these two-hour marathon discourses were under way.[7]

Documenting and disseminating Sathya Sai Baba's message became the goal and guiding principle of Kasturi's life. B. V. Raja Reddy, who was closely associated with him for decades, recalls:

> With no drop of verbal ambrosia falling from Baba's divine lips left unlettered, Professor Kasturi made sure that any delicious delicacy of a delivery from the divine lips would be feasted through his ears and then shared in full with his immediate neighbors and others. Blessed with a sharp intelligence, sturdy physique and a retentive memory, he was the unassailable and humble Kasturi.[8]

The guru gave his speeches in his own Telugu mother-tongue[9] and the hagiographer—notwithstanding his knowledge of other Dravidian languages—had to make great efforts to study and master "the most melodious of Indian languages."[10] As he admits in his autobiography, in December 1951 his understanding of Telugu was still halting and inchoate and he could neither read nor write the Telugu script: in order to record his master's words he utilized the Kannada script.[11] Kasturi says that "for a few years, this forced me into pitiable dumbness. When I picked up courage at last the tongue perpetrated bungles and bloomers, malapropisms and solecisms, each of which rewarded me with a lesson from Baba on Telugu conjugation and declension, syntax and style."[12] In the 1950s he was given Telugu lessons by the headmaster of the Middle School of Puttaparthi and in time, even thanks to the help of the guru, who insisted that he should speak to him only in Telugu, he was able to master the language and wade through the Telugu classics.[13]

The series of the guru's public discourses in English translation is called *Sathya Sai Speaks* and the first eleven volumes of it, comprising Sathya Sai Baba's speeches from 1953 to 1972, were all edited and translated by Kasturi from his precious notes. Throughout the 1950s and most of the 1960s, his memos were the only source from which he could work in order to prepare his English versions.[14] Prior to the publication of the speeches—in both *Sanathana Sarathi* and *Sathya Sai Speaks*—the guru would personally read and control every line and, if dissatisfied with Kasturi's editing, would indicate corrections. Changes, however, were usually limited to minor points and stylistic improvements.[15] Even when Kasturi wrote short prefaces to the volumes of *Sathya Sai Speaks*, sometimes in the form of short poems, he would always submit his writings to the guru for approval.[16]

Robert Priddy's idea that the hagiographer "acted as a kind of 'spin doctor' and even 'ghost writer' for Sathya Sai Baba"[17] is unfounded given that he never substituted himself for his master. The opinion voiced by M. Krishna, an ex-devotee who was close to the guru from 1950 to 1957,[18] that the latter's lectures "were mostly thoughts borrowed from Mr. Kasturi"[19] is also far-fetched. If the proximity with a learned man like the hagiographer must have had its impact upon the guru, the suggestion that Kasturi acted as a kind of *éminence grise* and that the Swami's discourses were borrowed from him is unjustified. The hagiographer was literally in awe of the guru's purported omniscience, constantly craving to record his "revelations" and words of wisdom. In 1958, in one of his poems he celebrated the "alchemic potency" of the Swami's discourses with these words: "Every word a Manthra, every phrase a Sutra; A Gayathri each sentence, Upanishad, a speech; Every hour a minute, a minute but a second."[20]

The early discourses of Sathya Sai Baba that Kasturi compiled are especially important since they convey the essential features of his moral and spiritual teachings. Whereas in the first five years, in the period 1953–57, the guru delivered just five speeches (the first three in Prasanthi Nilayam in October 1953, February 1955, and August 1956; the fourth in Venkatagiri in April 1957; and the fifth in Tirupati in July 1957), starting from 1958 he intensified his public discourses. Thus, in the subsequent five years he delivered fourteen speeches in 1958, six in 1959, ten in 1960, twenty-eight in 1961, and twenty-four in 1962, for a total of eighty-two, with an average of more than sixteen discourses per year.[21] Thirty-four of these eighty-two speeches took place outside Puttaparthi, with Kasturi always by his side, during the guru's tours of North India (in Lucknow in April 1961; in Badrinath and Nainital in June 1961) and his visits to towns and villages of Andhra Pradesh and other southern states (in particular, he held five speeches in Madras, three in Bangalore, three in Venkatagiri, and two in Tirupati).

The number of the guru's discourses increased throughout the decades, to the point that to date forty-two volumes of *Sathya Sai Speaks* have been edited, which comprise Sathya Sai Baba's speeches up to 2009. All in all, the Swami delivered more than a thousand public discourses during his avatāric career. Though Kasturi stated that his translations were a poor rendering of the guru's sublime words and that "English is too blunt and too blatant a tool to unravel the subtle treasures of Avataric wisdom,"[22] he still thought that "even when Swami's Telugu nectar is diluted and deformed by translation into English the call does not lose either its urgency or its intimacy."[23]

Besides being the compiler of the *Sathya Sai Speaks* series, from the mid-1950s until December 1971, the guru appointed him as the consecutive interpreter of his public speeches from Telugu into English.[24] He acted as Sathya Sai Baba's official interpreter on a myriad of occasions: at Prasanthi Nilayam and throughout India as well as during the guru's trip to East Africa in 1968. This was an arduous assignment, however, given that "the sentence structure in English is so different from the Telugu that the translator has to begin his version from the last few words and travel all the way back to where the core is generally expressed."[25] The hagiographer devotes an entire chapter of his autobiography to the subject.[26] Here is how it begins:

> I do not remember when I was charged with the well nigh impossible assignment of translating His discourses into English. I believe it was at the Lakshmi Narayana Temple near Malabar

Figure 4.1. Sathya Sai Baba correcting N. Kasturi's English translation during one of his speeches.

> Hill, Bombay. Thereafter, through the years, I was offered the unenviable opportunity until I failed dramatically to interpret His words before a gathering of twenty thousand at Madras.[27]

Kasturi writes that the guru would often come to his rescue:

> As soon as He stops, I begin the English. While I am on, Baba watches and scrutinizes. He leaves no word or idiom or phrase unturned. When a suggestion for Sadhana which He emphasized is handed out anemically by me, He wants me to repeat it more powerfully. He assists the memory when I miss one or two of the five or six categories or concepts He mentions. When a word sticks in my throat, He releases it. When the right word plays hide and seek, He redeems it. He is the thesaurus ready with the exact equivalent.[28]

At times, the professor would translate the guru's Telugu speeches into other South Indian languages such as Malayalam, Kannada, and Tamil. He never loses occasion to underline the transformative quality of the guru's talks, which are not to be understood as ordinary speeches but as an outpouring of wisdom saturated with love: "He has said that it is not a 'lecture' at all; it is . . . a 'mixture' prepared and prescribed by the physician to cleanse, cure and make us 'whole'—some. He calls them Sambhasan, Dialogue, Conversation."[29]

Once, during the first World Conference held at Dharmakshetra in Bombay in May 1968, Sathya Sai Baba's opening sentence happened to be in classical Sanskrit, and the master continued talking in Sanskrit for ten long minutes, which took Kasturi completely by surprise and left him utterly speechless. The guru then reverted to Telugu and publicly reprimanded the Brahmin Kasturi for having neglected the study of the sacred language of Bharat.[30] Though he never studied it in school, the professor read and understood elementary Sanskrit and knew several Sanskrit scriptures by heart, such as the *Bhagavadgītā* and a few *Upaniṣad*s. Nonetheless, he could neither speak Sanskrit nor engage in an instantaneous translation from it.[31] When during the Dasara festivals held in Prasanthi Nilayam in the 1950s and 1960s Sanskrit and Telugu pundits—including the guru's elder brother Seshama Rāju—composed elaborate Sanskrit poems in the master's honor, Kasturi could only offer him his English compositions.[32] From time to time, Sathya Sai Baba would also scold Kasturi for neglecting the repetition of the sacred *gāyatrī mantra*.[33]

In December 1971, in Madras, the professor had to translate Sathya Sai Baba's inaugural speech at the All India Conference of the Office Bearers of the thousands of units of the Sri Sathya Sai Seva Organization. However, he was unable to grasp the very introductory poem with which the guru began his discourse and which contained the English words "automatic light." Although the guru repeated the line twice, he could not figure out its meaning and was therefore asked to leave and sit down among the audience. Dr. S. Bhagavantham, the renowned Indian physicist, was asked to take his place, although he was no more successful in unraveling the meaning of the verse.[34] From then onward and for many years, Bhagavantham substituted Kasturi as the official interpreter of Sathya Sai Baba's Telugu discourses into English.

Kasturi as Editor of *Sanathana Sarathi* and Translator into English of Sathya Sai Baba's Writings

In January 1958, the guru summoned Kasturi to quit his work at the All India Radio Station in Bangalore and come back to Puttaparthi to become the editor of his new monthly newsletter, which he designated as *Sanathana Sarathi*, the "Eternal Charioteer," identifying himself with Kṛṣṇa in the *Bhagavadgītā*.[35] Kasturi was to be its editor all his life up until his death in August 1987.[36] In the inaugural editorial, the guru announced that "from this day . . . the Sanathana Sarathi will lead the army (spiritual texts and scriptures) against the evil forces of injustice, disorder, falsehood and wickedness, led by the demon Ego. This Sarathi will fight for the firm establishment of peace in the world."[37] Along these lines, Kasturi wrote:

> This day the Sanathana Sarathi starts the campaign against falsehood, injustice, viciousness and evil, which are all, the vile minions of egoism. The army is the Vedas, the Upanishads and the Sastras; the goal is the welfare of the world. When the drums of Victory resound, Humanity would have achieved Happiness and Peace.[38]

The first number of the newsletter was released on February 1958, on the auspicious day of Mahāśivarātri, and was printed by a press at Dharmavaram in a few hundred copies. For about five years the newsletter was bilingual, half in Telugu and half in English. The hagiographer recalls that, when in Bangalore, the guru "visited the Vichara Darpana Press on Avenue Road . . . myself and Raja Reddy accompanying Him, and bought a small foot-worked treadle Printing Machine with a platen of 14 inches diameter, a roller made up of some non-descript mould, and a case of English and Telugu Types."[39] Starting in 1963, however, the Telugu and English versions were published separately.

The *Sanathana Sarathi* monthly was most important since it became the chief vehicle through which the guru spread his message. His writings and the transcription of his discourses occupied the major space of its thirty-two pages,[40] alongside other articles written by devotees who shared their own experiences of the Avatar and general information on the guru's journeys, Prasanthi Nilayam's festivals, etc. Sathya Sai Baba was a regular contributor, with at least four pages every month: he wrote continuously in *Sanathana Sarathi* for twenty-five years.[41]

As noted it was here, as a series of articles written upon specific subjects, that his installments of the future *Vahini Series* appeared.[42] With reference to the guru's commentary on the *Bṛhadāraṇyaka Upaniṣad*, Kasturi writes:

> I am certain that Baba had never read it or consulted others who could talk on it. And there was no copy available anywhere within miles. But forty minutes after He moved out with the pen and the notebook as His sole possessions, I could descend the eighteen steps from His room with a ten-page dissertation on the truths this Upanishad enshrined![43]

The hagiographer remembers that, before turning the sheets into his hands, Sathya Sai Baba would read him the script and elucidate the ideas that he did not understand, explaining them in easy Telugu.[44] For Kasturi, it was a major task and a great penance[45] to wear the costume of the newsletter's editor. Already in the first years, 2,500 copies of *Sanathana Sarathi* were printed monthly and the hagiographer was kept busy most of the day and even a few hours at night.[46] With no professional help of any kind, Kasturi was responsible for the whole process of correcting proofs,[47] editing, printing, pasting, and parceling each and every issue, to be posted on the sixteenth of every month. The people at the ashram could see him diligently and tirelessly typing away on his typewriter, oblivious to the clutter and confusion around. Mrs. Geeta Ram, who was a girl at the time, recalls:

> Once hundreds of copies had been made in English, Professor Kasturi . . . would himself type-set the whole text of Swami's articles in Telugu. The whole process . . . would be repeated so many times. And after the sheets were printed, the ink would still be wet. They would then have to be spread all over the floor to dry, so the ink would not smear. Later, the pages were carefully collated, stapled together, packed and addressed in preparation for mailing—all done by hand. Although there were a few volunteers to help him, I remember Professor Kasturi doing all these jobs, month in and month out, for so many years. This was truly his labor of love for Swami.[48]

But of course the most cumbersome of all responsibilities was translating the guru's writings from Telugu into English. Kasturi was impressed by their scope and depth: "The most complicated metaphysical conundrum is resolved by a parable or a proverb. Depths of Vedic wisdom or Christian theology or Muslim mysticism are illumined for us by Him and indelibly mirrored in phrases and metaphors."[49] Although the Swami would help him by giving him "long lessons in Telugu every month for many years with His monthly installments of the Vahini series for the Sanathana Sarathi,"[50] the task constituted a constant challenge for him and he was well aware of his shortcomings.[51]

In 2004, Bill Aitken criticized Kasturi's English renderings for being too literal and heavy-going, with a sugary tone and a flowery turn of phrase, remarking that the narrative is repetitious, with a tone that is reminiscent of Victorian morality.[52] Moreover, he observes that "these articles were written in the vernacular (Telugu), largely for a peasant audience. However, the style obscures much of the wisdom. . . . When read in the original, as part of *Sanathan Sarathi* . . . these writings astonish with their range and depth."[53]

I think that this criticism is way too harsh. To go to the extent of saying that Kasturi's style concealed much of Sathya Sai Baba's "wisdom" is an overstatement. The fact is that he strove to be literal, since he wished to convey the exact meaning of his guru's teachings in the most careful way. This was his major concern, and he should rather be praised for it. In his preface to *Dhyana Vahini*, he wrote:

> Baba's Telugu is sweet and simple and goes straight to the heart. To translate it into English is indeed to squeeze out much of its native nectarine taste. But for those unacquainted with Telugu, this is the best means of listening to His Directions and so this book is presented to all such aspirants.[54]

To be sure, he did not endeavor to be literarily elegant but to convey his guru's instructions as precisely as possible. His English translations were always double-checked by the Swami for final approval and nothing was published without his authorization. As a professor of the Sri Sathya Sai University, M. Nanjundaiah, recalls: "[P]rof. Kasturi . . . had access to Swami and could directly interact with Him to seek clarifications about His discourses and writings."[55] His repetitious, flowery style is typical of the hagiographic genre, for instance, of the *Carita* for which he was to become famous. Kasturi viewed it as a time-honored feature of the Hindu tradition—a virtue and not a flaw—and he was undoubtedly influenced by it even while translating his guru's writings. It is true that at times his tone is reminiscent of Victorian morality but, as noticed already, this was a characteristic of much of the neo-Hindu discourse that was part and parcel of Kasturi's background.

It must also be noted that he had little time to do the job, being forced to translate the Swami's writings rather quickly. Despite the rush and all difficulties, the hagiographer succeeded in editing and translating into English the entire corpus of the guru's discourses and writings up to the 1970s and even beyond. His translations are the ones that still continue to be published nowadays, being widely appreciated by Indians and Westerners alike.

Smriti Srinivas has carefully analyzed the various images displayed on the *Sanathana Sarathi*'s covers, being revelatory of the developments that characterized the Sathya Sai Baba movement over time.[56] From 1958 to 1963, the covers largely featured Kṛṣṇa as Arjuna's charioteer, although they also included images of the guru himself, of Shirdi Sai Baba, and of Śiva's *liṅga*. From 1964 up to 1970, while the movement obtained growing support among the Indian middle and upper classes/castes, the cover was dominated by a blending of regional and pan-Indian associations. Kasturi notes that the newsletter "had on its cover page for about ten years simple drawings of spiritual significance."[57] But in February 1970, during the Mahāśivarātri festival, "Baba drew with a pen . . . a figure with the holy symbols of the five major religions of the world, with the Lotus Pillar in the Centre, indicating the Sadhak struggling through any one of those paths and achieving success. That drawing was made into a block. This has since been accepted as illustrating the universality of the Sai Message."[58] Kasturi further observes that this symbol conveys the guru's message that "[t]here is only one Religion, the Religion of Love."[59] Thus, in the 1970s the newsletter's cover shifted to a stark and simple design which only bore its title and the logo of the Sai Organization, emblem of its universalism.[60] In an effort to strengthen the movement's all-embracing nature, in 1981 and up to 1995 the *Sanathana Sarathi*'s cover came to feature the outline of the Sarva Dharma Stupa[61] on the bottom left—the ashram's fifty-feet-high pillar with a lotus flower at the top, symbolizing the unity of all world religions, which was built in 1975 on the occasion of the guru's fiftieth birthday—with the newsletter's name next to it.

All in all, during the almost thirty years of Kasturi's editorship from 1958 to 1987, *Sanathana Sarathi* grew out of a local, regional, and even national space to reach an ever more global, cosmopolitan audience. It was devoid of commercial motives, carried no advertisements, and for decades had an annual subscription fee of Rupees 20. The newsletter's expansion was to continue and strengthen itself in the years following the hagiographer's death. If already by 1975 *Sanathana Sarathi* was published in eleven languages—Telugu, English, Tamil, Malayalam, Kannada, Marathi, Gujarati, Bengali, Hindi, Assamese, and Nepali—in subsequent years international editions of it were released in Chinese, German, Greek, Hungarian, Italian, Japanese, Portuguese, Romanian, Russian, and Spanish from their respective country headquarters. Nowadays, the newsletter is published in English, Telugu and more than twenty-five Indian and foreign languages.

Kasturi as the Guru's Personal Secretary: The Chiseled Child's Intimacy with Him

At Prasanthi Nilayam, Kasturi acted as a personal secretary to his Swami, running all sorts of errands and carrying messages to and from the guru.[62] Through him, the master would even send money to devotees who were in need.[63] If answers were required to some of the three hundred letters that Sathya Sai Baba received weekly from India and all over the world, he would direct his hagiographer to write them on his behalf.[64] Usually, however, the guru would take care of the letters himself. John S. Hislop writes: "There is an endless flow of letters coming to Swami. Swami reads all the letters and, about 10 a.m., the letters are burned. Swami does everything himself, so everything is done right."[65] All that Kasturi did needed the Swami's approval, since he was never supposed to take any personal initiative without his consent; when this occasionally happened, the guru would severely reprimand him.

At the ashram, Kasturi volunteered to undertake all sorts of services. In the early years, there being few adult men around, he would carry out any number of errands such as cleaning the village drains and roads and carrying pots of water from the well near the eastern gate of the ashram to the kitchen at the far western end.[66] Once, in the late 1950s, the postmaster general at Hyderabad came up with the proposal of starting a post office at Prasanthi Nilayam, provided that a pensioner of some local authority or government authority would be willing to become the post master. The need for a local post office had especially emerged with the starting of *Sanathana Sarathi*. It so happened that Kasturi was the only person in the ashram qualified to take the job. Swallowing his ego as professor and former principal of a college, he volunteered to do it and for more than eight months he acted as the postmaster of Prasanthi Nilayam. In his autobiography he observes:

> Baba had a dig at my dutifulness. "I do not like a Principal and a Ph.D. to be spoken of as a Postmaster!" I knew He was watching to see if His statement disparaging the status I had assumed was receiving any approbation from me. I only replied, "Anyone should be proud, Swami, when he is addressed as Postmaster to Prasanthi Nilayam."[67]

Around the end of the 1960s, Kasturi was even appointed chairman of Prasanthi Nilayam township.[68] Most importantly, every day for decades, in the mornings and in the afternoons, he would be together with his beloved Swami for hours on end. Nobody was ever as close to the guru as Kasturi was. Prof. Anil Kumar Kamaraju,[69] a prominent figure within the guru's movement since 1980 and the interpreter of his discourses for more than twenty years, recalls:

> His level of communication was celestial. He was the only man who could communicate with Swami at that religious, philosophical, *Vedantic*, Himalayan plane of thoughts. I don't think anybody could do that—not even Sri Kamavadhani.[70] . . . Believe me, Swami would ask Professor Kasturi how His speech was! He would not ask anybody else! Swami would find in him an intellectual, a scholar, a man of great wisdom and a true seeker. . . . That interaction and sacred bonding was something extraordinary![71]

Sathya Sai Baba could rely on him for anything, from the most delicate tasks to the most ordinary ones, from acting as his ambassador throughout the country to warn devotees against quacks claiming to be his agents, to making announcements on the loudspeakers of the ashram in six languages—English, Telugu, Kannada, Malayalam, Tamil, and Hindi, one after the other—at festival times.[72] Howard Levin has written that Kasturi, as the "man of announcements" in Prasanthi Nilayam, "had a way of pausing when delivering a message from Sai Baba that would always cause my heart to flutter with anxiety, anticipating some devastating news."[73]

On his part, the hagiographer would be keen to inform the guru about what happened in the world, that is, what he had heard with his tiny transistor glued to his ear at 1:30 every afternoon. The Swami used to say: "See, My newspaper is coming! He is going to give Me news."[74] In the 1960s and 1970s, when the Sathya Sai Organization was taking shape, Kasturi used to go up to the Mandir to the guru's room soon after the end of the morning *bhajans*, around 9:30, and be in conversation with the Swami for an hour or two, during which time they would discuss matters relating to the Sai movement. Kasturi was unquestionably one of the main protagonists of the expansion and success of the organization, both in India and abroad, and for many years acted as the president of the Sathya Sai Organization of Karnataka, which brought him to travel extensively throughout the state.

Not only was Kasturi the closest person to the guru at Prasanthi Nilayam, he was also the constant companion of Sathya Sai Baba in all his most important trips and travels, be it the visit to Tirupati or Kashmir, Kanyakumari or Bombay, Srinagar or Simla, Rishikesh or Rajahmundry, Badrinath or Trivandrum, Goa or Coimbatore, Delhi or Dwarka or even East Africa.[75] He would often joke, saying: "I am the luggage of Swami. I am like a suitcase, which has no freewill. I go wherever He takes me!"[76]

The guru was fond of Kasturi from the early days and this is testified to by the many letters and cards that Sathya Sai Baba wrote to him, also containing poems and prayers written especially for him.[77] Kasturi's proximity to the guru as well as to the latter's parents, especially to Sathya Sai Baba's mother Easwaramma, determined a unique intimacy between the two. Kasturi's daughter Padma recalls: "Whenever somebody brought sweets to Him, Swami would keep a few for my father saying, 'Aye, this is for Kasturi. Let him enjoy it!' The intimacy that existed between them had to be seen to be believed. It was a relationship that was legendary in so many ways."[78] Along the years, the guru made many gifts to his hagiographer. When I met Padma in Prasanthi Nilayam in February 2016, I could see how these memorabilia filled the walls of her tiny apartment.

Figure 4.2. Padma, Kasturi's daughter, in her small apartment. Prasanthi Nilayam, February 11, 2016.

As Kasturi writes in his autobiography: "Mine is, let me confide in you, a Love Story."[79] In one of his lectures to overseas devotees, he remarked: "Sometimes in a meeting when I speak in His presence, Swami introduces me as 'mana Kasturi,' 'My Kasturi,' and I would be so happy. My mother would be delighted when she heard Swami say that."[80]

Generally, the guru used to be very free with him, and Kasturi himself felt at ease with the master. Whereas most people were scared and tight-lipped when in Sathya Sai Baba's presence, Kasturi was the only one who dared cut a joke, and the guru appreciated his humor and clever, entertaining responses.[81] So confident was the guru with him that on occasions he would tease him, saying that Kasturi was a lady's name: they joked together, and everyone present was delighted to witness their bond of love.[82] Kasturi's daughter remembers:

> [Their relationship] was very, very close—I could say like a father and a son; and even friends. Swami used to like him very much. He would give him good food and would ask him to eat with Him.[83]

Moreover:

> At that time, the intimacy was so much that I can say—at least for myself—that I didn't feel the Divinity in Him. The relation was different then. He was like a family member—He used to come home and talk to us and play with the children.[84]

On the solemn occasion of Sathya Sai Baba's birthday, a select few were chosen to apply oil to the guru's head. If the first ones to have the honor of anointing him were always his parents, the second ones were invariably Kasturi and his wife.[85] In turn, in 1956 the guru celebrated with due pomp his friend's sixtieth birthday, to give joy to the hagiographer's mother as well as to Kasturi and his wife. A priest was called from Bukkapatnam for Vedic recitals, musicians came from Mysore, and many All India Radio fans and friends of Kasturi gathered from Bangalore. The guru oversaw the whole ceremony and allowed the professor and his wife to adorn his feet with flowers as they chanted the 1,008 names of their lord. Finally, the Swami's hand moved in circular motion and out came a golden marriage thread (*maṅgalasūtra*)[86] and a medallion: the hagiographer tied the golden thread round his wife's neck while she placed the golden pendant over his head. Meanwhile, the guru shook his purportedly empty hand over their heads and blessed them with a shower of rice grains, *kuṃkum,* and turmeric, all considered to be most auspicious.[87] In his autobiography, Kasturi writes: "We were being wedded anew to heavenly vows. He placed in her arms a silk sari and in mine, a silk dhoti. This was compassion at its superlative sweetness. . . . The ceremony which marked my Sixtieth Birthday was indeed so lit by Divine Grace that it was beyond understanding."[88]

On one occasion, Kasturi himself mothered his lord, who would rest as a child, comfortable and calm, in the lap of his *bhakta*:

> We were at Chebrole[89] that evening. During dinner, He announced that we were to leave soon for Madras. His face was flushed and He was in evident hurry. . . . I found myself on the back seat [of the car with Baba]. . . . Baba showed an inclination to stretch rather uncomfortably on the space available. . . . I sat stroking the hair and soothing the brow until dawn broke on the outskirts of Madras.[90]

The uniqueness of Kasturi's intimate relation with Sathya Sai Baba brought devotees to speculate that in his next life he would be reborn as the mother of Prema Sai Baba, the third and final incarnation. As already noted, it appears that the guru himself had told this to the hagiographer.[91]

More than once when the guru left Puttaparthi on his travels, Easwaramma, who was always anxious about her son, asked Kasturi to protect him—as when he left for his North Indian tour in July 1957—or find where he was and bring him back home safe and sound.[92] On one such occasion, the hagiographer promised her to shield her son with the all-powerful *gāyatrī mantra*: she had heard wild stories of animosity between top-ranking monks and rivalry among monastic orders and was afraid that someone might want to hurt her Sathya.[93] When in December 1970 the Swami was in Goa with Kasturi, he sent him back to Puttaparthi to reassure his mother, who was downcast due to exaggerated reports in the press of the guru being critically ill. Kasturi reports: "Baba persuaded me to leave His Presence, with the argument, 'When *you* go among them and tell them personally, Easwaramma will have no hesitation to believe that I am well. For, she knows you would not go away from me unless I am well healed.' "[94]

Like Easwaramma, most devotees looked at Kasturi as a mediator and even intercessor between themselves and the guru, a person who could recommend their case to Sathya Sai Baba or intercede on their behalf and obtain an interview for them.[95] Although the hagiographer always made it clear that no third person could negotiate on behalf of devotees since the guru could not be advised or persuaded by anyone—the idea being that the Swami is in full control and calls to himself whomever he wants[96]—still there were cases in which it came almost natural to him to intercede for others.[97] At times, the guru would sharply censure him for such "gatekeeper to god" endeavors. Prof. Nanjundaiah recalls:

> One day when Kasturi was going to His Presence . . . as was his daily routine, an old-time friend who was aware of his proximity to Bhagavan caught him and started coaxing him. "You should recommend my case to Swami . . . Bhagavan should give me an interview. Please don't say 'No'! You must do this. . . ." Professor Kasturi, kind-hearted that he was, could not afford to hurt him nor could he reply in the affirmative, so, with an indirect reply, "I have to go to Swami," he moved on and went upstairs. After he saw Swami, He . . . asked: "What happened when you were coming up to me?" Professor Kasturi couldn't immediately get Him. Swami again queried, "What happened on the way?" Then, as if suddenly recollected, Kasturi exclaimed, "Oh, that Swami! One old friend met me on the way." "What did he tell you?", the Lord probed further. Kasturi said, "Swami, You know everything. He wanted an interview from You. He told me to recommend his case." Then, immediately Swami said: "O ho! Recommendation! You have grown so big in Prasanthi Nilayam as to recommend other people's cases to Swami! O ho!" [Kasturi answered:] "No Swami, I am an ordinary fellow; just a dust of Your Lotus Feet. Can I recommend anyone to You, Swami? That gentleman thought so many things and told me to do this." Professor Kasturi explained and implored. Still, Bhagavan commanded, "Go and tell him: I am nobody here, an absolutely ordinary person. Can any person recommend about others to Swami? Swami is God. Please don't expect me to do such things. I am really no one here." "Tell him and return." But when Kasturi went down to pass this message onto his

> friend the whole episode took an unexpected turn. That person was stone-deaf. And when Kasturi softly, with a serious face, communicated Swami's message, that gentleman thought his friend was only being too clever, and given his closeness to Bhagavan, he had really acquired for him a Divine audience. He began to rejoice. Kasturi, then, had to repeat His message, twice or thrice, and as loudly as possible, and as a result not only that particular gentleman but everyone around heard it carefully and clearly.[98]

In order to foster discipline and a contemplative attitude, at the ashram the guru was always keen that all men and women should adhere to general rules of conduct. Thus, he requested males and females to keep separate—during meals, *darśans*, *bhajans*, etc.—and limit their interactions to a minimum: anyone who would not conform to this basic rule would be asked to leave Prasanthi Nilayam. On the point of discipline and ethics, he was all the more demanding with those who were closest to him. On occasions, the master could be quite severe with the hagiographer, ignoring him for days or speaking harsh words to him. When Kasturi or any other close devotee did something wrong, the guru would not look at them or speak to them for days, and this would cause them great pain. Indulal H. Shah states: "Only when we come nearer to Baba can we see how strict and disciplinarian He is. He would condemn even the slightest drawback in the conduct of those who come close to Him. . . . If the devotee does not improve but goes on with his errant ways, Bhagavan Baba would be quick to react and His sympathy will give place to a stern indifference."[99]

Indeed, the guru demanded discipline from his *bhakta*s and would often scold them for their unrestraint. As he once said to some young Americans: "In America you think freedom means: 'I can go where I want to go, do what I want, have as many girlfriends as I like, sleep late as I want.' Our Indian dogs—same freedom! The end of wisdom is freedom. Happiness lies not in doing what you like, but liking what you have to do."[100] For Kasturi it was not at all easy to go through the hardships of his guru's discipline,[101] and he insisted on remarking that "Baba does not compromise, collude condone or conceal, as most Gurus and monastic heads do."[102] With reference to the guru's strictness, Diana Baskin's observation is worth quoting:

> The old-timers had warned me that, sooner or later, every sincere devotee had to expect a severe test from Swami. No one is spared. He always tests your weakest points. Many people could not withstand and surmount the testing and ended up at the breaking point, leaving Swami.[103]

Ex-devotee M. Krishna notices that "generally speaking there will be very few people who will continuously be with Swami after eight or ten years. Somehow or other they will fall off. . . . In those days [the 1950s] . . . he never accepted any criticism. As far as I know him, he will all the more resent criticism now when he has become an international figure."[104] Kasturi confirms that through the years many people left the guru, being "unable to stand the rigor of the discipline He enforces."[105] Sri Rama Brahmam once told Anil Kumar Kamaraju: "To be with Swami is walking on fire without getting burnt, walking on sword without being cut."[106]

The hagiographer compared Sathya Sai Baba's rigorous discipline to an alchemical transubstantiation:

> [I]n order to transform our metal into the precious one, He melts us in the crucible of life, and He draws out all the dregs, making us fit for His purpose. Whoever the culprit, however insignificant the fault—whether it is downright disobedience or an uppish untimely raising of the eyebrow—however aged or learned or "high-placed" the person, castigation will descend on him, prompt and peremptory, so that he is helped to repent and reconstruct his character and conduct.[107]

Arnold Schulman reports that "all [devotees] live in terror of Baba,"[108] their fear also implying a numinous experience, namely, the feeling of being confronted with god when in the guru's presence, whose rewards and punishments cannot be avoided. Kasturi himself writes that Baba has to be "not only loved, adored, approached for grace and gifts, but more than all 'feared.' "[109] Moreover:

> You fear when you are with Him. The closer you are with Him, the more afraid you are. Imagine a gathering of fifty thousand people whispering to each other, adding up to a big noise,

> and when Swami appears, pin-drop silence! That is creating a sense of awe, fear. It is only Divinity that will produce such silence. . . . Even now, after about 36 years of being in the presence of Swami, if someone comes after this talk and says "Swami calls you," I begin to think: "Probably He didn't like my telling you something, probably He may say: 'Why are you making these people laugh.' I don't know what mistake I have committed! Maybe I will be asked to get out! I will be asked to stop talking! Some punishment awaits me!" Like that I fear. My heart goes thud, thud.[110]

Fear of god is not to be confused with ordinary fear (*bhaya*), which the guru of Puttaparthi is thought to dispel. As he frequently used to say: "Why fear when I am here?"[111]

Kasturi devotes an entire chapter of his autobiography, titled "The Chiseled Child," to narrating episodes in which the guru exposed and punished his shortcomings so as to teach him a lesson, reduce his ego, and make him grow along the spiritual path. For instance, the master warned him not to accept that people reverentially touch his feet, since this would inflate his ego.[112] The hagiographer's aim is to offer a repertoire of behavioral patterns—as well as of ideas and intentions—that the guru's pupil should altogether avoid or learn to counter: in other words, these *exempla* are more than just a lesson in humility since they bear a normative, disciplining function, teaching how one ought *not* to behave oneself. Kasturi used to talk about his "foolish pride" even to groups of foreign devotees, and once pointed out: "Taking advantage of closeness to Him, feeling it is my due, because I am a big scholar, because I am indispensable to His glory, such swelling of the head will result in being sent out!"[113]

His longest period of punishment lasted several weeks, during which time the master ignored him or prevented him from approaching him. It happened after the professor had returned from a tour of Northeast India, where he had given talks on the guru and his message. His fault, the Swami later told him, had been that of accepting to be publicly presented as a "prominent personality granting interviews" during his stay in Orissa, thus priding himself as if he were the master.[114] Kasturi writes: "[B]aba knew that my ego felt internally elated when the 'personalities' were ushered in for the interview. It revealed a deep spiritual flaw and Baba graciously undertook to correct it."[115] In fact, this was but a momentary weakness on the hagiographer's part since Kasturi was a humble man who wouldn't ever dream of arrogance. This is proven by the fact that he never took advantage of his proximity to the master. The rare times when he tried to talk about personal problems or family issues with him, the guru would tell him: "What is the use of your stay with Me for so many years? You are still attached."[116] Yet, the Swami cared for him and periodically asked him about family matters.

Countering the high epithets with which devotees liked to honor him,[117] sometimes the guru would jokingly call Kasturi "buffalo" or "monkey"[118] (*kapi* instead of *kavi*, poet) and, in his old age, "the chaste old woman," "the '97 model," and "the ramshackle car."[119] These epithets were not meant as derogatory, being rather indicative of the intimacy between Kasturi and his master who, as we know, had praised him as the reincarnation of Nannaya Bhaṭṭa, the foremost of Telugu poets, as early as 1958.

Kasturi as Public Speaker

Another role in which the hagiographer excelled from his early days was that of public speaker, either in English or in a South Indian language. In his autobiography, he confesses of being "afflicted by a chronic willingness to accept lecture engagements."[120] On countless occasions the guru asked him to deliver talks to devotees, especially Westerners, both in his presence as well as in his absence, and Kasturi loved to do it, since talking about the glory of his lord was his sustenance and favorite pastime.[121] As his grandson Ramesh recalls: "Whenever he was sick, with cold or fever, Swami used to tell him: *Poyi lecture cheyi, ade neeku biksha* meaning, 'Go and speak about Swami, that lecture is your medicinal mixture.' "[122]

At the ashram, the guru commissioned him to deliver English lectures to overseas devotees on a regular basis, typically after morning *darśan*. His talks centered on the Avatar and his teachings, and the disciplines one should practice in order to progress along the spiritual path.[123] All who have heard him speak agree that he was a formidable orator and storyteller: his sweet voice touched the hearts and with his subtle humor he could keep his audiences spellbound for hours. His talks brilliantly fused together devotion, humility, and humor, as I myself can testify having listened to several of Kasturi's talks back in the 1980s. Prof. Anil Kumar

Figure 4.3. N. Kasturi delivering a lecture at Sathya Sai Baba's presence.

Kamaraju remembers: "There was no parallel! You may perhaps call this an expression of audacity, but I am sincere when I make the statement: 'If Baba is number one in story-telling, Kasturi would be number two!' His expressions had so much power and color. His simplicity, humility and endearing nature towards all was really great!"[124] As a devotee from the United Kingdom puts it: "[H]e emanated love, with humility. And we were spellbound with love for him!"[125]

Kasturi's skill as a speaker also took a more traditional form. As early as the late 1950s the hagiographer composed a *Sai Bhagavatham*, a poem of more than three hundred lines on the life and message of Sathya Sai Baba, which took the *Bhāgavata Purāṇa* as its inspirational model. He originally wrote it in Kannada and subsequently prepared versions of it in Malayalam,[126] Tamil, Telugu, and English.[127] In the original Kannada, every line ends in a word rhyming with the last syllable of "Jay Sathya Sanathana Sarathi."[128] The guru himself encouraged him to utilize this "Annunciation Song," as the hagiographer called it, in his talks.[129]

Significantly, in the English version of the poem Kasturi extols the guru as Śiva-Śakti, Kṛṣṇa, Rāma, Jehovah, Buddha, and Jesus Christ and declares that "His breath reveals the genuine Christ—On the self-same Cross in every blade of grass,"[130] which is reminiscent of the guru's "materialization" of a wooden cross with a figure of Jesus on it for J. S. Hislop. Kasturi's son M. V. N. Murthy would often sing the verses of the *Sai Bhagavatham* in either Kannada or Tamil in the traditional *gamaka* style,[131] and the hagiographer would offer his commentary to the verses by elaborating on their meaning: this form of communication was much valued, especially by Indian audiences, and father and son spread the gospel of their lord at many venues, in Prasanthi Nilayam as well as throughout South India, reciting it and commenting upon it several hundred times. In Kasturi's autobiography *Loving God*, one can read the English version of

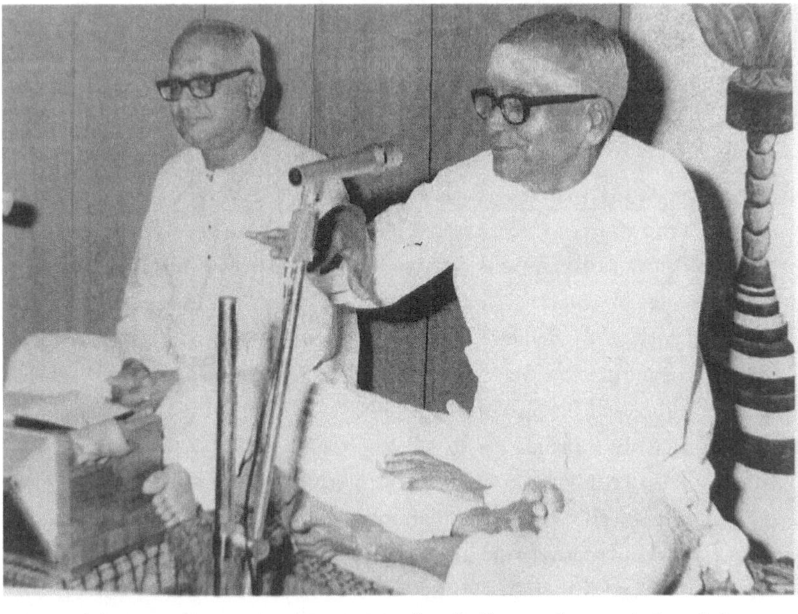

Figure 4.4. Kasturi's son M. V. N. Murthy (left) together with his father performing the recital and commentary of the *Sai Bhagavatham.*

the *Sai Bhagavatham* in just 136 lines, which he duly comments upon.[132] Like his father, M. V. N. Murthy was an ardent devotee of Sathya Sai Baba. In the 1960s and 1970s, while working for the Geological Survey of India, he spread the guru's message in Arunachal Pradesh, Assam, and other States of Northeastern India, and eventually settled in Prasanthi Nilayam on June 6, 1981.

Over the years, the hagiographer was able to establish thousands of personal contacts with all sorts of people from all walks of life, Indians as well as Westerners. If the guru presented himself as the "mother" of his devotees, and his ashram as their "mother's house," he would also say that Kasturi was their "mother-in-law," to whom they should refer for their practical needs.[133] The door of his small apartment was always open and he was available to all, ready to help and share his knowledge about his beloved guru with everyone. His network of relations with Westerners and Indians alike was strengthened by his habit of corresponding via mail with many people.[134]

Kasturi's Other Books on the Guru and His Autobiography *Loving God*

Besides his magnum opus *Sathyam Sivam Sundaram*, Kasturi authored other important works on Sathya Sai Baba, confirming his skills as a theologian. He also penned several poems on the guru[135] and compiled anthologies of his master's teachings such as *Teachings of Sri Satya Sai Baba* (Lakemont, GA: CSA Press, 1974), *Chinna Katha: Stories and Parables* (Prasanthi Nilayam: Sri Sathya Sai Books and Publications, 1975), and *Sadhana: The Inward Path. Quotations from the Divine Discourses of Bhagavan Sri Sathya Sai Baba* (Bangalore: Sri Sathya Sai Education and Publication Foundation, 1976; Rev. ed. 1978).[136] Alongside several articles, which he published on *Sanathana Sarathi* and in collective volumes,[137] he was a prolific book writer up to his last years.

Prof. Anil Kumar Kamaraju remarks that "he was no ordinary man, a scholar par excellence and a matchless writer. He knew Upanishadic, Ramakrishna and Aurobindo literature through and through, but never took the opportunity to showcase his scholarship."[138] The hagiographer points out that it was Sathya Sai Baba who exhorted him to study the *Upaniṣads*, the *Bhagavadgītā*, and, above all, the *Bhāgavata Purāṇa* and the *Uddhavagītā* incorporated therein. Moreover, the guru prodded him to study and recite the *Rudrādhyāya*, also known as *Śatarudrīya* or the "Hundred names of Rudra," sixteenth chapter of the *Vājasaneyī Saṃhitā* within the *White Yajurveda* recension, and told him: "It is only when you know the implications of that hymn that you can understand Me."[139]

In all of his works Kasturi's primary concern was to offer cogent, comprehensive answers to three essential questions: (1) Who is Sathya Sai Baba, that is, what is the master's true identity?[140] (2) What are the contents of his teachings and the overall purpose of his universal mission and movement? (3) What must be the response of devotees to the guru's call, that is, the spiritual values and lifestyle that his followers must cultivate, individually as well as collectively?

One of the first things he wrote, which later encouraged him to compose the *Sai Bhagavatham*, was a list of 108 names of Sathya Sai Baba in Kannada "for the use of devotees while meditatively worshipping the Lotus Feet of Bhagavan."[141] He first recited and explained the names when the sculpted pair of the guru's feet were installed on the left bank of the Kaveri River at Srirangapatna, near the city of Mysore. This invocation of the master by his epithets—each ending with the word *caraṇa*, "feet," symbolizing the most sacred repository of the guru's power and grace—is eloquent as a full theological treatise since the hagiographer utilizes the whole field of religious experience to honor the guru as the supreme godhead, recognizing him as none other than Shirdi Sai Baba, his prior incarnation: the names are both *vaiṣṇava* and *śaiva* and deal with the *saguṇa* or personal aspects of divinity as well as the *nirguṇa* or formless nature of the Absolute.

In the mid-1960s, Kasturi published a revised version of a list of 108 Sanskrit names in the guru's honor that one Seshagiri Rao[142] together with other devotees had composed when the master was still in his teens.[143] This revised version became the official list of the guru's names, which is in use even today. The hagiographer recalls:

> I consulted Baba for some of the Names seemed inappropriate. Baba spotted a few and directed me to substitute other Names in their place. Believe me, one of the Names omitted was Sankara[144] Amsa (a part, portion or limb of Sankara), and the substitute He gave me, was, Sankara![145]

The text was published in 1966 by the Sri Sathya Sai Education and Publication Foundation with the title *Garland of 108 Precious Gems: Ashtothara Sathanama Rathnamala*, and in 1979 it had reached its fourth edition.[146] Along the decades it has been reedited many times, since devotees recite the 108 names daily as part of their *sādhanā*. Most importantly, the text features Kasturi's thorough and perspicuous commentary on each name, in which he emphasizes the *sarvadaivatvasvarūpa* of Sathya Sai Baba's reality, the fundamental axiom that he embodies all names and forms of divinity and that, since he is all gods in one, he answers to any name. The hagiographer's exegesis of each epithet offers the best proof of his competence as a theologian in his own right.

In September 1963, Kasturi wrote the booklet *Siva Sakthi Swarupa* (Bombay: Parijat Prakashan, with a foreword by Dinesh N. Desai).[147] He published it just two months after the guru's momentous declaration of July 6, day of Gurupūrṇimā, when he revealed to a huge gathering of ecstatic devotees that he was the *avatāra* of Śiva-Śakti within the context of a triadic avatāric descent, the first one being Shirdi Sai Baba as Śiva and the third and final one being the future Prema Sai Baba as Śakti. In fact, he had given a hint at being Śiva-Śakti already in November 1958, when he purportedly saved a little girl's life by "appearing" on the route between Puttaparthi and Bangalore as a villager bearing the name of Joḍi Ādipalli Somāppa.[148] This is why the twentieth of his 108 names celebrates him as *Oṃ Śrī Joḍi Ādipalli Somāppāya Namaḥ*.[149] The guru explained that Ādipalli, the primeval village, stood for Kailāsa, the divine residence that is Joḍi meaning belonging to two, Somāppa meaning Śiva (*appā*, the father) with Umā (*sa* + Umā), his inseparable Śakti. In his book, Kasturi offers a detailed account of the guru's weeklong paralysis of his left side and of how he instantly freed himself of it. He further elaborates on the "historic" revelation of the guru's divine identity and its theological implications, in the framework of the story of sage Bharadvāja's visit to lord Śiva. Being all the time at the guru's side he was an eyewitness to all that happened, which, as he confides to his readers, was the most sensational experience of his life. Kasturi adopts an effective rhetorical device that adds to the suspense and awe of its subject matter, construing the narrative as a dialogue between himself and an initially skeptical questioner who is gradually won over by his testimony. Kasturi reveals to his fictitious interlocutor that the guru is indeed Sathyam Sivam Sundaram, "as I have named the book about Him, which I wrote in 1961."[150] He remarks how Sathya Sai Baba himself, in his discourse of July 7, 1963, stated:

> Sathyam is the function of the Intellect, Sivam of the Consciousness and Sundaram of the Heart; Sathyam is Splendor, and Sivam the recognition of the Truth inside it and Sundaram, the nature of that Truth; Sathyam is Jnana, Sivam is Karma and Sundaram is Bhakthi.[151]

Kasturi glorifies him as "the synthesis of all antitheses, the harmony behind all apparent discordances . . . the inner Principle as well as the outer Force."[152]

Five years later, in 1968, the hagiographer wrote an account of his guru's first and only trip outside India, when he accompanied Sathya Sai Baba on his summer tour of Kenya and Uganda, which lasted two weeks: the guru and his small party landed in Nairobi airport on June 30, 1968. His booklet was published in London by Sai Publications and was originally titled *Sathya Sai Baba: The Light of Love in Africa.*[153] The text is divided into two parts: the first (pp. 7–56), in seven chapters, offers a detailed account of the guru's day by day meetings and tours, while the second (pp. 59–113) records the seven discourses he delivered during his sojourn, comprising interactive sessions of questions and answers with spiritual aspirants and with members of the Rotary and Lions clubs in Kampala.[154] While chronicling Sathya Sai Baba's encounters and visits to places of interest—such as the guru's trip to the Ngorongoro crater and to the Murchison Falls National Park—Kasturi focuses on the principle of pure love (*preman*), based upon the recognition of the oneness of all people and faiths. He concentrates attention on the theological relevance of his guru's mission, who has not come to speak on behalf of any religion nor to collect followers for any particular sect or creed. He underlines the universal import of the present *avatāra,* who has no plan to attract devotees into his fold or any fold but has come to awaken mankind to a universal unitary faith, to the path and duty (*dharma*) of love.[155] The hagiographer interprets the African trip as the concrete sign of the expansion of the guru's mission to the world.[156]

Basing himself on a discourse that his guru delivered on November 23, 1968,[157] Kasturi that same year edited a short but far-reaching text, only ten pages long, on the significance of the Swami's mission, explaining why the Avatar had manifested. The booklet is titled *Sathya Sai Baba Announces His Mission and Why the Avatar Has Come, November 23, 1968.*[158] In 2010, David Gries and Phil Gosselin have painstakingly searched and identified the actual sources of Kasturi's narration, which is in fact quite different from the speech that the guru delivered in 1968 on the day of his birthday, since the hagiographer creatively construed it by synthesizing excerpts taken from no less than eighteen discourses which the guru held between 1963 and 1965.[159] Kasturi's careful harmonization of Sathya Sai Baba's utterances offers one more proof of his skill as a theologian and shows his decisive role in the construction of a unified canon. This solemn and powerful text, which is viewed as a veritable landmark by devotees,[160] neatly summarizes the main features of the guru's avatāric mission.

On Christmas of 1982, day of his eighty-fifth birthday, his lengthy autobiography titled *Loving God: Eighty Five Years Under the Watchful Eye of the Lord* (Prasanthi Nilayam: Sri Sathya Sai Books & Publications) was released with the Swami's blessings.[161] On this occasion and without prior notice, the guru asked the renowned journalist V. K. Narasimhan (1912–2000) to deliver a short talk on Kasturi. Narasimhan praised with touching words the hagiographer's life and works, presenting him as a luminous example for all devotees to follow. Sathya Sai Baba was very pleased with his speech, and whispered into his ear "very good, very good."[162] Kasturi must have valued such "consecration" as the best birthday gift he could ever receive. Divided into fifteen chapters for a total of 390 pages, *Loving God* offers an invaluable account of his life, rich and detailed, and is by all standards a mine of information. It is a precious source for delving into the hagiographer's self-understanding of his life-trajectory, both prior and after his decisive meeting with Sathya Sai Baba in 1948, even though to his formative years and brilliant career up to age fifty (from 1897 to 1947) he dedicates only the initial four chapters. To be sure, the emphasis of *Loving God* is on the years from 1948 onward and the hagiographer's unique relationship with the guru of Puttaparthi. His prose is elegant and entertaining, his English being remarkably clear and readable. He scrutinizes himself as if from a distance, with no self-indulgence but rather being slightly self-mocking. Throughout the book he recognizes his shortcomings: his self-criticism vis-à-vis the supreme model represented by his guru-god is the leitmotif of the autobiography. Even where he writes of his earlier life as a teacher and of his literary achievements as a Kannada litterateur, he keeps a characteristically low profile.

Significantly, the cover of the book shows not Kasturi but a close-up image of Sathya Sai Baba signed by the latter with the words "With Love, Baba." All the pictures within the book are of the hagiographer together with his beloved Swami, and on the back cover is a saying of the guru, which he chose as especially meaningful: "See in Me, yourself, for I see Myself in you all. You are My life, My breath, My soul. You are My forms, all. When I love you, I love Myself; when you love yourselves, you love Me! I have separated Myself from Myself, so that I may love Myself. My beloved ones, you are My Own Self." In the preface, he states that he was prompted to write his autobiography by an approving smile by his lord when someone whispered to him in the guru's presence that a bunch of his reminiscences would be welcomed by many. He argues: "Since the four parts of *Sathyam Sivam Sundaram* relate most of what I have yearned to communicate, this book has become a Personal Testament."[163]

For many years, his "New Year's resolution" had been to keep a written record of his activities, feelings, and experiences of the thirty-four years that he spent at Prasanthi Nilayam—the "second half" of his life, which, paraphrasing *Bhagavadgītā* 2.29, he called the era of *āścarya* or "astonishing marvel"[164]—but unfortunately he never succeeded in such endeavor.[165] Perhaps, he came to view his autobiography as a partial remedy to the absence of such diary. It should be added that a brief summary of Kasturi's life in his own words, tracing his journey from Ramakrishna Paramahamsa to Sathya Sai Baba, was published with the title *Gurudev* in 1985, on the occasion of the guru's sixtieth birthday (Prasanthi Nilayam: Sri Sathya Sai Books and Publications, 2005).

On May 6, 1984, the anniversary of Sathya Sai Baba's mother's death—from 1983 on, annually celebrated as Easwaramma Day—Kasturi released *Easwaramma: The Chosen Mother* (Prasanthi Nilayam: Sri Sathya Sai Books and Publications). The book, divided in seventeen chapters for a total of 191 pages, is the hagiographer's tribute to the mother of the Avatar represented as a poor, illiterate, most kind, and devout woman. Her original name was Namagiryamma and she was the eldest daughter of the younger sister of Ratnākaram Kondama Rāju, Veṅkaṭa Subbamma, and of one Meesaraganda Subba Rāju of Kolimigundla, a village in Kurnool district. Apparently, it was Ratnākaram Kondama Rāju, Sathya Sai Baba's grandfather, who first started calling her Easwaramma, meaning mother of god (Īśvara); he had become convinced of his grandson's divinity from when Sathya was a little boy.[166] Kasturi, however, writes that she was so named because she was born after her father constructed a temple to Īśvara.[167]

In the foreword, the hagiographer confesses his inability to present a fuller portrait of Easwaramma in spite of the twenty-four years he spent at Puttaparthi close to her: she was too noncommunicative and "laid bare her heart to me only on the occasions when she needed some pestering doubt cleared, some knotty tension loosened, some deep apprehension exorcised, some rumor explained."[168] Married to Pedda Veṅkappa Rāju at the age of fourteen, her son Sathyanārāyaṇa, the future Sathya Sai Baba, was her fourth child (and her eighth pregnancy).[169]

While chronicling what he envisions as the main events of her life—all inextricably related to the guru's career—Kasturi takes pains to articulate two points that are decisive in order to justify the divinity of his lord: (1) the guru resolved upon his birth by deciding who should be his mother, that is to say, his *māyā,* as indicated by the book's title; and (2) his conception was not human but divine, without any carnal intercourse, on analogy with the legendary births of other *avatāra*s as well as of the Buddha and, most importantly, of Jesus. Already on page twenty, he quotes Easwaramma and her prodigious son on the latter's miraculous conception:

> [Easwaramma]: "That morning when I was at the well drawing water, a big ball of blue light came rolling towards me and I fainted and fell. I felt, it glided into me." Swami turned to Rama Sarma[170] with a smile: "There you have the answer! I was not begotten. It was Pravesa [spiritual birth], not Prasava [biological birth]."[171]

Throughout the book, the hagiographer extols the saintly virtues of this simple woman—depicted as another Virgin Mary[172]—and her motherly apprehension for her son, whom she came to recognize as a divine phenomenon from the 1940s. Her apprehension for him is documented even in the last years of her life: "Why don't they [devotees] leave him alone? Look how they make him work. He doesn't sleep, he doesn't eat enough. All they care about is themselves. They want to kill him. He doesn't eat because he doesn't like their cooking. He likes my cooking."[173] Kasturi interprets Easwaramma's life as a journey, a day by day *sādhanā* that led her "from multiplicity to unity . . . from egoism to detachment . . . from unconcern to the love that cares and shares, from Maya to the Master."[174]

Along the decades, the life of the *gṛham ammāyi*—the "mother of the house" as her son called her, with no acknowledgment of any filial tie—unfolded in what Kasturi efficaciously terms "the fast multiplying multi-lingual, multi-racial, multi-creedal, global family of Sai."[175] There can be little doubt that the hagiographer's choice of writing a book on the guru's mother—and not on his father or other family members—was influenced by the exemplary model of the mother of Jesus, which he knew all too well that Western devotees of Sathya Sai Baba would find irresistible, inevitably establishing an equivalence between the two "chosen mothers."

On November 23, 1985, on the occasion of the guru's sixtieth birthday, which was attended by around four hundred thousand devotees from all over the world, in concomitance with the 4th World Conference of the Sri Sathya Sai Organizations, Kasturi offered to his Swami his last opus titled *Prasanthi: Pathway to Peace. As Learnt at the Lotus Feet of Bhagavan* (Prasanthi Nilayam: Sri Sathya Sai Books and Publications, 1985). Divided in four parts for a total of 118 pages, each section is introduced by a line taken from *Bhagavadgītā* 4.34 and, accordingly, the first focuses on the path of surrender (*praṇipāta*), the second on the path of inquiry (*paripraśna*), the third on the path of service (*sevā*), and the fourth and final one on the path that leads to the realization of the Absolute (*tat*) through meditation (*dhyāna*). Kasturi did so to explicitly link Sathya Sai Baba to Shirdi Sai Baba (thus lending support to the thesis of the latter's "Hinduness"), given that in the *Śrī Sāī Saccarita* this verse is commented upon by the Shirdi *faqīr* in an ingenious, unheard of way, by interpreting that the wise ones (*jñānins*) teach ignorance (*ajñāna*) rather than knowledge (*jñāna*), postulating the presence in the text of the negative particle *a* preceding the noun.

Shirdi Sai Baba exhibited a familiarity with Vedānta metaphysics that no one suspected he had. The Sanskrit verse runs as follows: *tad viddhi praṇipātena paripraśnena sevayā | upadekṣyanti te jñānam jñāninas tattvadarśinaḥ*. Here is a standard translation: "Learn to know this (*tat*, i.e., knowledge) by obeisance [to those who can teach it], By questioning [them], by serving [them]; They will teach thee knowledge, Those who have knowledge, who see the truth."[176] It is indeed possible to read *te ajñānam* instead of *te jñānam*, given that according to the rule of vowel *sandhi* (lit. "juncture"), final *e* followed by an initial short *a* results in the single vowel *e*, with the elision of *a*.[177]

In this book which is his final, remarkable synthesis, Kasturi presents the pathway toward the highest peace (*praśānti*), which coincides with Sathya Sai Baba. Following the lesson of the *Bhagavadgītā*, he examines from his own Vedāntic perspective a series of interrelated topics, in an effort to harmonize the paths (*mārga*) of action, devotion, and knowledge. The hagiographer's main points can be summarized thus: (1) The guru's life is *the* model one must follow. He is the incarnation of truth (*satya*) and of the supreme *Brahman*—the formless and nameless "It," responding to all names—to whom all must look for guidance and to whom all must surrender; (2) Love of god, *bhakti,* is of fundamental importance and one must follow its nine limbs (*navāṅgāni*) and engage in the remembrance of god's names and in the singing of his glories (*nāmasmaraṇa*, *japa*, *bhajana*, *saṃkīrtana*);[178] (3) Mankind must acknowledge the *Veda*s as the treasure house of wisdom and perform the rites and sacrifices (*yajña*) prescribed therein: they convey the sublime teaching that life is to be donated (*datta*) and that the secret of existence lies in selfless action (*naiṣkarmya*) and service (*sevā*) to all fellow beings, ultimately relinquishing all attachments; (4) The path of knowledge (*jñāna*) by means of Upaniṣadic self-inquiry and meditation (*dhyāna,* in particular through the contemplation of the light of a flame, *jyotis*) is necessary in order to overcome worldly illusion and realize one's ātmic identity. In the ultimate experience of nonduality (*advaita*) everyone and everything is recognized as none other than the supreme I, and Kasturi ends his book with these solemn words:

> I and I are I
>
> Prasanthi is the destiny to which every Yoga leads. The Yoga that fosters, fashions and fulfils all Yogas is the Prema Yoga, the Sai Yoga. This is the unique mission of this unique Avatar. Its uniqueness consists in the universality of its Love, Wisdom, Power and Joy. No other Personification of the Divine had this horizon-less dimension, and this spontaneous liberality of Grace, this unquestioning compassion for the foolish, the fumbling and the frenzied. Let us envelop ourselves in Silence and silence our clamorous mind, disputatious reason, and listen to the Voice of Sai, the Divine Guru who has Prasanthi as the Boon. There is neither Thou nor That in Prasanthi. There is but one all comprehensive I.[179]

All in all, it is fair to conclude that, through his writings and the multiple roles he played in the Sathya Sai Baba movement, the hagiographer exercised a tremendous influence over hundreds of thousands of people, Westerners as well as Indians. Here is a telling excerpt from a letter of thanks he received from an American devotee in 1971:

> Who or what I am is of no importance; what is important is that through the Door you opened for me, I have entered the temple of Baba to bow at His Feet and know the Ananda of His Existence. . . . I write to Him and He answers in the heart I have opened to Him because you helped me to understand Him. . . . [T]hrough your efforts, His words have reached me that I might comprehend them to whatever degree. Thank you, my brother, thank you.[180]

5

A Conversation with Professor Kasturi

After an extended field research in the village of Shirdi and the surrounding area, I reached Prasanthi Nilayam on October 31, 1985. I was twenty-three years old and this was my third visit to Sathya Sai Baba's ashram. As in my past trips to Puttaparthi of November 1982 and February 1985, I and other Westerners had the opportunity of attending Kasturi's lectures on the guru's life and teachings. He used to deliver his talks in the morning after *bhajans*, in a ground floor room near the ashram's main entrance, which was invariably packed with people who eagerly waited to hear him speak.

The hagiographer's English was fluent. He had a soft voice, a dramatic presence and charm, and a sense of theatrical fun in storytelling. I remember his gesticulations with those ever-bending, waving fingers that made his hands look like a cobra dancing to its charmer's flute. With his rising tones, deliberate halts, and humorous anecdotes he captivated his audience, to the extent that the listeners were like fish on the hook, caught hanging upon his every word and gesture. His subtle humor was his distinguishing mark.[1] Here is how M. N. Rao vividly describes him:

> Kasturi is the grand-old-man of Prasanthi Nilayam. With thick glasses and a geriatric hunch, out-sized scholarly head with a wide forehead plastered with *vibhuthi,* walking dignified with support from a walking stick or a human shoulder—that is the venerable Kasturi in 1985, the jolly walker with a ready toothless smile still going strong.[2]

Quite tall and broad-shouldered, he always wore a spotless *dhotī* and on the top of it a clean, white robe, right up to his knees. On his forehead, he invariably had the marks of *vibhūti* standing out, with in the middle a red *kuṃkum* spot.

On Thursday, November 7, 1985, at the end of his morning lecture, I took the courage to go up to him and present myself. Professor Kasturi was almost eighty-eight years old at the time. I explained to him that I came from Venice, Italy, that I was doing research on the life and teachings of Shirdi Sai Baba for my BA thesis, and that I had arrived at Puttaparthi directly from Shirdi where I was able to interview various people on the subject and, most importantly, a few old villagers who had known the *faqīr* in their youth. I then expressed to him my wish to interview him as part of my study. I told him that I had read his books wherein he strove to prove the continuity and veritable identity of the two Sai Babas, and that I hoped to deepen my understanding relative to the peculiar "three-in-one" *avatāric* descent of Shirdi Sai Baba, Sathya Sai Baba, and the future Prema Sai Baba.

The hagiographer appeared pleased at my request, and said he would be delighted to discuss these issues with me. Significantly, the first word he uttered when I said "Shirdi Sai Baba" was "Kabīrpanthī," a term that identifies the follower of the spiritual path supposedly founded by Kabīr, the popular fifteenth-century poet and mystic of Benares upholder of *nirguṇabhakti,* devotion to the formless divine principle.[3] Though there is no historical evidence of any connection between the Kabīrpanth and the Shirdi *faqīr,* scattered references in the latter's hagiographic sources identify him with Kabīr. Shirdi Sai Baba himself is reported saying that he was Kabīr in one of his previous lives, that Kabīr was his creed or religion, and also that Kabīr had been his guru.

Professor Kasturi emphasized to me that Shirdi Sai Baba had to be understood in the light of the god Dattātreya, and he added that I should read the book *Dattātreya: The Way and the Goal,* by Sri Jaya Chamarajendra Wadiyar Bahadur[4] (London: George Allen & Unwin, 1957; Reprint, Delhi: Motilal Banarsidass, 1982). As kind a person as he was, he immediately agreed to grant me an interview even though he had not been well during the past week, suffering from severe back pain. As his daughter points out: "He had a big heart. . . . All were the same to him. He considered everybody his children. He felt that everybody had the right to possess what Swami gave!"[5] He invited me to come see him the next day in the afternoon after *darśan,* around 5 p.m., at his small apartment—South Block

Figure 5.1. Prof. N. Kasturi leaving the lecture hall after his morning talk, Prasanthi Nilayam, November 1985.

1, no. 8—located just behind the Mandir. The interview was taped on a microcassette recorder and what follows is its faithful transcription. The conversation was in English, with no need of any interpreter. Kasturi and I were alone and there was no interruption of our dialogue.

The Interview: Friday, November 8, 1985

I: Sai Ram.[6] Good afternoon, Professor Kasturi, and thank you so much for allowing me the privilege of this conversation with you. Right from the start, I would like to ask you the following question: What do you think is the most important point one needs to consider when approaching the issue of Shirdi Sai Baba's identity and, in turn, of Sathya Sai Baba's link or oneness with him?

Kasturi: The answer is Dattātreya. From Dattātreya, also known as Datta, a tradition of *avadhūta*s can be traced. There is a tradition of *avadhūta*s in our country.[7] Shirdi Sai Baba was an *avadhūta*. *Avadhūta* means one who has destroyed all desires. *Dhū* means dust, so an *avadhūta* is one who has reduced everything to dust.[8] Concerning Dattātreya and this movement of *avadhūta*s, it should be noted that there are many Dattātreya temples all over the country. And Swami[9] has asked a number of people to go and reside in particular Dattātreya temples, saying: "You go and remain there, don't move from there." So here you see Swami's connection with Dattātreya. He often remembers and emphasizes it.

I: I am here reminded of the episode you were mentioning yesterday during your lecture, when Swami was in Ooty.[10] Could you tell me about it in more detail?

Kasturi: That's when Swami said: "I shall show you my real form." I myself was not present there. I know that Swami had just arrived at a local rest-house after coming down the Nilgiri Hills, and a group of students who accompanied him wanted to take his photograph. They had a Polaroid camera with them. After they had taken two or three pictures of him, Swami told them: "Wait, wait, I shall give you my real form." Swami stood straight and when the student was about to click one lady moved forward to adjust his robe, because the robe was a little too high and she wanted to put it right over his foot, but then Swami loudly said: "No, no, don't touch me!" And then, in the photo of the Polaroid camera it was not Swami that came out but Dattātreya with his three heads, with the cow behind him and the four dogs surrounding him.

I: This is the way Dattātreya is represented in the iconography, isn't it?

Kasturi: Yes, the picture came out like this. Therefore, you see how Swami is linked to the Dattātreya tradition. And Dattātreya is also mentioned in some of the *bhajan*s which we sing here: *Oṃ Sāī Datta, Oṃ Sāī Datta*; *Datta Guru, Datta Guru, Dattātreya Guru*; etcetera. These names are often used.

I: So what you wish to emphasize is that Sathya Sai Baba is an *avatāra* of Dattātreya, isn't it?

Kasturi: Yes, because he is all the three gods at the same time: Brahmā, Viṣṇu, and Śiva.

I: The supreme *trimūrti*?[11]

Kasturi: Yes, precisely.

I: Sathya Sai Baba has said that he belongs to the Bharadvāja *gotra* and to the Āpastamba *sūtra*. Could you explain what this actually means, what is its significance?

Kasturi: Swami has indeed said that he belongs to this *sūtra* and *gotra*. This means that he was born into a family that has this *sūtra* and *gotra*. *Gotra* means that he descends by tradition from a certain seer, a certain *ṛṣi*. Every *gotra* has its own *ṛṣi*. Yet the three higher castes alone have a *gotra*, namely Brahmins, Kṣatriyas, and Vaiśyas. *Gotra* literally means cowshed; this is to say that any member of a *gotra* belongs to a particular clan. For example, I belong to the Kauṇḍinya *gotra,* the clan which originated from a *ṛṣi* called Kauṇḍinya. Therefore, also my son will be of the Kauṇḍinya *gotra* and like that this has been going on generation after generation. It is the claim to belong to a particular *ṛṣi's* clan. *Sūtra* is a commentary on the Scriptures written by a certain individual. So, Swami belongs to the clan of Bharadvāja and for all rituals and rites he relies upon the commentary written by Āpastamba, who was another *ṛṣi*.

I: I see, so this is the explanation.

Kasturi: Yes. Swami said he would take birth into a family which has Bharadvāja as his *ṛṣi*. You must have read about the story Swami told of Śiva and Śakti, of the dance of Śiva and Śakti.

I: Yes, I have read about it in your book *Sathyam Sivam Sundaram*.

Kasturi: In the speech Swami gave on *Gurupūrṇimā* day, when he publicly cured himself of a stroke, he narrated how *ṛṣi* Bharadvāja once performed a sacrifice, a *yāga,* and wanted lord Śiva to attend in it. Then Śiva and Śakti promised him that they would come. And so he has now come as Śiva-Śakti, in order to fulfill the promise. So, this explains his link to Bharadvāja and Āpastamba. Concerning Dattātreya, please note that there are a number of people who worship him as their patron god.[12]

I: Is Dattātreya popular throughout India?

Kasturi: I sometimes speak about Swami being Dattātreya himself. And in order to prove this identity I utilize *stotra*s, hymns of praise, which concern Dattātreya and his worship, such as those composed by Śaṅkara[13] and other mystics and poets. There are many qualities belonging to Dattātreya that we can find in Swami. For example, in some *stotra*s it is said that he takes various forms—*bahurūpa*—that is, he appears in various forms.[14] And Swami also appears in various forms. Sometimes, he will say: "I have been to your house and you didn't give Me anything, although I begged to you."

I: This reminds me of Shirdi Sai Baba.[15]

Kasturi: Yes, it's the same. I remember an episode of when I was the principal of a College about two hundred miles off from here.[16] When we came to Puttaparthi, Swami told my wife: "What?! I came and shouted in front of your door, crying: 'Oh, oh,' and you said: 'No, no! The master of the house is not at home now, so I can't give you anything.' Then I went and shouted in front of the principal's office—that is, my office!—but he also didn't care for Me." So, you see, like that Swami appears in various ways.[17] There were some people from Bombay that once came here and Swami told them: "Look! When I once came to your house begging for something you gave me an inferior type of grain, the one you keep aside to be given to beggars. You gave me that inferior type!" And when they protested and said: "No, no, we didn't do that Swami," he brought the grain out of thin air and showed it to them saying: "This is the stuff that you especially keep in a place in your house so that your children or somebody may give it to any beggar that comes near your door." So, *bahurūpa,* in various forms he appears, as Dattātreya. Then there is another line of glory, a special characteristic of Dattātreya which you find in Swami: *tatkṣaṇāt sarvagāmin*, "Immediately he appears in a number of places at the same time." Appearing in a number of places at the same time is a characteristic which you will not find in the *sahasranāmastotra*s of other gods, that is, in the hymns of the thousand names of other deities.

I: So this is a special feature of Dattātreya?

Kasturi: Yes. This is an attribute of Dattātreya only. Of course, of all the gods it is said that they are *sarvavyāpin,* that is, omnipresent, as well as omnipotent, wholly blissful, and all that. But this kind of attribute, *tatkṣaṇāt sarvagāmin,* "going to a number of places at the same time," is a unique attribute of Dattātreya. Another characteristic which is peculiar of Dattātreya and which we also find in Swami as well as in Shirdi Sai Baba is the following: "By your command fire comes down and storms stop." You might remember that episode in the life of Shirdi Sai Baba when flames got up very high and he, by saying, "Calm down, calm down," had them subside.[18] And then, think of this other attribute of Dattātreya: "Sometimes a *yogī,* sometimes a *bhogī,* sometimes a *vairāgī,*" that is, *bhogī* means a person who bases his life on worldly things. At times he renounces the world as a *yogī*, at other times he binds himself to the world as a *bhogī*.[19] He also appears as a *vairāgī*, that is, as a person having renounced all things. These traits may be found in Shirdi Baba. For instance, at the time of his evening procession, when he was led to the place[20] where he used to sleep at alternate nights, he would wear special things and would be adorned with a crown, that is, a royal umbrella, etcetera.[21] And also here in Puttaparthi, processions are celebrated with great pomp. So *yogī* and *bhogī*, both he is. And Swami also says that he will grant both *bhukti* and *mukti*, worldly enjoyments as well as liberation, freedom from rebirth.[22]

I: The sources report that Shirdi Sai Baba granted children to childless couples as well as worldly prosperity to many people.[23]

Kasturi: Yes, people prayed to him in order to attain prosperity, mundane happiness. Even here, there is no barrier or separation: *bhukti* and *mukti*, both he will grant. And he himself has got *bhukti* and *mukti* since he is both a *yogī* and a *bhogī*. . . . This is something really great. And then there is another attribute which is peculiar of Dattātreya and of Swami as well, namely that he is very competent in elaborating upon the meaning of the Scriptures and upon the nature of the Absolute.

I: You mean to say that he offers commentaries to the Scriptures?

Kasturi: He gives the inner meaning of Scriptures. This is what is meant by the words *brahmapravacanavidhāne atiketuḥ*: "He is very expert in elaborating the nature and significance of the Absolute *Brahman*." This of course is not a characteristic which is attributed to Brahmā, Viṣṇu, or Śiva, since they don't explain themselves. But this *avatāra* has come precisely in order to explain. In Shirdi also, Sai Baba used to expound the meaning of texts, as when he explained a *śloka*, a verse of the *Bhagavadgītā*.[24] And by means of parables and stories, he illustrated the nature of the Supreme.[25] And here as well, Swami does the same by explaining the highest possible knowledge, *kevalajñāna.*[26] And actually, another important attribute of Dattātreya and of both these two, Shirdi Sai Baba and Sathya Sai Baba, is the following: *kevalavidyānidhi,* which means "He is the treasure-house of all facets of knowledge."

I: In the sense that he knows everything?

KASTURI: Yes. Architecture, music, Sanskrit and all languages, history, medicine, etcetera. He knows everything.[27]

I: What about the teaching? What do you think was the most important teaching which Shirdi Baba gave in his times, and which Sathya Sai Baba nowadays carries on?

KASTURI: It was the concept of unity. The unity of all creation.

I: Was this the most important?

KASTURI: Yes. And here it is the same. Unity is divinity.

I: Usually *avatāra*s are considered to be manifestations of god Viṣṇu, like Rāma and Kṛṣṇa. But Sathya Sai Baba has declared that he is also an *avatāra* of Śiva. Is this to be explained with the fact that he is a manifestation of Dattātreya?

KASTURI: Yes, yes. He is all three. That is to say, he is the source[28] of all three together. Dattātreya is not only Śiva and Viṣṇu but also Brahmā, all three in one. That's why it is important to emphasize the Dattātreya aspect of Swami. Here is another attribute of Dattātreya for you: *svakṛtanigamārthān līlānaravapus,* which means "He himself creates meanings for the *Vedas*."[29] That is to say, he offers new meanings, new interpretations of the *Vedas* for the modern man, and this is precisely what Swami does. As a matter of fact, Swami has explained the reason why he has incarnated, both in his discourses and in his songs.[30] And the reason he has given is of course the traditional one: morality has gone down and there is the need to revive it;[31] people have lost love and are sunk in hatred, etcetera.

So, in order to save them, he incarnates himself. Indeed, good men are not able to survive in an atmosphere of wickedness and so, in order to protect them, he comes down on earth. And then there is one other reason given for his incarnation, which is not found in any other *avatāra* with the exception of Dattātreya. And this is to reveal the true significance of the Scriptures: this is what Swami has said. And this is precisely a special qualification of Dattātreya as well as of Shirdi Sai Baba.[32] Another characteristic of Dattātreya which you find in Swami is the following: "One may be poor, may be a wise or a fool, he may even be stone-hearted, but nonetheless all are equally dear to him."[33] And this is true here as well as everywhere. One more attribute of Dattātreya which you see operating in Swami is remarkable: "He is able to transform people through gems, *maṇi,* as well as through *mantras*." This is a very important feature. That is to say, through the gift of precious gems or jewels—such as this ring I'm wearing and that Swami gave to me—as well as by giving *mantras* for recitation he is able to save people, to raise them up. It is also said that he affects the transformation of people through superhuman powers, *aiśvaryas,* and through various blessings and boons. But *maṇi* is especially mentioned as one of Dattātreya's gifts.

I: I know that Shirdi Sai Baba often used to give money to his devotees.

Kasturi: Yes [laughing]. But please note that here I'm not referring to the English word "money" but to the Sanskrit word *maṇi,* "gem."

I: Yes, of course. In any case, by *maṇi* you mean all sorts of valuable stones, of precious gifts, don't you?

Kasturi: Yes, gifts like this one you can see here [he shows it to me].

I: Is this a rosary, a *japamālā*?

Kasturi: No, no, this is not a *japamālā*. It is a garland of nine precious stones, a *navaratnamālā*.

I: Ah, it's really marvelous! I would like to ask you one other question. Apparently, Shirdi Sai Baba spoke of Kabīr as being his guru[34] and even claimed to have been Kabīr in one of his previous births.[35] It is reported that when he was interrogated by a legal officer who asked him what his creed or religion was he answered "Kabīr." Now, Kabīr was the famous fifteenth-century poet-saint of Benares, the vanquisher of caste and religious divisions in the name of *nirguṇabhakti,* a devotion devoid of attributes. Why do you think Shirdi Sai Baba said so? What is in your opinion the significance of this link?

Kasturi: Kabīr was also part of the Dattātreya group. For instance, you must have heard of Akkaḷkoṭ Mahārāj and of Māṇikprabhu; these were all *avadhūta*s who had some kind of inner contact with other spiritual beings.

I: Yes, I have heard about them as well as of other *avadhūta*s such as Gajānan Mahārāj from Shegaon, in the Vidarbha region of Maharashtra. With all of them Shirdi Sai Baba was supposedly in spiritual contact. Do you mean to say that they are all linked to Dattātreya?

Kasturi: Yes, precisely.

I: Were you in some way connected to Meher Baba before coming to Sathya Sai Baba? I have read in your preface to the first volume of *Sathyam Sivam Sundaram* that you came in contact with him.[36]

Kasturi: Not much really. I just met him once, that's all. This happened when he was staying near Bangalore, in a big establishment. But I did not have any particular contacts with him.

I: What did you think of him?

Kasturi: Well, I figured that he was dodging his mission. He kept silence for many years and the idea was that one day, when he would begin to speak, the whole world would change. But nothing ever happened. Have you ever seen this [he hands me the pages of a magazine article]? It is an interview which Swami gave to Mister R. K. Karanjia, a Bombay journalist of the magazine *Blitz*. He was a communist. He had read about Swami and thought he would verify for himself who he really was, so he came down here to Puttaparthi. He asked: "Swamiji, we would like to know something about your triple incarnation, past, present and future; that is, from Shirdi Sai Baba to Sathya Sai Baba up to the Prema Sai Baba to come, as according to your prophecy." Swami replied: "First of all, you must grasp the complete oneness of the three incarnations with those of the past, like Rāma and Kṛṣṇa. This is a difficult task: if people cannot understand the present, how can they comprehend the past? Every incarnation is full and complete in relation to the time, the environment, and the task. There is no distinction between the ways and the various appearances of God, such as Rāma, Kṛṣṇa or Sai. Rāma came to feed the root of truth." Then Mister Karanjia asked: "By the present *avatāra* you mean Sai Baba?" And Swami replied: "Yes, I incarnate from age to age." Karanjia further inquired: "But skeptics wonder why God should assume a human form. And why this task had to be divided into the three separate incarnations of Shirdi, Sathya and Prema Sai Baba?" Swami answered: "The previous *avatāra*, Shirdi Sai Baba, laid the basis for secular integration and gave mankind the message that duty, that is, work, is God." These lines that I have read to you are just an excerpt taken from this long interview. It is very insightful and if you want you can take it with you and return it to me in three or four days.

I: Thanks a lot, Professor Kasturi, but I already have a copy of this interview.

Kasturi: Swami likes to say that in the previous *avatāra* everything was cooked. Now, in this present *avatāra,* he has come to serve what was cooked. "That is why I have got to do it with so much love," Swami says. Because, you see, when a mother is busy cooking she becomes very angry if somebody interrupts her: therefore, the time of Shirdi Sai Baba was the cooking stage, whereas this is the serving stage. Moreover, Swami tells us: "The mission of the present *avatāra* is to make everybody realize that the same God or divinity resides in everyone. People should respect, love, and help each other irrespective of color and creed. Thus, all work can become an act of worship. Finally, the Prema Sai incarnation[37] shall promote the gospel that not only does God reside in everybody, but that everybody himself is God. That will be the final wisdom which will enable every man and woman to rise to be God. Thus these three *avatāra*s carry the triple message of work, worship, and wisdom."

I: So this is the essential message that Swami conveyed to Mister Karanjia?

Kasturi: Yes, to Karanjia and to all.

I: In the literature on Shirdi Sai Baba, one comes across the figures of an anonymous *faqīr* and of the enigmatic Veṅkuśā, who are presented as being the foster father and the guru of young Sai Baba respectively. By reading your books, I've learned what Sathya Sai Baba has said about Shirdi Sai Baba's birth and childhood. But has he ever given more details about his foster family and especially Veṅkuśā?

Kasturi: No, but in Swami's life there is one Veṅkāvadhūta. He didn't belong to Swami's family, mind you. He was a wandering ascetic, an *avadhūta,* and once, while roaming about, he came to these areas. He passed away about eighty miles from here, in the state of Karnataka. Swami's grandfather, Kondama Rāju, followed him. And this Veṅkāvadhūta promised him that God would be born in his family, that God would take *avatāra* in his family. He prophesized and promised this to him. And in the place in which he is now buried—you can go there and see his tomb if you are interested[38]—local people believe that he, Veṅkāvadhūta, was none other than Veṅkuśā.[39]

I: I see, so this would be the connection, the link between Shirdi Sai Baba and Sathya Sai Baba . . .

Kasturi: Yes. The idea is that Veṅkuśā, after his sojourn in Maharashtra, wandered about and got Swami's grandfather as one of his disciples or, let us say, admirers. Swami's grandfather was staying and going with him for some time. Then, when Veṅkuśā regained his old habits and manners of wandering, he gave him up.[40] I have written about him in my book *Easwaramma*: in it you will find out more information about Veṅkāvadhūta and Veṅkuśā.[41]

I: Wonderful, thank you. In your books I have read that Sathya Sai Baba's sister and even his parents were granted visions of Shirdi Sai Baba and of various places in Shirdi. This would have taken place when Sathya was very young, precisely in order to confirm his connection, his identity with Shirdi Sai Baba.

Kasturi: Yes, yes. But it was Swami's mother, not the sister.[42] The sister got a picture from Swami; she's got it even now! It is folded, since it was found behind or underneath a bag of *jowar*.[43] Besides the mother, there was also another lady who was granted visions by Swami, inside his own house. Swami told her: "Come, and I will show you Shirdi." And then she could actually see Shirdi Sai Baba sitting on his rock!

I: Along the years several devotees of Shirdi Sai Baba, who knew him in the flesh, have come here to worship Sathya Sai Baba, recognizing his identity with him. For instance, I'm reminded of the *rānī* of Chincholi.[44] By the way, is she still alive?

Kasturi: No, she passed away. The only one who was in Shirdi in Sai Baba's times and is still alive, residing in Puttaparthi, is an old lady called Peḍḍaboṭṭu.[45]

I: Is she the one who is known as Shirdi Mā?

KASTURI: Yes, Shirdi Mā. You should go visit her at her house. She has written a book about her experiences with Shirdi Sai Baba and you might ask her a copy. It is written in Telugu, however. If you go see her and say "Shirdi Sai Baba" to her, she will understand that you want information on him and she might respond to you.[46]

I: But she speaks only Telugu, doesn't she?

KASTURI: Yes [laughing], she speaks only Telugu.

I: In conclusion, is there anything you would like to add about Dattātreya, Shirdi Sai Baba or Sathya Sai Baba which you feel is important?

KASTURI: No, nothing else. I have told you all the important points.

I: Dear Professor Kasturi, thank you so much for sharing all this information and precious memories. It has been an honor to have this opportunity to talk to you. Sai Ram.

KASTURI: Sai Ram.

Our conversation lasted about an hour, and we could still hear the *bhajan*s being sung in the Mandir. The hagiographer accompanied me to the door and we said goodbye. I remember asking for his blessings and he simply smiled. That was the last time I saw him. Indeed, this interview was one of Professor Kasturi's last testimonies before his death, which occurred on August 14, 1987, after a brief illness.

While at the ashram, I carried with me in a small cellophane package the eight mini-cassettes with all the interviews I had collected in Shirdi and Prasanthi Nilayam—including the one with the hagiographer—hoping that the Swami might bless them during *darśan*. On Thursday afternoon of November 14, during *bhajan*s, I was sitting in first line in front of the

Mandir and it so happened that Sathya Sai Baba came out of his room for one more *darśan*. He walked straight toward me and graciously blessed me and my precious envelope. On this occasion he played a *līlā,* a trick. He repeatedly asked me, "What is this?" and when I replied, "Interviews with old devotees of Shirdi," he remained silent for a few moments and slapped me on my left shoulder. Unexpectedly, he then took the package from my hand and asked: "For me?" and while saying so he turned and started moving away. I had not anticipated that he could do this and for a second—a very long second!—my heart sank and I thought I had lost my invaluable "treasure." Terrified at the idea of losing the tapes, I replied: "No, no Swami, for a blessing!" He then stepped back and, with a benign smile, returned the package to me with perfect nonchalance. It was a real lesson in detachment and a most powerful exchange, which I will never forget.

Observations on Some Key Issues

In my meeting with Kasturi and in the interview that followed, the hagiographer touched upon many important points, which deserve to be given further thought, and also explained and contextualized more fully, since in some cases he implicitly acknowledged that I knew the details of what he was talking about and therefore didn't find it necessary to expand on the matter. What follows are some brief clarifications and addenda which I hope will be useful in order to better appreciate Kasturi's words and the main issues involved.

On Shirdi Sai Baba's Place of Birth, Early Years, and Guru

Kasturi summarizes the "revelations" that Sathya Sai Baba made in the 1940s to B. C. Subbannachar and V. C. Kondappa, his former teachers in Bukkapatnam, in Part 1 of *Sathyam Sivam Sundaram.*[47] Kondappa narrates the story of Shirdi Sai Baba's birth and childhood as given by the guru in the 102 verses (*ślokas*) of his book *Sri Sayeeshuni Charitra,* published in 1944.[48] Both Swami Sai Sharan Anand and V. B. Kher have taken into serious consideration Sathya Sai Baba's reconstruction, and Kher even accepts as historically probable the conclusion that Shirdi Sai Baba was born in the village of Pathri (located 150 kilometers southeast of Devgiri/Daulatabad and three kilometers southwest of the confluence of the Vidarbha and Godavari rivers) within a Yajurvedi Deshastha Brahmin family, and that his father gave him away to a *faqīr* when he was a child.[49] This theory seems to have been first voiced by Mhalsapati (d. 1922),[50] one of the oldest and most intimate devotees of Shirdi Sai Baba, who stated that this was told to him by the saint.

In a speech that Sathya Sai Baba delivered five years after my conversation with Kasturi, on September 28, 1990, he said that at age four Shirdi Sai Baba was taken by the *faqīr*'s wife to a high-souled pious scholar named Veṅkuśā, at whose ashram he stayed for twelve years.[51] The name of Veṅkuśā and the hypothesis that the future Sai Baba spent some years with him at his hermitage in a locale known as Selu/Sailu in Maharashtra is well attested to in the sources on the Shirdi saint and was long ago popularized by B. V. Narasimhaswami (1874–1956),[52] the single most influential figure behind the extraordinary growth of devotion to Shirdi Sai Baba starting from the 1940s. Narasimhaswami depended upon the testimony of the Citpavan Brahmin Ganpatrao Dattatreya Sahasrabuddhe, better known as Das Ganu (1868–1962), a devotee of the saint, who had been quite close to him.[53] Apparently, Shirdi Sai Baba mentioned the name of Veṅkuśā on more than one occasion. Noticeably, when he was once asked by a magistrate who his guru was he replied that his name was Veṅkuśā. Moreover, two weeks before his death, in the first days of October 1918, he is reported saying:

> My fakir's wife left me with "Venkusa" at Selu. I stayed with him 12 years, and left Selu. This brick (which Baba always lovingly used to support his arm or head) is my Guru's gift, my life companion. It is not the brick that is broken now—but my Karma (prarabdha) that has snapped. I cannot survive the breaking of the brick.[54]

Alternatively, the name of Shirdi Sai Baba's master might have been Veṅku Shāh, thus identifying him as a Sufi saint (*pīr*).[55] It should be noted that even followers of Shirdi Sai Baba have come to believe that this Veṅkāvadhūta was none other than his mysterious master Veṅkuśā/Veṅku Shāh, in the company of whom he would have spent twelve years in the village of Selu/Sailu.[56] The whole matter is inevitably controversial, however, there being no historical evidence. Besides this hypothesis, through the years other theories on the identity of Sai Baba's master have been put forward. For instance, Swami Sai Sharan Anand has argued that to him the saint of Shirdi would have told that the name of his guru was Roshan Shāh Miya/Mian.[57]

Be that as it may, Kasturi clearly favored the identification of Veṅkuśā with Veṅkāvadhūta, the guru and family deity of Kondama Rāju (1840–1952), Sathya Sai Baba's grandfather.[58] Apparently, Kondama Rāju and his wife Lakshmamma (1852–1931) named their two sons "Veṅka" after him, Pedda Veṅkama Rāju (1885–1963)—Sathya Sai Baba's father—and Chinna Veṅkama Rāju (1898–1978). This Veṅkāvadhūta was well known in the area, being revered as a divine embodiment in hundreds of villages even beyond the Anantapur district. His name implies that he was an ascetic of a radical kind, most probably consecrated to the god Veṅkaṭeś-vara of Tirupati. According to local hagiography, this holy man would have hailed from Maharashtra, would have lived a long, itinerant life, and would have finally settled at Hussainpur in the then Kingdom of Mysore in today's Karnataka, close to the border of Andhra Pradesh. His tomb is housed within the local Veṅkāvadhūta temple.[59] It is noteworthy that Kasturi, from the very first pages of his autobiography, extols the oneness of Sathya Sai Baba and Veṅkaṭeśvara, the god of his ancestors.[60]

In 1998, Ranganathan Padmanaban was told by one Rāma Rāo, the then priest of the Veṅkāvadhūta temple in Hussainpur, that Veṅkāvadhūta had gone into *jīvasamādhi*, meaning that he had willingly left the body, about three hundred years ago.[61] In such case, Sathya Sai Baba's grandfather Kondama Rāju could have never met him.[62] On the other hand, Prof. A. V. Narasimha Murthy, former head of the Department of Ancient History & Archaeology at the University of Mysore, who visited the site in 2010, reports that Veṅkāvadhūta died in Hussainpur around 1900.[63] If this is true, Kondama Rāju, who is said to have been born in 1840 and who lived to be an ultracentenarian, could have possibly met Veṅkāvadhūta sometime in the second half of the nineteenth century. Veṅkāvadhūta's promise that god would manifest himself in his family was firmly believed by Kondama Rāju, who came to recognize in his young nephew Sathyanārāyaṇa the fulfillment of the *avadhūta*'s words.[64]

For Kasturi, the "discovery" that Veṅkuśā was both Shirdi Sai Baba's master and he who announced the coming of the *avatāra*, that is, the reincarnation of his divine pupil as Sathya Sai Baba of Puttaparthi, was a sublime *līlā* and a wonderful way to square the circle and demonstrate the actual oneness of the two Babas.

Shirdi Sai Baba and Kabīr

The belief that Shirdi Sai Baba was Kabīr is widespread, both within[65] the circles of the saint's devotees as well as without[66] them. He himself in December 1910 stated that he had been Kabīr in one of his previous lives and used to spin yarn.[67] It is also reported that in his early days the saint "used to dance with tinkles tied to his feet singing rapturously songs of Kabir."[68] The idea that Shirdi Sai Baba was the reincarnation of Kabīr and that his purported guru Veṅkuśā was Kabīr's guru, that is, the fifteenth-century saint Rāmānanda reborn, was upheld by Das Ganu through his hagiography of the Shirdi saint, chap. 26 of his *Bhaktasārāmṛta*.[69] This influential devotee was a performer of popular song-sermons (*kīrtankar*) and through his hymns and hagiographical account he played an important role in spreading the *faqīr*'s renown, especially in urban areas.[70]

When Shirdi Sai Baba was interrogated by a magistrate—an already-mentioned episode, which Das Ganu reported to Narasimhaswami in 1936—to the question what was his creed or religion the saint answered that it was Kabīr.[71] This utterance is especially significant[72] and Arthur Osborne's comment to it is worth quoting: "[B]y giving his [Kabīr's] name, Sai Baba intimated that he also stood above the religions, at their source, and guided his followers on both paths [of Hinduism and Islām]."[73] To complete the picture of the saint's link to Kabīr, the *faqīr* would have further stated that Kabīr was his guru: "Kabir was my Guru. I put up at that tree foot, for that reason. God will bless those who burn incense here on Thursdays and Fridays."[74] There is a belief in Shirdi that Kabīr's tomb—whose body became flowers—is located at the foot of a margosa tree and this site is known as the Guru Sthān, the place of the guru.[75]

Nothing is known of Kabīr, the reconstructions of the so-called historical Kabīr—vis-à-vis the hagiographical interpretations of him—being merely conjectural. V. B. Kher has argued that "there is a marked difference in the approach of Kabir and that of Sai Baba," since whereas the former was a strong protester against both Hindu and Islāmic traditions, to the extent that he was condemned by both Islāmic and Hindu leaders, the latter's "approach to both these religions is syncretic."[76] This observation, however, misses the point, since it fails to recognize what is really at stake: Shirdi Sai Baba's appropriation of Kabīr mirrored the latter's hagiographical representation. In Maharashtra, Kabīr has been understood as the paradigm of a spiritual faith advocating the oneness of god, above and beyond castes and the barriers of institutionalized religions, and this image of Kabīr has been dominating Indian culture up to our times.[77]

To be sure, the idea of Kabīr as an apostle of Hindu-Muslim unity emerged in modern India and was functional to the building of a unified nation. Sai Baba fits within this same pattern and was interpreted along these lines (whereas nowadays when the Hindu Right is rampant such role has been deemphasized). One might say that there was a parallel enjoyment of Kabīr and Sai Baba: Muslims and Hindus alike considered them to be one of theirs. Interestingly, the late–nineteenth-century *Censuses of India* show that hundreds of thousands of people declared themselves to be both Hindu and Muslim, reflecting their awareness of a composite, nondual identity, which was precisely the ideal that Shirdi Sai Baba incarnated. My contention is that Kabīr's legacy stands out as the most authoritative paradigm for understanding the Shirdi *faqīr*. Kabīr was a legendary model, both for Shirdi Sai Baba and the devotees that surrounded him.

The Hindu construction of the *faqīr*'s integrative persona, beginning with his origins and early years—his being born to Brahmin parents who abandoned him in his infancy; his being raised by a Muslim couple; his being initiated by a Brahmin guru—mirrors Kabīr's hagiographical prototype.[78] Moreover, a comparison of Shirdi Sai Baba's teachings and cryptic language with the vast collection of poem-songs attributed to Kabīr shows similarities and an identity of views on fundamentals (oneness of god, be it Allāh or Rām, primacy of the guru, equality and rejection of caste, etc.).[79] Even the disputes that arose between Hindus and Muslims over Shirdi Sai Baba's body at the time of his death are reminiscent of the legends relative to Kabīr's postmortem.

In view of these parallelisms, it is only natural that Kabīr figured both in Shirdi Sai Baba's self-representation, that is, in the idea that he had of himself, as well as in the understanding that many of the *faqīr*'s followers had and have of him and his "religion."[80] A Marathi hagiographic source on Kabīr that the saint of Shirdi might possibly have been familiar with is the one found in the *Bhaktavijaya* (lit. "Victory of the Devotees") composed by Mahīpati (1715–1790) in 1762, partly based on the *Bhaktamāl* of Nabhadās, in which Kabīr is identified as an *avatāra* of Śuka, the principal narrator of the *Bhāgavata Purāṇa*.[81] Cheap editions of so-called Kabīr verses had an ample circulation during Shirdi Sai Baba's times and many *bhakta*s knew them by heart. Indira Kher explains the very name "Sai" of the Shirdi *faqīr* by having recourse to Kabīr: "The saint-poet Kabir has used the word 'Sai' in his compositions in the sense of Lord or God."[82]

Sathya Sai Baba referred several times to Kabīr in his discourses.[83] Typically, within the Sathya Sai Baba Organization Shirdi Sai Baba has been represented as a champion of universalism and equality, on analogy with Kabīr. It is said that Shirdi Sai Baba was "a prophet of Modern India and a hundred years back he put into practice the principles of democracy, socialism and secularism which form the bulwark of our constitution today. That is Sai Baba's philosophy."[84]

By stating that the most important teaching of Sathya Sai Baba as well as Shirdi Sai Baba is the concept of unity since unity is divinity, Kasturi not only encapsulates his guru's fundamental teaching of *ekatva/advaita* or oneness/nondualism, but also highlights his universalism, which is to be understood as an expansion of the integrative spirituality of the Shirdi saint, advocating Hindu-Muslim unity.[85] With reference to Shirdi Sai Baba, B. V. Narasimhawami already in the 1950s observed: "This unity of religions is not a new idea. Eknath, Namdev, Kabir and others had worked at it each in his own way. Guru Nanak was also in his own way working for the same. It was left to Baba to complete their work."[86] It should be noted that "Unity is Divinity" was a favorite expression of the guru of Puttaparthi. The fourth world conference of the Sathya Sai Organization, which was held in Rome in October 1983, was significantly titled "Unity is Divinity. Purity is Enlightenment."[87]

On Sathya Sai Baba as the Reincarnation of Shirdi Sai Baba

Kasturi aimed at convincing everyone of the truth of Sathya Sai Baba's foundational claim of being the reincarnation of Shirdi Sai Baba.[88] As he wrote in *Sathyam Sivam Sundaram*:

> Those who are conversant with the Leelas [lit. "plays," wondrous actions] of Shirdi Sai Baba and also the Leelas of Sri Sathya Sai Baba may note certain differences in style, language and technique, but, as was mentioned by Yogi Suddhananda Bharathiar of Madras who has seen and who has been inspired by both Babas, "There is an unmistakable identity of Mission and Message."[89]

After Kasturi, anyone who has written about Sathya Sai Baba from a devotional perspective has inevitably taken pains to articulate the latter's sameness with the Shirdi saint, this being crucial in the construction of the guru's identity and in the legitimation and promotion of his figure as an *avatāra.*[90]

It should be noted that the belief in Shirdi Sai Baba's future incarnations is attested to in the *faqīr*'s own sources as one of his solemn assurances to devotees.[91] In his *Life of Sai Baba*, which he wrote in the 1950s, Narasimhaswami states:

> He [Shirdi Sai Baba] mentioned numerous births of his own in the past, and said that he would be born again. . . . He said that as long as any pupil of his was still undeveloped, he would be reborn again and again with him until he took him to God. . . . It is a series of Avatars.[92]

By dedicating a chapter to the description of Shirdi Sai Baba's *līlās* in southern India, especially in Andhra Pradesh, he gave implicit support to the *faqīr*'s assertion.[93] Though he rejected the claims of three or four people who had declared themselves to be Sai Baba, he nonetheless took pains to go meet at least two of them, only to discover their "hollowness" and "worthlessness:"

> This sort of claim has been put forward in various places at various times . . . to the knowledge of this author himself three or four came forward with such claims. For instance a young man at Karur professed to be Sai Baba. . . . Some others also put forward similar claims. A girl at Bangalore put forward such a claim . . . invariably on investigation, it has been noted that any person, claiming to be Sai Baba, does not show even a very small fraction of Baba's nature.[94]

In his *Life of Sai Baba*, Narasimhaswami does not mention the youth of Puttaparthi. The following statement of his, however, could well refer to Sathya Sai Baba:

> Mere power to read thought, mere clairvoyance, mere production of articles from empty box or hands and mere devotion to Sai or God, will not constitute one into an Avatar of Sai. So, we might conclude this chapter by saying that Sai left no successor to his seat, that there was no seat to succeed to (as God's seat can never be vacant) and that there is no person living who

> can be recognized by all as having the entire Sai spirit or Soul in his body, that is, who can be regarded as the Avatar of Sai.[95]

What is certain is that Narasimhaswami did visit young Sathya in Puttaparthi. To his brother Seshama Rāju, he said: "Though we do *prachar* (propagation) of Sai Baba, we have not been as effective as this boy has been in spreading the name of Sai Baba. Whether he is an incarnation or not of Sai Baba, only time will tell."[96]

Along the decades, various groups of Shirdi Sai Baba followers have objected to the guru of Puttaparthi's affirmation of being the reincarnation of their lord. Indeed, only a minority of Shirdi Sai Baba's devotees have become devotees of Sathya Sai Baba, recognizing the truth of his claim. As I myself noticed in the mid-1980s:

> [T]he majority of Shirdi Sai Baba's *bhakta*s have not shifted their devotion to the present Satya Sai. Many of them ignore him or are critical of him: when I was doing research at Shirdi, people preferred to avoid the issue altogether.[97]

In January 2006, some devotees of Shirdi Sai Baba even filed a suit in the court at Rahata, in the Ahmednagar district of Maharashtra, asking it to restrain Sathya Sai Baba's followers from claiming that their guru is the reincarnation of the Shirdi saint.[98] But of course this is not an issue that might ever be settled in a court of justice: the controversy over Sathya Sai Baba's claim will never end, being a matter of faith.[99] Ultimately, the originator of the reincarnation/*avatāra* theory was Shirdi Sai Baba himself through his promises that he would be reborn again and again so as to be together with his dear devotees and guide them toward salvation.

The "proofs" that Kasturi mentions regarding the guru's link and identity with Shirdi Sai Baba are a picture of the saint, which he would have "materialized" for his sister Veṅkamma (1918–1993), and a vision of the village of Shirdi and of the *faqīr* himself, which he would have granted to Subbamma, the wife of Puttaparthi's Karnam, who was like a foster mother for young Sathya. Both these incidents date back to the 1940s and are duly recorded by the hagiographer in Part 1 of *Sathyam Sivam Sundaram*:

> Venkamma, the "sister" was pestering Baba for a picture of Shirdi Sai Baba, about whom so many songs were composed for the *Bhajan* by Baba, and it seems, He told her that He

> would be giving it by a certain Thursday. But, Baba went off to Uravakonda on the day previous to the Thursday indicated, and she too had forgotten all about it, for she was sure she would get it someday and was not very particular about it. When night fell and all were asleep at Puttaparthi, someone called out, "Ammayi," "Ammayi" outside the front door, but the sister did not go and open the door, since the call did not persist. She argued it must be someone calling the neighbor. When she laid herself down after the sitting up, she heard a grating sound, behind one of the bags of *jowar* in the same room; she imagined it to be a rat or a snake; it was distinct and loud; so, she lit a lamp and searched and, lo! something was sticking out behind the bag, white, sharp, a piece of rolled paper, a picture of Shirdi Sai Baba, mysteriously presented to her by Baba, who was at Uravakonda at the time! She has the picture still![100]
>
> . . . .
>
> At this, Smt. Subbamma and the Penukonda party were taken to Peddavenkappa Raju's house, where Baba was at the time. Baba asked Subbamma, if she would like to see the Shirdi Samadhi, and on her saying, "Yes," He took her inside the house to an inner room and said, "Look" and lo! there, she could see the Samadhi with all the flowers, incense-stick with smoke and fragrance complete, and an attendant sitting in one corner, murmuring some Manthra to himself! Baba told her, "This side, see the Anjaneya Temple, and in the far distance, see that Margosa tree," and it appeared to her as if she was in some vast open space looking at the scene in Shirdi the entire landscape spreading out before her for miles and miles to the horizon in the distance.[101]

On this latter occasion, young Sathya would have granted the same vision, including a panoramic view of Shirdi and of the *faqīr*'s tomb, to various other people including his father. Besides the guru's mother, whom Kasturi in our conversation explicitly mentions as having been granted a vision of Shirdi, other individuals claimed to have had a similar experience. Among these were Sathya Sai Baba's uncle Chinna Veṅkama Rāju, his cousin Krishnama Rāju, and Chinna Babaiah, a humble weaver of Puttaparthi.[102]

The Miracle of the Dattātreya Photo: Characteristics of Dattātreya that Agree with Sathya Sai Baba's Persona

Purported miracles related to the taking of photos and the guru's own "materialization" of photos are common in Sathya Sai Baba's hagiographic literature.[103] The case of the Polaroid picture, in which the guru came out as the three-headed deity Dattātreya, took place in the Madhumalai forest of the Wild Life Sanctuary, near the Nilgiri mountains, on March 7, 1978, day of Mahāśivarātri. Apparently, it was one of the guru's executives, the retired Colonel S. O. Joga Rao of the Indian Army Engineers, who begged him to show his "divine form." The lady who moved forward to adjust the guru's robe just when a student was about to take his picture was Mrs. Brij Ratanlal, a close devotee who was often permitted to travel with Sathya Sai Baba. The guru's peremptory order that she should not touch him was later explained by the Swami, who told Mrs. Brij Ratanlal that his power in assuming the form of Dattātreya—like a high voltage electric current—

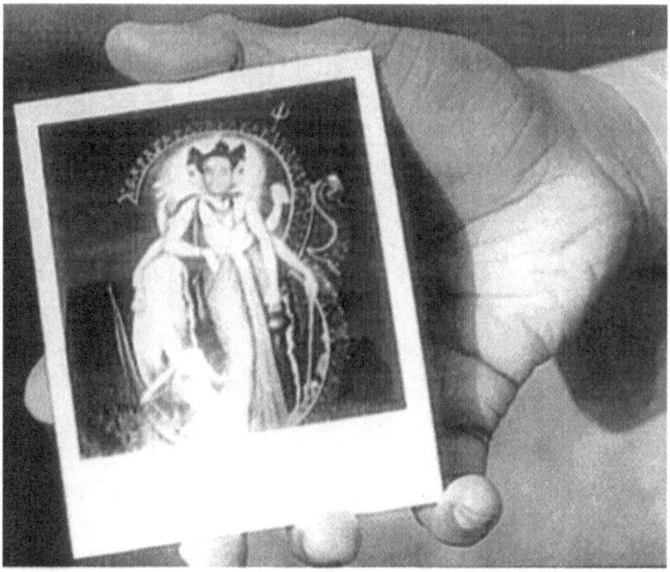

Figure 5.2. The Polaroid photo of Dattātreya showing Sathya Sai Baba's countenance as his central face.

would have killed her if she had come in contact with him.[104] As per the modern iconography of the deity,[105] the black and white Polaroid picture shows Dattātreya with three heads and six arms bearing the emblems of Brahmā, Viṣṇu, and Śiva. He wears a flowing garment covering his waist and legs whereas his torso is naked and a rosary adorns his neck. The lower left arm bent at the elbow rests on the back of a white cow while four dogs stand in the background. The deity and the cow are encircled by the symbol of the *oṃ* and most importantly Dattātreya's central face, which represents Viṣṇu, his primary identity, shows the countenance of a smiling Sathya Sai Baba.

Kasturi referred to this episode in two of his books: *Loving God* and *Easwaramma*. In *Loving God*, he writes: "He has revealed that His Reality is Datta Deva or Dattatreya or the Trinity in One as conceived in Hindu mythology. Once when cameras were clicking all around Him, He told one of the photographers: 'Here! Click now. I shall give you my Real Form!' And the picture was of the Trinity. So, the Feet are of Datta Deva."[106] In *Easwaramma*, he further remarks:

> Though Sri Sathya Sai Baba has declared and revealed that He is the embodiment of all the Names and Forms man has attributed to the Omniwill, on one occasion, in a playful but profoundly meaningful mood, He offered to disclose His reality, through a photograph He permitted a young man to take. The film showed not His Form as we know it but the form of Dattatreya, a Deity representing the Hindu Trinity, Brahma, Vishnu and Shiva, in one body. The three were so highly propitiated by the penance of the sage Atri and the chastity of his wife Anasuya, that they granted them the boon of a three-headed Son who would bring them the renown of being hailed as the Lord's parents. Dattatreya means "granted to Atri." He also has the celebrated name of Anasuya-putra, "the son of Anasuya," He who saved Anasuya from perdition.[107]

A characteristic of Dattātreya is his love of music and to be sure devotional hymns (*bhajans*) have always played an important role in Sathya Sai Baba's life and teachings. Yet it should be noted that Dattātreya does not figure prominently in the anthologies of the guru's *bhajan*s sung at Prasanthi Nilayam. Notwithstanding what Kasturi says, references to him are scarce. Here is the text of the second Dattātreya *bhajan* mentioned by the hagiographer: *Datta Guru, Datta Guru, Dattātreya Guru*; *Sāī Nātha, Dīna Nātha, Brahma Rūpa Guru*; *Alakha Nirañjana Bhava Bhaya Bhañjana Dattātreya Guru*; *Dattātreya Guru, Sāī Nātha Guru, Dīna Nātha Guru*. It is translated thus: "Chant the Holy Names of Noble Teacher Dattatreya and Lord Sai Nath. Reciting ever pure and spotless names of Noble Teacher Lord Dattatreya and Lord Sai Nath, destroys the fear and bondage of birth and death."[108] In the list of the guru's 1,008 names, only the 359th explicitly extols him as Dattātreya: *Oṃ Śrī Sāī Dattātreyāya Namaḥ*.[109]

On the other hand, Sathya Sai Baba was often celebrated as the incarnation of the triad of Brahmā, Viṣṇu, and Śiva. Thus, the forty-fifth of his 108 names worships him as *śrīmūrtitrayasvarūpa*, "He who has the triadic form as his own nature." Here is Kasturi's revealing commentary:

> *Moorthi-traya* means the three entities of Divinity; each entity demarcated for one function. The Three *Moorthis* or Forms denoted as Baba's *Swarupa* (real nature) are Brahma, Vishnu and Siva, the Entities responsible for Creation, Preservation and Destruction; Emergence, Existence and Mergence; Source, Stream and Sea; *Srishty*, *Sthiti* and *Laya*. Baba has all Three, is all Three. He creates objects from nothing. He preserves objects without diminution or decline (vide: His granting containers full of *Vibhoothi* or *Kumkum* which never become empty, however fast you use them). He dissolves objects into nothing. Since He is all three He is called also Dattatreya. He is "*Thatkshanaath Sarva Gami*" (reaching everywhere immediately) and "*Thyagi*" (detached), "*Bhogi*" (consuming objects, as the Indweller of all who consume), "*Divyayogi*" (the Divine Unifier) and "*Dayalu*" (full of Mercy and Grace). Sai Baba is the Incarnation of the Dattatreya form of Sri Narayana and so Sathya Sai Baba is *Moorthi-thraya-Swarupa*. He creates; He preserves; He subsumes.[110]

Kasturi mentions the *tatkṣaṇāt sarvagāmin* attribute of Dattātreya as one of the guru's peculiar characteristics already in Part 1 of *Sathyam Sivam Sundaram*:

> A villager had quarreled with his brother about a sharing of produce and he came over to Puttaparthi, hoping to remain there itself, on the charity of the pilgrims. Baba chastised him

> for being a burden on others, when with a little more patience and love, he could be happy with his brother in his own village. He assured him that His Grace will be on him, wherever he was and sent him away to his own place. He took it sadly to heart, as if Baba had driven him out; and so, he laid himself across the rails on a dark night and hoped that the wheels of an advancing train would end his misery. But, Baba's Grace is all pervading. He "hurried" to him on the railroad line, and pushed him aside, just in time. Persons around Him at Puttaparthi could see Him pushing something heavy, for His Gestures were of that type! And, Baba, came to, with an exclamation against the villager who had so foolishly interpreted His advice! The villager Bhimaiah, by name, felt, as he later explained to me, that Baba held His hand and dragged him down the slope of the bund on which he lay. Tearful with repentance and sorrow, he returned immediately to Puttaparthi, before joining his brother in his village! Bhimaiah must have felt that the Dattatreya in the famous *stotra*, "*Dattatreya tathkshanaath sarvagami, Thyagi bhogi divya yogi dayaluh*" was absolutely correct, so far as this Sathya Sai Avathar of Dattatreya was concerned. Even now, when devotees ask Bhimaiah why he put Baba to the bother of a trans-corporeal journey by his foolhardiness, he hangs his head down in shame, and pleads that we should not pursue a matter that is painful to him.[111]

Kasturi also insists on another peculiar trait of Dattātreya, namely, that of providing the inner meaning of Scriptures. Indeed, as the supreme guru, Dattātreya is commonly extolled as *jñānamūrti,* the embodiment of knowledge. The hagiographer claims that this is precisely what Sathya Sai Baba does. He argues that the Swami's explanations are not confined to the Hindu Scriptures[112] but extend to all world Scriptures and philosophies. Thus, he observes that "He quotes from Moses and Max Müller, from Johnson and Jayadev, Woodroffe and Vasistha with equal ease. His parables range from China to California. His illustrative stories and fables are taken from far-flung human communities and their culture."[113] In this way, Kasturi aims at emphasizing the universalist scope of his guru's mission, who has come to reveal the quintessential truths contained in the sacred texts of mankind. It is noteworthy that in his autobiography he quotes a poem that Sathya Sai Baba used to sing: in it, the guru says that the reinterpretation of the scriptures of *all* people as a means to cultivating the virtues they propagate is one of his avatāric tasks in order to recast the human mind.[114] The hagiographer reiterated this point in one of his lectures to overseas devotees:

> Swami says, "*kala sandhigdha vigraha sooktulaiyunta bhashyartha guptamu telupukoraku*." I have come in order to correct the misinterpretation of scriptures, that has been perpetrated by commentators, and to give the world the true meaning of the scriptures. This is something new. When I heard Him sing this poem, it sounded unique. . . . Swami knows the inner meaning of all scriptures. He says, "I have come to clarify Vedas for Hindus, Bible for Christians, Koran for Muslims, to tell them that the water underground is the same in all, though on top each may appear different." That is why Swami is able to quote from scriptures of different religions.[115]

Moreover:

> The fourth one [the fourth purpose of the Avatar], [is] "*bhashyartha guptamu telupukoraku*," to tell about the inner significance of scriptures. No previous *Avatar* has said this before! The commentaries of scriptures are confusing. The commentators have not understood the secret meaning of various scriptures. Not only Hindus, but even those of other religions. "*bhashyartha guptamu*," *bhashya* is commentary, *artha* is meaning, *gupta* is secret.[116]

And here is Kasturi's exegesis of this purportedly unique characteristic of his lord:

> This is a special aspect of Swami, relevant for this particular age. He has come to give the authentic meaning of all scriptures. Swami's Avatar has happened at a time when we have a number of scriptures, faiths, creeds by which people are kept apart. People carry scriptural books as they carry flags when they go to war, and declare this is the truth and not the

> other one. So, every religion or creed has become a flag to carry. . . . Swami says, the world is now suffering from creedal conflicts. . . . So, a new teaching has to come. That is why in the whole of India, probably in the whole world, Prasanthi Nilayam is the only place where in the innermost shrine of the temple of God, symbols of all religions are kept . . . they are all different facets of truth. Swami says, "I have come to tell people not to fight on silly exterior things, the rites and beliefs, but to go to the fundamental teaching of love, service, honesty, respect for elders, respect for wisdom of the past and so on, which is the real essence of all religions. It is to emphasize this that I have come as an Avatar."[117]

While delving upon Dattātreya's peculiar names and characteristics, Kasturi is quick to equate the god's ability to transform people through the gift of gems (*maṇis*) with the guru's "materialization" of rings and jewels, through which he is believed to trigger a spiritual transformation in the recipient. Dattātreya is especially linked with the *maṇipūracakra* (lit. "wheel of the jeweled city"), one of the six yogic psycho-energetic centers located at the navel and depicted as a ten-petaled lotus: the syllable *da*—the deity's *bīja* or "seminal," most sacred *mantra*—is inscribed in one of its petals.[118] With reference to Dattātreya's characterization as an ascetic, *Yogasūtra* 2.37 states that when non-stealing/non-covetousness (*asteya*) is established, all jewels (*ratna*) present themselves, that is, naturally come to the *yogin*. In his commentary to the twenty-eighth of Sathya Sai Baba's 108 names—*Oṃ Śrī Ratnākara Vaṃśodbhavāya Namaḥ*—the hagiographer writes:

> Ratnakara means the sea, which is the treasure house of pearls and corals, two of the nine Rathnas or gems. It also means the earth, which is the source of the seven other precious stones. We who are benefitting by the gems of advice and inspiration, gems of grace, gems of glory and wisdom from Baba must be filled with joy and wonder that the family name of the Rajus of Puttaparthi is appropriately Ratnakara (Source of gems).
>
> Baba has said that for the Avathar, the Lord selects the appropriate family and place. The Ratnakara family had a Rathna in Kondamaraju, the centenarian saint and another gem

> in Peddavenkappa Raju, born by the grace of the great saint Venka Avadhutha and named after him. . . . They systematically observed the Satyanarayana Vratha to propitiate God as Satyanarayana, and this gem among Avathars, "Satya" Sai Baba came down, into their lap and into our lives.[119]

On Dattātreya and Kabīr as Associated Figures

In the integrative religiosity of the Deccan, Dattātreya and Kabīr were associated and even accommodated to one another for centuries via the pan-Indian movement of the Nāth *yogin*s as well as through the activities of the saint-poets, both Hindu and Muslim. The Nāths mixed freely and exchanged beliefs and practices with other religious sects and adepts, such as the Sufis and the *nirguṇa bhakta*s. Charlotte Vaudeville has even suggested that "it is very likely that his [Kabīr's] own ancestral tradition was a form of Nāthism."[120] The texts, which are couched in the form of a dialogue/debate between Gorakhnāth, unanimously revered as one of the most outstanding Nāth adepts, and Dattātreya or Kabīr prove the interrelatedness between these figures.[121] Significantly, the author of the *Yogasaṅgrāma* Shaikh Mohammad (1560–1650)—disciple of the Sufi Cānda Bodhle who was revered as an incarnation of Dattātreya—"has been generally regarded as the Marathi reincarnation of Sant Kabir."[122] Moreover, it should be noted that within the corpus of sayings attributed to Kabīr, Dattātreya is mentioned in two *ramainī*s of his *Bījak*.[123]

Charles Sidney John White (b. 1929), who visited Sathya Sai Baba in 1970, being accompanied to the guru's ashram by Howard Murphet, was to my knowledge the first scholar to underline the relevance of the figures of Dattātreya and Kabīr for an understanding of both Shirdi Sai Baba and Sathya Sai Baba. His 1972 article titled "The Sai Baba Movement: Approaches to the Study of Indian Saints," was by all standards a seminal contribution.[124] Howard Murphet writes: "I discussed Dr. White's article with some of Baba's most erudite and devoted followers. Most of them seemed to think that there was something in White's ideas—some elusive link between our present *Avatar*, Dattatreya, Kabir and, possibly Gorakhnath. But none could explain what it was."[125] Evidently, Kasturi was not among these "most erudite and devoted followers," given that the hagiographer explicitly presented Sathya Sai Baba as an *avatāra* of Dattātreya already in Part 1 of *Sathyam Sivam Sundaram* which was released in November 1961. Following his master, he came to elaborate the theological equation Sathya Sai Baba = Dattātreya at least from the late 1950s if not earlier. As he told me during our conversation, he viewed Kabīr as part and parcel of "the Dattātreya group," a divine manifestation exhibiting a composite kind of spirituality of which Dattātreya was for centuries the prototype.

On Sathya Sai Baba's "Materialization" of Gems and Rings

If I remember correctly, the gold ring that Kasturi wore and which he showed to me during the interview had nine beautiful stones of different colors. It was possibly the same one about which he writes in his autobiography: "[H]e [Sathya Sai Baba] waved His right palm in a circle and produced what struck me as a small lump of light. It was a gold ring set with nine precious gems, extolled in legends as capable of winning for the wearer the boons the nine planets can grant; pearl, ruby, topaz, diamond, emerald, lapis lazuli, coral, sapphire and zircon, three each in three sections. He put it on my finger. It was a perfect fit."[126]

In the course of our conversation, the hagiographer implied that the guru had "materialized" the ring for him out of thin air. His "materializations" of hard objects such as rings were frequent and took place mainly during private interviews. The guru explained:

> In the world, the metal, the stone, the jeweler are all separate, as is the one who will take the ring, and they must be brought together. Whereas, in the world of Swami, the metal, the stone, the jeweler and the one who will take the ring are all one, and that One is God. In the world, time is needed. But God is beyond time. Immediately the ring is ready.[127]

Here is Sathya Sai Baba's reason for these gifts: "I give rings, rosaries, etc. to signalize the bond between Me and the receiver; when calamity befalls, the article comes to Me in a flash and returns with my grace of protection; the grace is available to all who call on Me in any Name or Form, not merely to those who wear the gifts."[128]

Apparently, the guru had "materialized" the garland of nine precious stones (*navaratnamālā*) especially for the hagiographer. The nine gems are believed to represent the nine planets and to ward off evil influences: the ruby stands for the sun, the pearl for the moon, the red coral for Mars, the yellow sapphire for Jupiter, the emerald for Mercury, the blue sapphire for Saturn, the diamond for Venus, the hessonite for Rahu, that is, the Dragon's Node, and the cat's eye for Ketu, that is, the Dragon's Antinode.

On the actual value and genuineness of these stones and rings there has always been discussion, some declaring them to be worthless trinkets and others to be most precious items. It is impossible to give one general answer, since each case should be considered separately. Obviously, devotees view these items as priceless gifts of grace, and some of them have also noted their economic value. For instance, Howard Levin writes: "One devotee I met actually had the diamond ring Sai Baba materialized for him appraised at Tiffany's in New York City. The appraiser said it was ten and a half carats, worth between ninety and one hundred thousand dollars."[129] Undoubtedly, Kasturi's ring and *navaratnamālā* were quite valuable. Here is Arnold Schulman's own experience in the late 1960s, with reference to a ring with the guru's picture painted on porcelain in the center, surrounded by sixteen stones, that Sathya Sai Baba "materialized" for him a few days before he left the ashram:

> The inspector [at the customs of San Francisco's airport] studied the ring carefully, then gave it to another inspector to look at. They both agreed the ring was worthless.
>
> A few days later, though, when he [Schulman] returned to New York, he called the Metropolitan Museum of Art to ask for the name of the most reliable jewelry appraisers they could recommend. On their recommendation, he took the ring to the Commonwealth Appraisal Corporation, where the ring was described as: "Lady's 18K gold and white sapphire ring, oval top circled with sixteen faceted white sapphires, total weight approximately 2.40 carats, center set with oval cloisonné enamel depicting a dignitary seated in a chair. Value: $125.00."[130]

Calculating inflation, the value of this ring in 2020 would amount to around $900.00.

Contemporaries of Shirdi Sai Baba Revered as *Avatāras* of Dattātreya

Undoubtedly, Shirdi Sai Baba was worshipped as an *avatāra* of Dattātreya by many of his followers during his lifetime.[131] But there were also other ascetics of the *avadhūta* type who were revered as incarnations of Dattātreya in Shirdi Sai Baba's days. There is a popular belief that these saints constituted a group, a holy network of sorts, and were and still are in spiritual contact with one another.[132] Kasturi, besides Kabīr (whom he comprised in this same group though not being a contemporary of Shirdi Sai Baba), mentions the names of Akkaḷkoṭ Mahārāj and Māṇikprabhu.

Also known as Swami Samarth, the saint of Akkaḷkoṭ (d. 1878) in the Solapur district of Maharashtra is popularly revered as an *avatāra* of Dattātreya. His followers extol him as the third "historical" *avatāra,* after the founding figures of Śrīpād Śrīvallabh and Nṛsiṃha Sarasvatī. On occasions, Shirdi Sai Baba identified himself with Akkaḷkoṭ Mahārāj and many Hindu devotees were and are convinced that Sai Baba was his spiritual successor.[133] To be sure, there were similarities between the two, such as their eccentric behavior—their "childlike" (*bāla*) and "mad" (*unmatta*) aspects—and their baffling utterances. The possibility that Akkaḷkoṭ Mahārāj and Shirdi Sai Baba knew each other cannot be ruled out.[134] There exist at least two different subtraditions of followers of Akkaḷkoṭ Mahārāj: one has developed in and around the area of Akkaḷkoṭ and the other is centered in Diṇḍorī, a village near Nasik.[135]

Māṇikprabhu (1817–1865), an older contemporary of Akkaḷkoṭ Mahārāj, was the saint of Māṇiknagar near Gulbarga. Like the devotees of the Swami of Akkaḷkoṭ, the followers of Māṇikprabhu worship him as the third *avatāra* of Dattātreya, after Śrīpād Śrīvallabh and Nṛsiṃha Sarasvatī. Founder of the *Sakalamatsampradāya,* Māṇikprabhu disregarded affiliations of religion, caste, and creed and accepted all faiths as paths leading to the one ultimate goal. It is noteworthy that among his devotees is a large proportion of Muslims.[136] There is a belief that before settling in the village of Shirdi, Sai Baba would have met him.[137]

Besides Akkaḷkoṭ Mahārāj and Māṇikprabhu, Shirdi Sai Baba is linked to Gajānan Mahārāj (d. 1910) of Shegaon, Vāsudevānanda Sarasvatī (1854–1914) of Garudeshvar, and Nārāyaṇ Mahārāj (1885–1945) of Kedgaon, all revered as *avatāra*s of Dattātreya. Gajānan Mahārāj, which I mention in the conversation with Kasturi, is a popular *avadhūta* believed to be linked to both Akkaḷkoṭ Mahārāj and Shirdi Sai Baba. In 1910, the very day he passed away in Shegaon—in the Khamgaon *tālukā* of Buldana district, in Vidarbha—Sai Baba at Shirdi is supposed to have exclaimed: "My Gajanan is gone."[138] He came to be addressed as Gajānan since he used to constantly chant the *mantra gaṇ gaṇ gaṇāt bote* or *gaṇāṅgunā gaṇāt bote* in honor of the elephant-headed god Gaṇeśa.[139]

Meher Baba

The Parsi holy man Merwan Sheriar Irani (1894–1969), to become famous as Meher Baba, first met Shirdi Sai Baba in December 1915. Apparently, the latter greeted him by addressing him as Parvardigar, "god-almighty-sustainer." From around 1922, after having reached full enlightenment at Sakori under the guidance of Upāsni Mahārāj (1870–1941)—the foremost Hindu disciple of Shirdi Sai Baba—Meher Baba presented himself as the Avatar of the age, the Highest of the High.

He claimed that Shirdi Sai Baba actively helped him in his avatāric mission and that the Shirdi saint was one of the five *qutb*s or perfect masters of his times, together with two Sufi saints—Tajuddin Baba (1861–1925) of Nagpur and the female ascetic Babajan (d. 1931) of Pune—and two Hindu saints, the above-cited Nārāyaṇ Mahārāj of Kedgaon and Upāsni Mahārāj of Sakori.

As the Avatar of the age, Meher Baba promised to usher humanity into a golden age of love and universal brotherhood. His vow of silence began on July 10, 1925. From 1927 to 1954, he stopped writing, using an alphabet board to convey his messages; from 1954 until his death in 1969, he communicated only through gestures. Kasturi clearly had a negative opinion of him, which reflected that of his guru. Once, when he was asked if Meher Baba was an *avatāra,* Sathya Sai Baba is reported to have said: "Meher Baba was a joker. He lost his voice in an automobile accident. Is this mauna (silence)?"[140] His communication through an alphabet board was also criticized by the guru of Puttaparthi as unworthy of being called silence. But Meher Baba's silence was unrelated to his car accident: he was seriously injured twice, in 1952 (in the USA) and in 1956 (in India), after which his ability to walk became limited. It is noteworthy that Meher Baba already in 1963 referred to Sathya Sai Baba as being a Tantric and using Tantra for his reputed miracles.[141] On his part, the guru of Puttaparthi claimed: "I need no tantra and no yantra to perform the so-called miracles which are natural to my state."[142]

With regard to his silence, the Parsi holy man had solemnly declared: "When I break my Silence, the world will come to know that *I am the One whom they were waiting for*. . . . The only incomparable miracle I will perform is when I speak . . . I will uncage myself; and then you will know my Divine Strength! . . . All will know me when I manifest."[143] To be sure, all Meher Baba's followers had great expectations with regard to his breaking of silence. However, the master died on January 31, 1969, without uttering any audible word. Allan Y. Cohen writes:

> Even among his worldwide family, the breaking of Baba's Silence is still a mystery. A few feel that Baba broke his Silence but the Word was heard only by the most spiritually advanced. Others explain that Baba has always been speaking through his Silence. Many think that Baba spoke but that the result of his speaking will be gradual, taking time to manifest in a new humanity. Still others believe that Baba has not yet broken his Silence.[144]

In his autobiography, Kasturi mentions a curious episode in which a confused Suddhananda Bharati, an octogenarian *yogin* and poet from Tamil Nadu, concluded a gathering in Sathya Sai Baba's honor with a full-throated *Jay! Meher Baba kī jay!* (Hail, hail to Meher Baba!) instead of *Jay! Sathya Sai Baba kī jay!* (Hail, hail to Sathya Sai Baba!), which is indicative of the Parsi holy man's renown.[145]

R. K. Karanjia's Interview with Sathya Sai Baba

Rustom Khurshedji Karanjia (1912–2008) was the founder and owner editor of *Blitz*, a weekly tabloid published in Bombay with focus on investigative journalism, which he had launched back in 1941. The magazine was Left-leaning and pro–Soviet Union, and reflected R. K. Karanjia's communist and Marxist ideology. The interview with Sathya Sai Baba was published in *Blitz* in September 1976: it lasted two and a half hours and it was the longest-ever interview that the guru granted to any journalist.[146]

Kasturi considered this interview to be of the highest importance for a correct understanding of his beloved Swami. In particular, he regarded the excerpts he read to me as decisive in order to rightly approach the theological mystery of the triadic characterization and function of the triune *avatāra* of Shirdi Sai Baba, Sathya Sai Baba, and Prema Sai Baba. Significantly, the hagiographer writes about R. K. Karanjia and his interview with his master both toward the end of *Sathyam Sivam Sundaram, Part IV*, as well as in his last book *Prasanthi: Pathway to Peace*.[147]

One of the themes upon which the guru insisted from the early days was the spiritual oneness of all *avatāra*s, despite their differences. This, he argued, was something very difficult for humans to grasp.[148] The preliminary difficulty for all creatures was to recognize the presence of a divine incarnation in their midst, men and women being deluded by his/her human appearance, that is, his/her own "power of illusion" (*māyā*). He taught that all *avatāra*s, such as the popular Rāma and Kṛṣṇa, were really one and the same notwithstanding their differences, which he explained as essentially due to the changed historical circumstances and the peculiar subjectivities of each of them, meaning their outward appearance, personal habits, teaching methods, etc. He acknowledged the fact that it was not at all easy to recognize the identity of even Shirdi Sai Baba and Sathya Sai Baba, though being close in time, and in this way he evidently wished to answer the question of why along the years only a minority of Shirdi Sai Baba devotees had accepted him as the reincarnation of their lord.

A case in point with regard to differences in teaching methods was that Shirdi Sai Baba did not follow the traditional Hindu mode of instruction consisting in a formal initiation (*dīkṣā*) through a *mantra.* As his own guru did not teach this way, he never taught any kind of *mantra.*[149] His rejection of Hindu rituals involving the use of *mantra*s appears to have been consonant with Kabīrian literature.[150] According to his Brahmin devotee Ganpatrao G. Narke, a geology professor, "in Baba's school, the Guru does not teach [through *mantras*]. He radiates or pours influence. That influence is poured in and absorbed with full benefit by the soul which has completely surrendered itself."[151]

Another peculiar usage of Shirdi Sai Baba was his habit of asking for money from his devotees, as I mention in the conversation with Kasturi. Apparently it was starting around 1908 that he began requesting *dakṣiṇā,* a monetary fee, from several people. Many visitors were scandalized by his behavior and one complained that he "never saw any saint talking of money all the hours of the day."[152] The Shirdi *faqīr* did not keep the money with him, however. Every evening he redistributed the accumulated sums among devotees, especially the poor.[153] Moreover, a symbolic meaning was attached to the number of coins or rupees he asked for: number one stood for the individual soul (*jīva*) or *Brahman,* number two for the twin virtues of faith (*niṣṭhā*) and patience (*saburī*), number five symbolized the senses (*indriya*), number nine the nine characteristics of *bhakti* beginning with hearing (*śravaṇa*) and ending with taking refuge in god or the guru (*śaraṇāgati*), etc.[154]

In his writings, Kasturi reiterated the point of the oneness of all *avatāras* typically by quoting the words of his master. Here are two telling instances:

> The Avathars of Sri Rama and Krishna are so different in the various incidents of their earthly careers; they also emphasized different aspects of ethical behavior and philosophical belief; they differed in methods of teaching and uplifting; it is all difference in emphasis rather than in basic things. It is difficult to get convinced that Sri Rama is Sri Krishna, but, few have doubts on that score. So, too, those who can delve deep into these mysteries can understand that the same Power has now assumed, another human form.[155]
>
> . . . .
>
> Rama and Krishna are Avathars of the same Lord, but their characteristics are different; so too how can you realize the identity between this Sariram [body] and the Shirdi Sariram! Those who worship Shirdi Sai have not understood Him and you too have not understood Me. It is only those who have understood both that can pronounce judgment, is it not![156]

Even Padma, Kasturi's daughter, underlined Sathya Sai Baba's oneness with all past *avatāras* and quoted the assuring words of her master:

> I ate so much butter in my previous Krishna Avatar that I have got disgusted with it. In the Rama Avatar I was born from the sweet *payasam* (a sweet rice porridge—a common sacrament). Therefore, now I do not like sweets. In this Avatar I like *paan* and *supari* (betel leaf and nut). For the next Avatar I will have to think of some other thing.[157]

With reference to the guru's metaphor of fixing a meal and that Shirdi Sai Baba represented the cooking stage whereas Sathya Sai Baba represents the stage of serving the food to all hungry creatures, it should be noted that the Swami utilized it from the early days, as Kasturi mentions it already in Part 1 of *Sathyam Sivam Sundaram*:

> Sathya Sai Baba Himself says that He is not as hard or as angry *now* at ignorance, negligence, disobedience or superciliousness as He was in His previous Manifestation. He explains this difference by means of a parable: "The mother is usually hard when the children enter the kitchen and disturb the cooking; but, while serving the food, she is all smiles and patience. I am now distributing the dishes cooked then; wherever you may be, if you are hungry, and if you sit with a plate, I shall serve you and feed you to your heart's content!"[158]

Kasturi himself often referred to this metaphor of Shirdi Sai Baba preparing the meal and Sathya Sai Baba serving it and feeding his devotees.[159] On the Swami's motto "Work is worship," it should be noted that this was a cornerstone teaching from the time of the *Bhagavadgītā*, elaborated upon by both Vivekananda and Sivananda. It was also the motto of the Intermediate D.R.M. College of Davangere, of which Kasturi was principal in the late 1940s.

After his meeting with Sathya Sai Baba, Karanjia's skepticism was shattered. He became a staunch devotee of the guru and abandoned his communist ideology and anti-Hindu secularism. In the book he wrote about him, *God Lives in India*, he exalted his "spiritual socialism." In later years, Karanjia became a sympathizer of the right-wing *Bharatiya Janata Party* (BJP).

6

Understanding Sathya Sai Baba in the Light of Dattātreya

Dattātreya: An Overview

Dattātreya is a multifaceted deity, in origin possibly a Tantric antinomian *yogin* later sanitized and adapted to the devotional milieu of the *Purāṇas*.[1] The mythical accounts present him as the son of the *ṛṣi* Atri (lit. "the Devourer," son of Brahmā and author of Vedic hymns) and of his wife Anasūyā (lit. "the Non-envious one"). The stories of the god's birth are related to Atri's power of austerity (*tapas*) and to Anasūyā's power of chastity (*satitva*). Purāṇic tales report that due to the help offered by Anasūyā to the *trimūrti*,[2] to her and her husband was bestowed the grace that the divine triad would take birth as their sons: thus were born the three brothers Soma (another name of the moon, Candra), Datta/Dattātreya (lit. "the Given/Granted one belonging to Atri's race"), and Durvāsas (lit. "the Ill-clothed," an ascetic famous for his bad temper), *avatāras* of Brahmā, Viṣṇu, and Śiva respectively.

In the *Purāṇas*, Dattātreya is magnified as an *avatāra* of Viṣṇu (*Bhāgavata Purāṇa* 1.3.11)[3] and a great *yogin* and teacher (*Mārkaṇḍeya Purāṇa*, ch. 17–19, 37–43).[4] Already in the *Mahābhārata* he is portrayed as a powerful *ṛṣi* granting boons, notably one thousand arms to Arjuna Kārtavīrya who had propitiated him by means of austerities.[5] From his very inception, Dattātreya proves to be an assimilative god. Though he is represented as a manifestation of Viṣṇu, he evidences Tantric characteristics more attuned to a *śaiva* or even *śākta* background than to a *vaiṣṇava* one:

important sites associated with the deity's worship—such as Māhur and Kolhāpur in Maharashtra—were *śaktipīṭhas* in origin. As an alter-ego of Śiva, in the *Mārkaṇḍeya Purāṇa* he figures as a "lord of Yoga" (*yogīśvara*) imparting his art to his disciple Alarka, while at the same time indulging in such impure behavior as drinking intoxicants and making love. The same *Purāṇa*, on the other hand, emphasizes Dattātreya's brāhmaṇical purity, pointing out that his fondness for meat and sex is merely an outward appearance, a way of disguising his sanctity and leading astray the unworthy ones.

Another Purāṇic source for Dattātreya is *Bhāgavata Purāṇa* 11.7.24–11.9.33,[6] where we find a dialogue between King Yadu and a young Brahmin ascetic, a *bālāvadhūta* traditionally identified as Datta. The latter teaches the secret of happiness, which lies in perfect detachment (*vairāgya*) acquired through the careful observation of the laws of nature. Dattātreya presents a list of twenty-four gurus comprising the five elements, the sun and the moon, the sea, twelve animals (pigeon, python, moth, bee, elephant, honey gatherer, deer, fish, osprey, serpent, spider, and wasp), the prostitute Piṅgalā (Dattātreya is the patron god of prostitutes), a child, a maiden, and an arrow maker.[7]

Dattātreya is, significantly, linked to Śaṅkara, the father of Advaita Vedānta. In Śaṅkara's hagiographies it is said that at the end of his life the immortal *yogin* took him by the hand to a cave, from which they were never seen to emerge: from then onward, he remained in the company of Datta in perennial contemplation/conversation on the truths of nondualism.[8] Dattātreya's connection with Śaṅkara's monastic order is further evidenced by the fact that he is the tutelary deity of the Jūnā division (*akhāṛā*) of the Daśanāmī *saṃnyāsins*.[9]

In so-called minor *Upaniṣads* such as the *Yoga Upaniṣads*, the *Saṃnyāsa Upaniṣads*, and the late *Dattātreya Upaniṣad* (focusing on the deity's *mantras* beginning with *daṃ/draṃ*), Dattātreya is glorified as a teacher of nondualist Yoga and as the highest renouncer (*paramahaṃsa*, *avadhūta*) beyond all rules and regulations. The medieval *Nāradaparivrājaka Upaniṣad* portrays Dattātreya along with other figures as one who has no visible emblem and keeps his conduct concealed, who acts as if he were a child, an intoxicated lunatic, and a demon (*bālonmattapiśācavad*).

Though Dattātreya's presence is traceable throughout India and as far as Kashmir and Nepāl (Bhaktapur), his heartland is the Marāṭhī cultural area.[10] Here, the oldest testimony of his presence—single-headed and yet four-armed—is in the literature of the monotheistic sect of the

Mahānubhāvs, a monastic community conceived as heterodox by brāhmaṇical authorities and often subject to persecutions.[11] This tradition is believed to have been founded by Dattātreya himself, revered as being eternally present in all four *yugas*, and later refounded in the thirteenth century by one Cakradhar, a Brahmin hailing from Gujarat. Like the more popular *bhakti* movement of the Vārkarī poet-saints (*santkavis*) devoted to god Viṭṭhala/Viṭhobā of Paṇḍharpur, the Mahānubhāvs were seminal in the origin and development of Marāṭhī literature. They believe in five manifestations of the one god whom they call Parameśvar (lit. "supreme lord"). These are the "five Kṛṣṇas" (*pañcakṛṣṇas*) comprising two deities—Kṛṣṇa and Dattātreya—and three sect figures: Cakradhar (d. 1274), the veritable founder of the sect, Guṇḍam Rāul (d. 1287–88), Cakradhar's guru, and Cāṅgdev Raul, Guṇḍam Rāul's guru. The adoption of Kṛṣṇa and Dattātreya exemplifies an inextricable fusion of devotion and asceticism, of *bhakti* and *yoga*. In Mahānubhāv texts concerning Dattātreya, such as the *Dattātreyabalkrīḍā*, the *Dattātreya Māhātmya* and the *Ātmatīrthprakāś*, we find the essence of their teaching: severest asceticism coupled with pure love and service to the guru. This is also seen in the *Sahyādralīlā*, which tells the incense-burner story of Arjuna Kārtavīrya who took live coals in his hands for worshipping his master Dattātreya.[12] This narrative puts together the two traditions about Kārtavīrya: self-mortification through which he propitiates the deity (thanks to which he gets his boons, notably one thousand arms as in the *Mahābhārata*) and loving service (as it is told in the *Mārkaṇḍeya Purāṇa* where he serves Dattātreya as a humble disciple).

The Mahānubhāvs appear to have received Dattātreya through the medium of the Western Nāths, a pan-Indian *śaiva* yogic tradition which became widespread from around the twelfth century.[13] The deity's association with the *Nāthsampradāya* is a distinctive characteristic of the Deccan region. Though James Mallinson argues that "the formalization of that association dates to approximately the 18th century, when texts such as the Marathi *Navanāthabhaktisāra* symbolically united the Nāth Sampradāya with the Mahānubhāv sect by identifying nine Nāths with nine Nārāyaṇas,"[14] the Marāṭhī scholar Ramchandra Chintaman Dhere long ago pointed out the seminal connections between Nāths and Mahānubhāvs, suggesting that both Cāṅgdev Raul and Guṇḍam Rāul were Nāth *yogins* and adepts of the Dattātreya movement.[15] This is the reason Mahānubhāvs excluded Dattātreya (together with Kṛṣṇa) from their rejection of all the other gods of the Hindu pantheon.

Dattātreya is mentioned in several texts of the Nāth tradition and has an important place in the Western pantheon of the "nine Nāths" (*navnāth*),[16] being revered as an immortal and one of the originators of the movement along with Gorakhnāth and Matsyendranāth/Macchindranāth. In Nāth sacred geography, Mount Girnār located in the Junagadh District of Gujarat is an especially relevant locale. The legend that Gorakhnāth got instruction from Dattātreya atop this mountain has made it a major pilgrimage site for both Nāth ascetics and Dattātreya devotees. In Maharashtra, perhaps the oldest site associated with Dattātreya is a Mahānubhāv pilgrimage place where Datta ascetics known as the "wearers of the twisted locks of hair" (*jaṭādharas*) meet: the Ātmatīrth at Pāñcāleśvar, on the south bank of the Godāvarī River east of Paiṭhaṇ.

In the Marāṭhī cultural area the advent of the *Dattasampradāya* (lit. "the tradition of the Datta [followers]") dates to the middle of the sixteenth century, when the Marāṭhī *Gurucaritra* or "Life of the Master" was composed by Sarasvatī Gaṅgādhar.[17] Construed in the form of a dialogue and divided into fifty-one chapters containing more than seven thousand verses (*ovīs*), this hagiography presents the miraculous lives of the Brahmin gurus Śrīpād Śrīvallabh (c. 1323–1353) and Nṛsiṃha Sarasvatī (c. 1378–1458), the two seminal figures venerated as the first "historical" *avatāras* of Dattātreya.[18] In a lucid narrative style, which has acquired a quasi-Vedic status due to its purported mantric power, the *Gurucaritra* emphasizes the need for unconditional surrender to the guru in order to earn his grace and focuses upon brāhmaṇical ritual orthodoxy,[19] that is, on what it envisages as the proper action, in an effort to counter Islāmic dominance as well as Tantric excesses. As Mugdha Yeolekar writes:

> The universe of the *Gurucaritra* consists of stories about the everyday life of ordinary people. It focuses on such topics as healing and health, children, instructions on cooking food, pilgrimages, rites of passage, and ideals for married men and women. Further, the narrative builds from the perspective of disciples whose lives are bettered because of their unwavering devotion to their *guru*.[20]

To this day, the *Gurucaritra* is undoubtedly the most popular sacred text in the Dattātreya tradition, its reading being regarded as most powerful and wish-fulfilling.[21] Nṛsiṃha Sarasvatī, the founder of the *Dattasampradāya*, appears to have been a Brahmin ascetic who had been ordained in the Sarasvatī order of the Śaṅkaran *daśanāmin* renunciants. Constantly on the move, he finally settled in the village of Gāṇagāpūr, about fifty miles southeast of Solāpur (presently in Northern Karnataka). This is the major pilgrimage center of the tradition, along with other sites such as Narsobācī Vāḍī, Audumbar, Kuravpūr, and Pīṭhāpūr.

If the *Dattasampradāya* originated as a revivalistic, brāhmaṇical movement which further expanded itself in several sub-branches, the deity came to be appropriated by a variety of social and religious strata across society. Today as in the past, its holy spots are famous as places of exorcism where people thought to be affected by evil spirits (*bhūta*s) and demons (*preta*s, *piśāca*s)—especially women—come in the hope of being liberated. Exorcist practices connected with malevolent possession (*bhūt-bādhā*) are traditionally regarded as impure and non-brāhmaṇical. Like the Dattātreya temples which are believed to be especially powerful (*jāgṛta*, lit. "awake"), along the centuries both Brahmin gurus and *pīr*s revered as Datta incarnations have been regarded as mighty exorcists, beginning with Śrīpād Śrīvallabh and Nṛsiṃha Sarasvatī themselves.[22]

Even though Dattātreya's identification with the *trimūrti* appears to be earlier,[23] it is from the time of the *Gurucaritra* that his iconography incorporating the triad of Brahmā, Viṣṇu, and Śiva emerges. He is represented as an ascetic, often naked, either standing or seated in a yogic posture, with three heads (*trimukhī*)[24]—the central one generally being that of Viṣṇu, his focal identity—and six arms holding the emblems of the *trimūrti*: the water-pot and the rosary of Brahmā, the mace and the conch of Viṣṇu, the drum and the trident of Śiva. He is surrounded by three or four dogs, symbol of extreme impurity and nonetheless said to represent the *Veda*s, as well as by a cow, symbol of mother earth and of brāhmaṇical purity. The icon recapitulates Dattātreya's integrative force, embracing all polarities as the manifestation of the fullness of the godhead.[25] On the other hand, the one-headed (*ekmukhī*) iconography of the deity is rarer and thought to be older.[26]

In Gāṇagāpūr and other holy spots such as Narsobācī Vāḍī, Audumbar, and Girnār Dattātreya's presence is attested to in the noniconic form of the *pādukā*s, the sandals worn by him or one of his incarnations, emblem of the wandering ascetic and of the deity's unfathomable omnipresence. Indeed, Dattātreya is believed to be eternal and to manifest himself under a variety of forms. Attaining his vision, that is, recognizing his presence,

Figure 6.1. The three-headed god Dattātreya.

is thought to be extremely difficult, a rare grace. Dattātreya is said to be unforeseeable in his transcendence, abruptly appearing as well as vanishing from site. As the prototype of the *avadhūta,* he is beyond caste and purity codes and a rule unto himself.

In the Vārkarī tradition, Eknāth[27] (1533–1599), his syncretic guru Janārdan[28]—whose teacher Cānda Bodhle[29] was possibly a Sufi—and the encyclopaedic Dāsopant (1551–1615) were all linked to Dattātreya and characterized by an integrative religiosity and liberal attitude.[30] The hagiographer Mahīpati offers accounts of the *darśans* the deity granted to Eknāth, appearing as a Muslim *faqīr* riding upon a horse and as a Muslim mendicant (*malaṅg*; *Bhaktavijaya* 45.74–123; *Bhaktalīlāmṛt* 13.164–205).

Mahīpati also tells stories of the meetings between Eknāth and Dāsopant, in which Dattātreya manifests himself to the latter as the guardian of Eknāth's house (*Bhaktalīlāmṛt* 22.48–65; 22.79–101).[31] In one of his lyrics Tukārām (1598–1649), the most beloved of Maharashtrian poet-saints author of a Dattātreya *ārtī* which is still sung today, beautifully portrays the god:

> I fall prostrate before the one with three heads and six
> hands;
> A bag of alms hanging from his shoulder;
> Dogs in front of him.
> He bathes in the Gaṅgā daily.
> A staff and water-pot are in his hands;
> On his feet are clanking wooden sandals;
> On his head a splendrous coil of hair;
> On his body beautiful ashes.
> Tukā says: I bow to him who is clad in space.[32]

In nineteenth- and twentieth-century Maharashtra up to the present, several personalities have been identified as *avatāra*s of Dattātreya, both within and without the *Dattasampradāya* and its sub-branches: *vaiṣṇava* and *śaiva* ascetics (often of Nāth inspiration) as well as *pīr*s and eclectic figures of Sufi background. All of these, often exhibiting a bizarre, antinomian character, are believed to grant both liberation (*mukti*) as well as mundane enjoyments (*bhukti*). Indeed, saints in whom powers (*siddhi*s) and liberating knowledge (*jñāna*) are harmonized are typically revered as manifestations of Dattātreya. Among them, one of the most popular and who has produced literary works in both Marāṭhī and Sanskrit is the orthodox Brahmin Vāsudevānanda Sarasvatī (1854–1914), also known as Ṭembe Svāmī, to whom are ascribed texts such as the *Dvisāhasrī* (1889), the *Datta Purāṇa* (1892), and the *Datta Māhātmya* (1901). Das Ganu narrates an incident which is worth quoting since it shows how Vāsudevānanda Sarasvatī, despite his conservative views,[33] acknowledged the saintliness of Shirdi Sai Baba above and beyond caste distinctions:

> I went on a pilgrimage to Puri and on the way, one Tembe Swami (Vasudevanand Saraswathi) whom I had known already met me and asked me if I was going to Shirdi. I said, "Yes,

> not immediately but a few months later." Then he gave me a coconut saying, "Present this as mine to Sai Baba." I took it and kept it in my bag. During my further travels, my companions took it out and then ate it up. When I went to Shirdi, as soon as I approached Sai Baba, he said, "Here is the thief. Where is the coconut given by my brother?"[34]

Vāsudevānanda Sarasvatī was thought to be in spiritual contact with Shirdi Sai Baba and this link was explained by positing that they were both Dattātreya *avatāra*s, their different social and religious milieus notwithstanding. Even after their death, the *faqīr* was believed to have placed one of his disciples under his care.[35] Nowadays, Vāsudevānanda Sarasvatī's pupils and grand-pupils exercise a noticeable influence in the religious life of the region.[36]

The earliest formulation of Haṭha Yoga, with which Nāth *yogin*s are especially associated, is found in the *Dattātreyayogaśāstra* (ca. thirteenth century) and to Dattātreya are attributed a number of Tantric works centered upon ritual practice, among which are a *Dattātreyakalpa,* a *Dattātreyapūjāpaddhati,* and a *Dattātreya Tantra.* Besides these, the most popular texts ascribed to the deity are three: the *Jīvanmuktagītā* ("The Song of the Liberated-in-Life"), a *śaiva* nondualist text in only twenty-four stanzas; the *Avadhūtagītā* ("The Song of the Free"), a nondualist text of possibly Nāth inspiration[37] in 289 stanzas divided into eight chapters; and the "Section on Knowledge" (*jñānakhaṇḍa*) of the *Tripurārahasya* ("The Secret of [the goddess] Tripurā"), a *śākta* nondualist text from South India in 2,163 stanzas, divided into twenty-two chapters. These works are all late compositions, presumably dating to the seventeenth or eighteenth centuries.

The god is thought to be always present on earth and to be the fulfiller of all desires, the supreme "giver" (*datta*) of liberation from *saṃsāra* and of worldly enjoyments (health, wealth, offspring, etc.). Thus, he is extolled as *smartṛgāmin*, "one who instantly goes to those who devoutly remember him." Taking concrete interest in the needs of their devotees, Dattātreya *avatāra*s are credited with the performance of all sorts of miraculous feats and this is precisely what makes them so popular among the masses.[38]

The god embodies in a paradigmatic fashion the roles of the immortal guru, supreme *yogin,* and eternal *avatāra* all in one. He is first of all the guru-god, the "guru of gurus" (*guruṇām guru*), and the foremost quality that his followers are required to cultivate is *gurubhakti*.[39] In this regard, the intensity of Shirdi Sai Baba's words on the greatness of his guru and his total surrender to him are consistent with the "way of the guru" (*guru-vāda*) that is so characteristic of the Dattātreya movement:

> Even as I am relating this to you, love surges in my heart. The Guru then took me to his school, showing for me the same loving concern as the mother-bird who clasps her young ones under her wings. And oh, how fascinating was the Guru's school! So much so that I forgot my fond attachment to my parents; the chain of delusion, attachment was broken and I was liberated, quite effortlessly. Bonds which are undesirable were totally snapped and the bondage that obstructs spiritual inclination was severed. I felt like embracing the Guru, storing up his image in the eyes themselves. Unless his image lives in the eyes all the time, the eyes will be but two balls of flesh. Or, I would rather be blind without his image. Such was the great importance of the Guru's school to me. Can there be anyone so unfortunate who, having once stepped into this school, would want to go back! My house, my family, my parents—Gururaya[40] became everything to me. All my sense-organs, including the mind, had left their places and come to stay in my eyes alone, for the purpose of meditating upon the Guru. When Guru alone is the object of meditation for the eyes and all else is as Guru himself, so that there is nothing separate from him, then it is called single-minded meditation. When thus meditating on the form of the Guru, the workings of the intellect cease. Therefore, ultimately, only make an obeisance to him, observing speechless silence.[41]

Surrender to the master is the cornerstone of Sufi practice, which naturally led to a fusion of Hindu and Islāmic horizons. As B. V. Narasimhaswami points out: "In Sufism the Guru is the only God that the pupil is to have in his mind. He must be swallowed up in the contemplation of his Guru and in the appreciation of his love, and think of nothing else."[42] This is also a recurring theme in the poem-songs ascribed to Kabīr.[43] Shirdi Sai Baba taught that one should never give up his/her guru: "Whatever may be the merits of other Gurus, we must never give up our own."[44] Finally, one must come to realize that one's beloved guru-god is none other than the Sadguru, the *gurutattva* ("guru principle") that abides within oneself.

Dattātreya stands out as a composite deity par excellence, accommodating from the outset *vaiṣṇava, śaiva,* and *śākta* traits. Through the centuries he has been appropriated by a variety of religious groups—Hindu, Islāmic, and even Jaina—which have reelaborated his mythical origins and functions. From at least the sixteenth century, Dattātreya has emerged in Maharashtra as the supreme godhead, encompassing the *trimūrti* of Brahmā, Viṣṇu, and Śiva. Devotion to him cuts through social strata and sectarian affiliations. Among his adepts we find high-caste Brahmins, *daśanāmin saṃnyāsin*s, Tantriks, Devī worshippers, *avadhūta*s, Mahānubhāvs, *faqīr*s, untouchables, and prostitutes. Precisely this synthetic spirituality, which rejects rigid distinctions such as the dual "essentialization" of Hinduism and Islām, is what constitutes the uniqueness of this fascinating, Protean deity.

Shirdi Sai Baba as Dattātreya

In the Marāṭhī cultural area, Hindus have tended to appropriate and sanitize figures they thought to be impure or non-Hindu by utilizing the "Dattātreya tool," that is, by viewing them as manifestations of the deity. Thus, it is widely believed that Dattātreya may incarnate in *faqīr*s.[45] This is what has happened in the case of Shirdi Sai Baba, who was thoroughly "Hinduized" by the Hindu majority soon after his death in 1918. In his *Śrī Sāī Saccarita* (ch. 4, v. 29), Govind R. Dabholkar clearly identifies the Shirdi saint with Dattātreya: "As Gangapur and Narsimhawadi, as Audumbar and Bhillawadi, so is Shirdi a famous place of pilgrimage on the banks of the holy river Godavari."[46] It is noteworthy that the Committee of the Sri Sai Baba Sansthan of Shirdi acknowledges with pride the fact that devotees consider the *Śrī Sāī Saccarita* as the modern *Gurucaritra*. The *Gurucaritra* is regarded as the model of the *Śrī Sāī Saccarita*, its study (*pārāyaṇa*) being "equally meritorious and efficacious."[47] Moreover, Hindu sources are ready to point out that the *Gurucaritra* was the favored book of the saint.[48]

Shirdi Sai Baba himself openly claimed to be Dattātreya.[49] Once he is reported to have told a devotee: "Are you puffed up? Where was male progeny in your destiny? (In answer to the prayer you offered before Datta at Gangapur) I tore up this body and gave you a son."[50] In another episode we read:

> In 1911, on Datta Jayanti day,[51] Balawant Kohojkar went to Baba at Shirdi. At 5 p.m.:
>
> Baba: "I am having pangs of labor and cannot bear the pain." So saying, he drove everyone out of the mosque. He was evidently identifying himself with Anasuya. A little later, Baba called all people in. Kohojkar went first and on Baba's *gadi* [seat] saw not Baba, but a small charming three-headed baby, i.e. Datta. In a moment, Datta disappeared and Baba was seen instead.[52]

At the same time, the saint presented himself as a humble servant/slave of god (*Yade Haqq*), never claiming to be god or an *avatāra*.[53] He did not pose himself as a guru either. As Narasimhaswami writes: "To most people . . . Baba did not appear to be a Guru at all, and he seldom declared himself to be a Guru."[54] To one Abdul Rangari who visited him in 1913 and asked why he let Hindus worship him with sandal paste smeared on his hand and face, he answered by saying *jaisa desh vaisa vesh*, "When in Rome, do as the Romans do," meaning that if Hindus wished to worship him as their god it was their right to do it, even though he himself was but a devotee of god.[55] Notwithstanding Sai Baba's annoyance and frequent hard words at being worshipped through ceremonial *ārtīs*, the fact is that along the years he condescended to his *bhaktas*' heartfelt wish to offer him both an individual and congregational *pūjā,* finally giving up all resistance and letting them have it their own way.

With his Hindu devotees, he identified himself with almost every deity of their pantheon, impressing on them the lesson of the unity of god and implicitly confirming them in the idea that he was a divine incarnation. The Gujarati Brahmin Vaman Prangovind Patel, alias Swami Sai Sharan Anand (1889–1982), who first met Shirdi Sai Baba in December 1911, remarks: "Sai Baba convinced every visitor—whatever his chosen deity: a god, goddess, incarnation or holy person—that he was fully identified with that chosen deity."[56] In order to comprehend the saint's assimilative force, one must contextualize it within the *longue durée* of the Deccan's composite culture.[57] Given such integrative milieu, many followers such as

S. B. Dhumal—in accordance with the *Śrī Sāī Saccarita* (ch. 7, v. 13)—came to the conclusion that Shirdi Sai Baba, just like Kabīr, "is neither Hindu nor Muslim but above both."[58]

All in all, it should come as no surprise that contemporary *sampradāya*s and groups that worship Dattātreya as their "chosen deity" (*iṣṭadevatā*) exhibit ambivalent, even contradictory tendencies. If on the one hand they express an open, inclusive spirituality that accommodates even Islāmic tenets, on the other they are the catalyst of brāhmaṇical pride and ritual orthodoxy,[59] which from time to time has given rise to clashes with low-castes, *dalit*s, and the Muslim "minority," such as in the controversy over the control of a disputed shrine in the mountainous locale of Baba Budhan Giri in the Chikmagalur district of Southern Karnataka.[60]

Sathya Sai Baba as Dattātreya

In Sathya Sai Baba's public discourses as well as in his writings, mention of Datta/Dattātreya is rare. I have been able to identify only two loci, one in a speech he held in October 1969 in Prasanthi Nilayam and another one in his paraphrase and commentary to the *Bhāgavata Purāṇa*, that is, in his *Bhagavatha Vahini*. The first is a mere reference in passing:

> Most of the Names of the Divine have but two letters or syllables; the significance of the number two (Rama, Krishna, Hara, Hari, Datta, Sakti, Kali, etc.)[61] is that the first syllable represents *Agni* (Fire principle),[62] which burns up accumulated demerit or sin, and the second represents the *Amrita* principle, the Restorative, the Refreshing, the Reformation force. The two processes are necessary; removal of obstructions and construction of the structure.[63]

In the second case, Dattātreya is mentioned in a list of *avatāra*s enumerated by sage Śuka[64] who is said to explain his advent thus:

> The consort of the sage Athri, Anasuya by name, prayed that the Lord may be born as the child of her womb and the Lord replied, "Granted" (Datta). Since the father's name was Athri, He was called Datta-athreya, Dattathreya. He showered on

> Karthaveeryarjuna and Yadu, emperors of high renown endowed with all glory, the great treasure of Yogic wisdom. It is in this Form that God, in the beginning of this Kalpa or Age, moved about as the four child sages, Sanaka, Sanandana, Sanathkumara and Sanathana. They were ever at the age of five, so innocent that they wore no clothes, so divine that they spread Wisdom and Peace around them.[65]

The guru of Puttaparthi mentioned Dattātreya's mother Anasūyā on another relevant occasion. This was in a discourse he delivered on July 3, 1993, day of Guru Pūrṇimā, less than a month from the most tragic episode, which haunted Prasanthi Nilayam, when on June 6 four persons were shot dead by the police after they had stabbed four devotees in the guru's living quarters, killing two.[66] While attributing the dreadful event to the evil effects of jealousy (*asūya*), he said:

> There are three off-springs for Jealousy (Asuya). They are Dwesha (Hatred), Krodha (Anger) and Lobha (Greed). There are three children begotten by Anasuya (The one who is totally free from Jealousy). They are: Brahma, Vishnu and Maheshwara, symbolizing Forbearance (Sahana), Prema (Love) and Saanubhoothi (Compassion). This is the difference between Asuya and Anasuya. The former gives birth to demonic qualities. The latter begets Divine qualities. The demonic qualities produced by Asuya (Jealousy) result in the destruction of the discriminating power and lead men to have no sense of what is temporary and what is permanent. Consequently they pursue evil ways.[67]

At the same time, the guru delved into the meaning of the *trimūrti* of Brahmā, Viṣṇu, and Śiva, often glossed as the Trinity, on numerous occasions. Typically, he would either focus attention upon the complementary functions of the holy triad while at the same time stressing their unity, or elaborate upon the correspondence of the *trimūrti* with other triads such as the sacred syllable *oṃ* (*a* + *u* + *m*)[68] and the waking, dreaming, and deep sleep states (along the lines of the *Māṇḍūkya Upaniṣad*). While discussing the meaning of the term *Bhagavan* (lit. "prosperous," "glorious") designating god, he once stated that the syllable *bha* means creation

(Brahmā), the syllable *ga* protection (Viṣṇu), and the syllable *va* change or transformation (Śiva): "Bhagavan is capable of all three. . . . That is My secret."[69] Here are two representative examples of his teaching, in which he symptomatically links the *trimūrti*/Trinity to the notions of *avatāra* and guru:

> At the conclusion of every aeon the process of involution is completed in the Deluge; then, evolution starts again and as Brahma, He creates beings again. He enlightens every one with a spark of His own Glory and fosters on the path of fulfillment every one of them, as Vishnu. It is he again, who as Siva, concludes the process by the destruction of all. Thus, you can see that there is no limit to His Might, no end to His Potency. There can be no boundaries for His achievements. He incarnates in countless ways; He comes as an Incarnation of a Kala (fragment) of His, or an Amsa (part) of His; He comes as an Inner inspirer for some definite Purpose; He comes to close an epoch and inaugurate another (Yugavathar). The narrative of these Incarnations is the Bhagavatha.
>
> The One Divine Principle works through three Forms, as Brahma, Vishnu and Siva, in order to manipulate and complete the process of becoming a being, called Srishti. The three are fundamentally of the same essence; there is no higher or lower; all three are equally Divine. Associated with Creation, He is Brahma; with Protection, He is Vishnu; with Dissolution, He is Siva. When He comes down assuming special form on special occasions for a specific purpose, He is known as Avathara.[70]

> Vishnu (symbolic of the waking stage) is in the Head, where all the senses function—the sense of perception through which knowledge is acquired. The senses of sight, hearing, smell, taste and touch are all active. Brahma (symbolic of the dream stage), the other facet of the Trinity, is in the Throat region. In the dream, a multiplicity of events and things are produced and projected. Siva (symbolic of the deep sleep stage) is in the Heart. The gross and the subtle bodies merge in the causal, the senses, the mind and the intellect are inactive in this Stage. Siva is white in color, Brahma is red and Vishnu blue. All the

> three are in each one. They are the Gurus whom you must seek and serve for achieving awareness of the Reality.[71]

Already in December 1960, on the occasion of Vaikuṇṭha Ekādaśī,[72] Sathya Sai Baba remarked that Brahmā, Viṣṇu, and Śiva, the three aspects of the Absolute *Brahman,* are to be understood as inseparably united to their energies or *śakti*s, Sarasvatī, Lakṣmī, and Pārvatī, which are not to be naively pictured as the "wives" of the "Trinity." Most importantly, the guru explicitly equated the *trimūrti* with Śiva-Śakti, Śiva being interpreted as incorporating the male triad itself: man's goal is to achieve unity with it.[73] In another speech he held in 1967, he underlined how his *avatāra*hood was to be understood as encompassing the triad of *śakti*s—*mahāśakti, māyāśakti,* and *yogaśakti*—as one indivisible whole, implicitly portraying himself as the fullest divine incarnation, as Śiva-Śakti and the *trimūrti.*[74] From his very youth, he spoke of himself as "the essential embodiment of the Trinity" of Brahmā, Viṣṇu, and Śiva, as recorded in the *Sri Sai Sathakamu.*[75] In the "revelations" given therein about Shirdi Sai Baba's parents, the test to which Śiva puts Shirdi Sai Baba's mother—the chaste Devagiriamma—that she should please him sexually, is reminiscent of the Purāṇic story of Dattātreya's mother Anasūyā.[76] Śiva's request for female company is a Tantric element that is akin to Dattātreya's portrayal, given that the latter is the patron lord of prostitutes.

In conversations with devotees he occasionally identified himself as a manifestation of Dattātreya, even "materializing" images of the deity in order to confirm his identity with "the symbol of the Unity of the Trinity in Hindu Mythology," as Kasturi puts it.[77] In the 1940s he is said to have "materialized" a photo of Dattātreya and in the early 1950s a ten-inch marble image of the god for Kasturi's daughter.[78] Whenever the subject of Dattātreya was brought up, either by him or by one of his followers—especially at times of the year such as Dattajayantī—he would speak about the "Trinity" of Brahmā, Viṣṇu, and Śiva and their functions.[79] The hagiographer reports that when a pupil of a Dattātreya adept (*upāsaka*) came to visit the guru in Prasanthi Nilayam, the latter immediately confirmed to him that he was indeed lord Dattātreya. Here is the story in full as narrated in Part 1 of *Sathyam Sivam Sundaram*:

> While on this point of the Dattatreya aspect of Baba, I am tempted to quote here the experience of a friend, a Professor of

> Philosophy. He had contacts with a Dattatreya Upasaka, disciple of Gandhavali Brahma Chaitanya Maharaja,[80] and he was studying various texts under the old man. Once, the Upasaka told him about Sri Sathya Sai Baba as the incarnation of Dattatreya and asked him to go to Puttaparthi and receive His Blessings. "I cannot go because I am too old to undertake the journey"; "but you should go and have His Darshan," he insisted. He came to Puttaparthi and when he was called in by Baba for the interview, the very first words with which Baba began the conversation were, "Come on! Have your *Namaskaram*. This is the Dattatreya *Peetham*[81] for you!" Dattatreya is extolled in the *Puranas* as "He who goes to every place at the same instant," in answer to calls, prayers, supplications from any quarter for intercession and solace, and strength and relief![82]

For V. K. Gokak, the guru of Puttaparthi once "materialized" a pendant bearing the portrait of Śrī Pant Mahārāj of Bāḷekundrī (1855–1905), an *avadhūta* popularly revered as an incarnation of Dattātreya to whom Gokak's father was devoted. Here is Howard Murphet's account of this episode:

> On an early visit to Dr. Gokak's home Baba saw on the wall for the first time a portrait of an Indian saint, Shri Panta Maharaja of Balekundri, and asked about its presence there. The Vice-Chancellor replied to Baba that the saint had been his father's guru, and that he, himself, held the holy man in great reverence. Baba: "Have you a smaller portrait of him to carry when you're travelling?" Dr. Gokak: "No." Baba: "Would you like one?" Dr. Gokak: "Yes, Swami, very much." Baba waved his hand, for a little longer than usual, remarking: "He is coming." Turning the palm up, he handed the doctor a small enamel pendant. It bore a miniature replica of the saint's portrait.[83]

But, as noted already, the most striking "revelations" of Sathya Sai Baba as Dattātreya took place in the 1970s during two of his travels. The first happened on Thursday, December 10, 1970 (on the verge of Dattajayantī, which that year fell on December 12), when while in Goa he produced out of thin air a picture of the three-headed god showing his own head thrice in lieu of the heads of Brahmā, Viṣṇu, and Śiva. The "materialization" took place soon after he had spectacularly rid himself of a painful appendicitis attack. At the time, he was in his room with the doctors who "asked Him some spiritual complexities, and He clarified them."[84] M. N. Rao specifies: "As though to enlighten the doctors, He materialized a scroll of Dathathreya, with three faces of Baba in place of the trinity!"[85] The second and most theatrical "revelation" took place on March 7, 1978 (day of Mahāśivarātri), when while in the Madhumalai forest of the Wild Life Sanctuary near the Nilgiri Mountains a picture taken of him with a Polaroid camera showed the modern icon of the three-headed deity, the central face of Dattātreya being Sathya Sai Baba's face. Here is how B. N. Narasimha Murthy, who succeeded Kasturi as the guru's official biographer, narrates this episode in volume 5 of *Sathyam Sivam Sundaram*:

> Finally, Baba asked the student to click His photograph. The lower part of His orange robe had been caught in the twigs of a bush. Before the camera clicked, Smt. Ratanlal rushed forward to set right the folds of the robe. Everyone was astonished when Bhagawan shouted at her loudly, "Don't touch Me!" and she retreated quickly. After the camera clicked, Baba held the photo coming out of the camera and gave it to Joga Rao. As he held it in his palm, the picture developed gradually.
>
> But what did he see? In the place where he had expected to see Baba's form in orange robe, there stood a young figure in the black and white photo. The form, which wore a white flowing garment, had three heads and six hands! Each arm was holding an insignia of Divinity. The lower left arm bent at the elbow, was resting on the back of a majestic young cow. There were four dogs in the background. The face in the centre was that of Baba! It was the form of Dattatreya as described in *Puranas*, the integrated form of the Trinity—*Brahma*, *Vishnu* and *Maheshwara*! Baba had answered Joga Rao's question. That was His real form! After all eyes had feasted on that incredible creation and all hearts had registered the rare revelation, the photo vanished. Bhagawan confirmed while speaking to the students at Brindavan the next morning that it was indeed His true form.[86] He also clarified that Smt. Ratanlal would not have survived if she had touched Him then![87]

His identification with Dattātreya could not have been argued more emphatically. When Jacob Copeman and Aya Ikegame write that "affiliations are not only claimed explicitly but also suggested in more subtle ways . . . many devotees view Sathya Sai Baba's fondness for animals as evidence of a further affiliation with Dattatreya,"[88] they are wrong and right at the same time: wrong because the guru's identification with Dattātreya was utterly explicit, and right because devotees—beginning with Kasturi—were encouraged by Sathya Sai Baba's self-definitions to popularize his claims. As they poignantly argue: "[H]ere the guru, as signifier, to employ Derridean terminology, is not fixed to a signified but points beyond itself to other signifiers in an indefinite referral of signifier to signified."[89] Moreover: "This is a kind of semiotic or associational uncontainability; the guru as collector of associations."[90] To be sure, being a "floating signifier, lacking determination," the guru "can participate in so many domains while generating a sense of omnipotentiality."[91]

There are several aspects of the guru's teachings that assimilate him to Dattātreya, and recent scholarship documents the fact that many Hindus, especially in Andhra, regard him as a Dattātreya incarnation.[92] Charles S. J. White was wrong when in 1974 he wrote that "the god Dattātreya, familiar in the cult of saints in Maharashtra, figured in some aspects of the cult of Shirdi Sāi Bābā, Upasani Bābā, and Mātā Godāvarī . . . but not in that of the fourth saint, Sathya Sāi Bābā."[93] The first and most obvious similarity is Sathya Sai Baba's emphasis on the guru's relevance, presenting himself as the ultimate divine master, the guru of gurus.[94] Indeed, he claimed to be India's foremost guru: "This [Prasanthi Nilayam] is like an ashram in olden times. You're all my chelas (disciples). None of you are new to me. All old friends. I know the past, present, and future of each and every one of you. All the gurus in India are like so many teachers in a school. Swamiji is like the principal!"[95] On more than one occasion, he has been identified with Dattātreya precisely in his role as teacher.[96] As seen in the previous chapter, Kasturi repeatedly notes that his beloved Swami not only offers new interpretations of the *Vedas*, like Dattātreya, but also reinterprets the scriptures of all people. The worship of the guru-god is a fundamental characteristic of Dattātreya theology and of the *Dattasampradāya* as a whole, given that all the gurus of its lineages are revered as incarnations of the deity. All devotees regard their guru as god incarnate, as both the means to salvation and the goal.[97] As the hagiographer writes:

"He [Sathya Sai Baba] accompanies us, all the while, as the Guru though He is also the Guri (the Goal)."[98]

The *incipit* of the first devotional song (*bhajan*) with which the lord of Puttaparthi inaugurated his mission in either October 1940 or 1943, is revealing in its programmatic character: *Mānasa Bhajare Guru-caraṇam / Dustarabhavasāgarataraṇam* ("Worship in thy mind the guru's feet: [these alone] carry over the ocean of existence, hard to overcome!"). Kasturi observes: "[H]e has come to help mankind cross the Ocean of flux (Change). . . . His insistence on each individual discovering Him as the core of his own being is designed to save and to liberate him. See Him in you and in all."[99] It should be noted that according to devotee M. L. Leela (1927–1999), who was a testimony of Sathya Sai Baba's early years in the 1940s, the closing line of this *bhajan* originally ran *Oṃ Śrī Datta Anasūyāputra Sāī Bābājī Veṅkuśārā*, "*Oṃ* Lord Datta, the son of Anasūyā, [who is] the Revered Sāī Bābā, [the son, i.e., pupil] of Veṅkuśā."[100] If this is true, young Sathya Sai Baba would have identified Shirdi Sai Baba—and himself—with Datta and would have acknowledged Veṅkuśā as Shirdi Sai Baba's guru at the very beginning of his mission, at the time of his solemn declaration, when he was just either thirteen or sixteen years old.

The theme of the guru and of *gurubhakti* has always been dominant in Sathya Sai Baba's teachings. The disciple must be loyal to the master and never forsake him. The idea is that it is not the pupil who chooses the guru but it is the guru who calls the pupil to himself. Diana Baskin notes:

> I realized that one has to remain with one teacher with wholehearted commitment. In fact, Swami once told my husband, Robert, that the greatest failing of His Western devotees was a lack of steady commitment. Dig one deep hole instead of many shallow holes, Swami says.[101]

It is no accident that the very day he proclaimed himself to be Sai Baba he commanded his *bhaktas* to worship him on every *guruvār*, every Thursday, "the day of the guru."[102] Indeed, the day of the week that is most sacred among devotees—as in all Dattātreya circles—is Thursday: on this day, *bhajan* sessions and *pūjās* are held in all Sathya Sai Baba Centers worldwide. Moreover, one of the most important religious festivals celebrated in Prasanthi Nilayam has always been Guru Pūrṇimā, falling on the full moon day of the month of *āṣāḍha* (July–August).[103] In one of his early discourses, the saint of Puttaparthi recalled Shirdi Sai Baba's refusal of giving a *mantropadeśa* to an elderly lady, Radhabai Deshmukh,[104] in order to underline that what is solely needed is the guru. His words are consonant with the lesson of the primacy of the guru which is taught by all Dattātreya *avatāras*:

> Baba asked her to go to some *Guru* and get initiated into the name; she said, "I know of no other." Baba asked her the meaning of the sloka [verse] "*Gurur Brahma Gurur Vishnur Gurur Devo Maheswarah, Guru-saakshaath Parambrahma Thasmai Sri Gurave namah*."[105] He asked her, "Why not take the *Guru*'s name, then? Why demand another name from the *Guru*? If the *Guru* is God, obeying His orders, walking in the path He has shown, these are as effective as the *japam* (repetition) of the name." Once you have secured a *Guru,* leave everything to him, even the desire to achieve liberation. He knows you more than you yourself ever can. He will direct you as much as is good for you. Your duty is only to obey and to smother the tendency to drift away from him. You may ask, how are we to earn our food, if we attach ourselves to a *Guru* like this? Be convinced that the Lord will not let you starve; He will give you not merely money, but also *Amrita,* not only food but the nectar of immortality.[106]

Similarly, Sathya Sai Baba revealed that once Kasturi, while in Benares, had implored him to give him a *mantra,* and for this reason he fasted and was in tears. The guru remarked: "But I was laughing all the time at his foolish request. Imagine asking for a mantra after securing Him, whom all mantras promise to secure for you!"[107]

By the same token, he invited everyone not to seek human gurus but to discover the supreme Sadguru, god, within oneself. Moreover:

> I ask only for purity of heart, to shower Grace. Do not posit distance between you and Me; do not interpose the formalities of the *Guru-sishya* (Preceptor-disciple) relationship, or even the altitudinal distinctions of the God-Devotee relationship, between you and Me. I am neither Guru nor God; I am you;

> You are I; that is the Truth. There is no distinction. That which appears so is the delusion. You are waves; I am the Ocean.[108]

While many Hindus, following a stereotyped pattern, revered and still revere him as Kalkin, the tenth eschatological *avatāra* of Viṣṇu,[109] he is more often perceived as an eternal *avatāra* since he incorporates the *trimūrti* in each of his three descents as Shirdi Sai Baba, Sathya Sai Baba, and the future Prema Sai Baba: given the fullness of his divinity, he is thought to be ever-present on earth, albeit invisibly.

Like Dattātreya, he is a teacher of Yoga and meditation along the lines of Śaṅkara's nondualism[110] though he himself is not a *yogin,* having never engaged in any kind of *tapas* or contemplative practice.[111] As M. V. Krishnayya notes: "He is . . . an ascetic and yogi of a special kind . . . he defies the traditional look of simplicity and austerity."[112] As the ultimate *avatāra,* Sathya Sai Baba qualified himself as the lord of *yogīs*[113] and the source of Yoga, its embodiment, and emphasized that he should not be confused as a Yoga adept. His speeches offer a clear indication of the importance he attributed to exercises such as meditation (*dhyāna*) and yogic *sādhanā* in general.[114] He especially recommended meditation upon light (*jyotir*). The use of light or fire as one's focus of attention is a well-known technique,[115] resorted to by both *yogins* and Sufi adepts: inside his mosque, every day and night, Shirdi Sai Baba used to sit in front of his sacred fire (*dhūnī*) for hours, absorbed in silent contemplation.

On June 29, 1959, the guru planted within the ashram's precincts a *vaṭa* tree.[116] To this day, devotees flock to it to practice meditation, the tree being thought to be charged with great spiritual energy given that the guru installed at its root a *yantra,* a thick copper plate fifteen inches long and ten inches wide upon which special *mantras* and mystic markings were etched. Through the implementation of this "meditation tree," Sathya Sai Baba established himself as a "lord of *yoga*" (*yogeśvara*), on analogy with Śiva Dakṣiṇāmūrti and, of course, Dattātreya.[117] The guru's utilization of a magic *yantra* links him to Tantrism. He himself noted that the present *kaliyuga,* the last and most degenerate of the four world ages, "is the age of Tantra."[118]

Another characteristic that links the guru of Puttaparthi to Dattātreya, duly underlined by Kasturi in our conversation, is his being a giver of both worldly enjoyments (*bhukti*) and the *summum bonum* of liberation (*mukti*).[119] He is said to behave sometimes as a *vairāgin* and sometimes as a *bhogin*, and the hagiographer once noted that he is "a very sensuous man."[120] Being both a *yogin* and a *bhogin* is a peculiar trait of Dattātreya *avatāras*. The deity is revered as "one who instantly goes to those who devoutly remember him" (*smartṛgāmin*), and Sathya Sai Baba's numerous trances, especially in his early years, were understood as sudden "travels" in which he "left" Puttaparthi to rescue his endangered *bhaktas*. As he once told an American devotee, speaking of himself in the third person: "He never sleeps even for a second as all the time He is ready to rush forward to help devotees in distress. . . . He again and again relieves His devotees by taking on Himself their ailments."[121] The raison d'être of Sathya Sai Baba's plethora of miracles from the early days is said to be the material and spiritual welfare of his *bhaktas*, since his compassionate concern is for each concrete individual and the fulfillment of his/her physical, psychological, and spiritual aspirations.[122] Along these lines, already at the end of the 1940s Sathya Sai Baba's grandfather Ratnākaram Kondama Rāju told Kasturi that he considered his grandson to be a special type of *avadhūta*: "This grandson too is an Avadhootha, but he is *in* the world, *for* the world."[123] Lawrence Babb rightly observes that Sathya Sai Baba "is thoroughly in the world, a social deity . . . par excellence. Through his magic he has made the world into an arena for his sanctity, and of course he has also encouraged the belief that the world can be made a better place by means of education and charitable service."[124] His activities of social service through the implementation of schools, hospitals, water supplies to villages, etc. were and are understood as part and parcel of his simultaneous concern for the material and spiritual well-being of all.

One more feature that assimilates him to Dattātreya and the *avadhūta* typology was his occasional childish (*bāla*) and apparently insane (*unmatta*) behavior.[125] His frequent unpredictability, alternating playful and grave moods, forced everyone to be on their guard at all times. He would often keep his devotees suspended in a space of indecision[126] and one of his mottos was: "Love my uncertainty."[127] Once, he noted: "[N]o scripture has laid down how a Prophet or spiritual master must behave. No guidelines by which you can judge them. They are free by themselves. They are unlimited and uncontrolled. You cannot lay down rules for them. Each one guides people in his own way."[128] Professor C. T. K. Chari thought that Sathya Sai Baba had a split personality, and his nephew Varadu, an ex-devotee of the guru, observed: "One moment he is that great soul that no one can fathom, another moment he is the rustic/crude villager."[129]

In his final years, when his health was rapidly deteriorating, the guru would sometimes not contain himself and cry in public, being touched by the devotion of his students and followers.[130] This was something that took devotees by surprise given that the guru had never been seen crying. For instance, during the celebrations of his birthday, on November 23, 2010, the guru wept like a child. A close follower commented after the guru's death: "Swami was not a distant, dry, unemotional Upanishadic or Platonic God. He was an intensely emotional and hypersensitive God who would respond to the pull of a deeply emotional plea or prayer from a devotee. . . . [H]e gave far more importance to emotions than dry analytical thought. And sometimes he too became emotional, especially during the last years of his life."[131] The crying of gods and *avatāra*s such as Kṛṣṇa and Rāma—out of sorrow or compassion—is well attested to in Hindu religions.[132] Already in October 1988, the guru told Erlendur Haraldsson that he is "also human," and referred to a hip injury he had recently suffered.[133] Even Kasturi told Haraldsson the same: "Divine he is, but also very human."[134] With regard to the fact that even divine incarnations cry, noteworthy are Rāmakṛṣṇa's words: "Assuming a human body, the Incarnation falls victim to disease, grief, hunger, thirst, and all such things, like ordinary mortals. Rāma wept for Sita. 'Brahman weeps, entrapped in the snare of the five elements.' "[135]

The guru's daily "materialization" of miracle-working ash or *vibhūti*—an off-white fine ash, bearing a slight fragrance—is another quality that links him to Dattātreya, given that the deity, much like all ascetics, is especially fond of *vibhūti*. Chapter 29 of the *Gurucaritra* is devoted to the wonderful powers of *vibhūti,* usually made of cow dung (*gomaya*) or taken from crematory grounds (*śmaśāna*): whoever comes in contact with it is said to be instantly purified and to attain the knowledge of *Brahman* and liberation. Throughout the text the holy ash is used by Dattātreya *avatāra*s as a means to cure a variety of illnesses, by smearing it on the forehead or sprinkling it on the bodies of devotees. Likewise, Sathya Sai Baba's *vibhūti* is thought to cure all sorts of diseases, afford protection, and grant liberation (*mokṣa pradātam*, as devotees sing). His followers often mix it with water and drink it as a medicine. Even Shirdi Sai Baba used to give his followers ash (*udī*) which he took from his *dhūnī*, both as a token of grace and as a healing substance. Up until 1979, on the occasion of religious holidays such as Mahāśivarātri and Dasara, Sathya Sai Baba used to perform the ceremonial bathing in ashes (*vibhūtyabhiṣeka*) of a silver statue of the Shirdi saint. Churning his arm in a supposedly empty urn held above the statue by an attendant—often Kasturi himself—he "materialized" huge quantities of *vibhūti* to the point of covering the image in a heap of ashes. Here is Samuel H. Sandweiss's report:

> Following the ceremony [*Mahāśivarātri*], I had a conversation with Professor Kasturi, who has been with Baba some thirty years. He said that when Baba places his hand in the empty urn, it immediately and completely fills with *vibuthi*. In fact, Baba leans over to warn the man holding the urn to prepare for the sudden increase in weight. He churns his hand inside

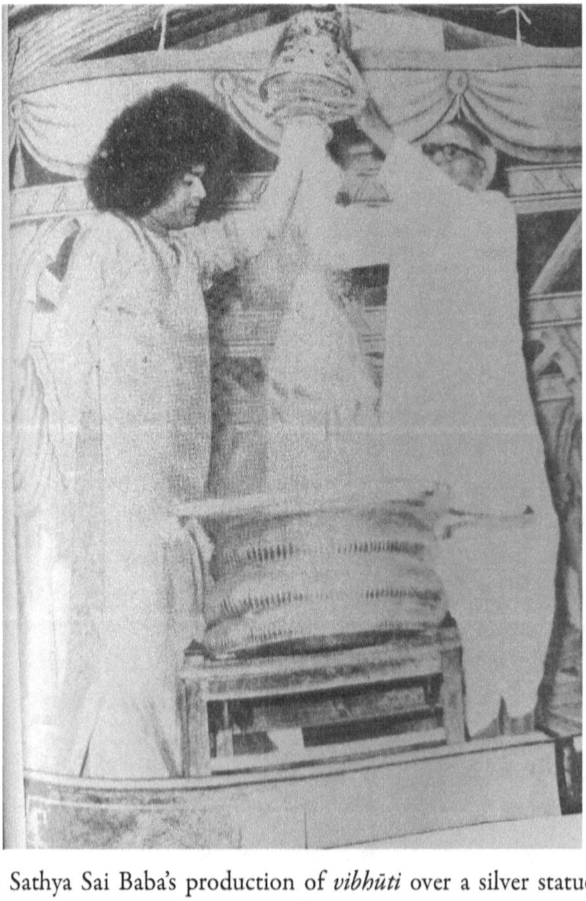

Figure 6.2. Sathya Sai Baba's production of *vibhūti* over a silver statue of Shirdi Sai Baba; N. Kasturi holds the supposedly empty urn.

> the urn until it is emptied, then replaces it with his other hand and the whole process is repeated, the urn again instantaneously filling with *vibuthi*. This is repeated until five or six times the amount of *vibuthi* that the urn could normally hold has been created. Professor Kasturi has been fortunate enough to hold the urn during many different *Mahashivarathris*. He says the moment is so spiritually intense that he completely loses contact with the crowd and is filled only with Baba's presence and the sacredness of the miracle. When asked whether he had ever inspected the urn to make sure it was empty before the miracle, he simply laughed and said, "Of course."[136]

When the guru was in a state of trance, *vibhūti* could be seen emerging from his forehead as well as from his face, mouth, thumbs, and toes. *Vibhūti* has even been reported to ooze out from the guru's portraits, in India and abroad.

Sathya Sai Baba's emphasis on his avatāric role as preserver of the *Veda*s through his fostering of *yajña*s and the promotion of schools of Vedic recitation, may also be regarded as a relevant aspect of his "Dattātreya nature." The *Dattasampradāya* plays a significant role in contemporary Vedic revivalism in Maharashtra, the deity being extolled as the upholder of brāhmaṇical purity and ritual orthodoxy. The importance that Sathya Sai Baba attributed to the *Veda*s can be appreciated by the frequency with which he spoke about them in his early discourses.[137] Conversely and perhaps more interestingly, like Dattātreya, the guru of Puttaparthi—characteristically in his early years—was linked to such impure features as possession and exorcism. As was Dattātreya, he himself was thought to be possessed and to behave "like a demon" (*piśācavad*). As M. V. Krishnayya writes: "He was possessed by Narasimha, the man-lion *avatāra* of Viṣṇu, and he was bitten by a scorpion. He was treated for hysteria but traditional exorcisms were of no use."[138]

Kasturi himself witnessed a few "scalp squeezes" performed by Sathya Sai Baba.[139] Apparently, Shirdi Sai Baba performed similar acts and B. V. Narasimhaswami states that "sometimes he pressed his hand heavily on the head of a devotee as though he was crushing out some of the lower impulses."[140] The guru of Puttaparthi exorcised people in many dramatic and unusual ways, to the point that those who were "suspected of being possessed by evil spirits would be brought to Puttaparthi for relief, many of them being women."[141] He is even said to have warded off a malignant influence that was causing trouble in the adjacent hamlet of Karnatanagapalli, which he explained was due to the locals' "disturbance" of a *pir,* a small golden hand-shaped article held to be the "representative" of Allāh by the Muslim community. He instructed the villagers to dig at a particular spot, where the *pir* could be found, and sure enough a copper plate, silver umbrella, and a *pir* were discovered there.[142] Moreover, he would have freed the people of the nearby village of Kammavaripalle from the disease of *naara kurupulu*[143] by burying four coconuts on the four sides of the village and by advising locals to sprinkle *vibhūti* all around it,[144] a ritual that calls to mind a well-known episode in the life of Shirdi Sai Baba, when he is said to have averted a cholera epidemic by grinding wheat and having it thrown on the village boundary along the side of the local brook.[145]

Another peculiar characteristic that assimilates him to Dattātreya was his fondness for "impure" dogs from his early days, the deity being typically surrounded by dogs in the iconography.[146] The guru often mentioned the dog in his discourses: he pointed out how humans must learn faithfulness and gratitude from him and that dogs can even be trained to relish vegetarian food.[147] He honored two of his faithful dogs by giving them burial (*samādhi*) in the sacred quadrangle behind the Old Mandir, on which spot a *tulsī*[148] was later planted.[149]

On January 13, 1986, just two months after my conversation with Kasturi, the guru inaugurated a temple of Dattātreya within the area housing the tombs of his parents. Through it he wished to signify that he originated from the *trimūrti,* his human parents having been the chosen instruments of a divine plan. Collocated under an *audumbar* tree[150]—which is especially sacred to Dattātreya—the three-headed god bears the emblems of Brahmā, Viṣṇu, and Śiva and is surrounded by three dogs and a cow, with the nine masters of the *Navnāthsampradāya* of which he is considered to be the *ādiguru*[151] encircling him (in clockwise order: Macchindranāth, Gorakhnāth, Jālandharnāth, Kānīfnāth, Charpatināth, Nāganāth, Bhartṛrināth, Revaṇanāth, and Gahinīnāth).[152] Dattātreya is seated with his right leg resting on the left knee,[153] which is reminiscent of Shirdi Sai Baba's characteristic pose with his right arm resting on his right thigh or lap, the right foot on the opposite knee, and the head slightly inclined in a pensive attitude. The saint's left hand lies on the foot of the crossed leg.

Figure 6.3. Sathya Sai Baba at the inauguration of the Dattātreya temple in Puttaparthi in January 1986.

Such a posture represents sovereignty, being the prerogative of gods and kings, and it "appears to be intentional, perhaps in an attempt to signify the true royalty of *faqīri* life (reflection of God's absolute sovereignty) versus the false one of human lordship."[154] In his youth, Sathya Sai Baba had himself photographed in this same posture, in an effort to stress his identity with the Shirdi saint.[155]

The fact that Dattātreya has always been marginal in the repertoire of Prasanthi Nilayam's *bhajans* and that the Dattajayantī festival has never been celebrated at the guru's ashram are to be explained with the fact that Dattātreya is a minor deity, and Sathya Sai Baba never wished to identify (and confine) himself with any sectarian tradition such as the

Figure 6.4. Left: Dattātreya's icon in Puttaparthi's temple. The deity's posture recalls Shirdi Sai Baba's typical posture (center), which young Sathya Sai Baba consciously mirrored (right).

Dattasampradāya, but always aimed at representing himself as the universal godhead incorporating all deities, beginning with such pan-Indian gods as Viṣṇu-Kṛṣṇa, Śiva, and the goddess.[156] This notwithstanding, it is indisputable that besides his solemn declaration of being Śiva-Śakti—which has been his dominant self-representation among Hindus—a parallel identification, which he has constantly nurtured, has been that of the *trimūrti* of Brahmā, Viṣṇu, and Śiva, which the icon of Dattātreya effectively recapitulates in his three-headed form. Posters representing Sathya Sai Baba's identity with either Śiva-Śakti or Dattātreya are easily found in the devotional shops surrounding the guru's ashram.[157] With regard to the Śiva-Śakti model, M. N. Rao observes: "At an exclusive session in July 1984, Swami had underlined the three-in-one phenomenon of the Sai Baba trinity. All the three have the same Sayeeswara divinity. The first born is more of Siva, the second of both Siva and Sakthi and the third more of Sakthi."[158]

Similarly, the triune Dattātreya model is aimed at showing how the supreme *Brahman*, namely, the "Sai principle," reveals itself through the three *mūrti*s of Brahmā, Viṣṇu, and Śiva. In each of these forms the other two are co-implicated, each member of the triad being inseparable from the others, the difference being one of emphasis. The Śiva-Śakti and the *trimūrti*/Dattātreya theological models coexist and, as Sathya Sai Baba has argued on several occasions, they are to be understood as one and the same given that the "Śiva principle" encompasses the male triad (Brahmā, Viṣṇu, and Śiva) and the "Śakti principle" the female triad (Sarasvatī, Lakṣmī, and Pārvatī). Historically, it appears that the *trimūrti* is related to the synthetic, dual icons of Harihara and Ardhanārīśvara (lit. "the lord who is half female"), that is, Śiva-Śakti. The Harihara icon is the logical antecedent of the *trimūrti,* which will subsequently be extended to include Brahmā. Through Dattātreya's "Trinitarian" paradigm, Sathya Sai Baba affirmed the fullness of his divinity establishing himself as the root and goal of all world religions. The Dattātreya icon was thus a most resourceful tool capable of simultaneously recapitulating the Sai Baba triune *avatāra*hood and expanding the guru's universalist claim even beyond India and Hinduism.

Dattātreya was familiar to Kasturi even before meeting the guru of Puttaparthi, given that the deity had been adopted by the Wadiyar dynasty of the *mahārāja*s of Mysore (1799–1947). As the hagiographer pointed out to me when we first met, Sri Jaya Chamarajendra Wadiyar Bahadur (1919–1974), the last *mahārāja,* wrote a fine monograph on Dattātreya back in 1957, and in the 1960s Kasturi himself penned a short biography on Krishnaraja Wadiyar IV (1884–1940) who was revered as another Aśoka and whose "dharmic governance" was extolled as *rāmarājya,* "the reign of Rama." By the end of the 1950s if not earlier, the hagiographer acknowledged Sathya Sai Baba as an *avatāra* of Dattātreya as he explicitly states in Part 1 of *Sathyam Sivam Sundaram* (first released in 1961): "This Sathya Sai Avathar of Dattatreya."[159] As I documented in the preceding chapter, such identification is scattered throughout his writings, notably in *Garland of 108 Precious Gems, Easwaramma,* and the autobiography *Loving God.* And yet this crucial idea was perhaps never argued as thoroughly and systematically as in our conversation of November 1985. During the decades of his discipleship, the guru's identification with Dattātreya and the *trimūrti* of Brahmā, Viṣṇu, and Śiva led Kasturi to theologically probe into such identity, bringing him to expand the Dattātreya paradigm in his construction of a universalist canon. We know that in the late 1970s, on the occasion of Dattajayantī, Kasturi's son M. V. N. Murthy even went on a pilgrimage to the famous Dattātreya temple located on a peak of Mount Girnār, which proves the strong devotion to this deity within Kasturi's family.[160]

The Title of Kasturi's Magnum Opus and Its Trinitarian Import

The very title of Kasturi's biography, *Sathyam Sivam Sundaram* or *Truth Goodness Beauty*, is suggestive of the Trinity and its perichoretical/relational nature. It evokes what classical philosophy calls the transcendental attributes, that is to say, the properties of being, which Christian theology has attributed to Christ's incarnation, affirming that these three are harmoniously embodied in him. Truth (*verum*), goodness (*bonum*), and beauty (*pulchrum*) are thought to cooperate with one another in a way that reflects the Trinity, since their source and medium is none other than the triune god—Father, Son, and Holy Spirit. As Andrew Fellows writes:

> There is no act of God where all three persons are not at work. So it is with Goodness, Beauty and Truth—where one is reflected the other two will always be present because they function as a unity. You never have one without the others. When you encounter real Goodness it will also be true (it will not deny the truth) and it will also be beautiful. The same applies to Truth—if something is true, it will also be good and it will be beautiful.[161]

The concepts of beauty, goodness, and truth, in this order, are at the core of the Trinitarian theology of Hans Urs von Balthasar (1905–1988), one of the major theologians of our times. The Biblical text that grounds the structure of his trilogy in fifteen volumes—*The Glory of the Lord*, *Theo-Drama*, and *Theo-Logic*—is *John* 1.14: "and we saw his glory, such glory as befits the Father's only Son, full of grace and truth."[162]

It is remarkable that while the guru declared himself to be Śiva-Śakti on July 6, 1963, on the subsequent day of July 7 he also claimed to be the holy triad of *Sathyam Sivam Sundaram*, confirming the essential oneness of the Śiva-Śakti and *trimūrti* models:

> There is no *Sathyam* (Truth), without *Sivam* (Goodness); there is no *Sivam*, without *Sundaram* (Beauty). Truth alone can confer *Mangalam* (Auspiciousness) and *Mangalam* alone

> is the real beauty; Joy is beauty; falsehood and grief are ugly, because they are unnatural. *Buddhi, chittham* and *hridayam* (intellect, sub-conscious mind and heart)—these are the three centres in the individual where reside *jnana, karma* and *bhakti*. The effulgence of *Sathyam* will reveal *Sivam*; do *karma* (action) which is approved by the higher wisdom, not *karma* which is born of ignorance. Then, all *karma* will be *Sivam* (auspicious, beneficial, blessed). The experience of that *Sivam* is what is called *Sundaram*; for it covers real *Aananda*. That is why My Life is named "Sathyam Sivam Sundaram."[163]

Thus, at his momentous disclosure of July 1963, he overtly identified himself with the triad that Kasturi had chosen as the auspicious title of his biography two years earlier in 1961.[164] From early times, both Kasturi and his master correlated *Sathyam Sivam Sundaram* to the Vedāntic triad of *sat cit ānanda,* being, awareness, and bliss. As the hagiographer wrote in the front page of his magnum opus:

> He is the sub-stratum, the substance; the separate and the sum; the Sath; the SATHYAM.
>
> He is the awareness, the activity, consciousness, feeling; the willing and the doing—the Chith; the SIVAM.
>
> He is the light, the splendour; the harmony, the melody, the Ananda; the SUNDARAM.[165]

Kasturi's conviction is that in the Sadguru Sathya Sai Baba the "Trinitarian" *Brahman* has gloriously revealed itself as truth/being, goodness/awareness, and beauty/bliss. Already by the end of the nineteenth century, an equivalence had been established in India between the Christian Trinity and the notions of *sat, cit,* and *ānanda*. Keshub Chandra Sen (1838–1884), the *Brahmo Samāj* reformer, was apparently the first to associate the Father, Son, and Holy Spirit with the Vedāntic triad and, inspired by such correspondence, the Benedictine monks Jules Monchanin (1895–1957) and Henry Le Saux (1910–1973) established in 1950 in Shantivanam, Tamil Nadu, the Saccidānanda ashram dedicated to the Trinity. The triadic model upon which such correlation rested was that of the *trimūrti.* The Western fascination with the *trimūrti* and the insisted comparison of this integrative concept with the Trinity has a long history which dates back to at least the sixteenth century, when the Portuguese writer Duarte Barbosa (1480–1521) superimposed the Christian doctrine of the one god in three persons to the Hindu triad. As I have elsewhere noted:

> The European assessment of the *trimūrti* brought about a process of re-enculturation, through which the Hindu self-understanding of the concept was subject to inevitable transformations. Particularly in the 20th century, the *trimūrti* scheme has become increasingly popular, part and parcel of the Vedāntic inclusivistic framework of neo-Hinduism.[166]

Right from its most revealing title, Kasturi's hagiography cleverly articulates Sathya Sai Baba's triadic identity, wishing to demonstrate how the Avatar, while firmly rooted in Hinduism, namely, being regarded as its fulfillment, is by no means restricted to it. His characterization as *sat, cit,* and *ānanda* or pure *Brahman,* while confirming the indigenous Vedānta reading (the guru as the incarnation of the "classical" *trimūrti* of Brahmā, Viṣṇu, and Śiva, that is, of Dattātreya), makes him simultaneously palatable via its Trinitarian translation to a global, Westernized audience, projecting him as the Father, Son, and Holy Spirit worshipped by Christians.

Clearly, *Sathyam Sivam Sundaram* is to be understood as a synonym of Dattātreya, one more name of the one who is believed to encompass all names and who in his transcendence has no name. In his commentary to the guru's 108 names, Kasturi writes: "As Vyaktha (Manifested) He is Sathya Sai Baba, as unmanifested He is Niraakaara, the formless Datta-Sakthi, Narayana-Siva-Brahma Sakthi."[167] Significantly, the guru said of himself: "I, assume all Names, the Peace; I, assume all Forms, the Good; I, Being, Awareness, Bliss, the One; Sathyam, Sivam, Sundaram."[168] He even adopted the hagiographer's triad in his naming of the main regional centers outside Puttaparthi:

> In the strategy for spreading His message across India, He had made Prasanthi Nilayam His headquarters with four regional centers—Sathyam at Bombay, Sivam at Hyderabad, Sundaram at Madras, and another at Bangalore.[169]

Sathyam Sivam Sundaram and the Triad of *karman, bhakti,* and *jñāna*: The Triune Sai Baba as the *trimūrti*

On November 23, 1966, as he had done already on July 7, 1963, Sathya Sai Baba referred *Sathyam Sivam Sundaram* to another well-known triad and, as Kasturi writes, those who were identifying the three terms with *sat, cit,* and *ānanda* opened their eyes at the novel meaning:

> Follow the Karma-marga [Path of action] with the harmony and charm of Sundaram; follow the Bhakthi-marga [Path of devotion] with the exhilaration and exaltation of Sivam; follow the Jnana-marga [Path of knowledge] with the directness and steadfastness of Sathyam.[170]

Sathyam, Sivam, and *Sundaram,* albeit in reverse order, are here linked to the three paths of *karman, bhakti,* and *jñāna,* which immediately call to mind the *Bhagavadgītā,* whose eighteen chapters are traditionally understood as the unsurpassed synthesis of the three *mārgas*, which all lead to liberation (*mokṣa*). As seen in chapter 4, in his paraphrase of the guru's discourse of July 7, 1963, Kasturi identifies *Sathyam* with *jñāna, Sivam* with *karman,* and *Sundaram* with *bhakti.* One should not regard these different identifications as contradictory, however. In fact, there is no one-to-one, rigid correspondence between the triads. The elements of each triad are understood to be inextricably interrelated in their ultimate oneness. What the guru's words wish to convey is that all triads are to be conceived as a harmonious whole and that they represent one and the same reality. Sathya Sai Baba's underlying idea is that ultimately *karman, bhakti,* and *jñāna,* just like the *Bhagavadgītā,* constitute one indivisible whole:

> They are like the confluence of the three holy rivers at Prayag, the Ganga, the Yamuna, and the unseen underground Saraswati. Ganga is the *Bhakti-marga* . . . ; Yamuna is the *Karma-marga* . . . ; Saraswati is the *Jnana-marga.* . . . The three Paths are like the wheels of a tricycle . . . *Bhakti* and *Jnana* are two wheels in one line at the back and the forward one is Karma.[171]

Like *sat cit ānanda,* this triad highlights the constitutive interrelatedness of the triune *Sathyam Sivam Sundaram. Karman, bhakti,* and *jñāna* apply to the triune Sai Baba incarnation, as the guru of Puttaparthi indicated in his interview to the journalist R. K. Karanjia as well as on various other occasions. That Kasturi during our meeting made it a point to read to me some key excerpts taken from his guru's answers to Karanjia proves the prime importance he attributed to such disclosure in his systematic articulation of Sathya Sai Baba as an *avatāra* of Dattātreya. Through his skillful analysis of the seminal verse of *Bhagavadgītā* 4.34 in his last book of 1985 titled *Prasanthi: Pathway to Peace*, the hagiographer illustrated Sathya Sai Baba's nature and message as the balanced integration of the paths of *karman, bhakti,* and *jñāna.*

To Karanjia, the guru preliminarily pointed out the harmonious "oneness" (*ekatva*) of the three Sai Baba incarnations so as to highlight that each of them was/is/will be "full" (*pūrṇa*), that is, that in each of them the Absolute *Brahman* was/is/will be incarnated as the triad of Brahmā, Viṣṇu, and Śiva together with their respective Śaktis, the differences among them being merely of degree or emphasis, not of substance. As he told the journalist with regard to all *avatāras*: "Their tasks and powers . . . differ according to the time, the situation and the environment, but they belong to and derive from, one and the same Dharma Swarup or Divine Body."[172]

From an analysis of Sathya Sai Baba's statements and Kasturi's overall discourse, a triadic structure can be uncovered that spans across the centuries, revealing an innovative theological vision inspired by the *trimūrti*/Dattātreya paradigm. In the first incarnation as Shirdi Sai Baba, the Brahmā aspect of *Brahman* was given prominence,[173] while in the second incarnation as Sathya Sai Baba, the Viṣṇu aspect of *Brahman* is thought to prevail. Finally, in the third incarnation of the future Prema Sai Baba, the Śiva aspect of *Brahman* will be accentuated. In the first incarnation of Shirdi Sai Baba—who in the threefold division of time represents the past—the aspect and function of the creator god Brahmā is underlined. Brahmā is especially linked to the law of *karman* at both a cosmological and human level, the deity being the emblem of inexorable fate (*daiva*). As Brahmā, Shirdi Sai Baba is said to have carefully predisposed all things, this being expressed by the metaphor of the "cooking of the food," meaning the stage of preparing the different types of spiritual nourishment needed by the faithful. This complex work of preparation is understood to set the avatāric mission in motion. The saint of Shirdi is represented as having been especially involved in action or *karman,* the *karmamārga* having been his foremost teaching given that the recognition and practice of the proper way of life coincided with each community's duty (*dharma*). As Sathya Sai Baba told Karanjia: "The previous Avatar, Shirdi Baba, laid the base for secular integration and gave mankind the message of Duty that is Work."[174] Rachel Dwyer has rightly observed that "Sai Baba . . . is regarded as 'secular' . . . in that he is held in equally high regard by Hindus and Muslims."[175] It is a fact that through his authoritative example and praxis, the saint of Shirdi was able to achieve harmony and integration between the Hindu and Muslim communities. Kasturi reports that from his early days the guru poignantly observed that "then [at Shirdi], the emphasis was more on community . . . then, it was more on Karma."[176] He more than once explained Shirdi Sai Baba's wrath and bursts of temper through a telling parable:

> While I was in Shirdi, I was like a mother, doing the cooking. When the mother is in the kitchen, she doesn't want to be disturbed. If the children play there, and the husband disrupts her, there will be spiritual curfew there in the kitchen. Yes, she will fire at you. She doesn't want to be disturbed since she is so busy in the kitchen. That is why Shirdi Sai was known for His anger. He used to manhandle people. If you didn't follow Him—finished! One or two blows, that side and this side, because that was the serious cooking stage.[177]

The maternal side of the *avatāra* is meant to highlight his androgynous character given that he is inseparable from his Śakti, which in Brahmā's case is his consort Sarasvatī. Shirdi Sai Baba's representation as "the old man" wearing a beard is reminiscent of the way Brahmā is depicted in traditional iconography, as an aged man with a white beard implying his sagelike portrayal.[178]

In the present Sathya Sai Baba incarnation, the emphasis is placed on Viṣṇu who is typically regarded as Dattātreya's basic identity. The guru's identification with Viṣṇu-Kṛṣṇa was especially emphasized in his early days, as his very name Sathyanārāyaṇa and the mythology surrounding his advent testify (such as Veṅkāvadhūta's prophecy and his grandfather's premonitory dream).[179] Viṣṇu-Kṛṣṇa's intimate relationship with his followers is based upon devotion, *bhakti,* and this is no doubt the dominant characteristic of Sathya Sai Baba's teaching. As he himself stated: "[N]ow [the emphasis] is on the individual; . . . now it is mostly on Bhakthi."[180] As he told Karanjia, his mission has expanded to the whole of humanity as it is aimed to make each and everyone realize that the same god resides in all. All people should come to love each other, irrespective of color and creed, so that every work can become an act of worship.[181] The guru's call to worship the god that dwells in every human being, that is, he himself who abides in the heart of all creatures, resonates with *Bhagavadgītā* 15.15, where Kṛṣṇa reveals to Arjuna that he abides in the heart of each and every one, he being their inner controller (*antaryāmin*). Thus, the universality of Sathya Sai Baba's avatāric mission is said to be characterized by worship or the *bhaktimārga*, since each individual needs to be awakened through the devotional path to experience god's presence within himself/herself. The guru would repeatedly say that he is "all love, now,"[182] his function being that of "serving the food" to the hungry humanity, a nurturing task that is consonant with Viṣṇu as the maintainer/upholder of the cosmos and of the welfare of all creatures. As Kasturi writes, quoting the words of his master: "While serving the food, she [the mother] is all smiles and patience. I am now distributing the dishes cooked then [during Shirdi Sai Baba's times]; wherever you may be, if you are hungry, and if you sit with a plate, I shall serve you and feed you to your heart's content!"[183] Moreover:

> But now, I have come to feed the hungry, and serve everyone the feast I got ready then. So, I have to speak soft and kind, so that you may eat happily and digest easily the banquet of the spirit![184]
>
> And this now is the Parthi stage. Parthi Sai is full of Love. He is serving food. One has to serve food with smiles. The housewife also needs to serve with smiles and happiness. If she is so serious, with her face all wrinkled up, the fellow will not feel to eat at all, except to have a glass of water. So as you serve, you need to smile. Then the other person will be encouraged to eat more and more.[185]

It is noteworthy that in the early days Sathya Sai Baba, homologizing Kasturi to his avatāric role, used to say that the hagiographer would be called on to "serve" the story of his life only at the right time, when there would be enough "hunger for the meal."[186]

In the future incarnation of Prema Sai Baba the emphasis will be placed on Śiva, whose function is to bring this illusory *saṃsāra* to an end.

This will be achieved through wisdom or *jñāna,* which Sathya Sai Baba explained as consisting in the final realization that not only does god reside in everyone, but that everyone *is* god.[187] Ultimately, there is not the least difference between the *avatāra* and his devotee, the latter having attained the pinnacle of *jñāna,* the nondual condition of supreme "nondifference" (*ananyatā*). This will be the time when the "spiritual food" prepared by the divine mother will be enjoyed, thus, assimilated/experienced, being wholly digested by her children. Indeed, "it is not enough if the food is served; one has to enjoy the food."[188] Having brought the mission to completion the *avatāra* will "wash the vessels," that is, bring this eon to its final consummation true to his annihilative function as Śiva.[189] As was mentioned in chapter 2, that Prema Sai Baba would lead his devotees along the path of *jñāna* was prophesized by the guru already in the *Sri Sayeeshuni Charitra,* composed in 1944: "Sai will enter *samadhi* after uniting disparate religions and giving happiness to the country. He will enter *samadhi* and take birth again after some years and give devotees the path of *jnana* (knowledge)."[190] Recently, even Madhusudhan Rao Naidu has stressed the characterization of Prema Sai Baba as a *jñānin,* saying that he will communicate through silence.[191] The emphasis on *jñāna* and on the Śiva facet of the *trimūrti* also resonates with the *avatāra*'s name, given that *preman* or pure love is thought to be inseparable from wisdom and that Śiva, especially in South India, is ultimately conceptualized as love. As is constantly repeated in Śaiva Siddhānta circles, "Śiva is love" (*Aṉpe civam*). The devotees' final realization of their true identity coincides with the *avatāra*'s final task of giving himself totally to his creatures.

The guru of Puttaparthi always reminded his devotees that love is at the root of everything and that it is the very nature of god and of the triune Sai Baba *avatāra.*[192] As he liked to say: "Ego lives by getting and forgetting, love lives by giving and forgiving."[193] Through giving and forgiving, the illusory ego (*ahaṃkāra*) is said to melt away revealing the pure *sat cit ānanda.* Kasturi notes: "'My hand knows only the act of giving,' He [Sathya Sai Baba] says. He never uses for Himself anything that He creates. His time is taken up in work for mankind, for man's uplift and liberation; He exhorts us also to grow in love."[194] Theologically, this definition of love as giving expresses the very nature of Dattātreya, as he is the one *avatāra* that has been "given" (*datta*) to Atri and to humanity as a whole and whose characteristic is to donate everything to his devotees—*bhukti, mukti,* and ultimately himself—forgiving through his grace (*kṛpā*) all their evils and sins (*pāpa*).[195] The practice of service (*sevā*) on which Sathya Sai Baba insisted so much must be understood as the natural outcome of this pure, unconditional love since it teaches the fundamental lesson of generosity. The guru taught that one should never be tired of serving, since in the act of service one's very nature is expressed and revealed.[196]

Through the act of giving one is called to utterly exceed himself/herself. One must offer himself/herself totally to the deity and his/her fellow men, with no residue, as when the camphor is burnt in the final *ārtī* ceremony, since only by losing one's life may one fulfill it and realize the divine. As Jesus admonished: "Whoever cares for his own safety is lost; but if a man will let himself be lost for my sake, he will find his true self" (*Matthew* 16.25). In Dattātreya's theology, the idea is that god *is* giving and that his gift is limitless since he is the paradigm of the excess of love (*preman*), untiringly sacrificing himself and going beyond himself. This is the profound reason why Dattātreya is the paradigm of the supreme renunciant, renunciation being the veritable essence of the Absolute. Only excess saves, only by surpassing/consuming oneself can one achieve communion with him: this is understood to be the secret of life. Ultimately, one discovers his/her true self by discarding the ego. The guru of Puttaparthi pointed out that the cross, symbol of Christianity, carries the message of the elimination of the 'I.' One must cut the 'I' feeling clean across and let his/her ego die on the cross.[197] Only by accepting this dynamic of loss by sacrificing one's life for the good of others without expecting anything in return can one harmonize himself/herself with god's mystery. As the cross teaches, this existential attitude leads to the experience of death. Indeed, man can surrender and go beyond himself/herself precisely because there is death.[198] It is only in this experience of pure love, in the joyful, ongoing act of giving and giving up one's life that man can unburden himself/herself and recognize his/her ātmic identity. Along these lines, it is noteworthy that many devotees believe that Prema Sai Baba will resemble Christ in his countenance and this is precisely one more way of universalizing their savior-like figure, linking his advent to Christ's second coming.

The progression through the three interdependent stages of *karman, bhakti,* and *jñāna* which characterizes the triune Sai Baba *avatāra* mirrors the spiritual development that all devotees must undergo. This threefold progression was reiterated by the guru in a talk he held on December 29, 1985. Here is how Howard Levin summarizes it:

> He began the evening program with a talk on the three stages of spiritual life, Karma, Bhakti and Jnana. He compared the three to the three hands on a clock. He said that the clock has the second hand, the minute hand, and the hour hand. Karma, the yoga of work, was the second hand. Bhakti, the yoga of devotion was the minute hand, and Jnana, the yoga of wisdom, was the hour hand. He added that when someone asks for the time he always asks what is the hour. No one ever asks simply for the minute or the second. In the same way, he said, we would all have to progress through the three stages. Through Karma yoga we develop Bhakti. Through Bhakti we develop Jnana. Jnana or wisdom is the final goal. It is the "hour" that everyone wants to know. So ultimately we all have to progress to the stage of Jnana, the wisdom of knowing one's self as God.[199]

The Swami further noticed: "The dusty fair-weather District Board road of Karma leads to the metalled State Government road of Bhakthi and this leads to the nice Asphalted National Highway of Jnana."[200] Along these lines, Kasturi remarks: "But just as a fruit undergoes three stages of development, fruiting, maturity and ripeness, man too has to pass through Karma, Upasana and Jnana. When the Jnana stage is reached, sweetness fills the fruit and man is full of Bliss. Baba is the Sun which matures and ripens the fruit and fills it with Ananda."[201]

The idea is that there is nothing but god and that knowledge coincides with giving thanks to him and sacrificing/donating one's life with gratitude by effacing the ego. As the German philosopher Martin Heidegger (1889–1976) was fond of saying, quoting a seventeenth-century Pietist phrase: *Denken ist danken*, "To think is to thank." To further stress the theological imperative of giving, Kasturi utilized the famous three *da*-s of *Bṛhadāraṇyaka Upaniṣad* 5.2, *dāmyata datta dayadhvam*, "restrain yourself, give, be compassionate," through which lord Prajāpati teaches the meaning of the "thunder's voice" calling for the cultivation of self-control, charity, and compassion to gods, men, and demons respectively. Though the "thunder's voice" was originally not intended to denote Dattātreya, the *bīja-mantra da* is thought to convey the deity's presence and power. Both the hagiographer and his master were no doubt well aware of the *da* syllable as signifier of Dattātreya.[202] Here are Kasturi's words:

> When there is thunder, it is God's voice! The Upanishads tell us, that thunder says "Da Da Da." *Damaya, Datta, Dayadhwam.* Control your passions, be charitable, be compassionate. So, the devotional type hears God's voice in the thunder, sees the body of God in the sky, beauty of God in the flower, hears prayer in the sound every tree makes. He acclaims God's glory that way! If everything is God, what about "*asat*"? There is no "*asat*," no "unreality" at all! We think all is unreal but it is suffused with God. There is God's voice, God's beauty, God's truth, God's glory, God's might in everything, in everyone and everywhere.[203]

In two of his public speeches, the guru of Puttaparthi interpreted the *da* of men as meaning *dharma,* possibly viewing the act of giving as a universal law (*sāmānyadharma*) to which all humans must conform themselves, regarding it as their primary duty and destiny:

> The *Upanishads* say that thunder teaches *Da, Da, Da, Daya* (compassion) to the ogres, *Dama* (self-control) to the gods and *Dharma* to men. Now, since man is all three—part ogre, part god, part man—he must practice all three himself; *daya* (be kind to all), *dama* (be the master of your mind and the senses) and *dharma* (be constantly alert on the path of fight); that is the advice given from the sky in the voice of thunder.[204]

> The *Upanishads* say that the thunder teaches a three-fold lesson, *da da* and *da—daya, dama* and *dharma*—to the persons entangled in these three *gunas. Dama* (self-control) to the *Satwic* who craves for *Ananda* (bliss); *dharma* (right conduct, ideals of righteousness) to the *Rajasic,* who craves for adventure, heroism and activity; and *daya* (compassion, based on Love, which enables attachment and sublimates greed) to those dominated by the *Tamasic* qualities like craving for objective pleasures through attachment to senses.[205]

As Sathya Sai Baba told Karanjia, his spiritual revolution was based on the universal religion of the three w's of work, worship, and wisdom, that is to say, of *karman, bhakti,* and *jñāna,* "in the context of the absolute equality of human brotherhood."[206] Grounded in the *trimūrti*/Dattātreya paradigm, he stressed the perfect oneness of the three *avatāra*s utilizing the analogy of the seed, the tree, and the fruit: "Let us take the example of FRUIT. It begins with the SEED which grows into the TREE and from it comes the FRUIT. WORK can be compared to the SEED, WORSHIP to the TREE and WISDOM to the FRUIT. . . . Thus the three Avatars carry the triple message of WORK, WORSHIP and WISDOM."[207] Already in the 1960s, he used to say that work, worship, and wisdom was the order of spiritual progress, these being the three paths to God.[208] Moreover:

> After all, in spiritual terms, all mankind belongs to one and the same class, caste or religion. The divine principles in each and all of them derive from one and the same God. This fundamental oneness has to be made manifest to them through direct contact with spiritual realities and the persuasive expanding power of love, till they become part of the universal religion of Work, Worship and Wisdom.[209]

In conclusion, Dattātreya is a discreet and yet constant presence in Sathya Sai Baba's avatāric career. All along, Kasturi has been well aware of this and has meticulously taken pains to articulate the Dattātreya identity of his beloved Swami. The deity surfaces along the way at crucial junctures, given that the "Hindu Trinity" plays unique theological functions. The ability to span through the dichotomies can be said to be the defining characteristic of Sathya Sai Baba and this is precisely the quintessential characteristic of Dattātreya, since the deity is understood to transcend all boundaries in a dynamic, unending process of inclusion. Mirroring the deity, the guru's extensible personality knew no limits. Because of its in-built character of bridging opposite poles, the triadic Dattātreya exhibits an even greater universalist potential than Śiva-Śakti, allowing an understanding of the triune Sai Baba *avatāra* as the comprehensive divine principle of Hinduism, Islām, Christianity, and, by extension, all world religions. In the holy man's ascendance to the role of universal guru-god the utilization and expansion of Dattātreya's assimilative paradigm was attuned to Vivekānanda's Vedāntic inclusivism, which it strengthened through the force of its "Trinitarian" scheme. Historically, Dattātreya's integrative icon may be regarded as a powerful antecedent of the inclusivist model, which Vivekānanda so efficaciously theorized in promoting Hinduism to the Western world. One more proof of how the roots of Vivekānanda's inclusivism lie deep in the assimilative character of premodern Hindu *sampradāyas*.

By asserting himself as the pinnacle of a hierarchical inclusivism, Sathya Sai Baba proclaimed that all gods—Hindu and non-Hindu—as well as the founders of all religions such as the Buddha, Jesus, Mohammed, Guru Nanak, etc. were comprehended in himself, were but different facets of his glory. The Dattātreya integrative icon was and is especially suited to enfold diverse spiritual experiences and religions, and through it Sathya Sai Baba effectively expanded his reach. With respect to the

Figure 6.5. Sculpture of Dattātreya in the Sri Sathya Sai Sanjeevani hospital recently built in Naya Raipur, Chhattisgarh.

modern and contemporary masters who were his competitors in the spiritual market, he adopted two types of responses: (1) if he acknowledged their guru-ship (as in the cases of Ramakrishna, Vivekananda, Aurobindo, Ramana Maharshi,[210] Sivananda, and Anandamayi Ma)[211] he considered them as realized persons who were in communion with him; (2) if he did not acknowledge their guru-ship (as in the cases of Meher Baba, Maharishi Mahesh Yogi,[212] and Muktananda)[213] he simply disregarded them (he usually avoided giving critical judgments about other gurus in public). In the first case he reiterated the logic of hierarchical inclusivism while in the second he excluded them altogether from the guru category (as either impostors or ordinary men, victims of self-deception). Like Ramakrishna,[214] he advised digging only one well in order to find water, that is, stay on one path, one teacher.[215] By presenting himself as the Sadguru, the assumption was that having once secured him a devotee was not to waste time looking for other, inferior teachers. In 1970, when Howard Levin first got to the master's ashram he was told by Tal Brooke: "You've made it, you know. You're one of the chosen apostles. Don't blow it. This is your big chance. This is the Second Coming of Christ!"[216]

It is noteworthy that one of the few gurus who paid homage to Sathya Sai Baba in Puttaparthi in the last decade of his life was Parama Pujya Sri Ganapathi Sachchidananda Swamiji (b. 1942), pontiff of Avadhoota Datta Peetham at the Sri Ganapathi Sachchidananda Ashram in Mysore, revered by his followers as an *avatāra* of Dattātreya.[217]

Sathya Sai Baba viewed himself to be above and beyond all gurus and movements who had become popular in the West and this is one of the reasons why—disappointing his Western followers to whom he had repeatedly promised he would visit their countries—he consciously avoided visiting Europe and the United States[218] (though he sent emissaries such as V. K. Gokak and S. Bhagavantham, to organize and promote his movement especially in the United States).[219] Not wanting to be confused with other gurus who traveled to the West in order to affirm themselves,[220] he marked his difference—the weight of his *gurutva* and self-asserted traditionalism—by remaining based in his ashram in Prasanthi Nilayam.[221]

Finally, Sathya Sai Baba was inevitably exclusivist in his inclusivism: exclusivism was part and parcel of his inclusivism given that the ultimate, supreme being could not but coincide with he himself. Though he emphasized equality on an ontological plane by saying that everyone is god and that the only difference between him and everyone else is merely epistemological (ordinary people not being aware of their divinity due to the operating force of *māyā*),[222] on the phenomenal plane he represented himself as the fullest divine descent, that is, as *stricto sensu* the *pūrṇāvatāra* of the age. By having his *darśan,* devotees believed they were witnessing the transcendent principle (*brahmatattva*) graciously descended on earth and simultaneously measured their abysmal difference from him as ordinary creatures enmeshed in their karmic ties. As Jacob Copeman and Aya Ikegame observe, "such a paradoxical message of accessibility and unattainability is a crucial mechanism in maintaining the authority and charisma of the guru."[223]

Through the powerful tool of the Dattātreya icon, Sathya Sai Baba embraced and bridged in his extensible persona Hinduism and Islām (strengthening his appropriation of Shirdi Sai Baba while at the same time minimizing his Sufi trait),[224] the *trimūrti* and the Trinity, that is, Hinduism and Christianity (expanding his universalism by presenting himself simultaneously as the supreme *Brahman* and the Holy Father), this-worldliness and other-worldliness, thus, the goals of *bhukti* and *mukti,* the domains of Brahminical purity and Tantric impurity, caste hierarchy and equality, tradition and modernity, and even the male and female genders through his purported androgynous nature.[225]

By exploiting the deity's postsectarian potential, the guru has been able to promote himself as both the ultimate *avatāra* and mankind's godhead, simultaneously fostering the immemorial heritage of the *Veda*s—by portraying himself as the source of the *śruti* and of *varṇāśramadharma*—and an egalitarian religion of universal love, understood as the comprehensive consummation of *sanātanadharma.* He was able to do so by rearticulating the ritual element, by minimizing its impact for a new, global audience while solemnly celebrating its sacredness. At the same time, the guru maximized the importance of the ethical dimension—private and public, eminently via social service—and of mystical experience, not any more constrained within the boundaries of renunciation (*saṃnyāsa*), it being open to all through the promotion of a lay spirituality.

In this way, Sathya Sai Baba succeeded in disseminating his fame worldwide by what Thomas J. Csordas has described as a "portable practice" and a "transposable message."[226] The protean Dattātreya paradigm is the key to understanding the guru's utmost freedom and unpredictability, his peculiar skill in accommodating tradition and innovation, strict discipline and a liberal approach. Tulasi Srinivas rightly points out that Sathya Sai

Baba has been capable of developing an innovative form of engaged cosmopolitanism rooted in a form of social inclusivity, given that his movement

> draws seamlessly from several great strands of religion in the subcontinent—Sufi mysticism and popular Hinduism in its Vedanta form, contemporary Christian teachings and indigenous healing rituals—to weave a constantly evolving Indic urban syncretism in which the problems of dogma, creed, and literature appear to magically fade into the background as also problems of division of caste, class, nationality and religion.[227]

This has been made possible precisely via the exploitation of the Dattātreya integrative paradigm, which stands at the very root of the guru's syncretistic ability of spanning through the dichotomies. Mirroring Dattātreya's 'integrative machine,' Sathya Sai Baba was perceived by devotees as the fountainhead of all possible meanings, allowing them to reflectively choose from his manifold identities and teachings the ones which appeared to be best suited for their spiritual uplift.[228] Along these lines, he was extolled as being both "with attributes" (*saguṇa*) and "without attributes" (*nirguṇa*), and as Kasturi remarked: "Just as when all colors merge, it becomes colorless white, when all Kalyana [beautiful] gunas assemble in One Divine Person, He is really Nirguna, attributeless."[229]

In each of the many roles he skillfully played, the hagiographer was successful in promoting Sathya Sai Baba's figure to both a Western audience as well as to a largely urban, Westernized Hindu middle and upper class by explaining his avatārahood and teachings in ways that everyone could understand. Along the decades, though challenged by the presence of an increasingly cosmopolitan public, he was able to translate the essential features of his guru's discourses and practices through a brilliant rhetoric that even non-Hindus could easily relate to. As a British devotee put it: "For the foreigners, he was a special Ambassador of Swami's Message. We absolutely adulated him. He was the *pi* to the equation! Swami was the equation, but he was the *pi*! It multiplied with him because he spoke such beautiful English; we understood it from him."[230] The Dattātreya/"Trinitarian" paradigm was a most efficacious instrument through which the hagiographer supported Sathya Sai Baba's claim to divinity as extending beyond India to embrace the whole of mankind, albeit remaining rooted within a Vedāntic theological horizon. As Hugh B. Urban writes:

> Sai Baba . . . offers a powerful vision for the preservation of traditional religious values, social structure and national identity in the face of the seemingly relentless expansion of largely Western-dominated global capitalist marketplace. Indeed as his biographer [Kasturi] very clearly puts it, Sai Baba has become incarnate not only to combat these global evils and revive the traditional Hindu spirit but also to redeem those of us in the material West from the evils of our own corrupt and godless society.[231]

The triune Sai Baba incarnation articulates the ingrained dialectics of Dattātreya as the *trimūrti*/"Trinity." At the phenomenal level, it conceives of god not as a static being but as constitutively relational, as love incarnated in the person of the *avatāra* that communicates himself to all beings and to whom all beings respond by abiding in his *preman*. Within Hinduism, this perspective is especially appealing to the more popular and *bhakti*-oriented forms of Vedānta, which are willing to concede some degree of reality to the world and to human individuality, thus safeguarding an ontology of relation.

On the other hand, in Śaṅkara's more elitist Advaita Vedānta the "lord" or personal god, Īśvara, is the "relational" aspect of *Brahman* with respect to the illusory projection of names and forms (*nāmarūpa*). Pertaining to the relative/conventional (*vyāvahārika*) level of truth/reality, Īśvara is devoid of ontological status and is himself ultimately *māyā* given that in the Absolute there can be no relations. Īśvara is therefore thought to have a preparatory, pedagogical function favoring the dawning of the recognition of the supreme truth/reality (*pāramārthika*). Śaṅkara's Vedānta theorizes a triad through which the Absolute "manifests" itself: Īśvara, the guru, and the *ātman*. But once the recognition of *Brahman* dawns, one realizes that nothing had really ever existed apart from it, and the phenomenal world "dissolves" as in a dream. Whereas for Śaṅkara this personal god is ultimately an illusory mask of *Brahman*, in the theistic schools of Vedānta he is recognized as a real manifestation of the Absolute bearing the functions of the *trimūrti*, that is, in charge of the origination, maintenance, and annihilation of the cosmos.[232] In Kasturi's and the guru's discourses, the triune Sai Baba *avatāra* has been vedāntically accommodated both ways, depending on the metaphysical orientation and spiritual receptivity of their audiences.

7

Narayan Kasturi's Last Years

In the last years of his life Kasturi had to face terrible losses, family disappointments,[1] and the inexorable deterioration of his health. According to his daughter Padma, he bore these psychological and physical hardships with composure, never complaining about them with his beloved Swami and never asking that he come to his or his dears' rescue: a word of him or just having his *darśan* was enough to console him and give him strength. Meanwhile, he continued to lecture and write incessantly and his activism mirrors the expansion of the guru's movement. By 1985, there were more than four hundred Sathya Sai Baba centers spread all over the world, excluding India: 149 in the Western Hemisphere (of which almost one hundred in the United States), seventy-two in Europe (of which forty-five were in the UK), 136 in Southeast Asia (of which seventy-eight were in Malaysia), twenty-five in South Africa, twenty-seven in the rest of Africa, and fifteen in Madagascar.[2]

After the publication of his autobiography *Loving God*, released in December 1982, the hagiographer published *Easwaramma: The Chosen Mother* in May 1984 and *Prasanthi: Pathway to Peace* in November 1985, which was to be his last opus. Kasturi was well aware that his end was approaching[3] and by daily besmearing his forehead with ash (*vibhūti*) had educated himself to be ready for death. In one of his lectures to overseas devotees, he narrated a telling episode:

> Once I was sitting in Whitefield in the verandah, Swami was there with some college students and others. Swami wanted me to speak to the students. I was sitting in a corner where

> there was not much light. I had ash drawn on my forehead as I have it now and Swami said "Yeh! Come under the light, otherwise people will think that you have a bandage." The white ash all over the forehead looked like a bandage! I came under the light. Speaking to students, I said, "Yes, the white ash is a bandage to remove bondage! To remind you that death is awaiting, that nothing is permanent, that all your property, possession, fame, honor, scholarship and medals you have won, titles you have accumulated are just a bit of ash! Bondage to property, bondage to family. The ash is all that remains in the end. Swami says, death does not ask any questions. It may come at any time and you must be ready. The camera clicks, and if you are not ready, what is the use? Be always ready for death."[4]

Significantly, he closed his autobiography with these words: "I have no knowledge of the years when I was last on earth. But I must congratulate myself that, this time, I have had good schooling. Now! I am waiting to receive my School Leaving Certificate—namely, the signal to leap into the warm lap of Sai, for the final rest in Him."[5]

The Death of Kasturi's Son

Preceded by the passing away of his son-in-law, Padma's husband Balachandran, at the beginning of the 1980s, in June 1983, at age eighty-five, Kasturi had to face the tragedy of seeing his eldest son M. Venkata Narayana Murthy die at sixty of a brain tumor. A highly reputed geologist of the Geological Survey of India, Murthy had retired in 1981 as deputy director general of southern India and had come to live in Prasanthi Nilayam in June of that same year, so as to be close to his parents and to Sathya Sai Baba, to whom he was wholly devoted.[6] During the two years he lived at the ashram, he dedicated himself to serving his mother and father[7] and to scrupulously following the instructions of his guru, on whose teachings he wrote an insightful book titled *The Greatest Adventure: Essays on the Sai Avatar and His Message* (Prasanthi Nilayam: Sai Sathya Sai Books and Publications, 1983).[8] According to the testimony of his sister, Murthy was very brave in facing his terminal illness and "didn't want to ask Swami to cure him through some miracle. He used to say, 'If I have to suffer, I will

Figure 7.1. Kasturi and Sathya Sai Baba on Christmas day of 1982, the hagiographer's birthday; on this day Kasturi's autobiography *Loving God* was released.

suffer happily. It is His blessing.' "[9] He died at the hospital of Bangalore soon after being operated on, on June 12, 1983. His family was devastated.[10] Outwardly, Kasturi's reaction was calm and he is reported to have said: "His station has come. My station is yet to come."[11] H. K. Ranganath, an ex-student of his, observes that by this time Kasturi "had reached a state of *Sthitaprajna* (a state of equanimity unperturbed by worldly callings)."[12] Regarding the death of the hagiographer's son, however, ex-devotee Eileen Weed reports quite a different story:

> Once his daughter [Padma] told me a story of something terrible Swami did to Kasturi. I forgot further details, but it had to do when Kasturi's only son died. Swami had told Kasturi

> to do something like take him to a certain doctor, Kasturi did it but the son died anyway; later, Sai told everyone that Kasturi did not follow his (Sai's) advice and that is why the son died. At that time, it seems Kasturi was boiling with rage and ordered his entire family out—his wife, daughter, grandsons, etc.—and ordered them never, ever to see Sai again. "Only I will stay, you should never come again because of this terrible deceit Sai did to us, telling such a lie." Well, the family never listened and didn't go away, but what struck me with the story was that Kasturi himself wanted to remain serving Sai, though he was totally hurt and boiling inside! Maybe he didn't want to experience more lose-face and lose the only reputation he gained in all those years. Just imagine a father's tragic despair when his god lied to everyone so sb [Sai Baba] could save his own face.[13]

Though it is not possible to establish the trustworthiness of this account—Padma in her book of memories *Twameva Matha*[14] is silent about it—I don't think it to be fabricated. That the guru told Kasturi that his son should be seen by a particular doctor is plausible, given that he frequently advised his devotees in these matters. That he blamed the hagiographer for not having followed his advice is also quite possible since he often reprimanded the people of his entourage for their purported negligence, even when they did what he had asked them to do. A strict disciplinarian, the guru would frequently scold the ashram residents for not carrying out his instructions thoroughly and appropriately.[15] Kasturi's first reaction of rage toward his master when his son died strikes me as a realistic trait: it was the anger of a hurt lover who felt abandoned and even betrayed by his beloved. It evidences the psychological difficulties and crises that characterize the asymmetrical relation between a disciple and his/her guru, even if the *śiṣya* is the master's hagiographer and foremost devotee.

If Kasturi was hurt at what he perceived was his guru's deceit, it is nonetheless impossible to prove that the latter "lied" to him, since the exact circumstances and details of his "advice" inevitably escape us. What is certain is that not only did no one in Kasturi's family ever leave Sathya Sai Baba—to this day, all of its members are devotees—but that he himself remained totally faithful to him. As he wrote in his autobiography:

> Death, disease, desertion, divorce, derision—no one of these, thanks to Swami, could deflect or distort my faith. During these years I have observed many fellow pilgrims succumb and fall behind, unable to plod forward through such gusts which they exaggerate as formidable.[16]

The idea that on the surface he continued to be devoted to his Swami out of fear of losing his "reputation" is unconvincing. I rather think that the pious *bhakta* Kasturi—even while mad at his master, being desperate at the loss of his son—came to justify the Swami's behavior, convincing himself that ultimately the guru could not but be right and he wrong. He must have rationalized the whole episode as part and parcel of his son's inescapable *karman* and as yet one more way through which the master, in his unfathomable design, chiseled his *śiṣya* by testing his surrender to him.[17] As his daughter writes: "Swami used to be generally very free with him but at times very strict. He found it very difficult to go through the hardships of the strictness of Swami. But always, after a few days everything would be normal."[18] Perhaps the guru later offered Kasturi his own explanation of what had happened, as he did on other occasions when he reprimanded him.[19]

The Death of Kasturi's Wife

In the latter part of his life, the hagiographer had also to take care of his wife Rajamma, who in 1974 had had a paralytic stroke and from then onward could move only with assistance. She stayed mostly in Prasanthi Nilayam being confined to her tiny apartment.[20] Despite the situation, she never complained but accepted her fate as god's will, being fully devoted to her Swami. With the help of a nurse, for eleven years Kasturi lovingly assisted her. In the midst of all this, the marital life of his daughter—who at the time resided with him in Prasanthi Nilayam—was beset with ongoing problems and she often complained about them, both with her father and with Sathya Sai Baba. One day, when Kasturi returned home after one of his usual lectures to foreign devotees, she burst out: "What is this? You go and talk for hours on how Swami helped this person or rescued those people, but what has He done for you? Your wife is sick. For 11 years she has been lying on the bed and see my marital problems!"[21] Apparently, the hagiographer listened to her calmly and replied:

> It is ok for you to talk in this vein, but I don't want Swami to do anything for me or my family. Whatever He does, He is Perfect, He is God. I have that faith in Him. Whomever He does it to, I consider them as my own. I do not have any attachment with you, my wife and family. From your point of view what you are saying is appreciable, but I do not have the feeling at all that He must do some miracle to me, my family, or my people.[22]

Actually, the guru used to regularly ask Kasturi about the well-being of his family and always showed concern for his health.[23] Nonetheless, the hagiographer appeared to be detached and stoic in his final years, though he continued taking care of his dear ones and being active in the ashram's life. Finally, on January 4, 1985, at 10:30 a.m.—while he was giving a lecture to overseas devotees—Kasturi's wife passed away. Padma recalls:

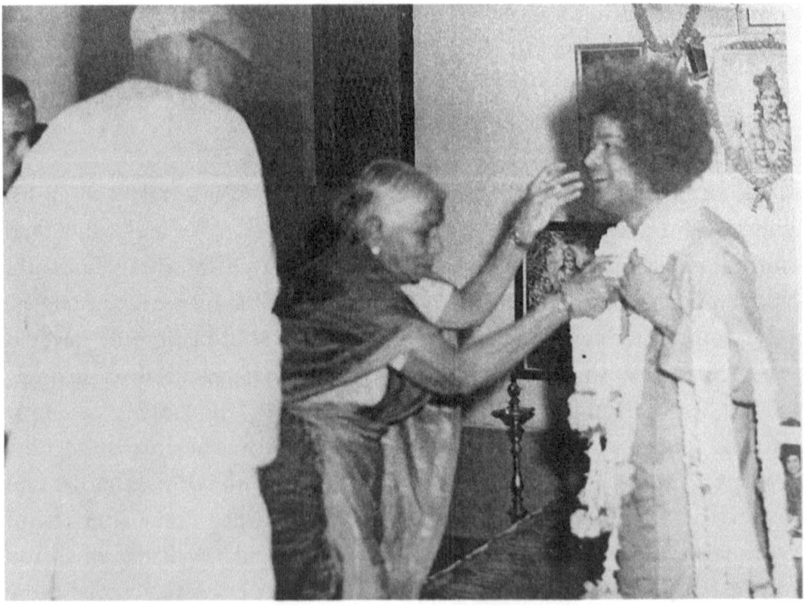

Figure 7.2. Kasturi's wife Rajamma, together with her husband, offering a garland to her lord.

> Swami immediately sent all the *bhajan* singers and Veda group saying, "She has served me for more than thirty-five years. All of you go and do *bhajan*." There was a big funeral procession with Veda chanting and *bhajan* by the ladies and men. I think all her *karma* was washed away in those eleven years of suffering.[24]

The Worsening of Kasturi's Conditions: His Declaration, "I am Atma"

For the last two and a half years of his life, the hagiographer was left alone with his daughter and his grandson Ramesh.[25] When I interviewed Kasturi on November 8, 1985, he was already not too well, suffering from severe back pain, though he considered himself blessed to be still alive at age eighty-seven.[26] In 1986, his back pain worsened to the point that he couldn't climb the stairs and walk up to the Mandir to have the *darśan* of his lord and was forced to his bed. Sathya Sai Baba eagerly inquired about him and came to visit Kasturi at his tiny apartment in the South Block a couple of times, consoling him and "materializing" *vibhūti* for him. The hagiographer pleaded with his lord, saying "Swami, give me a thump on my back. I am sure I will be all right." But the guru told him: "No, no. Take rest. Come for Darshan in a wheelchair."[27] Thus, from then onward he was taken to the Mandir on a wheelchair every day. He would be placed right in front of the door of the Swami's interview room. One morning, seeing him on his wheelchair, the guru smiled at him and jokingly said: "What Kasturi? No election, no selection and you have become a Chairman!"[28] On another occasion, pointing to the hagiographer's body, he remarked: " 'Kasturi! This is a 19th century model!' And pointing towards the interview room, added: 'Even this repair workshop cannot fix this model now.' The guru then looked deep into his eyes and asked, 'Kasturi, are you afraid?' 'No, Swami' was his reply. He then advised him: 'Take Swami's name. Don't worry!' "[29]

Despite his back problems and the fact of being forced to his bed most of the time—he was even hospitalized for a period—Kasturi continued to give lectures to overseas devotees. Here is the testimony of a devotee from the United Kingdom, Julian Wontner, in a letter he wrote to Peggy Mason dated April 18, 1988:

> I was so worried when I heard he had been ill as I got to Prasanthi Nilayam in November 1986 for the visit of the Italian Prime Minister Craxi;[30] so it was with the humblest and greatest joy that I could go to that lecture room to listen that morning when Baba gave him permission to resume his talks, even if he had to be carried to his chair. After the weeks of torture and pain on his back in hospital, Baba had healed him and gave him back his lifeline—his devoted students.
>
> We sat around his feet like mice in a kindergarten eager for him to star upon his stage again. He held us spellbound not only for one hour but I think one hour and a half, and he was so carried away he was still in full steam when someone dared to point out the time. Oh deary me, he was like a little child who had been allowed a sip of cream and in a flash had finished the lot. We scrambled to our feet and helped him out and despite his crouched infirm back and his venerable age he seemed like an ancient leprechaun or Merlin's uncle who really, secretly they said to themselves, was ageless. Such was this literary gnome whose books run along every ones shelves recounting thank goodness, for all time, the fascinating stories of Baba's life. So many of us are eternally grateful. His magic spell wafts like Baba's perfume through the secret niches in our hearts. Forever reminding us to listen to that Serene Sound of Silence. Swamiji, Baba.[31]

Kasturi also never stopped doing his work as editor of *Sanathana Sarathi*: he would dictate to Ramesh, his daughter's eldest son, and the young boy would write on the typewriter in lieu of him. When he once told the guru that he thought he couldn't manage to continue be the journal's editor anymore, Sathya Sai Baba insisted that he should not give up: "You were the editor, you are the editor, and you will be the editor till your last breath."[32]

In April 1987, the hagiographer had an attack of jaundice and became very weak. At the time, the guru happened to be in Whitefield and when the news was conveyed to him he sent him *vibhūti* through one of his aides. Nothing seemed to work, however, and Kasturi became more and more debilitated: his voice lost its usual power and his speech became feeble. Doctors said he was low on sugar and wanted to administer him glucose, but he insisted on seeking the guru's permission first. Only after

Sathya Sai Baba had been informed of his conditions did he accept following the doctors' treatments. Nonetheless, he didn't show any sign of recovery and his frame became even frailer.

Meanwhile, some people who had returned to Prasanthi Nilayam from Whitefield reported to him that his beloved lord was not well and had not given *darśan* for three-four days. As was customary, the guru's illness was explained as due to his taking upon himself the sickness of a devotee. On hearing that his Swami was sick, Kasturi immediately broke down in tears and pleaded with his daughter that he wanted to leave immediately by car for Whitefield, so as to go see his guru. Lying on his bed, he told her: "You take me early in the morning. Swami must be coming out at about 9 o'clock. I will have just one glimpse, at least, and then we can be back. I do not want anything else. Everybody is saying He has become very weak. I have to see my Swami somehow."[33] He was not in a condition to travel, however, and though she arranged a taxi for him—being moved by his burning desire and heartbreaking pleas—she was in a dilemma, since she realized that driving him all the way to Whitefield meant taking a huge risk. Against his will, she decided to inform Doctor Alreja and Mr. Kutumba Rao, who acted as the ashram's caretaker. As Padma puts it, "Though he was my father, he was also the 'property of Prasanthi Nilayam.' "[34] Doctor Alreja and Mr. Kutumba Rao discussed the issue and came to the conclusion that it was far too risky to allow him to leave in his conditions and didn't give permission. Though they tried to persuade him that staying home was the best thing to do, the hagiographer was distraught and cried the whole night lamenting his fate.[35]

The next day, with his unsteady hand, he decided to write a brief letter to the guru and to send it to him via Mr. Kutumba Rao who was leaving for Whitefield.[36] And the guru immediately replied to him. Here is his short message, dated April 1987:

> Kasturi! Accept My blessings. Do not have fear of any kind. Swami is always with you, in you, and around you. Be brave. Think of Him only. Give up thinking of anything else. The body is a water bubble. Do not worry about it. Spend your time thinking of God. Yours truly, Baba.[37]

Kasturi rejoiced at reading his lord's message though the agony of his unfulfilled *darśan* remained and he had to bear it until the month of

June, when Sathya Sai Baba finally returned to Puttaparthi. Many years before, on November 23, 1962, the guru had taught Kasturi a beautiful prayer on how he should patiently wait for him, and the hagiographer must have surely thought about it:

> Hoping You'll guide me—
>   this day or the day after—
> I await your call from day to day.
> Hoping You'll give darshan,
>   but afraid you may not,
> I'm all alert from hour to hour.
> Hoping You'll come to me straight
> This very instant,
> I'm watching and praying ever anon.
> Hoping You'll smile at me
>   at last, though not at first,
> I'm longingly gazing with thirsty eyes.
> I shall stand and stay, in deep distress
> Until my day of bliss does dawn;
> I am Yours, Your own, though exiled
>   far.
> Dear Father mine! Do heal Your
>   Child.[38]

It is a fact that the *bhakta* Kasturi always had a hard time bearing physical separation from his lord. Even back in the 1970s, the guru used to blame him for not realizing his omnipresence, beyond the physical plane. Once, during a Dasara speech the guru referred to him and said: "This Kasturi told you all those stories about My omnipresence. But shall I tell you what he does! When I am away from Puttaparthi for just a few days he sends me letters lamenting that he cannot bear the separation. He wants to touch My Feet. He says that my feet are everywhere but he complains that he has lost touch with them!"[39]

Now that he was approaching the end, he desperately pined to see his beloved. Before returning to Prasanthi Nilayam, as if responding to the hagiographer's intense yearning, the guru wrote him another message dated June 1987, reiterating his instruction to fix his mind upon him:

> Kasturi, accept My blessings. Sai is always with you, in you, and around you. Be in bliss. Do not think of anything else. Be always in the thought of God. That is the main Sadhana that you have to do now. I will come back soon. Wait for Sai. Yours, Baba.[40]

When the guru finally returned to Prasanthi Nilayam, the hagiographer eagerly went in his wheelchair to the Mandir for *darśan*. And when Sathya Sai Baba came near to him, he warned him in Telugu with the words: *nee asthamana samayam osthavundi*, meaning, "Your evening time is approaching, be ready."[41] On June 24, Kasturi wrote in an almost illegible handwriting what were to be his last words. He signed and dated this message for the book of the Malaysian devotee J. Jagadeesan[42] titled *Sai Baba: The Journey Within. Journey to God, Part III* (to be published in 1989): "Within and within, as we spread thinner and thinner and our thoughts become His creation and He . . ."[43]

Kasturi's health was now deteriorating by the day to the point that, despite his heartfelt desire to be in the guru's presence, by the month of July he could not make it to the Mandir anymore. Here is the testimony of J. Jagadeesan, dated June, 1987:

> I visited Prof. Kasturi in his room and I could just but barely conceal a gasp of sheer astonishment, shock, sorrow—for there he was, lying listlessly on his bed in the verandah of his apartment,—a frail, shadow of a great, grand old figure that I and many had grown to love. Only the twinkle of joy and love in his eyes remained of his old self. "Ah! Jegadish," he whispered. He could hardly speak—or move much of his body. I held his hands and looked at his beautiful face.[44]

He almost stopped eating, saying that food was not nourishment but rather punishment for him.[45] When his daughter sent word to the Swami about his conditions through the ashram's priest Sri Karunyananda and of his eagerness to have *darśan,* the guru said that he would soon come visit him. From that day, the hagiographer waited for him eagerly and whenever there was the slightest sound of footsteps in the room, he would expectantly ask: "Is that Swami?," "Has he come?". Padma says that it was heartrending to see how much he clamored for his beloved lord: a condition that is known as *virahabhakti* or "love in separation." In *virahabhakti,* the devotee identifies himself/herself with the intense emotions experienced by Rādhā and the other female cowherds (*gopī*) when they were separated from their lord Kṛṣṇa.[46] Ultimately, the highest distress caused by being separated from one's beloved, known as *paramaviraha,* is regarded in the *Nāradabhaktisūtras* (v. 82) as the highest form of *bhakti.* The idea is that the intense agony of the *bhakta* who eagerly awaits the return of his lord is itself the highest grace and the expression of the purest *preman.*

Meanwhile, the days passed, and during the holiday of *Gurupūrṇimā* a decisive event is said to have happened. Apparently, Kasturi experienced himself as *ātman*: it was not a purely intellectual conviction but the ultimate realization. Thus, it is believed that on the sacred day of *Gurupūrṇimā* the guru granted him "liberation while living" (*jīvanmukti*). On Saturday, July 11, while Sathya Sai Baba was delivering his discourse[47] inside the Poornachandra Auditorium and Padma sat on the steps of her father's apartment with her ears glued to the loudspeakers which conveyed the guru's booming voice, Kasturi from his bed called his grandson Ramesh and told him: "See, I am Atma. Kasturi is dead. Go and inform everybody."[48] The boy got frightened and immediately called his mother. To Padma, Kasturi repeated the very same words, adding that he should not be forced to take food anymore. She was shocked at hearing her father's announcement of being *ātman,* that is, of having experienced realization, and narrates that this event brought back to her memory something that had happened years before:

> Long ago, when Swami was in Whitefield, one Sri Gunjuru Narayana Sastri, who had the *Suka Naadi*[49] with him, came to Brindavan. He read out the *naadis* of some devotees. As he was reading my father's *naadi,* he said that my father was a *yogabhrashta* (a yogi in his previous birth) but because of some minor fault he had been born again. He said that in his last days he would experience *Nirvikalpa Samadhi*[50] (the realization of the ultimate *Brahman*).
>
> When this was read my father had a hearty laugh, "All this is bogus, Swami. How can I have *Nirvikalpa Samadhi*?" Swami replied: "Why not? Why can't you reach that state?"[51] When my father said that he was "Atma," and "Kasturi is dead,"

> I remembered His words. I thought he might have reached that state.[52]

In all evidence, Kasturi's purported last words and his daughter's selective remembrance have the function of sanctifying the hagiographer, pointing out that he was destined to a glorious end and that he did in fact achieve *mokṣa* in his final days. Having said this, I don't think that these narratives, which brought to the "hagiographication" of the hagiographer, should be regarded as a fabrication. Padma's testimony strikes me as realistic. And there is no reason to doubt that the well-known astrologer (*jyotiṣa*) Sri Gunjuru Narayana Sastri of the Sri Lakshminarasimha Jyotishalaya of Bangalore did in fact read Kasturi's *nāḍī*s, giving out his prediction. Sometime during the 1970s, this same astrologer claimed to have traced within the *Śuka Nāḍī* a *Sāī Caritāmṛta Grantha*, a manuscript prophesying Sathya Sai Baba's life, offering a variety of details on his family, personality, and present and future accomplishments. Along with other earlier "prophecies,"[53] it became quite popular among devotees.[54] We know that Sri Gunjuru Narayana Sastri visited Sathya Sai Baba's ashram and had the opportunity of meeting the guru and his entourage:[55] it was probably on such occasion that he read out Kasturi's *nāḍī*s.

The incredulity and sarcasm of the hagiographer at hearing the astrologer's prediction of him reaching *nirvikalpasamādhi* strikes me as a plausible reaction, reflecting Kasturi's personality. To be sure, he did not recognize himself in the *jyotiṣa*'s portrayal since he had never been a meditative, "yogic" type of person, being rather a practical, action-oriented man. Yet Kasturi himself believed in astrology. In the third part of his magnum opus he writes:

> There are certain remarkable ancient astrological texts called *Nadis* in South India and *Bhrgu Samhithas* in North India. They contain details of the lives of numerous persons, even of people who lived beyond the seas. The hereditary custodians of these manuscripts read out the relevant portions of the life of the person who comes to consult them. The late Dr. K. M. Munshi wrote some years ago in the Bhavan's Journal that the details recorded regarding his life in some of these manuscripts astounded him. The record mentions the exact time and place where he was to propose to Smt. Leelavathi

> Munshi. Sri Sharma, a former Chief Minister of Haryana State, states that the predictions recorded about him in *Bhrgu Samhithas* showed that he would meet God in human incarnation at Prasanthi Nilayam. Sri Sharma says that it was a job for him to find out where Prasanthi Nilayam was. . . . Whenever there is a reference in these texts to Baba, He is referred to as "the Father of all worlds, the supreme physician who cures at lightning speed and founder of *Patasalas*, institutions of higher learning and hospitals."[56]

That the guru did not rule out the possibility that the *jyotiṣa*'s prediction could come true is also credible. A traditionalist as he was, he took astrology seriously and was keen on performing rituals (such as marriages) and relevant actions (such as leaving for a journey) at the appropriate day and time, adhering to the auspicious (*amṛt, śubh, lābh,* and *car*) and inauspicious (*udveg, kāl, rogh*) time-periods (*caughaḍiyā*) within the twenty-four hours. He even advised Western devotees in such matters. Once, he told Howard Levin: "Go to Anantapur before seven-thirty. Seven-thirty to nine is not a good time to travel on Mondays."[57] With reference to numerology, the guru valued the auspiciousness of the number nine: his license plate numbers, summed together, would always amount to nine or multiples of nine. But of course Kasturi viewed his lord as being beyond the influence of the nine planets and argued that "His Anugraha (grace) can overcome the Navagraha (Nine planets) and transmute Manava (Man) into Madhava (God)."[58]

The prediction that the hagiographer would attain *nirvikalpasamādhi* in his last days resonates with a statement said to be found in the *Sāī Caritāmṛta Grantha*: "[A]ll *rishis* declare . . . that he [Sathya Sai Baba] is one in the *Nirvikalpa Samadhi* state."[59] Sri Gunjuru Narayana Sastri's interpretation of the *Śuka Nāḍī* texts was aimed at highlighting that Kasturi would reach the very same blissful condition that was inborn to his master and that he would ultimately merge with him.

By all evidence, the goal of these combined narratives—be they factual or not—is to sanctify Kasturi and to show how in the end he was capable of transcending his attachment to the master's form: by interiorizing the guru he attained spiritual oneness with him. The idea is that such final achievement was made possible because of his total surrender to the love of his life, his dear Bhagavan. Thus, we are told that from the momentous day of his realization of being *ātman* he stopped talking and was in silence, in a state of apparent bliss. Kasturi's daughter poignantly specifies that "he did not even crave for Him as pathetically as before. He was just immersed in himself. Maybe that was the realization."[60] Moreover:

> [F]ather was totally with himself, oblivious to every external sound or stimulus. . . . I thought, maybe, he is going through that transcendental liberating experience, because after that "I am the *Atma*" moment, he only wanted silence; never liked us conversing with people who came to meet him. When somebody suggested that we play *Vishnusahasranama* (the thousand names of Lord Vishnu), he out-rightly refused. He wanted absolute serenity and silence around him at all times.[61]

Kasturi's Last Days; His Death on August 14, 1987

Around the end of July, the guru sent a message to Padma saying that it would not be good for him to come to their apartment because crowds would gather and cause lots of disturbance. He told her to ask the doctors to admit her father at the local General Hospital and promised that he would come there to see him. On August 7, Kasturi had problems with urination and was taken to the hospital, as per the guru's advice. True to his word, the following day Sathya Sai Baba came to visit him. He gave him *vibhūti,* helped him drink one full glass of water, and before leaving reiterated his instruction to him: "Don't think of anything. Think of Swami only."[62] He told the doctors that he was not to be disturbed and to put a "Visitors Not Allowed" sign on the door: only Padma and her son Ramesh were to be allowed in to take care of him. Kasturi's daughter emphasizes that her father was completely in a different plane[63] and that he didn't want any sort of sound or even light. He "didn't like even us, mother and son, talking to each other. 'No . . . Silence,' he would indicate but never utter a syllable. . . . We maintained the ambience as quiet as possible."[64]

On the afternoon of August 13, Kasturi's conditions worsened. He started bleeding due to liver complications and when the doctors asked the guru whether blood should be transfused he said to give him just slow glucose and that nothing else needed to be done since his time was approaching. The next day, Friday, August 14, was to be the fatal one. In the morning, Kasturi was semiconscious and breathed with great difficulty. When word was sent to the guru through Dr. Alreja, he said not to worry and assured that he would soon come to the hospital. While giving *darśan* on the Mandir's verandah he is reported to have praised his hagiographer with these words: "From the very first day when he saw Me to the very last his faith in Me was not shaken though he went through a series of problems."[65] When the morning *bhajan*s ended, however, Sathya Sai Baba instead of directing himself to the hospital went straight to the college hostel to see the students who were rehearsing a drama. B. N. Narasimha Murthy, who was with him at the time, recalls: "Swami came to see the rehearsal of the drama to be staged by the boys on the first anniversary of the MBA course, and He seemed deeply engrossed watching the performance. But at 11:30, He suddenly stood up and said: 'I have to go, Kasturi is not well,' and went to the General Hospital."[66] In no time the guru reached the bedside of his dear devotee where Padma and Ramesh were eagerly waiting for him. He gently called into his ear "Kasturi, Kasturi," and the latter immediately opened his eyes and started to fold his palms wanting to offer his salutations (*namaskāra*). But the master caught hold of his hands and "materialized" *vibhūti* for him, applying it to his forehead and throat, and told his daughter to mix the rest of the holy ash in water and to feed it to her father. He then stroked Kasturi's fragile bodily frame and lovingly closed his eyes, emphasizing that no one should touch his body anymore.[67] He also recommended that there shouldn't be any noise in the room.[68] He ordered Padma and Ramesh to prostrate themselves and "take *namaskāra,*" implying that from then onward they would be under his care.[69] When he left the room, he told the doctors and their staff: "Only one hour more. A grand procession with a band must be arranged since he was world famous."[70] He instructed them to go to Kasturi's room and to do *nāmasmaraṇa* by repeating the *mantra Oṃ Śrī Sāī Rām*. By now the hagiographer's breathing had become smooth and slow and his face was calm. Padma mixed the guru's *vibhūti* in some Ganges water that had been purposefully brought from Benares and everyone took turns to administer it to him. Suddenly, the woman doctor who regularly checked Kasturi's pulse started chanting *Gaṇeśa Śaraṇam*, "Surrender to Gaṇeśa."[71] Padma looked at her in astonishment, and she said: "Everything is over." The hagiographer had breathed his last at 12:30 p.m., just as the guru had predicted. He was eighty-nine years old.

The guru ordered that the body be kept in a room in the Guest House next to the General Hospital, that is, in a public space so that people could come and pay their homage to him. Through Sri Karunyananda, he sent a garland to be placed over Kasturi's body and commanded that *bhajans* be sang there until 7 p.m. He also instructed that the room should be locked at 9 p.m., with no one remaining inside, and reopened at 6 a.m. the next morning. All his directions were scrupulously followed, although some expressed reservations fearing that leaving the body without custody might expose the corpse to the risk of being infested by ants. But the guru said: "No ants will come. I will take care of it. You just lock it now and open again only at 6 in the morning."[72] Through one Mr. Chiranjeevi Rao, he asked Padma if it would be all right to use a band for her father's funeral, as this was not the custom in their caste.[73] She replied: "He is Swami's Kasturi. Let Swami do whatever he likes. I have no objection or suggestions."[74] By evening, the hagiographer's relatives arrived in Prasanthi Nilayam to attend the funeral rites: Padma's other two sons Prasad and Rajaram[75] from Bangalore along with their families, and M. V. N. Murthy's son Vasanth[76] from Madras. The next morning at 6, Padma and Dr. Shanta went to the Guest House and the latter opened the room where Kasturi's body was kept.[77] They were both astonished to find out that the ambience was permeated with a wonderful fragrance and that the hagiographer's face was shining and looked lively. That morning the guru told the students in the Mandir: "I was there with him the whole night."[78] Dr. Shanta kept a diary of these happenings, starting from the day when Kasturi was taken to the hospital, on August 7. It is a precious testimony, which is worth quoting in full:

The Fountain of Death Makes the Water of Life Play

> Mr. Kasturigaru[79] was admitted to the hospital on August 7th 1987. Swami sent message to me to take care of him. He was passing blood from the rectum. We started conservative line of treatment. I.V. drips, haemostat injections, etc. On the 13th he passed blood clots. I was a bit worried. I went and informed Swami—asked Him whether I can arrange for blood transfusion. Swami said that he Himself will come and see him.
>
> Swami, as He was entering, told me to completely stop the tap from which occasionally water drops were falling. I closed it. Swami said, "It should be as silent as possible when patient is there." Then Swami came and stood in front of Kasturigaru . . . and told him. "Kasturi, see who has come. You go

on looking at Me only. Don't think of any other thing,—you think of Me." Kasturigaru was looking at Swami with a smile on his face. Swami materialized Vibhuti, gave it to the hands of Padma, daughter of Kasturigaru. Swami told her to mix it in water and to give that in sips. Swami came out. I kept one photo of Swami, where Swami was standing. Kasturigaru was staring at the photo.

Swami came downstairs, in the central hall of the hospital He started talking to Dr. Chari, "Chari, you must arrange for double band—music band—as Kasturi is very famous, popular in Karnataka. He was a well-known Radio Artist. They will announce in the All-India Radio. Funeral should be very, very grand." Dr. Chari replied, "Yes, Swami."

After a few minutes, Swami said, "Chari, only one music band will do." Then Dr. Chari said: "Yes, Swami." Swami asked him: "Do you know why? Our doctors will start the first music band. They chant Om Sri Sai Ram in such a way that though the soul does not want to go, it will leave the body immediately." Swami enjoyed His joke, and laughed loudly, mischievously, looking at us. We looked at each other. Then He told us, "Yes, you can start now. Go to his room and start chanting."

We went up and started chanting Om Sri Sai Ram. Eyes of Kasturigaru which were staring at Swami's photo closed slowly and peacefully. He breathed his last. A humourous send-off by Bhagawan to a humourist.[80]

After death, the body was shifted to the Old Travelers' Bungalow. Evening after bhajan Swami sent one flower garland with Karunyanandaji. He came put it on the body and went away. I got a message that "at 9.00 p.m. I must go and close the door of the Old Travelers' Bungalow and keep the keys with me. Morning 6.00 a.m., I must go and open the doors." I did according to the instructions. Morning when I went and opened the door, nice fragrance pushed me aside and came out. I was astonished to get good fragrance from the dead body. The body was looking as fresh as a live body. Swami in the Verandah mentioned about the incident—told that Swami was there with Mr. Kasturi, throughout night.

> Kasturigaru had served Bhagawan closely and physically. His soul after death also had the physical nearness. He was doubly blessed.[81]

Kasturi's Funeral Rites and *kapālamokṣa*

Kasturi's funeral was solemnly celebrated on the morning of August 15, Independence Day. The guru instructed that the ashram's canteen be closed and that all the colleges' staffs and students join the funeral procession after finishing the flag-hoisting ceremony. A band led the procession from the General Hospital to the bed of the Chitravathi River where the body was to be cremated,[82] with the accompaniment of Vedic recitations and the singing of *bhajans*. The crowd of devotees was so huge and overwhelming that local authorities, fearing a stampede, requested all women to leave the procession and stay in the ashram. The guru watched the whole ceremony standing on the balcony of the Prasanthi Nilayam Mandir. The cremation rite (*agnisaṃskāra*)[83] was performed by M. V. N. Murthy's son Vasanth.[84]

As soon as it was over, Sri Karunyananda came to Padma and told her: "*Amma*, your father was a superlatively great man. He attained 'Kapala moksha,' the kind of liberation-release that happens when the 'atma' or the 'life-force' floats away from the body breaking the centre of the skull. I am fortunate to be able to see this."[85] The narrative of the hagiographer's sanctity reaches here its climax. By means of *kapālamokṣa* or "liberation through the skull," the soul of the '*yogin*' Kasturi is believed to have attained definite release from the bondage of the physical body, achieving the blissful condition of oneness with *Brahman*. As it is said in *Kaṭha Upaniṣad* 6.15–17:

> When the knots are all cut,
> that bind one's heart on earth;
> Then a mortal becomes immortal—
> For such is the teaching.
> One hundred and one, the veins of the heart.
> One of them runs up to the crown of the head.[86]
> Going up by it, he reaches the immortal.
> The rest, in their ascent, spread out in all directions.
> A person the size of a thumb in the body,[87]

> always resides within the hearts of men;
> One should draw him out of the body with
> determination,
> like a reed from the grass sheath.[88]

A few hours later, Sathya Sai Baba authoritatively confirmed Sri Karunyananda's words. Padma writes:

> That evening the whole family was seated in the first row for Darshan. Swami came to me and said, "He has attained what he had to attain. You do not have to do any ceremonies. On the thirteenth day, I Myself will arrange for Narayana Seva. Ask Vasanth to collect the ashes and immerse them in the sea at Madras. Almost all the rivers merge in the sea."[89] Of course, the river "Kasturi" merged in the ocean "Swami." He gave padnamaskaram to all of us.[90]

The idea is that Kasturi attained oneness with *Brahman*, meaning liberation, and therefore there was no need to perform the ordinary rituals which are meant to "create a body" (*preta*) for the deceased in the next world and unite him with his ancestors (preventing his spirit from wandering homelessly and bothering the living as a hungry ghost). Thus, Kasturi's family was dispensed from the customary rules for mourning, such as purification ceremonies, offerings, etc.[91] Narayana Seva or "service of god," is a day consecrated to the feeding of the poor. After someone's death, it is customary to offer food to the poor in memory of the deceased. At Prasanthi Nilayam, Narayana Seva usually precedes the Dasara festival, and on this day the guru himself served food to hundreds of people.[92]

The story of the hagiographer's last days and post-mortem is intended as exemplary of a devotee's trajectory, leading to one's merging in *Brahman*/Sathya Sai Baba: as Kasturi led an ideal life, his destiny was to exit *saṃsāra* and achieve divinity. This process began well during Kasturi's life—he being unanimously revered as the guru's foremost disciple and a living legend—and was brought to completion immediately after his death with the explicit approval and support of Sathya Sai Baba, who declared him to be a world-famous personality (implicitly affirming his own worldwide, divine fame). Professor Anil Kumar describes the hagiographer as at the same time a unique figure and a universal, inspirational model: "[L]ike there is only one Luke, one Matthew or Mark; or one Meera, Shabari or Hanuman; or even one Arjuna or Vyasa, there will always be one Kasturi; but the mesmerizing fragrance of his personality will, for generations, mould the minds and motivate the hearts of millions in leading them towards their true goal."[93]

If one of Sathya Sai Baba's frequent mottos was "My life is my message," in Kasturi's case it can symmetrically be said that "the guru's message was his life."[94] And this in a twofold sense, he having been simultaneously the one who spelled out his lord's life and message for the masses through his hagiographical opus, and the one who consecrated his existence to serve his master and live up to his teachings. If objectively *Sathyam Sivam Sundaram* constituted his highest achievement—the narrative of his hero's deeds and words establishing the model to which devotees were and are expected to conform their lives—subjectively, his very existence came to be regarded as illustrative of a disciple's dedicated life.

The conviction among devotees is that Kasturi was the guru's preferred tool, having been uniquely graced by Sathya Sai Baba. Not only did he understand him intellectually and was capable of illuminating his life and teachings by beautifully writing about him, but most importantly he exercised and exemplified the guru's *upadeśa* in his daily life, being an inspiration for all. Along the years, his constant dedication to his Swami brought him to "reflect" his lord in thoughts, words, and deeds. His "hierarchical intimacy" with the guru—as Lawrence A. Babb has aptly called it—was so strong that Sathya Sai Baba functioned as a kind of mirror in which he was able to recognize his own true self.[95] In both precept and practice, he was no doubt the most powerful instrument in the dissemination of his guru's renown and in the elucidation of his teachings and mission, contributing like no other to the growth of the Sathya Sai Baba organization and the construction of a unified theological canon.

It is fair to conclude that Kasturi's life was characterized by an extraordinary, unremitting love for his guru. As he confided in his autobiography: "Love is my *sadhana*, my path, my *mantram*, my fast and my feast, my silence and my speech."[96] Moreover: "I am clinging to my Beloved, and I hope that the Beloved will accept me. I love Sai not for the reason that I get back the love but because I know that He is the most lovable person on earth. My dearest *sadhana* is to present my Beloved to all whom He loves."[97] Throughout his long life, Kasturi was an adept along the paths of disinterested action (*naiṣkarmya*) and *gurubhakti*. The burning love for his Swami—worshipped as the "Trinity" of Brahmā, Viṣṇu, and Śiva, that is to say, as Dattātreya—inspired him to engage in *sevā* by cultivating the recognition of his lord's presence in all creatures, in the awareness that service and *bhakti* are inseparable.[98] Echoing his lord, the hagiographer knew that authentic *bhakti* is not as easy as is often surmised, since it may often degenerate into emotionalism and hysteria. It must be based on *jñāna* or wisdom,[99] that is, controlled by discriminative reason and translated into action: "That is why Swami insists on *jnana*. To translate *bhakti* based on *jnana* into action is very difficult."[100] Kasturi's wise heart, his unsullied *preman,* is precisely what is believed to have finally led him to achieve the pinnacle of *jñāna,* his "river" merging into the "ocean" of Sathya Sai Baba.[101]

Kasturi's death was mourned in all Sathya Sai Baba centers throughout the world and was widely reported in Indian media. In particular, the All India Radio as well as the main newspapers of South India devoted ample coverage, remembering him as an avant-garde figure of Kannada literature as well as a pioneering radio broadcaster.[102] The newly appointed editor of the *Sanathana Sarathi* newsletter, V. K. Narasimhan, solemnly announced the demise of his legendary predecessor in the September 1987 issue:

Unto Sai a Witness

> "Death is the denouement of the drama of life," wrote Prof. Kasturi in 1981. That denouement came to him on August 14 at noon, a few minutes after Bhagavan Baba saw him in the Sathya Sai Hospital at Prasanthi Nilayam. He was 90.[103]
>
> Bhagavan Baba, who was overseeing a students' rehearsal in the College Auditorium, abruptly stopped it at 11:30 a.m. and went straight to the hospital. Reaching the bedside of Prof. Kasturi, Swami called him: "Kasturi!" Prof. Kasturi opened his eyes for a moment and looked at the Lord. Bhagavan materialized *vibhuti* and placed it in Kasturi's mouth. Kasturi closed his eyes and a serene peace enveloped him. Swami told those at the bedside to do *Namasmarana.* An hour later his spirit merged in the Lotus Feet of the Lord. Streams of devotees paid their last respects to him at the hospital.

> The next morning his mortal remains were cremated on the bed of the Chitravathi river.
>
> For over forty years he rendered devoted service to Bhagavan as writer, editor, companion and tireless propagator of Swami's life and message. Millions of devotees all over the world got acquainted with Bhagavan's life and teachings through the four volumes of *Sathyam Sivam Sundaram* (on the life of Bhagavan) and the 11 volumes of *Sathya Sai Speaks*, besides the *Vahini Series*.
>
> Prof. Kasturi was a witness to the innumerable miracles of Swami and he could bear authentic testimony to the glory and magnificence of the Avatar as few others could. He had traveled with Bhagavan all over India. Vivid accounts of his intimate experiences with Swami are given in his autobiography, *Loving God*, which was released by Swami on Christmas day in 1982.
>
> Kasturi continued to work right up to his last illness, giving of his best to *Sanathana Sarathi*, which Swami launched in 1957 with Kasturi as the Editor.
>
> After 1982 Kasturi brought out two books, one on the Lord's mother *Easwaramma*, and the other on the essence of Swami's message in a book entitled *Prasanthi*.
>
> It could be truly said of Kasturi: "Of such is the Kingdom of Heaven."[104]

Kasturi's death preceded that of his lord of almost twenty-four years since Sathya Sai Baba died of cardio-respiratory failure on April 24, 2011, at Puttaparthi's Super Specialty Hospital: he was eighty-five years old. The guru, however, had repeatedly prophesized that he would discard his body at ninety-four, ninety-five, or ninety-six, when his mission would be accomplished.[105] The leaders of the Organization have tried to "solve" this discrepancy by arguing that he would have meant the traditional lunar years, not calendar years.[106] Another theory that is current among a group of devotees is that the god-man is still active in his "subtle body" (*sūkṣmaśarīra*) and that he will continue to operate through it until the prophesized date of his demise, sometime between 2020 and 2022, after which the third Sai Baba, Prema Sai Baba, will manifest himself and carry on the avatāric mission.[107]

All in all, though Kasturi did not live to see the developments of the Sathya Sai Organization and the subsequent phases in the avatāric career of his lord, who was sixty-one years old at the time of his demise, it is impossible to overestimate the value of his contribution to the growth and direction of the guru's movement. His role was indisputably decisive and second only to Sathya Sai Baba's own leadership. Regarded as a legendary figure by devotees, his death marked the end of an era: no one within the god-man's entourage at Prasanthi Nilayam could ever replace him or match his moral and intellectual stature.

8

Epilogue

Narayan Kasturi's Legacy Lives On

> Baba is the Kalpataru come on earth;
> we need not travel in travail.
> The Tree covers every sky.
> We are in Its shade where we are.
> We approach the Tree to fulfill our wish
> but we seldom realize what the Tree does to us.
> It induces us to cling it forever.
>
> —Kasturi, *Loving God*

The hagiographer did not live to witness the worldwide expansion of his hero's fame in the 1990s and onward, and the concomitant accusations of sexual abuse and financial mishandlings voiced against him in the press and on the internet.[1] The most tragic episode, which haunted Prasanthi Nilayam, took place six years after his death, on June 6, 1993, when four youths were killed by the police after they fatally stabbed two of Sathya Sai Baba's disciples and injured two others in the guru's living quarters. The motives behind this bloodshed were never satisfactorily explained.[2] Despite various allegations against the guru—sleight of hand, fraud, and sexual overtures to young men[3]—he succeeded in expanding his celebrity and fabulously rich "kingdom." To be sure, Sathya Sai Baba has become a national glory, one of the most successful "trademarks" of India's spirituality.

Kasturi has been instrumental in promoting his Swami as a universal god-man rooted in Hinduism and yet beyond it. In these concluding remarks, I focus attention on three aspects of the Sathya Sai Baba movement, which Kasturi contributed to shape and which nowadays continue to inspire the lives of devotees, in India and all over the world. These are: the movement's peculiar universalism leading to an experience of wholeness (*ekatva*) through the promotion of self-awareness and introspection; its conceptualization of *darśan* and the crucial role of media in fostering *bhakti*; its promotion of social service and education as *the* way of putting the guru's teachings into practice and achieving liberating knowledge. Altogether, they constitute the theological vision and pragmatic agenda of both Sathya Sai Baba and his hagiographer, which the latter painstakingly championed through his tireless activism. This unified, flexible canon may be regarded as Kasturi's long-lasting legacy.

Universalism

Over time, Kasturi had become competent as no other in extracting what he regarded as the "essence" (*sāra*) of his guru's teachings, and was always keen to offer it to his readers and listeners via his books and lectures. In this regard, his last years' lectures to overseas devotees are revealing. On one of these occasions he emphatically stated: "This is the only place where all religions are considered to be facets of the same truth. There is nothing like 'All religions.' Religion has no plural. There is only one religion."[4] He especially insisted on the singularity of religion. During another of his talks, he observed: "His [Sathya Sai Baba's] message of 'sathya, dharma, shanti and prema,' and there is only one religion, the religion of love, there is only one God, He is omnipresent, stimulated unification of humanity!"[5] Kasturi echoed his master, who in one of his discourses said: "Like the seven blind men who spoke of an elephant as a pillar, fan, rope, or wall because they contacted one part, religions speak of a part and assert that their vision is total."[6]

The adoption of the Vivekanandian inclusivism of all religions, graphically represented by the *sarvadharma* emblem, led both the guru and his hagiographer to push their universalist rhetoric forward, beyond the recognition of the pluralism of religions understood as different paths leading to the same ineffable goal. The conviction that religion is universal—and not religions, meaning, its lower, particularized fragmentation—may have been due to the influence of the Theosophical Society.[7] The ideas of the Theosophical Society, with its headquarters in Adyar, Madras, were part and parcel of the neo-Hindu spirituality of the twentieth century, determining close interactions between Europeans, Americans, and the rising Indian middle class. The fact that prominent devotees of Sathya Sai Baba such as Howard Murphet and Diana Baskin were linked to it is noteworthy. Smriti Srinivas has observed that "a theosophical universalism . . . is central to the spread of the organization and the cult within and without India."[8] It should be noted that several twentieth-century Western Indologists subscribed to a theosophical worldview. Toward the end of his life, the Italian scholar Giuseppe Tucci (1894–1984) argued that "religion is universal, not religions. It is necessary to reach to cosmic religion, our Euro-Asiatic religion."[9] Even Friedrich Max Müller, the founder of the Science of Religion (*Religionswissenschaft*), maintained in Kantian fashion that there is but one religion or transcendental truth—its acme being Advaita Vedānta—and that all historical religions including Christianity contain elements of it in varying degrees.[10] That the essence of this cosmic religion, coinciding with the "Sai religion,"[11] is pure love (*preman*) or the brotherhood of man and the fatherhood of god, was Sathya Sai Baba's constant teaching: "The cultivation of Love alone can convince man of this Truth, that there is only one Caste, the Caste of Humanity, and only one Religion, the Religion of Love."[12]

The claim is made that cultural dichotomies such as East/West, India/rest of the world, etc. and all fixed juxtapositions of religious identities such as Christian versus Hindu, Islāmic versus Buddhist, etc. are ultimately illusory superimpositions. Already in his early discourses the guru remarked: "Don't confuse religion with social custom; religion is the Mother."[13] Moreover: "Now, Hindu Dharma, Christian Dharma, Muslim Dharma are identified with external conformities, mostly superstition and mumblery."[14] The idea is that a Sathya Sai Baba devotee should be able to move beyond compartmentalized religions and realize his/her oneness with the divine, that is, with the guru, himself identified with all forms of godhead[15] as well as with the whole of mankind. When Sophie Hawkins writes that "the universalist teachings of the oneness of god mask the fact that this one, omnipresent god is indeed Sai himself,"[16] she is wrong since the universalist teachings of both Sathya Sai Baba and the hagiographer did not disguise such correlation but rather tended to emphasize it. The guru proclaimed himself to be the one, omnipresent god from his early discourses: "There is no Name I do not bear; there is no Form that is not Mine"; "You are all my limbs, nourished by me; you constitute the Sai Body"; "You are I and I am you."[17] Only pure, selfless love is said to lead to such nondual (*advaita*) realization. As noted, the guru taught that "it is good to be born in a church, but it is not good to die in it."[18] The seed of nondual universalism moving beyond institutionalized religions originated with Shirdi Sai Baba himself. As I elsewhere wrote:

> In Sai Baba's training and experience, Sufism and *bhakti* were not two separate blocs. His personality is the result of a complex, nondual process of identity development, freely combining Sufi and Hindu elements. . . . Sai Baba's teaching of universalism and oneness drew on an integrative culture that had been constitutive of the Deccan for centuries. As he himself pointed out, Kabīr's legacy stands as the most authoritative paradigm for understanding his figure.[19]

And nonetheless, as Smriti Srnivas has observed, Sathya Sai Baba's—and Kasturi's—universalism is in all evidence grounded in Indic religiosity. She rightly emphasizes the guru's ambivalence, his "ability to move from a construction of Indian culture involving universal values to an inner and philological reading of scriptural traditions, from an emphasis on Vedic truths to pragmatic formulae, from an insistence on cultural roots to a theosophical universalism."[20] This capacity of simultaneously spanning through the dichotomies is the salient characteristic of the guru and his movement, which finds in the theology of Dattātreya its inspirational source, duly adapted and reframed to make it applicable to a truly global enterprise. Through it, Sathya Sai Baba was successful in creating an adaptable canon that allowed him to constantly reposition himself, encompassing the whole world without ever leaving his native village. Like Dattātreya, he could claim to be omnipresent without stepping outside of his ashram: "[I] am everywhere at all times. I need not go or come back."[21] Moreover: "I can go forward and backward in time, and learn of anything I wish. Time and space can impose no limitation on Me."[22] He stretched beyond his Indic boundaries by saying that he didn't belong to Andhra Pradesh or even to India,[23] and preached the one religion of love to his planetary audience without ever abandoning his Hindu heritage. The implementation of *sanātanadharma* is thought to be achieved precisely via this kind of rooted universalism. This is a characteristic of what Angela Rudert has called New Age gurus, who "synthesize, adapt, re-frame, re-position, and re-package for *their age*. In the process of embracing the particularly Indian and universally applicable, New Age gurus also redefine, and sometimes go beyond, boundaries to include new conversation partners, incorporate new ideas, *and* sometimes to include new adherents. And finally, they do all this without abandoning Indian spiritual heritage."[24]

Having acknowledged the guru's ability—and ambiguity—of reconciling a universalist élan with Hindu traditionalism, I still think there is something more radical in Kasturi's and Sathya Sai Baba's attitude, which can be realized if seen in the light of Dattātreya as the highest renouncer (*avadhūta*). To be sure, the *avadhūta* is the model of *mokṣa,* since he recapitulates in himself absolute freedom. My understanding is that when the hagiographer posits his guru as the savior of mankind, ushering humanity into the era of the religion of love, he is thinking of Sathya Sai Baba as the ultimate *avadhūta* who, in his antinomian autarky, goes beyond *all* institutionalized religions and thus must inevitably transcend Hinduism itself together with its rituals, norms, codes of conduct, caste ideology, etc. Though the rhetoric of inclusivity often conceals a centralized power and, as Lise McKean observes, "spirituality is Janus-faced in its effects" and "universalist claims occult the inequalities of class, caste, and gender hierarchies,"[25] still, this ideal goal must be acknowledged in all of its transformative, even transgressive potential. In this radical kind of universalism, the various religions and multifarious "names and forms" of the divine are not merely assimilated/incorporated but transcended. By emulating hagiographical models that are characteristic of Shirdi Sai Baba, Sathya Sai Baba advocated an inclusivist strategy of "both/and," while simultaneously superseding it via a supra-logical, transcending strategy of "neither/nor."[26] The paradoxical assumption is that the fulfillment of *sanātana-dharma* requires that it ultimately be bypassed and exceeded, since pure love, *preman,* knows no rules and regulations, "no reason and no season," as the guru liked to say.[27] Kasturi's claim is that Sathya Sai Baba incarnates the universal freedom of the *avadhūta* taken to its maximal extension, in a cosmopolitan dimension beyond the cultural boundaries of India and Hinduism: this is the utopian conviction that the hagiographer fostered and which constitutes his legacy.

After Kasturi's death, the constituency of the Sathya Sai Baba Organization has continued to grow, both in India and abroad. Smriti Srinivas reports that in 2001 there was an estimate of around nine thousand official

Sathya Sai Baba Centers present in India and two thousand others disseminated throughout the world in more than 130 countries.[28] She points out that the god-man's following can be distinguished into two main groups: urban middle-class and upper-class Indian nationals and non-Indian devotees together with Indians of the diaspora.[29] The fact that outside India the guru's transnational movement has been able to draw people from all over the globe as well as Indian immigrants is indicative of its ductile charisma given that most contemporary guru movements either attract mainly Indian immigrants or draw Westerners to their fold.[30] The difference with the Shirdi Sai Baba's constituency—despite its similar universalist claim and composite, nonsectarian spirituality—is striking in this regard, given that outside India the number of Shirdi Sai Baba's non-Indian followers is small: his devotees are 90 percent Indians and their absolute majority is Hindu (among them, only a small number revere Sathya Sai Baba as an incarnation of Shirdi Sai Baba).[31] Thus, whereas in the case of the saint of Shirdi Western *bhakta*s are few and their role is negligible, in Sathya Sai Baba's constituency their number is high and their role in the movement significant.

I think that this contrast is to be largely explained by the difference in function that the ritual element has played and still plays in the two constituencies. Whereas devotion to Shirdi Sai Baba has been spreading outside India in much the same way that it spread within the country,[32] that is, through the construction of temples that Indian immigrants have built for him (in Malaysia, Singapore, Australia, New Zealand, the United States, Canada, etc.), in the Sathya Sai Baba movement no dedicated temples have ever been erected to the self-proclaimed *avatāra,* neither in India nor outside of it. This trait is part and parcel of Sathya Sai Baba's and Kasturi's universalist strategy, given that the guru was always contrary to building temples in his honor. In India, the guru would visit and frequently consecrate temples of Shirdi Sai Baba but not of himself: to my knowledge, with the possible exception of the Guindy Mandir near Madras (Chennai), erected in 1946 (his first spiritual center, housing an image of Shirdi Sai Baba), Sathya Sai Baba temples have never been built. If the ritual dimension, and specifically that of temple ritual, is *the* way through which Shirdi Sai Baba's figure has been exported to the Western world, the Sathya Sai Baba Organization has succeeded in expanding its constituency abroad precisely by minimizing its impact.[33] As Karline McLain observes in her recent book on the afterlife of the Shirdi saint, the "Shirdi Sai Baba temples in North America typically have not been successful in attracting many devotees who are not ethnically South Asian, in spite of their inclusive theology and rhetoric."[34]

The Sathya Sai Baba Centers worldwide organize their Thursday weekly gatherings in either public or private spaces, which are not infrequently devotees' homes. At these congregational meetings, the guru's teachings are read and meditated upon and worship is performed through the singing of devotional hymns (*bhajans*) in both Sanskrit and whatever be the local language spoken by the followers. If English is the main *lingua franca* in use, the movement's nonreliance on Sanskrit as the mandatory sacred language indicates its capacity to accommodate itself to various cultural contexts, cutting across class and caste barriers. To my knowledge, only the ceremony of *ārtī,* which closes every meeting, is sung in Sanskrit and it is only at this point that a ritual practice that consciously mimics the Hindu *pūjā* as enacted in Prasanthi Nilayam is performed, though many adaptations of it have been devised along the years and the man or woman who devoutly waves the camphor flame in front of Sathya Sai Baba's image/chair may belong to whatever nationality and social class. A testimonial to the ambivalent inclinations of Western devotees is found in a report of the movement's American Council, written in 2000, for improving the Sathya Sai Baba Centers: "Many people wanted more English devotional songs and fewer Sanskrit *bhajans*. They wanted less ritual (e.g., *arati*, Sanskrit prayers, prostration). And yet, many Western devotees thrive on the Eastern ways of doing things and would rather not switch styles."[35]

Over the years, the Sathya Sai Baba movement has succeeded in adapting itself to the different needs and sensibilities of its followers, both in India and abroad. Its avoidance of rigid rules and sectarian dogmatism, its careful balance between any given cultural context and the ways and forms of expressing devotion to the guru, has proven to be its strength. As Norris W. Palmer observes:

> In some centers this requirement of balance has meant following Swami's mandate that at every *satsang* [meeting] at which overseas devotees are present, at least one *bhajan* must be sung in the native tongue of that devotee, and that the spiritual significance of Sai Programs is to be explained in newcomer orientation workshops to ward off the possible appearance of cultism.[36]

In this way, the movement has been capable of attracting a large following of people who are not ethnically Hindus or South Asians but who have nonetheless adopted the guru of Puttaparthi as their personal god.[37] Sathya Sai Baba and his hagiographer were effective in promoting a more and more de-ethnicized Hinduism,[38] a universalist discourse, which they substantiated through a set of theological principles and ethical codes that placed minimal requirements on devotees and could easily be adopted globally. If by emphasizing Hindu orthopraxis, that is, the ritual dimension, Shirdi Sai Baba has developed into an ethnic guru-god and one of the main deities of the Hindu diaspora, by emphasizing the ethical dimension of the "universal religion of love," Sathya Sai Baba has elevated himself to the status of supreme god and savior-of-mankind figure, who purportedly transcends the boundaries of his own religion and culture. Moreover, such cosmopolitan openness and potential for expansion is theologically enhanced by the prophecy of his future incarnation as Prema Sai Baba.

Although Sathya Sai Baba's and Kasturi's universalist/ecumenical message goes to the paradoxical extreme of distancing itself from Hinduism,[39] what we see going on even today in the guru's headquarter of Prasanthi Nilayam is the daily performance of *nāgarasankīrtan*s, *bhajan*s, and Vedic recitations and rituals led by both pundits and students of his schools. It was the Swami's explicit will, up to the end of his life, that Vedic rituals be performed at the ashram as well as throughout India and even abroad, and that they should be open to Westerners.[40] The practice of *pūjā* and the singing of Sanskrit and Hindi *bhajan*s is a defining characteristic of Sathya Sai Baba Centers throughout India. Moreover, if it is true that outside India many Western devotees wish to deemphasize the "Indianness" of their lord and thus want to worship him having minimal recourse to Hindu ritual, it is also true that for many other Westerners the recitation of Sanskrit *mantra*s and *bhajan*s and the performance of the *ārtī,* etc. are perceived as fundamental aspects of their identity as Sathya Sai Baba followers. In short, what the charismatic guru and his foresighted hagiographer have taken pains to articulate is an open canon, capable of adapting itself to the different needs and expectations of the movement's cosmopolitan constituency.[41] They have surely been successful at this, and once again the Dattātreya paradigm appears as the key to appreciating the god-man's discourse in its capacity to include the local and the foreign, the national and the transnational, ethnicity and universality, with Prasanthi Nilayam standing all along as the uncontested center of spiritual authority, attracting people from all corners of the globe. Indeed, because of the presence in Prasanthi Nilayam of men and women from all over the world, devotees think of it as a United Nations of sorts.

When talking to overseas followers, Kasturi was always keen to stress the point that Sathya Sai Baba was not to be understood as the founder of a new cult. Here are some of his statements:

> Swami has not come to establish a cult of His own. He does not want to be worshipped. That is a very rare, very unique thing in this Avatar. He said in a letter which He wrote when He was young, "*naku vooroo ledu, peroo ledu.*" "I have no place, I have no name." Call Me by any name, I will answer.[42]

> He does not want to be a cult figure. He has come to strengthen the roots of all religions, to establish the validity of all paths to God, like reaching the Everest by the southern path or any other path.[43]

> Swami is not for a cult. What He wants is to take us on the road to God, to merge in our source, He takes us to the goal, step by step.[44]

> He has said not to have His picture displayed in human values classes held all over the country and abroad . . . no one need to have a uniform. There are some gurus whose followers must wear a particular type of dress.[45] But, so far as Swami is concerned, no uniform dress, no uniform mantra, no uniform religion even![46]

The guru voiced this same argument on numerous occasions already in his early discourses: "I have not come to set afoot a new cult"; "I do not call upon you to cultivate faith in Me or to worship Me; cultivate faith in yourselves and worship the Lord who is utilizing you as his instrument."[47] Sathya Sai Baba's strategy has been that of positing himself as the inner core/truth of each and all religions, hence the pointlessness of erecting temples to him. By presenting himself as the rescuer of all faiths come to earth to revive the *dharma* of Hinduism and of all religions,[48] he placed himself above all creeds as their underlying spirit, their veritable pristine source. Ultimately, he claimed to be beyond name and form.[49] As Kasturi effectively articulates in the last book he wrote, *Prasanthi: Pathway to Peace*, the guru is not to be conceived as an individual but rather as a principle (*tattva*), an "it," meaning, pure *Brahman*. Thus, Sathya Sai Baba would have once shown John S. Hislop, who accompanied him on a road journey, his "true self" limitless as the sky and unfathomable as the depths of the ocean, a "formless form" containing everything within itself:

> At some point in the journey, perhaps about halfway, Baba was talking and I turned to look. My breathing stopped and I was transfixed! What transfixed my movements and stopped my breathing now, was his face—the Baba I knew was not there! Instead there was a face of extraordinary beauty—quite different in shape and cast of features of our beloved Sai. Never in my life . . . have I seen a face of such exquisite beauty. It was beyond imagination and concept, beyond experience. And his color was blue . . . deep blue, like velvet blue that sometimes can be seen in a dark sky, like blue that I have at times seen from the deck of a ship thousands of miles from shore on the Pacific Ocean. "Swami, what was that blue color?" He replied, "Oh! That? Whenever there is something of unfathomable depth it appears to be deep blue."[50]

The guru aimed at presenting himself as the unfathomable *grund* of godhead, the nameless/formless transcendent principle, and this is the reason why Kasturi, in his faithful exegesis, insisted that Sathya Sai Baba should not be confused with the founder of a new faith or with one of the many gurus available on the marketplace of spirituality. Correspondingly, the god-man taught that devotees should not change their religion and "convert" to Sai Baba or Hinduism.[51] By claiming to mystically contain all religions within himself, of being the enlivening spirit of them all, the lord of Puttaparthi inevitably exceeded all individualized cult figures. He thus established himself as the universal god from whom all deities and religions derive their partial/circumscribed truth and authority.

Through his inclusivist strategy, Sathya Sai Baba asserted himself as the uncontainable god of gods, above and beyond particularized faiths. As Sophie Hawkins writes: "Sai Baba's role is consistently perceived in global terms by devotees: as 'world teacher, planetary Christ,' the 'Cosmic Emperor' . . . of 'all nations, all cultures, all languages.'"[52] Through such resourceful theological setup, in which he posited himself as both the means and the goal, he was able to declare himself not to be a cult figure while all along proposing his "impersonal persona" as the supreme "object" of worship for all humanity. In this way he could pretend not to be confined to Hinduism while claiming that all people, notwithstanding their own religion, should recognize him as their final goal. Finally, the idea is that the only fitting temple of Sathya Sai Baba—understood as a purely spiritual principle—is the "temple of the heart," the inner sanctum of each and all creatures. As he solemnly declared: "I am the divinity that is your reality."[53] Such mystical dimension resonates with the prophesized advent of Prema Sai Baba, who, as the guru foretold, will lead mankind to the final realization that not only does god reside in everyone but that everyone *is* god.

Throughout the decades, this all-encompassing strategy—setting Sathya Sai Baba above and beyond all other gurus—proved rewarding in expanding the god-man's transnational movement and Kasturi, as always, was its most enthusiastic spokesman. The hagiographer tirelessly insisted that his Swami's universalism be understood in spiritual terms, not by erecting stone temples or establishing a Sathya Sai Baba church or religion but by coming to realize his abiding presence first and foremost in one's heart. He fully subscribed to what Jesus told the Samaritan woman in John 4.24: "God is spirit, and those who worship him must worship in spirit and in truth," and firmly believed that with Sathya Sai Baba's advent the time of the "religion of the spirit" had finally come. By expanding the guru's universalist theology via the comprehensive passe-partout of the triune Dattātreya, he efficaciously promoted his lord as the ultimate hypostasis of *Brahman* which transcends all names and forms and yet is immanent everywhere, filling the entire cosmos.

The Experience of *darśan*: Old and New Media

The experience of *darśan* was and still is the alpha and omega in the worship of the guru-god. Seeing Sathya Sai Baba and being seen by him—in an exchange of gazes and counter-gazes of mutual recognition—was the crowning of a pilgrimage to Prasanthi Nilayam, the foundation upon which one's relation with the god-man rested, and from which physical contact with him (*sparśana,* such as touching his feet) and conversation with him (*sambhāṣaṇa,* as in the interviews which he granted) could eventually be derived. *Darśan* is truly the most crucial element in the life of a *bhakta,* since it kindles and fosters devotion.[54] Even Kasturi—though convinced of the guru's omnipresence—pined for just catching a glimpse of his form up to the last days of his life, the separation from his lord being intolerable to him.

Mediating the Swami's presence or, in other words, spanning the dichotomy between visibility and invisibility, seeing and non-seeing, was one of the hagiographer's tasks in order to promote his guru's fame, which he accomplished through his magnum opus *Sathyam Sivam Sundaram,* as well as through his other publications and tireless activities as lecturer, teacher, president of the Sathya Sai Baba Organization, etc. His objective was twofold: to attract people to Puttaparthi's ashram, so that they could experience the transformative power of the guru's physical presence, and at the same time to convince them that the *avatāra* was not confined to Prasanthi Nilayam. He would articulate Sathya Sai Baba's omnipresence by narrating many miracles of his appearing to devotees living thousands of kilometers away and of *vibhūti* and other substances emanating from his pictures. He writes:

> He announces His presence by signs, by fragrances, by flashes of light, by the swinging of pictures and of garlands, by the formation of Pranava on pictures, by foot prints marked out on the floor. For example, He has, for the sake of the people who find it difficult or costly to make the journey to Puttaparthi, manifested Himself clearly inside the marble Linga of an old Siva Temple at Kothanaghatta.[55]

Not only was the guru said to manifest himself in far-off places. He was also believed to offer personal instruction by granting "inner views," most commonly through dreams so as to solve devotees' doubts. These "inner views" were said to correspond to the interviews the god-man granted daily to a fortunate few. Significantly, Kasturi writes that Sathya Sai Baba's interview room was popularly known in Telugu as the *korike* room, the wish-fulfilling room.[56]

Through his narratives of the guru's magic, Kasturi favored a spatial and temporal displacement, which hinted at the illusory nature of space and time. He was able to convince his audience that the god-man was not bound by either of them, being present everywhere and at all times both visibly and/or invisibly.[57] He writes: "He can be in more than one place at the same time, as He did in December 1964 when He was both at Venkatagiri in Andhra and Manjeri in Kerala."[58] As Smriti Srinivas has shown, fostering the belief in miraculous encounters—which is one of the leitmotivs of Kasturi's hagiography and of all devotional sources on Sathya Sai Baba—was a crucial endeavor since it overcame the problem of distance: the belief in the guru's "nomadic charisma" greatly contributed to his success in attracting followers outside of India as well as Indian immigrants.[59] All the guru's devotees, be they residing in Prasanthi Nilayam or elsewhere, lived and live in an atmosphere saturated with magic: a truly enchanted world, which coexists with modernity and carries with itself an implicit critique of rationality.[60] The role of magic and of the forces of the imaginary in the construction of reality is paramount in the Sathya Sai Baba movement. As Bruce Kapferer observes, through magical practice, "people are able to establish their own original relation to existential reality and to reorient themselves into surrounding realities."[61] Modern magical practices must not be viewed as relics of the past but understood in the contexts of their use, given that traditional continuities are a function of the political and social structures of the present.[62]

Kasturi put his plural competences at work by thoroughly utilizing the media that were available to him in the service of the *avatāra.* His objective was to reach out to the whole world. Not only was he a skillful writer, a meticulous editor and translator, and a passionate, entertaining lecturer. He was also a poet, a humorist, a theatrical actor, and a journalist who had accumulated experience by working for various magazines, newspapers, and the *All India Radio.* Remembering his days at the *All India Radio*, Kasturi writes: "I did my best to justify His selecting me for that job. Simultaneously, I prayed to Him to bless me with another role, where I could broadcast His Advent and His Message."[63] He even acted as consultant and screenwriter for the first films[64] that were produced on the guru (such as the ones of Richard Bock), and through the telling of the *Sai Bhagavatha* poem together with his son Murthy he played a role akin to that of a traditional *kīrtankār,* a song-sermon performer.

No one understood better than Kasturi the importance of promoting his hero's figure by putting to use the media he was most familiar with, first and foremost the written word. Starting in the early 1960s, through his publications he was able to disseminate Sathya Sai Baba's life and teachings to an increasing number of people, in India and throughout the globe, literally reaching millions of readers. He also offered the mediated *darśan* of the god-man through the use of black-and-white and colored photos and pictures, which were part and parcel of his official hagiography and of various other works which he either penned (such as his autobiography) or edited/translated (via the covers of the *Vahini Series* as well as the guru's photos published in the *Sanathana Sarathi* newsletter). This of course was Sathya Sai Baba's own strategy, given that all the objects and pictures of himself and other gods that he "materialized" for his devotees were understood to convey his power and omnipresence. Indeed, even Shirdi Sai Baba recommended his followers to worship his picture saying that he abided therein. Thus, we read: "Baba gave my grandfather a picture of himself and said: 'Take this picture home with you. Know that I am in the picture in your home and henceforth don't come to Shirdi.' "[65]

Figure 8.1. Sathya Sai Baba and Kasturi on the day of the guru's birthday.

Though Kasturi did not live to see the emergence of computer technology and the revolution of digital and visual media distributed over the internet, there is no doubt that he would not have missed the opportunity to put the World Wide Web to use in order to spread the "good news" of his lord, as the official Sathya Sai Baba Organization has effectively done and does through its extensive websites, which have become the primary mode of disseminating the guru's message.[66] Kasturi appreciated all new means of communication, and already in his 1966 commentary to one of the guru's 108 names—the nineteenth, *Oṃ Śrī Yaśaḥkāya Śirḍī Vāsine Namaḥ*—he remarked:

> In the Sathya Sai form, the "Yasah" or fame is spreading faster and farther; for, now, the new means of communication are being used to the fullest extent.[67]

Nowadays, the amount of information about Sathya Sai Baba available on line is staggering. And yet, it should be noted that the guru himself was highly critical of the internet. The major reason for this was that he could exercise no control over the discordant mass of information provided on him by the Web, which starting in the 1990s increased the global awareness of the allegations voiced against the Swami. As Norris W. Palmer observes, "The free flow of information via the Internet provides an indication of the degree to which geopolitical borders are meaningless."[68] From his headquarters in Prasanthi Nilayam, the guru could in no way govern and correct such unending flow of information, and even less could he stop it or prevent it. In a discourse he held during the Dasara festival of October 15, 1999, he spoke about the role of the internet in spreading what he called "false propaganda," arguing that he had nothing to do with it:

> All the trials and tribulations faced in this world are due to the so-called development in science and technology. It is not technology but it is "tricknology." Do not become a slave to such technology. . . . Swami has nothing to do with Internet. Not only now, even in future also you should not indulge in such wrong activities.[69]

The guru had an ambivalent attitude toward science. He criticized it—positing himself as a traditionalist—and yet recognized many of its achievements. It is fair to say that he maintained an overall negative opinion about it. Paraphrasing the *Rāmāyaṇa* epic, he once said that the demon Rāvaṇa's greatest error was that he robbed *prakṛti,* that is, nature (Sītā), from *prakṛti*'s master (Rāma):

> Your scientists are committing the same mistake today and are bound to drag all who fete them and follow them into perdition. Sitha is Nature, Prakrthi; the daughter of the Earth, found in a furrow. Ravana kidnapped Prakrthi; Science is exploiting Nature and proud that it has conquered Her. But, Ravana did not pay heed to Nature's Lord, Rama. Science does not revere life; it is not humble, not afraid to insult and injure Prakrthi. It denies Rama, Prakrthi's Lord.[70]

But of course, despite the guru's critical attitude toward the new media,[71] the Sathya Sai Baba Organization as all other major god-man's movements could not but "embark" itself on the ship of the Web and surf through its perilous waves: this is so true that the Swami's devotees call the cyberspace "Saiberspace."[72] Entering the internet arena was a vital need for the movement, not only in order to face the competition[73] of other gurus and promote the message of its lord, but also to counter the accusations voiced against him by his opponents in the global market of spirituality.[74] The Swami's discourses can all be freely downloaded from the official Sathya Sai Baba website. The competent *bhakta*s who are in charge of what their god defined as the new "tricknologies"[75]—an ironic neologism, given the guru's fame as a trickster—are walking in Kasturi's steps and are no doubt to be regarded as the hagiographer's natural heirs, the dangers and ambiguities of the internet's "open government" notwithstanding. Indeed, most of Kasturi's works, starting with the four volumes of *Sathyam Sivam Sundaram*, have been made available on the Web and can easily be downloaded for the benefit of devotees all over the world. The hagiographer would have certainly welcomed as a dream come true the unprecedented opportunities offered by the open access of texts and the transferring of visual images and audio recordings from the locale of their production to an infinite number of places and cultural milieus worldwide.

Mention must here be made of the creation in 2017 of the Shri Sathya Sai Archives Building, which had received the Swami's prior blessings and consent. Its treasures include thousands of hours of audio recordings and video recordings of the guru (taken by professionals as well as countless individuals), images and photos of him from the 1940s onward, and circa five thousand manuscripts written by Sathya Sai Baba, which comprise handwritten letters (even the "historical" one he wrote to his brother Seshama Raju, and which was in Kasturi's possession), poems, songs, articles for *Sanathana Sarathi*, etc. All these documents are presently being digitized so as to preserve them for posterity.

Even within the context of the new media, it is important to highlight the three types of *darśan* that were and are most valued by *bhakta*s: (1) in the first place, the experience of physical proximity with the guru at his ashram in Prasanthi Nilayam, regarded as a decisive turning point since it was thought to trigger the transformation of an individual[76] (after the guru's death in April 2011,[77] most powerful is thought to be the pilgrimage to his tomb or *samādhi*); (2) the mediated *darśan*[78] that the internet, a film/television broadcast, a *mūrti,* a picture, a photo, or the god-man's voice—preserved and disseminated through Radio Sai Global Harmony, which was inaugurated with the guru's blessings—instantly provide, and which are also believed to convey his actual presence, being charged by his power (*śakti*); (3) the realization of the god-man's omnipresence—in oneself, in others, and everywhere—achieved through a combination of *sevā* and meditative practices: a state of inner communion that is regarded as the culmination of one's *sādhanā* given that it transcends the subject-object dichotomy. Everything and everyone is then experienced as being saturated with him, and the *darśan* of the lord becomes a constant, uninterrupted experience: indeed, there is only him! Of course, this third modality of "seeing/recognizing the divine" was and is reserved to only a handful of virtuosi.

In his last days, Kasturi was believed to have had access to this highest realization, that is, the interiorization of the "Sai principle" leading to *mokṣa*. By emphasizing the guru's magical omnipresence throughout his works, he endeavored to intellectually predispose all devotees to this ultimate experience that all are expected to achieve sooner or later. From the 1950s, the hagiographer saw it as his special *dharma* to inform everyone of the god-man's life and teachings, whereas the actual transformation of the people's minds was inevitably left to the will (*saṃkalpa*) of the ubiquitous *avatāra*. Sophie Hawkins rightly points out that "Sai Baba was seen to be multi-locational (omnipresent) long before virtual technology was popularly available,"[79] and this dissemination of the guru's purported omnipresence was largely dependent on Kasturi's painstaking efforts.

The god-man's mediated *darśan,* be it through films/photos on the internet or popular posters—in which his image is, variously, combined with Shirdi Sai Baba, Jesus, the Buddha, and all the gods of the Hindu pantheon—mirrors his continual shift between the real and the mythic.[80] Spiritual commodities travel far and wide at the speed of a click in the digital world,[81] and the life of the guru's images binds together the material and the virtual, one's life at home and sacred Puttaparthi, the holy man's personal immanence and his imagined transcendence.[82] As Kasturi well knew, what makes these images come alive is devotion: devotees "charge" the guru's images with power, *śakti,* making them into veritable visual "texts" and "hagiographic machines." Inspired by them, countless stories of Sathya Sai Baba's divinity are (re)created/fantasized and relived/brought back to memory, and these stories are the substance upon which *bhakti* thrives. As Sophie Hawkins writes: "The images, through their figural representing of Sai, are then implicit markers of a space wherein the dualisms of myth and history, sacred and secular, local and global, subject and object, etc., are co-presently validated."[83]

Education and Service to Society

Through the Ramakrishna Mission, Kasturi had enthusiastically dedicated himself to the service of society and to a variety of educational activities from his early years, prior to his meeting the guru of Puttaparthi. To him, it came natural to full-heartedly embrace Sathya Sai Baba's *sevā* projects and educational concerns, which he envisioned as the followup to his work with his students in college as an adept of Vivekananda's *karmayoga.* The hagiographer knew well that his vocation was to devote himself to *karman,* "love in action," since he was not made for a life of renunciation, of passive and solitary contemplation.[84] In this he was attuned to the neo-Hindu perspective of his Swami who, though falling into the category of the renouncer, always had the student (*brahmacārin*) and the lay householder (*gṛhastha*) as the main targets of his mission.[85] In the guru's teaching, the call to renunciation (*saṃnyāsa*) was either minimized or subsumed under the *naiṣkarmya* doctrine of the *Bhagavadgītā,* reinterpreted along Vivekanandian lines as selfless service to be rendered to society at large, as per his dictum "heads in the forest, hands in society."[86] When in 1977 the island of Divi Seema in Andhra Pradesh was hit hard by a six-meter high wave which killed thousands, eighty-year-old Kasturi was among the Seva Dals who moved to the area to offer food and shelter to the local population. When the emergency was over, even before looking at a photo album documenting the work devotees had done there, the guru asked: "Where is the photo of Kasturi visiting that small hut where he consoled the old people?"[87]

In his discourses the Swami taught that the practice of *sevā* was to be understood as the natural outcome of *bhakti,* since it inspired the recognition of god's presence in one's fellow beings. For both Sathya Sai Baba and Shirdi Sai Baba, devotion to the guru was the precondition to the outpouring of grace, which led to the recognition of god, the *guru-tattva,* present in each and every person. The final experience of oneness is said to be achieved through the cultivation of selfless service in which the relational element, the bond of love with the "other"—understood to be none else than the guru—is essential.[88] The theological assumption is that only god can worship god. In order to recognize oneself and one's neighbor as god, that is to say, as *ātman,* the royal path is said to be none other than *preman,* selfless love. As Sathya Sai Baba pointed out:

> When you have freed yourselves of Vibhakthi [separation], Bhakthi manifests. . . . Krishna [in the *Bhagavadgītā*] did not insist on man thinking of Him only and of no other. What he meant was, "You have to give up the thought of 'the other;' there is no Anya, other, any one different. All are one. When you have discarded all thoughts of 'the other,' the loving God loves you as His own."[89]

The etymological understanding of Datta/Dattātreya as "the given" (to Atri and to the whole of humanity) leads to an understanding of life as an oblation to god and one's fellow beings: the secret of existence, its raison d'être, resides ultimately in donating it, in "giving and forgiving" as the guru used to say.[90] Here, the weight attributed to the relational element which is linked to the reconceptualization of the *trimūrti* (Dattātreya as the Trinity) is a clear indication of the influence of Christian theology, at least at the ordinary (*vyāvahārika*) level of experience.[91]

Under the constant supervision of its leader, over the decades the Sathya Sai Baba Organization has undertaken a variety of projects in the fields of education and social service—primarily in India but also overseas—especially through its schools (from elementary education to university, implementing its Education in Human Values program) and the helping of the poor and the sick (providing food, building high-tech hospitals where people are cured free of charge, etc.).[92] Smriti Srinivas has cogently described the guru's teachings and *sevā* projects in terms of a "bio-civic ethics."[93] As she argues, devotion to Sathya Sai Baba is "a sensory moral praxis that establishes a meaningful and transformative relationship between the body-self and civic space—a sphere of embodied citizenship."[94] The idea is that the guru's ethical codes and spirit of service should be implemented in all public spheres, in politics as well as economy.[95] As Norris W. Palmer notes:

> The Trust concerns itself mainly with benevolent projects within India and is said to have established an impressive record in providing education, health care, relief to the most destitute, and, more recently, potable water to hundreds of thousands, all without cost to those receiving the benefits. The many institutions in and around Prasanthi Nilayam . . . are representative examples of the interests of the Trust, and projects of a similar nature dot the landscape of southern India.[96]

As a professor and educator, Kasturi put his professional skills at the service of his lord who untiringly reminded students and devotees alike that "the end of education is character."[97] The god-man underlined that "education that does not confer humility and discrimination is a sheer waste of precious time,"[98] and constantly reminded people that his avatāric mission of bringing about the reestablishment of morality and righteousness (*dharmasthāpana*) required that it be undertaken through a reform of the educational system, for—in the hagiographer's words—"every year . . . [schools] pump into the stream of national life the perfidious poison of irreverence, indiscipline, inefficiency, and rootless culture."[99]

Every two weeks Kasturi used to give lectures to the students of Sathya Sai Baba's institutes in and around Prasanthi Nilayam,[100] strengthening his moral lessons through stories culled from the guru's life or from his personal interaction with him. The students regarded the hagiographer as being second only to their master in authority and wisdom, and through his communicative competence he was able to hold his young listeners spellbound. Periodically, Kasturi even went on tours throughout Andhra

Pradesh giving lectures to thousands of students of the guru's colleges and schools. As per his guru's order, he instructed a multitude of Bal Vikas, Junior Seva Dals, and Seva Dals and played a pivotal role as organizer and speaker at the annual Summer Schools which for many years were held at the ashram and saw the participation of Indians and Westerners alike. Moreover, all of the hagiographer's books circulated widely among Sathya Sai Baba's students and *sevā* workers, functioning as powerful instruments for the implementation of the guru's ethics.

Through their painstaking endeavor, Kasturi and the god-man were successful in promoting the Sathya Sai Baba Organization as a transnational movement active in a variety of overlapping fields such as education, social assistance, and medicine. For both of them, the Ramakrishna Mission and the neo-Hindu gurus of the colonial period were inspirational models, being to a greater or lesser extent influenced by the social activism of Christian missionaries.[101] The engagement of the Sathya Sai Baba Organization in the global civil society is similar to that of other contemporary religious movements.[102] As Angela Rudert has pointed out, some of the most successful god-men and god-women of today "act much like CEOs in a powerful new role beyond their role as spiritual guide to aspirants,"[103] and "transnational religious organizations bear many similarities to corporate organizations and non-governmental organizations (NGOs) in the way they thrive in this non-state space."[104] Already at the end of the 1990s, Sophie Hawkins remarked that

> Sai Baba seems to mimic to great success the globalising strategies of multinationals—advertising a global product locally without foregoing the situated ideologies of its production. Indeed, the movement itself rests on a liberal multi-nationalism, where other national identities are invited to participate on Sai Baba's (Indian) playing field, so long as the host's rules of the game are respected.[105]

Although neither Sathya Sai Baba nor Kasturi was ever linked to any one political movement or party, I have noted that the guru managed to have a significant following among prominent political figures, regional as well as national. The guru himself possessed appreciable political skills. M. Krishna, an ex-devotee, recalls:

> Even in those days [the 1950s] some of us who were very close used to . . . discuss him and say that he was more of a politician than a guru . . . because of the terrific mind he has got. He is a great politician. He knows how to get things done when he wants something from you, how to talk to you nicely, and once his need for you is over, how to keep you at arm's length. Even in those days he was an expert at that art. He knew all the tactics of "divide and rule."[106]

Along the years, his power of attraction of even international political leaders bears testimony to his global appeal.[107] The fact that many Indian "big-men" were and are his devotees has determined an ongoing exchange of political and economic favors, the guru's blessings and public endorsement being a way to secure recognition, consensus, and even votes.[108] Indeed, despite having been accused of many things, the guru has always been defended by the Indian elites and the government. In December 2001, the then–prime minister A. B. Vajpayee and other political authorities expressed through a public letter their anguish for the "wild, reckless and concocted allegations made by certain vested interests and people against Bhagawan Sri Sathya Sai Baba."[109] They argued that responsible media should ascertain the truth before printing calumnies, "especially when the person is revered globally as an embodiment of love and selfless service to humanity."[110] Such a situation, as Norris W. Palmer notes, "has the twin effects of leaving his detractors angry about lack of due process and his proponents angry about unsubstantiated libel without recourse."[111]

If Kasturi was not directly involved in his guru's dealings with politicians, nonetheless he was keen in remembering a few of them in his hagiography, especially when they contributed to spreading the name and fame of his lord. By mentioning relevant figures such as the *rāja* of Venkatagiri Velugoti Sarvagna Kumar Krishna Yachendra, B. Ramakrishna Rao, and K. M. Munshi the hagiographer simultaneously gratified their egos—"immortalizing" them as significant individuals deserving a place in the official account of the *avatāra*'s life—and contributed to strengthening the alliance between them and the god-man. Moreover, in his role as Sathya Sai Baba's secretary Kasturi had countless occasions to interact with a vast array of social and political authorities. In his contacts with them, he gave ample proof of his savoir faire and diplomatic skills, always scrupulously following his lord's instructions.

Finally, the hagiographer was the representative of Sathya Sai Baba's ideal devotee, that is to say, of one who endeavors to achieve liberating knowledge (*jñāna*) by means of selfless service rather than through the elitist, most arduous path of renunciation and asceticism. By studying the writings of Kasturi—"the first one to unfold to the humanity at large the grandeur of Sri Sathya Sai Avatar's unique mission on earth and reveal that He is the incarnation of Love and Truth"[112]—Satya Pal Ruhela claims to have discovered the six most significant points that constitute the guru's "philosophy": (1) his rejection of atheism, since no instruction that refuses to acknowledge god's existence can be safe and sustaining; (2) the idea that *jñāna* alone confers liberation (*mokṣa*), *bhakti* and *karma* being regarded as its indispensable pathways; (3) his advocacy of Advaita Vedānta, given that only pure nondualism "satisfies the most complex demands of the intellect and reconciles all the discoveries of science";[113] (4) the idea that man is the crown of creation and that he/she must realize god's immanence in the universe; (5) the elevation of man to a higher level of consciousness, so that he/she may attain a state of equanimity leading to oneness with god; (6) the idea that the real "I" is none other than Sathyam Sivam Sundaram: each individual is in fact the *ātman,* and this is why "you resent when the deformities and defects of the physical vehicle are attributed to you."[114]

To be sure, the hagiographer ended his last work *Prasanthi: Pathway to Peace* with the affirmation of the nondual *ātman-Brahman* as the sole reality, beyond all illusory dualisms: "There is neither Thou nor That in Prasanthi [the highest peace, the Absolute *Brahman*]. There is but one all comprehensive I."[115] This ultimate truth of *advaita* coincides with what the guru himself revealed to his students in a telling dialogue:

> Baba asked the boys pointing to Himself, "Who am I?"
>
> The answer came almost immediately; "God!" shouted many boys simultaneously.
>
> . . . But Baba smiled and said, "Not correct!"
>
> . . . One of the boys said, "Swami, You are *Shiva Shakti swaroopa*!"
>
> All looked at Bhagawan expectantly. . . . He said, "Not correct!"

> . . . One of the students made bold to say, "Swami, You are Sri Krishna come again!"
>
> Baba laughed aloud and repeated, "Not correct!"
>
> "Swami, You are *Sarva Devata swaroopa*!" said one of the elderly devotees.
>
> "Not correct!"
>
> . . . One of the devotees pleaded, "Swami, please tell us who You are!"
>
> "I am I!" declared Bhagawan. . . . " 'I' is the basis of everything. To say 'I am this or that,' is *dwaita bhavam*—duality. 'I am I' means *adwaitam* or *ekatwam*—oneness. That is the ultimate truth. It is this 'I,' which is called by various names—God, Atma, Brahman, Krishna, Rama, Shiva, Allah or Yahweh."[116]

Apparently, Kasturi's "great saying" (*mahāvākya*) was not a mere intellectual conviction given that in the last days of his life he is said to have experienced self-realization, achieving the wisdom of *ātmajñāna* with the concomitant dissolution (*laya*) of the mind, as per his guru's dictum that the true "diamond," namely, the spiritual reality of the *ātman,* coincides with the experience of "die-mind." Though in Prasanthi Nilayam rumors circulated that Kasturi would soon be reborn as the mother of the future Prema Sai Baba,[117] the belief sanctioned by Sathya Sai Baba's final assurance is that the hagiographer "merged in him," that is, attained *mokṣa,* putting a definite end to the painful cycle of transmigration (*saṃsāra*). Ultimately, for all devotees as well as for the guru, Kasturi's exemplary life-trajectory was his uttermost legacy to the world, the excellence of the pupil being the best advertisement of the divinity of his beloved Swami.

Notes

Introduction

1. For a fine collection of articles and a detailed bibliography on Indian hagiographical writing, see F. Mallison, ed., *Constructions hagiographiques dans le monde indien. Entre mythe et histoire* (Paris: Librairie Honoré Champion, 2001). See also W. M. Callewaert and R. Snell, eds., *According to Tradition: Hagiographical Writing in India* (Wiesbaden: Harrassowitz, 1994); P. Granoff and K. Shinohara, eds., *Monks and Magicians: Religious Biographies in Asia* (Oakville, Ontario: Mosaic Press, 1988). Still useful for its comprehensive approach and breadth of analysis of the hagiographic discourse is F. E. Reynolds and D. Capps, eds., *The Biographical Process: A Study in the History and Psychology of Religion* (Berlin: Walter de Gruyter, 1976).

2. For a rare case of a hagiography without miracles, see P. Granoff, "The Miracle of a Hagiography Without Miracles: Some Comments on the Jain Lives of the Pratyekabuddha Karakaṇḍa," *Journal of Indian Philosophy* 16 (1986): 1–15.

3. Among the poet-saints of Maharashtra, an interesting case of a woman hagiographer is that of Janābāī (d. 1350); see C. Shelke, "Janābāī as a Mystic and Hagiographer," in *The Banyan Tree: Essays on Early Literature in New Indo-Aryan Languages (Proceedings of the Seventh International Conference on Early Literature in New Indo-Aryan Languages, Venice, 1997)*, Vol. 1. ed. M. Offredi (New Delhi: Manohar, 2000), 283–98.

4. For an introduction to Hindu hagiography and its genres, see R. Barz, "Hagiography," in *Brill's Encyclopedia of Hinduism*, ed. K. A. Jacobsen, H. Basu, A. Malinar, V. Narayanan (Leiden: Brill Online, 2013).

5. On Purāṇic literature, see L. Rocher, *The Purāṇas* (Wiesbaden: Otto Harrassowitz, 1986). On the variety of *Purāṇas*—Brahminical, folk, and even beyond Hinduism—see W. Doniger, ed., *Purāṇa Perennis: Reciprocity and Transformation in Hindu and Jaina Texts* (Albany: State University of New York

Press, 1993). A useful Purāṇic reader is the one by C. Dimmitt and J. A. B. van Buitenen, eds. and trans., *Classical Hindu Mythology: A Reader in the Sanskrit Purāṇas* (Philadelphia: Temple University Press, 1978).

6. On folk narrative, see K. Narayan, *Storytellers, Saints, and Scoundrels: Folk Narrative in Hindu Religious Teaching* (Philadelphia: University of Pennsylvania Press, 1989). See also R. C. Dhere, "Folk Perception and Saints Perception," in *Folk Culture, Folk Religion, and Oral Tradition as a Component in Maharashtrian Culture*, ed. G.-D. Sontheimer (New Delhi: Manohar, 1995), 245–58.

7. For an appraisal of the *Carita* genre with reference to the poet-saints of Maharashtra, see J. E. Abbott and N. R. Godbole, trans., *Stories of Indian Saints: Translation of Mahipati's Marathi* Bhaktavijaya. Intro. G. V. Tagare. 2 Vols. in 1 (Delhi: Motilal Banarsidass, 1982 [Poona, 1933]). For an excellent study of a Marāṭhī hagiography presenting the life of the mad saint Guṇḍam Rāuḷ (d. 1287/1288), one of the five manifestations of the supreme god Parameśvar according to the Mahānubhāv sect, see A. Feldhaus, *The Deeds of God in Ṛddhipur*. With introductory essays by Anne Feldhaus and Eleanor Zelliot (New York: Oxford University Press, 1984).

8. On Puttaparthi's foundational myth and Sathya Sai Baba's appropriation of it, see A. Rigopoulos, "The Construction of a Cultic Center Through Narrative: The Founding Myth of the Village of Puttaparthi and Sathya Sāī Bābā," *History of Religions* 54, no. 2 (Nov. 2014): 117–50.

9. On a saint's career and her final achievement of divine status, see C. Clémentin-Ojha, *La divinité conquise. Carrière d'une sainte* (Nanterre: Société d'ethnologie, 1990).

10. See E. Bryant, "Krishna in the Tenth Book of the *Bhagavata Purana*," in *Krishna: A Sourcebook*, ed. E. Bryant (New York: Oxford University Press, 2007), 111–36.

11. See L. A. Babb, "Sathya Sai Baba's Saintly Play," in *Saints and Virtues*, ed. J. S. Hawley (Berkeley: University of California Press, 1987), 168–86.

12. F. Mallison, "Introduction," in Ead., *Constructions hagiographiques dans le monde indien*, xvii (my translation).

13. N. Kasturi, *Loving God. Eighty Five Years Under the Watchful Eye of the Lord* (Prasanthi Nilayam: Sri Sathya Sai Books and Publications, 1982), 72.

14. On these issues, see P. Granoff, "The Politics of Religious Biography: The Biography of Balibhadra the Usurper," *Bulletin d'Études Indiennes* 9 (1991): 75–91.

15. A good example is the eighteenth-century Marāṭhī hagiographer Mahīpati (1715–1790); see S. G. Tulpule, *Classical Marāṭhī Literature: From the Beginning to A.D. 1818* (Wiesbaden: Otto Harrassowitz, 1979), 429–32; J. Keune, "Gathering the Bhaktas in Marāṭhī," *Journal of Vaishnava Studies* 15, no. 2 (2007): 169–88.

16. See T. K. Stewart, *Perceptions of the Divine: The Biographies of Chaitanya* (Chicago: The University of Chicago Press, 1985).

17. R. Rinehart, *One Lifetime, Many Lives: The Experience of Modern Hindu Hagiography* (Atlanta: Scholars Press, 1999), 185. On the hagiographic genre in modern Hinduism, see ibid., 1–16.

18. See, for instance, M. Kheirabadi, *Sri Satya Sai Baba*, introductory essay by Martin E. Marty (Philadelphia: Chelsea House, 2005).

19. For a first assessment, see L. A. Babb, *Redemptive Encounters: Three Modern Styles in the Hindu Tradition* (Berkeley: University of California Press, 1986), 159–74. On the role of supernatural powers in Vedānta hagiographies, see P. Granoff, "Scholars and Wonder-workers: Some Remarks on the Role of the Supernatural in Philosophical Contests in Vedanta Hagiographies," *Journal of the American Oriental Society* 105, no. 3 (1985): 459–69.

20. For a comparison with the representation of charisma in the hagiography of Sahajānanda (1781–1830), the founder of the Swaminarayan tradition, see P. Schreiner, "Institutionalization of Charisma: The Case of Sahajānanda," in *Charisma and Canon: Essays on the Religious History of the Indian Subcontinent*, ed. V. Dalmia, A. Malinar, and M. Christof (New York: Oxford University Press, 2001), 155–70. On the narration of charisma in the hagiography of a modern saint of the Caitanya tradition, see A. Malinar, "Rādhāramaṇa Caraṇa Dās und die Caitanya-Nachfolge in Orissa: Zur Textualisierung von Charisma," in *Toḥfa-e-Dil. Festschrift für Helmuth Nespital*, ed. D. Lönne (Reinbek: Verlag für Orientalistische Fachpublikationen, 2001), 295–313.

21. He was a Brahmin servant of the Bombay Government and his last appointment was as a magistrate in the Bandra suburb of Bombay. Though he lacked an academic education he was a poet at heart, well-versed in the classics of Maharashtrian literature such as the *Jñāneśvarī* of Jñāndev and the *Eknāthī Bhāgavata* of Eknāth. Shirdi Sai Baba nicknamed him Hemadpant after the learned thirteenth-century court poet and author of the Yādava dynasty. On G. R. Dabholkar and his opus, see B. V. Narasimhaswami, *Life of Sai Baba* (Madras: All India Sai Samaj, 1980–1985 [1955–1956]), vol. 2, 212–27; K. McLain, *The Afterlife of Sai Baba: Competing Visions of a Global Saint* (Seattle and London: University of Washington Press, 2016), 31–35; K. R. D. Shepherd, *Sai Baba of Shirdi: A Biographical Investigation* (New Delhi: Sterling, 2015), 59–67.

22. Apparently Shirdi Sai Baba spoke these words in 1916, two years prior to his death.

23. G. R. Dabholkar (Hemadpant), *Shri Sai Satcharita: The Life and Teachings of Shirdi Sai Baba*, trans. I. Kher (New Delhi: Sterling, 1999), 23 (chap. 2, vv. 75–76).

24. See ibid., ix. The *Eknāthī Bhāgavata* is Eknāth's Marāṭhī commentary on the eleventh book of the *Bhāgavata Purāṇa*. Completed in Benares in 1573, it is a voluminous work in more than eighteen thousand stanzas.

25. For its English translation, see V. C. Kondappa, *Sai's Story: As Revealed by Sathya Sai to His Teacher*, foreword B. Subbannachar (Bangalore: Sai Towers, 2004).

26. See ibid., i. On V. C. Kondappa, see R. Padmanaban, "V. C. Kondappa: The Teacher Biographer," *Spiritual Impressions* 1, no. 2 (May–June 2001): 56–60.

27. See R. Padmanaban, *Love Is My Form: A Biographical Series on Sri Sathya Sai Baba*. Vol. 1: *The Advent (1926–1950)* (Bangalore: Sai Towers, 2000), 199. See also ibid., 201–203.

28. The *Sri Sai Sathakamu* was composed in 1944 by Manchiraju Thammiraju, the mathematics teacher of Sathya Sai Baba; see ibid., 138. On Telugu *śatakas*, see Bh. Krishnamurti, "Shift of Authority in Written and Oral Texts: The Case of Telugu," in D. Shulman, ed., *Syllables of Sky: Studies in South Indian Civilization in Honour of Velcheru Narayana Rao* (Delhi: Oxford University Press, 1995), 84–85.

29. Barz, *Hagiography*, 10.

30. Ibid.

31. See P. Schalk, ed., *Geschichten und Geschichte. Historiographie und Hagiographie in der asiatischen Religionsgeschichte* (Uppsala: Uppsala University Library, 2010).

32. J.-Y. Tilliette, "Introduction," in *Les fonctions des saints dans le monde occidental (III*e*–XIII*e *siècle). Actes du colloque organisé par l'École française de Rome avec le concours de l'Université de Rome "La Sapienza," Rome 27–29 octobre 1988* (Rome: École française de Rome, Palais Farnèse, 1991), 5 (my translation). With reference to the Indian context, see D. N. Lorenzen, "The Social Ideologies of Hagiography: Śaṅkara, Tukārām and Kabīr," in *Religion and Society in Maharashtra*, ed. M. Israel and N. K. Wagle (Toronto: University of Toronto Centre for South Asian Studies, 1987), 92–114. On the hagiographies of Śaṅkara (c. 700 CE), the seminal founder of the Advaita Vedānta tradition, see Id., "The Life of Śaṅkarācārya," in Reynolds, Capps, *The Biographical Process*, 87–107; M. Piantelli, *Śaṅkara e la rinascita del brāhmanesimo* (Fossano: Editrice Esperienze, 1974), 5–106. See also Govindanātha, *Il poema di Śaṅkara*. Śrīśaṅkarācāryacarita, ed. M. Piantelli (Torino: Promolibri, 1994); Y. Sawai, *The Faith of Ascetics and Lay Smārtas: A Study of Śaṅkara Tradition in Śriṅgeri* (Vienna: De Nobili Research Library, 1992); W. Cenkner, *A Tradition of Teachers: Śaṅkara and the Jagadgurus Today* (Delhi: Motilal Banarsidass, 1983).

33. On these issues, an exemplary study is the one carried out by Philip Lutgendorf on the *Rāmcaritmānas* of Tulsīdās: *The Life of a Text: Performing the*

Rāmcaritmānas *of Tulsidas* (Berkeley and Los Angeles: University of California Press, 1991).

Chapter 1

1. He recalls: "I had an unpronounceable name given by my parents, 'Kasturi Ranganatha Sharma.' Awful! Nine syllables. My mother could not pronounce it. Whenever I anticipated punishment, by the time she finished pronouncing it, I would run away! I changed my name into mere Kasturi"; H. M. Shivaram, ed., *Sathya Sai Baba: God in Action. Talks by Prof. N. Kasturi* (Prasanthi Nilayam: Sri Sathya Sai Sadhana Trust, 2015), 176. He paid twelve rupees to have his name reduced; ibid., 162. See also Padmamma, *Twameva Matha* (Bangalore: Sadguru Screens, 2009), 100.

2. In later years, Kasturi would say: "I am a Tamil settler in Kerala State, who came into Kannada area, and finally found harbor in Telugu land. . . . My ancestors' Tamil land, my interval in Kerala, my profession in Karnataka and my final in Andhra"; Shivaram, *Sathya Sai Baba: God in Action*, 34. See also Kasturi, *Loving God*, 200. Kasturi's father was eighteen and his mother twelve when they got married; see ibid., 4.

3. Shivaram, *Sathya Sai Baba: God in Action*, 200. On the Ranganathaswamy Temple, the country's largest *vaiṣṇava* sanctuary, situated on the river island of Shrirangam where Viṣṇu is depicted asleep on the cosmic serpent Śeṣa, see V. N. Hari Rao, *History of the Srirangam Temple* (Tirupathi: Sri Venkateshwara Historical Series, 1976); R. K. Das, *Temples of Tamilnad* (Bombay: Bharatiya Vidya Bhavan, 1964).

4. His grandmother, however, did not like this abnormality and scissored the extra four to make the baby look normal; see Kasturi, *Loving God*, 5.

5. He once noted: "My tongue and ear accustomed for years to love and loll in the Dravidian family of languages . . . Malayalam, Tamil and Telugu—dared not venture into the Indo-European language, Hindi"; ibid., 296–97.

6. He was the Karyakar or Executive of the temple of Parthasarathi (lit. "Charioteer of Partha/Arjuna," i.e., Kṛṣṇa) of Thrippunithura. From the eleventh day of his earthly career and for many years as a child, Kasturi was brought here by his mother for blessings; see ibid., 3.

7. Padmamma, *Twameva Matha*, 100.

8. Kasturi recalls: "He told us stories of the Paramahamsa [Ramakrishna] and his Apostles so picturesquely that we always asked for more. He persuaded us to learn by heart that part of one of Vivekananda's electrifying speeches which culminates with the prayer, 'God! Make me a Man!' Gurudev [Ramakrishna] was my prop and Providence until the fifties of my life"; Kasturi, *Loving God*, 336–37.

9. For an introduction to Vivekananda's life and teachings, see D. H. Killingley, "Vivekananda," in *Brill's Encyclopedia of Hinduism*, ed. K. A. Jacobsen, H. Basu, A. Malinar, and V. Narayanan (Brill Online, 2012). See also A. P. Sen, *Swami Vivekananda* (New York: Oxford University Press, 2013) and A. Raghuramaraju, ed., *Debating Vivekananda: A Reader* (New York: Oxford University Press, 2014). For an insider's perspective, see Swami Nikhilananda, *Vivekananda: A Biography* (New York: Ramakrishna-Vivekananda Center, 1953). For an overview of Vivekananda's writings, see M. R. Paranjape, ed., *Swami Vivekananda: A Contemporary Reader* (New Delhi: Routledge, 2015); A. P. Sen, ed., *The Indispensable Vivekananda: An Anthology for Our Times* (Delhi: Permanent Black, 2006). Swami (Skt. *svāmin*) means "lord," "master," and is an honorific term commonly addressed to a guru.

10. For an introduction to Ramakrishna, see A. P. Sen, "Ramakrishna," in *Brill's Encyclopedia of Hinduism*, ed. K. A. Jacobsen, H. Basu, A. Malinar, and V. Narayanan (Brill Online, 2012). On Ramakrishna's life, see *Life of Sri Ramakrishna. Compiled from Various Authentic Sources*, with a Foreword by M. K. Gandhi (Calcutta: Advaita Ashrama, 1964 [1924]). See also the controversial monograph by J. J. Kripal, *Kālī's Child: The Mystic and the Erotic in the Life and Teachings of Ramakrishna* (Chicago: Chicago University Press, 1998). An insiders' response to it is provided by Swami Tyagananda and P. Vrajaprana, *Interpreting Ramakrishna: Kālī's Child Revisited* (Delhi: Motilal Banarsidass, 2010). For an anthology of the *guru*'s teachings, see M. Gupta ("M"), *The Gospel of Sri Ramakrishna* (Sri Sri Ramakrishna Kathamrita), translated from the Bengali by Swami Nikhilananda, foreword by Aldous Huxley (New York: Ramakrishna-Vivekananda Center, 1942; available at http://www.vedanta-nl.org/GOSPEL.pdf). On Ramakrishna, Vivekananda, and the spirits of the age, see P. van der Veer, *Imperial Encounters: Religion and Modernity in India and Britain* (Delhi: Permanent Black, 2006), 55–82.

11. N. Kasturi, *Gurudev* (Prasanthi Nilayam: Sri Sathya Sai Books and Publications, 2005), 1–2. For this famous speech, see Swami Vivekananda, *My Master*, with an appended extract from the *Theistic Quarterly Review* (New York: Baker and Taylor, 1901^3).

12. She was an only child, like Kasturi, and having lost her father in her infancy she was raised by her grandfather. Her mother tongue was also Tamil; see Kasturi, *Loving God*, 165.

13. Kasturi describes him as "a prodigious Sanskrit Pundit, a pillar of Bharathiya Culture, a model Guru, an encyclopedic scholar and an ideal Brahmin"; ibid., 33. On K. V. Rangaswami Iyengar and the History Department of the University College, see http://www.historiatrivandrum.com/docs/downloads/history.pdf.

14. On the Ramakrishna Mission, see G. Beckerlegge, "Ramakrishna Math and Mission," in *Brill's Encyclopedia of Hinduism*, ed. K. A. Jacobsen, H. Basu, A. Malinar, and V. Narayanan (Brill Online, 2012). See also the articles by G. Beckerlegge and H. Rüstau in A. Copley, ed., *Gurus and Their Followers: New Religious Reform Movements in Colonial India* (New Delhi: Oxford University Press, 2000), 59–106.

15. His father-in-law's father-in-law warned him: "Do not be a lawyer! Do not cheat! Teach! The teacher alone can be happy, in this world and the next"; Kasturi, *Loving God*, 38. In 1919, Kasturi definitely left his native village: he was to come back to Thrippunithura for a short visit only in 1968, along with his guru Sathya Sai Baba; ibid., 1.

16. Paramahaṃsa (lit. "exalted swan") is a title given to the highest category of ascetics. It was conferred on Ramakrishna by his followers.

17. Kasturi, *Loving God*, 46. Kasturi's wife Rajamma as well as Sathya Sai Baba had a negative opinion of lawyers, depicted as liars and "brothers of Ravanasura" [the demon Rāvaṇa]; Padmamma, *Twameva Matha*, 97–98.

18. A learned Vedāntin and a prominent personality within the Ramakrishna Order, he was initiated by Swami Brahmananda and later sent to France, where in 1947 he established the Centre Védantique Ramakrishna at Gretz, near Paris. Swami Siddheswarananda had also great regard for Ramana Maharshi, whom he visited at his ashram in the 1930s. On Swami Siddheswarananda's life, see M. Lallement, *Swâmi Siddheswarânanda et son temps*, tomes 3 (Paris: Les Éditions du Petit Véhicule, 2006–2007). He wrote several books, and his last writings have been collected in Swami Siddheswarananda, *The Metaphysical Intuition: Seeing God with Open Eyes. Commentaries on the Bhagavad Gita* (Rhinebeck, NY: Monkfish, 2006).

19. M. V. N. Murthy, *The Greatest Adventure: Essays on the Sai Avatar and His Message* (Prasanthi Nilayam: Sri Sathya Sai Books and Publications, 1983), 1.

20. The founder of the Ramakrishna-Vivekananda Center of New York, of which he remained the head until his death in 1973. An accomplished writer, Swami Nikhilananda's most important contribution was the translation in 1942 of the *Sri Sri Rāmakrishna Kathāmrita* from Bengali into English under the title *The Gospel of Sri Ramakrishna*. Kasturi notes: "I knew him very well. He was with me in Mysore and then he was posted to New York. A very learned person who has translated Ramakrishna's Gospel and written some books on *Vedanta*"; Shivaram, *Sathya Sai Baba: God in Action*, 134.

21. Kasturi remembers: "I was with Ramana Maharishi, who was *jnana* himself, and then I came to Swami [Sathya Sai Baba]. Ramana Maharishi asked me to delve into things, 'Who is this I?' You have to go and sit in a corner and enquire who you are. That is one way"; ibid., 253. Elsewhere, he states that he

stayed with Ramana Maharshi for three days; Kasturi, *Loving God*, 68. It should be noted that at the time when Ramana Maharshi passed away in Tiruvannamalai, i.e., April 14, 1950, at around 9 p.m., Sathya Sai Baba in Puttaparthi fell into a trance and said that Ramana Maharshi had reached his feet: nearly two kilograms of *vibhūti* poured out from the sole of his right foot; see Padmanaban, *Love is My Form*, 497, 501.

22. He gave his first speech in Kannada in the early 1920s, at the Conference of the Landholders of Coorg in the town of Ammathi.

23. See Kasturi, *Loving God*, 379.

24. Shivaram, *Sathya Sai Baba: God in Action*, 133. See also Kasturi, *Gurudev*, 6–7. For an introduction to *mantras*, see S. Timalsina, "Mantra," in *Brill's Encyclopedia of Hinduism*, ed. K. A. Jacobsen, H. Basu, A. Malinar, and V. Narayanan (Brill Online, 2012); H. G. Coward and D. J. Goa, *Mantra: Hearing the Divine in India and America* (New York: Columbia University Press, 2005).

25. "He Is My Swami"—Part 1, http://media.radiosai.org/journals/Vol_05/01MAY07/14-h2h_special.htm, 6.

26. R. H. Davis, *The Bhagavad Gita: A Biography* (Princeton: Princeton University Press, 2015), 112–13. Vivekananda became a paradigm for all those gurus who adopted the *Bhagavadgītā* for promoting universal messages, in India and throughout the world.

27. See Kasturi, *Loving God*, 71. He would argue: "Then active people, 'karmayogis,' who are engaged in activity: 'mrutyorma amrutamgamaya,' from death lead me to immortality, is their prayer. For example, myself. I do not reason out things. . . . I am interested in service activity. How does an active person escape death and go to immortality? That is what I am after"; Shivaram, *Sathya Sai Baba: God in Action*, 42.

28. The German indologist Paul Hacker (1913–1979) has argued that Vivekananda's altruism and call for *sevā*—motivated by his identification of god with mankind—was not due to Christian influence but rather to the influence of European positivism; see W. Halbfass, ed., *Philology and Confrontation: Paul Hacker on Traditional and Modern Vedānta* (Albany: State University of New York Press, 1995), 330. On Vivekananda and *sevā*, see G. Beckerlegge, *Swami Vivekananda's Legacy of Service: A Study of the Ramakrishna Math and Mission* (New Delhi: Oxford University Press, 2006). On neo-Hinduism and social service, see G. Beckerlegge, "*Sevā*: The Focus of a Fragmented but Gradually Coalescing Field of Study," *Religions of South Asia* 9, no. 2 (2015): 208–39; A. O. Fort, "*Jīvanmukti* and Social Service in Advaita and Neo-Vedānta," in *Beyond Orientalism: The Work of Wilhelm Halbfass and Its Impact on Indian and Cross-Cultural Studies*, ed. E. Franco and K. Preisendanz (Amsterdam/Atlanta: Rodopi, 1997), 489–504; W. Halbfass, "Practical Vedānta," in *Representing Hinduism: The Construction of Religious Traditions and National Identity*, ed. V. Dalmia and H. von Stietencron (New Delhi: Sage, 1995), 211–23. On his part, Ramakrishna showed little interest in

social service and viewed one's engagement in the world as a form of attachment to it; see C. T. Jackson, *Vedanta for the West: The Ramakrishna Movement in the United States* (Bloomington: Indiana University Press, 1994), 75–80; A. Bharati, *The Ochre Robe* (Santa Barbara: Ross-Erikson, 1980), 95. On Vivekananda's sanitization of Ramakrishna's message and Tantric practices in terms of a Hindu universal spirituality, see van der Veer, *Imperial Encounters*, 46–48, 70–74.

29. Bill Aitken's remark that Kasturi, given his "middle-class" status, was "not directly familiar" with the sufferings of the poor is a mistaken assumption; see B. Aitken, *Sri Sathya Sai Baba: A Life* (New Delhi: Penguin, 2004), 78.

30. Lit. "people of god." The term was coined by M. K. Gandhi.

31. Shivaram, *Sathya Sai Baba: God in Action*, 132. For an overview on Vivekananda's Hinduism and religious nationalism, see W. Halbfass, *India and Europe: An Essay in Understanding* (Albany: State University of New York Press, 1988), 228–42; Halbfass, *Philology and Confrontation: Paul Hacker on Traditional and Modern Vedānta*, 319–36.

32. Along these lines, years later Kasturi would argue:

> According to Vivekananda, the olden days of Brahmins are theocracy of the present. The Kshatriyas of olden days, are the armies of the present. The Vaisyas of olden days are the merchant class of the present. The Shudras of olden days are the workers and farmers of the present. So this Age requires some special method for spiritual uplift and Swami [Sathya Sai Baba] has said, "namasmarana," remembering the name of God, is the special method for this age. Whenever you see someone, remember the name of God. There is no higher thing. It is all Sai Ram. (Shivaram, *Sathya Sai Baba: God in Action*, 126)

On the significance of *nāmasmaraṇa*, see *Kalyana Kalpataru, The Divine Name Number*, vol. 5, n. 1 (Gorakhpur: Gita Press, 1938).

33. Kasturi's son M. Venkata Narayana Murthy recalls: "Since my father used to take me along with him on the many extra-curricular activities (dramas, *hari-katha*, literacy classes, scouting), I could develop a taste of these during my boyhood itself and use their influence on me during my later years" (Murthy, *The Greatest Adventure*, 1)." See also the testimony of Kasturi's daughter Padma in "He Is My Swami"—Part 1, http://media.radiosai.org/journals/Vol_05/01MAY07/14-h2h_special.htm, 6; Padmamma, *Twameva Matha*, 103.

34. On the social and political relevance of mythological drama in the 1920s, see N. Bhatia, *Acts of Authority / Acts of Resistance: Theater and Politics in Colonial and Postcolonial India* (Ann Arbor: The University of Michigan Press, 2004), 43–50. On the performance of plays and *harikathās* aimed at social reform, see A. Schultz, *Singing a Hindu Nation: Marathi Devotional Performance and Nationalism* (New York: Oxford University Press, 2013), 50–76. On Western

influence over Indian theatre/music drama from the mid-nineteenth century onward, see ibid., 22, 29, 31, 33–34.

35. See H. K. Nanjunda Swamy, *Where the Angels Roamed*. English Adaptation of *Nenapina Nandana* (Kannada) of Dr. H. K. Ranganath (Bangalore: Alex Price Publication, 2002), 54.

36. Kasturi, *Loving God*, 58–59. On Kasturi's community service, see Nanjunda Swamy, *Where the Angels Roamed*, 55.

37. Kuvempu's monumental epic *Shri Ramayana Darshanam* was translated into English by Shankar Mokashi-Punekar in 2004 (New Delhi: Sahitya Akademi).

38. Kasturi, *Loving God*, 50.

39. Ibid., 54.

40. Ibid., 58–59, 379.

41. The name of Kasturi's house in Mysore was *Kalpataru*, i.e., the wish-fulfilling tree. H. K. Ranganath further recalls:

> I became another son-like in their house. He was my professor in college, my boss in *Akashavani*, and the director of all my stage activities over the next ten years. I had a role to play in his *Harikathas*. I accompanied him in his travels and sat in front row during his lectures. I got the first chance to read his manuscripts and was an essential participant in his endless practical jokes. At home I became the favorite of all the members of the family—his mother, wife, first son Narayana Murthy, second son Venkatadri and of course, daughter, little Padma. (Nanjunda Swamy, *Where the Angels Roamed*, 53)

42. Ibid., 53–54. See also ibid., 113.

43. Kasturi, *Loving God*, 338.

44. Ibid., 306–307.

45. L. S. Seshagiri Rao, "Kasturi N.," in *Encyclopaedia of Indian Literature*, ed. A. Datta (New Delhi: Sahitya Akademi, 2010 [1989]), vol. III, 2004.

46. M. N. Rao, *Sathya Sai Baba: God as Man* (Tustin, CA: Sathya Sai Baba Society and Sathya Sai Book Center of America, 1985), 89.

47. Already in the 1920s, Kasturi had published a history of the British occupation of India: N. Kasturi, *History of the British Occupation of India. Being a Summary of* Rise of the Christian Power in India *by Major B. D. Basu, Vols. I to V* (Calcutta: R. Chatterjee, n. d.). In 1935, as a lecturer in the department of history of Mysore University, he published an article titled "Tipu Sultan's Projected Confederacy against the British, 1790."

48. In accordance with his Vivekanandian orientation, Kasturi viewed Aśoka as the champion of tolerance and as the upholder of the goodness of all religions. This brought him to choose the Mauryan emperor as the subject of his

monograph; see N. Kasturi, *Ashoka*, ed. K. V. Puttappa. *Mysore University Kannada Granthamale*, 25 (Mysore: Wesley Press, 1952). On Kasturi's understanding of Aśoka's teachings, see Shivaram, *Sathya Sai Baba: God in Action*, 125. Aśoka was also the name of Kasturi's house in Bangalore, near Wilson Garden; see Kasturi, *Loving God*, 166.

49. H. K. Ranganath remembers:

> When he was creating one of these works he would become extremely restless as "a cat on a hot tin roof." "These are birth pangs" he would say. Once the book was completed, he would be bouncing around like a new born colt. "Will you ever have an easy delivery?" we would ask. His reply used to be "No author can have an easy delivery. If anyone says he does, either he is a liar or his work is worthless." (Nanjunda Swamy, *Where the Angels Roamed*, 56)

50. Nonetheless, in retrospect, he admitted: "Some of my hits used to throw one over the other, and I used to feel proud. People kept away from me because they were afraid that I may ridicule them!! My head was getting swollen, and I used my cleverness to hurt other people"; Kasturi, *Loving God*, 19.

51. He first represented his plays in the "quadrangle" of Maharaja's College: its "thirty feet long, twenty feet wide and three feet high ornate stage"; Nanjunda Swamy, *Where the Angels Roamed*, 66. Kasturi laid the foundation for Kannada impromptu theatre and some of his works are staged even today; see H. K. Ranganath, *The Karnatak Theatre*. With a Foreword by Wrangler D. C. Pavate (Dharwar: Karnatak University, 1960), 210. Kasturi also wrote plays in English (*Headmaster's Daughter*) and Malayalam (*Shahajahan*). Unfortunately, many of his Kannada plays such as *Gundurayana gulige*, *Mankasura vadhe*, *Nandanar*, *Shambhu*, and *Tiruppanalvar* remain unpublished.

52. For an anthology of Kasturi's works, see Y. V. Gundu Rao, ed., *Best of Kasturi* (Bangalore: Ankita Pustaka, 2005).

53. These ten characters are the protagonist's mother, wife, neighbor, boss, mentor, three of his friends, a milk vendor, and the narrator. *Gundayana*, a comedy based on *Chakradristi*, was successfully staged in Bangalore in August 2015.

54. Kasturi, *Loving God*, 60.

55. Seshagiri Rao, *Kasturi N.*, 2004.

56. See N. Kasturi, *Anarthakosha* (Bangalore: Ankita Pustaka, 2012). For recent, enthusiastic comments posted by readers, see http://vasukir.blogspot.it/2012/10/anartha-kosha.html.

57. See Vijayakumar M. Boratti, "*Paapachchi* (*Alice*) in the Kannada Netherworld," in *Alice. In a World of Wonderlands: The Translations of Lewis Carroll's Masterpiece*, ed. J. A. Lindseth (New Castle, DE: Oak Knoll Press, 2015), vol.

1, 324–25; vol. 2, 316–17; vol. 3, 560–61; P. Baliga, "Translating for Children: Changing Notions of Autonomy and Gender (*Katha Yatra: The Story Festival*; November 2014. *Translations and Migrations*)," http://www.bhaashaa.org/download/Full%20Papers%20for%20Our%20First%20issue.pdf (70–73); K. S. Umapathi, "Children's Literature in Kannada," *International Library Review* 13, no. 4 (1981): 435–43. On translating Western classics into Indian languages, see M. Chandran and S. Mathur, eds., *Textual Travels: Theory and Practice of Translation in India* (New Delhi: Routledge, 2015).

58. Together with Shankara Bhatta, he translated Pillai's political novel *Randidangazhi* or *Two Measures* (1948). Its Kannada title is *Eradu balla* (Reprint, 1996).

59. On the Kuṟavañci or Kuṟatti, the wandering female fortuneteller of the Kuravar hill tribe, see I. V. Peterson, "The Drama of the Kuṟavañci Fortune-teller: Land, Landscape, and Social Relations in an Eighteenth-century Tamil Genre," in *Tamil Geographies: Cultural Constructions of Space and Place in South India*, ed. M. A. Selby and I. V. Peterson (Albany: State University of New York Press, 2008), 59–86. Dr. M. Shivaram ran the *Koravanji* magazine for twenty-five years, from 1942 to 1967. On Kasturi's contribution, see N. Kasturi, *Koravanji Kasturi* (Bangalore: Aparanji Prakashan, 1996). In 2011, thanks to lexicographer G. Venkatasubbaiah, all issues of *Koravanji*, comprising around 1,200 pages, were made available on a single CD co-produced by the Koravanji-Aparanji Trust, the Bharatiya Vidya Bhavan, and the Department of Kannada and Culture.

60. See http://www.thehindu.com/news/national/karnataka/spotted-by-koravanji-as-a-student/article6826047.ece; https://m.yourstory.com/2016/01/republic-day-early-works-cartoonist-r-k-laxman.

61. Kasturi, *Loving God*, 61.

62. Unfortunately, most of the plays and *kathā*s that he wrote for the radio have not been preserved.

63. Nanjunda Swamy, *Where the Angels Roamed*, 74–75.

64. Ibid., 56.

65. Kasturi, *Loving God*, 62. Kasturi recalls how he was invited to speak over the air and how he stumbled on the words Akash Vani as equivalent to Radio Broadcast; ibid., 212. H. K. Ranganath writes: "I know for certain that it was he who gave the name *Akashavani* to it"; Nanjunda Swamy, *Where the Angels Roamed*, 55. According to other sources, however, it was the Bengali poet Rabindranath Tagore (1861–1941) who first coined the expression Akash Vani in the 1930s. On the Akash Vani radio, see A. Virmani, *Atlas historique de l'Inde. Du VIe siècle av. J.-C. au XXIe siècle*. Préface de Sanjay Subrahmanyam (Paris: Éditions Autrement, 2012), 77.

66. Nanjunda Swamy, *Where the Angels Roamed*, 8.

67. See ibid., 57.

68. Ibid., 53.

69. See Kasturi, *Loving God*, 307; Shivaram, *Sathya Sai Baba: God in Action*, 19. Kasturi was also appointed as the representative for the Kannada language at a literary valedictory program in Delhi. For an assessment of Kasturi's literary achievements, see the *Festschrift* in his honor on the centenary of his birth: N. B. Chandra Mohan and K. Subba Rao, eds., *Kastūri śatakam* (Bangalore: B. S. Rajaram, Canvas Creatives Pvt. Ltd., 1996). It comprises articles written by scholars and friends of Kasturi, among whom are L. S. Seshagiri Rao, Neelattahalli Kasturi, H. K. Ranganath, A. S. Venugopala Rao, A. R. Mitra, Vimala Sheshadri, and G. S. Shivarudrappa. For a biographical account, see A. S. Venugopala Rao, *Nā. Kastūri: Nārāyaṇa Raṅganātha Kastūri-baduku-baraha. Amrtotsava male* 29 (Bangalore: Kannada Sahitya Parishat, 1990). See also G. R. Garg, *International Encyclopaedia of Indian Literature. Vol. IV: Kannada* (Delhi: Mittal Publications, 1987), 71; Seshagiri Rao, *Kasturi N.*, 2004; *Who's Who of Indian Writers: Compiled by Sahitya Akademi* (New Delhi: Sahitya Akademi, 1961), 159.

70. Venkatadri was born in 1929, whereas Kasturi's elder son, M. Venkata Narayana Murthy, was born in 1923. At the time of his brother's death M. Venkata Narayana Murthy was in Scotland, at the University of Glasgow, pursuing a PhD in geology: a staunch devotee of Sathya Sai Baba, he had a brilliant career as a geologist, being appointed Deputy Director General of the Geological Survey of India. Both the brothers' names evidence Kasturi's and his wife's devotion to god Veṅkaṭeśvara of Tirupati—one of the major sacred sites of Southern India—to whom they went on pilgrimage at the time of Venkata Narayana Murthy's birth as well as ten years later, so as to have him initiated into the *gāyatrī mantra*; see Kasturi, *Loving God*, 6–7; Shivaram, *Sathya Sai Baba: God in Action*, 116. Kasturi and his wife also had a daughter, Padma, who was born in 1934. Nowadays she lives in a tiny apartment within the precincts of Prasanthi Nilayam, filled with the memorabilia of her father and of Sathya Sai Baba, and I had the privilege of meeting her in February 2016. In his autobiography, however, Kasturi writes that he had four children, not three; perhaps he/she died at birth or in his/her infancy; see Kasturi, *Loving God*, 27. On Kasturi's family, see Padma's recent book *Twameva Matha*. She also authored a short article on her father in Chandra Mohan and Subba Rao, *Kastūri śatakam*.

71. In Kasturi's words: "My younger son, who was studying in an engineering college, who, his professors were saying will get a top rank, fell ill from typhoid long before the medical world could successfully treat it and save! He passed away"; Shivaram, *Sathya Sai Baba: God in Action*, 19. Kasturi's daughter Padma recalls: "The atmosphere in the house was always gloomy—with my mother crying, my grandmother in deep grief, and my father silent in agony"; Padmamma, *Twameva Matha*, 2–3. Kasturi's wife would tell Sathya Sai Baba: "Swami, formerly I was like [the devotee] Prahlada, always remembering Him [Venkateshwara] with love, but now I am like [the demon] Hiranyakashipu—uttering the same Name with hatred"; ibid., 4.

72. The site's fortunes were fostered by the patronage of the Vijayanagar kings between the fourteenth and sixteenth centuries. On Veṅkaṭeśvara, see V. Narayanan, "Veṅkaṭeśvara," in *Brill's Encyclopedia of Hinduism*. Vol. 1 *Regions, Pilgrimage, Deities*, ed. K. A. Jacobsen, H. Basu, A. Malinar, and V. Narayanan (Leiden: Brill, 2009), 781–85. See also K. Neelima, *Tirupati: A Guide to Life* (Noida: Random House India, 2012); C. S. Vasudevan, *Temples of Andhra Pradesh* (Delhi: Bharatiya Kala Prakashan, 2000), 151–228.

73. A tributary of the Pennar River, the Chitravathi originates at Chikballapur in Karnataka and flows along the western and southern boundaries of Puttaparthi. Though it can swell in the monsoon season, even flooding the village, in the summer it dries up and vanishes into its sandy bed. On the river's current pollution, see http://hubpages.com/entertainment/Chitravati-The-painful-story-of-pollution-of-a-sathya-sai-baba-holy-river.

74. According to Sathya Sai Baba, Puttaparthi had a population of only 100 to 150 people when he was young; see Sri Sathya Sai Baba, *His Story as Told by Himself. A Compilation from the Divine Discourses of Bhagavan Sri Sathya Sai Baba* (Prasanthi Nilayam: Sri Sathya Sai Sadhana Trust, 2014), 29, 189. In 1961, the *Census of India* reports that the population of the village was 3,471 and it was made up of the following communities: caste Hindus—mainly Kapu, Bhatrāju, and Boya—scheduled castes (387) and scheduled tribes (64). The means of livelihood were agriculture and traditional occupations; *Census of India 1961*. Vol. II, *Andhra Pradesh*, Part VII-B (10) *Fairs and Festivals* (10. Anantapur District). Superintendent of Census Operations: A. Chandra Sekhar, Indian Administrative Service (Delhi: Manager of Publications, 1965), 128.

75. On sacred ash, a characteristic emblem of asceticism, see A. Rigopoulos, "Vibhūti," in *Brill's Encyclopedia of Hinduism*. Vol. 5. *Religious Symbols; Hinduism and Migration: Contemporary Communities Outside South Asia; Some Modern Religious Groups and Teachers*, ed. K. A. Jacobsen, H. Basu, A. Malinar, and V. Narayanan (Leiden: Brill, 2013), 181–83. On Sathya Sai Baba's *vibhūti*, see S. C. Bhatnagar, ed., *Sai Vibhuti Prasadam and Its Significance (Based on Sai's Teachings)*. A Humble Offering to Bhagavan Sri Sathya Sai Baba (Prasanthi Nilayam: Sri Sathya Sai Sadhana Trust, 2011).

76. He was identified as a *faqīr* (lit. "poor man"), a Muslim mendicant subsisting on alms. For an introduction to his figure, see A. Rigopoulos, "Shirdi Sai Baba," in *Brill's Encyclopedia of Hinduism*. Vol. 5, 641–50. For comprehensive studies, see C. B. Satpathy, *New Findings on Shirdi Sai Baba* (New Delhi: Sterling, 2019); K. R. D. Shepherd, *Sai Baba: Faqir of Shirdi* (New Delhi: Sterling, 2017); K. McLain, *The Afterlife of Sai Baba: Competing Visions of a Global Saint* (Seattle and London: University of Washington Press, 2016); K. R. D. Shepherd, *Sai Baba of Shirdi: A Biographical Investigation* (New Delhi: Sterling, 2015); M. Warren, *Unravelling the Enigma: Shirdi Sai Baba in the Light of Sufism* (New

Delhi: Sterling, 1999; revised ed., 2004); Swami Sai Sharan Anand, *Shri Sai Baba*, trans. from Gujarati by V. B. Kher (New Delhi: Sterling, 1997); A. Rigopoulos, *The Life and Teachings of Sai Baba of Shirdi* (Albany: State University of New York Press, 1993); M. V. Kamath and V. B. Kher, *Sai Baba of Shirdi: A Unique Saint* (Bombay: Jaico, 1991). See also V. B. Kher, *Sai Baba: His Divine Glimpses*, foreword by M. V. Kamath (New Delhi: New Dawn, 2001).

77. Shivaram, *Sathya Sai Baba: God in Action*, 19.

78. Ramakrishna taught that all supernatural powers (*siddhis*) were obstacles along the spiritual path; see Shrî Râmakrishna, *Alla ricerca di Dio*. Parole raccolte e annotate da Jean Herbert (Roma: Ubaldini Editore, 1963), 145–49. On the notion of *camatkāra*, see A. Pelissero, *Estetica indiana* (Brescia: Morcelliana, 2019), 45–55.

79. See M. Piantelli, "Prefazione," in H. Murphet, *Sai Baba l'uomo dei miracoli* (Torino: Edizioni Sadhana, 1972), 7–12. In 1980, to a visitor who asked him what he thought of Sathya Sai Baba's "materializations" and "dematerializations," the Vedāntin teacher Nisargadatta Maharaj (1897–1981) said: "It's just for show. Forget about it"; Nisargadatta Maharaj, *Non Dualismo*. Prefazione di Giuseppe Genna (Milano: il Saggiatore, 2017), 384 (my translation). On the issue of powers, see K. A. Jacobsen, ed., *Yoga Powers: Extraordinary Capacities Attained Through Meditation and Concentration* (Leiden: Brill, 2012).

80. Kasturi, *Loving God*, 67. See also N. Kasturi, *Sathyam Sivam Sundaram, Part IV* (Prasanthi Nilayam: Sri Sathya Sai Books and Publications, 1981), 91.

81. Shivaram, *Sathya Sai Baba: God in Action*, 83.

82. Balachandran was the only son to his parents and his family was not very orthodox, which was something that Kasturi appreciated; Padmamma, *Twameva Matha*, 5. For a description of the traditional practice of *vadhūparīkṣā* or "evaluation of the bride to be," see Nanjunda Swamy, *Where the Angels Roamed*, 160–62.

83. In the 1940s and 1950s, the young guru frequently visited the homes of his devotees in Bangalore. He also visited the house of the sisters of the Rani of Chincholi; see Kasturi, *Loving God*, 107–108.

84. Lit. "vision." The transformative experience of seeing the divine and being seen by it; see K. Valpey, "*Pūjā* and *darśana*," in *Brill's Encyclopedia of Hinduism*. Vol. II. *Sacred Texts and Languages, Ritual Traditions, Arts, Concepts*, ed. K. A. Jacobsen, H. Basu, A. Malinar, and V. Narayanan (Leiden: Brill, 2010), 380–94.

85. Kasturi, *Loving God*, 67.

86. Ibid., 68.

87. See Padmamma, *Twameva Matha*, viii.

88. "He Is My Swami"—Part 1, http://media.radiosai.org/journals/Vol_05/01MAY07/14-h2h_special.htm, 3.

89. Kasturi, *Loving God*, 70.

90. Ibid.

91. He and his wife were early devotees who first met the guru in 1945. Their house was located on Richmond Road.

92. Kasturi, *Loving God*, 71.

93. Ibid., 71–72.

94. Ibid., 74.

95. Kasturi states that Sathya Sai Baba looked younger: "He did not convince me, as having been born in 1926. The year must be nearer 1932, I felt"; ibid., 76. In school records the guru's date of birth is recorded as October 4, 1929, against the traditionally recognized date of November 23, 1926; see Padmanaban, *Love Is My Form*, 68, 132. Nonetheless, Padmanaban notes that "it has long been a practice in the schools to record a date of birth as being much later than the 'actual' date of birth—in order to facilitate career prospects"; ibid., 68.

96. Shivaram, Sathya Sai Baba: *God in Action*, 18.

97. Kasturi, *Loving God*, 337.

98. Ibid., 339.

99. See N. Kasturi, *Sathyam Sivam Sundaram, Part I (1926–1960). Bhagavan Sri Sathya Sai Baba* (Prasanthi Nilayam: Sri Sathya Sai Books and Publications, 1980), 93–94.

100. See "Souljourns—Part 2, Vijaya Kumari" (https://www.youtube.com/watch?v=rDLJAe5HBfA), minutes 5–8. This interview was recorded in Whitefield, Bangalore, at the beginning of 2013.

101. See "He Is My Swami"—Part 1, http://media.radiosai.org/journals/Vol_05/01MAY07/14-h2h_special.htm, 7–8. According to Mrs. Vijayakumari, Kasturi became a staunch *bhakta* with no more doubts only when he started translating the guru's discourses; see "Souljourns—Part 2, Vijaya Kumari" (https://www.youtube.com/watch?v=rDLJAe5HBfA), minute 7.

102. He would often claim having been to Shirdi during his trances. On Vijayadaśamī, the day when Shirdi Sai Baba died, he would always fall into a trance and "visit" Shirdi; see Kasturi, *Loving God*, 96–97; Padmamma, *Twameva Matha*, 15.

103. On Hindu marriage and the social and religious construction of the married person, see G. Pfeffer, "Kinship and Marriage," in *Brill's Encyclopedia of Hinduism*, ed. K. A. Jacobsen, H. Basu, A. Malinar, and V. Narayanan (Brill Online, 2012).

104. The reminiscences of Kasturi's son M. Venkata Narayana Murthy are noteworthy:

> The first tragedy in the house occurred when I was in Glasgow; my younger brother, a brilliant student of the Engineering College, died. I had to bear this tragedy alone, far away from home, but when I

> returned home, smiles had returned, for, you [Sathya Sai Baba] had taken direct charge. When father wrote to me about his having secured you, and how you were helping my people to overcome the pangs of the tragedy, I was happy. But, I was confused, with my new born pride of having become a scientist with a Ph.D., when he described the miracles he witnessed. I had the good fortune of having your *Darshan*, *Sparshan* [contact, i.e., especially touching the guru's feet] and *Sambhashan* [a talk exchange] on my return in early 1949 and I recall how sweet you were to me. (Murthy, *The Greatest Adventure*, 2)

On the motivations for guru seeking, see M. Warrier, "*Guru* Choice and Spiritual Seeking in Contemporary India," *International Journal of Hindu Studies* 7, no. 1–3 (2003): 37–39.

105. See Kasturi, *Loving God*, 74 ff. See also Rao, *Sathya Sai Baba: God as Man*, 89; Padmanaban, *Love Is My Form*, 523–27 (with pictures of the marriage). Kasturi's daughter reports that her wedding was celebrated on October 20, 1950, day of Dasara; see Padmamma, *Twameva Matha*, 8–16. This date is problematic, however, since there were no Dasara celebrations that year, Prasanthi Nilayam being under construction; see Kasturi, *Loving God*, 114. Celebrations were conducted only one month later, on November 23, 1950, along with the guru's birthday and the inauguration of Prasanthi Nilayam; see Padmanaban, *Love Is My Form*, 529 n. 32. Yet even the 1948 date is troublesome: Ranganathan Padmanaban writes that the Dasara festival was not celebrated that year as Sathya Sai Baba stayed at the residence of his devotee D. Sakamma in Bangalore between August and October; see ibid., 452–53 (the author, however, contradicts himself, stating that in 1948 the guru delivered an invitation for Dasara to the Rani of Chicholi; ibid., 463). At any rate, Padma's married life turned out to be unhappy and fraught with hardships and her husband had to face many difficulties at finding suitable jobs. Whenever her life at home became unbearable, Padma came to Puttaparthi with her three children and found shelter at Sathya Sai Baba's feet; see Padmamma, *Twameva Matha*. On the letters the guru wrote to Padmamma in her times of distress, see https://soundcloud.com/kg-sreeganeshan/interview-padma-kasturi.

106. Also spelled Dassera/Dussera, from Sanskrit *daśahara* ("the tenth day [festival]"). It is the culmination of the "nine night" (Navaratri) festival, celebrating the goddess Durgā's defeat of the buffalo-demon Mahiṣāsura. It is also known as Vijayadaśamī since it coincides with the climax of the Rama Lila festival, on the tenth day (*daśamī*) of which Rāma's victory (*vijaya*) over the demon Rāvaṇa is celebrated.

107. Sathya Sai Baba gave the following message to the wedded couple:

> The path of the wife is Dharmam. The path of the husband is Brahman. May you develop a mutual love for both the paths and live a life of mutual understanding. Justify the adage that every marriage is the union of Siva and Shakthi forces. Lead an exemplary life to show the way to contemporary boys and girls, and win a good name to the home of your birth and to the new home acquired. Utilize your physical bodies for the selfless divine services. Try to move closer to Param Jyothi and attain enlightenment through Wisdom! Amma! Endeavor to justify the attributes of your married status as . . . Gruhalakshmi! Dharma Pathni! Illalu! and safeguard them at all costs! (Padmanaban, *Love is My Form*, 527)

108. The college is named after the donor Sri Dharma Rathnakara Rajanahalli Maddurayappa of Davangere.

109. See Kasturi, *Loving God*, 111–13.

110. "Sai's kasturi . . . A Phantasmagoric Fragrance Forever," at http://www.saibabaofindia.com/sais_kasturi_heart2heart.htm, 14. See also Nanjunda Swamy, *Where the Angels Roamed*, 53.

111. According to real value, it was worth about seventy rupees. Kasturi considered it fit, neither thick nor thin; see Kasturi, *Loving God*, 366.

112. See ibid., 120–21. The Sri Sathya Sai Institute of Higher Learning (Deemed University) was inaugurated in Prasanthi Nilayam three decades later, on November 22, 1981, in the presence of the then chief justice of India, Justice Y. V. Chandrachud, and other dignitaries and heads of State. Kasturi had written only incomplete theses—"The Last Rajas of Coorg," which was very near to completion, plus a few chapters on "Factory Laws in India" and a few dozen files on "The Dutch Merchants at Cochin"—and had not been able to secure a PhD from either the Madras or Mysore universities. In 1940, he published a short article titled "The Last Rajas of Coorg" in *The Half-Yearly Journal of the Mysore University: Section B—Science 1*, 1: 75–79.

113. On the guru's first visit to their home, Kasturi composed two songs in his honor; see Padmamma, *Twameva Matha*, 115. Both Kasturi's wife Rajamma and his mother Janakamma were devoted to Sathya Sai Baba. Janakamma lived to be more than eighty years old—she passed away in the mid-1960s, in the month of May—and the guru was always fond of her and Rajamma; see ibid., 97–101. Kasturi narrates having had a vivid dream of his mother six months after she passed away, in which she instructed him to read the *Bhagavatam*, that is, the *Bhāgavata Purāṇa*; see Kasturi, *Loving God*, 359–60.

114. In September 1956, Sathya Sai Baba convinced Kasturi, despite his reluctance, to put his talents to use and become the Producer of Programs for the newly established All India Radio Station in Bangalore. The Akash Vani welcomed

Kasturi as her old lover: for fifteen months he greatly enjoyed the post, until in January 1958 his guru called him back to Puttaparthi to become the editor of his monthly newsletter *Sanathana Sarathi*; ibid., 190–95.

115. Padmamma, *Twameva Matha*, 105.

116. Kasturi, *Loving God*, 187.

117. He edited a couple of books together with Adya Rangacharya (1904–1984), who wrote under the pen name Shriranga: Shriranga and N. Kasturi, eds., *Ekanka Natakagalu* (Bangalore: Sharat Agencies, 1957); Shriranga and N. Kasturi, eds., *Cheppudu Matalu and Other Kannada Plays in Telugu*, trans. T. Ramachandra (Madras: The Southern Languages Book Trust, 1960). In the 1960s, Kasturi even published a short biography in Kannada on Krishnaraja Wadiyar IV (1884–1940), the famous *mahārāja* of Mysore: *Shri Krishnarajendra Odeyaravaru* (Mysore: Samsthanada Vayaskara Shikshanasamiti, n.d.).

118. Kasturi, *Loving God*, 357.

119. On the criticism of Sathya Sai Baba by "rationalists" and followers of Ramakrishna, see ibid., 299–300.

120. Ibid., 380, 388–89.

121. Kasturi, *Sathyam Sivam Sundaram, Part I (1926–1960)*, iii.

122. See Kasturi, *Loving God*, 307. G. P. Rajaratnam translated several writings of Sathya Sai Baba into Kannada.

123. Once, in a conversation with John S. Hislop, the guru of Puttaparthi mentioned how Ramakrishna succeeded in transforming Vivekananda:

> HISLOP: Baba said Ramakrishna Paramahansa merely touched Vivekananda and transformed him?
>
> SAI: Yes. But it was temporary. After a while it fell away. Vivekananda's strong temper rose again, and he had to work out his own sadhana. What Ramakrishna accomplished was to reverse the trend of Vivekananda's life from downwards into material life, to upward into spiritual sadhana. Without that, Vivekananda would have continued into materialistic life. (J. S. Hislop, *Conversations with Bhagavan Sri Sathya Sai Baba* [Bangalore: Sri Sathya Sai Baba Society of America, 1979], 99–100)

124. See Kasturi, *Loving God*, 230.

125. Ibid., 100. Sathya Sai Baba held Ramakrishna in high esteem, viewing him as a true Paramahamsa; see H. Levin, *Good Chances*. Introduction by Elsie Cowan (Prasanthi Nilayam: Sai Towers, 1998), 143. Once, the guru presided over an anniversary celebration of the Ramakrishna Mission in Bangalore; see S. Balu, *Living Divinity* (London: Sawbridge Enterprises, 1981), 233.

126. B. V. Narasimhaswami, *Sri Sai Baba's Charters and Sayings,* foreword by M. B. Rege (Madras: All India Sai Samaj, 1942), 8.

127. See Kasturi, *Loving God*, 366.

128. See ibid., 282, 375.

129. Kasturi, *Gurudev*, 4.

130. See Shivaram, *Sathya Sai Baba: God in Action*, 134, 248. With regard to Ramakrishna's spiritual development, Sathya Sai Baba noted: "Ramakrishna started as a devotee of God. There was Mother Kali and himself. They were separate. A duality existed. At one point he engaged in a certain action, and Mother Kali never appeared to him again. Towards the end he merged in God and was God-realized"; Hislop, *Conversations with Bhagavan Sri Sathya Sai Baba*, 133. Moreover: "The concentration of Ramakrishna Paramahamsa was naturally so strong that he grew something of a tail when meditating on Hanuman, the monkey. His body was just a changing bubble, his concentration was so strong"; ibid., 168.

131. It is noteworthy that in his early public discourses Sathya Sai Baba mentioned Ramakrishna twenty times; see D. Gries and E. Gries, eds., *An Index of Sathya Sai Speaks, Volumes I–XI. Covering Discourses by Bhagavan Sri Sathya Sai Baba 1953–1982* (Tustin, CA: Sathya Sai Book Center of America, 1993), 157, 273, 277–78.

132. See Kasturi, *Sathyam Sivam Sundaram, Part I (1926–1960)*, 235; Kasturi, *Loving God*, 221–22, 257, 370.

133. See ibid., 342, 356, 379, 387.

Chapter 2

1. On its authoritative status, see Smriti Srinivas, *In the Presence of Sai Baba: Body, City, and Memory in a Global Religious Movement* (Leiden: Brill, 2008), 50 n. 2; Tulasi Srinivas, *Winged Faith: Rethinking Globalization and Religious Pluralism Through the Sathya Sai Movement* (New York: Columbia University Press, 2010), 53, 62, 357 n. 62.

2. See Kasturi, *Loving God*, 227, 389.

3. See Tulasi Srinivas, "Sathya Sai Baba," in *Brill's Encyclopedia of Hinduism*, ed. K. A. Jacobsen, H. Basu, A. Malinar, and V. Narayanan (Brill Online, 2012), 3; Ead., *Winged Faith*, 53.

4. See L. A. Babb, *Redemptive Encounters: Three Modern Styles in the Hindu Tradition* (Berkeley: University of California Press, 1986), 162 n. 2; Tulasi Srinivas, *Winged Faith*, 357 n. 62.

5. See Kasturi, *Loving God*, 89. For an English translation of the *Śrī Sāī Saccarita*, see G. R. Dabholkar (Hemadpant), *Shri Sai Satcharita: The Life and Teachings of Shirdi Sai Baba*, trans. I. Kher (New Delhi: Sterling, 1999). On

Dabholkar's original wish to write a book on the Shirdi saint and the latter's consent to his project, see ibid., 1–33. Kasturi visited Shirdi at least once in his lifetime: his daughter accompanied him and they stayed there three days; Padmamma, *Twameva Matha*, 73.

6. Kasturi, *Loving God*, 89. The Pandhari bhajan group created by the young Sathya was so called in honor of the god Viṭṭhal of Pandharpur. In this way, the guru of Puttaparthi exhibited his link to the Marāṭhī religious tradition and to his "prior incarnation," the village of Shirdi being extolled as a modern Pandharpur. On the Pandhari bhajans, see Sri Sathya Sai Baba, *His Story as Told by Himself*, 27–32; S. C. Bhatnagar, ed., *Sai Speaks About His Childhood (Based on Sai's Discourses).* A Humble Offering to Bhagawan Sri Sathya Sai Baba on His 85th Auspicious Birthday (Prasanthi Nilayam: Sri Sathya Sai Sadhana Trust, 2011), 155–60. For an excellent portrayal of Viṭṭhal, see R. C. Dhere, *The Rise of a Folk God: Viṭṭhal of Pandharpur* (New York: Oxford University Press, 2011).

7. See N. Kasturi, *Sathyam Sivam Sundaram, Part II. The Life of Bhagavan Sri Sathya Sai Baba* (Prasanthi Nilayam: Sri Sathya Sai Books and Publications, 1981), 142–43; Kasturi, *Loving God*, 381. By the same token, Kasturi would glorify his master as "the Kavimkaveenaam, the Poet of Poets, an appellation ascribed to God in the Vedas"; N. Kasturi, *Sathyam Sivam Sundaram, Part III* (Prasanthi Nilayam: Sri Sathya Sai Books and Publications, 1981), 105. On the "poet of poets," see Sri Sathya Sai Baba, *His Story as Told by Himself*, 73–87.

8. On these issues, see S. Aravamudan, *Guru English: South Asian Religion in a Cosmopolitan Language* (Princeton: Princeton University Press), 2006.

9. As M. N. Rao observes:

> Kasturi is a prolific writer with a facile pen and a photographic memory; a literary caricaturist and a juggler in vocabulary; and a linguist who understood early in life, Baba's language. He was fortunate to be chosen as the instrument to help spread Baba's message to the English speaking world through the four excellent biographic volumes of "Sathyam Sivam Sundaram"; through the simultaneous rendering of Baba's divine discourses into English; and through English translations of Baba's writings. (Rao, *Sathya Sai Baba: God as Man*, 90)

10. See K. P. Prentiss, *The Embodiment of Bhakti* (New York: Oxford University Press, 1999), 7.

11. See Kasturi, *Loving God*, 187; Kasturi, *Sathyam Sivam Sundaram, Part I (1926–1960)*, 294.

12. A. Schulman, *Baba* (New York: Viking Press, 1973 [1971]), 119.

13. Ibid., 120.

14. Ibid., 119.

15. Tulasi Srinivas, *Sathya Sai Baba*, 3.

16. See primarily Padmanaban, *Love Is My Form*, which in its thoroughly researched six hundred pages offers a variety of documented primary sources on the first twenty-five years of Sathya Sai Baba's life, such as his official school records and certificates, various letters written by him, and the sale deeds concerning the sites of the so-called Old Mandir and of the Prasanthi Nilayam ashram. For a video on Ranganathan Padmanaban and an interview with him with details concerning his painstaking research on Sathya Sai Baba's early years, see https://vimeo.com/139318585; https://www.youtube.com/watch?v=kR5NPvBsZQY. See also R. Padmanaban, "Baba Develops a Professional Photographer: The Material Is No Different From the Spiritual for Baba," *Spiritual Impressions* 1, no. 2 (May–June 2001): 22–23.

17. Aitken, *Sri Sathya Sai Baba*, 78. Bill Aitken remarks that "in his narrative . . . he [Kasturi] prefers to dodge the sociological realities of rural poverty and take refuge behind the smokescreen of ancient quick-fix mythology"; ibid. Moreover: "Professor Kasturi skirts the ground realities . . . in favor of mythological euphoria"; ibid., 213. However, it is a mistake to expect a scientific treatment from the author of a *Carita* whose aim is essentially devotional. For an interview with Bill Aitken on his book, see https://www.youtube.com/watch?v=6Nr8g96VrpI. By Bill Aitken see also "Sathya Sai Baba: A Non-devotee's Perspective," in *Divine Grace: Sathya Sai Baba. An India Today Impact Presentation*, The India Today Group, 2011, 48.

18. Kasturi, *Sathyam Sivam Sundaram, Part IV*, 169. See also Kasturi, *Sathyam Sivam Sundaram, Part II*, 143. Over the years, Kasturi has repeatedly stressed this point. Robert Priddy writes: "Kasturi told me how Baba had told him that people would think the history was all some sort of 'Arabian Nights Entertainment,' some imaginative fairy tale concocted between himself and Kasturi! Baba added that they should let the message spread by word of mouth awhile yet. In good time there would be enough hunger for the meal; then Kasturi would be called on to serve it"; R. Priddy, *Source of the Dream: My Way to Sathya Sai Baba* (York Beach, ME: Samuel Weiser, 1998), 224.

19. Ibid., 225–26. Previously, Sathya Sai Baba had told Kasturi that he could not be understood through books but only through personal experience.

20. With the noticeable exception of the Telugu poem *Sri Sayeeshuni Charitra*, written by Sathya Sai Baba's school teacher V. C. Kondappa, which was published in 1944. The author presents young Sathya's narration of the first sixteen unknown years of Shirdi Sai Baba, strengthening his claim to be none other than the Shirdi saint. For an English translation, see V. C. Kondappa, *Sai's Story: As Revealed by Sathya Sai to His Teacher* (Bangalore: Sai Towers, 2004). See also Padmanaban, *Love Is My Form*, 199; R. Padmanaban, "V. C. Kondappa: The Teacher Biographer," *Spiritual Impressions* 1, no. 2 (May–June 2001): 56–60. In writing his biography, Kasturi made ample use of this text.

21. The celebration of the guru's birthday as a major festival was inaugurated on November 23, 1946; see Padmanaban, *Love Is My Form*, 331.

22. See M. J. Spurr, *Sathya Sai Baba as Avatar. "His Story" and the History of an Idea.* PhD Diss. University of Canterbury, Christchurch, New Zealand, 2007, 37.

23. Thus, Bill Aitken observes: "No one reading *Sathyam Sivam Sundaram* . . . would guess that . . . Puttaparthi lies in the heart of the region gripped by Naxalism, modern India's defiant rural agitation against feudal exploitation by landlords. Kasturi, like all gospel writers, is committed to giving us the good news"; Aitken, *Sri Sathya Sai Baba*, 78. For an overview of the Naxalite rebellions which interested Andhra Pradesh especially during the decade 1980–90, see I. Saint-Mézard, *Atlas de l'Inde. Une nouvelle puissance mondiale* (Paris: Éditions Autrement, 2016), 66–67.

24. Also spelled *ānā,* it was a currency unit formerly used in India, equal to 1/16 of a rupee. It was subdivided into four *paisa* or twelve *pies.*

25. Bhatnagar, *Sai Speaks About His Childhood*, 185. Hilda Charlton, an early American devotee who met the guru of Puttaparthi in the mid-1960s, recalls:

> At one time . . . he said to me, "I'll give you three siddhis [extraordinary powers]." As the days went by . . . I cornered him and I said, "Baba, what were those three siddhis that you're going to give me?" He said, "*Prema siddhi*," which is love, "*Shanti siddhi*," which is peace, and "*Anandam siddhi*," which is bliss. I looked at him and I said, "Those aren't siddhis, Baba." I've never seen Baba so strict in my life. He pulled up another inch, which made him then five foot three, and he said, "If you want lesser things, go to a lesser teacher." I went away and thought about it, and I thought, "My God, he's giving me God. God is bliss." . . . I went to him and I said, "Excuse me, Baba, that was my fault." He said, "Not your fault. My fault. Swami's fault." How sweet and humble—such humility, such wonder he is, such love he shows for everybody. (H. Charlton, *Saints Alive* [Woodstock, NY: Golden Quest, 1989], ch. 2)

26. Kasturi, *Sathyam Sivam Sundaram, Part I (1926–1960)*, 30–31.

27. Kasturi, *Loving God*, 226–27.

28. Gupta, *The Gospel of Sri Ramakrishna*, 132–33, 305–306.

29. See Kasturi, *Loving God*, 227–28, 299. On Vivekananda's seminal Yoga teachings in the West, see E. De Michelis, *A History of Modern Yoga: Patanjali and Western Esotericism* (London/New York: Continuum, 2004), 91–126, 149–80; S. Strauss, *Positioning Yoga* (Oxford/New York: Berg, 2005). See also Syman, *The Subtle Body: The Story of Yoga in America* (New York: Farrar, Strauss, and

Giroux, 2010), 62–79; C. L. Albanese, *A Republic of Mind and Spirit: A Cultural History of American Metaphysical Religion* (New Haven/London: Yale University Press, 2007), 354–58.

30. N. Kasturi, *Garland of 108 Precious Gems: Ashtothara Sathanama Rathnamala* (Prasanthi Nilayam: Sri Sathya Sai Education and Publication Foundation, 1979), 78–79.

31. See http://www.gandhistudycentre.org/pdf/truth.pdf.

32. Tulasi Srinivas reports the words of a devotee: "I like Narayana Kasturi's book best. He is Baba's first, best *bhakta* (devotee). So nicely he writes about the Swami's childhood years and different miracles"; Srinivas, *Winged Faith*, 81–82.

33. See D. A. Swallow, "Ashes and Powers: Myth, Rite, and Miracle in an Indian God-man's Cult," *Modern Asian Studies* 16, no. 1 (1982): 126.

34. One of the earliest documented "materializations" is a photo of Shirdi Sai Baba with Kṛṣṇa, Rāma, Śiva, and Hanuman in the background; see Padmanaban, *Love Is My Form*, 136. On Sathya Sai Baba's alleged miracles, see E. Haraldsson, *Modern Miracles: Sathya Sai Baba: The Story of a Modern Day Prophet* (Guildford: White Crow Books, 2013); B. Steel, *The Powers of Sathya Sai Baba* (Delhi: BR Publishing Corporation, 1999); B. Steel, *The Sathya Sai Baba Compendium: A Guide to the First Seventy Years* (York Beach, ME: Samuel Weiser, 1997), 129–71. For study cases on some nineteenth- and twentieth-century miracle workers, see C. G. Dempsey and S. J. Raj, eds., *Miracle as Modern Conundrum in South Asian Religious Traditions* (Albany: State University of New York Press, 2008).

35. Babb, *Redemptive Encounters*, 161–62.

36. On the supernatural in literature and in a fairy tale such as *Hänsel und Gretel*, see F. Orlando, *Il soprannaturale letterario. Storia, logica e forme*, edited by S. Brugnolo, L. Pellegrini, and V. Sturli. Preface by Thomas Pavel (Torino: Einaudi, 2017).

37. Kasturi observed: "When I wrote the book *Sathyam Sivam Sundaram* people said, I was off my head! But, now they say that I am not sufficiently off my head!"; Shivaram, *Sathya Sai Baba: God in Action*, 209.

38. Priddy, *Source of the Dream*, 225.

39. Following the guru typology proposed by Meera Nanda, Sathya Sai Baba is a "type 1 guru," whose appeal is dependent on the miracles he is said to perform; see M. Nanda, *The God Market: How Globalisation Is Making India more Hindu* (Delhi: Random House, 2009).

40. Balu, *Living Divinity*, 305.

41. See Kasturi, *Sathyam Sivam Sundaram, Part I (1926–1960)*, 62; Kasturi, *Loving God*, 173.

42. Kasturi, *Sathyam Sivam Sundaram, Part I (1926–1960)*, 108.

43. Sri Sathya Sai Baba, *His Story as Told by Himself*, 126. This prayer was composed by Rabindranath Tagore and its singing began daily sessions in

schools established by Annie Besant (1847–1933) of the Theosophical Society. It was to become the forerunner of the national anthem; see Padmanaban, *Love Is My Form*, 126.

44. In other words, he will die. The *samādhi* is a memorial marking the tomb of a saint or of a renouncer (*saṃnyāsin*).

45. Kondappa, *Sai's Story*, 9. See also ibid., 21.

46. See Kasturi, *Sathyam Sivam Sundaram, Part I (1926–1960)*, 75–77, 83, 87, 104, 114, 125–26, 240. See also Kasturi, *Loving God*, 247. As early as January 1946, Sathya Sai Baba wrote a letter to one Madhoji Rao saying that he made no distinction between rich and poor; see Padmanaban, *Love Is My Form*, 276. On the guru's equality, see also ibid., 331.

47. Ibid., 271.

48. See Peddabottu, *Autobiography*, trans. Dr. Sathya Sai Shree Lakshmi (Hyderabad: Visual Graphix & Printing, 2013), 214–15.

49. In 1960, many people living in surrounding villages were still hostile toward him, see D. Roumanoff, *Candide au pays des Gourous. Journal d'un explorateur de l'Inde spirituelle.* Préface de Michel Hulin (Croissy-Beaubourg: Dervy-Livres, 1990), 143.

50. The hereditary chieftain and revenue official in charge of land records and the collection of taxes.

51. See Schulman, *Baba*, 135–36; Kasturi, *Easwaramma: The Chosen Mother* (Prasanthi Nilayam: Sri Sathya Sai Books and Publications Trust, 1984), 35–36.

52. Ibid., 77–78; Sri Sathya Sai Baba, *His Story as Told by Himself*, 179; Bhatnagar, *Sai Speaks About His Childhood*, 293–95; Schulman, *Baba*, 135.

53. See Balu, *Living Divinity*, 34; Bhatnagar, *Sai Speaks About His Childhood*, 292–93.

54. See Kasturi, *Sathyam Sivam Sundaram, Part I (1926–1960)*, 59–60; Padmanaban, *Love Is My Form*, 237, 264 n. 10; Roumanoff, *Candide au pays des Gourous*, 134.

55. See Padmamma, *Twameva Matha*, 11. See also Balu, *Living Divinity*, 149.

56. Sathya Sai Baba's elder brother Seshama Raju wished that Sathya be trained to become a big officer and was skeptical of his divinity; see Padmanaban, *Love Is My Form*, 88. On the other hand, Kasturi notes how in the mid-1950s the guru's father Pedda Venkama Raju was devoted to his son, whom he respectfully addressed as Bhagawan Sri Sri Sathya Sai Baba; see Kasturi, *Loving God*, 188.

57. Kasturi writes that "a few press comments that rose from ignorance pained him"; Kasturi, *Sathyam Sivam Sundaram, Part II*, 8.

58. Padmanaban, *Love Is My Form*, 349.

59. Ibid., 350–51.

60. The guru claimed that his was an immaculate conception; see Sri Sathya Sai Baba, *His Story as Told by Himself*, 182.

61. The interpretive writings of sage Āpastamba on the *Vedas*, that is, his school of Vedic exegesis.

62. Sage Bharadvāja's spiritual lineage. For an in-depth analysis of Sathya Sai Baba's *gotra* and *sūtra,* see Spurr, *Sathya Sai Baba as Avatar*, 97–114. The guru claimed that even Shirdi Sai Baba belonged to this same *gotra* and *sūtra*; see N. Kasturi, *The Light of Love: An Account of Bhagawan Sri Sathya Sai Baba's Visit to East Africa and His Divine Discourses* (Prasanthi Nilayam: Sri Sathya Sai Sadhana Trust, 2014), 67. See also Kasturi, *Garland of 108 Precious Gems*, 32.

63. Although Kasturi speaks of October 20, 1940, as the date of the "Grand Declaration," the correct date appears to be October 20, 1943; see Padmanaban, *Love Is My Form*, 149, 160 n. 64.

64. Ibid., 117.

65. The eldest son of the couple, Seshama Rāju (1911–1985), was to become a Telugu scholar and teacher and lived a retired life in Puttaparthi until his death. The second- and third-born were girls, Veṅkamma (1918–1993) and Parvathamma (1920–1996), who also lived in the village all their lives. The youngest son, Jānakīrām Rāju (1931–2005), was educated up to high school and was for decades an influential member of the Sri Sathya Sai Central Trust, which was founded in 1972 with Sathya Sai Baba as chairman. On Sathya Sai Baba's brothers and sisters, see Padmanaban, *Love Is My Form*, 88. Apparently, Easwaramma suffered four miscarriages before having Sathyanārāyaṇa. She prayed to the village gods, fasted, and performed the auspicious *satyanārāyaṇapūjā,* the worship of Satyanārāyaṇa, that is, Viṣṇu: she finally gave birth to a child and he was named Sathyanārāyaṇa as a thanksgiving to Viṣṇu for answering her prayers; see ibid., 17. For the Ratnākaram family tree, see ibid., 22–23. On the *satyanārāyaṇapūjā,* see Dabholkar, *Shri Sai Satcharita: The Life and Teachings of Shirdi Sai Baba*, 213 (chap. 13, v. 181).

66. In South Indian villages, cross cousin marriage was and still is a common pattern. The effect of such marriages is to bind people in relatively small, tight-knit kin groups. The younger sister of Ratnākaram Kondama Rāju, Veṅkaṭa Subbamma, married one Meesaraganda Subba Rāju of Kolimigundla, a village in Kurnool district. They had six children, three sons and three daughters. Their eldest daughter was Easwaramma. When she was fourteen, Ratnākaram Kondama Rāju arranged the marriage between her and Pedda Veṅkama Rāju, his firstborn son.

67. This family name is quite common and means "sea," "ocean," lit. "jewel-mine."

68. See Sri Sathya Sai Baba, *His Story as Told by Himself*, 39, 49, 57–58; Hislop, *Conversations with Bhagavan Sri Sathya Sai Baba*, 143.

69. See Sri Sathya Sai Baba, *His Story as Told by Himself*, 18. The guru's habits were always frugal; see Padmanaban, *Love Is My Form*, 209, 562.

70. See Sri Sathya Sai Baba, *His Story as Told by Himself*, 183.

71. See Kondappa, *Sai's Story*, 7. See also Rao, *Sathya Sai Baba: God as Man*, 4; Padmanaban, *Love Is My Form*, 11, 24 n. 6.

72. See E. Thurston and K. Rangachari, *Castes and Tribes of Southern India*, vol. 1 (Madras: Government Press, 1909), 223–30; H. V. Nanjundayya and Rao Bahadur L. K. Ananthakrishna Iyer, *The Mysore Tribes and Castes*, vol. 2 (University of Mysore, 1928), 259–76.

73. See Sri Sathya Sai Baba, *His Story as Told by Himself*, 15–25, 167–76. Young Sathya often used to stay at his grandfather's house, located in a street where the hunting community of the Boyas lived. Contrary to Hindu custom, the old man didn't live together with his sons but chose to stay in a separate cottage; see Schulman, *Baba*, 121–22.

74. See Levin, *Good Chances*, 83–85. On the importance of *bhajans* in the guru's worship, see Smriti Srinivas, *In The Presence of Sai Baba*, 304–307. In his work, Kasturi recalls his lord's eminence as a playwright, see *Sathyam Sivam Sundaram, Part III*, 129.

75. The occasional presence of serial production numbers on wristwatches and other items said to have been "materialized" by Sathya Sai Baba has given rise to controversy between devotees and anti-guru activists; see S. P. Ruhela, *Sri Sathya Sai Baba and the Press (1972–1996)* (New Delhi: Umang Paperbacks, 1997), 1–6 (ch. 1, "Controversy about the Seiko Watch [1972]").

76. See Steel, *The Sathya Sai Baba Compendium*, 147–48; Padmanaban, *Love Is My Form*, 170, 205, 213, 255, 275, 279, 313, 319, 345, 357, 370, 379, 509, 523; A. K. Kamaraju, *Memories and Memoirs: Four Decades of Journey with God* (Prasanthi Nilayam: Sri Sathya Sai Books and Publications Trust, 2015), 152.

77. In the early days, the guru's relation with devotees was patterned along the lines of Kṛṣṇa *bhakti*; see Tulasi Srinivas, *Winged Faith*, 63. On Kṛṣṇa *bhakti*, see B. Holdrege, *Bhakti and Embodiment: Fashioning Divine Bodies and Devotional Bodies in Kṛṣṇa Bhakti* (London: Routledge, 2013).

78. See A. Rigopoulos, "A Modern Kalpavṛkṣa: Sathya Sai Baba and the Wish-Fulfilling Tree," in *Roots of Wisdom, Branches of Devotion: Plant Life in South Asian Traditions*, ed. F. M. Ferrari and T. Dähnhardt (Sheffield/Bristol: Equinox, 2016), 10–18.

79. See D. Baskin, *Divine Memories of Sathya Sai Baba* (San Diego: Birth Day, 1990), 226, 248. On the guru's unpredictability as being central to the understanding of the divine, see Spurr, *Sathya Sai Baba as Avatar*, 58–60.

80. Starting in 1944, through the skillful organization of one Seshagiri Rao and his daughter Sundaramma, who was a talented singer, organized *bhajans* evolved in a big way in Bangalore. The first twenty-four-hour *bhajan* session (*akhaṇḍabhajan*) was held in 1946; see Padmanaban, *Love Is My Form*, 213,

278–79, 315, 319, 323, 387. See also the testimony of Nikhil Koushik at https://www.youtube.com/watch?v=wFMJ_H0jdNY. In Bangalore, the young guru performed his first surgical operation, "materializing" the instruments necessary to cut out a duodenal ulcer; see Schulman, *Baba*, 134–35.

81. See Padmanaban, *Love Is My Form*, 289. The hagiographer reports how Sathya Sai Baba appeared to him in lieu of Veṅkaṭeśvara when he once visited Tirupati; see Kasturi, *Loving God*, 6–7. See also ibid., 307, and Balu, *Living Divinity*, 170.

82. See Kasturi, *Sathyam Sivam Sundaram, Part I (1926–1960)*, 271. On Puttaparthi's foundational myth and its exaltation as being as sacred as Tirupati, see A. Rigopoulos, "The Construction of a Cultic Center Through Narrative: The Founding Myth of the Village of Puttaparthi and Sathya Sai Baba," in *History of Religions* 54, no. 2 (Nov. 2014): 117–50. On Tirupati's sacredness in the guru's own words, see Kamaraju, *Memories and Memoirs*, 42.

83. See Balu, *Living Divinity*, 113.

84. See Bhatnagar, *Sai Speaks About His Childhood*, 339–40. On Puttaparthi's glory, see also ibid., 9–20.

85. Arnold Schulman writes:

> Many people (none of whom would consent to be quoted) told the writer that one of the important motivating factors in Baba's decision to build an ashram was that he already had acquired the necessary backing of high-ranking government officials to have the ashram incorporated as a separate township, thereby escaping the *karnam,* who, it is said, kept asking for higher and higher taxes. (Schulman, *Baba*, 136–37)

On the meaning of *praśānti*, which echoes *Bhagavadgītā* 18.62c, see Shivaram, *Sathya Sai Baba: God in Action*, 127.

86. See Padmanaban, *Love Is My Form*, 550–51. Shirdi Sai Baba is depicted as wearing an ochre robe and an ochre headdress, clearly in an effort to Hinduize him. In fact, the *faqīr* used to wear a white robe (*kafnī*) which is the typical attire of Sufi adepts. Nonetheless, Mhalsapati, the earliest devotee who first addressed him as "Sai"—a term of Persian origin often attributed to Muslim ascetics, meaning "saint"—states that when he arrived in Shirdi he wore an ochre dress and cap; see Kher, *Sai Baba: His Divine Glimpses*, 19; R. B. M. W. Pradhan, *Shri Sai Baba of Shirdi: A Glimpse of Indian Spirituality* (Shirdi: Shree Sai Baba Sansthan, 1982), 28. In Shirdi and in the publications of the Shirdi Sai Baba Sansthan, the *faqīr* is often portrayed in an ochre/orange robe; see ibid. On the color of Shirdi Sai Baba's robe—white, orange, and even green—see Shepherd, *Sai Baba: Faqir of Shirdi*, 64; V. Chitluri, *Baba's Rinanubandh: Leelas during His Sojourn in Shirdi*

(New Delhi: Sterling, 2007), 42. On the evolution of Sathya Sai Baba's robe, see Padmanaban, *Love Is My Form*, 187, 432.

87. See Roumanoff, *Candide au pays des Gourous*, 139.

88. Kasturi, *Loving God*, 162.

89. Kasturi, *Sathyam Sivam Sundaram, Part I (1926–1960)*, 98–99.

90. Ibid., 105. On the history and origin of Prasanthi Mandir *bhajans,* see https://www.youtube.com/watch?v=Gmm4I_Al0CE.

91. *Sai Suprabhatam: Learning Sanskrit Through Sri Sathya Sai Suprabhatam* (Prasanthi Nilayam: Sri Sathya Sai Students and Staff Welfare Society, 2009), 35. The *Sai Suprabhatam* was composed by the Telugu Pundit Dhupati Thirumalacharlu, a staunch devotee of the guru whom he first met in Venkatagiri in 1950. Soon afterward, Dhupati Thirumalacharlu transferred to Puttaparthi where he served Sathya Sai Baba for more than three decades; see ibid., 2; Padmanaban, *Love Is My Form*, 513, 519. Dhupati Thirumalacharlu also wrote a book in Telugu on Sathya Sai Baba: *Sri Sathya Sai Bala Ramayanam* (Venkatagiri, 1957).

92. Kasturi, *Sathyam Sivam Sundaram, Part I (1926–1960)*, 96.

93. Ibid., 95. On this meditation tree and its symbolism, see Rigopoulos, *A Modern Kalpavṛkṣa: Sathya Sai Baba and the Wish-Fulfilling Tree*, 18–22.

94. On the "materialization" of *liṅgas* by the guru of Puttaparthi, see Steel, *The Sathya Sai Baba Compendium*, 110–19; Padmanaban, *Love Is My Form*, 345, 349. On the suspicion of it being a conjuring trick, see Roumanoff, *Candide au pays des Gourous*, 144–45.

95. The Divine Life Society, a nonsectarian center for the development of spiritual knowledge, was founded by Swami Sivananda in 1936. On the DLS and its more recent evolutions, see V. Altglas, "Indian Gurus and the Quest for Self-perfection Among the Educated Middle-Classes," in *Salvation Goods and Religious Markets: Theory and Applications*, ed. J. Stolz (Bern: Peter Lang, 2008), 211–34; Ead., *"N'importe quelle échelle, du moment que ça monte" . . . La globalisation du religieux: Modes de diffusion et d'appropriation des pratiques et des valeurs se référant à l'hindouisme. Étude du Siddha Yoga et des Centres Sivananda en France et en Angleterre, Tomes I–III* (PhD Diss., École Pratique des Hautes Études, Paris, 2004); S. Strauss, "Locating Yoga: Ethnography and Transnational Practice," in *Constructing the Field: Ethnographic Fieldwork in the Contemporary World*, ed. V. Amit (New York: Routledge, 2000), 162–94. See also D. M. Miller, "The Divine Life Society Movement," in *Religion in Modern India*, ed. R. D. Baird (Delhi: Manohar, 1981), 81–112.

96. For an account of a devotee who witnessed the event, see Vijayakumari, *Anyathā Saranam Nasthi: Other Than You Refuge There Is None* (Ekrattuthangal, Chennai: Sai Shri Ram Printers, 2000), 262–65. She writes: "Some carried on negative propaganda about Swami, distributed leaflets, and said that He had no place for the poor, but only for the rich, and that He performed only magic

but not truth"; ibid., 265. On the guru presiding over the All-India Divine Life Society Conference at Venkatagiri, see also Balu, *Living Divinity*, 36.

97. Kasturi, *Sathyam Sivam Sundaram, Part I (1926–1960)*, 125. Apparently, Swami Satchidananda, who later witnessed an "extra-corporeal" journey of Sathya Sai Baba, got convinced of his *avatāra*hood "whatever others may take Baba to be"; ibid., 130–34.

98. Ibid., 128.

99. Ibid., 127–28. See also Kasturi, *Loving God*, 212. For the full discourse that the guru held in Venkatagiri, see Sathya Sai Baba, *Sathya Sai Speaks, Vol. 1. Discourses of Bhagawan Sri Sathya Sai Baba (Delivered during 1953–1960)* (Prasanthi Nilayam: Sri Sathya Sai Sadhana Trust, 2015), 20–22. The DLS monk Swami Sadananda would have told Kasturi that "silly stories about Baba have to be scotched and my brother Sanyasins have to be appraised of the Divinity of Baba"; Kasturi, *Sathyam Sivam Sundaram, Part I (1926–1960)*, 135.

100. Kasturi accompanied the guru, having obtained his permission. He was to travel with him on most of his trips. For an account of this 1957 tour, see http://sathyasaiwithstudents.blogspot.it/2013/08/a-north-indian-tour-with-sri-sathya-sai.html#.WMOfhtP2bwo. Sathya Sai Baba was to make further visits to North India in the 1960s, '70s, and '80s.

101. A seminal figure in the worldwide popularization and transnationalization of modern Yoga, alongside B. K. S. Iyengar (1918–2014). On Kuppuswami Iyer, alias Swami Sivananda, a physician who hailed from a distinguished Brahmin family of Tamil Nadu, see S. Strauss, "Sivananda and the Divine Life Society," in *Brill's Encyclopedia of Hinduism*, ed. K. A. Jacobsen, H. Basu, A. Malinar, and V. Narayanan (Brill Online, 2012); M. Fracchia, *Swami Sivananda e la Divine Life Society. Analisi della figura e del ruolo del guru e della sua istituzione nella riforma neo-hindu e nella diffusione dello yoga in Occidente* (MA Thesis, Università degli Studi di Padova/Università Ca' Foscari Venezia, 2009). See also J. S. Alter, *Yoga in Modern India: The Body Between Science and Philosophy* (Princeton: Princeton University Press, 2004), 63–64.

102. The idea of inviting him to Rishikesh was Swami Satchidananda's and Swami Sadananda's: they hoped he would heal their master; see Kasturi, *Loving God*, 195–96; Kasturi, *Easwaramma*, 122.

103. See Kasturi, *Sathyam Sivam Sundaram, Part I (1926–1960)*, 142–44. For another testimony to the guru's meeting with Swami Purushottamananda, see Roumanoff, *Candide au pays des Gourous*, 140.

104. On special occasions, the guru transferred his power of "materialization" to others. Recalling his youth, when several people in the village were against him, he noted:

> One day, someone invited Me for lunch in their house. They wanted to kill Me by mixing poison in the food. They were jealous of My

> reputation that was growing more and more day by day. By the time I returned from their house after taking food there, the color of My body turned blue and froth started coming out of My mouth. Then, I instructed Easwaramma to wave her hand in a circular motion. When she did so, vibhuti appeared in her hands. She wondered, "How it happened! I have seen vibhuti appearing when Swami waved His hand in a circular motion. But, how did it appear in my hands?" In fact, it was I who granted that power to her for that short period. She then mixed the vibhuti in a glass of water and gave it to Me to drink. The moment I drank that water the effect of the poison disappeared miraculously. (Sri Sathya Sai Baba, *His Story as Told by Himself*, 179)

105. See also Rao, *Sathya Sai Baba: God as Man*, 264–68. In the 1960s, the frequency of his trances reduced, and his last public trance took place in 1969, on the day of Mahāśivarātri, when he brought out a *liṅga* from his mouth; see Padmanaban, *Love Is My Form*, 141.

106. Among the many places in his hagiography where he discusses this topic, see Kasturi, *Sathyam Sivam Sundaram, Part I (1926–1960)*, 139.

107. Hislop, *Conversations with Bhagavan Sri Sathya Sai Baba*, 132.

108. See Kasturi, *Loving God*, 370; Shivaram, *Sathya Sai Baba: God in Action*, 236–37; Kasturi, *Sathyam Sivam Sundaram, Part II*, 205; Roumanoff, *Candide au pays des Gourous*, 134.

109. L. Siegel, *Net of Magic: Wonders and Deceptions in India* (Chicago and London: The University of Chicago Press, 1991), 334–35.

110. Sathya Sai Baba, *Sathya Sai Speaks, Vol. 2. Discourses of Bhagawan Sri Sathya Sai Baba Delivered During 1961–62* (Prasanthi Nilayam: Sri Sathya Sai Books and Publications, 2008), 127. It should be noted that besides the guru of Puttaparthi there were several other figures who, starting from the 1940s, pretended to be the reincarnation of Shirdi Sai Baba. In the 1960s one of these lived in Secunderabad; see Narasimhaswami, *Life of Sai Baba*, vol. 4, 175–84; Roumanoff, *Candide au pays des Gourous*, 130.

111. See Kasturi, *Garland of 108 Precious Gems*, 26. On the belief that Shirdi Sai Baba would reincarnate soon, see Dabholkar, *Shri Sai Satcharita: The Life and Teachings of Shirdi Sai Baba*, 717 (ch. 43, vv. 139, 144); Rigopoulos, *The Life and Teachings of Sai Baba of Shirdi*, 244–49. On the persistence of such belief among Shirdi Sai Baba followers, see P. Malyala, "Sri Shirdi Sai Baba—Avatar," in *Sri Sai Leela*, Newsletter of the Sri Shirdi Sai Baba Temple of Monroeville, PA (2012): 4.

112. See Rigopoulos, *The Life and Teachings of Sai Baba of Shirdi*, 367–73. On Sathya Sai Baba's understanding of religion and on his link to all religions, see Gries and Gries, *An Index of Sathya Sai Speaks, Volumes I–XI*, 160–61, 281–82.

113. As when, on July 6, 1968, in Kampala, Uganda, he gave this reply at the beginning of a session of questions and answers: "Again, Sai Baba [of Shirdi] was not a Muslim. He was a Brahmin by birth, of the Apastamba Sutra and the Bharadwaja Gotra"; Kasturi, *The Light of Love*, 67.

114. See Kasturi, *Sathyam Sivam Sundaram, Part I (1926–1960)*, 13. See also Kasturi, *Garland of 108 Precious Gems*, 32; Aitken, *Sri Sathya Sai Baba*, 88.

115. See Kasturi, *Sathyam Sivam Sundaram, Part I (1926–1960)*, 263.

116. The first hospital in Prasanthi Nilayam, the Sri Sathya Sai General Hospital, was inaugurated in October 1957; ibid., 118.

117. *Divine Grace: Sathya Sai Baba*, 1.

118. See Kasturi, *Sathyam Sivam Sundaram, Part I (1926–1960)*, 89, 108, 134, 145, 235, 239, 271. On *sanātanadharma* as a programmatic expression of traditionalist self-assertion, see Halbfass, *India and Europe*, 343–47. For an early-twentieth-century *sanātanadharma* manual in English, see *Sanâtana Dharma: An Elementary Text-Book of Hindu Religion and Ethics* (Benares: Central Hindu College, 1916). On the complex, multifaceted notion of *dharma* and its early history, see A. Hiltebeitel, *Dharma: Its Early History in Law, Religion, and Narrative* (New York: Oxford University Press, 2011); P. Olivelle, ed., *Dharma: Studies in Its Semantic, Cultural, and Religious History* (Delhi: Motilal Banarsidass, 2009).

119. Tulasi Srinivas, *Winged Faith*, 62.

120. The guru knew English and spoke it with his Western *bhaktas* especially when he met them in his interview room, though as an early devotee noted, "His English wasn't as good then [in the mid-1960s] as it is now [in the early 1980s]"; see Charlton, *Saints Alive*, ch. 2. Sathya Sai Baba had studied English during his schooldays in Kamalapuram, Bukkapatnam, and Uravakonda.

121. For instance, Kasturi informs us that for more than a year Sathya Sai Baba's articles dwelled on the subject of *dhyāna* or meditation; see *Sathyam Sivam Sundaram, Part I (1926–1960)*, 258.

122. See Padmanaban, *Love Is My Form*, 391, 394.

123. Sathya Sai Baba, *Sathya Sai Speaks, Vol. 1*, 1.

124. With reference to the guru's first public speech, Kasturi recalls: "Fortunately, I had my pen in my pocket and someone lent me sheets of paper. I could secure His words and put them together"; Kasturi, *Loving God*, 172.

125. See Kasturi, *Sathyam Sivam Sundaram, Part I (1926–1960)*, 192–93.

126. Ibid., 272.

127. He held several important positions in the political and administrative sphere. During the early 1950s, he was chief minister of the old Hyderabad State, and as such helped create the modern State of Andhra Pradesh in 1956. He was later appointed governor of Kerala and governor of Uttar Pradesh. On B. Ramakrishna Rao and his link to Sathya Sai Baba, see H. Murphet, *Sai Baba: Man of Miracles* (New Delhi: Macmillan, 1981), 171–77.

128. As Bill Aitken aptly notes: "To be part of any governor's entourage is an accolade of respectability in the eyes of the public. Only a few years earlier, like Shirdi Baba, the Puttaparthi saint had to be content with petty officials at the base of India's pyramid of political authority"; Aitken, *Sri Sathya Sai Baba*, 99.

129. This highly influential thinker and exegete, founder of the Daśanāmī order of renunciants (*saṃnyāsin*), was an orthodox Brahmin who hailed from the village of Kalati in Kerala. For an introduction, see Th. A. Forsthoefel, "Śaṅkara," in *Brill's Encyclopedia of Hinduism*, ed. K. A. Jacobsen, H. Basu, A. Malinar, and V. Narayanan (Brill Online, 2012).

130. Kasturi, *Sathyam Sivam Sundaram, Part I (1926–1960)*, 286.

131. Padmamma, *Twameva Matha*, 104.

132. Like Swami Vivekananda, Sivananda preached a universalist message according to which Hinduism, as the mother of all religions and the spiritual guru of humanity, comprised the essence of all faiths. Significantly, both the Ramakrishna Mission and the Divine Life Society were the promoters of a variety of charitable and educational activities. The guru of Puttaparthi shared these same neo-Hindu convictions and strategies.

133. Shivaram, *Sathya Sai Baba: God in Action*, 252.

134. D. M. Knipe, *Vedic Voices: Intimate Narratives of a Living Andhra Tradition* (New York: Oxford University Press, 2015), 182.

135. Kasturi, *Loving God*, 196–97.

136. H. Levin, *Heart to Heart: "A Sequel to Good Chances"* (Bangalore: Sai Towers, 1996), 54.

137. See G. Yocum, "The Coronation of a Guru: Charisma, Politics, and Philosophy in Contemporary India," in *A Sacred Thread: Modern Transmission of Hindu Traditions in India and Abroad*, ed. R. B. Williams (Chambersburg, PA: Anima Publications, 1992), 84.

138. See Padmanaban, *Love Is My Form*, 245, 293, 299, 303, 327, 330–31, 367, 371, 412–23, 435–45, 457–71, 483–84, 505–19; Sri Sathya Sai Baba, *His Story as Told by Himself*, 185, 189. Already in the 1940s the guru used to visit the *rāja* of Venkatagiri; Rao, *Sathya Sai Baba: God as Man*, 194.

139. On Subbamma's devotion for young Sathya, who welcomed him and his first devotees in her house and cooked his meals, see Sri Sathya Sai Baba, *His Story as Told by Himself*, 137–65.

140. As Arnold Schulman rightly points out, the wife's *Karnam* "by sponsoring Sathya, made his holiness much easier to accept among those who had doubted it"; Schulman, *Baba*, 132.

141. H. Murphet, *Sai Baba: Invitation to Glory* (New Delhi: MacMillan, 1989 [1982]), 75.

142. Haraldsson, *Modern Miracles*, 84. For an interview with V. V. Rajagopal Yachendra, see ibid., 75–85.

143. Kasturi, *Loving God*, 196.

144. See N. Kasturi, *Sathyam Sivam Sundaram. Part I. The Life of Bhagavan Sri Sathya Sai Baba* (Prasanthi Nilayam: Sri Sathya Sai Books and Publications, 1983), 107.

145. Ch. Jaffrelot and G. Tarabout, "Les transformations de l'hindouisme," in Ch. Jaffrelot, ed., *L'Inde contemporaine. De 1990 à aujourd'hui* (Paris: Fayard/Pluriel, 2014), 202.

146. Aitken, *Sri Sathya Sai Baba*, 98.

147. Kasturi, *Sathyam Sivam Sundaram, Part I (1926–1960)*, 137. It is noticeable that in his book *Lives of Saints* (Shivanandanagar: The Divine Life Society, 1999)—which has a final chapter on the saints of recent times—Sivananda does not mention either Shirdi Sai Baba or Sathya Sai Baba (though he dedicates chapters to Dattātreya, Kabīr, and Akkaḷkoṭ Mahārāj). All in all, there have been very few encounters between Sathya Sai Baba and other gurus. One of these was with Swami Muktānanda (1908–1982), the founder of the Siddha Yoga movement, who paid a brief visit to him at Prasanthi Nilayam in the 1970s.

148. The *locus classicus* of the *avatāra* doctrine—though the term *avatāra* is never used—are the solemn words of Kṛṣṇa to Arjuna in *Bhagavadgītā* 4.7–8: "For whenever of the right (*dharma*) a languishing appears, son of Bharata, a rising up of unright (*adharma*), then I send Myself forth. For protection of the good, and for destruction of evil-doers, to make a firm footing for the right, I come into being in age after age"; F. Edgerton, trans., *The Bhagavad Gītā* (New York: Harper Torchbooks, 1964), 23. On the concept of *avatāra* and the crucial understanding of Sathya Sai Baba as the ultimate divine incarnation, see Spurr, *Sathya Sai Baba as Avatar*. On Sathya Sai Baba's self-proclaimed *avatāra*hood, see Gries and Gries, *An Index of Sathya Sai Speaks, Volumes I–XI*, 281–82.

149. In 1960, Daniel Roumanoff noted that the guru expressed himself in a complicated language, using many Sanskrit terms. At times, he had the impression that he said what was essential and that his teaching was elementary; at others, that he distorted everything; Roumanoff, *Candide au pays des Gourous*, 142.

150. On the concept of neo-Hinduism vis-à-vis traditional Hinduism, see Halbfass, *Philology and Confrontation: Paul Hacker on Traditional and Modern Vedānta*, 227–72; Halbfass, *India and Europe*, 217–46.

151. As Norris W. Palmer remarks: "Baba's statements are primordialist. He conflates being Hindu with being Indian and calls for the reassertion of a properly robust Indian—that is, Hindu—identity"; N. W. Palmer, "Baba's World: A Global Guru and His Movement," in *Gurus in America*, ed. Th. A. Forsthoefel and C. A. Humes (Albany: State University of New York Press, 2005), 105.

152. Steel, *The Sathya Sai Baba Compendium*, 213.

153. This term was coined by the German indologist Paul Hacker. On Swami Vivekananda's inclusivism, see Halbfass, *Philology and Confrontation*, 11, 244–55; Halbfass, *India and Europe*, 403–18. And yet inclusivism was an ancient

practice in India and not an invention of Vivekananda; see A. Rigopoulos, "Tolerance in Swami Vivekānanda's Neo-Hinduism," *Philosophy and Social Criticism* 45, no. 4 (2019): 438–60. On Vivekananda's universalism and its impact in the United States, see S. E. Gregg, *Swami Vivekananda and Non-Hindu Traditions: A Universal Advaita* (London and New York: Routledge, 2019); V. Narayanan, "United States," in *Brill's Encyclopedia of Hinduism*, ed. K. A. Jacobsen, H. Basu, A. Malinar, and V. Narayanan (Brill Online, 2012). On Vivekananda and modernity, see W. Radice, ed., *Swami Vivekananda and the Modernization of Hinduism* (New Delhi: Oxford University Press, 1998).

154. Halbfass, *India and Europe*, 238.

155. Gries and Gries, *An Index of Sathya Sai Speaks, Volumes I–XI*, 160.

156. See P. P. Arya, *Attaining God Here and Now: Path of Bhakti Expounded in* Narada Bhakti Sutras (Chandigarh: Umang Printers, 2010).

157. Kasturi, *Sathyam Sivam Sundaram, Part I (1926–1960)*, 235. See also ibid., 59–60, 279–81.

158. See Shivaram, *Sathya Sai Baba: God in Action*, 100–103.

159. Kasturi, *Garland of 108 Precious Gems*, 88–89.

160. See Kasturi, *Sathyam Sivam Sundaram, Part I (1926–1960)*, 273.

161. See Shivaram, *Sathya Sai Baba: God in Action*, 132–33, 167, 195.

162. During one of his public speeches he said: "Himalayas are the head of India, Cape Comorin the feet, Bombay the stomach, Prasanthi Nilayam the heart"; Gries and Gries, *An Index of Sathya Sai Speaks, Volumes I–XI*, 91.

163. H. B. Urban, "Avatar for Our Age: Sathya Sai Baba and the Cultural Contradictions of Late Capitalism," *Religion* 33 (2003): 89. On the guru's ideas on women, see Gries and Gries, *An Index of Sathya Sai Speaks, Volumes I–XI*, 217–18. As early as 1949, Sathya Sai Baba taught: "Ladies are under the mistaken notion that they are born to tend to their families, that they are puppets in the hands of men and that the kitchen is their only sanctuary. Woman is as much an empress with full powers as she is a housewife. The sorrows and pleasures of family life never stand in the way of devotion"; Padmanaban, *Love Is My Form*, 487.

164. R. K. Karanjia, *God Lives in India* (Puttaparthi: Saindra, 1994), 62. In his early public discourses Sathya Sai Baba mentioned Vivekananda eight times; see Gries and Gries, *An Index of Sathya Sai Speaks, Volumes I–XI*, 277–78.

165. Babb, *Redemptive Encounters*, 174.

166. See Shivaram, *Sathya Sai Baba: God in Action*, 234–35.

167. See S. P. Ruhela, "Sai Baba: A Biographical Sketch," in *Sai Baba and His Message: A Challenge to Behavioural Sciences*, ed. S. P. Ruhela and D. Robinson (Delhi: Vikas Publishing House, 1982), 18.

168. Shivaram, *Sathya Sai Baba: God in Action*, 240.

169. The guru of Puttaparthi adopted this statement from M. K. Gandhi; see E. Easwaran, *Gandhi, the Man* (Tomales, CA: Nilgiri Press, 1997), 140. Apparently, when Gandhi was assassinated in Delhi on January 30, 1948, around

5:30 p.m., Sathya Sai Baba who was in Puttaparthi clairvoyantly knew about it and told one of his devotees; see Padmanaban, *Love Is My Form*, 427, 453.

170. See Gries and Gries, *An Index of Sathya Sai Speaks, Volumes I–XI*, 285. Shirdi Sai Baba was also against religious conversion or "changing one's father"; see Narasimhaswami, *Sri Sai Baba's Charters and Sayings*, 263; Id., *Life of Sai Baba*, vol. 3, 82–83; vol. 4, 87, 107. See also Rigopoulos, *The Life and Teachings of Sai Baba of Shirdi*, 367–68.

171. See Padmanaban, *Love Is My Form*, 311, 323.

172. See Sri Sathya Sai Baba, *His Story as Told by Himself*, 9, 154–55. There are testimonies that he didn't treat the so-called untouchables separately but many times visited their slum, without the elders' knowledge; see Padmanaban, *Love Is My Form*, 42. See also ibid., 80.

173. Kondappa, *Sai's Story*, 18.

174. Aitken, *Sri Sathya Sai Baba: A Life*, 54.

175. See Babb, *Redemptive Encounters*, 172.

176. As he stated in one of his 1960s discourses:

> The cry of equality now being used as a slogan is a vain and meaningless cry, for, how can men, inheriting a multiplicity of impulses, skills, qualities, tendencies, attitudes and even diseases from their ancestors and from their past be all of the same stamp? And in spite of all this advertisement for the supposed equality, you find more misunderstandings and factions now than at any previous period of history. Those who promote inequality are those who most loudly proclaim this modern doctrine of equality. (Sathya Sai Baba, *Sathya Sai Speaks, Vol. 3. Discourses of Bhagawan Sri Sathya Sai Baba [Delivered During 1963]* [Prasanthi Nilayam: Sri Sathya Sai Books & Publications, 2008], 129–30, n. 17 "Lakshya Puja," Aug. 2, 1963)

177. On these issues, see W. Halbfass, *Tradition and Reflection: Explorations in Indian Thought* (Albany: State University of New York Press, 1991), 347–406.

178. Shivaram, *Sathya Sai Baba: God in Action*, 132. Even V. K. Gokak describes Sathya Sai Baba's mission as "the revolution of revolutions," aimed at transforming the individual as well as society; see Karanjia, *God Lives in India*, 39.

179. Ibid., 40.

180. P. Bilimoria, "Sri Aurobindo and Sri Sathya Sai Baba on Sruti (Vedas)," *Darshana International* 33, 4/132 (1993): 2. On how modern and/or traditional Sathya Sai Baba and his movement are, see J. E. Llewellyn, "Gurus and Groups," in R. Rinehart, *Contemporary Hinduism: Ritual, Culture, and Practice* (Santa Barbara/Denver/Oxford: ABC CLIO, 2004), 232–37.

181. See Swallow, *Ashes and Powers*, 157; Babb, *Redemptive Encounters*, 200–201; Urban, *Avatar for Our Age*.

182. See Palmer, *Baba's World*, 105–108, 119–20.

183. Apparently his first encounter with nondual Vedānta was through such medieval texts as the *Yogavāsiṣṭha* and the *Aṣṭāvakragītā*. On these issues, see J. Madaio, "Rethinking Neo-Vedānta: Swami Vivekananda and the Selective Historiography of Advaita Vedānta," *Religions* 8, no. 101 (2017): 1–12.

184. Sri Sathya Sai Baba, *His Story as Told by Himself*, 8–9.

185. See Hislop, *Conversations with Bhagavan Sri Sathya Sai Baba*, 89. On the guru's rejection of Marxist ideology, see S. P. Ruhela, "Educational Reconstruction in the Sai Age," in Ruhela and Robinson, *Sai Baba and His Message*, 175–76.

186. See Smriti Srinivas, "The Advent of the Avatar: The Urban Following of Sathya Sai Baba and Its Construction of Tradition," in *Charisma and Canon: Essays on the Religious History of the Indian Subcontinent*, ed. V. Dalmia, A. Malinar, and M. Christof (New York: Oxford University Press, 2001), 308 n. 9; Tulasi Srinivas, *Winged Faith*, 260.

187. See http://www.sssbpt.info/ssspeaks/volume33/sss33-08.pdf.

188. Karanjia, *God Lives in India*, 35–50.

189. On these issues, see Spurr, *Sathya Sai Baba as Avatar*, 315–17.

190. J. P. Waghorne, "Global Gurus and the Third Stream of American Religiosity: Between Hindu Nationalism and Liberal Pluralism," in *Political Hinduism: The Religious Imagination in Public Spheres*, ed. V. Lal (New Delhi: Oxford University Press, 2009), 144. Nonetheless, it is noteworthy that in recent years Vivekananda has been appropriated by right wing political movements such as the VHP.

191. See Gries and Gries, *An Index of Sathya Sai Speaks, Volumes I–XI*, 91–92. On Vivekananda's religious nationalism, see Halbfass, *Philology and Confrontation*, 319–33.

192. Gries and Gries, *An Index of Sathya Sai Speaks, Volumes I–XI*, 129. Apparently, these were the words with which F. Max Müller answered a question posed to him by Swami Vivekananda when they met in London, "When do you propose to visit India?" On Max Müller's idea that Vedānta expresses the universal truth of religion as such, in harmony with Vivekananda's neo-Hinduism, see van der Veer, *Imperial Encounters*, 78–79, 106–16. To corroborate his claim to divinity, Sathya Sai Baba once cited the authority of another Western orientalist, Horace Hayman Wilson (1786–1860): "As Wilson translated the Padma Purana, he came across a reference of a visionary, 5'4 in height, manifesting himself in Parthi [Puttaparthi]"; http://www.eaisai.com/baba/docs/pv960617.html. Kasturi reports that he also quoted from the works of Sir John Woodroffe, i.e. Arthur

Avalon (1865–1936), a pioneering writer on Hindu Tantrism and the translator of important Tantric texts; see Kasturi, *Gurudev*, 21; Kasturi, *Sathyam Sivam Sundaram, Part I (1926–1960)*, 234.

193. S. Hawkins, "Bordering Realism: The Aesthetics of Sai Baba's Mediated Universe," in *Image Journeys: Audio-Visual Media and Cultural Change in India*, ed. Ch. Brosius and M. Butcher (New Delhi: Sage, 1999), 154. See also ibid., 158.

194. Kasturi, *Sathyam Sivam Sundaram, Part II*, 20.

195. See also Kasturi, *Sathyam Sivam Sundaram, Part III*, 105–106; Padmanaban, *Love Is My Form*, 473–74.

196. Kasturi, *Garland of 108 Precious Gems*, 55–56. See also V. K. Gokak, *Bhagavan Sri Sathya Sai Baba: The Man and the Avatar (An Interpretation)* (New Delhi: Abhinav Publications, 1983 [1975]), 305. The Sino-Indian border conflict lasted about a month and ended on November 21, 1962, when China declared a ceasefire, simultaneously announcing its unilateral withdrawal. On the Sino-Indian war and its causes, see P. K. Chakravorty, "Sino-Indian War of 1962," *Indian Historical Review* 44, no. 2 (2017): 285–312; A. D. Abitbol, "Causes of the 1962 Sino-Indian War: A Systems Level Approach," *Josef Korbel Journal of Advanced International Studies* 1 (2009): 74–88.

197. From when he was a ten-year-old boy, Sathya Sai Baba was fond of singing *bhajans* in honor of Viṭṭhal of Pandharpur. He started what was then called the Pandhari *bhajan* group, which also enacted the Pandhari dance; Padmanaban, *Love Is My Form*, 34–36. For a review of the guru's own reminiscences, see Sri Sathya Sai Baba, *His Story as Told by Himself*, 27–32.

198. On the purported significance of this sacrifice, see E. B. Fanibunda, *Vision of the Divine* (Prasanthi Nilayam: Shri Sathya Sai Books and Publications, 1987 [1976]), 57–89. See also G. V. Subba Rao, "Esoteric Significance of the Veda Purusha Jnana Yajna," *Sanathana Sarathi* 40, no. 12 (Dec. 1997): 335–36.

199. Kasturi recalls: "He [Sathya Sai Baba] went on with preparations for the Dasara festivities in 1965, in spite of the campaigns and counter campaigns of the Indo-Pakistan conflict. He announced that the hostilities will cease in time, and quite dramatically, to the surprise of the combatants and many leaders in both countries and in the United Nations Organization, cease-fire was declared, with two days to spare, before Dasara began"; Kasturi, *Garland of 108 Precious Gems*, 56.

200. Its celebration has continued along the years. See, for instance, the Ati Rudra Maha Yajna held in 2006, presented as a powerful prayer for universal peace; http://media.radiosai.org/journals/Vol_04/01SEP06/CoverStory_Army.htm.

201. Kasturi, *Sathyam Sivam Sundaram, Part II*, 36.

202. Ibid., 37.

203. Ibid., 37–38.

204. Ibid., 40.

205. Ibid., 40–41.

206. Ibid., 43.

207. See Padmamma, *Twameva Matha*, 26–30.

208. He once stated that "if Shankaracharya had not restored the Vedantic vision, India would have become another China"; Gries and Gries, *An Index of Sathya Sai Speaks, Volumes I–XI*, 28. On the frequency with which Sathya Sai Baba cited Śaṅkara from the time of his early speeches, see ibid., 168–69. On the guru's *advaitabhakti* orientation, see S. R. Savkur, *Reflections on Adi Shankara's Bhaja Govindam (Based on Teachings of Bhagawan Sri Sathya Sai Baba)* (Prasanthi Nilayam: Sri Sathya Sai Sadhana Trust, 2012). On his early fondness for Śaṅkara's *Bhaja Govindam*, see Padmanaban, *Love Is My Form*, 219.

209. Kasturi, *Garland of 108 Precious Gems*, 80.

210. Kasturi, *Sathyam Sivam Sundaram, Part II*, 54.

211. Ibid., 58.

212. Schulman, *Baba*, 166. See also ibid., 105; Kasturi, *Sathyam Sivam Sundaram, Part I (1926–1960)*, 211.

213. See Roumanoff, *Candide au pays des Gourous*, 134–35.

214. See Rigopoulos, *The Life and Teachings of Sai Baba of Shirdi*, 91–94; Warren, *Unravelling the Enigma*, 45–46; Shepherd, *Sai Baba of Shirdi: A Biographical Investigation*, 111–13.

215. This important festival falls on the full moon day of the month of *āṣāḍh* (July–August). On this auspicious day, Hindus honor their teachers.

216. On another occasion, when in the early 1970s he happened to be paralyzed from the waist down, he explained his illness by saying that some "very powerful yogis" were testing him to determine if he really was the *avatāra*; see Baskin, *Divine Memories of Sathya Sai Baba*, 108–10.

217. In the 1970s, the guru stated: "I must admit that, occasionally, I take upon Myself the ailments of My devotees, but these only pass through My body without having any effect on Me"; Kasturi, *Sathyam Sivam Sundaram, Part IV*, 164.

218. For an analysis of this claim and of the Bharadvāja myth, see Swallow, *Ashes and Powers*, 123–58. On Sathya Sai Baba as being both Śiva and Śakti, see L. A. Babb, "Sathya Sai Baba's Saintly Play," in *Saints and Virtues*, ed. J. Stratton Hawley (Berkeley: University of California Press, 1987), 168–86. By the same author, see also *Redemptive Encounters*, 159–201.

219. Apparently, Sathya Sai Baba had prophesized his future incarnation as Prema Sai Baba already in 1960; see Kasturi, *Sathyam Sivam Sundaram, Part II*, 203. For references on Prema Sai Baba, see Steel, *The Sathya Sai Baba Compendium*, 204–205. On the oneness of the Sai Babas' triple incarnation, see Bhatnagar, *Sai Speaks About His Childhood*, 95–99.

220. For a thorough presentation of Sathya Sai Baba's illness—diagnosed as cerebral thrombosis—and eventful declaration, see N. Kasturi, *Siva Sakthi Swarupa* (Prasanthi Nilayam: Sri Sathya Sai Sadhana Trust, 2012). The booklet

was originally published by Kasturi in the same year, 1963. Therein, Shirdi Sai Baba is presented as the *avatāra* of Śiva, not Śakti, and the future Prema Sai Baba as the *avatāra* of Śakti, not Śiva. The same is reported in *Sathya Sai Speaks, Vol. 3*, 118. It appears that in *Sathyam Sivam Sundaram, Part II*, Kasturi did not quote his guru's words correctly and thus inverted the two. On this issue, see Smriti Srinivas, *In the Presence of Sai Baba*, 60–61.

221. For this speech, see Sathya Sai Baba, *Sathya Sai Speaks, Vol. 3*, 113–20.

222. For an investigation of this purported bilocation, see Haraldsson, *Modern Miracles*, 271–87.

223. See Kasturi, *Sathyam Sivam Sundaram, Part II*, 151, 172.

224. Kasturi, *Sathyam Sivam Sundaram, Part IV*, 164.

225. See Kasturi, *Sathyam Sivam Sundaram, Part II*, 146–53.

226. See Rigopoulos, *The Life and Teachings of Sai Baba of Shirdi*, 15–18, 197, 305.

227. Kasturi, *Sathyam Sivam Sundaram, Part II*, 137.

228. For a review of Sathya Sai Baba's statements on Ramakrishna and Vivekananda, see Sathya Sai Baba, *Sai Vani: Avatar on Mahapurushas. Based on the Writings and Divine Discourses of Bhagavan Sri Sathya Sai Baba* (Prasanthi Nilayam: Sai Publications, 2015), 223–43, 261–68.

229. He advocated M. K. Gandhi's dictum: "My India is the India of villages"; Gries and Gries, *An Index of Sathya Sai Speaks, Volumes I–XI*, 90.

230. See Kasturi, *Sathyam Sivam Sundaram, Part II*, 167.

231. See Kasturi, *Garland of 108 Precious Gems*, 22–23.

232. Daniel Roumanoff, for instance, suspected that the guru's "materializations" were tricks and criticized his fondness for luxury and silk robes, which he found lascivious. His impressions were ambivalent, however, since he also noted that the guru's manners were simple and that he readily sat on the floor in his room and on the ground in the garden; Roumanoff, *Candide au pays des Gourous*, 138, 141–42, 145.

233. Kasturi, *Sathyam Sivam Sundaram, Part II*, 205.

234. Ibid.

235. It was formally constituted into a separate township a year later, on August 5, 1967; ibid., 253.

236. In 1953, he would have brought back to life one V. Radhakrishna "whose body had started decomposing"; Gokak, *Bhagavan Sri Sathya Sai Baba*, 303. On this episode, see Murphet, *Sai Baba: Man of Miracles*, 131–34; Haraldsson, *Modern Miracles*, 248–51. For the testimony of a follower of Ramana Maharshi, see F. Taleyarkhan, *Sages, Saints and Arunachala Ramana*. Foreword by Dr. Sarvepalli Radhakrishnan. Introduction by Shri Sri Prakasa (Madras: Orient Longmans, 1970), 166–68.

237. Sathya Sai Baba's *sarvadharma* emblem recalls the "mastery in servitude" emblem of the Parsi holy man Meher Baba (1894–1969), which first appeared on the title page of the latter's book *God Speaks: The Theme of Creation and Its Purpose* (New York: Dodd, Mead, 1955). Some kind of symbolic drawing possibly reminiscent of the *sarvadharma* was already familiar in Ramakrishna's circle of devotees. We read: "On the wall hung an oil painting . . . in which Sri Ramakrishna was pointing out to Keshab [Chandra Sen] the harmony of Christianity, Islam, Buddhism, Hinduism, and other religions. On seeing the picture Keshab had once said, 'Blessed is the man who conceived the idea'"; see Gupta, *The Gospel of Sri Ramakrishna*, 159.

238. See Kasturi, *Sathyam Sivam Sundaram, Part I (1926–1960)*, 100. On the *sarvadharma* emblem, see Steel, *The Sathya Sai Baba Compendium*, 224–26.

239. He first met Sathya Sai Baba in 1959, when the latter "materialized" a copy of the *Bhagavadgītā* in Telugu script for him. On Bhagavantham's link to the guru of Puttaparthi, see Murphet, *Sai Baba: Man of Miracles*, 177–82. For an interview dated Christmas 1978 with S. Bhagavantham, Howard Murphet, Samuel Sandweiss, and two other American devotees, see https://www.youtube.com/watch?v=kVzxmUv9ZJU.

240. This important organization was founded in the United States in 1875 by the occultist of Russian origin Helena Petrovna Blavatsky and Colonel Henry S. Olcott. In 1878, Blavatsky moved to India, taking the headquarters of the society with her to Adyar, a suburb of Madras. On the hypothesis of an influence of the Theosophical Society on Sathya Sai Baba's self-consciousness as the ultimate divine incarnation, see Spurr, *Sathya Sai Baba as Avatar*, 328–31.

241. He first met the guru in 1965. Sathya Sai Baba claimed that the first Westerner that ever came in contact with him was the alleged psychic and telepathist Wolf Messing (1899–1974). He would have accidentally met him in 1937 at the Kamalapuram railway station, during his school days (there appears to be a chronological discrepancy, however, since young Sathya joined the Board Middle School in Kamalapuram only in 1940; see Padmanaban, *Love Is My Form*, 128). Just by looking at him, the Polish mentalist would have realized the boy's divinity; see Sathya Sai Baba, *Sai Vani*, 190–93; Sri Sathya Sai Baba, *His Story as Told by Himself*, 68–71; Padmanaban, *Love Is My Form*, 48. See also Spurr, *Sathya Sai Baba as Avatar*, 334–36.

242. Kasturi, *Sathyam Sivam Sundaram, Part II*, 251.

243. See https://www.youtube.com/watch?v=kVzxmUv9ZJU, minutes 24–27. See also Murphet, *Sai Baba: Invitation to Glory*, 173–86.

244. Kasturi, *Sathyam Sivam Sundaram, Part II*, 252–53.

245. Schulman, *Baba*, 82, 168. On the Beatles in India with Maharishi Mahesh Yogi see L. H. Lapham, *With the Beatles* (Hoboken: Melville House,

2005); https://www.youtube.com/watch?v=YpGME3Iv7Yg. In the 1960s, Maharishi Mahesh Yogi had been sent away by the Daśanāmī monks of the Badarī Nārāyaṇa monastery because of his pretense to become the head (*jagadguru*) of the Pūrṇagiripīṭha.

246. He was a captain in the British Army and served for several years with the Royal Engineers. Later, he was commissioned captain in the U.S. Air Force rescue organization. He had experience as editor and publisher of technical journals in Australia and Canada and in the late 1970s became the advertising manager of a publishing house in Los Angeles. He first heard of Sathya Sai Baba in 1964. He wrote a few books on the guru, one of which is a collection of articles on the Swami which also contains letters from both him and Kasturi: *My Beloved. The Love and Teaching of Bhagavan Sri Sathya Sai Baba* (Prasanthi Nilayam: Sri Sathya Sai Baba Books and Publications, 1981). Apparently, he experienced the saint's presence even in Los Angeles: "Baba sits before him, converses with him, teaches him, answers his questions, as clearly as if He is concretely present. . . . When Penn sends the typescripts to me for perusal or publication, I have often asked Baba for further clarification and never once has He disavowed His authorship"; Kasturi, *Sathyam Sivam Sundaram, Part II*, 256. Charles Penn claimed that the guru had resurrected him; see Steel, *The Sathya Sai Baba Compendium*, 154, 156. For an article of his, see Ch. Penn, "At His Blue Lotus Feet," in *Golden Age 1980* (Prasanthi Nilayam: Sri Sathya Sai Books and Publications Trust, 1980), 46–50.

247. In Puttaparthi, Sathya Sai Baba encouraged her to train the ashram's residents and the boys of the Sathya Sai Veda Shastra Pathasala in Yoga and meditation. Kasturi writes:

> He was Himself present on the two days, ready to elaborate the reasons she gave for choosing the Flame as the focus of meditation and to clarify other points which she felt essential for the course. Contemplation on the Flame is the ancient Vedic prescription, where the Lord is described as a "straight streak of lightning brilliance, in the center of the heart." Baba has the Param-jyothi or the Supreme Light, as the crest and crown of the Yoga-danda on the Prasanthi Flag. In the Nilayam, during the pre-dawn hours of meditation, a lamp, with its steady Flame, clear and bright, is used for concentration. (Kasturi, *Sathyam Sivam Sundaram, Part II*, 257–58)

248. She first met Sathya Sai Baba in 1966. She had studied Yoga in India with the "father of modern Yoga" Sri Tirumalai Krishnamacharya (1888–1989), and later established a Yoga ashram at Tecate, Mexico, on the United States border.

She wrote the book *Sai Baba and Sai Yoga* (New Delhi: MacMillan India, 1975). On Indra Devi's seminal role in the popularization of Hatha Yoga in America in the late 1940s, see Syman, *The Subtle Body*, 179–97. For a biographical account, see M. Goldberg, *The Goddess Pose: The Audacious Life of Indra Devi, the Woman Who Helped Bring Yoga to the West* (London: Corsair, 2015).

249. Kasturi, *Sathyam Sivam Sundaram, Part II*, 262. The guru remarked that the hands that serve are holier than the lips that pray and, accordingly, the motto of Seva Dals was and is "Work is Worship." A periodical for Seva Dal volunteers was soon created, called *Sri Sathya Sai Seva Dal.*

250. Ibid., 266.

251. See Smriti Srinivas, *The Advent of the Avatar.*

252. On these issues, see A. Rigopoulos, *Guru: Il fondamento della civiltà dell'India. Con la prima traduzione italiana del "Canto sul Maestro"* (Roma: Carocci, 2009), 189–213.

253. Though it decreased in the following decades, the performance of Vedic rituals in Prasanthi Nilayam continued throughout Sathya Sai Baba's life. On the occasion of his seventieth birthday, on November 23, 1995, three of the invited seventy Brahmin pundits came from the famed Konasima area of the Godavari delta. As David M. Knipe reports:

> [They] provided effusive descriptions of their invited week in Puttaparti . . . not forgetting emoluments for lending Veda to the party. "I had not seen him before," said a beaming Cayanulu. "For seven days I recited Veda in his presence. That was wonderful! I was given new clothes, Rs. 5,000, Rs. 1,000 for travel, and my wife . . . received a new sari, gold bangles, a pressure cooker. Until I went to see him I was feeling weakness but I recited with great ease. My daughters pointed out that all this was due to his blessings, because I had darsan of him." Lanka's son . . . went to his free hospital for heart bypass surgery. At his death the Sathya Sai Baba Trust was reported to be worth at least $8.9 billion.
>
> Mitranarayana also talks about Puttaparti but without obsequious tones. "Sathya Sai Baba offered me Rs. 40,000 to sponsor a yajna. I asked about the animal sacrifice that is dictated by Veda and Baba accepted on the grounds of those Vedic sanctions. But I thought what if we are in the midst of the sacrifice and he dismisses us with full fee. We would be committing the sin of an incomplete sacrifice. How many other yajna would I have to perform as compensation?" Mitranarayana did not trust the famous saint to keep his word and therefore excused himself. (Knipe, *Vedic Voices*, 183)

254. Kasturi, *Sathyam Sivam Sundaram, Part II*, 36. On the guru as Vedapuruṣa, see also Kasturi, *Loving God*, 300; Balu, *Living Divinity*, 123. Moreover, see S. D. Kulkarni, *Shri Satya Sai, the Fount of Vedic Culture: Vedas are the Heritage of Mankind* (Bombay: Shri Bhagawana Vedavyasa Itihasa Samsodhana Mandira, 1992).

255. Taleyarkhan, *Sages, Saints, and Arunachala Ramana*, 167.

256. See E. Goldberg, *The Lord Who Is Half Woman: Ardhanārīśvara in Indian and Feminist Perspective* (Albany: State University of New York Press, 2002).

257. See Kasturi, *Easwaramma*, 144–45. On Sathya Sai Baba as Śiva-Śakti, see also Kondappa's early account, *Sai's Story*, 16.

258. See Shri Sathya Sai Baba, "Who Is Sai," in Ruhela and Robinson, *Sai Baba and his Message*, 33; Gries and Gries, *An Index of Sathya Sai Speaks, Volumes I–XI*, 288; Balu, *Living Divinity*, 85–86.

259. Schulman, *Baba*, 167. See also Shivaram, *Sathya Sai Baba: God in Action*, 66, 212, 230.

260. See Padmanaban, *Love Is My Form*, 277, 523.

261. See Sri Sathya Sai Baba, *His Story as Told by Himself*, 90–96.

262. The stepdaughter of Desikacharya Rajagopalacharya (1900–1993), an important figure of the Theosophical Society and of the entourage of the spiritual philosopher Jiddu Krishnamurti (1895–1986). For decades, D. Rajagopalacharya was the editor of Krishnamurti's teachings and helped manage his foundation. Apparently, Krishnamurti secretly met Sathya Sai Baba in the early 1980s, at which occasion Krishnamurti presented him a rose; see Baskin, *Divine Memories of Sathya Sai Baba*, 283–84.

263. Ibid., 43. See also Padmanaban, *Love Is My Form*, 39, 72–75, 79, 295, 299, 379, 560, 568 n. 3; N. Purnaiya, *The Divine Leelas of Sri Satya Sai Baba* (Bangalore: House of Seva, 1976), 7.

264. Sathya Sai Baba announced that he would be reborn in Mandya near Mysore as early as the mid-1940s; see Padmanaban, *Love Is My Form*, 197.

265. See Balu, *Living Divinity*, 29.

266. See https://robertpriddy.wordpress.com/2015/01/10/souljourns-narasimha-murthys-secret-of-prema-sai.

267. See Kasturi, *Loving God*, 335, 362–63.

268. http://www.saibabaofindia.com/sais_kasturi_heart2heart.htm, 22.

269. S. H. Sandweiss, *Spirit and the Mind* (San Diego: Birth Day, 1985), 170.

270. P. Mason and R. Laing, *Sathya Sai Baba: Embodiment of Love* (London: Sawbridge, 1982), 225.

271. Tulasi Srinivas, *Winged Faith*, 74.

272. In September 1893, at the World's Parliament of Religions, held in Chicago, Swami Vivekananda had interpreted the Parliament as the fulfillment

of Kṛṣṇa's statement in *Bhagavadgītā* 4.11, which he rendered thus: "Whosoever comes to Me, through whatever form, I reach him; all men are struggling through paths which in the end lead to Me." On Vivekananda and the *Bhagavadgītā*, see H. W. French, "Swami Vivekananda's Use of the Bhagavadgita," in *Modern Indian Interpreters of the Bhagavadgita*, ed. R. N. Minor (Albany: State University of New York Press, 1986), 131–46.

273. Gries and Gries, *An Index of Sathya Sai Speaks, Volumes I–XI*, 92. The guru stated: "India is the engine that hauls, through the steam of Prema, all other nations, along the twin rails of Sathya and Dharma towards the terminus, Santhi"; Kasturi, *Garland of 108 Precious Gems*, 45.

274. Kasturi, *Sathyam Sivam Sundaram, Part II*, 235–36.

275. Gries and Gries, *An Index of Sathya Sai Speaks, Volumes I–XI*, 91.

276. Ibid., 92.

277. Ibid.

278. See ibid., 129.

279. Kasturi, *Garland of 108 Precious Gems*, 94.

280. Kasturi, *Sathyam Sivam Sundaram, Part II*, 215. See also Kasturi, *Sathyam Sivam Sundaram, Part III*, 150.

281. Ibid., 93.

282. Ibid.

283. Tulasi Srinivas, *Winged Faith*, 260.

284. Kasturi, *Sathyam Sivam Sundaram, Part III*, 2.

285. On Sathya Sai Baba's capacity to attract the urban middle classes and the political elites, see Jaffrelot and Tarabout, *Les transformations de l'hindouisme*, 202–203.

286. See J. Copeman and A. Ikegame, "The Multifarious Guru: An Introduction," in *The Guru in South Asia: New Interdisciplinary Perspectives*, ed. J. Copeman and A. Ikegame (London and New York: Routledge, 2012), 37. For a general survey on the guru as a domain crosser, see Rigopoulos, *Guru*, 161–224.

287. He even represented India at the PEN International World Conference held in Japan in 1957 and at the Biennial Conference of Poets held in Belgium in 1961.

288. S. Minajagi, *Vinayaka Krishna Gokak (Vinayaka)* (New Delhi: Sahitya Akademi, 1999), 25.

289. By V. K. Gokak see also *The Advent of Sathya Sai* (Gauhati: Sri Sathya Sai Prakashan, 1977).

290. Kamaraju, *Memories and Memoirs*, 89.

291. For his precious testimony, significantly titled "Satya Sai Baba et les *siddhi*," see Roumanoff, *Candide au pays des Gourous*, 129–47.

292. Haraldsson, "True to His Nation," in *Golden Age, 1980*, 255–56.

293. On the bodily practices in the guru's cosmopolitan ashram and their multiple interpretations, see Tulasi Srinivas, "Relics of Faith: Fleshly Desires, Ascetic Disciplines, and Devotional Affect in the Transnational Sathya Sai Movement," in *Routledge Handbook of Body Studies*, ed. B. S. Turner (London and New York: Routledge, 2012), 185–205. By the same author, see also *Winged Faith*, 228–30.

294. By 1975, it was circulating in both Hindi and Bengali. Howard Murphet's three other books are: *Sai Baba Avatar: A New Journey into Power and Glory* (San Diego: Birth Day, 1977); *Sai Baba: Invitation to Glory*; *Where the Road Ends* (N. S. W. Australia: Butterfly Books, 1993). For an article of his, see "The Finger of God," in *Golden Age, 1980*, 35–40.

Chapter 3

1. Kasturi, *Sathyam Sivam Sundaram, Part III*, 13.

2. The first Sathya Sai Baba center outside India was inaugurated in Ceylon/Sri Lanka in 1967.

3. The first Sathya Sai Baba center in the United States was established in 1969 in California. In the same year, a center was opened in the United Kingdom.

4. N. Kasturi, *Sathyam Sivam Sundaram: The Life of Bhagavan Sri Sathya Sai Baba*, editorially revised in collaboration with N. Kasturi by Charles Penn et al. (Tustin, CA: Sathya Sai Book Center of America, 1988).

5. He was also present at the World Conference and gave a speech in which he affirmed his belief in Sathya Sai Baba's divinity; see V. Balu, *The Glory of Puttaparthi* (Delhi: Motilal Banarsidass, 1990), 13. Before he met the guru, however, he considered him to be a charlatan.

6. Kasturi, *Sathyam Sivam Sundaram, Part III*, 9. Given the solemnity of this disclosure, the hagiographer also quotes the Telugu original: *Sarvadaivathwaswaroopalanu Dharinchina Manavaakarame Ee Aakaramu*.

7. Ibid., 5. In his autobiography, Kasturi quotes a telling statement of Reiner Seeman on the Swami's claimed *avatāra*hood: "One is forced quickly to recognize that Baba has entered the arena as Avatar not to make Himself seen, but rather to meet our Divinity"; Kasturi, *Loving God*, 251. "It is God drawing Itself to Itself," comments the hagiographer; ibid. Reiner Seeman was the author of "Versuch zu einer Theorie des Avatāra. Mensch gewordener Gott oder Gott gewordener Mensch?" *Numen* 33, no. 1 (1986): 90–140.

8. On the guru's visit to East Africa and its social and political implications, see Smriti Srinivas, *In the Presence of Sai Baba*, 259–71.

9. Hislop, *Conversations with Bhagavan Sri Sathya Sai Baba*, 127.

10. Kasturi, *Garland of 108 Precious Gems*, 87.

11. Kasturi, *Siva Sakthi Swarupa*, 65. See also Gries and Gries, *An Index of Sathya Sai Speaks, Volumes I–XI*, 288.

12. Though he closed his last speech in Kampala on July 8, 1968, saying that he would come again next year and stay longer, this never happened; see Sathya Sai Baba, *Sathya Sai Speaks, Vol. 8. Discourses of Bhagawan Sri Sathya Sai Baba Delivered in 1968 (Including Six Discourses Given During Dasara)* (Prasanthi Nilayam: Sri Sathya Sai Sadhana Trust, 2010), 177.

13. On various occasions the guru told his American and European devotees that he would visit their countries, and careful arrangements were made to receive him; with reference to Italy, see the booklet edited by Antonio Craxi, *Incontri in attesa di Sathya Sai Baba* (Milano, 1981).

14. The founder of the Self-Realization Fellowship in 1925 in Encinitas, California, and the author of the *Autobiography of a Yogi* (1st ed. New York 1946), which proved exceptionally popular. For an introduction to Mukunda Lal Ghosh alias Paramahamsa Yogananda, see S. Gandhi, "Yogananda and the Self-Realization Fellowship," in *Brill's Encyclopedia of Hinduism*, ed. K. A. Jacobsen, H. Basu, A. Malinar, and V. Narayanan (Brill Online, 2012). See also A. P. Foxen, *Biography of a Yogi: Paramahansa Yogananda and the Origins of Modern Yoga* (New York: Oxford University Press, 2017). It should be noted that Sathya Sai Baba did not recognize the immortality of Babaji, the mysterious figure whom Yogananda revered as the *ādiguru* who revived the ancient discipline of *kriyāyoga*: "Nobody lives forever in this physical body. After twenty-one days in samadhi, the body will drop away"; Levin, *Good Chances*, 83.

15. See Schulman, *Baba*, 110.

16. In 1972, Idi Amin Dada ordered the expulsion of all Asians. On Sathya Sai Baba's trip to Uganda and his meeting with Idi Amin Dada, see the *Souljourns* interview with Navin Patel recorded in Leicester, England, in April 2016: https://www.youtube.com/watch?v=2BX4z26kJSQ.

17. Kasturi writes that Munshi "could not suppress his tears of joy and gratitude, when he said, 'I was pained to see around me the quick decline of faith in God and earnestness in religion, and I was on the brink of despair when I contemplated the future of this ancient land. But as I look upon Bhagavan Sri Sathya Sai Baba, and witness the transformation He is effecting in the hearts of millions, I am heartened and happy' "; Kasturi, *Sathyam Sivam Sundaram, Part III*, 31.

18. Ibid., 32.

19. Kasturi, *Garland of 108 Precious Gems*, 39.

20. In the guru's words: "The most essential message of Indian culture and spirituality is '*Sathyam vada, Dharmam cara*' (speak truth and practice righteousness). This message has to be translated into action by one and all"; Sri Sathya Sai Baba, *His Story as Told by Himself*, 46.

21. The guru's overall conservatism on fundamentals emerges throughout Kasturi's narrative as when he praises traditional village life and criticizes town life; see his paragraph "Save Villages from Cities," Kasturi, *Sathyam Sivam Sundaram, Part IV*, 60–61.

22. Gokak, *Bhagavan Sri Sathya Sai Baba*, 307.

23. Kasturi, *Loving God*, 168.

24. Sathya Sai Baba performed the spiritual remarriage of this American couple when they turned sixty. In 1969, they were the first to set up a Sathya Sai Baba Center in their house in Tustin, California, and later established the Sathya Sai Book Center of America. Walter Cowan is famous among devotees since it is claimed that the holy man "resurrected" him when he "died" at Puttaparthi on Christmas Day 1971; see Steel, *The Sathya Sai Baba Compendium*, 154–55; Baskin, *Divine Memories of Sathya Sai Baba*, 52–53, 62–63; Levin, *Good Chances*, 171–72; Levin, *Heart to Heart*, 2; Haraldsson, *Modern Miracles*, 243–51.

25. A prominent American devotee, he first came to Sathya Sai Baba in January 1968, after being told of the guru of Puttaparthi by Diana Baskin's mother, Mrs. Rajagopalacharya. That same year, he taped two conversations with him and made careful notes of others, later published as *Conversations with Sathya Sai Baba*, a book that was instrumental in spreading the holy man's renown. John S. Hislop, whom Sathya Sai Baba defined as "my best foreign devotee" (Baskin, *Divine Memories of Sathya Sai Baba*, 207), has been the closest Western follower of Sathya Sai Baba, having had the privilege of numerous private conversations with him. Another important book authored by Hislop is *My Baba and I* (San Diego: Birth Day, 1985); see Baskin, *Divine Memories of Sathya Sai Baba*, 74–75. In 1974, he was appointed the first president of the Sathya Sai Baba Council of America and he greatly contributed to the development of Sathya Sai Baba Centers in the United States. Hislop and the Sathya Sai Baba Organization of America were the veritable engine of the international Sathya Sai Baba movement. For an article of his, see J. S. Hislop, "The International Problem," in *Golden Age 1980*, 172–74.

26. A teacher, dancer, and healer who taught classes in meditation and prayer in New York for twenty-three years, she said she could always feel Sathya Sai Baba's presence in her classes. A student of Buddhist philosophy, she spent some years in Sri Lanka and later pursued studies in goddess worship in Delhi. She first came to Sathya Sai Baba at the end of 1964: while visiting Shirdi, she heard about him and decided to go see him in Puttaparthi. She lived at Prasanthi Nilayam and Whitefield for nearly two years. She talks about her experiences with the guru in chapter 2 of her *Saints Alive*, as well as in her autobiography *Hell-Bent for Heaven: The Autobiography of Hilda Charlton* (Woodstock, NY: Golden Quest, 1990). By Hilda Charlton, see also "Sathya Sai Baba: God-Man," in *Golden Age 1980*, 230–31.

27. A successful American playwright, screenwriter, and actor, he received Oscar nominations in 1963 and 1969 for best original screenplays. In his career, he also received three Writers Guild nominations for best screenplay and a Writers Guild award. In 1994, he was the recipient of a Humanitas Prize award. Schulman was the first Westerner, along with Howard Murphet, to write an informative and well-researched book on the guru of Puttaparthi: *Baba* (New York: Viking Press, 1971). Although it sympathizes with Sathya Sai Baba it does not bear the hagiographic overtones of much of the guru's literature, and Schulman never became an active devotee. For Kasturi's remarks on Schulman, see *Sathyam Sivam Sundaram, Part IV*, 90. In an interview recorded in 2011 ("The Writer Speaks: Arnold Schulman," https://www.youtube.com/watch?v=5JxCPB-ti-c), Schulman recalls (minutes 82–83):

> Travelling is everything to me. . . . I have spent several months living with former cannibals in New Guinea, I spent a couple of months in the Peruvian Amazon jungle and with headhunters in Borneo. . . . I loved that, and I was maybe twenty times in India and I wrote a book about this holy man, in 1971, that nobody had ever heard of, his name is Sai Baba, and last week or the week before all the papers, even the LA Times and the BBC had a huge article about him. . . . he died. His [wealth] was worth 9 billion dollars and he has hundreds, hundreds of millions of followers all over the world, and when I was there there were like fifty people or so. . . . These things have happened to me.

28. Kasturi, *Sathyam Sivam Sundaram, Part III*, 79–80.

29. Some years later, just before Christmas 1984, the guru "materialized" a picture of Jesus "as he truly was" at age twenty-nine; see P. Phipps, *Sathya Sai Baba and Jesus Christ: A Gospel for the Golden Age* (Auckland: Sathya Sai Publications of New Zealand, 1994), 71.

30. The guru, however, did not identify himself often with Kalki. For an instance of such identification, see Padmanaban, *Love Is My Form*, 175. On this belief, see S. P. Ruhela, *Sri Sathya Sai as Kalki Avatar* (Delhi: BR Publishing Corporation, 1996).

31. Kasturi, *Sathyam Sivam Sundaram, Part III*, 86.

32. Ibid., 101–102.

33. Shri Sathya Sai Baba, "Why I Incarnate," in Ruhela and Robinson, *Sai Baba and His Message*, 26. See also Kasturi, *Garland of 108 Precious Gems*, 90.

34. Referring to a beautiful ring with nine gems in its setting that the guru had "materialized" for him around the end of the 1970s, John S. Hislop writes:

> That night at the hotel in Bangalore my wife and I admired the ring, but in the morning to my great distress one gem, the pearl, was missing. A thorough search of floor and bed failed to locate the missing pearl. As soon as we arrived at Brindavan I asked Swami if I could speak with Him for a moment. He kindly motioned to come to the inner room. I took opportunity to touch the Lotus Feet and then said, "In some way I have displeased Swami, for He has already taken one of the gems from the ring." I showed the ring to Him. He put His hand on my shoulder and laughingly said, "No, no, nothing like that. When I made the ring a thought came to mind (to wonder) if this was the right ring for you. And with the imperfect concentration, the ring was imperfect and not fully permanent! What would you like?" "I would like a ring in which I could see Swamiji," I replied. With that, in a movement which by now many devotees have observed, Swami put the gemstone ring between thumb and forefinger, blew His breath upon it and lo and behold a new ring was there, a heavy golden ring with a large oval setting in which was installed a beautiful portrait of Sri Sathya Sai Baba. (John S. Hislop, "Three Stories," in *Golden Age 1980*, 175)

35. Kasturi, *Sathyam Sivam Sundaram, Part III*, 103.

36. Howard Murphet, who saw the Shirdi Sai Baba statue in Guindy in 1968, writes that "like Michael Angelo's marble Moses in a little church in Rome, it gave me, personally, the immediate impression that it was alive"; Murphet, *Sai Baba: Man of Miracles*, 116.

37. Kasturi, *Sathyam Sivam Sundaram, Part III*, 106. See also Gries and Gries, *An Index of Sathya Sai Speaks, Volumes I–XI*, 29.

38. With regard to the first three types, Kasturi defines the *nyāsaputra*s as the children "born in order to realize the value of some deposit that they had made with you in the previous life which you had misappropriated and misused," the *ṛṇaputra*s as the ones "born in order to recover un-discharged loans given by them to the man who has now come as the father," and the *suputra*s as the ones "born as a consequence of the blessings of God"; Kasturi, *Sathyam Sivam Sundaram, Part III*, 111.

39. Ibid., 121. The quote is taken from the book *Sri Aurobindo on Himself and on the Mother* (Pondicherry: Sri Aurobindo Ashram, 1953), 208. See also Kasturi, *Loving God*, 285; Rao, *Sathya Sai Baba: God as Man*, 307–308. On Aurobindo Ghose's statement and Sathya Sai Baba's appropriation of it, see Spurr, *Sathya Sai Baba as Avatar*, 336–38. The guru of Puttaparthi once observed: "I am *Lokanath* [Lord of the Collectivity] and Sri Aurobindo *Vyaktinath* [Lord of the Individual]"; Balu, *The Glory of Puttaparthi*, 304. For a biographical account

on Aurobindo Ghose, see P. Heehs, *The Lives of Sri Aurobindo* (New York: Columbia University Press, 2008).

40. On the *Veda* pundits and *ahitagni*s of the Godavari delta, see the recent study by David M. Knipe, *Vedic Voices.*

41. Kasturi, *Sathyam Sivam Sundaram, Part III*, 122.

42. Ibid., 155.

43. Ibid.

44. The ceremony of circling a tray of lights before a deity or a holy man at the end of worship, while chanting a hymn.

45. The dust (*reṇu*) of the lord's feet (*śrīpāda*), that is, of Veṅkaṭeśvara's feet.

46. Kasturi, *Sathyam Sivam Sundaram, Part III*, 161. The guru would often claim to be the god of Tirupati; see Haraldsson, *Modern Miracles*, 184.

47. Kasturi, *Sathyam Sivam Sundaram, Part III*, 178. On the crucial theological relevance of the divine triad, see ch. 6.

48. Here, Sathya Sai Baba implicitly identifies himself with Kṛṣṇa. On Kṛṣṇa's call to Arjuna to promote the "welfare of the world" (*lokasaṃgraha*), see *Bhagavadgītā* 3.20, 3.25.

49. Kasturi, *Sathyam Sivam Sundaram, Part III*, 179.

50. For the guru's own explanation of his recovery from what the doctors considered as sure death, see Hislop, *Conversations with Bhagavan Sri Sathya Sai Baba*, 141–42. On Sathya Sai Baba's trip to Goa, see also Levin, *Good Chances*, 108–23; Baskin, *Divine Memories of Sathya Sai Baba*, 149–53. On his taking upon himself the pain and illnesses of his devotees, see ibid., 127, 148–49.

51. Kasturi, *Sathyam Sivam Sundaram, Part III*, 196. See also Rao, *Sathya Sai Baba: God as Man*, 225.

52. See Kasturi, *Sathyam-Sivam-Sundaram. Part I. The Life of Bhagavan Sri Sathya Sai Baba*, between pages 198 and 199.

53. On his love of dogs, see Sri Sathya Sai Baba, *His Story as Told by Himself*, 131–35. On his love of cats, see Kasturi, *Sathyam Sivam Sundaram, Part IV*, 30–31.

54. Kasturi, *Sathyam Sivam Sundaram, Part III*, 199–200.

55. Ibid., 204.

56. See R. Sorabji, *Gandhi and the Stoics: Modern Experiments on Ancient Values* (Chicago: The University of Chicago Press, 2012), 105–108.

57. Kasturi, *Sathyam Sivam Sundaram, Part III*, 212.

58. Ibid., 213.

59. Ibid., 223.

60. Ibid., 12.

61. By the 1930s, he held a reputation as one of Gujarat's most distinguished litterateurs.

62. M. Bhagavan, "The Hindutva Underground: Hindu Nationalism and the Indian National Congress in Late Colonial and Early Postcolonial India,"

in *Religion and Identity in South Asia and Beyond: Essays in Honor of Patrick Olivelle*, ed. S. E. Lindquist (London and New York: Anthem Press, 2013), 342.

63. See G. J. Larson, *India's Agony over Religion* (Albany: State University of New York Press, 1995), 176, 275, 284.

64. As early as 1961, he remarked that limiting the *avatāra* Rāma to Ayodhya was to deny his glory. A CIA secret report approved for release in the year 2000 noted that "the [Sathya] Sai Baba movement could help provide stability to a troubled country, and his influence may also counterbalance the appeal of Hindu chauvinists and ethnic separatists"; "Cultural Trends Study: India's Sai Baba Movement"; www.cia.gov/library/readingroom/docs/CIA-RDP96-00792R000400280002-2.pdf.

65. A chartered accountant since 1942, he was a dedicated follower of M. K. Gandhi and the secretary of the Indian National Congress for the Bombay Region from 1951 to 1960. He first met Sathya Sai Baba in 1965 and served as chairman of the World Council of Sathya Sai Organisations for many years. He authored several books on Sathya Sai Baba and his movement, among which are the following: *Sixteen Spiritual Summers* (Prasanthi Nilayam: Sri Sathya Sai Books and Publications Trust, 1980); *We Devotees* (Prasanthi Nilayam: Sri Sathya Sai Books and Publications Trust, 1983); *Spiritual Blueprints of My Journey* (Bombay: Sarla Charity Trust, 1993).

66. I. H. Shah, "Sri Sathya Sai Seva Organisation: Aims and Accomplishments," in *Golden Age 1980*, 219, 221.

67. Though the guru pointed out to Schulman that what he really wanted was him, not a book:

> "You don't understand," Baba said. "I only told you 'Write the book' because I wanted you. Understand? You. Not a book. The book is publicity. I don't need publicity. I don't want publicity. I want you. I want your faith. I want your love. Everybody who comes here to see me thinks they have arranged it, but *I* arranged it. When the time is ready I call all of those who need me to me, when they are ready. No one can get here to see me otherwise. I want your soul, because it is time now for you to stop vacillating." (Schulman, *Baba*, 105)

68. American devotee Susan Salguero offers interesting memories of the guru and Prasanthi Nilayam between 1978 and 1980; see S. Salguero, *When God Came Walking: 1978–1980 with Sathya Sai Baba* (Ojai, CA: StarBright Books, 2014).

69. As for instance at the valedictory ceremony of the 1978 Summer Course. On this occasion, when a Vedic pundit from Shimoga, Karnataka, was asked if he thought of Sathya Sai Baba as an *avatāra,* he answered in the affirmative by quoting *Bhagavadgītā* 10.41: "Whatever being shows supernal-manifestations

(*vibhūti*), or majesty or vigor, be thou assured that that in every case is sprung from a fraction of My glory" (Edgerton, *The Bhagavad Gītā*, 54); see also Balu, *Living Divinity*, 91.

70. For a testimony dating to the early 1970s, see Levin, *Good Chances*, 40–41. Apparently, Sathya Sai Baba enjoyed hearing what he called "those Yogananda [English] songs."

71. Kasturi, *Garland of 108 Precious Gems*, v.

72. On these issues, see the seminal article by Agehananda Bharati, "The Hindu Renaissance and its Apologetic Patterns," *Journal of Asian Studies* 29, no. 2 (1970): 267–87. On the contemporary relevance of *yajña*s in both India and the West and the novel functions and meanings that the promoters of these rituals attach to them, see S. Bechler, "Globalized Religion: The Vedic Sacrifice (*Yajña*) in Transcultural Public Spheres," in *Experiencing Globalization: Religion in Contemporary Contexts*, ed. D. M. Nault, B. Dawei, E. Voulgarakis, R. Paterson, and C. Andres-Miguel Suva (London/New York: Anthem Press, 2014), 59–77.

73. Levin, *Good Chances*, 116.

74. Kasturi, *Loving God*, 385.

75. See A. Kent, *Divinity and Diversity: A Hindu Revitalization Movement in Malaysia* (Honolulu: University of Hawai'i Press, 2005), 39.

76. Hawkins, *Bordering Realism*, 143.

77. See Kasturi, *Sathyam Sivam Sundaram, Part IV*, 61–62. Sathya Sai Baba remarked that "in the Tibetan monastery where Jesus spent many years, His name is recorded as Isa, which means 'Lord of all living beings' "; ibid., 61.

78. See R. Laing, "The Second Coming Has Come!" in *Golden Age 1980*, 15–22; Rev. R. E. Pipes, "The Oneness of Jesus Christ and Sathya Sai Baba," ibid., 57–63; Rev. C. J. Rossner, "The Priest and the Avatar," ibid., 104–22. On the alleged similarities between Sathya Sai Baba and Christ, see Murphet, *Sai Baba: Invitation to Glory*, 126–38.

79. See Tulasi Srinivas, *Winged Faith*, 86.

80. Gries and Gries, *An Index of Sathya Sai Speaks, Volumes I–XI*, 186.

81. Ibid. Even in one of his early discourses held in July 1958, the guru stated: "[M]an is divine, take it from Me; he is really here on a holy mission, for a divine purpose. To consider him as mean, weak, or sinful is a great mistake. That is itself a great sin"; Sathya Sai Baba, *Sathya Sai Speaks, Vol. 1*, 57 (11. "Discrimination and Detachment").

82. Kasturi, *Garland of 108 Precious Gems*, 54.

83. Swami Vivekananda, *The Complete Works of Swami Vivekananda*, 8 Vols. (Calcutta: Advaita Ashrama, 1970–73), Vol. 2, 295.

84. Ibid., Vol. 1, 11. Vivekananda's outlook reflected Ramakrishna's own conviction; see Gupta, *The Gospel of Sri Ramakrishna*, 152–53, 175, 303, 317. Paul Hacker has pointed out that Vivekananda "never made an effort to learn

about Christian doctrine and spirituality thoroughly and patiently. His statements on Christianity remain at the surface; they are often distorted and sometimes on a rather low level"; Halbfass, *Philology and Confrontation*, 332–33.

85. See S. P. Ruhela, *Sai Trinity: Shirdi Sai, Sathya Sai, Prema Sai Incarnations* (Faridabad: Sai Age Publications, 1993), 116.

86. Sandweiss, *Spirit and the Mind*, 237.

87. See Balu, *Living Divinity*, 84.

88. See Gupta, *The Gospel of Sri Ramakrishna*, 51–52.

89. Vivekananda, *The Complete Works of Swami Vivekananda*, Vol. 2, 143.

90. See the guru's speech of December 25, 1978, titled "Isa," in Sathya Sai Baba, *Sai Vani*, 126–27; Kasturi, *Sathyam Sivam Sundaram, Part IV*, 61.

91. See N. Notovitch, *The Unknown Life of Jesus: The Original Text of Nicolas Notovitch's 1887 Discovery* (Sanger, CA: Quill Driver Books, 2004 [New York: 1890]). In fact, the original Hemis manuscript was never found and Notovitch's accounts were soon exposed as fabrications. For a critical assessment, see B. N. Rice, "The Apocryphal Tale of Jesus' Journey to India: Nicolas Notovitch and the *Life of Saint Issa* Revisited," in *Fakes, Forgeries, and Fictions: Writing Ancient and Modern Christian Apocrypha*, ed. T. Burke. Proceedings from the 2015 York University Christian Apocrypha Symposium. Foreword by Andrew Gregory (Eugene, OR: Cascade Books, 2017), 265–84.

92. Hislop, *Conversations with Bhagavan Sri Sathya Sai Baba*, 110.

93. See Kasturi, *Loving God*, 387.

94. Sathya Sai Baba, *Sai Vani*, 140–41. See also Kasturi, *Loving God*, 1–2, 268, 321, 334–35; Gries and Gries, *An Index of Sathya Sai Speaks, Volumes I–XI*, 28; Levin, *Heart to Heart*, 128; Balu, *Living Divinity*, 82–83. On the influence that a speech by the American follower Tal Brooke might have had on the guru's declaration (in which he referred to the *Book of Revelation* 19.11–16), see Spurr, *Sathya Sai Baba as Avatar*, 338–39; Levin, *Good Chances*, 56–57. A few years later, Brooke became disillusioned with Sathya Sai Baba and converted to Christianity. He was the author of one of the first books that vehemently criticized the guru: *Sai Baba, Lord of the Air* (Berkhamsted: Lion Publishing, 1976), later revised and titled *Avatar of Night*. For an anthology of Sathya Sai Baba's numerous sayings on Jesus, see Sathya Sai Baba, *Sai Vani*, 105–46. On Christ and Christianity in the holy man's discourses, see Gries and Gries, *An Index of Sathya Sai Speaks, Volumes I–XI*, 28–29.

95. See for instance Kasturi, *Sathyam Sivam Sundaram, Part III*, 8. See also Kasturi, *Loving God*, 266, 270, 363. That Sathya Sai Baba is all the names and forms of god is reiterated throughout the hagiographer's works.

96. The famous dictum of *Ṛgveda* 1.164.46: "They have called him Indra, Mitra, Varuṇa, Agni and also the celestial great-winged Garutmān; for, although

one, the wise speak of him diversely (*ekaṃ sad viprā bahudhā vadanti*): they call him Agni, Yama, Mātariśvan."

97. See Kasturi, *Garland of 108 Precious Gems*, 97–98. As he elsewhere argues: "One can elaborate on how Muslims ('We are now understanding the Holy Quran better'), Christians ('The Comforter, the Father revealed to St. John, is here'), Jews ('Prophet Isaiah 56–7'), Buddhists, Parsis, Sikhs, Jains—all find solace and light in Him"; Kasturi, *Loving God*, 321. On the guru and his Muslim devotees, see Murphet, *Sai Baba: Invitation to Glory*, 139–48.

98. See Rigopoulos, *Tolerance in Swami Vivekānanda's Neo-Hinduism*. For one more testimonial to Sathya Sai Baba's universalism, see Kamaraju, *Memories and Memoirs*, 109–14.

99. Levin, *Good Chances*, 82. On Sathya Sai Baba's educational enterprise, see Rao, *Sathya Sai Baba: God as Man*, 357–77.

100. Hislop, *Conversations with Bhagavan Sri Sathya Sai Baba*, 42.

101. Kasturi, *Sathyam Sivam Sundaram, Part III*, 214.

102. Babb, *Redemptive Encounters*, 169.

103. *The Song He Sings* is an English translation of a Telugu song that young Sathya wrote back in 1945. In 1946, the guru's Telugu poems were devoutly collected and published by the *rāja* of Venkatagiri under the title *Songs by Baba*.

104. Kasturi, *Sathyam Sivam Sundaram, Part IV*, 6–7.

105. Ibid., 10. On hypocrisy being the worst sin, see Kasturi, *Loving God*, 346. Young Sathya, like Kasturi, had also been a Boy Scout "eager to use the chance to direct the 'good turns' of scouting towards the path of *sadhana*"; Kasturi, *Sathyam Sivam Sundaram, Part IV*, 6.

106. Ibid., 15.

107. Ibid., 18.

108. Ibid.

109. Ibid., 21.

110. Ibid., 22.

111. Ibid., 48–49.

112. Around the year 2000, its treasury was estimated to be somewhere between $1.5 and $2 billion; see Palmer, *Baba's World*, 114.

113. Kasturi quotes his guru's words:

> Parents, politicians and teachers are all responsible for the extent to which the educational system has deteriorated. . . . In education . . . borrowed ideals, imported systems and fickle loyalties have brought disaster in their train. . . . When the students of this college become leaders and teachers, the number of persons able to

> voyage happily on an even keel over the turbulent sea of life will increase. . . . Truth, justice, love and grace shall soon return to earth. The re-organization of education is one of the means towards this end. (Kasturi, *Sathyam Sivam Sundaram, Part IV*, 24)

114. Ibid., 25.

115. The value of being loyal to one's motherland was always underlined by the guru. Thus, the *avatāra* Rāma "holds up the ideal of a patriot, eager to serve his native land"; see Gries and Gries, *An Index of Sathya Sai Speaks, Volumes I–XI*, 143.

116. Kasturi writes: "He seldom misses an opportunity to bless the members of the armed forces, for He likes them to know, more and more, the glory of the land that they have vowed to defend"; Kasturi, *Sathyam Sivam Sundaram, Part IV*, 31–32.

117. Ibid., 51–52.

118. Ibid., 20.

119. For details on this first summer course, see Levin, *Heart to Heart*, 28–37.

120. The fourteen volumes of the *Summer Showers Series*, compiled from discourses given by Sathya Sai Baba during the Summer Courses on Indian Culture and Spirituality, are published by the Sri Sathya Sai Books and Publications Trust; see http://www.sssbpt.info/english/showers.html.

121. On the guru's composure when his mother passed away, see also Levin, *Heart to Heart*, 33.

122. Shivaram, *Sathya Sai Baba: God in Action*, 165.

123. See Gries and Gries, *An Index of Sathya Sai Speaks, Volumes I–XI*, 34.

124. This "materialization" took place just before the Swami's production of a *liṅga* in Bandipur Forest, in the Chamarajanagar District of Karnataka, about eighty kilometers from Mysore.

125. Hislop, *My Baba and I*, 19.

126. Kasturi, *Sathyam Sivam Sundaram, Part IV*, 32. See also Hislop, *Conversations with Bhagavan Sri Sathya Sai Baba*, 104–105; Fanibunda, *Vision of the Divine*, 49; Shivaram, *Sathya Sai Baba: God in Action*, 15–17.

127. See Kasturi, *Sathyam Sivam Sundaram, Part IV*, 57. For an article of his, see F. G. Baranowski, "A Date with the Celestial," in *The Splendour of Sathya Sai* (Hyderabad: Sri Prasanthi Society, 1995), 55–58.

128. On this occasion he produced a *jyotirliṅga* and declared twice to the assembled devotees that "you who have experienced the sublimity and splendor of this divine event, have acquired thereby, merit enormous enough to save you from the cycle of birth and death"; see Baskin, *Divine Memories of Sathya Sai Baba*, 172.

129. The temple of the flute-playing lord as cowherd, Kṛṣṇa Gopāla. It is especially sacred being linked to the myth of Puttaparthi's origins; see Rigopoulos, *The Construction of a Cultic Center Through Narrative.*

130. See Balu, *Living Divinity*, 42–43.

131. On Sathya Sai Baba's allowing translation of *mantras* in any language, saying that what counts is the heart, see Steel, *The Sathya Sai Baba Compendium*, 264.

132. Kasturi, *Sathyam Sivam Sundaram, Part IV*, 66.

133. For an excellent introduction to the most famous of all Indian scriptures, see Davis, *The Bhagavad Gita: A Biography.*

134. Kasturi, *Sathyam Sivam Sundaram, Part IV*, 66–67.

135. Ibid., 88.

136. Shivaram, *Sathya Sai Baba: God in Action*, 83.

137. Sri Sathya Sai Baba, *Sree Gurucharanam. A Compilation of Divine Discourses of Bhagavan Sri Sathya Sai Baba During Guru Poornima (1956–1998)* (Prasanthi Nilayam: Sri Sathya Sai Books & Publications, 2000), 49.

138. An unusual episode is reported by Shakuntala Balu:

> Sri Sathya Sai Baba moved his hand in the familiar circular way and Swami Shraddhananda pounced on it and caught it and said, "Don't give me those peppermints!" Dr. Gadhia was aghast, but Sri Sathya Sai Baba remained unperturbed . . . in this moment of extreme provocation, he was full of love and spoke gently to the aggressive *swami*, "Let me give the peppermints to those who want them. Then I will talk to you." . . . Shraddhananda emerged from the interview exultant, tears of joy streaming down his face. Later, when he was more composed, Shraddhananda said, "Baba is a great soul. He is divine. For, when he opened his shirt, I saw my *guru*. Yes, Guru Nityananda on his chest!" (Balu, *Living Divinity*, 196)

139. On Sathya Sai Baba as *satyabodhaka*, see Kasturi's lecture to overseas devotees titled "The Teacher of Truth," in Shivaram, *Sathya Sai Baba: God in Action*, 229–35.

140. By 1975, the newsletter was published in eleven languages: Telugu, English, Tamil, Malayalam, Kannada, Marathi, Gujarati, Bengali, Hindi, Assamese and Nepali.

141. Kasturi extols Sathya Sai Baba as the remover of all doubts in his commentary to the ninety-eighth of the guru's 108 names, *Oṃ Śrī Sakala Saṃśaya Harāya Namaḥ*; Kasturi, *Garland of 108 Precious Gems*, 100–101.

142. In Part 1, Kasturi states that "Baba has written five series of articles under the titles Prema Vahini, Dhyana Vahini, Prasanthi Vahini, Jnana Vahini and Sandehanivarini. His is simple, direct, spoken Telugu and so when one reads the articles, one can picture Baba Himself talking in His intimate and inspiring way to the reader"; Kasturi, *Sathyam Sivam Sundaram, Part I (1926–1960)*, 256.

143. For an appreciation of Sathya Sai Baba's commentaries on the *Upaniṣads*, see K. G. Witz, *The Supreme Wisdom of the Upaniṣads: An Introduction* (Delhi: Motilal Banarsidass, 1998).

144. Kasturi, *Sathyam Sivam Sundaram, Part IV*, 123.

145. Ibid., 132.

146. Levin, *Heart to Heart*, 3. Howard Levin first came to Sathya Sai Baba's ashram on June 5, 1970. For his testimony and the testimony of other American devotees who first came to Prasanthi Nilayam in the early 1970s, see www.youtube.com/watch?v=HpV8fhK0QFg (Summer 2019 meeting of Sathya Sai Baba devotees at Feathered Pipe Ranch, Helena, Montana).

147. Kasturi, *Sathyam Sivam Sundaram, Part IV*, 166.

148. See Kasturi, *Loving God*, 261; Kasturi, *Sathyam Sivam Sundaram, Part I (1926–1960)*, 233.

149. Babb, *Redemptive Encounters*, 171.

150. Kasturi, *Sathyam Sivam Sundaram, Part IV*, 157–59. On Sathya Sai Baba as being both *saguṇa* and *nirguṇa,* see Kasturi, *Garland of 108 Precious Gems*, 95.

151. For an appreciation of the strength of the guru's fingers and the dexterity of his hands, see Levin, *Good Chances*, 84–85; Roumanoff, *Candide au pays des Gourous*, 146; Padmanaban, *Love Is My Form*, 201, 275, 563. For instance, he would pluck coconut leaves, split them, and skillfully weave them in different shapes—often in that of a deer—which he offered to devotees as bookmarks. In February 2016, I saw the one he donated to Padmamma, Kasturi's daughter, back in 1957. The deer's tail was missing ("It came away along the years," said Padmamma, adding that "the tail is symbolic of the ego") and its caption read "Creation." On the tail as symbol of the ego, see Shivaram, *Sathya Sai Baba: God in Action*, 9. As Ramakrishna once told Keshab Chandra Sen (1838–1884): "[A]s long as man wears the tail of ignorance, he can only live in the world; but, when the tail drops off, he can live either in the knowledge of God or in the world, whichever he pleases"; C. Isherwood, *Ramakrishna and His Disciples* (London: Methuen, 1965), 161. On this particular gift to Padmamma, see https://soundcloud.com/kg-sreeganeshan/interview-padma-kasturi (minute 1); http://www.saibabaofindia.com/he_is_my_swami_5.htm, 1–2.

152. One of the most vocal denouncers was the rationalist Abraham Kovoor (1898–1978), who calls Sathya Sai Baba a fake in his book *Bygone Godmen! Encounters with Spiritual Frauds* (Bombay: Jaico, 1976). A collection of data

against the guru, titled *The Findings*, was made public in 2000 by former devotees David and Faye Bailey; see http://www.exbaba.com/findings.html. Against Sathya Sai Baba, see also K. Shepherd, *Investigating the Sai Baba Movement: A Clarification of Misrepresented Saints and Opportunism* (Dorset: Citizen Initiative, 2005), 269–301. On the skeptical reception of the guru of Puttaparthi, see Tulasi Srinivas, *Winged Faith*, 232–81; Haraldsson, *Modern Miracles*, 315–31.

153. Belief in the existence of demons and evil spirits (*rākṣasas*, *bhūtas*, *piśācas*) was and still is the rule in village India.

154. Kasturi, *Sathyam Sivam Sundaram, Part IV*, 171. A group of rationalists planned a demonstration against Sathya Sai Baba as early as 1947; see Padmanaban, *Love Is My Form*, 391, 394.

155. Kasturi took the imagery of diving from his master. In one of his first discourses, dated July 1958, the guru stated: "Come to Me gladly; dive into the sea and discover its depth; there is no use dipping near the shore and swearing that the sea is shallow and has no pearls. Dive deep and you will secure your desire"; Sathya Sai Baba, *Sathya Sai Speaks, Vol. 1*, 58. Ramakrishna used this same imagery: "[D]ive deep. Can a man get pearls by floating or swimming on the surface? He must dive deep"; Gupta, *The Gospel of Sri Ramakrishna*, 323. See also ibid., 391.

156. See his short article "Parapsychology and Sathya Sai Baba," in *Golden Age 1980*, 257–58.

157. The guru, however, did not allow them to conduct clinical tests on him. By Erlendur Haraldsson, see his 2013 revised edition of *Modern Miracles*. The psychology professor writes that in spite of his long-lasting and painstaking effort, he could find no evidence of fraud.

158. Kasturi, *Sathyam Sivam Sundaram, Part IV*, 171–72.

159. See S. H. Sandweiss, *Sai Baba: The Holy Man . . . and the Psychiatrist* (San Diego: Birth Day, 1975) and Id., *Spirit and the Mind*. See also his article "A Garland for Baba," in *Golden Age 1980*, 84–87. He set up a Sathya Sai Baba Center at his home in San Diego, California.

160. Kasturi, *Sathyam Sivam Sundaram, Part IV*, 173.

161. Ibid., 172.

162. Ibid., 173.

163. Ibid.

164. Even Western devotees underlined that it was not true that the guru was partial to the rich; see Baskin, *Divine Memories of Sathya Sai Baba*, 80.

165. Kasturi, *Sathyam Sivam Sundaram, Part IV*, 173. In 1976, the guru claimed to "never see or make any distinction between the rich and the poor"; see Karanjia, *God Lives in India*, 63. See also ibid., 13–14, 35–50.

166. She wrote several popular books on the guru of Puttaparthi, the first of which was *Sai Baba: The Ultimate Experience* (Los Angeles: Aura Books,

1985). For her bibliography, see Steel, *The Sathya Sai Baba Compendium*, 312. Along with her husband, she was active in setting up the American Sathya Sai Organization together with John S. Hislop. For an article of hers, see Ph. Krystal, "The Guide Within," in *The Splendour of Sathya Sai*, 121–23.

167. A former aerospace engineer advisor to the U.S. Air Force, Al Drucker (1927–2016) later trained as a natural healer. For the story of Drucker's dramatic introduction to Sathya Sai Baba, see his article "God Is Always with You," in *Golden Age 1980*, 138–43. He edited the text *Sai Baba Gita: The Way to Self-Realisation and Liberation in This Age* (Crestone, CO: Atma Press, 1993), which is the American edition of Sathya Sai Baba, *Discourses on the Bhagavad-Gita*, comp. and ed. A. Drucker (Prasanthi Nilayan: Sri Sathya Sai Books and Publications, 1988).

168. Though he first arrived in Puttaparthi in 1974, he was given his first interview only after fifteen years of visits to the ashram. He was the owner of the famous Hard Rock Café in London and other cities. When he sold his chain of Hard Rock Cafés, he donated to the guru $59 million—half the sale price—for building the Super Speciality Hospital in Puttaparthi. On Isaac Tigrett and the Hard Rock Café's support of Sathya Sai Baba, see M. L. Chibber, *Sai Baba's Mahavakya on Leadership: Book for Youth, Parents, and Teachers* (Faber, VA: Leela Press, 1995), 50–51.

169. A wealthy Californian businessman, he was actively involved in the establishment of the Sathya Sai Organization in the United States, along with John S. Hislop. For many years he has also been a trustee of the Sathya Sai Book Center of America.

170. In the late 1960s as well as in the 1970s and 1980s, the American devotee Richard Bock together with his wife Janet produced several documentary films on the guru, which were instrumental in popularizing his figure: among these, *The Message I Bring* (Prasanthi Nilayam: Sri Sathya Sai Books & Publication Trust, n.d.; Video-CD of a film taken in 1968); *Aura of Divinity* (Prasanthi Nilayam: Sri Sathya Sai Books & Publication Trust, n.d.; Video-CD of a film taken in the 1970s); *Truth Is My Name* (Prasanthi Nilayam: Sri Sathya Sai Books & Publication Trust, n.d.; Video-CD of films taken in the 1970s and 1980s). See also their book *The Jesus Mystery of Lost Years and Unknown Travels* (Los Angeles: Aura Books, 1980). By R. Bock, see "Communicating Divinity," in *Golden Age 1980*, 147–49, in which he recalls how he first heard Sathya Sai Baba's name from his friend Ravi Shankar (1920–2012), the renown sitar player. In the 1970s, Ravi Shankar performed a few times in the presence of Sathya Sai Baba; see his short article "A Tribute to Baba," ibid., 150. On Ravi Shankar's first meeting with the guru of Puttaparthi, see Baskin, *Divine Memories of Sathya Sai Baba*, 65–66.

171. Already in their seventies when they first arrived in Prasanthi Nilayam, they were the founders of the Sathya Sai Organization in the UK. A collection of their articles on the guru was published with the title *Sathya Sai Baba: Embodi-*

ment of Love (London: Sawbridge, 1982). Ron Laing viewed Sathya Sai Baba as the manifestation of Christ. For an article by Peggy Mason, see "Coming Home," in *Golden Age 1980*, 126–32. In the UK, Peggy Mason edited the Sathya Sai Newsletter till the end of her life in the mid-1990s.

172. Hislop, *Conversations with Bhagavan Sri Sathya Sai Baba*, 57–58.

173. Kasturi, *Sathyam Sivam Sundaram, Part IV*, 165.

174. B. N. Narasimha Murthy states that even in the early 1960s there were derogatory newspaper articles on the guru and many people accused him of favoring the rich; see https://vimeo.com/97850716 (minutes 10, 12).

175. On the accusations of sexual abuses, see A. K. Menon and A. Malik, "Test of Faith," *India Today* 25, no. 49 (2000): 41–45.

176. On the miraculous in Jesus's life, see J. P. Meier, *A Marginal Jew: Rethinking the Historical Jesus. Vol. 2. Mentor, Message, and Miracles* (New York: Doubleday, 1994).

177. Premanand, who never met Sathya Sai Baba, maintained that the guru's so-called miracles were but conjuring tricks; see his books *The Lure of Miracles* (Podanur: Indian CSICOP, 1982) and *Sathya Sai Baba and the Gold Control Act* (Podanur: Indian CSICOP, 1986). See also Siegel, *Net of Magic*, 340–45.

178. Haraldsson, *Modern Miracles*, 37.

179. When Dr. Karlis Osis described to Doug Henning an incident in which the enamel stone with the guru's picture disappeared from his ring, Henning commented that this was beyond the skills of magicians; see ibid., 345.

180. Schulman, *Baba*, 165.

181. See Shivaram, *Sathya Sai Baba: God in Action*, 69.

182. Karanjia, *God Lives in India*, 41.

183. See for instance P. P. R. Sawhny, *Shri Satya Sai Baba's Divine Mission of Love, Self-Realisation and Eternal Bliss for All Mankinds* (New Delhi: Lakherwal Press, 1979).

184. See Smriti Srinivas, *In the Presence of Sai Baba*, 208–15. On Prasanthi Nilayam's sacred architecture, see also Tulasi Srinivas, "Building Faith: Religious Pluralism, Pedagogical Urbanism, and Governance in the Sathya Sai Sacred City," *International Journal of Hindu Studies* 13, no. 3 (2010): 301–36.

185. This photograph was taken by an American satellite, the Earth Resources Orbiting Sensor, on November 29, 1972; see *Prasanthi Nilayam Information Booklet*. Compiled by Public Relations Office, Sri Sathya Sai Central Trust, Prasanthi Nilayam (Prasanthi Nilayam: Sri Sathya Sai Sadhana Trust, 2015), 4. For this story, see Balu, *Living Divinity*, 65–68.

186. In the words of the Swami: "Each person gives his point of view, and finally values are derived from this. . . . Each one listens eagerly and many will give their point of view. The Bible, the Koran, the Gita, Swami's books may

be used"; Hislop, *Conversations with Sathya Sai Baba*, 158–59. On world religions and their purported unity, see K. Raghavan, *Guide to Indian Culture and Spirituality. Based on the Divine Teachings of Bhagawan Sri Sri Sri Sathya Sai Baba* (Prasanthi Nilayam: Sri Sathya Sai Books and Publications, 1990), 63–84. For a sample of the texts utilized within the organization at the beginning of the 1980s, see *Lessons for Study Circle* (Prasanthi Nilayam: World Council Sri Sathya Sai Organisations, 1982). On the theory and practice of study circles, see J. Roof, *Pathways to God: A Study Guide to the Teachings of Sathya Sai Baba* (Faber, VA: Leela Press, 1991).

187. Krystal, *Sai Baba: The Ultimate Experience*, 43.

188. *Service and Spirituality: The Sathya Sai Movement in Malaysia* (Kuala Lumpur: Sri Sathya Sai Central Council of Malaysia, 1985), 117. On the EHV program at the beginning of the 1980s, see *The Path Divine. For Sri Sathya Sai Bal Vikas, Group III.* Education in Human Values Series (Prasanthi Nilayam: Sri Sathya Sai Bal Vikas Education Trust), 1983. For an overview, see C. Romano, *Teoria e pratica del "Sathya Sai Education in Human Values Program"* (BA thesis, Università Ca' Foscari, Venezia, 1999). On the implementation of EHV programs, see E. Arweck, "Common Values for the Common School? Using Two Values Education Programmes to Promote 'Spiritual and Moral Development,' " *Journal of Moral Education* (2005): 325–42. See also Y. Sankar, "Education in Crisis: A Value-Based Model of Education Provides Some Guidance," *Interchange* (2004): 127–51.

189. On the Third World Conference, see V. Balu and S. Balu, *Divine Glory* (Delhi: Sri Satguru Publications, 1999), 4–16.

190. See *The Divinity Within. Based on Spiritual Museum at Sri Sathya Sai Arts, Science & Commerce College, Whitefield, Bangalore.* Under the Auspices of Sri Sathya Sai Central Trust, India (Bombay: India Book House Education Trust, 1978).

191. Shri Sathya Sai Baba, *Sathya Sai Vahini* (Prasanthi Nilayam: Sri Sathya Sai Books and Publications, 1981), 98.

192. Swami Vivekananda, *The Complete Works of Swami Vivekananda*, Vol. 3, 56.

193. On Aurobindo Ghose and Sarvepalli Radhakrishnan, see Halbfass, *India and Europe*, 248–56. S. Radhakrishnan had taught philosophy at the Maharaja's College of Mysore in the period 1918–1921, just a few years before Kasturi was appointed there in 1928; for an introduction to S. Radhakrishnan's life and thought, see M. Hawley, "Sarvepalli Radhakrishnan (1888–1975)," *Internet Encyclopedia of Philosophy* (http://www.iep.utm.edu/radhakri/#SH1d). Aurobindo had come to the conclusion that Hinduism had a glorious, eternal (*sanātana*) destiny: "That which we call the Hindu religion is really the eternal religion, because it is the universal religion which embraces all others"; Aurobindo Ghose, "Uttarpara Speech," in *Karmayogin: Political Writings and Speeches 1909–1910* (Pondicherry:

Sri Aurobindo Ashram Press, 1997), 11. On Aurobindo's reception in the West, see M. Castagnetto Alessio, *Il loto e la spada. Il pensiero di Aurobindo Ghose e la sua ricezione in Occidente* (Milano: Franco Angeli, 2020).

194. As Paul Hacker observed: "Vivekananda taught that Ramakrishna was the living commentary to all of the sacred texts of the Hindus; he encompassed within himself all that which had been lived in the millennia of Hindu religious life; with his birth, the Golden Age, the 'Age of Truth,' had dawned once again" (L. Schmithausen, ed., *Writings of Paul Hacker: Kleine Schriften* [Wiesbaden: Otto Harrassowitz, 1978], 567).

195. Halbfass, *India and Europe*, 238.

196. Kasturi, *Sathyam Sivam Sundaram, Part I (1926–1960)*, iv.

197. "He Is My Swami"—Part 1, http://media.radiosai.org/journals/Vol_05/01MAY07/14-h2h_special.htm, 1.

198. Tulasi Srinivas, *Winged Faith*, 357 n. 62.

199. Kasturi, *Sathyam Sivam Sundaram, Part I. The Life of Bhagavan Sri Sathya Sai Baba* (Prasanthi Nilayam: Sri Sathya Sai Books & Publications, 1982), iii.

200. See B. N. Narasimha Murthy, *Sathyam Sivam Sundaram. Volume 5. Life Story of Bhagawan Sri Sathya Sai Baba 1980–85* (Prasanthi Nilayam: Sri Sathya Sai Sadhana Trust, 2014 [2005]).

201. See B. N. Narasimha Murthy, *Sathyam Sivam Sundaram. Volume 6. Life Story of Bhagawan Sri Sathya Sai Baba 1986–1993* (Prasanthi Nilayam: Sri Sathya Sai Sadhana Trust, 2007); B. N. Narasimha Murthy, *Sathyam Sivam Sundaram. Volume 7. Life Story of Bhagawan Sri Sathya Sai Baba 1994–2001* (Prasanthi Nilayam: Sri Sathya Sai Sadhana Trust, 2010).

202. "Sai's kasturi . . . A Phantasmagoric Fragrance Forever," in *Heart-2Heart—Radio Sai Listeners' Journal*, 9–10 (http://media.radiosai.org/journals/Vol_06/01JAN08/03-coverstory.htm).

203. B. N. Narasimha Murthy speaks of himself, of his activities and life-long devotion to Sathya Sai Baba in an interview with Ted Henry and Jody Cleary recorded in January 2013 in Muddenahalli; see https://vimeo.com/97850716.

204. A village situated seven kilometers away from Chikballapur, in the Chikballapur district of Karnataka. Muddenahalli is fifty-five kilometers from Bangalore via Yelahanka and Devanahalli.

205. He originally joined the Brindavan Campus in 1996 to pursue a Bachelor's degree in chemistry. On these recent developments, see B. N. Narasimha Murthy, ed., *Sri Sathya Sai Uvacha, Vol. 1. Divine Discourses of Bhagawan Sri Sathya Sai Baba in the Subtle Body (May to September 2014)* (Muddenahalli: Sri Sathya Sai Premamruta Prakashana, 2014). For further information, see the website Sri Sathya Sai Vrinda (http://saivrinda.org).

206. See http://www.saiprakashana.online. On how it all started in Madhusudhan Rao Naidu's own words, see Narasimha Murthy, *Sri Sathya Sai Uvacha, Vol. 1*, 22–27.

207. Lit. "good or true teacher." The supreme teacher who is identified with the qualityless Absolute, dwelling in one's own heart.

208. This extract of Narasimha Murthy's talk was publicized on the internet on July 16, 2019. I got the news through the *Sai Darshan Italia*, an Italian organization affiliated with Madhusudhan Rao Naidu's movement based in Muddenahalli.

209. https://www.saiprakashana.online/web/en.

210. See for instance the appeal to the Muddenahalli group by Prof. Anil Kumar Kamaraju; https://www.youtube.com/watch?v=TfySaF0Dyjg.

211. See the speech of Sri K. Chakravarthi, member-secretary of the Sri Sathya Sai Central Trust, held on April 24, 2017, sixth anniversary of the guru's death; https://www.youtube.com/watch?v=c7mk0SwKOyA&feature=youtube_gdata_player.

212. https://www.saiprakashana.online/web/en.

213. On Prema Sai Baba's advent, see S. P. Ruhela, *The Triple Incarnations of Sai Baba: Sri Shirdi Sai Baba, Sri Sathya Sai Baba, and Future Prema Sai Baba* (Gurgaon: Partridge India, 2015), 305–29.

214. Hislop, *Three Stories*, 177. John S. Hislop claimed that the portrait on the ring gradually changed over time.

Chapter 4

1. See Kasturi, *Loving God*, iii, 378. Arnold Schulman, who visited Puttaparthi in the late 1960s, writes that "Baba designated him his official biographer"; Schulman, *Baba*, 57. Moreover: "As a member of the innermost circle Kasturi has more prestige than anyone else in the ashram with the possible exception of Raj Reddy, the son of a maharaja, who is Baba's personal chauffeur and all around right-hand man"; ibid. A Malaysian devotee, J. Jagadeesan, states: "As Valmiki for Rama, as Vyasa for Krishna, so Kasturi for Sathya Sai"; J. Jagadeesan, *Sai Baba: The Journey Within. Journey to God, Part III* (Prasanthi Nilayam: Sri Sathya Sai Books and Publications, 1989), 4.

2. Kasturi, *Loving God*, 342.

3. Remembering his stay in the ashram in June 1972, Howard Levin writes: "When I got to Prasanthi Nilayam at nine P.M. that night all the lights were out. I found Mr. Kasturi hunched over his typewriter with only a candle for light"; Levin, *Heart to Heart*, 43.

4. Kasturi, *Loving God*, 172.

5. Referring to his own torrential speeches, the guru observed that "only the swift stream can flush the slime away"; N. Kasturi, "Baba–As Speaker," in *Sai Chandana: Book of Homage*, ed. V. K. Gokak (Prasanthi Nilayam: Sri Sathya Sai Institute of Higher Learning, 1985), 284.

6. Kasturi, *Loving God*, 262. The hagiographer took down his notes in both Telugu and Kannada, Kannada being the language he was most familiar with.

7. Priddy, *Source of the Dream*, 222.

8. http://www.saibabaofindia.com/sais_kasturi_heart2heart.htm, 19. On B. V. Raja Reddy, see Rao, *Sathya Sai Baba: God as Man*, 84–85.

9. Like many natives of Andhra Pradesh, Sathya Sai Baba knew Kannada and Tamil, and Kasturi records several instances in which he used these languages to express himself. He even gave a few public speeches in Kannada, but this was an exception to the rule; see Kasturi, *Loving God*, 108, 119, 165, 264–65. Kasturi claims that during interviews with devotees the guru could speak any language, "whether it is Swahili, Nepali, French, Adi, Marathi or Bantu"; ibid., 263. See also ibid., 258; Kasturi, *Gurudev*, 18.

10. Kasturi, *Loving God*, 258.

11. Ibid., 119. Sathya Sai Baba wrote letters to him in Kannada, though using the English script; see Padmamma, *Twameva Matha*, 90. See also http://www.saibabaofindia.com/sais_kasturi_heart2heart.htm, 8.

12. Kasturi, *Loving God*, 217. See also ibid., 303.

13. Ibid., 303–304.

14. The first tape recordings of the guru's speeches appeared in the 1970s.

15. See Priddy, *Source of the Dream*, 222–23.

16. Nowadays, there exist various editions of these English volumes: several Indian ones (Kasturi's original edition alongside revised, enlarged versions of it, of which the last was published in 2009 and subsequently reprinted) and an American edition of eleven volumes of select discourses, based on a different division of years, published by the Sathya Sai Book Center of America in January 1993. For an excellent index of this latter edition, see Gries and Gries, *An Index of Sathya Sai Speaks, Volumes I–XI*.

17. http://www.saibaba-x.org.uk/27/kasturi.html, 9.

18. He later converted to Christianity, becoming an active member of the Indian Methodist Church.

19. Haraldsson, *Modern Miracles*, 186.

20. Kasturi, *Loving God*, 249.

21. See Sathya Sai Baba, *Sathya Sai Speaks, Vol. 1*, and *Sathya Sai Speaks, Vol. 2*.

22. Kasturi, *Loving God*, 259.

23. Ibid., 252.

24. At Dasara of 1970, an attempt was made by Kasturi to deliver the English version of the guru's speech as a post hoc program, that is, a few hours later, but the experiment was a failure and had to be given up; ibid., 258–59.

25. Ibid., 259.

26. See ibid., 258–72.

27. Ibid., 258.

28. Ibid., 263. See also ibid., 262. For a telling instance in which Sathya Sai Baba publicly corrected Kasturi, who erroneously translated the term *prapañca* as "world" instead of "universe," see ibid., 267–68. Sometimes the guru would criticize Kasturi for his inadequate translation after its delivery, when they met in private; see http://www.saibabaofindia.com/sais_kasturi_heart2heart.htm, 19–20. On many occasions Kasturi translated the guru's Telugu when he granted private interviews to devotees and the Swami would take delight in correcting him whenever he missed a subtle nuance of his speech; see Jagadeesan, *Sai Baba: The Journey Within*, 37.

29. Kasturi, *Loving God*, 260.

30. See ibid., 265.

31. The guru would even correct his Sanskrit pronunciation of his 1008 names; see ibid., 209.

32. See ibid., 169, 248, 370–72.

33. See ibid., 225, 375, 382.

34. Here is Kasturi's explanation of the meaning of the guru's words:

> Baba described to us later . . . the symbolism inherent in his reference to "automatic light." They are the signal lights which direct the flow of traffic wherever many roads intersect, changing automatically at fixed intervals from red to yellow and from yellow to green. The codes of moral behavior and social conducts, of Dharma in short, are also traffic signals fixed by the Master to save humans from conflict and clash, from violence and war. Baba also spoke of traffic regulations laid down by Providence to prevent galaxies and planets, comets and constellations, from behaving chaotically in their cosmic gyrations. (Ibid., 261)

35. Ibid., 211–13. The title also refers to the relationship between the body (chariot) and the Self (charioteer), often highlighted by the guru.

36. In the first number of the newsletter, B. V. Raja Reddy figured as the editor. This, however, was only accidental, and Kasturi figured as the editor of *Sanathana Sarathi* starting with the second number; ibid., 212. At Kasturi's death in 1987, the editor became V. K. Narasimhan who had been deputy editor of *The Hindu* and editor of *Indian Express*, *Financial Express*, and *Deccan Herald*. On his faith in the guru whom he first met in December 1977, see V. K. Narasimhan, "What Sri Sathya Sai Baba Means to Me," in *Golden Age 1980*, 12–14.

37. Kasturi, *Loving God*, 213.

38. Kasturi, *Garland of 108 Precious Gems*, 83.

39. Kasturi, *Loving God*, 213.

40. "It had never more than 32 pages of crown 1/8 size or 30 of double crown size"; ibid., 224.

41. See ibid. Kasturi writes that the length of his article would be exactly the same, month after month: "The diction—sweet and satisfying, simple and sustaining—avoids pedantry and prolixity. The calligraphy is charming to the eye"; ibid.

42. As editor of the *Vahini Series*, Kasturi in his prefaces would often recall to his readers that the texts were first serialized in full in the *Sanathana Sarathi* newsletter; see Shri Sathya Sai Baba, *Sathya Sai Vahini*, i.

43. Kasturi, *Sathyam Sivam Sundaram, Part IV*, 119. See also Kasturi, *Gurudev*, 21. For the guru's commentary on this *Upaniṣad*, the earliest and longest among the Vedic *Upaniṣads*, see Shri Sathya Sai Baba, *Upanishad Vahini* (Prasanthi Nilayam: Sri Sathya Sai Education and Publication Foundation, 1975), 32–40.

44. See Kasturi, *Loving God*, 303.

45. See ibid., 215, and the chapter titled "Penance for Pen," ibid., 210–32.

46. See ibid., 220.

47. This was a most difficult task for him, a duel with the printer's devil as he called it, also because his Telugu lettering was perplexing and "Kannadic"; see ibid., 218–19.

48. http://www.saibabaofindia.com/sais_kasturi_heart2heart.htm, 18–19. On the hagiographer's toil in the preparation of the newsletter, see Kasturi, *Loving God*, 218–21.

49. Ibid., 224–25.

50. Ibid., 303.

51. See ibid., 217–18.

52. See Aitken, *Sri Sathya Sai Baba: A Life*, 122–23.

53. Ibid., 123.

54. Shri Sathya Sai Baba, *Dhyana Vahini* (Prasanthi Nilayam: Sri Sathya Sai Books and Publications, 1980), i–ii. On the quality of the guru's Telugu, see B. Rama Raju, "Sathya Sai as a Master of the Telugu Language and as a Writer," in *Sai Chandana: Book of Homage*, 287–94.

55. http://www.saibabaofindia.com/sais_kasturi_heart2heart.htm, 19.

56. See Smriti Srinivas, *In the Presence of Sai Baba*, 188–208.

57. Kasturi, *Loving God*, 224.

58. Ibid.

59. Ibid.

60. Starting in 1972, *Sanathana Sarathi* also became larger, about ten inches by six inches, and continues to be this size even nowadays.

61. Here is how the current Prasanthi Nilayam information booklet describes it:

> The pillar, with its concentric rings at the base, represents the unity of faiths, that all are seeking the one and the same God. The rising column signifies that humanity rises above differences to the blossoming of the "lotus of the heart," whose petals are at the top of the pillar. The flame or inner illumination is in the center of the lotus. Just as the lotus plant lives in water but does not get contaminated by it, so we should live in the world without getting engaged in it. The base of the pillar is surrounded by plaques with symbols of the five main religions and their inner significance, emphasizing the unity of faiths and humanity's spiritual journey. (*Prasanthi Nilayam Information Booklet*, 59–60)

On the Sarva Dharma Stupa see Steel, *The Sathya Sai Baba Compendium*, 224–26; Balu, *Living Divinity*, 38, 117.

62. See Schulman, *Baba*, 142; Levin, *Heart to Heart*, 42–43.

63. See https://www.youtube.com/watch?v=qw1WB6Kj88Y (minutes 1–2).

64. See Schulman, *Baba*, 79, 148.

65. Hislop, *Conversations with Bhagavan Sri Sathya Sai Baba*, 83.

66. See Kasturi, *Loving God*, 114, 340.

67. Ibid., 341. See also ibid., 221; http://www.saibabaofindia.com/sais_kasturi_heart2heart.htm, 17.

68. See Schulman, *Baba*, 110.

69. From 1963 to 1989, he was lecturer in botany at the Christian College of Guntur, Andhra Pradesh. Raised in a family of followers of the Brahmo Samaj, he first visited Prasanthi Nilayam in 1970 complying with his wife's wish, who hoped the guru would cure her from her illness; see http://www.saibabaofindia.com/sais_kasturi_heart2heart.htm, 13–14. He was appointed zonal convener of Sri Sathya Sai Organizations of Andhra Pradesh in 1980, vice president in 1984, and served as the state president from 1985 to 1989. He was then appointed principal of the Sri Sathya Sai University, Whitefield Campus, Bangalore. He served in this position from 1989 to 1995. Since 1995, he has been serving as the professor of bio sciences, Sri Sathya Sai University, Prasanthi Nilayam campus. He has written more than twenty books on Sathya Sai Baba and has traveled extensively, in India and throughout the world, giving talks on the guru's message. Among his many publications, see Kamaraju, *Memories and Memoirs*. He met Kasturi on his first visit to Puttaparthi: his children were thirsty and the hagiographer provided water for them, even though this caused him to be late for the guru's *darśan*. True to his *sevā* ideal, Kasturi observed: "To me, giving you water is more important than darshan"; ibid., 18.

70. A distinguished Vedic scholar who resided in Prasanthi Nilayam and was close to Sathya Sai Baba.

71. http://www.saibabaofindia.com/sais_kasturi_heart2heart.htm, 2–3.

72. See Kasturi, *Loving God*, 307–308, 386–87; http://www.saibabaofindia.com/sais_kasturi_heart2heart.htm, 17–18.

73. Levin, *Good Chances*, 110.

74. http://www.saibabaofindia.com/sais_kasturi_heart2heart.htm, 3.

75. Ibid., 20–22. See also Kasturi, *Loving God*, 248–49. Even during the fifteen months when he served as producer of programs for the All India Radio Station in Bangalore, Kasturi was allowed to take a long leave so as to accompany the guru on his first visit to North India; see ibid., 195–96.

76. http://www.saibabaofindia.com/sais_kasturi_heart2heart.htm, 22.

77. See Kasturi, *Loving God*, 81–84; Padmamma, *Twameva Matha*, 89–96. The guru also wrote letters to the hagiographer's mother, wife, son, and daughter.

78. Ibid., 4.

79. Kasturi, *Loving God*, 375.

80. Shivaram, *Sathya Sai Baba: God in Action*, 114.

81. See http://www.saibabaofindia.com/sais_kasturi_heart2heart.htm, 3.

82. See Jagadeesan, *Sai Baba: The Journey Within*, 36–37.

83. http://media.radiosai.org/journals/Vol_05/01MAY07/14-h2h_special.htm, 5 ("He Is My Swami"—Part 1).

84. Ibid., 8.

85. See Padmamma, *Twameva Matha*, 98.

86. The wife is expected to wear it at all times as long as her husband lives.

87. See Kasturi, *Loving God*, 207–10; http://www.saibabaofindia.com/sais_kasturi_heart2heart.htm, 12.

88. Kasturi, *Loving God*, 209–10.

89. A town in the Guntur district of Andhra Pradesh.

90. Kasturi, *Loving God*, 383–84. See also http://www.saibabaofindia.com/sais_kasturi_heart2heart.htm, 4.

91. See ibid. See also https://robertpriddy.wordpress.com/2015/01/10/soul-journs-narasimha-murthys-secret-of-prema-sai. S. P. Ruhela writes: "It was heard in Prasanthi Nilayam that Baba had said that late Prof. N. Kasturi . . . would be reborn so as to be the mother of Prema Sai Baba"; Ruhela, *Sai Trinity*, 115.

92. See Kasturi, *Loving God*, 189–90.

93. See ibid., 196–97; Kasturi, *Easwaramma*, 123.

94. Kasturi, *Loving God*, 386.

95. See, for instance, Schulman, *Baba*, 115, 142, 164; N. Roy, "Closer to God," in Ruhela and Robinson, *Sai Baba and His Message*, 262–63, 266. On analogy with Madhavrao Deshpande alias Shyama, a villager of Shirdi and a staunch *bhakta* of the first Sai Baba who often acted as an intermediary between the saint and the devotees; see Rigopoulos, *The Life and Teachings of Sai Baba of Shirdi*, 221, 230–31, 355. Kasturi was also identified with Bhagoji Shinde,

a leper who was a devotee of Shirdi Sai Baba and who is shown in a popular photograph—probably dating around 1912—holding the ceremonial umbrella (*chattrā*) over the saint's head. The reason for such identification is that Kasturi suffered from an eczema on his feet, which had brought to a discoloration of the skin that resembled leprosy, and would often hold the ceremonial umbrella over Sathya Sai Baba's head during processions; see Kasturi, *Loving God*, 309. For a photo of Kasturi carrying the *chattrā* over the guru's head, see ibid., 144–45.

96. See ibid., 354, 378–79.

97. He once helped a monk of the Ramakrishna Mission, Jagadananda Maharaj, to secure an interview with the guru; see http://www.saibabaofindia.com/sais_kasturi_heart2heart.htm, 14.

98. Ibid., 14–15. For another instance of the hagiographer being punished for trying to recommend someone, see Kasturi, *Loving God*, 351–53. Other devotees of Sathya Sai Baba's entourage were similarly reprimanded by the guru; see Kamaraju, *Memories and Memoirs*, 140–41.

99. Shah, *Sixteen Spiritual Summers*, 55.

100. Levin, *Good Chances*, 152. See also Baskin, *Divine Memories of Sathya Sai Baba*, 111, 124–25.

101. See Levin, *Heart to Heart*, 45–46, 54; Shivaram, *Sathya Sai Baba: God in Action*, 159–60. In 1957, while in Rishikesh, the guru commanded Kasturi to give up the bad habit of snuffing—to which he had been addicted for over three decades—and he promptly obeyed; see Kasturi, *Loving God*, 198–200. To set an example, when on his sixtieth birthday in November 1985 he asked his devotees to put a "ceiling on desires," the guru gave up his habit of chewing *paan*, a digestive combining betel leaf with areca nut of which he was fond and which he used to call "his red lipstick" since it causes profuse red colored salivation; see Roumanoff, *Candide au pays des Gourous*, 144. He gave the *paan* box to Kasturi, saying: "It is of no use for Me now, because I have sealed the desire on paan!"; http://www.saibabaofindia.com/he_is_my_swami_4.htm, 9.

102. Kasturi, *Loving God*, 387. See also ibid., 379.

103. Baskin, *Divine Memories of Sathya Sai Baba*, 236.

104. Haraldsson, *Modern Miracles*, 185.

105. Kasturi, *Loving God*, 387.

106. Kamaraju, *Memories and Memoirs*, 118. See also ibid., 126, 130–31.

107. Kasturi, *Gurudev*, 15.

108. Schulman, *Baba*, 119. On the guru's punishments, see Steel, *The Sathya Sai Baba Compendium*, 208.

109. Kasturi, *Loving God*, 105.

110. Shivaram, *Sathya Sai Baba: God in Action*, 47–48. In general, devotees were afraid of the guru because they felt he knew everything; Roumanoff, *Candide au pays des Gourous*, 132.

111. This saying was a favorite of Shirdi Sai Baba, from whom Sathya Sai Baba adopted it; see *Shirdi Diary of the Hon'ble Mr. G. S. Khaparde* (Bombay: Shri Sai Baba Sansthan, n.d.), 6; Narasimhaswami, *Sri Sai Baba's Charters and Sayings*, 5, 132–33. During the procession for the inauguration of the Prasanthi Nilayam Mandir in November 1950, Sathya Sai Baba "materialized" silver coins with images of Shirdi Sai Baba and himself inscribed on them with the phrase "Why fear when I am here?" written in English as well as in several Indian languages; see Padmanaban, *Love Is My Form*, 545.

112. See Kasturi, *Loving God*, 354–55.

113. See Shivaram, *Sathya Sai Baba: God in Action*, 8–9.

114. See Kasturi, *Loving God*, 346–51.

115. Ibid., 351.

116. Padmamma, *Twameva Matha*, 105.

117. Kasturi, *Loving God*, 378.

118. Kasturi's daughter Padma recalls that once the god-man "materialized" a stone monkey for her father. It happened during a discussion about the evolution of man, when the guru spoke of one species of monkeys that used to live on trees but had no tail. In order to prove his point he "created" a stone monkey of brown/beige color of about three inches in size, with no tail: "It had beautiful twinkling eyes and it was holding a fruit in its hand"; http://www.saibabaofindia.com/he_is_my_swami_4.htm, 10.

119. Kasturi, *Loving God*, 381.

120. Ibid., 379.

121. See for instance Levin, *Good Chances*, 53, 77.

122. http://www.saibabaofindia.com/sais_kasturi_heart2heart.htm, 18.

123. Kasturi, *Loving God*, 325–26. For a compilation of Kasturi's talks to foreign devotees at Prasanthi Nilayam, see Shivaram, *Sathya Sai Baba: God in Action*.

124. http://www.saibabaofindia.com/sais_kasturi_heart2heart.htm, 15. He emphatically concludes: "People may come and go, there may be many speakers and writers, any number in the past, numerous in the present and many more in the future, but none can equal Kasturi in the art of oration and narration. His poetic style, nectarine language, convincing candor, and his soft and tender, appealing and devoted voice. . . . Professor Kasturi is a legend, a personality too extraordinary to imitate or emulate" (ibid., 28).

125. Ibid., 16.

126. The hagiographer felt it was his duty to translate the *Sai Bhagavatham* in the language of Kerala, his mother tongue; see Kasturi, *Loving God*, 314.

127. The English version was prompted by the request of Western devotees to Kasturi's son Murthy to please sing the poem in a language they could understand; see ibid., 317. Kasturi notes that "whenever a group of such [over-

seas] visitors leaves for home, Bhagavan has graciously acceded to our request for giving the participants copies of the poem after a recital with illustrative explanations"; ibid., 326.

128. See ibid., 313.

129. See ibid., 315.

130. Kasturi, *The Annunciation Song* (Prasanthi Nilayam: Sri Sathya Sai Books and Publications, n. d.), 19.

131. A style of recital of Hindu epic stories. In the early 1940s, Kasturi's son learned to sing the *Mahābhārata* in the traditional *gamaka* style, a knowledge he acquired from Kasturi's friend and colleague Krishnagiri Krishnarao, a noted *gamaki*. Here is how the hagiographer himself describes the *gamaka* style: "[T]he art . . . of reading epic poetry in *ragas* [notes on which melodies are improvised] which can illumine the emotion or élan, the pathos or passion, the calm or conflict which the poet has encased in each stanza"; Kasturi, *Loving God*, 314. See also Padmamma, *Twameva Matha*, 101–102. Kasturi never sang the poem himself since he had no ear for music.

132. See Kasturi, *Loving God*, 317–26; Id., *The Annunciation Song*. In his autobiography he writes that "the poem in English . . . emerged after prayers to Bhagavan [Sathya Sai Baba] for guidance"; Kasturi, *Loving God*, 317–18. For a rare video of the hagiographer reading and explaining his "Annunciation Song" to Western devotees in December 1983, see www.youtube.com/watch?v=sndi-adTPH1c (www.youtube.com/watch?v=O-_aFlHf-7M with English subtitles). Herein, he starts his lecture from lines 45–47: "The Full Moon Hall where all the gods / That ever man adored / Do congregate to witness him!" Evidently, he had been reading and commenting the preceding lines in previous lectures.

133. See Levin, *Good Chances*, 49–50; https://www.youtube.com/watch?v=ah-MI9pzjPj8 (minute 52).

134. For a sample of letters written by Kasturi to an Australian American devotee, see Ch. Penn, *My Beloved*.

135. For an early poem that he dedicated to his guru back in October 1958, see http://www.vahini.org/Discourses/d3-kasturispoem.html#poem. Herein, the Swami is extolled as he who fuses creeds and imposes no doctrine. The last poem that Kasturi wrote is titled "The Road to Prasanthi"; see N. Kasturi, *Prasanthi: Pathway to Peace. As Learnt at the Lotus Feet of Bhagavan* (Prasanthi Nilayam: Sri Sathya Sai Books and Publications, 1985), iii–v.

136. In his 1976 Foreword to *Sadhana: The Inward Path*, he writes: "This work is one in a series that are being brought out in an effort to assemble together important facets of the Message from Bhagavan's Discourses and present them for deeper study, contemplation and practice"; Sathya Sai Baba, *Sadhana: The Inward Path. Quotations from the Divine Discourses of Bhagavan Sri Sathya Sai Baba* (Bangalore: Sri Sathya Sai Education and Publication Foundation, rev. ed. 1978), i.

137. See for instance the following: N. Kasturi, "The Interview He Grants," in *Garland of Golden Rose* (Prasanthi Nilayam: Sri Sathya Sai Trust, 1975), 50–53; N. Kasturi, "In the Altar of Your Heart," in Ruhela and Robinson, *Sai Baba and His Message*, 246–50; N. Kasturi, "Singular and Plural," in *Golden Age 1980*, 133–37; N. Kasturi, "Baba—As Speaker," in *Sai Chandana: Book of Homage*, 282–86; N. Kasturi, "What Is Truth," at http://media.radiosai.org/journals/Vol_03/05MAY01/truth.htm (originally published in *Sanathana Sarathi* in 1987). See also http://www.theprasanthireporter.org/category/from-kasturis-pen.

138. http://www.saibabaofindia.com/sais_kasturi_heart2heart.htm, 15.

139. Kasturi, *Gurudev*, 12. See also Padmamma, *Twameva Matha*, 104.

140. When Daniel Roumanoff posed this question to the guru in February 1960, the latter answered "*saṃkalpa*," meaning pure, divine will. The idea is that whatever he wills, it instantly happens; Roumanoff, *Candide au pays des Gourous*, 140.

141. Kasturi, *Loving God*, 311.

142. He first came to the guru in 1944, and in the same year he established a Bhajan Mandali in Bangalore, that is, a group singing devotional hymns; see Padmanaban, *Love Is My Form*, 201, 213, 315, 319, 323. At the inauguration of Prasanthi Nilayam in 1950, he along with the guru performed the milk *abhiṣeka* and *pūjā* to the *mūrti* of Shirdi Sai Baba; ibid., 553. He was to be the Mandir's first priest. Sathya Sai Baba assigned him the task of waving the flame during the closing *āratī* ceremony; see Kasturi, *Loving God*, 166. On Seshagiri Rao see also Rao, *Sathya Sai Baba: God as Man*, 83, 207, 232, 265.

143. Seshagiri Rao recited the guru's 108 names on the occasion of the Mahāśivarātri festival of 1949; see Vijayakumari, *Anyathā Saranam Nasthi*, 149.

144. Lit. 'the auspicious one," a name of Śiva.

145. Kasturi, *Loving God*, 330. *Oṃ Śrī Śaṅkarāya Namaḥ* is the thirtieth name in the list. For the hagiographer's commentary on it, see Kasturi, *Garland of 108 Precious Gems*, 35–36.

146. The 1966 date can be inferred from what Kasturi writes on pages 27–28: "3 years ago, when He most dramatically threw off the paralysis of a devotee which He had taken over, He announced that He was 'Siva-Sakthi' come in human form." Sathya Sai Baba announced that he was Śiva-Śakti on July 6, 1963.

147. The Sri Sathya Sai Books and Publications Trust reprinted it between April 2003 and October 2008. In February 2012, its first edition appeared published by the Sri Sathya Sai Sadhana Trust, Publications Division.

148. This little girl, Sudha Raghunathan, was the daughter of a couple who had come to Puttaparthi for the celebration of the guru's birthday. She was to become one of the country's leading Carnatic vocalists and the recipient of the prestigious Padma Shri Award by the Government of India. For her account of how Sathya Sai Baba saved her by appearing as Joḍi Ādipalli Somāppa, see S.

Raghunathan, "The Story of 'Jodi Adi Palli Somappa,'" in *Divine Grace: Sathya Sai Baba*, 54–55.

149. See Kasturi, *Garland of 108 Precious Gems*, 26–27.

150. Kasturi, *Siva Sakthi Swarupa*, 65.

151. Ibid. Actually, this is Kasturi's paraphrase of the guru's exact words; see Sathya Sai Baba, *Sathya Sai Speaks, Vol. 3,* 125.

152. Kasturi, *Siva Sakthi Swarupa*, 65.

153. For a recent edition, see Kasturi, *The Light of Love.*

154. Volume 8 of *Sathya Sai Speaks* records only three of the guru's discourses: the Nairobi discourse ("The Message I Bring," delivered on July 4) and two Kampala discourses ("The Way of the Wise" and "Light the Lamps of Love," delivered on July 7 and 8 respectively); see *Sathya Sai Speaks, Vol. 8*, 153–78. If in Kasturi's book the title of the first discourse is the same, the second and third are titled differently, as "The I of All I's" and "The Only Raft," respectively. Kasturi's rendering of the guru's second discourse and the *Sathya Sai Speaks* text differ to some extent.

155. Mario Mazzoleni, a Roman Catholic priest who in the 1990s was excommunicated from the Church for being a Sathya Sai Baba devotee, effectively articulates this position: "Sai Baba does not compete against religions. . . . He is a person on His own who transcends religion itself, and He is not interested in having initiates or followers. He does not add or remove a single iota from scriptures but rather explains them, showing how they have been distorted or forgotten"; Don M. Mazzoleni, *A Catholic Priest Meets Sai Baba* (Faber, VA: Leela Press, 1994), 83.

156. A prominent African devotee of the guru from the mid-1970s was Victor Kanu (d. 2011), former high commissioner of Sierra Leone in Great Britain, Norway, and Sweden; see V. Kanu, "My Spiritual Journey to Sathya Sai Baba," in *Golden Age 1980*, 163–69. He authored *Sai Baba, God Incarnate* (London: Sawbridge, 1981).

157. See *Sathya Sai Speaks, Vol. 8*, 301–10. Herein, Sathya Sai Baba's discourse is titled "Give the Giver the Gift."

158. Kasturi's account can also be found in Sandweiss, *Sai Baba: The Holy Man . . . and the Psychiatrist.*

159. See D. Gries and Ph. Gosselin, "The Sources of a Historic Discourse (July 2009, Updated in July 2010)," at http://www.saicast.org/1968/kasturi681123.pdf.

160. Based on Kasturi's narrative is a popular film produced by Richard Bock in 1968–69, titled *The Message I Bring.*

161. In order to explain the title of his autobiography, on November 17, 1986, Kasturi wrote these dedicatory words: "Loving God means loving every image of His, every manifestation of His 'imagination,' that is to say, all that lives. This is the lesson I am learning."

162. V. K. Narasimhan, who at Kasturi's death succeeded him as editor of *Sanathana Sarathi*, wrote a solemn tribute to him in the newsletter's issue of September 1987.

163. Kasturi, *Loving God*, iii.

164. Kasturi appropriately translates the *Bhagavadgītā* verse thus: "A certain person sees This as an astonishing marvel. Likewise, another person speaks about This as an astonishing marvel. Another hears of It as astonishing marvel. But, in spite of hearing thus-wise, none really understands This!" Here is his commentary: "I have *seen* Baba; I have been spoken to by Him and I have myself *spoken* to Him; I have *heard* from many. Nevertheless, He remains an astonishing marvel, eluding appraisal and overleaping human judgment!"; ibid., 106–107; see also ibid., 388.

165. Ibid., 382–83.

166. See Bhatnagar, *Sai Speaks About His Childhood*, 100–101.

167. See Kasturi, *Garland of 108 Precious Gems*, 34.

168. Kasturi, *Easwaramma*, vi. For a collection of the guru's sayings on his mother, see Bhatnagar, *Sai Speaks About His Childhood*, 100–14.

169. Apparently, her other four children had died in their infancy; see Kasturi, *Easwaramma*, 188.

170. A Brahmin scholar well versed in the *Purāṇa*s, who first put the question if his birth was to be understood as *praveśa*, a divine "entrance" into his mother's womb, or *prasava*, a natural conception.

171. Kasturi, *Easwaramma*, 20.

172. See ibid., 84. On Kasturi's parallelism of Easwaramma with the Virgin Mary, see ibid., 6.

173. Schulman, *Baba*, 116–17.

174. Kasturi, *Easwaramma*, v. The tombs of Easwaramma and her husband Pedda Veṅkama Rāju are placed side by side: this is known as the Samādhi Shrine and is located at the end of Samadhi Road in Puttaparthi, near the Ganesh Gate of Prasanthi Nilayam.

175. Ibid.

176. Edgerton, *The Bhagavad Gītā*, 26.

177. On this episode, see Dabholkar, *Shri Sai Satcharita: The Life and Teachings of Shirdi Sai Baba*, 643–58, 813–33; B. V. Narasimhaswami, *Devotees' Experiences of Sri Sai Baba, Parts I, II & III* (Mylapore, Chennai: All India Sai Samaj, 2006 [Madras, 1940]), 261–66; Narasimhaswami, *Life of Sai Baba,* vol. 2, 88–91; Narasimhaswami, *Sri Sai Baba's Charters and Sayings*, 63–69. For an analysis of Shirdi Sai Baba's exegesis, see A. Rigopoulos, "Silenzio, gesto, parola: i linguaggi dell'Assoluto del Sai Baba di Shirdi," in *I linguaggi dell'Assoluto*, ed. M. Raveri and L. V. Tarca (Milano-Udine: Mimesis, 2017), 268–83. See also Id., *The Life and Teachings of Sai Baba of Shirdi*, 128–32; Warren, *Unravelling the Enigma*, 356–59; Shepherd, *Sai Baba of Shirdi: A Biographical Investigation*, 162–67.

178. In an effort to highlight the sameness of the two Sai Babas, Kasturi remembers how in the early days his master's *bhajans* celebrated the god Viṭṭhal of Pandharpur, the most popular Maharashtrian deity. On Viṭṭhal and the Pandhari *bhajan* group set up by young Sathya, see Kasturi, *Loving God*, 88–90, 334.

179. Kasturi, *Prasanthi*, 118.

180. Kasturi, *Loving God*, 326.

Chapter 5

1. As Anil Kumar Kamaraju recalls: "[H]e had the knack of putting across his views to the listeners at large in a very subtle and humorous way which everyone could understand. The young and old would get immersed and enjoy in his humorous and witty way of talks"; Kamaraju, *Memories and Memoirs*, 61.

2. Rao, *Sathya Sai Baba: God as Man*, 87. Kasturi, however, didn't like walking with a stick. When at home, he used his grandchildren as walking stick by keeping his hands on their shoulders. Once, while holding on to his junior grandson he sneezed loudly. In his characteristic humorous vein, he told his grandson: "I was scared that you would fly in the air, so strong was my sneeze. That's why I had to hold on to you. Otherwise, who knows what would have happened to you!"; Chandra Mohan and Subba Rao, *Kastūri śatakam*, 160.

3. For an introduction to Kabīr's life and works, see M. Burger, "Kabīr," in *Brill's Encyclopedia of Hinduism*, ed. K. A. Jacobsen, H. Basu, A. Malinar, and V. Narayanan (Brill Online, 2012). On the Kabīrpanthīs, see Ead., "Kabīrpanthīs," in ibid.

4. The twenty-fifth and last ruling *mahārāja* of the Kingdom of Mysore from 1940 to 1950, Sri Jaya Chamarajendra Wadiyar Bahadur (1919–1974) was a noted philosopher, musicologist, political thinker, and philanthropist. He was the founder-president of the *Vishwa Hindu Parishad* (VHP) in 1964. For an account of his first visit to North Karnataka, see Nanjunda Swamy, *Where the Angels Roamed*, 189–92. On the Wadiyar/Wodeyar dynasty, see V. Sampath, *Splendours of Royal Mysore: The Untold Story of the Wodeyars* (New Delhi: Rupa, 2008).

5. Padmamma, *Twameva Matha*, 104.

6. Lit. "Sai as Ram." The principal expression of greeting among ashramites and Sathya Sai Baba's followers. The name *Ram* is interpreted as the divine principle dwelling in each heart as pure delight. It is both a *mantra* and an epithet bestowed upon the guru by devotees and constantly repeated along with the visualization of his form. Sathya Sai Baba taught: "Do not shout hello when meeting someone; sanctify the meeting with the remembrance of God; say Ram, Om, Hari Om, or Sai Ram"; Gries and Gries, *An Index of Sathya Sai Speaks, Volumes I–XI*, 168. Moreover, he noted:

> The name of Rama is very important. It is the most powerful name of God. Shaivites say Om Namah Shivaya, Vaishnavites say Om

> Namah Narayana. If you take out the Ra in Om Namah Narayana, you have Om Namah Nayana, which means death. If you take out the Ma in Om Namah Shivaya, you have Om Na Shivaya. This is also lifeless. So the life of the two mantras is the syllables Ra and Ma—this is Rama. (Levin, *Good Chances*, 83)

7. Dattātreya and his incarnations are commonly referred to as *avadhūtas* given their ascetic excellence. For an introduction to Hindu renunciation and the *avadhūta* typology, see P. Olivelle, trans., *Saṃnyāsa Upaniṣads: Hindu Scriptures on Asceticism and Renunciation* (New York: Oxford University Press, 1992), 19–112. On *avadhūtas* and the *Avadhūtagītā*, see A. Rigopoulos, *Dattātreya: The Immortal Guru, Yogin, and Avatāra. A Study of the Transformative and Inclusive Character of a Multi-Faceted Hindu Deity* (Albany: State University of New York Press, 1998), 51 n. 48, 57–87, 195–221. For a presentation of radical types of ascetics, see W. Donkin, *The Wayfarers: An Account of the Work of Meher Baba with the God-Intoxicated, and also with Advanced Souls, Sadhus, and the Poor* (San Francisco: Sufism Reoriented, 1969).

8. Literally, *avadhūta* means "shaking off/removing [worldly ties]." Kasturi appears to have had in mind *Avadhūtagītā* 8.8, where the syllable *dhū* is indicative of "him whose limbs are grey with dust" (*dhūlidhūsaragātrāṇi*). The guru of Puttaparthi defined *avadhūtas* thus: "They are not worried in the least. They have no relation with others. They pay no heed to past present or future. They move about on thorn and stone, silent, smiling to themselves, ever joyous, ever alert, seeking no comfort and no shelter, seeking no place to sleep or to take food, for *ananda* [bliss] is their *ahara* [food]"; see H. S. Youngs, *Translations by Baba* (Tustin, CA: Sathya Sai Book Center of America, 1975), 25.

9. During the conversation, Kasturi always referred to his guru as Swami, that is, "lord," "master" (Skt. *svāmin*).

10. A wonderful resort in the Nilgiri Hills, 2,270 meters high, in the State of Tamil Nadu. The guru used to spend part of the spring and summer here.

11. On the notion of *trimūrti* (lit. "having three forms"), its origin and development, see A. Rigopoulos, "Trimūrti," in *Brill's Encyclopedia of Hinduism*, ed. K. A. Jacobsen, H. Basu, A. Malinar, and V. Narayanan, vol. VI, 81–90. Among the earliest evidence of *trimūrti* worship in India are the cave temples patronized by the Pallava ruler Mahendra (circa 580–630).

12. Kasturi means that Dattātreya is the "chosen deity" (*iṣṭadevatā*) of many Hindus.

13. Among the more than four hundred works traditionally ascribed to Śaṅkara, there are a few hymns in Dattātreya's praise such as the *Dattātreyagurustavarāja*, the *Dattamahimākhyastotra*, and the *Dattabhujaṅgastotra*. On Śaṅkara's hymns, see R. E. Gussner, "A Stylometric Study of the Authorship of Seventeen Sanskrit Hymns Attributed to Śaṅkara," in *Journal of the American Oriental Society* 96, no.

2 (1976): 259–67. The famous *Bhaja Govindam* hymn is popular among Sathya Sai Baba's devotees; see Savkur, *Reflections on Adi Shankara's Bhaja Govindam*. On Dattātreya's link with Śaṅkara and the Daśanāmī order, see Rigopoulos, *Dattātreya*, 95–97. See also M. Clark, *The Daśanāmī-Saṃnyāsīs: The Integration of Ascetic Lineages into an Order* (Leiden: Brill, 2006), 58, 67, 90–91, 155 n. 32, 168 n. 74.

14. This and the following attributes of Dattātreya are taken from the *Purāṇas*. During our conversation, Kasturi held a book in his hands, possibly a *nāmastotra* anthology, and he sometimes read from it, though it was clear that he knew all these Dattātreya features by heart. I have not been able to identify any one hymn containing all the epithets he cites.

15. The sources report cases of Shirdi Sai Baba identifying himself with anonymous beggars as well as with animals, especially dogs; see Rigopoulos, *The Life and Teachings of Sai Baba of Shirdi*, 139, 179.

16. The college in Davangere, in central Karnataka.

17. Kasturi tells this story in his autobiography *Loving God*, 137–38. He insisted on the oneness of Shirdi Sai Baba and Sathya Sai Baba till the end of his life. When on November 28, 1986, he gifted a copy of the *Śrī Sāī Saccarita* to the Malaysian devotee J. Jagadeesan, he wrote the following dedication: "With prayers to Bhagawan for making you realize the identity of the two Sais"; Jagadeesan, *Sai Baba: The Journey Within*, 3.

18. See Dabholkar, *Shri Sai Satcharita: The Life and Teachings of Shirdi Sai Baba*, 177–78; Narasimhaswami, *Sri Sai Baba's Charters and Sayings*, 145.

19. See *Avadhūtagītā* 7.9–10.

20. The *cāvaḍī,* a rural assembly hall.

21. Shirdi Sai Baba's evening procession from the mosque to the *cāvaḍī* began on December 10, 1909. Usually, Bapusaheb Jog or Bhagoji Shinde, a leper, held the ceremonial umbrella over his head; see Rigopoulos, *The Life and Teachings of Sai Baba of Shirdi*, 142–44.

22. On the deity granting both *bhukti* and *mukti*, see Rigopoulos, *Dattātreya*, 76, 113, 128 n. 17, 140, 166 n. 87, 247 n. 81.

23. Progeny, especially male, is one of the most common graces that people seek from holy men. On Shirdi Sai Baba granting offspring to childless couples, see Rigopoulos, *The Life and Teachings of Sai Baba of Shirdi*, 68–69, 100, 110–12, 178, 190. On the saint's interest in the worldly affairs of his devotees and the help he gave them, see ibid., 337 ff.

24. Kasturi refers to Shirdi Sai Baba's explanation of *Bhagavadgītā* 4.34 to his close devotee Nanasaheb Chandorkar; see Dabholkar, *Shri Sai Satcharita: The Life and Teachings of Shirdi Sai Baba*, 813–33 (ch. 50).

25. On Shirdi Sai Baba's habit of telling parables and allegorical stories, see Rigopoulos, *The Life and Teachings of Sai Baba of Shirdi*, 136–37, 155, 181, 206, 353–66; Id., *Silenzio, gesto, parola: i linguaggi dell'Assoluto del Sai Baba di Shirdi*, 255–67.

26. Kasturi, *Sathyam Sivam Sundaram, Part IV*, 118.

27. In his lifetime Shirdi Sai Baba was also revered as a *sarvajña*, an omniscient person. The ninth and seventy-sixth of Sathya Sai Baba's 108 names extol him as "he who knows everything," *Oṃ Śrī Sarvajñāya Namaḥ*, and as "he whose form is knowledge," *Oṃ Śrī Jñānasvarūpāya Namaḥ*; for Kasturi's commentary, see *Garland of 108 Precious Gems*, 18, 81. Here is how the hagiographer declares his faith in the guru's omniscience:

> Baba stopped short of the fifth form in high school, when He was fourteen years of age. He did not read books or learn from any teacher. He is Wisdom incarnate. He is poet, pundit, linguist, educationist, artist, mystic—the best in each field. In His discourses He quotes freely from the Bible, the Koran, the poems of the Sufis, the dialogues of Socrates, the sayings of Johnson, the dicta of Herbert Spencer, Kant and Karl Marx, and from the myths and legends of ancient cultures. (Kasturi, *Sathyam Sivam Sundaram, Part IV*, 118)

On Sathya Sai Baba as *a sarvajña,* see also Kasturi, *Sathyam Sivam Sundaram, Part I (1926–1960)*, 234. Several scientists and intellectuals, such as S. Bhagavantham and V. K. Gokak, fell at the guru's feet convinced of his divine omniscience. Arthur Osborne, who later became a follower of Ramana Maharshi and settled in Tiruvannamalai, remarked: "Now . . . after meeting Sri Sathya Sai Baba, I know how wrong I have been in my estimation of such a scholarly personality, who is a mine of learning and philosophy of the most abstruse kind"; Balu, *The Glory of Puttaparthi*, 3.

28. The idea is that he is *Brahman*, the impersonal Absolute, which manifests itself in the three forms of the *trimūrti*.

29. Just when Kasturi was saying these words, the evening *bhajan* session started inside the Mandir with the chanting of the *Oṃ*. The first song, as per tradition in god Gaṇeśa's praise, was *Lambodara Gaṇanātha Gajānana* ("Pot-bellied, lord of the *gaṇa*s, elephant-faced"). Up until the end of our conversation, we could hear the melodious singing of *bhajan*s in the background.

30. On the characteristics of and reasons for his mission as an *avatāra*, see Gries and Gries, *An Index of Sathya Sai Speaks, Volumes I–XI*, 10–12. See also Steel, *The Sathya Sai Baba Compendium*, 36–38, 171–72. On the purpose of the *avatāra,* see Kasturi's three talks in Shivaram, *Sathya Sai Baba: God in Action*, 121–28, 155–66, 174–84.

31. When the hagiographer says "morality," he has in mind the notion of *dharma* and the *avatāra* theory of *Bhagavadgītā* 4.7–8.

32. Besides his exegesis of *Bhagavadgītā* 4.34, the sources report that through his teachings Shirdi Sai Baba inspired his devotee Das Ganu to write

commentaries on the *Īśa Upaniṣad* and the *Amṛtānubhava* of Jñāndev (d. 1296); see Dabholkar, *Shri Sai Satcharita: The Life and Teachings of Shirdi Sai Baba*, 324–33 (ch. 20, vv. 12-105); Rigopoulos, *The Life and Teachings of Sai Baba of Shirdi*, 132–34. For an overview of the texts he recommended his Hindu followers to read, see *ibid.*, 261–70.

33. The tenth name of Sathya Sai Baba's 108 names extols him as "he who is dear to all," *Oṃ Śrī Sarvajanapriyāya Namaḥ*. Likewise, the sixty-seventh and sixty-eighth names extol him as "the dear one" and "he who is dear to his devotees," *Oṃ Śrī Priyāya Namaḥ* and *Oṃ Śrī Bhaktapriyāya Namaḥ* respectively. For the hagiographer's commentary on these names, see Kasturi, *Garland of 108 Precious Gems*, 19, 67–68. On Sathya Sai Baba's "democracy," see Kasturi, *Sathyam Sivam Sundaram, Part II*, 167.

34. See Narasimhaswami, *Sri Sai Baba's Charters and Sayings*, 62.

35. Ibid., 207. See also Narasimhaswami, *Life of Sai Baba, vol. 4*, 103; Rigopoulos, *The Life and Teachings of Sai Baba of Shirdi*, 17–18; Kher, *Sai Baba: His Divine Glimpses*, 39.

36. See Kasturi, *Sathyam Sivam Sundaram, Part I (1926–1960)*, ii.

37. Less than two years before my conversation with Kasturi, the guru announced the birth of Prema Sai Baba's father: "On Nov. 28, '83 Sathya Sai Baba at Bangalore was in an unusually happy mood. On enquiry from the devotees around, he was reported as having made a significant revelation. Prema Sai's would-be father was just born on that day and Swami was happy on that account"; Rao, *Sathya Sai Baba: God as Man*, 115.

38. Unfortunately, at the time I did not have the opportunity to visit the Veṅkāvadhūta temple.

39. Kasturi pronounced the name as Veṅkūsa rather than Veṅkuśā, stretching the u vowel and placing the accent on it, with no palatalization of the s. He stretched and accented the u vowel possibly in an effort to highlight its similarity with Veṅkāvadhūta.

40. Not in the sense that he wasn't anymore devoted to him. Kasturi means that when Veṅkāvadhūta left the area and started roaming again, Kondama Rāju did not follow him in his wanderings.

41. See Kasturi, *Easwaramma*, 11–13.

42. See ibid., 52, 72–73.

43. *Jowar* is sorghum. Veṅkamma, the guru's sister, was very close to him; see Padmanaban, *Love Is My Form*, 88.

44. On the *rānī* of Chincholi and her connection to Shirdi Sai Baba and Sathya Sai Baba, see Kasturi, *Sathyam Sivam Sundaram, Part I (1926–1960)*, 183–84; Padmanaban, *Love Is My Form*, 457–73.

45. Lit. "big dot." The guru nicknamed her Peḍḍaboṭṭu because of the impressive *kuṃkum* dot she used to wear on her forehead. Also known as Shirdi Mā, her real name was Gali Sharada Devi (1888–1986). She met Sathya Sai Baba

for the first time in Uravakonda in 1940 and settled permanently in Prasanthi Nilayam in 1958. For an outline of her life, detailing her link to Shirdi Sai Baba, see Rao, *Sathya Sai Baba: God as Man*, 91–100. On Shirdi Mā, see also Padmanaban, *Love Is My Form*, 155–56. Back in 1917, during her last visit to Shirdi, the saint would have told her that he would be reborn in Andhra Pradesh and that she would stay with him forever.

46. In November 1985, Shirdi Mā, aged ninety-seven, was ill and confined to her bed. Though the hagiographer was so kind as to propose to accompany me to her house, I didn't have the chance to see her. She passed away the following year, on Christmas Day of 1986. The title of her Telugu book is *Sweeya Charithra* and it was issued in Prasanthi Nilayam in 1984. In 2003, it was translated into English by Sathya Sai Shree Lakshmi and titled *Autobiography*. Kasturi reports that Shirdi Mā often pressed Easwaramma to tell her about his son's miracles when he was a child; see Kasturi, *Easwaramma*, 25–27.

47. See Kasturi, *Sathyam Sivam Sundaram, Part I (1926–1960)*, 178–81.

48. See Kondappa, *Sai's Story*.

49. See Kher, *Sai Baba: His Divine Glimpses*, 1–14; Swami Sai Sharan Anand, *Shri Sai Baba*, 10–11. On Shirdi Sai Baba's purported Brahmin-ness, see Narasimhaswami, *Life of Sai Baba*, vol. 1, Appendix IV, x; ibid., vol. 3, 118; ibid., vol. 4, 104. For an overview of the Pathri issue, see Shepherd, *Sai Baba of Shirdi: A Biographical Investigation*, 74–77.

50. See ibid., 126–27.

51. See "Revelations about the Sai Avatar," *Sanathana Sarathi*, October 1990.

52. On his figure, see McLain, *The Afterlife of Sai Baba*, 91–132; Shepherd, *Sai Baba of Shirdi: A Biographical Investigation*, 68–74, 328–37.

53. Veṅkuśā was interpreted by Das Ganu as a diminutive of Veṅkaṭeśvara/Veṅkaṭeśa—"the lord (*īśvara/īśa*) of the Veṅkaṭa hill," a form of Viṣṇu also known as Bālājī ("the child [Kṛṣṇa]")—the popular god of Tirupati.

54. Narasimhaswami, *Sri Sai Baba's Charters and Sayings*, 61. See also ibid., 60–62, 256; Rigopoulos, *The Life and Teachings of Sai Baba of Shirdi*, 8. On his first arrival in Shirdi, presumably in 1872, see Satpathy, *New Findings on Shirdi Sai Baba*, 21–36.

55. See Warren, *Unravelling the Enigma*, 40.

56. See the article "Sri Venka Avadhoota," published by A. V. Narasimha Murthy on June 17, 2010, at http://www.ourkarnataka.com/Articles/starofmysore/venka009.htm; Sathya Sai Shree Lakshmi, *Venka Avadhoota* (Puttaparthi: Satya Sai Vedanadalayam Books and Publications, 2005). On this whole issue, see Warren, *Unravelling the Enigma*, 41, 370–74.

57. See Swami Sai Sharan Anand, *Shri Sai Baba*, 33. On the controversy relative to Shirdi Sai Baba's guru, see Kher, *Sai Baba: His Divine Glimpses*, 36–54.

58. On Sathya Sai Baba's grandfather, see Bhatnagar, *Sai Speaks About His Childhood*, 119–28.

59. See Sathya Sai Shree Lakshmi, *Venka Avadhoota.*

60. He writes: "In fact, Venkateshwara adored by millions for centuries is Bhagavan Baba Himself"; Kasturi, *Loving God*, 6.

61. On Veṅkāvadhūta's tomb and the saint's powerful presence, see Padmanaban, *Love Is My Form*, 25 n. 11.

62. See ibid., 12, 25 n. 11.

63. See http://www.ourkarnataka.com/Articles/starofmysore/venka009.htm; http://appmithistories.blogspot.it/2013/02/sri-venka-avadhoota.html.

64. See Rigopoulos, *The Construction of a Cultic Center Through Narrative*, 137–39.

65. See Narasimhaswami, *Life of Sai Baba*, vol. 1, 14, 168; Z. Taraporevala, *A Humble Tribute of Praise to Shri Sainath. Marathi Text of* Shri Sainath Stavanamanjari *by Das Ganu.* English Translation & International Phonetics (Bombay: Sai Dhun Enterprises, 1987), 60.

66. See K. Frøystad, "The Mediated Guru: Simplicity, Instantaneity, and Change in Middle-Class Religious Seeking," in Copeman and Ikegame, *The Guru in South Asia*, 190.

67. See *Shirdi Diary of the Hon'ble Mr. G. S. Khaparde*, 7; Narasimhaswami, *Sri Sai Baba's Charters and Sayings*, 207. See also Narasimhaswami, *Life of Sai Baba*, vol. 1, 56; ibid., vol. 3, 155; ibid., vol. 4, 103.

68. Ibid., vol. 1, 72. See also ibid., vol. 1, 19, 174; ibid., vol. 3, 155.

69. See McLain, *The Afterlife of Sai Baba*, 75–76, 80. Having gone on a field research trip to Selu in 1901, Das Ganu claimed that Veṅkuśā was the pseudonym under which one Gopalrao Deshmukh was known when he was the provincial governor of the Jintur province. On his tentative reconstruction and its critics, see Rigopoulos, *The Life and Teachings of Sai Baba of Shirdi*, 9–14.

70. See McLain, *The Afterlife of Sai Baba*, 54–90. See also Narasimhaswami, *Life of Sai Baba*, vol. 2, 122–54; Shepherd, *Sai Baba of Shirdi: A Biographical Investigation*, 221–26.

71. See Narasimhaswami, *Devotees' Experiences of Sri Sai Baba, Parts I, II & III*, 128–30; Shepherd, *Sai Baba of Shirdi: A Biographical Investigation*, 189–91.

72. See Kher, *Sai Baba: His Divine Glimpses*, xiii, 2–3.

73. A. Osborne, *The Incredible Sai Baba* (New Delhi: Orient Longmans, 1970 [1957]), 20. On Kabīr's explicit statement of being neither a Hindu nor a Muslim, see P. Caracchi, "Who Was a Hindu for Kabīr? Was Kabīr a Hindu?" in *Feeding the Self, Feeling the Way*, ed. A. Monti, M. Goglio, and E. Adami (Torino: L'Harmattan Italia, 2005), 19–60.

74. Narasimhaswami, *Sri Sai Baba's Charters and Sayings*, 62.

75. See ibid., 54. See also Narasimhaswami, *Life of Sai Baba*, vol. 3, 101–102, 156; McLain, *The Afterlife of Sai Baba*, 79.

76. Kher, *Sai Baba: His Divine Glimpses*, xiii. See also Shepherd, *Sai Baba of Shirdi: A Biographical Investigation*, 192–97, who follows along these lines.

776. See M. Hedayetullah, *Kabir: The Apostle of Hindu-Muslim Unity: Interaction of Hindu-Muslim Ideas in the Formation of the Bhakti Movement with Special Reference to Kabir, the Bhakta* (New Delhi: Motilal Banarsidass, 1977). See also H. Coward, "Tolerance and Responses to Religious Pluralism," in *Brill's Encyclopedia of Hinduism*, ed. K. A. Jacobsen, H. Basu, A. Malinar, and V. Narayanan (Brill Online, 2012).

78. See D. N. Lorenzen, *Who Invented Hinduism? Essays on Religion in History* (New Delhi: Yoda Press, 2006), 102–19; Id., *Kabir Legends and Ananta-Das's "Kabir-Parachai"* (Albany: State University of New York Press, 1991), 3–22.

79. See Rigopoulos, *The Life and Teachings of Sai Baba of Shirdi*, 15–18, 197, 297–305, 329–32, 349, 363–64, 371–72; Narasimhaswami, *Life of Sai Baba*, vol. 3, 155; K. S. Srivastava, *Sufism and Sai Baba* (New Delhi: APH Publishing Corporation, 2015), 243–55. For an appreciation of Kabīr's poetry, see W. M. Callewaert, *The Millennium Kabīr Vāṇī: A Collection of Pad-s*, in collaboration with S. Sharma and D. Taillieu (Delhi: Manohar, 2000). On Kabīr's language, see C. P. Zoller, "Kabir and Ritualized Language," *Acta Orientalia* 65 (2004): 33–68; S. McGregor, "Kabīr's Language: Notes on Data from Selected Texts," in *Images of Kabīr*, ed. M. Horstmann (New Delhi: Manohar, 2002), 73–84.

80. See N. V. Gunaji, *Shri Sai Satcharita* (Shirdi: Shirdi Sansthan, 1982), 3, 19–20; C. R. Ajgaonkar, "Saibaba and Kabir," *Shri Sai Leela* 62, no. 4 (July 1983): 21–22.

81. For an English translation, see J. E. Abbott and N. R. Godbole, trans., *Stories of Indian Saints: Translation of Mahipati's Marathi* Bhaktavijaya, intro. G. V. Tagare (Delhi: Motilal Banarsidass, 1982 [Poona, 1933]), 2 vols. in 1, 78–122, 178–86, 387–400.

82. Dabholkar, *Shri Sai Satcharita: The Life and Teachings of Shirdi Sai Baba*, 88.

83. For an overview, see Sathya Sai Baba, *Sai Vani*, 195–99; Gries and Gries, *An Index of Sathya Sai Speaks, Volumes I–XI*, 266.

84. See *The Divinity Within*, 28. On the ideas on Kabīr and his link to Shirdi Sai Baba in Sathya Sai Baba's circles, see Rao, *Sathya Sai Baba: God as Man*, 113–14.

85. On these issues, see Rigopoulos, *The Life and Teachings of Sai Baba of Shirdi*, 367–73; Shepherd, *Sai Baba of Shirdi: A Biographical Investigation*, 322–27.

86. Narasimhaswami, *Life of Sai Baba*, vol. 4, 109.

87. See A. Craxi, ed., *Atti del simposio internazionale "Unity Is Divinity Purity Is Enlightenment," Roma 30–31 ottobre 1983* (Pontevecchio Magenta: Organizzazione Sathya Sai Baba Italia, 1984). V. K. Gokak attended the conference as the guru's representative.

88. For a collection of the guru's sayings on the Shirdi saint and Kasturi's comments, see Bhatnagar, *Sai Speaks About His Childhood*, 266–88.

89. Kasturi, *Sathyam Sivam Sundaram, Part I (1926–1960)*, 193. On the identity of the two Babas in Kasturi's magnum opus, see especially ibid., 177–218. See also Kasturi, *Garland of 108 Precious Gems*, 88.

90. See Murphet, *Sai Baba: Man of Miracles*, 58–67; Rao, *Sathya Sai Baba: God as Man*, 119–31; Padmanaban, *Love Is My Form*, 455–91; A. D. Bharvani and V. Malhotra, *Shirdi Sai and Sathya Sai Are One and the Same* (Bombay: Sai Sahitya Samithi, 1983); G. R. Sholapurkar, *Foot-prints at Shirdi and Puttaparthi*. Foreword by V. K. Gokak (Delhi: Bharatiya Vidya Prakashan, 1989); R. T. Kakade and A. Veerabhadra Rao, *Shirdi to Puttaparthi* (Hyderabad: Ira Publications, 1990).

91. See Rigopoulos, *The Life and Teachings of Sai Baba of Shirdi*, 246.

92. Narasimhaswami, *Life of Sai Baba*, vol. 4, 64. See also ibid., vol. 2, 347–48.

93. See ibid., vol. 4, 175–84.

94. See ibid., vol. 2, 347.

95. Ibid.

96. Padmanaban, *Love Is My Form*, 156. B. V. Narasimhaswami wrote about his visit to Puttaparthi in *Sai Sudha*, the official magazine of the Shirdi Sai Samaj based in Madras.

97. Rigopoulos, *The Life and Teachings of Sai Baba of Shirdi*, 249.

98. See http://home.hetnet.nl/~ex_baba/engels/shortnews/Mumbai%20 Mirror.htm.

99. See S. P. Ruhela, *The Truth in Controversies About Sri Shirdi Sai Baba* (Delhi: Indian Publishers' Distributors, 2000), 66–92, 107–13.

100. Kasturi, *Sathyam Sivam Sundaram, Part I (1926–1960)*, 61–62. On this episode, see also Balu, *Living Divinity*, 33.

101. Kasturi, *Sathyam Sivam Sundaram, Part I (1926–1960)*, 69–70. On this episode, see also Rao, *Sathya Sai Baba: God as Man*, 116.

102. See Padmanaban, *Love Is My Form*, 170–71.

103. See Kasturi, *Sathyam Sivam Sundaram, Part I (1926–1960)*, 56, 163, 165; Kasturi, *Loving God*, 185; Schulman, *Baba*, 108; Hislop, *Conversations with Bhagavan Sri Sathya Sai Baba*, 22; Balu, *Living Divinity*, 33.

104. For more details, see Murphet, *Sai Baba: Invitation to Glory*, 80–85.

105. On Dattātreya's iconography, see Rigopoulos, *Dattātreya*, 223–48.

106. Kasturi, *Loving God*, 312.

107. Kasturi, *Easwaramma*, 5.

108. M. Patel and N. Patel, *Bhajanamavali (For Overseas Devotees)* (Bombay: St. Francis I.T.I., n.d.), 84. See also *Bhajanavali* (Prasanthi Nilayam: Sri Sathya Sai Books and Publications, 1983), 13. A popular *bhajan* glorifying Dattātreya that is nowadays sung in Prasanthi Nilayam is *Dattātreya Sadguru Deva*; see https://

www.youtube.com/watch?v=UnRYvBd9ac4.

109. See A. P. Narasappa, R. Narasappa, and R. Seethalakshmi, trans., *Sahasradalakamala (1008 Names of Bhagavan Sri Sathya Sai Baba).* With English Translation (Bangalore: Brindavan Printers, 1985), 38.

110. Kasturi, *Garland of 108 Precious Gems*, 48. Moreover, in commenting on Sathya Sai Baba's forty-ninth name *Oṃ Śrī Sarvādhārāya Namaḥ*, Kasturi points out: "Salutations to all Gods direct themselves to the one, to Kesava; for Kesava as Baba says, means 'He, whose one single hair represents the three: Brahma, Vishnu, and Siva' "; ibid., 51.

111. Kasturi, *Sathyam Sivam Sundaram, Part I (1926–1960)*, 249–50.

112. He writes: "He quotes from the Upanishads and reveals new significances in the utterances of the sages, to the astonishment of the savants who have too long been content with arid dialectics they have treasured"; Kasturi, *Sathyam Sivam Sundaram, Part IV*, 118.

113. Kasturi, *Gurudev*, 21–22.

114. See Kasturi, *Loving God*, 326–27.

115. Shivaram, *Sathya Sai Baba: God in Action*, 163.

116. Ibid., 128.

117. Ibid., 183.

118. See Rigopoulos, *Dattātreya*, 70; Dalādanamuni, *Dattalaharī. L'onda di Datta*, ed. A. Rigopoulos (Venezia: Cafoscarina, 1999), 34–35, 65, 71, 79, 85, 89, 105, 113.

119. Kasturi, *Garland of 108 Precious Gems*, 33–34.

120. Ch. Vaudeville, *A Weaver Named Kabir: Selected Verses, with a Detailed Biographical and Historical Introduction* (Delhi: Oxford University Press, 1993), 77.

121. See D. N. Lorenzen and U. Thukral, "Los Dialogos Religiosos entre Kabir y Gorakh," *Estudios de Asia y Africa* 126, XL, no. 1 (2005): 161–77; V. Bouillier, *Itinérance et vie monastique. Les ascètes Nāth Yogīs en Inde contemporaine* (Paris: Éditions de la Maison des sciences de l'homme, 2008), 14.

122. N. H. Kulkarnee, "Medieval Maharashtra and Muslim Saint-Poets," in *Medieval Bhakti Movements in India: Śrī Caitanya Quincentenary Commemoration Volume*, ed. N. N. Bhattacharyya (New Delhi: Munshiram Manoharlal, 1989), 217–18. On Shaikh Mohammad's synthetic mysticism having its roots in Kabīr's teachings, see S. G. Tulpule, *Classical Marāṭhī Literature: From the Beginning to A.D. 1818* (Wiesbaden: Otto Harrassowitz, 1979), 377–78. For an overview on the Muslim saint-poets of Maharashtra, see R. C. Dhere, *Musalmān Marāṭhī Santa-Kavī* (Pune: Jnanraj Prakashan, 1967).

123. See Rigopoulos, *Dattātreya*, 137.

124. See C. S. J. White, "The Sai Baba Movement: Approaches to the Study of Indian Saints," *Journal of Asian Studies* 31, no. 4 (1972): 863–78. With one of his students, Charles S. J. White also made a film of Sathya Sai Baba's activities; see Murphet, *Sai Baba: Invitation to Glory*, 83.

125. Ibid., 84.

126. Kasturi, *Loving God*, 123–24.

127. Hislop, *Conversations with Bhagavan Sri Sathya Sai Baba*, 103.

128. Gries and Gries, *An Index of Sathya Sai Speaks, Volumes I–XI*, 125. On the significance and multiple functions of the sacred objects "materialized" by the guru or linked with him, see Tulasi Srinivas, "Articles of Faith: Material Piety, Devotional Aesthetics and the Construction of a Moral Economy in the Transnational Sathya Sai Movement," *Visual Anthropology* 25, no. 4 (2012): 270–302.

129. Levin, *Heart to Heart*, 155.

130. Schulman, *Baba*, 173.

131. On Shirdi Sai Baba as an *avatāra* of Dattātreya, see chapter 6.

132. See C. B. Satpathy, *Shirdi Sai Baba and Other Perfect Masters* (New Delhi: Sterling, 2001); Narasimhaswami, *Life of Sai Baba*, vol. 1, 239.

133. See Rigopoulos, *The Life and Teachings of Sai Baba of Shirdi*, 135–36; Swami Sai Sharan Anand, *Shri Sai Baba*, 72–74.

134. On Akkaḷkoṭ Mahārāj and Shirdi Sai Baba, see Kher, *Sai Baba: His Divine Glimpses*, 103–14; Shepherd, *Sai Baba of Shirdi: A Biographical Investigation*, 93–97.

135. On Akkaḷkoṭ Mahārāj, see N. S. Karandikar, *Biography of Sri Swami Samarth Akkalkot Maharaj* (Bombay: Akkalkot Swami Math, 1978); V. R. Prabhu, ed., *Shree Swami Samarth Akkalkot Maharaj (As The Eternal Sage)* (Mumbai: Jaico, 1997). See also H. S. Joshi, *Origin and Development of Dattātreya Worship in India* (Baroda: The Maharaja Sayajirao University of Baroda Press, 1965), 136–42.

136. On Māṇikprabhu, see N. D. Sonde, *Shri Manik Prabhu: His Life and Mission* (Maniknagar: Shri Manik Prabhu Samsthan, 1995); Joshi, *Origin and Development of Dattātreya Worship in India*, 130–35.

137. See Kher, *Sai Baba: His Divine Glimpses*, xii.

138. See Rigopoulos, *The Life and Teachings of Sai Baba of Shirdi*, 138; Id., *Dattātreya*, 251.

139. On Gajānan Mahārāj, see K. R. Kulkarni, *The Saint of Shegaon: A Book of Poems on the Life of Shri Gajanan Maharaj* (Nagpur, 1969); Dasaganu, *Gajanan vijay*. An English Adaptation by N. B. Patil (Shegaon: Shree Gajanan Maharaj Sansthan, 1980).

140. Levin, *Good Chances*, 83.

141. See http://www.lordmeher.org/rev/index.jsp?pageBase=page.jsp&nextPage=4926.

142. Karanjia, *God Lives in India*, 31.

143. A. Y. Cohen, *The Mastery of Consciousness. An Introduction and Guide to Practical Mysticism and Methods of Spiritual Development as Given by Meher Baba* (London: Eel Pie, 1977), 146.

144. Ibid., 145–46. For a brief sketch of Meher Baba, see Rigopoulos, *The Life and Teachings of Sai Baba of Shirdi*, 208–10. For an in-depth study on his life and teachings, see K. R. D. Shepherd, *Meher Baba, an Iranian Liberal* (Cambridge: Anthropographia Publications, 1988). On Meher Baba's life and works, see also Donkin, *The Wayfarers*; N. Anzar, *The Beloved: The Life and Work of Meher Baba* (North Myrtle Beach, SC: Sheriar Press, 1974); T. Hopkinson and D. Hopkinson, *Much Silence: Meher Baba: His Life and Work* (New York: Dodd, Mead, 1974). On Meher Baba's teachings in his own words, see Meher Baba, *God Speaks*; Meher Baba, *Discourses* (San Francisco: Sufism Reoriented, 1967); C. B. Purdom, *God to Man and Man to God: The Discourses of Meher Baba* (North Myrtle Beach, SC: Sheriar Press, 1975).

145. See Kasturi, *Loving God*, 308–309.

146. For its full content, see Karanjia, *God Lives in India*. See also Sandweiss, *Spirit and the Mind*, 235–58 (ch. 28).

147. Kasturi, *Sathyam Sivam Sundaram, Part IV*, 172–73; Kasturi, *Prasanthi*, 52–53.

148. It should be noted that Ramakrishna taught exactly the same; see Shrî Râmakrishna, *Alla ricerca di Dio*, 261–62.

149. See Narasimhaswami, *Sri Sai Baba's Charters and Sayings*, 43. An exception has been recorded: "[B]aba did not give mantra Upadesa except in exceptional cases. Baba gave it to Mrs. G. S. K[haparde] thus: 'Go on saying Rajah Ram, Rajah Ram' "; Narasimhaswami, *Life of Sai Baba*, vol. 2, 312.

150. See Rigopoulos, *The Life and Teachings of Sai Baba of Shirdi*, 305.

151. Narasimhaswami, *Life of Sai Baba,* vol. 3, 119. See also ibid., vol. 4, 55–56. On these issues, see Rigopoulos, *Sāī Bābā of Śirdī and Yoga Powers*, 404–409.

152. Kher, *Sai Baba: His Divine Glimpses*, 75.

153. See Satpathy, *New Findings on Shirdi Sai Baba*, 58–59.

154. See Rigopoulos, *The Life and Teachings of Sai Baba of Shirdi*, 144–49, 184–85.

155. Kasturi, *Sathyam Sivam Sundaram, Part I (1926–1960)*, 194.

156. *Ibid.*, 243–44.

157. Padmamma, *Twameva Matha*, 38. See also ibid., 70.

158. Kasturi, *Sathyam Sivam Sundaram, Part I (1926–1960)*, 193. See also Bhatnagar, *Sai Speaks About His Childhood*, 98–99.

159. See his 1985 Preface to Shri Sathya Sai Baba, *Sandeha Nivarini: Dissolving Doubts* (Prasanthi Nilayam: Sri Sathya Sai Sadhana Trust, 2014).

Chapter 6

1. For a comprehensive survey on Dattātreya, see Rigopoulos, *Dattātreya*; P. N. Jośī, *Śrīdattātreyajñānkoś* (Bombay: Surekha Prakashan, 1974); Joshi,

Origin and Development of Dattātreya Worship in India; R. C. Dhere, *Datta Sampradāyācā Itihāsa* (Pune: Nilakanth Prakashan, 1964). See also M. Yeolekar, *Gurucaritra Pārāyaṇ: Social Praxis of Religious Reading* (PhD diss., Arizona State University, 2014).

2. Through her *śakti* Anasūyā had restored the sun's light previously obscured by the pious Śāṇḍilī. The latter wished to save her husband Kauśika, who had been cursed by sage Maṇḍavya that he would die at dawn.

3. Herein he figures as the sixth *avatāra* in a list comprising twenty-two descents.

4. These chapters tell the stories of Dattātreya and king Arjuna Kārtavīrya and of the deity teaching Yoga to Alarka.

5. See *Mahābhārata* 3.115.8 ff.; 12.49.30 ff.; 13.137.5–6; 13.138.12; 13.142.21. References are to the edition of the Bhandarkar Oriental Research Institute (BORI), which assigns the first two cases to an appendix as interpolations.

6. Corresponding to *Uddhavagītā* 2–4. For a parallel, see *Skanda Purāṇa* VI, *Nāgarakhaṇḍa* 184.11–185.91.

7. In 1943, while he was still studying in Uravakonda, young Sathya Sai Baba is reported to have explained to a local pundit, Narayana Sastri, the most complex passages of the *Haṃsagītā*, also known as *Uddhavagītā*, which is part of the *Bhāgavata Purāṇa* and contains the story of the *bālāvadhūta* and his twenty-four teachers; see Padmanaban, *Love Is My Form*, 100–101.

8. See Rigopoulos, *Dattātreya*, 95.

9. See ibid., 96–97. See also Clark, *The Daśanāmī-Saṃnyāsīs*, 58, 175 n. 102.

10. With extensions in Gujarat (Girnār and Garuḍesvar), Karnataka (Akkaḷkoṭ, Bāḷekundrī), and Andhra Pradesh (Pīṭhāpūr, Humaṇābād): all these places were sanctified by the presence of Dattātreya gurus. On the Dattātreya movement in Andhra Pradesh, see M. V. Krishnayya, "Dattatreya Worship in the Popular Hinduism of Coastal Andhra," in *Incompatible Visions: South Asian Religions in History and Culture. Essays in Honor of David M. Knipe*, ed. J. Blumenthal (Madison, WI: Center for South Asia, 2005), 171–83.

11. For an introduction to this seminal religious movement and its nonconformity to mainstream Hinduism, see A. Feldhaus, "Mahānubhāvs," in *Brill's Encyclopedia of Hinduism*, ed. K. A. Jacobsen, H. Basu, A. Malinar, and V. Narayanan (Brill Online, 2012); A. Rigopoulos, *The Mahānubhāvs* (London/New York/Delhi: Anthem Press, 2011).

12. Holding burning items in one's hands is often an extraordinary feat performed as a result of divine possession (*angāt yeṇe*).

13. See Krishnayya, *Dattatreya Worship in the Popular Hinduism of Coastal Andhra*, 174–75. For an introduction to the Nāth *yogins* and the

Nāthsampradāya, see J. Mallinson, "Nāth Sampradāya," in *Brill's Encyclopedia of Hinduism*, ed. K. A. Jacobsen, H. Basu, A. Malinar, and V. Narayanan (Brill Online, 2012).

14. Ibid., 4.

15. See Dhere, *Datta Sampradāyācā Itihāsa*, 58–66.

16. The first Sanskrit text to include a list of the nine Nāths is the *Gorakṣasiddhāntasaṃgraha* (ca. eighteenth century) which in turn cites the *Tantramahārṇava*, a work of doubtful antiquity, which includes Dattātreya in its list of Nāths.

17. On the *Gurucaritra* as guru, see J. G. Morse, "The Literary Guru: The Dual Emphasis on *bhakti* and *vidhi* in Western Indian Guru-Devotion," in Copeman and Ikegame, *The Guru in South Asia: New Interdisciplinary Perspectives*, 222–40.

18. Śrīpād Śrīvallabh was born in Pīṭhāpūr, in the East Godāvarī district of Andhra Pradesh, whereas Nṛsiṃha Sarasvatī was born in Kārañja, in the Akolā district of Maharashtra.

19. To one Dattātreya is ascribed the authorship of a *Dharmaśāstra*, a brāhmaṇical law book. Yādava Prakāśa (twelfth century), the teacher of the *viśiṣṭādvaitin* theologian Rāmānuja (d. 1137), in his *Yatidharmasamuccaya* quotes him as an authority on the rules of brāhmaṇical asceticism; see *Rules and Regulations of Brahmanical Asceticism:* Yatidharmasamuccaya *of Yādava Prakāśa*, ed. and trans. P. Olivelle (Albany: State University of New York Press, 1995), 30, 46, 48, 86, 124, 136, 148, 173.

20. Yeolekar, *Gurucaritra Pārāyaṇ*, 85–86.

21. In her study on the reading of the *Gurucaritra* in contemporary Maharashtra, Mugdha Yeolekar writes:

> In the process of reading the *Gurucaritra*, the readers re-traditionalize themselves so that they develop a renewed sense of what it means to be a Hindu in their urban contexts. And yet, they modernize by becoming highly intentional about how they interpret the narratives from the text and by taking a critical approach toward their tradition. (Ibid., 100)

22. See ibid., 83; Rigopoulos, *Dattātreya*, 122–25. On Dattātreya and possession, see A. Rigopoulos, "Forms of Possession in the Marāṭhī Cultural Area: The Cases of Khaṇḍobā and Dattātreya," in *Shamanic Cosmos: From India to the North Pole Star*, ed. R. Mastromattei and A. Rigopoulos (Delhi: D. K. Printworld, 1999), 207–20. On possession in South Asia, see F. M. Smith, *The Self Possessed: Deity and Spirit Possession in South Asian Literature and Civilization* (New York: Columbia University Press, 2006).

23. Apparently, he first came to be identified with the gods of the *trimūrti* standing side by side, an icon usually referred to as Hari-Hara-Pitāmaha. Already from around the eleventh-twelfth centuries, Dattātreya is sculptured as Viṣṇu seated in a yogic posture, his triple nature being indicated by the emblems of Brahmā, Viṣṇu, and Śiva.

24. Having many heads, arms, etc. is a theological statement of divine fullness and completeness; see D. M. Srinivasan, *Many Heads, Arms, and Eyes: Origin, Meaning, and Form of Multiplicity in Indian Art* (Leiden: Brill, 1997).

25. The triadic Dattātreya is also equated with the three *guṇa*s of *sattva, rajas,* and *tamas,* the constituents of the material world; see Sri Siddharameshwar Maharaj, *Embrasser l'immortalité:* Amrut laya. *Méthode pratique pour se libérer du faux* (Paris: Les Deux Océans, 2007), 260.

26. See H. N. Kunden, *Ekmukhī Śrīdatta* (Puṇe: Ulhas Cintamani Latkar, 1997).

27. For an introduction, see J. Keune, "Eknāth," in *Brill's Encyclopedia of Hinduism,* ed. K. A. Jacobsen, H. Basu, A. Malinar, and V. Narayanan (Brill Online, 2012).

28. He was instrumental in spreading Dattātreya's popularity beyond Maharashtra's borders, especially in Andhra Pradesh.

29. See D. Deák, "Maharashtra Saints and the Sufi Tradition: Eknath, Chand Bodhle, and the Datta Sampradaya," *Journal of Deccan Studies* 3, no. 2 (2005): 22–47.

30. See Rigopoulos, *Dattātreya,* 135–54. On Dāsopant's life, see the anonymous and incomplete *Dāsopantcaritra* dating to the seventeenth or eighteenth century; J. E. Abbott, trans., *Dasopant Digambar: Translation of the* Dasopant Charitra. Poet-Saints of Maharashtra Series, no. 4 (Puṇe: Scottish Mission Industries, 1927). In his *Padārṇava,* Dāsopant devotes about one thousand verses to Dattātreya.

31. For the *Bhaktavijaya* accounts, see Abbott and Godbole, *Stories of Indian Saints,* 160–64. For the stories in the *Bhaktalīlāmṛt* (lit. "Essence of the Saints' Divine Play," completed in 1774), see J. E. Abbott, trans., *The Life of Eknāth.* Śrī Eknāth Charita. *Translated from the* Bhaktalīlāmṛta (Puṇe 1927; Reprint, Delhi: Motilal Banarsidass, 1981), 18–22, 194–99. On Mahīpati, see J. Keune, "Gathering the Bhaktas in Marāṭhī," *Journal of Vaishnava Studies* 15, no. 2 (2007): 169–88.

32. Ch. Pain and E. Zelliot, "The God Dattatreya and the Datta Temples of Pune," in *The Experience of Hinduism: Essays on Religion in Maharashtra,* ed. E. Zelliot and M. Berntsen, trans. Charles Pain (Albany: State University of New York Press, 1988), 96.

33. On Vāsudevānanda Sarasvatī's orthodox views and his prohibiting women from reading the *Gurucaritra,* see Morse, *The Literary Guru,* 231, 234.

34. Narasimhaswami, *Devotees' Experiences of Sri Sai Baba*, 133. On this episode, see also Dabholkar, *Shri Sai Satcharita: The Life and Teachings of Shirdi Sai Baba*, 844–49 (ch. 51, verses 125–83); Swami Sai Sharan Anand, *Shri Sai Baba*, 208; McLain, *The Afterlife of Sai Baba*, 78.

35. See Narasimhaswami, *Life of Sai Baba*, vol. 3, 129.

36. *Avatāras* of Dattātreya are believed to manifest themselves throughout the subcontinent, especially in the South, and not exclusively in Maharashtra. A case in point between the nineteenth and twentieth centuries is that of Shrimat Pandurangashram Swami, who from 1864 until 1915 served as the head of the Shri Chitrapur Matha at Shirali, a village in the North Kanara district on India's west coast; see F. F. Conlon, "A Nineteenth-Century Indian Guru," in *Charisma and Sacred Biography*, ed. M. A. Williams, *Journal of the American Academy of Religion*, Thematic Studies 48, nos. 3–4 (1982): 145.

37. James Mallinson observes that the attribution of the *Avadhūtagītā* to Dattātreya "has led scholars, probably mistakenly, to associate the text with the Nāth Sampradāya." Yet, he adds that "whether or not this attribution is justified, its carefree attitude is mirrored by texts that certainly are the products of a Nāth milieu, such as the *Siddhasiddhāntapaddhati* and some of the verses of the *Gorakhbānī*"; Mallinson, *Nāth Sampradāya*, 17.

38. The figure of Shirdi Sai Baba is exemplary in this regard; see Rigopoulos, *The Life and Teachings of Sai Baba of Shirdi*, 337–51.

39. Significantly, the *Gurucaritra* has come to incorporate the Sanskrit *Gurugītā*; see A. Rigopoulos, "The *Guru-gītā* or 'Song of the Master' as Incorporated in the *Guru-caritra* of Sarasvatī Gaṅgādhar: Observations on Its Teachings and the *guru* Institute," in *Theory and Practice of Yoga: Essays in Honour of Gerald James Larson*, ed. K. A. Jacobsen (Leiden/Boston: Brill, 2005), 237–92. Along these lines, even one of Eknāth's hagiographies, the *Pratiṣṭhāncaritra* (circa 1700), focuses upon the saint's extreme *gurubhakti*. As Jon Keune writes: "It depicts scenes in which Eknāth gleefully cleans his *guru*'s toilet by hand, and Eknāth hides in order to consume the contents of his *guru*'s spittoon that his *guru* had ordered him to throw away—examples of Eknāth's conviction that everything associated with his *guru* is blessed"; Keune, *Eknāth*, 4.

40. Lit. "guru-king."

41. Dabholkar, *Shri Sai Satcharita: The Life and Teachings of Shirdi Sai Baba*, 521–22. See also Narasimhaswami, *Life of Sai Baba*, vol. 1, 168–70. On *gurubhakti*, see Swami Sai Sharan Anand, *Shri Sai Baba*, 31–50; Narasimhaswami, *Life of Sai Baba*, vol. 2, 107, 237–39; ibid., vol. 3, 73, 118–20, 125–26, 201; ibid., vol. 4, 11–12, 53–57, 96–97; M. B. Nimbalkar, *Shri Sai Baba's Teachings and Philosophy* (New Delhi: New Dawn, 2001), 115–25.

42. Narasimhaswami, *Life of Sai Baba*, vol. 3, 154.

43. See Rigopoulos, *The Life and Teachings of Sai Baba of Shirdi*, 299–301.

44. Narasimhaswami, *Life of Sai Baba*, vol. 4, 188.

45. V. B. Kher notes how Dattātreya became known as Shah Faqir to the Muslims; Kher, *Sai Baba: His Divine Glimpses*, 61. See also D. Deák, "Śahādat or Śahā Datta? Locating the Mysterious Fakir in the Marathi Texts," in *Muslim Cultures in the Indo-Iranian World during the Early-Modern and Modern Periods*, ed. D. Hermann and F. Speziale (Berlin: Klaus Schwarz Verlag, 2010), 501–32.

46. Dabholkar, *Shri Sai Satcharita: The Life and Teachings of Shirdi Sai Baba*, 57. See also Smriti Srinivas, *In the Presence of Sai Baba*, 46, 224; Krishnayya, *Dattatreya Worship in the Popular Hinduism of Coastal Andhra*, 176–78; *Dattatreya: Glory of the Divine in Man*. Dedicated to Lord Sainath of Shirdi. With the Blessings of Acharya Sri E. Bharadwaja, ed. R. S. Babu (Ongole: Sainath Printers, 1981).

47. See Gunaji, *Shri Sai Satcharita*, xvii. See also ibid., xx; Narasimhaswami, *Life of Sai Baba*, vol. 2, 214.

48. See *Shri Sai Leela Magazine* 17, no. 1–3 (1940); V. Chitluri, *Baba's Divine Symphony* (New Delhi: Sterling, 2014), 147. See also Dabholkar, *Shri Sai Satcharita: The Life and Teachings of Shirdi Sai Baba*, 289 (ch. 18, vv. 56–57).

49. See Joshi, *Origin and Development of Dattātreya Worship in India*, 158–59; Rigopoulos, *The Life and Teachings of Sai Baba of Shirdi*, 18–19, 113, 147, 178; Warren, *Unravelling the Enigma*, 126, 146–49. On the identification of the Shirdi *faqīr* with Dattātreya within the *Śrī Sāī Saccarita*, see Dabholkar, *Shri Sai Satcharita: The Life and Teachings of Shirdi Sai Baba*, 6, 57, 539, 866, 868, 877, 882 (ch. 1, v. 53; ch. 4, v. 29; ch. 33, between vv. 82 and 83; ch. 53, vv. 18, 31, 132, 200). On the saint's identification with the deity and the devotees' conviction that he was a Datta incarnation, see also A. R. Junnarkar, *Gūḍhramy Gurutrayī Śrī Sāī Śrī Upāsanī Śrī Godāī* (Sākurī: Śrī Upāsanī Kanyākumārī Sthān, 2017); Swami Sai Sharan Anand, *Shri Sai Baba*, 14–15, 317–18; Narasimhaswami, *Life of Sai Baba*, vol. 3, 30–31, 147; Chitluri, *Baba's Divine Symphony*, 60–62, 306–307.

50. Narasimhaswami, *Sri Sai Baba's Charters and Sayings*, 9.

51. The day on which Dattātreya's birthday is celebrated. It falls on the full moon day of the lunar month of Mārgaśīrṣa (November–December).

52. Narasimhaswami, *Sri Sai Baba's Charters and Sayings*, 153–54. See also Narasimhaswami, *Life of Sai Baba*, vol. 1, 60.

53. See for instance Chitluri, *Baba's Divine Symphony*, 38–39.

54. Narasimhaswami, *Life of Sai Baba*, vol. 2, 175.

55. See Shepherd, *Sai Baba of Shirdi: A Biographical Investigation*, 67, 180–181, 197.

56. Swami Sai Sharan Anand, *Shri Sai Baba*, 74. When he visited Shirdi in May 1913, the *faqīr* had him stay with him for nearly eleven months. See also Narasimhaswami, *Life of Sai Baba*, vol. 4, 101.

57. See ibid., 99–111. Another exemplary case is that of Banne Miyan of Aurangabad (d. 1921), a contemporary of Shirdi Sai Baba with whom the latter was linked; see N. Green, "Making a 'Muslim' Saint: Writing Customary Religion in an Indian Princely State," *Comparative Studies of South Asia, Africa and the Middle East* 25, no. 3 (2005): 617–33; Shepherd, *Sai Baba of Shirdi: A Biographical Investigation*, 88–92.

58. Narasimhaswami, *Life of Sai Baba*, vol. 4, 102–103.

59. See T. Lubin, "Science, Patriotism, and Mother Veda: Ritual Activism in Maharashtra," *International Journal of Hindu Studies* 5, no. 3 (2001): 81–105.

60. See Y. Sikand, *Sacred Spaces: Exploring Traditions of Shared Faith in India* (Delhi: Penguin, 2003), 53–68; Id., "Shared Hindu-Muslim Shrines in Karnataka: Challenges to Liminality," in *Lived Islam in South Asia: Adaptation, Accommodation, and Conflict*, ed. I. Ahmad and H. Reifeld (New Delhi: Social Science Press, 2004), 166–86. On these issues, see also K. Saptarshi, "Orthodoxy and Human Rights: The Story of a Clash," in Zelliot and Berntsen, *The Experience of Hinduism: Essays on Religion in Maharashtra*, 251–63.

61. Although the deities' names are given in parentheses, there is no doubt that Sathya Sai Baba uttered them; with reference to his mention of Datta, see also Gries and Gries, *An Index of Sathya Sai Speaks, volumes I–XI*, 35.

62. *Daṁ*, the sound *da* nasalized with the addition of the so-called *candrabindu*, is the sonic personification of Dattātreya, his all-powerful *mantra*. It is inscribed in the lotus of the *maṇipūracakra*, one of the seven psycho-energetic centers of Tantric Yoga located at the navel, which has *raṁ* as its *mantra*, the sonic personification of Agni.

63. Sathya Sai Baba, *Sathya Sai Speaks, Vol. 9*, 161 (n. 23, "Exercise in Futility").

64. Sathya Sai Baba, *Bhagavatha Vahini*, trans. N. Kasturi (Bangalore: Sri Sathya Sai Education and Publication Foundation, 1979), 71. See also ibid., 237.

65. Ibid., 72. See also ibid., 238.

66. The young *bhaktas* of Sathya Sai Baba who lost their lives, Sri N. Radhakrishnan and Sri Sai Kumar Mahajan, were ex-students in the guru's schools.

67. *Divine Message on Guru Poornima by Bhagawan Sri Sathya Sai Baba, 3rd July, 1993* (Bangalore: Sri Sathya Sai Publication Society, 1993), 4.

68. See also Kasturi, *Sathyam Sivam Sundaram, Part I (1926–1960)*, 103.

69. Ibid., 138.

70. Sathya Sai Baba, *Bhagavatha Vahini*, 188.

71. Sathya Sai Baba, *Sree Gurucharanam*, 74 (excerpt from *Sanathana Sarathi*, 1982).

72. A major annual *vaiṣṇava* festival held at the Śrīraṅgam temple in Tamil Nadu in the lunar month of Pauṣa (December–January).

73. See Sathya Sai Baba, *Sathya Sai Speaks, Vol. 1*, 193 (n. 35, "The Dangers of Doubt"). See also Gries and Gries, *An Index of Sathya Sai Speaks, volumes I–XI*, 205.

74. See Sathya Sai Baba, *Sathya Sai Speaks, Vol. 7. Discourses of Bhagavan Sri Sathya Sai Baba (Delivered During 1967)* (Prasanthi Nilayam: Sri Sathya Sai Sadhana Trust, 2012), 172 (n. 25, "Three-in-one Now"). On the three aspects of *śakti* denominated Mahasaraswati, Mahalakshmi, and Mahakali, each linked to one of the three *guṇa*s, see ibid., 192 (n. 30, "The Tiger in the Ring"). Kasturi himself extolled the guru as "the triune embodiment of Durga, Lakshmi, and Saraswathi"; Kasturi, *Loving God*, 167. See also Kasturi, *Garland of 108 Precious Gems*, 58; Kasturi, *Prasanthi*, 15.

75. Kondappa, *Sai's Story*, 14.

76. See ibid., 1–2; Rigopoulos, *Dattātreya*, 5–8.

77. Kasturi, *Sathyam Sivam Sundaram, Part I (1926–1960)*, 108–109. See also ibid., 165; Kasturi, *Garland of 108 Precious Gems*, 56–57; Balu, *Living Divinity*, 227–28.

78. See Padmanaban, *Love Is My Form*, 307; Padmamma, *Twameva Matha*, 21.

79. Kasturi, *Sathyam Sivam Sundaram, Part I (1926–1960)*, 224.

80. The Marāṭhī saint Brahma Chaitanya (1845–1913) was also known as Gondavalekar Mahārāj.

81. The pedestal on which the image of a deity is installed.

82. Kasturi, *Sathyam Sivam Sundaram, Part I (1926–1960)*, 250–51.

83. Murphet, *Sai Baba: Man of Miracles*, 184. On the holy man of Bāḷekundrī, a village in the Belgaum district of Karnataka, see I. Kher, *Avadhuta Yogi Pant Maharaj of Balekundri* (Bombay: Bharatiya Vidya Bhavan, 1994).

84. Kasturi, *Sathyam Sivam Sundaram, Part III*, 196.

85. Rao, *Sathya Sai Baba: God as Man*, 225.

86. As the guru told them: "Because I am with you in this human form, I move about among you as one of you. You therefore do not understand Me nor do you realize that I am *Dattatreya* amidst you"; Balu, *Living Divinity*, 129. To Howard Murphet's question "why he [Sathya Sai Baba] showed you Dattatreya instead of Rama or Krishna," Mr. Joga Rao answered: "Oh, Dattatreya is his true Form"; Murphet, *Sai Baba: Invitation to Glory*, 82.

87. B. N. Narasimha Murthy, *Sathyam Sivam Sundaram. Vol. 5. Life Story of Bhagawan Sri Sathya Sai Baba, 1980–85* (Prasanthi Nilayam: Sri Sathya Sai Sadhana Trust, 2014 [2005]), 105–106. Page 106-A shows a photo of this Polaroid picture, which the guru holds in his hand. Though Bill Aitken writes that "early devotees claim that often, when they had their photographs taken with Sathya Sai, the developed print would depict him in the form of Dattatreya"

(*Sri Sathya Sai Baba: A Life*, 54), as far as I know the sources report only the two above-mentioned cases.

88. Copeman and Ikegame, *The Multifarious Guru*, 16.

89. Ibid.

90. Ibid., 17.

91. Ibid., 38.

92. See Krishnayya, *Dattatreya Worship in the Popular Hinduism of Coastal Andhra*, 178. In a recent hagiography on Śrīpād Śrīvallabh produced in Andhra, Shirdi Sai Baba is taken to be an *avatāra* of Dattātreya via the utilization of Sathya Sai Baba's Bharadvāja myth and Śiva-Śakti portrayal; see S. Bhatt, Sripada Srivallabha Charitamrutam*: Biography of a Dattatreya Avatar* (Münster: Kulapati.de, 2019), 509–13.

93. C. S. J. White, "Swāmi Muktānanda and the Enlightenment Through Śakti-Pāt," *History of Religions* 13, no. 4 (May 1974): 310.

94. On Sathya Sai Baba as supreme guru and "teacher of truth" (*satya-bodhaka*), see Kasturi, *Loving God*, 243–44, 270, 325; Shivaram, *Sathya Sai Baba: God in Action*, 229–35. See also N. Kasturi, "The Teacher of Truth," in *Garland of Golden Rose* (Prasanthi Nilayam: Sri Sathya Sai Central Trust, 1975), 19–25.

95. Levin, *Good Chances*, 81. See also Kasturi, *Loving God*, 356–57.

96. See the article "National Conference of Bal Vikas Gurus," *Sanathana Sarathi* 37, no. 8 (August 1994): 208.

97. The *śiṣya* is required to make the right effort and follow the path indicated by the master. Once in May 1972, at the first Summer Course, when one British devotee asked him to "clean his mind," Sathya Sai Baba replied: "No, no, this is not my work. This is your work. I am only a sign post"; Levin, *Heart to Heart*, 34.

98. Kasturi, *Garland of 108 Precious Gems*, 83.

99. Ibid., 30.

100. See M. L. Leela, *Lokanatha Sai* (Madras: Sri Sathya Sai Mandali Trust, n.d.), 132. The closing line that is given in current *bhajan* books is the following: *Oṃkāraṃ Bābā Oṃkāraṃ Bābā Oṃkāraṃ Bābā Oṃ Namo Bābā*. M. L. Leela came from Madras (Chennai) and was the daughter of Lokanatha Mudaliar; see Padmanaban, *Love Is My Form*, 217–19, 230–31, 278, 361, 431, 473.

101. Baskin, *Divine Memories of Sathya Sai Baba*, 258.

102. See Padmanaban, *Love Is My Form*, 114.

103. See Gries and Gries, *An Index of Sathya Sai Speaks, volumes I–XI*, 78–80; Sathya Sai Baba, *Sree Gurucharanam*.

104. She had resolved to fast until the Shirdi saint would whisper a *mantra* in her ear. On this episode, see Shepherd, *Sai Baba of Shirdi: A Biographical Investigation*, 136–37.

105. The most famous verse of the *Gurugītā* hymn: "The guru is Brahmā, the guru is Viṣṇu, the guru is [Śiva] Maheśvara (lit. "the great lord")! The guru is indeed the Supreme *Brahman*: adoring salutations be paid to this venerable guru!" As noted, this Sanskrit hymn was incorporated in the Marāṭhī *Gurucaritra*: the guru who is Brahmā, Viṣṇu, and Śiva is none other than Dattātreya; see Rigopoulos, *The* Guru-gītā *or 'Song of the Master' as Incorporated in the* Guru-caritra *of Sarasvatī Gaṅgādhar.* For Sathya Sai Baba's exegesis of a *Gurugītā* verse, see Sathya Sai Baba, *Sree Gurucharanam*, 38–47.

106. Ibid., 5–6.

107. Kasturi, *Loving God*, 376. See also Padmamma, *Twameva Matha*, 109.

108. Sathya Sai Baba, *Sathya Sai Speaks, Vol. 10. Discourses of Bhagavan Sri Sathya Sai Baba (Delivered During 1970)*. Revised and Enlarged Edition (Prasanthi Nilayam: Sri Sathya Sai Sadhana Trust, 2011), 109 (n. 14 "*Guru* God," July 18, 1970).

109. Though he rarely presented himself as Kalkin, he once identified the triune Sai Baba descent with him:

> In the present *caturyuga*, the tenth *avatāra,* Kalki, has split into three aspects as the forms of Shirdi Sai, Sathya Sai and Prema Sai. This has not happened before and can only be seen in this Kaliyuga. Sai *avatāras* neither had taken place in earlier Kaliyugas nor will take place in future Kaliyugas. (K. Ramamurthy, *Sri Sathya Sai, Aanandadayi: Journey with Sai* [Prasanthi Nilayam: Sri Sathya Sai Publications, 2001], 67)

Kasturi reports that on a special occasion he gave a vision of himself as Kalkin riding on a white horse; see Kasturi, *Sathyam Sivam Sundaram, Part I (1926–1960)*, 65; Murphet, *Sai Baba: Invitation to Glory*, 192. See also "Souljourns—Part 2, Vijaya Kumari" (https://www.youtube.com/watch?v=rDLJAe5HBfA), minutes 18–21. The guru's white Maruti car was homologized by devotees with the white steed of Kalkin; see Hawkins, *Bordering Realism*, 142. On Sathya Sai Baba as Kalkin, see Ruhela, *Sri Sathya Sai as Kalki Avatar*; Spurr, *Sathya Sai Baba as Avatar*, 339–42. On Sathya Sai Baba as the "Yuga Avatara," see S. D. Kulkarni, *Shri Satya Sai, the Yugavatara: Scientific Analysis of Baba Phenomenon* (Bombay: Shri Bhagawana Vedavyasa Itihasa Samsodhana Mandira, 1990). On Kalkin, see A. Fadda, *"Il divino a cavallo tra distruzione e salvezza." Ipotesi su origini ed evoluzioni della figura del Kalkin Avatār* (MA thesis, Università degli Studi di Padova/Università Ca' Foscari Venezia, 2015).

110. From his early discourses, Sathya Sai Baba made constant reference to Śaṅkara; see Gries and Gries, *An Index of Sathya Sai Speaks, volumes I–XI*,

168–69. On the god-man's link to Śaṅkara, see also Kasturi, *Loving God*, 329–30.

111. As Kasturi once told to Mayah Balse: "He is God. He has done neither meditation nor Yoga. He has had no guru, all his superpowers have come to him almost overnight. There was no travail of the spirit or struggle as there is with a great number of Yogis"; M. Balse, *Mystics and Men of Miracles in India* (Delhi: Orient Paperbacks, 1978), 37. On Sathya Sai Baba and Yoga, see Smriti Srinivas, "Sathya Sai Baba and the Repertoire of Yoga," in *Gurus of Modern Yoga*, ed. M. Singleton and E. Goldberg (New York: Oxford University Press, 2014), 261–79. For an appreciation of the guru's teachings in his own words, see Sathya Sai Baba, *Sadhana: The Inward Path*.

112. Krishnayya, *Dattatreya Worship in the Popular Hinduism of Coastal Andhra*, 178.

113. See the hagiographer's commentary to the one hundredth of the guru's 108 names, *Oṃ Śrī Yogīśvarāya Namaḥ*; Kasturi, *Garland of 108 Precious Gems*, 102–103.

114. See Sathya Sai Baba, *Dhyana Vahini*; Id., *Sadhana: The Inward Path*. See also Devi, *Sai Baba and Sai Yoga*; Levin, *Good Chances*, 137–53; Steel, *The Sathya Sai Baba Compendium*, 125–28, 190–91, 276. On Yoga in Sathya Sai Baba's early discourses, see Gries and Gries, *An Index of Sathya Sai Speaks, volumes I–XI*, 223–24.

115. *Jyotirdhyāna* or *tejodhyāna* is one of three kinds of meditation described in the *Gheraṇḍasaṃhitā* (chap. 6, vv. 1, 15–17, 21).

116. *Ficus bengalensis*. The tree is known as *nyagrodha* in Sanskrit and as *marri ceṭṭu* or *vaṭamu* in Telugu.

117. See Rigopoulos, *A Modern* Kalpavṛkṣa, 18–22.

118. See Kasturi, *Sathyam Sivam Sundaram, Part I (1926–1960)*, 234.

119. He often insisted on this point; see Shivaram, *Sathya Sai Baba: God in Action*, 69–71.

120. Haraldsson, *Modern Miracles*, 369.

121. Ruhela, *Sai Baba: A Biographical Sketch*, 13.

122. On the guru of Puttaparthi as the wondrous "tree of plenty" conferring both *bhukti* and *mukti*, see Rigopoulos, *A Modern* Kalpavṛkṣa. See also Levin, *Good Chances*, 43.

123. Kasturi, *Loving God*, 85.

124. Babb, *Redemptive Encounters*, 201.

125. On his *bāla* aspects, see Kasturi, *Loving God*, 150–56; Padmamma, *Twameva Matha*, 40–41; Baskin, *Divine Memories of Sathya Sai Baba*, 93, 117–19; Levin, *Good Chances*, 80. On his *unmatta* aspects, see Spurr, *Sathya Sai Baba as Avatar*, 396.

126. See Levin, *Heart to Heart*, 149.

127. See Kasturi, *Sathyam Sivam Sundaram, Part III*, 35–36; Kasturi, *Loving God*, 155, 377; Shivaram, *Sathya Sai Baba: God in Action*, 7.

128. Ibid., 168.

129. Haraldsson, *Modern Miracles*, 365. For Mr. Varadu's testimony, see ibid., 159–73.

130. See https://www.youtube.com/watch?v=aatcu88uKNE; https://www.youtube.com/watch?v=hL_bB7PeEAg.

131. Haraldsson, *Modern Miracles*, 356.

132. On the religious significance and function of crying, see J. S. Hawley and K. Patton, eds., *Holy Tears: Weeping in the Religious Imagination* (Princeton, Princeton University Press, 2005).

133. Haraldsson, *Modern Miracles*, 299–300.

134. Ibid., 324.

135. Gupta, *The Gospel of Sri Ramakrishna*, 394. See also ibid., 461.

136. Sandweiss, *Spirit and the Mind*, 169. On this *abhiṣeka* (lit. "sprinkling") of *vibhūti,* see also Padmamma, *Twameva Matha*, 104; www.youtube.com/watch?v=pux1v6U6z-Y (minutes 7–8).

137. See Gries and Gries, *An Index of Sathya Sai Speaks, volumes I–XI*, 209–11. On ritual revivalism in Maharashtra and in the *Dattasampradāya*, see Lubin, *Science, Patriotism, and Mother Veda*.

138. Krishnayya, *Dattatreya Worship in the Popular Hinduism of Coastal Andhra*, 178. See also Kondappa, *Sai's Story*, 8; Padmanaban, *Love Is My Form*, 93–113.

139. Kasturi, *Loving God*, 161.

140. Narasimhaswami, *Life of Sai Baba*, vol. 3, 130. See also ibid., vol. 4, 35. On Sathya Sai Baba's dealings with an evil ghost, see Baskin, *Divine Memories of Sathya Sai Baba*, 97–102.

141. Padmanaban, *Love Is My Form*, 285. See also ibid., 166–67, 205; Peddabottu, *Autobiography*, 181.

142. See Padmanaban, *Love Is My Form*, 297.

143. A dreadful open sore, which fails to heal. It is said to develop from drinking unhygienic water.

144. See Padmanaban, *Love Is My Form*, 297–99. He is also said to have applied *vibhūti* to another coconut and to have dropped it into the village well, asking the locals to clean it.

145. See Dabholkar, *Shri Sai Satcharita: The Life and Teachings of Shirdi Sai Baba*, 11–14; Rigopoulos, *The Life and Teachings of Sai Baba of Shirdi*, 159–61.

146. See http://www.theprasanthireporter.org/2013/04/baba-and-the-animal-world ("From Kasturi's Pen; November 1958 issue of *Sanathana Sarathi*"); Pad-

manaban, *Love Is My Form*, 193, 269–71; Murphet, *Sai Baba: Invitation to Glory*, 83–84; Aitken, *Sri Sathya Sai Baba: A Life*, 54, 178; Baskin, *Divine Memories of Sathya Sai Baba*, 47, 50, 84–85, 93, 260–65; Levin, *Good Chances*, 38–39, 50; Narasimha Murthy, *Sathyam Sivam Sundaram, vol. 5*, 32–33.

147. Gries and Gries, *An Index of Sathya Sai Speaks, volumes I–XI*, 49; see also ibid., 263. On Sathya Sai Baba's mention of dogs in his analogies, see ibid., 234.

148. *Ocymum sanctum*. The sweet basil plant, sacred to Viṣṇu.

149. These were the Pomeranians Jack and Jill; see http://www.theprasanthi reporter.org/2013/04/baba-and-the-animal-world ("From Kasturi's Pen; November 1958 issue of *Sanathana Sarathi*"); Padmanaban, *Love Is My Form*, 271. Shirdi Sai Baba was also fond of dogs and identified himself with them; see Rigopoulos, *The Life and Teachings of Sai Baba of Shirdi*, 19, 41 n. 133, 86–87, 342–43.

150. On this particular tree and Dattātreya, see A. Rigopoulos, "The Sanctity of the *audumbar* in Mahārāṣṭra," in *Tīrthayātrā: Essays in Honour of Stefano Piano*, ed. P. Caracchi, A. S. Comba, A. Consolaro, and A. Pelissero (Alessandria: Edizioni dell'Orso, 2010), 349–65.

151. The first or primeval teacher.

152. On Dattātreya's connection to Nāthism see Rigopoulos, *Dattātreya*, 89–90, 99–100 ff., 197–98, 250–52. On the hypothesis of Shirdi Sai Baba's link to Nāthism, see Rigopoulos, *The Life and Teachings of Sai Baba of Shirdi*, 18, 39 n. 119; Shepherd, *Sai Baba of Shirdi: A Biographical Investigation*, 309–15. See also Rigopoulos, *Sāī Bābā of Śirḍī and Yoga Powers*.

153. For similar poses in the deity's iconography, see Rigopoulos, *Dattātreya*, 96; Jośī, *Śrīdattātreyajñānkoś*, between pages 24 and 25 (Gorakṣāsaha Śrīdatta, "Lord Datta with Gorakṣa"); http://www.kamat.com/indica/faiths/gods/13040.jpg.

154. Rigopoulos, *The Life and Teachings of Sai Baba of Shirdi*, 68.

155. See Sathya Sai Baba's photos in Kasturi, *Sathyam Sivam Sundaram, Part I (1926–1960)*, between pages 64 and 65; Padmanaban, *Love Is My Form*, 164, 192, 200, 202, 306.

156. This is evident both in the guru's self-representation and in Kasturi's portrayal; see Kasturi, *Loving God*, 162, 224, 321, 330, 335, 363.

157. For a popular print depicting Dattātreya, Shirdi Sai Baba, and Sathya Sai Baba as one and the same divine entity, see Tulasi Srinivas, *In the Presence of Sai Baba*, 73.

158. Rao, *Sathya Sai Baba: God as Man*, 115.

159. See Kasturi, *Sathyam Sivam Sundaram, Part I (1926–1960)*, 249–51. See also ibid., 293.

160. See Murthy, *The Greatest Adventure*, 5.

161. A. Fellows, "Recovering Goodness, Beauty, and Truth," in *L'Abri Papers* #AF02, http://www.labri.org/england/resources/05052008/AF02_Goodness_Beauty_3E64FE.pdf.

162. For an introduction to von Balthasar's theology, see A. Nichols, *A Key to Balthasar: Hans Urs von Balthasar on Beauty, Goodness, and Truth* (London: Darton, Longman & Todd, 2011). See also R. Gibellini, *La teologia del XX secolo*. Edizione attualizzata con una Appendice "Il passo del Duemila in teologia" (Brescia: Queriniana, 2014), 253–70, 676–78.

163. Sathya Sai Baba, *Sathya Sai Speaks, Vol. 3*, 125 (n. 16 "Protection of the Devotees," July 7, 1963).

164. He states: "He is Sathyam Sivam Sundaram, as I have named the book about Him, which I wrote in 1961. And, strangely enough, Baba in His Discourse on the 7th July dwelt on those three words!"; Kasturi, *Siva Sakthi Swarupa*, 65.

165. Kasturi, *Sathyam Sivam Sundaram, Part I (1926–1960)*. See also Kasturi, *Loving God*, 229. The guru would plainly announce: "Know me as the Teacher of Truth, as Sathyam, Sivam, Sundaram"; ibid., 231–32. As years went by, Kasturi became convinced that "all three were but facets of the Love He is: Love as thought is Truth, Sathyam; Love as action is Goodness, Sivam; Love as feeling is Beauty, Sundaram"; ibid., 232.

166. Rigopoulos, *Trimūrti*, 88.

167. Kasturi, *Garland of 108 Precious Gems*, 60.

168. Kasturi, *Loving God*, 229. Even in devotional hymns, the guru of Puttaparthi is extolled as Sathyam Sivam Sundaram; see Patel and Patel, *Bhajanamavali*, 235.

169. Rao, *Sathya Sai Baba: God as Man*, 276. See also Kasturi, *Sathyam Sivam Sundaram, Part IV*, 21; Shivaram, *Sathya Sai Baba: God in Action*, 185. Sivam, in Hyderabad, was inaugurated in 1974 on Ugadi Day; Sundaram, in Madras, was inaugurated in 1981.

170. Kasturi, *Sathyam Sivam Sundaram (Part II)*, 219. However, I was unable to trace this statement in the published collection of the guru's discourses.

171. Sathya Sai Baba, *Sathya Sai Speaks, Vol. 7*, 218–19 (n. 35, "The Tricycle"). Moreover:

> The sages discovered the truth "*Tat Twam Asi*" ("That Thou Art"). "That" is the Divine, out of which all "this" arose, of which all "this" is, into which all "this" merges. It can be known by the *Bhakti marga*—the path of dedication, of devotion and surrender of the Self. The "Thou," that is to say, the Individual can be understood by the *Karma marga*—the path of selfless activity, of the abnegation of the consequences of all activity, done in a spirit of adoration and with as much sincerity as an act of worship. Then, the process of

> identification of *Tat* and *Twam* (That and Thou) called the recognition of the *Asi* has to be consummated, through *Jnana marga*—the path of knowledge, of sharp and relentless discrimination. When *Bhakti* and *Karma* merge, it leads to *Jnana*. *Bhakti* sees everything as *Tat*; *Karma* wipes out the separateness of the *Twam*. So, the *Asi* (identification) process becomes easy. (Sathya Sai Baba, *Sathya Sai Speaks, Vol. 9*, 169; n. 24 "Assert With Every Breath," October 17, 1969)

172. Karanjia, *God Lives in India*, 18.

173. I think this remains true even though Sathya Sai Baba identified the Shirdi saint as an *avatāra* of Śiva in his reconstruction of his birth and early years; see Kondappa, *Sai's Story*; Rigopoulos, *The Life and Teachings of Sai Baba of Shirdi*, 21–27.

174. Karanjia, *God Lives in India*, 18.

175. R. Dwyer, *Filming the Gods: Religion and Indian Cinema* (London and New York: Routledge, 2006), 135.

176. Kasturi, *Sathyam Sivam Sundaram, Part I (1926–1960)*, 197.

177. Bhatnagar, *Sai Speaks About His Childhood*, 98. See also Kasturi, *Sathyam Sivam Sundaram, Part I (1926–1960)*, 193.

178. For an overview on Brahmā, see G. Bailey, "Brahmā," in *Brill's Encyclopedia of Hinduism, Vol. 1. Regions, Pilgrimage, Deities*, 499–512.

179. See Rigopoulos, *The Construction of a Cultic Center Through Narrative*, 137–39; Id., *A Modern* Kalpavṛkṣa, 5–12.

180. Kasturi, *Sathyam Sivam Sundaram, Part I (1926–1960)*, 197.

181. Karanjia, *God Lives in India*, 18.

182. Kasturi, *Loving God*, 137.

183. Kasturi, *Sathyam Sivam Sundaram, Part I (1926–1960)*, 193.

184. Kasturi, *Garland of 108 Precious Gems*, 67.

185. Bhatnagar, *Sai Speaks About His Childhood*, 98.

186. See Priddy, *Source of the Dream*, 224.

187. Karanjia, *God Lives in India*, 18.

188. Bhatnagar, *Sai Speaks About His Childhood*, 99.

189. S. Saraf, *Sai Vandana: Salutations to Lord Sai. Book of Homage* (Prasanthi Nilayam: Sri Sathya Sai Institute of Higher Learning, 1990), 142.

190. Kondappa, *Sai's Story*, 9.

191. Madhusudhan Rao Naidu, "Prema Sai: The Silent Teacher," https://saivrinda.org/?s=Prema+Sai. He claims that there will be three phases in Prema Sai Baba's life: in the first, though based in India, he will often travel; in the second, he will be based in one or more of his ashrams outside of India, though he will visit India from time to time; in the third, he will return to India and stay there.

192. See his teaching to Daniel Roumanoff back in 1960; Roumanoff, *Candide au pays des Gourous*, 139–40.

193. Karanjia, *God Lives in India*, 44. On the practice of *dāna* within the guru's movement, see A. Kent, "Divinity, Miracles, and Charity in the Sathya Sai Baba Movement of Malaysia," *Ethnos* 69, no. 1 (March 2004): 43–62.

194. Kasturi, *Garland of 108 Precious Gems*, 65.

195. On Dattātreya's giving and self-giving nature as an *avadhūta,* see D. Hudson, "Early Evidence of the *Pāñcarātra Āgama*," in *The Roots of Tantra*, ed. K. A. Harper and R. L. Brown (Albany: State University of New York Press, 2002), 154–55.

196. The favorite motto of the Italian poet Gabriele D'Annunzio (1863–1938) comes to mind: "Io ho quel che ho donato," "I have what I have given."

197. See Steel, *The Sathya Sai Baba Compendium*, 225.

198. This is the reason why death is identified with the guru. *Locus classicus* is the *Kaṭha Upaniṣad*, which presents the dialogue between Yama (Death) and the Brahmin boy Naciketas.

199. Levin, *Heart to Heart*, 144.

200. Kasturi, *Garland of 108 Precious Gems*, 79.

201. Ibid., 80.

202. On the significance of the three *da*-s of the *Bṛhadāraṇyaka Upaniṣad* in the *Śrī Sāī Saccarita*, see Dabholkar, *Shri Sai Satcharita: The Life and Teachings of Shirdi Sai Baba*, 228–29 (chap. 14, vv. 134–47). On the three *da*-s and Dattātreya's "hidden presence" in T. S. Eliot's fifth and last section of *The Waste Land—What the Thunder Said*, see Rigopoulos, *Dattātreya*, 257–59.

203. Kasturi, *Sathya Sai Baba: God in Action*, 38.

204. Sathya Sai Baba, *Sathya Sai Speaks, Vol. 5. Discourses of Bhagawan Sri Sathya Sai Baba Delivered During 1965* (Prasanthi Nilayam: Sri Sathya Sai Sadhana Trust, 2009), 102 (n. 13 "The Voice of Thunder," March 24, 1965).

205. Sathya Sai Baba, *Sathya Sai Speaks, Vol. 9*, 169 (n. 24 "Assert With Every Breath," October 17, 1969).

206. Karanjia, *God Lives in India*, 14.

207. Ibid., 18–19.

208. See Gries and Gries, *An Index of Sathya Sai Speaks, volumes I–XI*, 219.

209. Karanjia, *God Lives in India*, 42.

210. In the first *bhajan* he taught, the above-mentioned *Mānasa Bhajare Gurucaraṇam,* reference is made to the sacred Arunachala Mountain, popularly identified as Ramana Maharshi's site. It is reported that when the latter died in 1950, Sathya Sai Baba said that he "had attained his feet"; Haraldsson, *Modern Miracles*, 297 (Rev. ed., 2013).

211. See Roumanoff, *Candide au pays des Gourous*, 137.

212. See Piantelli, *Prefazione*, 11.

213. See Levin, *Good Chances*, 142–44.

214. See Shrî Râmakrishna, *Alla ricerca di Dio*, 203.

215. See Levin, *Good Chances*, 55, 105.

216. Ibid., 34.

217. See https://www.youtube.com/watch?v=WZoM_zzQHuE (minute 3:35). On Sri Ganapathi Sachchidananda Swamiji, see Krishnayya, *Dattatreya Worship in the Popular Hinduism of Coastal Andhra*, 178–80.

218. Lola Williamson argues that the movements founded by Paramahamsa Yogananda, Maharishi Mahesh Yogi, and Swami Muktananda (the Self-Realization Fellowship, the Transcendental Meditation, and the Siddha Yoga) together constitute a new religion in the United States; L. Williamson, *Transcendent in America: Hindu-Inspired Meditation Movements as New Religion* (New York/London: New York University Press, 2010).

219. According to V. K. Narasimhan, "There is one reason why Baba, despite the importunities of his non-Indian followers, has deliberately chosen not to go abroad. He has felt that unless India itself is made a real exemplar of the life of the spirit, there is no point in his going abroad to spread his message"; Narasimhan, *What Sri Sathya Sai Baba Means to Me*, 13.

220. Howard Levin records:

> On another occasion Danny showed Sai Baba the Hare Krishna magazine "Back to Godhead." Swami looked at it, thumbing through the pages. He leaned forward and spoke in a low voice, "They're doing bhajans in the streets of America, ladies and gents mixed." Then He leaned toward the gents, cupping His hand around one side of His mouth so the ladies could not hear. He said, "And they are naked!" He slapped His thigh and threw the magazine to Danny. "The streets of America are a mental institution," He said. (Levin, *Good Chances*, 140–41)

221. The hagiographer constantly emphasized Sathya Sai Baba's difference, saying that he was not like other gurus; see Kasturi, *Loving God*, 342–43. Back in the early days, Sathya Sai Baba had promised his mother that he would never abandon his native place; see Kasturi, *Easwaramma*, 63–64. He remarked that his roots were in Puttaparthi and that he would never transplant himself somewhere else; see Kasturi, *Sathyam Sivam Sundaram, Part I (1926–1960)*, 9–10; Kasturi, *Easwaramma*, 14. As he once told to Howard Levin: "Native place is best"; Levin, *Heart to Heart*, 87.

222. See Levin, *Good Chances*, 75; Id., *Heart to Heart*, 128.

223. Copeman and Ikegame, *The Multifarious Guru*, 25.

224. Though small, the numbers of his Muslim devotees both in India and abroad are not negligible. Tulasi Srinivas writes of having met several Muslim followers of the guru who came from predominantly Muslim countries; see Tulasi Srinivas, *Winged Faith*, 4, 117.

225. Apparently, even Sri Chandrasekharendra Saraswati (1894–1994), Shankaracarya of Kanchi, ordered his devotee M. S. Subbulakshmi and her husband to go to Prasanthi Nilayam where "Goddess Durga is present in the form of a man in Puttaparthi in flesh and blood"; https://www.youtube.com/watch?v=WZoM_zzQHuE (minute 0:19).

226. See Th. J. Csordas, "Introduction: Modalities of Transnational Transcendence," in *Transnational Transcendence: Essays on Religion and Globalization*, ed. Th. J. Csordas (Berkeley: University of California Press, 2009), 4.

227. Tulasi Srinivas, *Winged Faith*, 9.

228. On the flexibility and freedom of choice that characterizes most followers in their interaction with a guru, see Copeman and Ikegame, *The Multifarious Guru*, 35–36.

229. Kasturi, *Garland of 108 Precious Gems*, 95.

230. http://www.saibabaofindia.com/sais_kasturi_heart2heart.htm, 20.

231. Urban, *Avatar for Our Age*, 90.

232. On these issues and for a comparison with Trinitarian theology, see A. Rigopoulos, "Observations on Śaṅkara's Nondualism in the light of R. Panikkar's Thought," in *Fullness of Life*, ed. K. Acharya, M. Carrara Pavan, and W. Parker (Mumbai/New Delhi: Somaiya Publications, 2008), 13–41.

Chapter 7

1. In particular, Kasturi's daughter had to face marital and financial problems throughout her life. She used to seek refuge at Sathya Sai Baba's feet, and the guru helped her on numerous occasions, offering advice and material sustenance to her and her three children. She finally settled in Prasanthi Nilayam, living together with her father and her first son Ramesh, who did his Vedic schooling at the ashram; see Padmamma, *Twameva Matha*. Nowadays, Padma still lives at the ashram, in the Patashala Block of Prasanthi Nilayam.

2. See Smriti Srinivas, *The Advent of the Avatar*, 307 n. 7.

3. In his autobiography, he noted: "During the present sojourn on earth, I have circumambulated the God of the Gayathri [Sathya Sai Baba] eighty-five times. Sai may give me a few more rounds or He may not"; Kasturi, *Loving God*, 382. The hagiographer believed that Sathya Sai Baba had always protected him throughout his life, saving him from sure death when years before he was diagnosed with an advanced abdominal tuberculosis. The guru himself confirmed

that he had gifted him a bonus of more years with him; see ibid., 364. Kasturi was convinced that his Swami had saved him even at age eighty-two:

> I know that Sai has summoned Yama's [the god of death's] emissary back from my bed-side, three years ago, when I was hastened along, by a team of doctors in a hospital. Swami charges me facetiously, even now, with the crime of cheating "the hungry tongues of five" [Yama]. Who knows how often He has intervened against the executors of Karmic Judgments in order to keep me alive? He does not announce such grants of Grace. (Ibid., 382)

If not a misprint for fire, number five refers to the five elements (*mahābhūta*) in which, at the time of death, the body resolves itself. Thus, the famous saying *pañcatvaṃ gacchati*, "He goes to the fivefold state," meaning the five elements: earth, water, fire, air, and ether/space.

4. Shivaram, *Sathya Sai Baba: God in Action*, 128. Along the years, the guru taught him many lessons on the inevitability of death. Kasturi once narrated a telling episode of the early 1970s, when Sathya Sai Baba's brother-in-law, the elder sister's husband who was also his mother's brother, passed away of hydrophobia having been bitten by a mad dog. The whole village was in gloom and the hagiographer, overwhelmed by emotion, had started crying:

> Swami looked at me and said, "*yemayya Kasturi*! *kadayya, chachedi puttedi lekapote naketlayya time potundi*?" "What is this Kasturi! If there is to be no death and no birth, how can I pass my time?" Wonderful! We are born and we die as His pastime! He brings us into life and makes us play upon the stage. We are all puppets in His drama, in His story, in His plot. When He thinks He is getting tired of us, we exit! That is "*gati*." That opened my eyes. I thought this is a great moment, a great revelation. No one has said it before! In the midst of all this sorrow, He is the one unaffected director of the play. That is *Avatar*. (Ibid., 197–98)

On death and dying in Sathya Sai Baba's teachings, see Gries and Gries, *An Index of Sathya Sai Speaks, volumes I–XI*, 35–37; Schulman, *Baba*, 166–67; Steel, *The Sathya Sai Baba Compendium*, 56–57.

5. Kasturi, *Loving God*, 390.

6. It was the guru who directed him to choose geology as his subject of specialization; see Murthy, *The Greatest Adventure*, 1. His scientific contributions are numerous; see M. V. N. Murthy, *Mica Fields of India* (New Delhi, 1964); M. V. N. Murthy, ed., *Research Papers in Petrology by Officers of the Geological*

Survey of India (Delhi: Manager of Publications, 1964); M. V. N. Murthy, S. N. P. Vastava, and A. Dube, *Indian Meteorites* (Calcutta: Geological Survey of India, 1968); M. V. N. Murthy, ed., *Zircon: A Collection of Research Papers* (Delhi: Manager of Publications, 1969). On Sathya Sai Baba's guidance and protection of the hagiographer's son and his family, see Kasturi, *Loving God*, 367–68.

7. To his sister Padma he used to say: "Now, this is my turn to serve our parents. You have served them for many years and earned a good deal of *punya* (merit). Let me also earn some now"; Padmamma, *Twameva Matha*, 102.

8. He also authored the book *Who Is a Devotee of the Lord: Talks in Prasanthi Nilayam on the Ghagavad* [*sic*] *Gita (12th Chapter)* (Prasanthi Nilayam: Sri Sathya Sai Books and Publications, 2005). As a college student, Murthy had been influenced by M. K. Gandhi and in the early 1940s had taken part in the freedom struggle; see Padmamma, *Twameva Matha*, 101.

9. Ibid., 102. His last words to his wife Shyamala and all his dear ones before being operated on were: "I do not know whether I will come back alive or not. Sai Ram to you all"; ibid.

10. See Nanjunda Swamy, *Where the Angels Roamed*, 57.

11. Padmamma, *Twameva Matha*, 105. When Murthy was cremated in Bangalore, Kasturi was present and, to everyone's surprise, started repeating the solemn *asato mā* prayer: "From the unreal lead me to the real! From darkness lead me to light! From death lead me to immortality!" (*asato mā sad gamaya* | *tamaso mā jyotir gamaya* | *mṛtyor māmṛtaṃ gamaya* ||; *Bṛhadāraṇyaka Upaniṣad* 1.3.28).

12. Nanjunda Swamy, *Where the Angels Roamed*, 57.

13. https://robertpriddy.wordpress.com/tag/divya-weed.

14. Besides her book, worthy of notice are the transcripts of two interviews of Ms. Rajeshwari Patel to Padma Kasturi; see http://www.saibabaofindia.com/he_is_my_swami.htm; http://www.saibabaofindia.com/he_is_my_swami_2.htm; http://www.saibabaofindia.com/he_is_my_swami_3.htm; http://www.saibabaofindia.com/he_is_my_swami_4.htm; http://www.saibabaofindia.com/he_is_my_swami_5.htm.

15. See Levin, *Good Chances*, 87–88.

16. Kasturi, *Loving God*, 364.

17. The feeling of being tested or even forsaken by the guru is frequent in the devotional literature; see Levin, *Heart to Heart*, 93–98, 119, 132–33. At a certain point, Levin writes that he "never wanted to see Puttaparthi or Sai Baba again." Moreover:

> On the airplane I began to think that maybe it was all a big lie. Maybe Swami wasn't God. "But then why would he be doing all of this?" I asked myself. He certainly wasn't in it for the money. He doesn't go for any publicity, nor did he have ninety Rolls Royces like

> the Guru in Oregon [Bhagwan Shree Rajneesh/Osho]. He was really helping so many people. Why did I feel so beaten and defeated by him? I realized that it was my ego, struggling to survive. Sai Baba had systematically boxed my ego into a corner where it no longer had any "reality" to hang on to. (Ibid., 127)

18. Padmamma, *Twameva Matha*, 105.

19. See Kasturi, *Loving God*, 350–51.

20. On New Year's Day 1978, Kasturi asked American devotee and filmmaker Jack Lenchiner the courtesy to allow his bedridden wife to have the guru's *darśan* through a TV monitor of his; see https://www.youtube.com/watch?v=me0qX-pKFcw, minutes 6–7. See also https://vimeo.com/217396543.

21. http://www.saibabaofindia.com/sais_kasturi_heart2heart.htm, 23.

22. Ibid.

23. His daughter writes: "When my father was sixty, He asked him to cut down on his food intake. When he turned eighty, he made him eat more often asking my father to eat with Him and making sure he ate well!"; Padmamma, *Twameva Matha*, 105.

24. Ibid., 99. Thus, Rajamma's heartfelt prayer that she should die earlier than her husband was answered; on Kasturi's wife, see ibid., 97–99.

25. The spiritually inclined Ramesh married a German woman, Ananda, herself a devotee of the guru of Puttaparthi; see ibid., 30.

26. In one of his lectures to foreign devotees he remarked: "'I am already 87 years, and I will be stepping into 88th year from December' is what I feel, grudging the passing of time. Whenever I see the obituary column in a newspaper, I look at the age of the person and if the person has died at his 71st year, I am happy because I have survived up to 87th year. I look forward to approaching milestones and death"; Shivaram, *Sathya Sai Baba: God in Action*, 88–89.

27. Padmamma, *Twameva Matha*, 106.

28. http://www.saibabaofindia.com/sais_kasturi_heart2heart.htm, 23.

29. Ibid.

30. Antonio Craxi (1936–2017), the brother of Italian prime minister Bettino Craxi (1934–2000), was a prominent devotee who was instrumental in propagating Sathya Sai Baba's renown in Italy.

31. Wontner also writes that he was "honoured to have spent hours discussing LIFE in his little study, like schooldays with my house tutor or even at Oxford, a place he would have loved. He was a genius and a legend, and would have been wherever he went in this world."

32. Padmamma, *Twameva Matha*, 106. It should be noted that from the early 1980s the guru appointed the reputed journalist V. K. Narasimhan as coeditor of *Sanathana Sarathi.*

33. http://www.saibabaofindia.com/sais_kasturi_heart2heart.htm, 24.

34. Padmamma, *Twameva Matha*, 106.

35. In order to console him, they said: "Kasturi *garu*, this cab is not a good one; it is very shaky and uncomfortable. We will arrange a good car for you and inform Swami too, and then you can go"; http://www.saibabaofindia.com/sais_kasturi_heart2heart.htm, 24. In fact, the hagiographer never managed to leave Puttaparthi.

36. The letter "looked like a sorry scribble on a sheet of paper"; ibid.

37. Padmamma, *Twameva Matha*, 107.

38. Kasturi, *Loving God*, 83.

39. Ibid., 357. See also Shivaram, *Sathya Sai Baba: God in Action*, 201–202.

40. Padmamma, *Twameva Matha*, 107.

41. http://www.saibabaofindia.com/sais_kasturi_heart2heart.htm, 25. Freedom from the fear of death is the reward of pure devotion: one must concentrate all his/her thoughts exclusively on his/her "chosen deity" (*iṣṭadevatā*) or the guru; on these issues, see E. H. R. Jarow, *Tales for the Dying: The Death Narrative of the* Bhāgavata-Purāṇa (Albany: State University of New York Press, 2003).

42. Also spelled J. Jegathesan. A prominent government official, he first met Sathya Sai Baba in 1976 and was the promoter of the Sathya Sai Organization in Malaysia and of various service projects. He authored several books on the guru; see Steel, *The Sathya Sai Baba Compendium*, 98–99. For an article of his, see J. Jagadeesan, "Experiences with the Divine Presence," in *The Splendour of Sathya Sai*, 78–81.

43. Jagadeesan, *Sai Baba: The Journey Within*, 4. The hagiographer wrote this touching epitaph on the cover of Jagadeesan's manuscript, which the latter had left with him six months before; see ibid., 2. On Kasturi's last written words see also the testimony of his grandson Ramesh: http://media.radiosai.org/journals/vol_10/01DEC12/living-the-divine-presence-Prof-N-Kasturi-biographer-translator-of-sathya-sai-baba.htm.

44. Jagadeesan, *Sai Baba: The Journey Within*, 2.

45. His daughter observes that though he could not talk much he still liked playing with words and that "through his sickness he retained his sense of humour"; Padmamma, *Twameva Matha*, 107.

46. On *virahabhakti*, see F. E. Hardy, *Viraha Bhakti: The Early History of Kṛṣṇa Devotion in South India* (New York: Oxford University Press, 1983).

47. It is titled "God and you are One"; see http://www.sssbpt.info/ssspeaks/volume20/sss20-15.pdf. The guru's discourse was taped and can be listened to at http://www.radiosai.org/program/listen.php?f=DD_1987_07_11_GURU_POORNIMA.mp3. It ends with these words, which sound like an appeal to his hagiographer: "Proceed from *Dvaita* (dualism) to *Vishishtaadvaita* (partial non-dualism) and reach the stage of *Advaitic* (non-dual) consciousness. Do not

stay put in the stage where you are like a milestone. Having performed *sadhana,* studied the scriptures, met the saintly men and listened to the discourses, you should realize the fruits of spiritual experience."

48. Padmamma, *Twameva Matha*, 108. On countless occasions Kasturi had written and taught that the true nature of man is *ātman*. Once, during a talk to overseas devotees he mentioned the *Bhagavadgītā* and Kṛṣṇa's famous hymn to the *ātman* (2.19–25): "In the second chapter there is the teaching 'You are not killed. You are *Atma*.' That is the first lesson that Swami also teaches us, that we are *Atma*. That is why, when He addresses us, the first thing He says is '*divyatmaswarupulara*.' He tells us that we are all *Atma*"; Shivaram, *Sathya Sai Baba: God in Action*, 77. Moreover: "It comes like a flash. It stuns us! I am not Kasturi, I am not so and so, I am *Atma*. We have given up many bodies in the past and passed through a number of stages, like a caterpillar emerging from a cocoon as butterfly"; ibid., 232. On the crucial concept of experience, see Halbfass, *India and Europe*, 378–402. See also A. Tagliapietra, *Esperienza. Filosofia e storia di un'idea* (Milano: Raffaello Cortina, 2017).

49. In South India, *nāḍī* is the name given to palm leaf manuscripts believed to have been written by ancient sages such as Śuka. They are thought to contain the characteristics, family history, and life story of countless individuals. Many Hindus consult the astrologers who keep these *nāḍī* volumes since they believe they can trace the palm leaves that contain their biography and destiny.

50. Lit. "absorption without distinction." This technical term is used in Vedānta as synonymous of *asamprajñātasamādhi*, the "non conscious absorption" of classical Yoga. All mental fluctuations (*cittavṛtti*s) having stopped, the *yogin* abides in a state of objectless absorption in which only karmic residues are left. The distinction (*vikalpa*) of knower, act of knowing, and object known is dissolved.

51. Apparently, the guru's exact words were: "No, don't laugh. Why not? You might get it. Don't laugh at this"; http://www.saibabaofindia.com/sais_kasturi_heart2heart.htm, 25.

52. Padmamma, *Twameva Matha*, 108.

53. Already in 1960 one Dr. E. V. Sastry, member of the Indian Astro-Occult Research Association of New Delhi, claimed to have found in the *Nāḍī Grantha*s of Tamil Nadu a series of prophetical indications of Sathya Sai Baba's life and avatāric career. He reports that one of these texts, the *Brahma Nāḍī*, states that he is "like Dattatreya, an avatar conjoining the Trinity (Brahma, Vishnu, Shiva), together"; http://www.saibaba.ws/avatar/naadiinscriptions.htm. An article detailing Dr. E. V. Sastry's "findings" was published in February 1961 in *Sanathana Sarathi*, titled "Bhagavan's Sathya Sai Baba's 500-Year Old Horoscope." On modern astrologers and the appeal of *Nāḍī Grantha*s, see M. Gansten, "Modern Astrologers," in *Brill's Encyclopedia of Hinduism*, ed. K. A. Jacobsen, H. Basu, A. Malinar, and V. Narayanan (Brill Online, 2012).

54. See Balu, *Living Divinity*, 51–55. See also Ruhela, *Sri Sathya Sai as Kalki Avatar*, 68–70. Among other things, it is said that Kabīr returned to earth as Shirdi Sai Baba, confirming the belief in the identity of the medieval poet and mystic of Benares with the triune Sai Baba *avatāra*.

55. See Balu, *Living Divinity*, 55.

56. Kasturi, *Sathyam Sivam Sundaram, Part III*, 221–22.

57. Levin, *Heart to Heart*, 168. As early as 1944, Sathya Sai Baba warned his devotees against the influence of evil planets; see Padmanaban, *Love Is My Form*, 187. On inauspicious time and planets, see D. M. Knipe, "Softening the Cruelty of God: Folklore, Ritual and the Planet Śani (Saturn) in Southeast India," in *Syllables of Sky: Studies in South Indian Civilization in Honour of Velcheru Narayana Rao*, ed. D. Shulman (Delhi: Oxford University Press, 1995), 206–48.

58. Kasturi, *Garland of 108 Precious Gems*, 105.

59. Balu, *Living Divinity*, 52.

60. http://www.saibabaofindia.com/sais_kasturi_heart2heart.htm, 25.

61. Ibid.

62. Ibid., 26. See also Padmamma, *Twameva Matha*, 108. On liberating oneself from karmic bonds at the time of death, see A. Malinar, *The Bhagavadgītā: Doctrines and Contexts* (New York: Cambridge University Press, 2007), 136–44. See also F. Edgerton, "The Hour of Death," *Annals of the Bhandarkar Oriental Research Institute* 8 (1926–27): 219–49.

63. Kasturi's daughter speculates that perhaps her father "was immersed in the Mantra that Swami had given him a year before; in his dream He had fulfilled his long standing wish for a Mantra from Swami"; Padmamma, *Twameva Matha*, 109–10.

64. http://www.saibabaofindia.com/sais_kasturi_heart2heart.htm, 26. See also Padmamma, *Twameva Matha*, 109.

65. Ibid., 110. The guru added: "Death is certain to follow birth. Nobody is permanent. Even this body also"; ibid.

66. http://www.saibabaofindia.com/sais_kasturi_heart2heart.htm, 26.

67. As per the testimony of Kasturi's grandson Ramesh, see http://media.radiosai.org/journals/vol_10/01DEC12/living-the-divine-presence-Prof-N-Kasturi-biographer-translator-of-sathya-sai-baba.htm.

68. During his visit, the disturbing trickling of water from a tap in the bathroom could be heard and he asked Dr. Shanta to stop it.

69. He looked at them and with authority said *chesko*, "do it," pointing to his feet.

70. Padmamma, *Twameva Matha*, 111. Another source reports that he pronounced an almost identical statement: "We have to arrange a band for his funeral procession. He is a respectable world figure; the procession should be grand"; http://www.saibabaofindia.com/sais_kasturi_heart2heart.htm, 26.

71. The elephant-headed god, elder son of Śiva and Pārvatī, is the prime deity whom all Hindus worship since he is believed to be the reliever of obstacles, finally cutting all worldly bondages and bestowing liberation to those who seek his grace. This is the reason why the first prayer or devotional hymn is always addressed to Gaṇeśa.

72. http://www.saibabaofindia.com/sais_kasturi_heart2heart.htm, 26.

73. It must be recalled that Kasturi was a *vaiṣṇava* Brahmin belonging to the Kauṇḍinya *gotra*.

74. Padmamma, *Twameva Matha*, 111.

75. Sri B. S. Rajaram, Kasturi's grandson, contributed along with other relatives to the publication of Chandra Mohan and Subba Rao, *Kastūri śatakam*.

76. Kasturi's son Murthy had two sons: Sudhakar and Vasanth, who was the youngest. Sathya Sai Baba guided the life of both. He instructed Vasanth to choose entomology as the subject of his specialization for his MS at Gauhati University in Assam; see Kasturi, *Loving God*, 368.

77. It is reported that when Dr. Shanta opened the door, "she felt as if something or somebody was pushing her from inside"; http://www.saibabaofindia.com/sais_kasturi_heart2heart.htm, 27.

78. Ibid. See also Padmamma, *Twameva Matha*, 112.

79. *Gāru* is an honorific plural affix to singular names and nouns.

80. Indeed, even at the ashram, the hagiographer continued to exercise his humoristic side. As his daughter writes: "After reaching Swami's abode, my father *almost* gave up his old habits of 'humour' and 'criticism.' There was a touch of 'light humour' even in his talks about Swami"; Padmamma, *Twameva Matha*, 105. For a collection of articles on Sathya Sai Baba's sense of humor, see P. Mason, S. Lévy, and M. Veeravahu, eds., *Sai Humour* (Prasanthi Nilayam: Sri Sathya Sai Towers Hotels, 1996). The collection comprises two short articles by Kasturi taken from *Journey to God—Part 2* (Kuala Lumpur, 1981), by J. Jagadeesan, and Kasturi's autobiography *Loving God*: "Rain Rain Go Away" (61–63) and "The Divine Photographer" (75–77), respectively.

81. Padmamma, *Twameva Matha*, 112–13.

82. As the hagiographer once stated during a lecture to overseas devotees: "I belong to the caste where after death I will be reduced to ash. Not buried, but burnt. I become ash one day!"; Shivaram, *Sathya Sai Baba: God in Action*, 227.

83. Also known as *antyeṣṭi* or the last sacrifice. The dead body is washed and wrapped in white cloth, the big toes are tied together with a string and a red, yellow, or white mark (*tilaka*) is placed on the forehead. At the cremation ground near a river or water, the body is placed on the wooden pyre with feet facing south. The eldest son or the lead mourner bathes himself before leading the cremation ceremony. He circumambulates the pyre, says a eulogy or recites

a hymn, places sesame seeds or rice in the dead person's mouth, sprinkles the body and the pyre with clarified butter, and draws three lines signifying Yāma, the god of death, *kāla*, time, the god of cremation, and the dead person. Prior to lighting the pyre, an earthen pot is filled with water, and the lead mourner circles the body with it, before lobbing the pot over his shoulder so it breaks near the head. Once the pyre is ablaze, the lead mourner and the closest relatives may circumambulate it one or more times. The ceremony is concluded by the lead cremator with the ritual known as *kapālakriyā*, piercing the burning skull with a stave so as to break it and release the spirit.

84. American devotee and filmmaker Jack Lenchiner filmed Kasturi's funeral at the Chitravathi River; see https://www.youtube.com/watch?v=me0qX-pKFcw, minutes 13–14. This is perhaps the only testimony of the hagiographer's cremation and Mr. Lenchiner recently told me that he hopes to retrieve the video and put it online (personal communication, June 14, 2019). He owns a collection of videotapes since from around 1977 he was allowed to film Sathya Sai Baba's *darśans* and public discourses as well as Kasturi's speeches to overseas devotees.

85. http://www.saibabaofindia.com/sais_kasturi_heart2heart.htm, 27. Many people expressed to Kasturi's daughter similar sentiments of their good luck for having being able to attend the sacred ceremony. In her book, Padma reports that Sri Karunyananda and others told her: "Amma, he was a real yogi. His soul must have escaped from the *Brahmarandra* (head) because we saw the *kapala moksha*. We were all fortunate to see it"; Padmamma, *Twameva Matha*, 114. The *brahmarandhra* or "Brahmā's aperture" is the suture in the crown of the head. At death, the soul is supposed to leave the body by this route.

86. In Yoga, this vein or channel (*nāḍī*) is regarded as the subtle body's central and most important conduit and is called *suṣumnā*. This central channel of the spinal column is said to originate from the *cakra* or center at the base of the spine (*mūlādhāracakra*) and to end up in the *brahmarandhra* at the crown of the head, also known as *sahasrāracakra* since it is represented as a thousand-petalled lotus.

87. This is the *ātman,* the soul.

88. P. Olivelle, trans., *Upaniṣads* (New York: Oxford University Press, 1996), 246. *Kaṭha Upaniṣad* 6.16 occurs in *Chāndogya Upaniṣad* 8.6.6. On these issues see also *Bhagavadgītā* 8.5, 8.9–13 and the guru's commentary in *Geetha Vahini.* Discourses by Bhagavan Sri Sathya Sai Baba (Prasanthi Nilayam: Sri Sathya Sai Books and Publications, 1983), 76–80.

89. According to another source, the guru's words to Padma were: "He attained what he has to attain. So have no worries; you do not need to do any rituals either. He has merged in Swami"; http://www.saibabaofindia.com/sais_kasturi_heart2heart.htm, 27.

90. Padmamma, *Twameva Matha*, 114. A year later, in October 1988, while speaking to Erlendur Haraldsson, the guru praised Kasturi saying that he

was "a very gentle and spiritual man"; Haraldsson, *Modern Miracles*, 299 (2013 revised edition).

91. On Yama, *antyeṣṭi,* and the postmortem rituals, see G. G. Filippi, *Mṛtyu: Concept of Death in Indian Traditions. Transformation of the Body and Funeral Rites* (New Delhi: D. K. Printworld, 1996).

92. I. H. Shah observes: "The basic concept of feeding the poor has been lifted to the level of 'Narayana Seva' i.e. feeding Narayana or Bhagavan, the Indweller of all beings and here, the God in the poor. Even the way of performing the Seva has been transformed into a Sadhana"; Shah, *Sixteen Spiritual Summers*, 122.

93. http://www.saibabaofindia.com/sais_kasturi_heart2heart.htm, 28.

94. Significantly, one of Kasturi's lectures to foreign devotees is titled "Our Life Is His Message"; Shivaram, *Sathya Sai Baba: God in Action*, 155–66.

95. See Babb, *Redemptive Encounters*, 69–70, 183–85, 212–14. The charisma of the guru is thought to enable disciples to discover their true identity. A transaction is said to take place: the *bhakta* surrenders his/her ego and in exchange for his/her devotion receives the guru's love and comes to recognize his/her higher self, the *ātman*.

96. Kasturi, *Loving God*, 375.

97. Ibid., 377.

98. As he taught overseas devotees: "Swami means, Master, and we are servants. We serve Him through serving others, which makes Him pleased"; Shivaram, *Sathya Sai Baba: God in Action*, 61.

99. See ibid., 219.

100. Ibid., 250.

101. As Kasturi remarked: "This journey must end in '*jnana*,' knowledge. Then only it will be unshaken. . . . If you want to attain *Sat Chit Ananda*, you must move on from *bhakti* to *jnana*"; ibid., 219.

102. See for instance *The Indian Express* of Bangalore, with an article titled "Kasturi dead," published on August 17, 1987. Another article taken from this newspaper and dated August 18, 1987, is titled: "Litterateur who worked for adult education."

103. He would have turned ninety on December 25, 1987. Per Hindu tradition, however, the nine months of gestation are counted as the first year in a person's life.

104. V. K. Narasimhan, "Unto Sai a Witness," *Sanathana Sarathi* (September 1987): 260. See *Matthew* 19.14: "Let the children come to me; do not try to stop them; for the kingdom of Heaven belongs to such as these." See also *Luke* 18.16. V. K. Narasimhan authored a short article on Kasturi in Chandra Mohan and Subba Rao, *Kastūri śatakam*.

105. See Kasturi, *Garland of 108 Precious Gems*, 89; Kasturi, *Sathyam Sivam Sundaram, Part IV*, 164; Sathya Sai Baba, *Sathya Sai Speaks, Vol. 1*, 172; Hislop, *Conversations with Bhagavan Sri Sathya Sai Baba*, 104.

106. Their argument is as follows: Sathya Sai Baba lived 30,833 days. Lunar months average 27.21 days and there are 12 lunar months in a lunar year. Therefore, he lived about 1,133 lunar months, or 94.4 lunar years. In fact, the number of lunar years the guru lived can be made out to be anything between 89.5 and 94.4.

107. See https://vimeo.com/97850716.

Chapter 8

1. Financial and sexual misconduct are among the most frequent accusations against gurus and Sathya Sai Baba has been no exception. The Indian press has been replete with injunctions against him, and some of his staunchest critics are to be found in Indian journalism; see Ruhela, *Sri Sathya Sai Baba and the Press (1972–1996)*. Moreover, criticism abounds on the internet, notably from ex-devotees; see https://robertpriddy.wordpress.com. On the sexual life of gurus, see Copeman and Ikegame, *The Multifarious Guru*, 27–30.

2. At the time, police sources reported that three of the four assailants had links with the *Vishwa Hindu Parishad* and the *Rashtriya Swayamsevak Sangh*; see newspaper articles of *The Times of India* ("Sai Baba Escapes Bid on Life," dated June 8, 1993) and *The Hindu* ("Police Probing Puttaparthi Incident," dated June 7, 1993).

3. The guru used to "materialize" an oily liquid and apply it to the lower abdomen of young men, saying that it would help them control their sexual urge. While doing this, he would sometimes touch their penis and testicles. Daniel Roumanoff, who experienced such "treatment" back in 1960, thought that "his intentions are certainly not bad." And yet he noted that "his attitude seemed ambiguous and his ways too relaxed and easy going"; Roumanoff, *Candide au pays des Gourous*, 137–38; my translation.

4. Shivaram, *Sathya Sai Baba: God in Action*, 25.

5. Ibid., 240.

6. Gries and Gries, *An Index of Sathya Sai Speaks, volumes I–XI*, 160.

7. For an introduction to the Theosophical Society, see G. Viswanathan, "Theosophical Society," in *Brill's Encyclopedia of Hinduism*, ed. K. A. Jacobsen, H. Basu, A. Malinar, and V. Narayanan (Brill Online, 2012). See also the articles of M. Bevir, "Theosophy as a Political Movement," and C. Risseuw, "Thinking Culture Through Counter-culture: The Case of Theosophists in India and Ceylon and Their Ideas on Race and Hierarchy (1875–1947)," in Copley, *Gurus and Their Followers*, 159–205.

8. Smriti Srinivas, *The Advent of the Avatar*, 304.

9. R. Pisu, "Con il lama Tucci sul Tetto del Mondo. Parla il famoso orientalista e esploratore, che sta per compiere novant'anni," *La Stampa*, 20 ottobre 1983, 3; my translation. On Giuseppe Tucci and Theosophy, see A. Crisanti, *Giuseppe Tucci. Una biografia* (Milano: Unicopli, 2020), 120–26.

10. See van der Veer, *Imperial Encounters*, 78. *The Theosophist*, the Theosophical Society's journal founded by Helena Petrovna Blavatsky in 1879, has always had as its maxim the family motto of the Maharajahs of Benares: "There is no religion higher than truth" (*satyāt nāsti paro dharmaḥ*).

11. As the guru proclaimed in one of his discourses: "The Sai religion is the harmonious blending, through love, of all religions." Moreover: "The Sai religion (using religion in its literal sense of binding man to God) is the essence of all faiths and religions, including those like Islam, Christianity, and Judaism"; Gries and Gries, *An Index of Sathya Sai Speaks, volumes I–XI*, 285.

12. Fanibunda, *Vision of the Divine*, 107.

13. Gries and Gries, *An Index of Sathya Sai Speaks, volumes I–XI*, 160.

14. Ibid.

15. The idea that Sathya Sai Baba personified all deities was a leitmotiv from the guru's early days. See one of Kasturi's talks symptomatically titled "He Is All Forms of Godhead," in Shivaram, *Sathya Sai Baba: God in Action*, 100–103.

16. Hawkins, *Bordering Realism*, 158.

17. Gries and Gries, *An Index of Sathya Sai Speaks, volumes I–XI*, 285. On the guru's names, see Kasturi, *Sathyam Sivam Sundaram, Part III*, 215–24.

18. Ibid., 106. See also Gries and Gries, *An Index of Sathya Sai Speaks, volumes I–XI*, 29.

19. Rigopoulos, *Shirdi Sai Baba*, 649.

20. Smriti Srinivas, *In the Presence of Sai Baba*, 161. See also Ead., *The Advent of the Avatar*, 304–305, where she remarks that "in spite of this universalism, the casting of Sanathana Dharma is not in terms of an international religious synthesis, but a 'Vedic' and 'national' one."

21. Kasturi, *Sathyam Sivam Sundaram, Part IV*, 162.

22. Ibid., 163.

23. Kasturi, *Garland of 108 Precious Gems*, 45.

24. A. Rudert, "Research on Contemporary Indian Gurus: What's New About New Age Gurus?" *Religion Compass* 4, no. 10 (2010): 635.

25. L. McKean, *Divine Enterprise: Gurus and the Hindu Nationalist Movement* (Chicago: University of Chicago Press, 1996), 12.

26. See Sathya Sai Baba, *His Story as Told by Himself*, 123; J. Loar, "From Neither/Nor to Both/And: Reconfiguring the Life and Legacy of Shirdi Sai Baba in Hagiography," *International Journal of Hindu Studies* 22 (2018): 475–96.

27. He enjoyed singing the following song in English: "Love is my form, truth is my breath, bliss is my food. My life is my message, my message is my life: no reason for love, no season for love, no birth no death."

28. See Smriti Srinivas, *In the Presence of Sai Baba*, 1. In his 2005 article, however, Norris W. Palmer reports the existence of "roughly 1,200 Sai Centers worldwide"; Palmer, *Baba's World*, 115.

29. See Smriti Srinivas, *The Advent of the Avatar*, 295.

30. See Llewellyn, *Gurus and Groups*, 237. Llewellyn argues that "to a certain extent" the pattern of attracting Westerners as adherents is also a characteristic of the Sathya Sai Baba movement. But the truth is that the guru of Puttaparthi has always attracted large numbers of both Indians and Westerners. Even nowadays, the percentage of Indians (and Indian immigrants) who are his devotees is conspicuous and certainly higher than that of other popular neo-Hindu movements such as the Hare Krishnas. On the transnational character of the Sathya Sai Baba movement, see A. K. Sahoo and M. Kelly, "Social Movements in the Diasporic Context: The Sathya Sai Baba Movement," in *The Political Economy of South Asian Diaspora: Patterns of Socio-Economic Influence*, ed. G. Pillai (New York: Palgrave Macmillan, 2013), 143–66; Tulasi Srinivas, *Winged faith*; A. K. Sahoo, *Religion, Diaspora, and Transnational Networks: The Case of Sri Sathya Sai Baba Movement* (PhD diss., Shodhganga University of Hyderabad, 2006). On these issues, see also M. J. Spurr, "Modern Hindu Guru Movements," in *Hinduism in India: Modern and Contemporary Movements*, ed. W. Sweetman and A. Malik (New Delhi: Sage, 2016), 141–75.

31. The number of Muslim devotees and their presence in Shirdi has sensibly diminished over the years. In 2013, Shirdi had about thirty thousand residents and an estimated annual influx of eight million visitors; see K. A. Shinde and A. M. Pinkney, "Shirdi in Transition: Guru Devotion, Urbanisation, and Regional Pluralism in India," *South Asia: Journal of South Asian Studies* 36, no. 4 (2013): 554–70.

32. In India, the spread of the Shirdi Sai Baba movement has been staggering, especially starting from the 1970s, with the building of hundreds of temples dedicated to him. The maximum concentration of temples is in the states of Maharashtra and Andhra Pradesh (Shirdi Sai Baba's largest statue has recently been built in Machilipatnam), but his presence is ubiquitous throughout the subcontinent. In recent years, devotee C. B. Satpathy of New Delhi, with his Shri Shirdi Sai Heritage Foundation Trust, has built more than two hundred Shirdi Sai Baba temples throughout India and is a major force behind the globalization of the saint's movement; see K. McLain, "Praying for Peace and Amity: The Shri Shirdi Sai Heritage Foundation Trust," in *Public Hinduisms*, ed. J. Zavos, P. Kanungo, D. S. Reddy, M. Warrier, and R. B. Williams (New Delhi:

Sage, 2012), 190–209. On the development of modern Hindu temples in India, see J. P. Waghorne, *Diaspora of the Gods: Modern Hindu Temples in an Urban Middle-Class World* (New York: Oxford University Press, 2004).

33. On these issues, see J. P. Waghorne and N. Cutler, eds., *Gods of Flesh, Gods of Stone: The Embodiment of Divinity in India* (New York: Columbia University Press, 1985).

34. McLain, *The Afterlife of Sai Baba*, 212. On the Shirdi Sai Baba movement as a counterpoint to Hindu fundamentalism, promoting a composite vision of spiritual unity in diversity, see K. McLain, "Be United, Be Virtuous: Composite Culture and the Growth of Shirdi Sai Baba Devotion," *Nova Religio: The Journal of Alternative and Emergent Religions* 15, no. 2 (2011): 20–49.

35. Quoted in Palmer, *Baba's World*, 116. On the singing practices of Sathya Sai Baba's Swiss devotees and the peculiar mixture of Sanskrit *bhajan*s and Swiss songs, implying strategies of de-territorialization and re-territorialization, see V. Meier, "Song Choices of Swiss Sathya Sai Baba Devotees," *Diskus: The Journal of the British Association for the Study of Religions* 16, no. 1 (2014): 68–81.

36. Palmer, *Baba's World*, 116.

37. For an assessment of gurus' manifold strategies to adopt new devotees, see A. Lucia, "Innovative Gurus: Tradition and Change in Contemporary Hinduism," *International Journal of Hindu Studies* 18, no. 2 (2014): 221–63.

38. On the possibilities of a de-ethnicized Hinduism, see Waghorne, *Global Gurus and the Third Stream of American Religiosity*. On the god-man of Puttaparthi as global guru, see R. S. Weiss, "The Global Guru: Sai Baba and the Miracle of the Modern," *New Zealand Journal of Asian Studies* 7, no. 2 (2005): 5–19.

39. This tendency has been duly underlined by Tulasi Srinivas in her monograph *Winged Faith*, as well as in her article *Sathya Sai Baba*.

40. For example, in 2015 Sathya Sai Baba devotees held an Ati Rudra Mahā Yajña in Badrinath; see https://www.youtube.com/watch?v=RAZb76__EeE. Such Vedic revivalism is a widespread feature in contemporary Hinduism along with the promotion of traditional Vedic schools (*gurukula*); on these issues, see B. Larios, *Embodying the Vedas: Traditional Vedic Schools of Contemporary Maharashtra* (Berlin: Walter de Gruyter, 2017).

41. On the guru's semiotic flexibility and expansive embrace, see C. Bauman, "Sathya Sai Baba: At Home Abroad in Midwestern America," in *Public Hinduisms*, ed. J. Zavos, P. Kanungo, D. S. Reddy, M. Warrier, and R. B. Williams, 141–59.

42. Shivaram, *Sathya Sai Baba: God in Action*, 23. Sathya Sai Baba declared to have "no name at all" already in his school years; see Sathya Sai Baba, *His Story as Told by Himself*, 120, 123–24.

43. Shivaram, *Sathya Sai Baba: God in Action*, 235.

44. Ibid., 26.

45. Kasturi may have had in mind the Hare Krishna and the Bhagwan Shree Rajneesh/Osho movements.

46. Shivaram, *Sathya Sai Baba: God in Action*, 25.

47. Gries and Gries, *An Index of Sathya Sai Speaks, volumes I–XI*, 285.

48. Already in the early 1960s, he declared: "I come always for the sake of reviving Dharma"; ibid., 287. Moreover: "I do not identify with anything"; ibid., 286.

49. One of the hagiographer's lectures to overseas devotees is, significantly, titled "No Name, No Form"; see Shivaram, *Sathya Sai Baba: God in Action*, 20–27.

50. Hislop, *My Baba and I*, 38.

51. Gries and Gries, *An Index of Sathya Sai Speaks, volumes I–XI*, 285.

52. Hawkins, *Bordering Realism*, 153.

53. Gries and Gries, *An Index of Sathya Sai Speaks, volumes I–XI*, 286.

54. On *darśan,* see Valpey, Pūjā *and* darśana.

55. Kasturi, *Garland of 108 Precious Gems*, 23.

56. See Kasturi, *Loving God*, 122.

57. See Kasturi's lecture to foreign devotees titled "He Is Everywhere"; Shivaram, *Sathya Sai Baba: God in Action*, 94–99.

58. Kasturi, *Garland of 108 Precious Gems*, 89.

59. See Smriti Srinivas, *In the Presence of Sai Baba*, 76–104.

60. See Palmer, *Baba's World*, 108–109.

61. B. Kapferer, "Introduction. Outside All Reason: Magic, Sorcery, and Epistemology in Anthropology," in *Beyond Rationalism: Rethinking Magic, Witchcraft, and Sorcery*, ed. B. Kapferer (New York/Oxford: Berghahn Books, 2003), 23.

62. See Siegel, *Net of Magic*, 423–40. On the guru's magic vis-à-vis the rationalist critique of it, see Tulasi Srinivas, "Doubtful Illusions: Magic, Wonder, and the Politics of Virtue in the Sathya Sai Movement," *Journal of Asian and African Studies* (2015): 1–31.

63. Kasturi, *Loving God*, 193.

64. On the production of films and videos by the Sathya Sai Baba Organization, either centered on the god-man's life, for instance, a visual biography, or on the organization's charitable activities—"largely directed to a novitiate middle-class audience seeking rational justifications for their faith in Sai as a guru/avatar/messiah"—see Hawkins, *Bordering Realism*, 145–47. It should be noted that the guru's "prior incarnation," Shirdi Sai Baba, is something of a patron saint to the Indian film industry, see Dwyer, *Filming the Gods: Religion and Indian Cinema*, 93–95. In July 2017, a radio show was launched on Shirdi Sai Baba's teachings and experiences titled *Sāī kī Mahimā* (produced by Aushim Khetarpal), of which to date more than a hundred episodes have been broadcast.

65. Chitluri, *Baba's Divine Symphony*, 43. See also Dabholkar, *Shri Sai Satcharita: The Life and Teachings of Shirdi Sai Baba*, 545–46 (ch. 33, vv. 150–62), 668 (ch. 40, v. 107), 672 (ch. 40, v. 155), 732 (ch. 44, vv. 126–29), 757–59 (ch. 46, vv. 61–90), 840 (ch. 51, v. 74). On the idea that the image of Shirdi Sai Baba is as powerful as his bodily presence, see W. Elison, "Site, Sight, Cite: Conceptualizing Wayside Shrines as Visual Culture," *South Asia Multidisciplinary Academic Journal* 18 (2018): 1–25 (http://journals.openedition.org/samaj/4540); W. Elison, "Sai Baba of Bombay: A Saint, His Icon, and the Urban Geography of *Darshan*," *History of Religions* 54, no. 2 (2014): 151–87.

66. On the use of digital and visual media in the Sathya Sai Baba movement, see Hawkins, *Bordering Realism*, 145–47.

67. Kasturi, *Garland of 108 Precious Gems*, 26.

68. Palmer, *Baba's World*, 119. On these issues, see the collection of articles in A. K. Sahoo and J. G. De Kruijf, eds., *Indian Transnationalism Online: New Perspectives on Diaspora* (Farnham: Ashgate, 2014). See also H. Campbell, *Digital Religion: Understanding Religious Practice in New Media Worlds* (London: Routledge, 2013); S. Jacobs, "Communicating Hinduism in a Changing Media Context," *Religion Compass* 6, no. 2 (2012): 136–51.

69. Available at http://www.geocities.com/Athens/Olympus/9158/d15101999.html.

70. Kasturi, *Loving God*, 108–109. For an overview of the guru's early opinions on science and scientists, see Gries and Gries, *An Index of Sathya Sai Speaks, volumes I–XI*, 177–78.

71. Already in November 1980, the guru remarked that "one cause of the general deterioration in the world is rapid communication. This allows advertising and publicity to have a strong influence on people"; Steel, *The Sathya Sai Baba Compendium*, 261.

72. On the electronic presence of the *avatāra,* see Smriti Srinivas, *In the Presence of Sai Baba*, 104–10.

73. The competition is enhanced by the fact that through the internet guru seekers are offered an overwhelming variety of alternative paths and spiritual commodities. Spiritual hopping from one guru to another is a common characteristic of the contemporary religious consumer market.

74. On the social and political use of media, see A. Rajagopal, "Politics and Media," in *Brill's Encyclopedia of Hinduism*, ed. K. A. Jacobsen, H. Basu, A. Malinar, and V. Narayanan (Brill Online, 2012). See also U. Rao, "Media Hinduism," in Sweetman and Malik, *Hinduism in India: Modern and Contemporary Movements*, 123–40.

75. He coined this neologism earlier than 1999, since his statement that "modern technology is more aptly named modern tricknology" is found already

in a book edited by Mason, Lévy, and Veeravahu, *Sai Humour*, 110, published in 1995.

76. As a devotee remarked: "Having *darshan* in person just blows you. Experience that cannot be explained"; Hawkins, *Bordering Realism*, 150.

77. The guru's funeral was fully covered by Indian televisions: millions of people throughout the country were glued to the screen; see M. K. Das, "Televising Religion: A Study of Sathya Sai Baba's Funeral Broadcast in Gangtok, India," *Anthropological Notebooks* 21, no. 3 (2015): 83–104.

78. See Hawkins, *Bordering Realism*, 147–50. As Maya Warrier notes, "The more popular and successful *gurus* . . . can no longer sustain close personal ties with each individual devotee. Largely revolutionized media and communication systems mediate their relationship with devotees"; Warrier, *Guru Choice and Spiritual Seeking in Contemporary India*, 48.

79. Hawkins, *Bordering Realism*, 158.

80. On the place of posters of Hindu saints and deities in the practice of devotion, see H. D. Smith, "Impact of 'God Posters' on Hindus and Their Devotional Traditions," in *Media and the Transformation of Religion in South Asia*, ed. L. A. Babb and S. Wadley (Delhi: Motilal Banarsidass, 1997), 24–50.

81. See Warrier, *Guru Choice and Spiritual Seeking in Contemporary India*, 48–49.

82. On these issues, see R. H. Davis, *Lives of Indian Images* (Princeton: Princeton University Press, 1997).

83. Hawkins, *Bordering Realism*, 157.

84. Some Westerners, however, thought that Kasturi was a *saṃnyāsin*; see Roumanoff, *Candide au pays des Gourous*, 133.

85. As Smriti Srinivas observes: "It appears that the householder now encodes into himself/herself the roles of the priest and the renouncer and a distance is created from political power as a defining social value, even though many devotees have access to that power"; Srinivas, *The Advent of the Avatar*, 305.

86. Gries and Gries, *An Index of Sathya Sai Speaks, volumes I–XI*, 67.

87. Kamaraju, *Memories and Memoirs*, 50.

88. On the guru's relationality, see Bauman, *Sathya Sai Baba: At Home Abroad in Midwestern America*, 154–55.

89. Kasturi, *Loving God*, 236.

90. On giving and forgiving, see E. Bianchi, *Dono e perdono. Per un'etica della compassione* (Torino: Einaudi, 2014).

91. One is reminded of the seven corporal works of mercy in the Christian tradition (*Matthew* 25:31–46): to feed the hungry, to give water to the thirsty, to clothe the naked, to shelter the homeless, to visit the sick, to visit the imprisoned and to bury the dead. To these are linked the seven spiritual works of mercy: counseling the doubtful, instructing the ignorant, admonishing

the sinner, comforting the sorrowful, forgiving injuries, bearing wrongs patiently, and praying for the living and the dead. On the corporal works of mercy, see E. Bianchi, *Grammatica dell'amore. Fare misericordia agli altri* (Comunità di Bose: Edizioni Qiqayon, 2016).

92. See *Prasanthi Nilayam Information Booklet*, 22–45.

93. See Smriti Srinivas, *In the Presence of Sai Baba*, 111–61.

94. Ibid., 112.

95. See J. Hawley, *Reawakening the Spirit in Work: The Power of Dharmic Management* (San Francisco: Berrett-Koehler, 1993).

96. See Palmer, *Baba's World*, 114–15.

97. See Gries and Gries, *An Index of Sathya Sai Speaks, volumes I–XI*, 26. From his early discourses, the guru remarked that "character has lost priority in the educational system" and that "character is the most precious gift of education." Moreover: "Character, not knowledge, is power"; ibid.

98. Ibid., 54. The master stressed that "education must remove hatred between pilgrims on the various roads to God" and that "education practiced in ancient India was superior and more fruitful, for it equipped the student with a healthy spirit of self reliance and gave them mental peace and equipoise"; ibid.

99. Kasturi, *Sathyam Sivam Sundaram, Part III*, 38.

100. See Smriti Srinivas, *In the Presence of Sai Baba*, 152.

101. See Beckerlegge, "Swami Akhandananda's Sevavrata (Vow of Service) and the Earliest Expressions of Service to Humanity in the Ramakrishna Math and Mission," in Copley, *Gurus and Their Followers*, 59–82.

102. See J. Casanova, "2000 Presidential Address: Religion, the New Millennium, and Globalization," *Sociology of Religion* 62, no. 4 (2001): 415–41; G. M. Thomas, "Religions in Global Civil Society," ibid., 515–33.

103. Rudert, *Research on Contemporary Indian Gurus*, 636.

104. Ibid., 637.

105. Hawkins, *Bordering Realism*, 158.

106. Haraldsson, *Modern Miracles*, 185.

107. For an overview of high-ranking politicians, Indian as well as foreign, who over the years came to Puttaparthi to homage Sathya Sai Baba, see https://www.youtube.com/watch?v=7eQ5VHmB-JE.

108. See Palmer, *Baba's World*, 119. On the exchange of "gifts" (*dāna*) between gurus and affluent social and political figures and the interests that bind them to one another, see M. Mines and V. Gourishankar, "Leadership and Individuality in South Asia: The Case of the South Indian Big-man," *The Journal of Asian Studies* 49, no. 4 (1990): 761–86.

109. Quoted in http://en.wikipedia.org/wiki/Sathya_Sai_Baba.

110. Ibid.

111. Palmer, *Baba's World*, 119.

112. S. P. Ruhela, *In Search of Sai Divine: A Comprehensive Research Review of Writings and Researches on Sri Sathya Sai Baba Avatar* (New Delhi: Umang Paperbacks, 1996), 64.

113. Ibid., 65.

114. Ibid.

115. Kasturi, *Prasanthi*, 118. See also one of his lectures to overseas devotees, eloquently titled "I Am You and You Are I," Shivaram, *Sathya Sai Baba: God in Action*, 76–84.

116. Narasimha Murthy, *Sathyam Sivam Sundaram, vol.* 5, 1–2.

117. See Ruhela, *Sai Trinity: Shirdi Sai, Sathya Sai, Prema Sai Incarnations*, 115.

General Bibliography

Abbott, Justin E., trans. *Dasopant Digambar: Translation of the* Dasopant Charitra. Poet-Saints of Maharashtra Series, no. 4. Pune: Scottish Mission Industries, 1927.

———, trans. *The Life of Eknāth.* Śrī Eknāth Charita. *Translated from the* Bhaktalīlāmṛta. Puṇe 1927. Reprint, Delhi: Motilal Banarsidass, 1981.

Abbott, Justin E., and N. R. Godbole, trans. *Stories of Indian Saints: Translation of Mahipati's Marathi* Bhaktavijaya. Introduction by G. V. Tagare. 2 Vols. in 1. Poona, 1933. Reprint, Delhi: Motilal Banarsidass, 1982.

Abitbol, Aldo D. "Causes of the 1962 Sino-Indian War: A Systems Level Approach." *Josef Korbel Journal of Advanced International Studies* 1 (2009): 74–88.

Aitken, Bill [William McKay]. "Sathya Sai Baba: A Non-devotee's Perspective." *Divine Grace: Sathya Sai Baba. An India Today Impact Presentation.* The India Today Group, 2011, 48.

———. *Sri Sathya Sai Baba: A Life.* New Delhi: Penguin, 2004.

Ajgaonkar, C. R. "Saibaba and Kabir." *Shri Sai Leela* 62, no. 4 (July 1983): 21–22.

Albanese, Catherine L. *A Republic of Mind and Spirit: A Cultural History of American Metaphysical Religion.* New Haven/London: Yale University Press, 2007.

Alter, Joseph S. *Yoga in Modern India: The Body Between Science and Philosophy.* Princeton: Princeton University Press, 2004.

Altglas, Véronique. "Indian Gurus and the Quest for Self-perfection Among the Educated Middle-Classes." In *Salvation Goods and Religious Markets: Theory and Applications*, edited by J. Stolz, 211–34. Bern: Peter Lang, 2008.

———. *"N'importe quelle échelle, du moment que ça monte" . . . La globalisation du religieux: Modes de diffusion et d'appropriation des pratiques et des valeurs se référant à l'hindouisme. Étude du Siddha Yoga et des Centres Sivananda en France et en Angleterre.* Tomes I–III. PhD Diss., École Pratique des Hautes Études, Paris, 2004.

Anzar, Naosherwan. *The Beloved: The Life and Work of Meher Baba.* North Myrtle Beach, SC: Sheriar Press, 1974.

Aravamudan, Srinivas. *Guru English: South Asian Religion in a Cosmopolitan Language*. Princeton: Princeton University Press, 2006.

Arweck, Elisabeth. "Common Values for the Common School? Using Two Values Education Programmes to Promote 'Spiritual and Moral Development.' " *Journal of Moral Education* (2005): 325–42.

Arya, P. P. *Attaining God Here and Now: Path of Bhakti Expounded in* Narada Bhakti Sutras. Chandigarh: Umang Printers, 2010.

Aurobindo Ghose, Sri. *Sri Aurobindo on Himself and on the Mother*. Pondicherry: Sri Aurobindo Ashram, 1953.

———. "Uttarpara Speech." In *Karmayogin: Political Writings and Speeches 1909–1910*, 3–12. Pondicherry: Sri Aurobindo Ashram Press, 1997.

Babb, Lawrence A. *Redemptive Encounters: Three Modern Styles in the Hindu Tradition*. Berkeley: University of California Press, 1986.

———. "Sathya Sai Baba's Saintly Play." In *Saints and Virtues*, edited by J. Stratton Hawley, 168–86. Berkeley: University of California Press, 1987.

Babu, R. S., ed. *Dattatreya: Glory of the Divine in Man*. Dedicated to Lord Sainath of Shirdi. With the Blessings of Acharya Sri E. Bharadwaja. Ongole: Sainath Printers, 1981.

Bahadur, Sri Jaya Chamarajendra Wadiyar. *Dattātreya: The Way and the Goal*. London: George Allen and Unwin, 1957. Reprint, Delhi: Motilal Banarsidass, 1982.

Bailey, Greg. "Brahmā." In *Brill's Encyclopedia of Hinduism, Vol. 1. Regions, Pilgrimage, Deities*, edited by K. A. Jacobsen, H. Basu, A. Malinar, and V. Narayanan, 499–512. Leiden: Brill, 2009.

Balse, Mayah. *Mystics and Men of Miracles in India*. Delhi: Orient Paperbacks, 1978.

Balu, Shakuntala. *Living Divinity*. London: Sawbridge Enterprises, 1981.

Balu, V. *The Glory of Puttaparthi*. Delhi: Motilal Banarsidass, 1990.

Balu, V., and Shakuntala Balu. *Divine Glory*. Delhi: Sri Satguru Publications 1999.

Baranowski, F. G. "A Date with the Celestial." In *The Splendour of Sathya Sai*, 55–58. Hyderabad: Sri Prasanthi Society, 1995.

Barz, Richard. "Hagiography." In *Brill's Encyclopedia of Hinduism*, edited by K. A. Jacobsen, H. Basu, A. Malinar, and V. Narayanan. Brill Online, 2013.

Baskin, Diana. *Divine Memories of Sathya Sai Baba*. San Diego: Birth Day, 1990.

Bauman, Chad. "Sathya Sai Baba: At Home Abroad in Midwestern America." In *Public Hinduisms*, edited by J. Zavos, P. Kanungo, D. S. Reddy, M. Warrier, and R. B. Williams, 141–59. New Delhi: Sage, 2012.

Bechler, Silke. "Globalized Religion: The Vedic Sacrifice (*Yajña*) in Transcultural Public Spheres." In *Experiencing Globalization: Religion in Contemporary Contexts*, edited by D. M. Nault, B. Dawei, E. Voulgarakis, R. Paterson, and C. Andres-Miguel Suva, 59–77. London/New York: Anthem Press, 2014.

Beckerlegge, Gwilym. "Ramakrishna Math and Mission." In *Brill's Encyclopedia of Hinduism*, edited by K. A. Jacobsen, H. Basu, A. Malinar, and V. Narayanan. Brill Online, 2012.

———. "*Sevā*: The Focus of a Fragmented but Gradually Coalescing Field of Study." In *Religions of South Asia* 9, no. 2 (2015): 208–39.

———. "Swami Akhandananda's Sevavrata (Vow of Service) and the Earliest Expressions of Service to Humanity in the Ramakrishna Math and Mission." In *Gurus and Their Followers: New Religious Reform Movements in Colonial India*, edited by A. Copley, 59–82. New Delhi: Oxford University Press, 2000.

———. *Swami Vivekananda's Legacy of Service: A Study of the Ramakrishna Math and Mission*. New Delhi: Oxford University Press, 2006.

Bevir, Mark. "Theosophy as a Political Movement." In *Gurus and Their Followers: New Religious Reform Movements in Colonial India*, edited by A. Copley, 159–79. New Delhi: Oxford University Press, 2000.

Bhagavan, Manu. "The Hindutva Underground: Hindu Nationalism and the Indian National Congress in Late Colonial and Early Postcolonial India." In *Religion and Identity in South Asia and Beyond: Essays in Honor of Patrick Olivelle*, edited by S. E. Lindquist, 321–45. London/New York: Anthem Press, 2013.

"Bhagavan's Sathya Sai Baba's 500-Year Old Horoscope." In *Sanathana Sarathi*, February 1961.

Bhajanavali. Prasanthi Nilayam: Sri Sathya Sai Books and Publications, 1983.

Bharati, Agehananda. "The Hindu Renaissance and Its Apologetic Patterns." *Journal of Asian Studies* 29, no. 2 (1970): 267–87.

———. *The Ochre Robe*. Santa Barbara: Ross-Erikson, 1980.

Bharvani, A. D., and V. Malhotra. *Shirdi Sai and Sathya Sai Are One and the Same*. Bombay: Sai Sahitya Samithi, 1983.

Bhatia, Nandi. *Acts of Authority / Acts of Resistance: Theater and Politics in Colonial and Postcolonial India*. Ann Arbor: The University of Michigan Press, 2004.

Bhatnagar, S. C., ed. *Sai Speaks About His Childhood (Based on Sai's Discourses)*. A Humble Offering to Bhagawan Sri Sathya Sai Baba on His 85th Auspicious Birthday. Prasanthi Nilayam: Sri Sathya Sai Sadhana Trust, 2011.

———, ed. *Sai Vibhuti Prasadam and Its Significance (Based on Sai's Teachings)*. A Humble Offering to Bhagavan Sri Sathya Sai Baba. Prasanthi Nilayam: Sri Sathya Sai Sadhana Trust, 2011.

Bhatt, S. Sripada Srivallabha Charitamrutam*: Biography of a Dattatreya Avatar*. Münster: Kulapati.de, 2019.

Bianchi, Enzo. *Dono e perdono. Per un'etica della compassione*. Torino: Einaudi, 2014.

———. *Grammatica dell'amore. Fare misericordia agli altri.* Comunità di Bose: Edizioni Qiqajon, 2016.

Bilimoria, Purushottama. "Sri Aurobindo and Sri Sathya Sai Baba on Sruti (Vedas)." *Darshana International* 33, no. 4/132 (1993): 1–6.

Bock, Richard. "Communicating Divinity." In *Golden Age 1980*, 147–49. Prasanthi Nilayam: Sri Sathya Sai Books and Publications Trust, 1980.

Bock, Richard, and Janet Bock. *The Jesus Mystery of Lost Years and Unknown Travels.* Los Angeles: Aura Books, 1980.

Bouillier, Véronique. *Itinérance et vie monastique. Les ascètes Nāth Yogīs en Inde contemporaine.* Paris: Éditions de la Maison des sciences de l'homme, 2008.

Brooke, Tal. *Sai Baba, Lord of the Air.* Berkhamsted: Lion Publishing, 1976.

Bryant, Edwin. "Krishna in the Tenth Book of the *Bhagavata Purana*." In *Krishna: A Sourcebook*, edited by E. Bryant, 111–36. New York: Oxford University Press, 2007.

Burger, Maya. "Kabir." In *Brill's Encyclopedia of Hinduism*, edited by K. A. Jacobsen, H. Basu, A. Malinar, and V. Narayanan. Brill Online, 2012.

———. "Kabīrpanthīs." In *Brill's Encyclopedia of Hinduism*, edited by K. A. Jacobsen, H. Basu, A. Malinar, and V. Narayanan. Brill Online, 2012.

Callewaert, Winand M. *The Millennium Kabīr Vāṇī: A Collection of Pad-s.* In Collaboration with Swapna Sharma and Dieter Taillieu. Delhi: Manohar, 2000.

———, and Rupert Snell, eds. *According to Tradition: Hagiographical Writing in India.* Wiesbaden: Harrassowitz, 1994.

Campbell, Heidi. *Digital Religion: Understanding Religious Practice in New Media Worlds.* London: Routledge, 2013.

Caracchi, Pinuccia. "Who Was a Hindu for Kabīr? Was Kabīr a Hindu?" In *Feeding the Self, Feeling the Way*, edited by A. Monti, M. Goglio, and E. Adami, 19–60. Torino: L'Harmattan Italia, 2005.

Casanova, José. "2000 Presidential Address: Religion, the New Millennium, and Globalization." *Sociology of Religion* 62, no. 4 (2001): 415–41.

Castagnetto Alessio, Marco. *Il loto e la spada. Il pensiero di Aurobindo Ghose e la sua ricezione in Occidente.* Milano: Franco Angeli, 2020.

Cenkner, William. *A Tradition of Teachers: Śaṅkara and the Jagadgurus Today.* Delhi: Motilal Banarsidass, 1983.

Census of India 1961. Vol. II, *Andhra Pradesh,* Part VII-B (10) *Fairs and Festivals* (10. Anantapur District). Superintendent of Census Operations: A. Chandra Sekhar, Indian Administrative Service. Delhi: Manager of Publications, 1965.

Chakravorty, Prabir K. "Sino-Indian War of 1962." *Indian Historical Review* 44, no. 2 (2017): 285–312.

Chandran, Mini, and Suchitra Mathur, eds. *Textual Travels: Theory and Practice of Translation in India.* New Delhi: Routledge, 2015.

Charlton, Hilda. *Hell-Bent for Heaven: The Autobiography of Hilda Charlton.* Woodstock, NY: Golden Quest, 1990.

———. *Saints Alive.* Woodstock, NY: Golden Quest, 1989.

———. "Sathya Sai Baba: God-Man." In *Golden Age 1980*, 230–31. Prasanthi Nilayam: Sri Sathya Sai Books and Publications Trust, 1980.

Chibber, M. L. *Sai Baba's Mahavakya on Leadership: Book for Youth, Parents, and Teachers.* Faber, VA: Leela Press, 1995.

Chitluri, Vinny. *Baba's Divine Symphony.* New Delhi: Sterling, 2014.

———. *Baba's Rinanubandh: Leelas during His Sojourn in Shirdi.* New Delhi: Sterling, 2007.

Clark, Matthew. *The Daśanāmī-Saṃnyāsīs: The Integration of Ascetic Lineages into an Order.* Leiden: Brill, 2006.

Clémentin-Ojha, Catherine. *La divinité conquise. Carrière d'une sainte.* Nanterre: Société d'ethnologie, 1990.

Cohen, A. Y. *The Mastery of Consciousness. An Introduction and Guide to Practical Mysticism and Methods of Spiritual Development as Given by Meher Baba.* London: Eel Pie, 1977.

Conlon, Frank F. "A Nineteenth-Century Indian Guru." In *Charisma and Sacred Biography*, edited by M. A. Williams, 127–48. *Journal of the American Academy of Religion*, Thematic Studies, vol. 48, nos. 3–4, 1982.

Copeman, Jacob, and Aya Ikegame. "The Multifarious Guru: An Introduction." In *The Guru in South Asia: New Interdisciplinary Perspectives*, edited by J. Copeman and A. Ikegame, 1–45. London and New York: Routledge, 2012.

Coward, Harold G. "Tolerance and Responses to Religious Pluralism." In *Brill's Encyclopedia of Hinduism*, edited by K. A. Jacobsen, H. Basu, A. Malinar, and V. Narayanan. Brill Online, 2012.

Coward, Harold G., and David J. Goa. *Mantra: Hearing the Divine in India and America.* New York: Columbia University Press, 2005.

Craxi, Antonio, ed. *Atti del simposio internazionale "Unity is Divinity Purity is Enlightenment," Roma 30–31 ottobre 1983.* Pontevecchio Magenta: Organizzazione Sathya Sai Baba Italia, 1984.

———, ed. *Incontri in attesa di Sathya Sai Baba.* Milano, 1981.

Crisanti, Alice. *Giuseppe Tucci. Una biografia.* Milano: Unicopli, 2020.

Csordas, Thomas J. "Introduction: Modalities of Transnational Transcendence." In *Transnational Transcendence: Essays on Religion and Globalization*, edited by T. J. Csordas, 1–29. Berkeley: University of California Press, 2009.

"Cultural Trends Study: India's Sai Baba Movement." www.cia.gov/library/readingroom/docs/CIA-RDP96-00792R000400280002-2.pdf.

Dabholkar, Govind R. (Hemadpant). *Shri Sai Satcharita: The Life and Teachings of Shirdi Sai Baba.* Translated by I. Kher. New Delhi: Sterling, 1999.

Dalādanamuni. *Dattalaharī. L'onda di Datta*, edited by A. Rigopoulos. Venezia: Cafoscarina, 1999.

Das, Manoj Kumar. "Televising Religion: A Study of Sathya Sai Baba's Funeral Broadcast in Gangtok, India." *Anthropological Notebooks* 21, no. 3 (2015): 83–104.

Das, R. K. *Temples of Tamilnad*. Bombay: Bharatiya Vidya Bhavan, 1964.

Dasaganu. *Gajanan vijay*. An English Adaptation by N. B. Patil. Shegaon: Shree Gajanan Maharaj Sansthan, 1980.

Davis, Richard H. *Lives of Indian Images*. Princeton: Princeton University Press, 1997.

———. *The Bhagavad Gita: A Biography*. Princeton: Princeton University Press, 2015.

De Michelis, Elizabeth. *A History of Modern Yoga: Patanjali and Western Esotericism*. London/New York: Continuum, 2004.

Deák, Dušan. "Maharashtra Saints and the Sufi Tradition: Eknath, Chand Bodhle and the Datta Sampradaya." In *Journal of Deccan Studies* 3, no. 2 (2005): 22–47.

———. "Śahādat or Śahā Datta? Locating the Mysterious Fakir in the Marathi Texts." In *Muslim Cultures in the Indo-Iranian World during the Early-Modern and Modern Periods*, edited by D. Hermann and F. Speziale, 501–32. Berlin: Klaus Schwarz Verlag, 2010.

Dempsey, Corinne G., and Selva J. Raj, eds. *Miracle as Modern Conundrum in South Asian Religious Traditions*. Albany: State University of New York Press, 2008.

Devi, Indra. *Sai Baba and Sai Yoga*. New Delhi: MacMillan India, 1975.

Dhere, Ramchandra Chintaman. *Datta Sampradāyācā Itihāsa*. Pune: Nilakanth Prakashan, 1964.

———. "Folk Perception and Saints Perception." In *Folk Culture, Folk Religion, and Oral Tradition as a Component in Maharashtrian Culture*, edited by G.-D. Sontheimer, 245–58. New Delhi: Manohar, 1995.

———. *Musalmān Marāṭhī Santa-Kavī*. Pune: Jnanraj Prakashan, 1967.

———. *The Rise of a Folk God: Viṭṭhal of Pandharpur*. New York: Oxford University Press, 2011.

Dimmitt, Cornelia, and J. A. B. van Buitenen, eds., trans. *Classical Hindu Mythology: A Reader in the Sanskrit Purāṇas*. Philadelphia: Temple University Press, 1978.

Divine Grace: Sathya Sai Baba. An India Today Impact Presentation. The India Today Group, 2011.

Doniger, Wendy, ed. *Purāṇa Perennis: Reciprocity and Transformation in Hindu and Jaina Texts*. Albany: State University of New York Press, 1993.

Donkin, William. *The Wayfarers: An Account of the Work of Meher Baba with the God-Intoxicated, and also with Advanced Souls, Sadhus, and the Poor.* San Francisco: Sufism Reoriented, 1969.

Drucker, Al. "God Is Always with You." In *Golden Age 1980*, 138–43. Prasanthi Nilayam: Sri Sathya Sai Books and Publications Trust, 1980.

———, ed. *Sai Baba Gita: The Way to Self-Realisation and Liberation in this Age.* Crestone, CO: Atma Press, 1993 (American ed. of Sathya Sai Baba, *Discourses on the Bhagavad-Gita.* Compiled and Edited by A. Drucker. Prasanthi Nilayan: Sri Sathya Sai Books and Publications, 1988).

Dwyer, Rachel. *Filming the Gods: Religion and Indian Cinema.* London and New York: Routledge, 2006.

Easwaran, E. *Gandhi, the Man.* Tomales, CA: Nilgiri Press, 1997.

Edgerton, Franklin, trans. *The Bhagavad Gītā.* New York: Harper Torchbooks, 1964.

———. "The Hour of Death." *Annals of the Bhandarkar Oriental Research Institute* 8 (1926–27): 219–49.

Elison, William. "Sai Baba of Bombay: A Saint, His Icon, and the Urban Geography of *Darshan.*" *History of Religions* 54, no. 2 (2014): 151–87.

———. "Site, Sight, Cite: Conceptualizing Wayside Shrines as Visual Culture." *South Asia Multidisciplinary Academic Journal* 18 (2018): 1–25; http://journals.openedition.org/samaj/4540

Fadda, Antonio. *"Il divino a cavallo tra distruzione e salvezza." Ipotesi su origini ed evoluzioni della figura del Kalkin Avatār.* MA Thesis, Università degli Studi di Padova–Università Ca' Foscari Venezia, 2015.

Fanibunda, Eruch B. *Vision of the Divine.* Prasanthi Nilayam: Shri Sathya Sai Books and Publications, 1987 (1976).

Feldhaus, Anne. "Mahānubhāvs." In *Brill's Encyclopedia of Hinduism*, edited by K. A. Jacobsen, H. Basu, A. Malinar, and V. Narayanan. Brill Online, 2012.

———. *The Deeds of God in Ṛddhipur.* With introductory essays by Anne Feldhaus and Eleanor Zelliot. New York: Oxford University Press, 1984.

Fellows, A. "Recovering Goodness, Beauty, and Truth." In *L'Abri Papers* #AF02; http://www.labri.org/england/resources/05052008/AF02_Goodness_Beauty_3E64FE.pdf

Filippi, Gian Giuseppe. *Mṛtyu: Concept of Death in Indian Traditions. Transformation of the Body and Funeral Rites.* New Delhi: D. K. Printworld, 1996.

Forsthoefel, Thomas A. "Śaṅkara." In *Brill's Encyclopedia of Hinduism*, edited by K. A. Jacobsen, H. Basu, A. Malinar, and V. Narayanan. Brill Online, 2012.

Fort, Andrew O. "*Jīvanmukti* and Social Service in Advaita and Neo-Vedānta." In *Beyond Orientalism: The Work of Wilhelm Halbfass and Its Impact on*

Indian and Cross-Cultural Studies, edited by E. Franco and K. Preisendanz, 489–504. Amsterdam/Atlanta: Rodopi, 1997.

Foxen, Anya P. *Biography of a Yogi: Paramahansa Yogananda and the Origins of Modern Yoga*. New York: Oxford University Press, 2017.

Fracchia, Margherita. *Swami Sivananda e la* Divine Life Society. *Analisi della figura e del ruolo del guru e della sua istituzione nella riforma neo-hindu e nella diffusione dello yoga in Occidente*. MA Thesis, Università degli Studi di Padova–Università Ca' Foscari Venezia, 2009.

French, Harold W. "Swami Vivekananda's Use of the *Bhagavadgita*." In *Modern Indian Interpreters of the Bhagavadgita*, edited by R. N. Minor, 131–46. Albany: State University of New York Press, 1986.

Frøystad, Kathinka. "The Mediated Guru: Simplicity, Instantaneity, and Change in Middle-Class Religious Seeking." In *The Guru in South Asia: New Interdisciplinary Perspectives*, edited by J. Copeman and A. Ikegame, 181–201. London and New York: Routledge, 2012.

Gandhi, S. "Yogananda and the Self-Realization Fellowship." In *Brill's Encyclopedia of Hinduism*, edited by K. A. Jacobsen, H. Basu, A. Malinar, and V. Narayanan. Brill Online, 2012.

Gansten, Martin. "Modern Astrologers." In *Brill's Encyclopedia of Hinduism*, edited by K. A. Jacobsen, H. Basu, A. Malinar, and V. Narayanan. Brill Online, 2012.

Gibellini, Rosino. *La teologia del XX secolo*. Edizione attualizzata con una Appendice "Il passo del Duemila in teologia." Brescia: Queriniana, 2014^7.

Gokak, Vinayak Krishna. *Bhagavan Sri Sathya Sai Baba: The Man and the Avatar (An Interpretation)*. New Delhi: Abhinav Publications, 1983 (1975).

———. *The Advent of Sathya Sai*. Gauhati: Sri Sathya Sai Prakashan, 1977.

Goldberg, Ellen. *The Lord Who Is Half Woman: Ardhanārīśvara in Indian and Feminist Perspective*. Albany: State University of New York Press, 2002.

Goldberg, Michelle. *The Goddess Pose: The Audacious Life of Indra Devi, the Woman who Helped Bring Yoga to the West*. London: Corsair, 2015.

Govindanātha. *Il poema di Śaṅkara*. Śrīśaṅkarācāryacarita, edited by M. Piantelli. Torino: Promolibri, 1994.

Granoff, Phyllis. "Scholars and Wonder-workers: Some Remarks on the Role of the Supernatural in Philosophical Contests in Vedanta Hagiographies." *Journal of the American Oriental Society* 105, no. 3 (1985): 459–69.

———. "The Miracle of a Hagiography Without Miracles: Some Comments on the Jain Lives of the Pratyekabuddha Karakaṇḍa." *Journal of Indian Philosophy* 16 (1986): 1–15.

———. "The Politics of Religious Biography: The Biography of Balibhadra the Usurper." *Bulletin d'Études Indiennes* 9 (1991): 75–91.

Granoff, Phyllis, and Koichi Shinohara, eds. *Monks and Magicians: Religious Biographies in Asia*. Oakville, Ontario: Mosaic Press, 1988.

Green, Nile. "Making a 'Muslim' Saint: Writing Customary Religion in an Indian Princely State." *Comparative Studies of South Asia, Africa and the Middle East* 25, no. 3 (2005): 617–33.

Gregg, Stephen E. *Swami Vivekananda and Non-Hindu Traditions: A Universal Advaita.* London/New York: Routledge, 2019.

Gries, David, and Elaine Gries, eds. *An Index of Sathya Sai Speaks, volumes I–XI. Covering Discourses by Bhagavan Sri Sathya Sai Baba 1953–1982.* Tustin, CA: Sathya Sai Book Center of America, 1993.

Gunaji, Nagesh Vasudev. *Shri Sai Satcharita.* Shirdi: Shirdi Sansthan, 1982.

Gupta, Mahendranath ("M"). *The Gospel of Sri Ramakrishna* (Sri Sri Ramakrishna Kathamrita). Translated from the Bengali by Swami Nikhilananda. Foreword by Aldous Huxley. New York: Ramakrishna-Vivekananda Center, 1942.

Gussner, R. E. "A Stylometric Study of the Authorship of Seventeen Sanskrit Hymns Attributed to Śaṅkara." *Journal of the American Oriental Society* 96, no. 2 (1976): 259–67.

Halbfass, Wilhelm. *India and Europe: An Essay in Understanding.* Albany: State University of New York Press, 1988.

———. "Practical Vedānta." In *Representing Hinduism: The Construction of Religious Traditions and National Identity*, edited by V. Dalmia and H. von Stietencron, 211–23. New Delhi: Sage, 1995.

———. *Tradition and Reflection: Explorations in Indian Thought.* Albany: State University of New York Press, 1991.

———, ed. *Philology and Confrontation: Paul Hacker on Traditional and Modern Vedānta.* Albany: State University of New York Press, 1995.

Haraldsson, Erlendur. *Modern Miracles: An Investigative Report on Psychic Phenomena Associated with Sri Sathya Sai Baba.* Mamaroneck, NY: Hastings House, 1997 (Rev. ed.: *Modern Miracles: Sathya Sai Baba: The Story of a Modern Day Prophet.* Guildford: White Crow Books, 2013).

———. "True to His Nation." In *Golden Age, 1980*, 255–56. Prasanthi Nilayam: Sri Sathya Sai Books and Publications Trust, 1980.

Hardy, Friedhelm E. *Viraha Bhakti: The Early History of Kṛṣṇa Devotion in South India.* New York: Oxford University Press, 1983.

Hari Rao, V. N. *History of the Srirangam Temple.* Tirupathi: Sri Venkateshwara Historical Series, 1976.

Hawkins, Sophie. "Bordering Realism: The Aesthetics of Sai Baba's Mediated Universe." In *Image Journeys: Audio-Visual Media and Cultural Change in India*, edited by Ch. Brosius and M. Butcher, 139–62. New Delhi: Sage, 1999.

Hawley, Jack. *Reawakening the Spirit in Work: The Power of Dharmic Management.* San Francisco: Berrett-Koehler, 1993.

Hawley, John Stratton, and Kimberley Christine Patton, eds. *Holy Tears: Weeping in the Religious Imagination.* Princeton: Princeton University Press, 2005.

Hawley, Michael. "Sarvepalli Radhakrishnan (1888–1975)." In *Internet Encyclopedia of Philosophy*; http://www.iep.utm.edu/radhakri/#SH1d

Hedayetullah, Muhammad. *Kabir: The Apostle of Hindu-Muslim Unity: Interaction of Hindu-Muslim Ideas in the Formation of the Bhakti Movement with Special Reference to Kabir, the Bhakta.* New Delhi: Motilal Banarsidass, 1977.

Heehs, P. *The Lives of Sri Aurobindo*. New York: Columbia University Press, 2008.

Hiltebeitel, Alf. *Dharma: Its Early History in Law, Religion, and Narrative*. New York: Oxford University Press, 2011.

Hislop, John S. *Conversations with Bhagavan Sri Sathya Sai Baba*. Bangalore: Sri Sathya Sai Baba Society of America, 1979.

———. *My Baba and I*. San Diego: Birth Day, 1985.

———. "The International Problem." In *Golden Age 1980*, 172–74. Prasanthi Nilayam: Sri Sathya Sai Books and Publications Trust, 1980.

———. "Three Stories." In *Golden Age 1980*, 175–77. Prasanthi Nilayam: Sri Sathya Sai Books and Publications Trust, 1980.

Holdrege, Barbara. *Bhakti and Embodiment: Fashioning Divine Bodies and Devotional Bodies in Kṛṣṇa Bhakti*. London: Routledge, 2013.

Hopkinson, Tom, and Dorothy Hopkinson. *Much Silence: Meher Baba: His Life and Work*. New York: Dodd, Mead, 1974.

Hudson, Dennis. "Early Evidence of the *Pāñcarātra Āgama*." In *The Roots of Tantra*, edited by K. A. Harper and R. L. Brown, 133–67. Albany: State University of New York Press, 2002.

Isherwood, Christopher. *Ramakrishna and His Disciples*. London: Methuen, 1965.

Jackson, Carl T. *Vedanta for the West: The Ramakrishna Movement in the United States*. Bloomington: Indiana University Press, 1994.

Jacobs, Stephen. "Communicating Hinduism in a Changing Media Context," *Religion Compass* 6, no. 2 (2012): 136–51.

Jacobsen, Knut Axel, ed. *Yoga Powers: Extraordinary Capacities Attained Through Meditation and Concentration*. Leiden: Brill, 2012.

Jaffrelot, Christophe, and Gilles Tarabout. "Les transformations de l'hindouisme." In *L'Inde contemporaine. De 1990 à aujourd'hui*, edited by Ch. Jaffrelot. Paris: Fayard/Pluriel, 2014.

Jagadeesan, J. "Experiences with the Divine Presence." In *The Splendour of Sathya Sai*, 78–81. Hyderabad: Sri Prasanthi Society, 1995.

———. *Journey to God—Part 2*. Kuala Lumpur, 1981.

———. *Sai Baba: The Journey Within. Journey to God, Part III*. Prasanthi Nilayam: Sri Sathya Sai Books and Publications, 1989.

Jarow, E. H. Rick. *Tales for the Dying: The Death Narrative of the* Bhāgavata-Purāṇa. Albany: State University of New York Press, 2003.

Joshi, Hariprasad Shivprasad. *Origin and Development of Dattātreya Worship in India*. Baroda: The Maharaja Sayajirao University of Baroda Press, 1965.

Jośī, P. N. *Śrīdattātreyajñānkoś*. Bombay: Surekha Prakashan, 1974.

Junnarkar, Anil Raghunāth. *Gūḍhramy Gurutrayī Śrī Sāī Śrī Upāsanī Śrī Godāī*. Sākurī: Śrī Upāsanī Kanyākumārī Sthān, 2017.

Kakade, R. T., and A. Veerabhadra Rao. *Shirdi to Puttaparthi*. Hyderabad: Ira Publications, 1990.

Kalyana Kalpataru. *The Divine Name Number*, vol. 5, no. 1. Gorakhpur: Gita Press, 1938.

Kamaraju, Anil Kumar. *Memories and Memoirs: Four Decades of Journey with God*. Prasanthi Nilayam: Sri Sathya Sai Books and Publications Trust, 2015.

Kamath, M. V., and V. B. Kher. *Sai Baba of Shirdi: A Unique Saint*. Bombay: Jaico, 1991.

Kanu, Victor. "My Spiritual Journey to Sathya Sai Baba." In *Golden Age 1980*, 163–69. Prasanthi Nilayam: Sri Sathya Sai Books and Publications Trust, 1980.

———. *Sai Baba, God Incarnate*. London: Sawbridge, 1981.

Kapferer, Bruce. "Introduction. Outside All Reason: Magic, Sorcery, and Epistemology in Anthropology." In *Beyond Rationalism: Rethinking Magic, Witchcraft, and Sorcery*, edited by B. Kapferer, 1–30. New York/Oxford: Berghahn Books, 2003.

Karandikar, N. S. *Biography of Sri Swami Samarth Akkalkot Maharaj*. Bombay: Akkalkot Swami Math, 1978.

Karanjia, Rustom Khurshedji. *God Lives in India*. Puttaparthi: Saindra, 1994.

Kent, Alexandra. *Divinity and Diversity: A Hindu Revitalization Movement in Malaysia*. Honolulu: University of Hawai'i Press, 2005.

———. "Divinity, Miracles, and Charity in the Sathya Sai Baba Movement of Malaysia." *Ethnos* 69, no. 1 (March 2004): 43–62.

Keune, Jon. "Eknāth." In *Brill's Encyclopedia of Hinduism*, edited by K. A. Jacobsen, H. Basu, A. Malinar, and V. Narayanan. Brill Online, 2012.

———. "Gathering the Bhaktas in Marāṭhī." In *Journal of Vaishnava Studies* 15, no. 2 (2007): 169–88.

Kheirabadi, Masoud. *Sri Satya Sai Baba*. Introductory essay by Martin E. Marty. Spiritual Leaders and Thinkers Series. Philadelphia: Chelsea House, 2005.

Kher, Indira. *Avadhuta Yogi Pant Maharaj of Balekundri*. Bombay: Bharatiya Vidya Bhavan, 1994.

Kher, V. B. *Sai Baba: His Divine Glimpses*. Foreword by M. V. Kamath. New Delhi: New Dawn, 2001.

Killingley, D. H. "Vivekananda." In *Brill's Encyclopedia of Hinduism*, edited by K. A. Jacobsen, H. Basu, A. Malinar, and V. Narayanan. Brill Online, 2012.

Knipe, David M. "Softening the Cruelty of God: Folklore, Ritual, and the Planet Śani (Saturn) in Southeast India." In *Syllables of Sky: Studies in South Indian Civilization in Honour of Velcheru Narayana Rao*, edited by D. Shulman, 206–48. Delhi: Oxford University Press, 1995.

———. *Vedic Voices: Intimate Narratives of a Living Andhra Tradition*. New York: Oxford University Press, 2015.

Kondappa, V. C. *Sai's Story: As Revealed by Sathya Sai to His Teacher*. Foreword by B. Subbannachar. Bangalore: Sai Towers, 2004.

Kovoor, Abraham. *Bygone Godmen! Encounters with Spiritual Frauds*. Bombay: Jaico, 1976.

Kripal, Jeffrey J. *Kālī's Child: The Mystic and the Erotic in the Life and Teachings of Ramakrishna*. Chicago: Chicago University Press, 1998.

Krishnamurti, Bh. "Shift of Authority in Written and Oral Texts: The Case of Telugu." In *Syllables of Sky: Studies in South Indian Civilization in Honour of Velcheru Narayana Rao*, edited by D. Shulman, 76–102. Delhi: Oxford University Press, 1995.

Krishnayya, M. V. "Dattatreya Worship in the Popular Hinduism of Coastal Andhra." In *Incompatible Visions: South Asian Religions in History and Culture. Essays in Honor of David M. Knipe*, edited by J. Blumenthal, 171–83. Madison, WI: Center for South Asia, 2005.

Krystal, Phyllis. *Sai Baba: The Ultimate Experience*. Los Angeles: Aura Books, 1985.

———. "The Guide Within." In *The Splendour of Sathya Sai*, 121–23. Hyderabad: Sri Prasanthi Society, 1995.

Kulkarnee, Narayan H. "Medieval Maharashtra and Muslim Saint-Poets." In *Medieval Bhakti Movements in India: Śrī Caitanya Quincentenary Commemoration Volume*, edited by N. N. Bhattacharyya, 198–231. New Delhi: Munshiram Manoharlal, 1989.

Kulkarni, K. R. *The Saint of Shegaon: A Book of Poems on the Life of Shri Gajanan Maharaj*. Nagpur, 1969.

Kulkarni, S. D. *Shri Satya Sai, the Fount of Vedic Culture: Vedas are the Heritage of Mankind*. Bombay: Shri Bhagawana Vedavyasa Itihasa Samsodhana Mandira, 1992.

———. *Shri Satya Sai, the Yugavatara: Scientific Analysis of Baba Phenomenon*. Bombay: Shri Bhagawana Vedavyasa Itihasa Samsodhana Mandira, 1990.

Kunden, H. N. *Ekmukhī Śrīdatta*. Puṇe: Ulhas Cintamani Latkar, 1997.

Kuvempu. *Shri Ramayana Darshanam*. Translated by Shankar Mokashi-Punekar. New Delhi: Sahitya Akademi, 2004.

Laing, Ron. "The Second Coming Has Come!" In *Golden Age 1980*, 15–22. Prasanthi Nilayam: Sri Sathya Sai Books and Publications Trust, 1980.

Lallement, M. *Swâmi Siddheswarânanda et son temps*. Tomes 3. Paris: Les Éditions du Petit Véhicule, 2006–07.

Lapham, Lewis H. *With the Beatles*. Hoboken: Melville House, 2005.

Larios, Borayin. *Embodying the Vedas: Traditional Vedic Schools of Contemporary Maharashtra*. Berlin: Walter de Gruyter, 2017.

Larson, Gerald James. *India's Agony over Religion*. Albany: State University of New York Press, 1995.

Leela, M. L. *Lokanatha Sai.* Madras: Sri Sathya Sai Mandali Trust, n.d.

Lessons for Study Circle. Prasanthi Nilayam: World Council Sri Sathya Sai Organisations, 1982.

Levin, Howard. *Good Chances.* Introduction by Elsie Cowan. Prasanthi Nilayam: Sai Towers, 1998 (3rd Reprint).

———. *Heart to Heart: "A Sequel to* Good Chances.*"* Bangalore: Sai Towers, 1996.

Life of Sri Ramakrishna. Compiled from Various Authentic Sources. With a foreword by M. K. Gandhi. Calcutta: Advaita Ashrama, 1964 (1924).

Llewellyn, J. E. "Gurus and Groups." In *Contemporary Hinduism: Ritual, Culture, and Practice*, edited by R. Rinehart, 213–41. Santa Barbara/Denver/Oxford: ABC CLIO, 2004.

Loar, Jonathan. "From Neither/Nor to Both/And: Reconfiguring the Life and Legacy of Shirdi Sai Baba in Hagiography." *International Journal of Hindu Studies* 22 (2018): 475–96.

Lorenzen, David N. *Kabir Legends and Ananta-Das's "Kabir-Parachai."* Albany: State University of New York Press, 1991.

———. "The Life of Śaṅkarācārya." In *The Biographical Process: A Study in the History and Psychology of Religion*, edited by F. E. Reynolds and D. Capps, 87–107. Berlin: Walter de Gruyter, 1976.

———. "The Social Ideologies of Hagiography: Śaṅkara, Tukārām and Kabīr." In *Religion and Society in Maharashtra*, edited by M. Israel and N. K. Wagle, 92–114. Toronto: University of Toronto Centre for South Asian Studies, 1987.

———. *Who Invented Hinduism? Essays on Religion in History.* New Delhi: Yoda Press, 2006.

Lorenzen, David, and Uma Thukral. "Los Dialogos Religiosos entre Kabir y Gorakh." *Estudios de Asia y Africa* 126, XL, no. 1 (2005): 161–77.

Lubin, Timothy. "Science, Patriotism, and Mother Veda: Ritual Activism in Maharashtra." *International Journal of Hindu Studies* 5, no. 3 (2001): 81–105.

Lucia, Amanda. "Innovative Gurus: Tradition and Change in Contemporary Hinduism." *International Journal of Hindu Studies* 18, no. 2 (2014): 221–63.

Lutgendorf, Philip. *The Life of a Text: Performing the* Rāmcaritmānas *of Tulsidas.* Berkeley/Los Angeles: University of California Press, 1991.

Madaio, James. "Rethinking Neo-Vedānta: Swami Vivekananda and the Selective Historiography of Advaita Vedānta." *Religions* 8, 101 (2017): 1–12.

Malinar, Angelika. "Rādhāramaṇa Caraṇa Dās und die Caitanya-Nachfolge in Orissa: Zur Textualisierung von Charisma." In *Tohfa-e-Dil. Festschrift für Helmuth Nespital*, edited by D. Lönne, 295–313. Reinbek: Verlag für Orientalistische Fachpublikationen, 2001.

———. *The Bhagavadgītā: Doctrines and Contexts.* New York: Cambridge University Press, 2007.

Mallinson, James. "Nāth Sampradāya." In *Brill's Encyclopedia of Hinduism*, edited by K. A. Jacobsen, H. Basu, A. Malinar, and V. Narayanan. Brill Online, 2012.

Mallison, Françoise. "Introduction." In *Constructions hagiographiques dans le monde indien. Entre mythe et histoire*, edited by F. Mallison, vii–xxviii. Paris: Librairie Honoré Champion, 2001.

———, éd. *Constructions hagiographiques dans le monde indien. Entre mythe et histoire*. Paris: Librairie Honoré Champion, 2001.

Malyala, P. "Sri Shirdi Sai Baba—Avatar." *Sri Sai Leela*. Newsletter of the Sri Shirdi Sai Baba Temple of Monroeville, PA (2012): 4.

Mason, Peggy. "Coming Home." In *Golden Age 1980*, 126–32. Prasanthi Nilayam: Sri Sathya Sai Books and Publications Trust, 1980.

Mason, Peggy, and Ron Laing. *Sathya Sai Baba: Embodiment of Love*. London: Sawbridge, 1982.

Mason, Peggy, Sandra Lévy, and M. Veeravahu, eds. *Sai Humour*. Prasanthi Nilayam: Sri Sathya Sai Towers Hotels, 1996.

Mazzoleni, Mario. *A Catholic Priest Meets Sai Baba*. Faber, VA: Leela Press, 1994.

McGregor, Stuart. "Kabīr's Language: Notes on Data from Selected Texts." In *Images of Kabīr*, edited by M. Horstmann, 73–84. New Delhi: Manohar, 2002.

McKean, Lisa. *Divine Enterprise: Gurus and the Hindu Nationalist Movement*. Chicago: University of Chicago Press, 1996.

McLain, Karline. "Be United, Be Virtuous: Composite Culture and the Growth of Shirdi Sai Baba Devotion." *Nova Religio: The Journal of Alternative and Emergent Religions* 15, no. 2 (2011): 20–49.

———. "Praying for Peace and Amity: The Shri Shirdi Sai Heritage Foundation Trust." In *Public Hinduisms*, edited by J. Zavos, P. Kanungo, D. S. Reddy, M. Warrier, and R. B. Williams, 190–209. New Delhi: Sage, 2012.

———. *The Afterlife of Sai Baba: Competing Visions of a Global Saint*. Seattle and London: University of Washington Press, 2016.

Meher Baba. *Discourses*. San Francisco: Sufism Reoriented, 1967.

———. *God Speaks: The Theme of Creation and Its Purpose*. New York: Dodd, Mead, 1955.

Meier, John P. *A Marginal Jew: Rethinking the Historical Jesus. Vol. 2. Mentor, Message, and Miracles*. New York: Doubleday, 1994.

Meier, V. "Song Choices of Swiss Sathya Sai Baba Devotees." *Diskus: The Journal of the British Association for the Study of Religions* 16, no. 1 (2014): 68–81.

Menon, A. K., and A. Malik. "Test of Faith." *India Today* 25, no. 49 (2000): 41–45.

Miller, D. M. "The Divine Life Society Movement." In *Religion in Modern India*, edited by R. D. Baird, 81–112. Delhi: Manohar, 1981.

Minajagi, S. *Vinayaka Krishna Gokak (Vinayaka)*. New Delhi: Sahitya Akademi, 1999.

Mines, Mattison, and Vijayalakshmi Gourishankar. "Leadership and Individuality in South Asia: The Case of the South Indian Big-man." *The Journal of Asian Studies* 49, no. 4 (1990): 761–86.

Morse, J. G. "The Literary Guru: The Dual Emphasis on *bhakti* and *vidhi* in Western Indian Guru-Devotion." In *The Guru in South Asia: New Interdisciplinary Perspectives*, edited by J. Copeman and A. Ikegame, 222–40. London/New York: Routledge, 2012.

Murphet, Howard. *Sai Baba: Invitation to Glory*. New Delhi: MacMillan, 1989 (1982).

———. *Sai Baba: Man of Miracles*. New Delhi: Macmillan, 1981 (London 1971).

———. *Sai Baba Avatar: A New Journey into Power and Glory*. San Diego: Birth Day, 1977.

———. "The Finger of God." In *Golden Age, 1980*, 35–40. Prasanthi Nilayam: Sri Sathya Sai Books and Publications Trust, 1980.

———. *Where the Road Ends*. N. S. W. Australia: Butterfly Books, 1993.

Murthy, M. Venkata Narayana. *Mica Fields of India*. New Delhi, 1964.

———. *The Greatest Adventure: Essays on the Sai Avatar and His Message*. Prasanthi Nilayam: Sri Sathya Sai Books and Publications, 1983.

———. *Who Is a Devotee of the Lord: Talks in Prasanthi Nilayam on the Ghagavad* [sic] *Gita (12th Chapter)*. Prasanthi Nilayam: Sri Sathya Sai Books and Publications, 2005.

———, ed. *Research Papers in Petrology by Officers of the Geological Survey of India*. Delhi: Manager of Publications, 1964.

———, ed. *Zircon: A Collection of Research Papers*. Delhi: Manager of Publications, 1969.

Murthy, M., Venkata Narayana, S. N. P. Vastava, and A. Dube. *Indian Meteorites*. Calcutta: Geological Survey of India, 1968.

Nanda, Meera. *The God Market: How Globalisation Is Making India More Hindu*. Delhi: Random House, 2009.

Nanjundayya, H. V., and Rao Bahadur L. K. Ananthakrishna Iyer. *The Mysore Tribes and Castes*. 4 Vols. University of Mysore, 1928.

Narasappa A. P., R. Narasappa, and R. Seethalakshmi, trans. *Sahasradalakamala (1008 Names of Bhagavan Sri Sathya Sai Baba)*. With English translation. Bangalore: Brindavan Printers, 1985.

Narasimha Murthy, A. V. "Sri Venka Avadhoota"; http://www.ourkarnataka.com/Articles/starofmysore/venka009.htm (June 17, 2010)

Narasimha Murthy, B. N. *Sathya Sai Divya Anandam*. Muddenahalli: Sri Sathya Sai Premamruta Prakashana, 2013.

———. *Sathya Sai Divya Sannidhi*. Prasanthi Nilayam: Sri Sathya Sai Sadhana Trust, 2011.

———. *Sathyam Sivam Sundaram. Vol. 5. Life Story of Bhagawan Sri Sathya Sai Baba, 1980–85*. Prasanthi Nilayam: Sri Sathya Sai Sadhana Trust, 2014 (2005).

———. *Sathyam Sivam Sundaram. Vol. 6. Life Story of Bhagawan Sri Sathya Sai Baba 1986–1993*. Prasanthi Nilayam: Sri Sathya Sai Sadhana Trust, 2007.

———. *Sathyam Sivam Sundaram. Vol. 7. Life Story of Bhagawan Sri Sathya Sai Baba 1994–2001*. Prasanthi Nilayam: Sri Sathya Sai Sadhana Trust, 2010.

———. *Sri Sathya Sai Divya Kripashraya*. Prasanthi Nilayam: Sri Sathya Sai Sadhana Trust, 2010.

———, ed. *Sri Sathya Sai Uvacha, Vol. 1. Divine Discourses of Bhagawan Sri Sathya Sai Baba in the Subtle Body (May to September 2014)*. Muddenahalli: Sri Sathya Sai Premamruta Prakashana, 2014.

Narasimhan, V. K. "What Sri Sathya Sai Baba Means to Me." In *Golden Age 1980*, 12–14. Prasanthi Nilayam: Sri Sathya Sai Books and Publications Trust, 1980.

Narasimhaswami, B. V. *Devotees' Experiences of Sri Sai Baba, Parts I, II, & III*. Mylapore, Chennai: All India Sai Samaj, 2006 (Madras, 1940).

———. *Life of Sai Baba*. 4 Vols. Madras: All India Sai Samaj, 1980–85 (1955–56).

———. *Sri Sai Baba's Charters and Sayings*. Foreword by M. B. Rege. Madras: All India Sai Samaj, 1942.

Narayan, Kirin. *Storytellers, Saints, and Scoundrels: Folk Narrative in Hindu Religious Teaching*. Philadelphia: University of Pennsylvania Press, 1989.

Narayanan, Vasudha. "United States." In *Brill's Encyclopedia of Hinduism*, edited by K. A. Jacobsen, H. Basu, A. Malinar, and V. Narayanan. Brill Online, 2012.

———. "Veṅkaṭeśvara." In *Brill's Encyclopedia of Hinduism, Vol. 1. Regions, Pilgrimage, Deities*, edited by K. A. Jacobsen, H. Basu, A. Malinar, and V. Narayanan, 781–85. Leiden: Brill, 2009.

"National Conference of Bal Vikas Gurus." *Sanathana Sarathi* 37, no. 8 (August 1994): 208.

Neelima, Kota. *Tirupati: A Guide to Life*. Noida: Random House India, 2012.

Nichols, A. *A Key to Balthasar: Hans Urs von Balthasar on Beauty, Goodness, and Truth*. London: Darton, Longman and Todd, 2011.

Nikhilananda, Swami. *Vivekananda: A Biography*. New York: Ramakrishna-Vivekananda Center, 1953.

———, trans. *The Gospel of Sri Ramakrishna*. New York: Ramakrishna-Vivekananda Center, 1942.

Nimbalkar, M. B. *Shri Sai Baba's Teachings and Philosophy*. New Delhi: New Dawn, 2001.

Nisargadatta Maharaj. *Non Dualismo*. Prefazione di Giuseppe Genna. Milano: il Saggiatore, 2017.

Notovitch, Nicolas. *The Unknown Life of Jesus: The Original Text of Nicolas Notovitch's 1887 Discovery*. Sanger, CA: Quill Driver Books, 2004 (New York: 1890).

Olivelle, Patrick, ed., *Dharma: Studies in Its Semantic, Cultural, and Religious History*. Delhi: Motilal Banarsidass, 2009.

———, ed., trans. *Rules and Regulations of Brahmanical Asceticism:* Yatidharmasamuccaya *of Yādava Prakāśa*. Albany: State University of New York Press, 1995.

———, trans. *Saṃnyāsa Upaniṣads: Hindu Scriptures on Asceticism and Renunciation*. New York: Oxford University Press, 1992.

———, trans. *Upaniṣads*. New York: Oxford University Press, 1996.

Orlando, Francesco. *Il soprannaturale letterario. Storia, logica e forme*. Edited by S. Brugnolo, L. Pellegrini, and V. Sturli. Preface by Thomas Pavel. Torino: Einaudi, 2017.

Osborne, Arthur. *The Incredible Sai Baba*. New Delhi: Orient Longmans, 1970 (1957).

Osis, Karlis. "Parapsychology and Sathya Sai Baba." In *Golden Age 1980*, 257–58. Prasanthi Nilayam: Sri Sathya Sai Books and Publications Trust, 1980.

Padmanaban, Ranganathan. "Baba Develops a Professional Photographer: The Material Is No Different From the Spiritual for Baba." *Spiritual Impressions* 1, no. 2 (May–June 2001): 22–23.

———. *Love Is My Form: A Biographical Series on Sri Sathya Sai Baba*. Vol. 1: *The Advent (1926–1950)*. Bangalore: Sai Towers Publishing, 2000.

———. "V. C. Kondappa: The Teacher Biographer." *Spiritual Impressions* 1, no. 2 (May–June 2001): 56–60.

Pain, Charles, with Eleanor Zelliot. "The God Dattatreya and the Datta Temples of Pune." In *The Experience of Hinduism: Essays on Religion in Maharashtra*, edited by E. Zelliot and M. Berntsen, 95–108. Albany: State University of New York Press, 1988.

Palmer, Norris W. "Baba's World: A Global Guru and His Movement." In *Gurus in America*, edited by Th. A. Forsthoefel and C. A. Humes, 97–122. Albany: State University of New York Press, 2005.

Paranjape, Makarand R. ed. *Swami Vivekananda: A Contemporary Reader*. New Delhi: Routledge, 2015.

Patel, M., and N. Patel. *Bhajanamavali (For Overseas Devotees)*. Bombay: St. Francis I.T.I., n.d.

Peddabottu (Gali Sharada Devi). *Autobiography*. Translated by Dr. Sathya Sai Shree Lakshmi. Hyderabad: Visual Graphix & Printing, 2013.

Pelissero, Alberto. *Estetica indiana*. Brescia: Morcelliana, 2019.

Penn, Charles. "At His Blue Lotus Feet." In *Golden Age 1980*, 46–50. Prasanthi Nilayam: Sri Sathya Sai Books and Publications Trust, 1980.

———. *My Beloved. The Love and Teaching of Bhagavan Sri Sathya Sai Baba*. Prasanthi Nilayam: Sri Sathya Sai Baba Books and Publications, 1981.

Peterson, Indira Viswanathan. "The Drama of the Kuṟavañci Fortune-teller: Land, Landscape, and Social Relations in an Eighteenth-century Tamil Genre." In *Tamil Geographies: Cultural Constructions of Space and Place in South India*, edited by M. A. Selby and I. V. Peterson, 59–86. Albany: State University of New York Press, 2008.

Pfeffer, Georg. "Kinship and Marriage." In *Brill's Encyclopedia of Hinduism*, edited by K. A. Jacobsen, H. Basu, A. Malinar, and V. Narayanan. Brill Online, 2012.

Phipps, Peter. *Sathya Sai Baba and Jesus Christ: A Gospel for the Golden Age*. Auckland: Sathya Sai Publications of New Zealand, 1994.

Piantelli, Mario. "Prefazione." In H. Murphet, *Sai Baba l'uomo dei miracoli*, 7–12. Torino: Edizioni Sadhana, 1972.

———. *Śaṅkara e la rinascita del brāhmanesimo*. Fossano: Editrice Esperienze, 1974.

Pipes, R. E. "The Oneness of Jesus Christ and Sathya Sai Baba." In *Golden Age 1980*, 57–63. Prasanthi Nilayam: Sri Sathya Sai Books and Publications Trust, 1980.

Pisu, Renata. "Con il lama Tucci sul Tetto del Mondo. Parla il famoso orientalista e esploratore, che sta per compiere novant'anni." *La Stampa*, 20 ottobre 1983, 3.

Prabhu, V. R., ed. *Shree Swami Samarth Akkalkot Maharaj (As The Eternal Sage)*. Mumbai: Jaico Publishing House, 1997.

Pradhan, R. B. M. W. *Shri Sai Baba of Shirdi: A Glimpse of Indian Spirituality*. Shirdi: Shree Sai Baba Sansthan, 1982.

Prasanthi Nilayam Information Booklet. Compiled by Public Relations Office, Sri Sathya Sai Central Trust, Prasanthi Nilayam. Prasanthi Nilayam: Sri Sathya Sai Sadhana Trust, 2015.

Premanand, Basava. *Sathya Sai Baba and the Gold Control Act*. Podanur: Indian CSICOP, 1986.

———. *The Lure of Miracles*. Podanur: Indian CSICOP, 1982.

Prentiss, Karen P. *The Embodiment of Bhakti*. New York: Oxford University Press, 1999.

Priddy, Robert. *Source of the Dream: My Way to Sathya Sai Baba*. York Beach, ME: Samuel Weiser, 1998.

Purdom, Charles Benjamin. *God to Man and Man to God: The Discourses of Meher Baba*. North Myrtle Beach, SC: Sheriar Press, 1975.

Purnaiya, Nagamani. *The Divine Leelas of Sri Satya Sai Baba*. Bangalore: House of Seva, 1976.

Radice, William, ed. *Swami Vivekananda and the Modernization of Hinduism*. New Delhi: Oxford University Press, 1998.

Raghavan, K. *Guide to Indian Culture and Spirituality. Based on the Divine Teachings of Bhagawan Sri Sri Sri Sathya Sai Baba*. Prasanthi Nilayam: Sri Sathya Sai Books and Publications, 1990.

Raghunathan, S. "The Story of 'Jodi Adi Palli Somappa.'" *Divine Grace: Sathya Sai Baba. An India Today Impact Presentation*. The India Today Group, 2011, 54–55.

Raghuramaraju, Adluru, ed. *Debating Vivekananda: A Reader*. New York: Oxford University Press, 2014.

Rajagopal, Arvind. "Politics and Media." In *Brill's Encyclopedia of Hinduism*, edited by K. A. Jacobsen, H. Basu, A. Malinar, and V. Narayanan. Brill Online, 2012.

Rama Raju, B. "Sathya Sai as a Master of the Telugu Language and as a Writer." In *Sai Chandana: Book of Homage*, edited by V. K. Gokak, 287–94. Prasanthi Nilayam: Sri Sathya Sai Institute of Higher Learning, 1985.

Râmakrishna, Shrî. *Alla ricerca di Dio*. Parole raccolte e annotate da Jean Herbert. Roma: Ubaldini Editore, 1963.

Ramamurthy, K. *Sri Sathya Sai, Aanandadayi: Journey with Sai*. Prasanthi Nilayam: Sri Sathya Sai Publications, 2001.

Rao, M. N. *Sathya Sai Baba: God as Man*. Tustin, CA: Sathya Sai Baba Society and Sathya Sai Book Center of America, 1985.

Rao, Ursula. "Media Hinduism." In *Hinduism in India: Modern and Contemporary Movements*, edited by W. Sweetman and A. Malik, 123–40. New Delhi: Sage, 2016.

Reynolds, Frank E., and Donald Capps, eds. *The Biographical Process: A Study in the History and Psychology of Religion*. Berlin: Walter de Gruyter, 1976.

Rice, Bradley N. "The Apocryphal Tale of Jesus' Journey to India: Nicolas Notovitch and the *Life of Saint Issa* Revisited." In *Fakes, Forgeries, and Fictions: Writing Ancient and Modern Christian Apocrypha*, edited by T. Burke, 265–84. Proceedings of the 2015 York University Christian Apocrypha Symposium. Foreword by Andrew Gregory. Eugene, OR: Cascade Books, 2017.

Rigopoulos, Antonio. "A Modern *Kalpavṛkṣa*: Sathya Sāī Bābā and the Wish-Fulfilling Tree." In *Roots of Wisdom, Branches of Devotion: Plant Life in South Asian Traditions*, edited by F. M. Ferrari and Th. Dähnhardt, 3–28. Sheffield/Bristol: Equinox, 2016.

———. *Dattātreya: The Immortal Guru, Yogin, and Avatāra. A Study of the Transformative and Inclusive Character of a Multi-Faceted Hindu Deity*. Albany: State University of New York Press, 1998.

———. "Forms of Possession in the Marāṭhī Cultural Area: The Cases of Khaṇḍobā and Dattātreya." In *Shamanic Cosmos: From India to the North Pole Star*, edited by R. Mastromattei and A. Rigopoulos, 207–20. Delhi: D. K. Printworld, 1999.

———. *Guru: Il fondamento della civiltà dell'India*. Con la prima traduzione italiana del "Canto sul Maestro." Roma: Carocci, 2009.

———. "Observations on Śaṅkara's Nondualism in the Light of R. Panikkar's Thought." In *Fullness of Life*, edited by K. Acharya, M. Carrara Pavan, and W. Parker, 13–41. Mumbai/New Delhi: Somaiya, 2008.

———. "Sāī Bābā of Śirḍī and Yoga Powers." In *Yoga Powers: Extraordinary Capacities Attained Through Meditation and Concentration*, edited by K. A. Jacobsen, 381–426. Leiden: Brill, 2012.

———. "Shirdi Sai Baba." In *Brill's Encyclopedia of Hinduism*. Vol. 5. *Religious Symbols; Hinduism and Migration: Contemporary Communities Outside South Asia; Some Modern Religious Groups and Teachers*, edited by K. A. Jacobsen, H. Basu, A. Malinar, and V. Narayanan, 641–50. Leiden: Brill, 2013.

———. "Silenzio, gesto, parola: i linguaggi dell'Assoluto del Sai Baba di Shirdi." In *I linguaggi dell'Assoluto*, edited by M. Raveri and L. V. Tarca, 255–85. Milano/Udine: Mimesis, 2017.

———. "The Construction of a Cultic Center Through Narrative: The Founding Myth of the Village of Puttaparthi and Sathya Sāī Bābā." *History of Religions* 54, no. 2 (November 2014): 117–50.

———. "The *Guru-gītā* or 'Song of the Master' as Incorporated in the *Guru-caritra* of Sarasvatī Gaṅgādhar: Observations on Its Teachings and the *guru* Institute." In *Theory and Practice of Yoga: Essays in Honour of Gerald James Larson*, edited by K. A. Jacobsen, 237–92. Leiden/Boston: Brill, 2005.

———. *The Life and Teachings of Sai Baba of Shirdi*. Albany: State University of New York Press, 1993.

———. *The Mahānubhāvs*. London/New York/Delhi: Anthem Press, 2011.

———. "The Sanctity of the *audumbar* in Mahārāṣṭra." In *Tīrthayātrā: Essays in Honour of Stefano Piano*, edited by P. Caracchi, A. S. Comba, A. Consolaro, and A. Pelissero, 349–65. Alessandria: Edizioni dell'Orso, 2010.

———. "Tolerance in Swami Vivekānanda's Neo-Hinduism." *Philosophy and Social Criticism* 45, no. 4 (2019): 438–60.

———. "Trimūrti." In *Brill's Encyclopedia of Hinduism*. Vol. 6. *Index*, edited by K. A. Jacobsen, H. Basu, A. Malinar, and V. Narayanan, 81–90. Brill: Leiden, 2015.

———. "Vibhūti." In *Brill's Encyclopedia of Hinduism*. Vol. 5. *Religious Symbols; Hinduism and Migration: Contemporary Communities Outside South Asia; Some Modern Religious Groups and Teachers*, edited by K. A. Jacobsen, H. Basu, A. Malinar, and V. Narayanan, 181–83. Leiden: Brill, 2013.

Rinehart, Robin. *One Lifetime, Many Lives: The Experience of Modern Hindu Hagiography*. Atlanta: Scholars Press, 1999.

Risseuw, Carla. "Thinking Culture Through Counter-culture: The Case of Theosophists in India and Ceylon and Their Ideas on Race and Hierarchy (1875–1947)." In *Gurus and Their Followers: New Religious Reform Movements in Colonial India*, edited by A. Copley, 180–205. New Delhi: Oxford University Press, 2000.

Rocher, Ludo. *The Purāṇas*. Wiesbaden: Otto Harrassowitz, 1986.

Romano, Claudia. *Teoria e pratica del "Sathya Sai Education in Human Values Program."* BA Thesis, Università Ca' Foscari, Venezia, 1999.

Roof, J. *Pathways to God: A Study Guide to the Teachings of Sathya Sai Baba.* Faber, VA: Leela Press, 1991.

Rossner, C. J. "The Priest and the Avatar." In *Golden Age 1980*, 104–22. Prasanthi Nilayam: Sri Sathya Sai Books and Publications Trust, 1980.

Roumanoff, Daniel. *Candide au pays des Gourous. Journal d'un explorateur de l'Inde spirituelle.* Préface de Michel Hulin. Croissy-Beaubourg: Dervy-Livres, 1990.

Roy, Neeta. "Closer to God." In *Sai Baba and His Message: A Challenge to Behavioural Sciences*, edited by S. P. Ruhela and D. Robinson, 258–74. Delhi: Vikas, 1982.

Rudert, Angela. "Research on Contemporary Indian Gurus: What's New about New Age Gurus?" In *Religion Compass* 4, no. 10 (2010): 629–42.

Ruhela, Satya Pal. "Educational Reconstruction in the Sai Age." In *Sai Baba and His Message: A Challenge to Behavioural Sciences*, edited by S. P. Ruhela and D. Robinson, 171–94. Delhi: Vikas, 1982.

———. *In Search of Sai Divine: A Comprehensive Research Review of Writings and Researches on Sri Sathya Sai Baba Avatar.* New Delhi: Umang Paperbacks, 1996.

———. "Sai Baba: A Biographical Sketch." In *Sai Baba and His Message: A Challenge to Behavioural Sciences*, edited by S. P. Ruhela and D. Robinson, 1–22. Delhi: Vikas, 1982.

———. *Sai Trinity: Shirdi Sai, Sathya Sai, Prema Sai Incarnations.* Faridabad: Sai Age Publications, 1993.

———. *Sri Sathya Sai as Kalki Avatar.* Delhi: BR Publishing Corporation, 1996.

———. *Sri Sathya Sai Baba and the Press (1972–1996).* New Delhi: Umang Paperbacks, 1997.

———. *The Triple Incarnations of Sai Baba: Sri Shirdi Sai Baba, Sri Sathya Sai Baba, and Future Prema Sai Baba.* Gurgaon: Partridge India, 2015.

———. *The Truth in Controversies About Sri Shirdi Sai Baba.* Delhi: Indian Publishers' Distributors, 2000.

Rüstau, Hiltrud. "The Ramakrishna Mission: Its Female Aspect." In *Gurus and Their Followers: New Religious Reform Movements in Colonial India*, edited by A. Copley, 83–106. New Delhi: Oxford University Press, 2000.

Sahoo, Ajaya Kumar. *Religion, Diaspora, and Transnational Networks: The Case of Sri Sathya Sai Baba Movement.* PhD Diss., Shodhganga University of Hyderabad, 2006.

Sahoo, Ajaya Kumar, and Melissa Kelly. "Social Movements in the Diasporic Context: The Sathya Sai Baba Movement." In *The Political Economy of South Asian Diaspora: Patterns of Socio-Economic Influence*, edited by G. Pillai, 143–66. New York: Palgrave Macmillan, 2013.

Sahoo, Ajaya Kumar, and Johannes G. De Kruijf, eds. *Indian Transnationalism Online: New Perspectives on Diaspora.* Farnham: Ashgate, 2014.

Sai Sharan Anand, Swami. *Shri Sai Baba*. Translated from Gujarati by V. B. Kher. New Delhi: Sterling, 1997.

Sai Suprabhatam: Learning Sanskrit Through Sri Sathya Sai Suprabhatam. Prasanthi Nilayam: Sri Sathya Sai Students and Staff Welfare Society, 2009.

Saint-Mézard, Isabelle. *Atlas de l'Inde. Une nouvelle puissance mondiale*. Paris: Éditions Autrement, 2016.

Salguero, Susan. *When God Came Walking: 1978–1980 with Sathya Sai Baba*. Ojai, CA: StarBright Books, 2014.

Sampath, Vikram. *Splendours of Royal Mysore: The Untold Story of the Wodeyars*. New Delhi: Rupa, 2008.

Sanâtana Dharma: An Elementary Text-Book of Hindu Religion and Ethics. Benares: Central Hindu College, 1916.

Sandweiss, Samuel H. "A Garland for Baba." In *Golden Age 1980*, 84–87. Prasanthi Nilayam: Sri Sathya Sai Books and Publications Trust, 1980.

———. *Sai Baba: The Holy Man . . . and the Psychiatrist*. San Diego: Birth Day, 1975.

———. *Spirit and the Mind*. San Diego: Birth Day, 1985.

Sankar, Yassin. "Education in Crisis: A Value-Based Model of Education Provides Some Guidance." *Interchange* (2004): 127–51.

Saptarshi, Kumar. "Orthodoxy and Human Rights: The Story of a Clash." In *Experience of Hinduism: Essays on Religion in Maharashtra*, edited by E. Zelliot and M. Berntsen, 251–63. Albany: State University of New York Press, 1988.

Saraf, S. *Sai Vandana: Salutations to Lord Sai. Book of Homage*. Prasanthi Nilayam: Sri Sathya Sai Institute of Higher Learning, 1990.

Sathya Sai Baba, Shri. *Bhagavatha Vahini*. Translated by N. Kasturi. Bangalore: Sri Sathya Sai Education and Publication Foundation, 1979[3].

———. *Dhyana Vahini*. Prasanthi Nilayam: Sri Sathya Sai Books and Publications, 1980.

———. *Divine Message on Guru Poornima by Bhagawan Sri Sathya Sai Baba, 3rd July, 1993*. Bangalore: Sri Sathya Sai Publication Society, 1993.

———. *His Story as Told by Himself. A Compilation from the Divine Discourses of Bhagavan Sri Sathya Sai Baba*. Prasanthi Nilayam: Sri Sathya Sai Sadhana Trust, 2014.

———. "Revelations about the Sai Avatar." In *Sanathana Sarathi*, October 1990.

———. *Sadhana: The Inward Path. Quotations from the Divine Discourses of Bhagavan Sri Sathya Sai Baba*. Bangalore: Sri Sathya Sai Education and Publication Foundation, 1976 (Rev. ed. 1978).

———. *Sai Vani: Avatar on Mahapurushas*. Based on the Writings and Divine Discourses of Bhagavan Sri Sathya Sai Baba. Prasanthi Nilayam: Sai Publications, 2015.

———. *Sandeha Nivarini: Dissolving Doubts.* Prasanthi Nilayam: Sri Sathya Sai Sadhana Trust, 2014.

———. *Sathya Sai Speaks, vol. 1. Discourses of Bhagawan Sri Sathya Sai Baba (Delivered during 1953–1960).* Prasanthi Nilayam: Sri Sathya Sai Sadhana Trust, 2015 (2009).

———. *Sathya Sai Speaks, vol. 2. Discourses of Bhagawan Sri Sathya Sai Baba Delivered During 1961–62.* Prasanthi Nilayam: Sri Sathya Sai Books & Publications, 2008.

———. *Sathya Sai Speaks, vol. 3. Discourses of Bhagawan Sri Sathya Sai Baba (Delivered During 1963).* Prasanthi Nilayam: Sri Sathya Sai Books & Publications, 2008[2].

———. *Sathya Sai Speaks, vol. 5. Discourses of Bhagawan Sri Sathya Sai Baba Delivered During 1965.* Prasanthi Nilayam: Sri Sathya Sai Sadhana Trust, 2009[2].

———. *Sathya Sai Speaks, vol. 7. Discourses of Bhagavan Sri Sathya Sai Baba (Delivered During 1967).* Prasanthi Nilayam: Sri Sathya Sai Sadhana Trust, 2012.

———. *Sathya Sai Speaks, vol. 8. Discourses of Bhagawan Sri Sathya Sai Baba Delivered in 1968 (Including Six Discourses Given During Dasara).* Prasanthi Nilayam: Sri Sathya Sai Sadhana Trust, 2010.

———. *Sathya Sai Speaks, vol. 9. Discourses of Bhagawan Sri Sathya Sai Baba (Delivered during 1969, including Dasara Discourses).* Prasanthi Nilayam: Sri Sathya Sai Sadhana Trust, 2011.

———. *Sathya Sai Speaks, vol. 10. Discourses of Bhagavan Sri Sathya Sai Baba (Delivered During 1970).* Revised and Enlarged Edition. Prasanthi Nilayam: Sri Sathya Sai Sadhana Trust, 2011.

———. *Sathya Sai Vahini.* Prasanthi Nilayam: Sri Sathya Sai Books and Publications, 1981.

———. *Songs by Baba.* Compiled by Velugoti Sarvagna Kumar Krishna Yachendra Bahadur. Venkatagiri, 1946.

———. *Sree Gurucharanam. A Compilation of Divine Discourses of Bhagavan Sri Sathya Sai Baba During Guru Poornima (1956–1998).* Prasanthi Nilayam: Sri Sathya Sai Books & Publications, 2000.

———. *Upanishad Vahini.* Prasanthi Nilayam: Sri Sathya Sai Education and Publication Foundation, 1975.

———. "Who Is Sai." In *Sai Baba and His Message: A Challenge to Behavioural Sciences,* edited by S. P. Ruhela and D. Robinson, 30–33. Delhi: Vikas, 1982.

———. "Why I Incarnate." In *Sai Baba and His Message: A Challenge to Behavioural Sciences,* edited by S. P. Ruhela and D. Robinson, 23–29. Delhi: Vikas, 1982.

Sathya Sai Shree Lakshmi. *Venka Avadhoota.* Puttaparthi: Satya Sai Vedanadalayam Books and Publications, 2005.

Satpathy, Chandra Bhanu. *New Findings on Shirdi Sai Baba*. New Delhi: Sterling, 2019.

———. *Shirdi Sai Baba and Other Perfect Masters*. New Delhi: Sterling, 2001.

Savkur, Suresh Rao. *Reflections on Adi Shankara's Bhaja Govindam (Based on Teachings of Bhagawan Sri Sathya Sai Baba)*. Prasanthi Nilayam: Sri Sathya Sai Sadhana Trust, 2012.

Sawai, Yoshitsugu. *The Faith of Ascetics and Lay Smārtas: A Study of Śaṅkara Tradition in Śriṅgeri*. Vienna: De Nobili Research Library, 1992.

Sawhny, P. P. R. *Shri Satya Sai Baba's Divine Mission of Love, Self-Realisation and Eternal Bliss for All Mankinds*. New Delhi: Lakherwal Press, 1979.

Schalk, Peter, ed. *Geschichten und Geschichte. Historiographie und Hagiographie in der asiatischen Religionsgeschichte*. Uppsala: Uppsala University Library, 2010.

Schmithausen, Lambert, ed. *Writings of Paul Hacker: Kleine Schriften*. Wiesbaden: Otto Harrassowitz, 1978.

Schreiner, Peter. "Institutionalization of Charisma: The Case of Sahajānanda." In *Charisma and Canon: Essays on the Religious History of the Indian Subcontinent*, edited by V. Dalmia, A. Malinar, and M. Christof, 155–70. New York: Oxford University Press, 2001.

Schulman, Arnold. *Baba*. New York: Viking Press, 1973 (1971).

Schultz, Anna. *Singing a Hindu Nation: Marathi Devotional Performance and Nationalism*. New York: Oxford University Press, 2013.

Seeman, Reiner. "Versuch zu einer Theorie des Avatāra. Mensch gewordener Gott oder Gott gewordener Mensch?" *Numen* 33, no. 1 (1986): 90–140.

Sen, Amiya Prosad. "Ramakrishna." In *Brill's Encyclopedia of Hinduism*, edited by K. A. Jacobsen, H. Basu, A. Malinar, and V. Narayanan. Brill Online, 2012.

———. *Swami Vivekananda*. New York: Oxford University Press, 2013.

———, ed. *The Indispensable Vivekananda: An Anthology for Our Times*. Delhi: Permanent Black, 2006.

Service and Spirituality: The Sathya Sai Movement in Malaysia. Kuala Lumpur: Sri Sathya Sai Central Council of Malaysia, 1985.

Shah, Indulal H. *Sixteen Spiritual Summers*. Prasanthi Nilayam: Sri Sathya Sai Books and Publications Trust, 1980.

———. *Spiritual Blueprints of My Journey*. Bombay: Sarla Charity Trust, 1993.

———. "Sri Sathya Sai Seva Organisation: Aims and Accomplishments." In *Golden Age 1980*, 218–24. Prasanthi Nilayam: Sri Sathya Sai Books and Publications Trust, 1980.

———. *We Devotees*. Prasanthi Nilayam: Sri Sathya Sai Books and Publications Trust, 1983.

Shankar, Ravi. "A Tribute to Baba." In *Golden Age 1980*, 150. Prasanthi Nilayam: Sri Sathya Sai Books and Publications Trust, 1980.

Shelke, Christopher. "Janābāī as a Mystic and Hagiographer." In *The Banyan Tree: Essays on Early Literature in New Indo-Aryan Languages (Proceedings of the*

Seventh International Conference on Early Literature in New Indo-Aryan Languages, Venice, 1997), edited by M. Offredi, Vol. 1, 283–98. New Delhi: Manohar, 2000.

Shepherd, Kevin R. D. *Investigating the Sai Baba Movement: A Clarification of Misrepresented Saints and Opportunism*. Dorset: Citizen Initiative, 2005.

———. *Meher Baba, an Iranian Liberal*. Cambridge: Anthropographia Publications, 1988.

———. *Sai Baba: Faqir of Shirdi*. New Delhi: Sterling, 2017.

———. *Sai Baba of Shirdi: A Biographical Investigation*. New Delhi: Sterling, 2015.

Shinde, Kiran A., and Andrea Marion Pinkney, "Shirdi in Transition: Guru Devotion, Urbanisation and Regional Pluralism in India." In *South Asia: Journal of South Asian Studies* 36, 4 (2013): 554–70.

Shirdi Diary of the Hon'ble Mr. G. S. Khaparde. Bombay: Shri Sai Baba Sansthan, n.d.

Sholapurkar, G. R. *Foot-prints at Shirdi and Puttaparthi*. Foreword by V. K. Gokak. Delhi: Bharatiya Vidya Prakashan, 1989.

Shri Sai Leela Magazine 17, no. 1–3, 1940.

Siddharameshwar Maharaj, Sri. *Embrasser l'immortalité:* Amrut laya. *Méthode pratique pour se libérer du faux*. Paris: Les Deux Océans, 2007.

Siddheswarananda, Swami. *The Metaphysical Intuition: Seeing God with Open Eyes. Commentaries on the Bhagavad Gita*. Rhinebeck, N Y: Monkfish, 2006.

Siegel, Lee. *Net of Magic: Wonders and Deceptions in India*. Chicago/London: The University of Chicago Press, 1991.

Sikand, Yoginder. *Sacred Spaces: Exploring Traditions of Shared Faith in India*. Delhi: Penguin, 2003.

———. "Shared Hindu-Muslim Shrines in Karnataka: Challenges to Liminality." In *Lived Islam in South Asia: Adaptation, Accommodation, and Conflict*, edited by I. Ahmad and H. Reifeld, 166–86. New Delhi: Social Science Press, 2004.

Sivananda, Swami. *Lives of Saints*. Shivanandanagar: The Divine Life Society, 1999.

Smith, F. M. *The Self Possessed: Deity and Spirit Possession in South Asian Literature and Civilization*. New York: Columbia University Press, 2006.

Smith, H. Daniel. "Impact of 'God Posters' on Hindus and Their Devotional Traditions." In *Media and the Transformation of Religion in South Asia*, edited by L. A. Babb and S. Wadley, 24–50. Delhi: Motilal Banarsidass, 1997.

Sonde, Nagesh D. *Shri Manik Prabhu: His Life and Mission*. Maniknagar: Shri Manik Prabhu Samsthan, 1995.

Sorabji, Richard. *Gandhi and the Stoics: Modern Experiments on Ancient Values*. Chicago: The University of Chicago Press, 2012.

Spurr, Michael James. "Modern Hindu Guru Movements." In *Hinduism in India: Modern and Contemporary Movements*, edited by W. Sweetman and A. Malik, 141–75. New Delhi: Sage, 2016.

———. *Sathya Sai Baba as Avatar. "His Story" and the History of an Idea.* PhD Diss. University of Canterbury, Christchurch, New Zealand, 2007.

Srinivas, Smriti. *In the Presence of Sai Baba: Body, City, and Memory in a Global Religious Movement.* Leiden: Brill, 2008.

———. "Sathya Sai Baba and the Repertoire of Yoga." In *Gurus of Modern Yoga*, edited by M. Singleton and E. Goldberg, 261–79. New York: Oxford University Press, 2014.

———. "The Advent of the Avatar: The Urban Following of Sathya Sai Baba and Its Construction of Tradition." In *Charisma and Canon: Essays on the Religious History of the Indian Subcontinent*, edited by V. Dalmia, A. Malinar, and M. Christof, 293–309. New York: Oxford University Press, 2001.

Srinivas, Tulasi. "Articles of Faith: Material Piety, Devotional Aesthetics, and the Construction of a Moral Economy in the Transnational Sathya Sai Movement." *Visual Anthropology* 25, no. 4 (2012): 270–302.

———. "Building Faith: Religious Pluralism, Pedagogical Urbanism, and Governance in the Sathya Sai Sacred City." *International Journal of Hindu Studies* 13, no. 3 (2010): 301–36.

———. "Doubtful Illusions: Magic, Wonder, and the Politics of Virtue in the Sathya Sai Movement." *Journal of Asian and African Studies* (2015): 1–31.

———. "Relics of Faith: Fleshly Desires, Ascetic Disciplines, and Devotional Affect in the Transnational Sathya Sai Movement." In *Routledge Handbook of Body Studies*, edited by B. S. Turner, 185–205. London/New York: Routledge, 2012.

———. "Sathya Sai Baba." In *Brill's Encyclopedia of Hinduism*, edited by K. A. Jacobsen, H. Basu, A. Malinar, and V. Narayanan. Brill Online, 2012.

———. *Winged Faith: Rethinking Globalization and Religious Pluralism Through the Sathya Sai Movement.* New York: Columbia University Press, 2010.

Srinivasan, Doris Meth. *Many Heads, Arms, and Eyes: Origin, Meaning, and Form of Multiplicity in Indian Art.* Leiden: Brill, 1997.

Srivastava, Kamal Shankar. *Sufism and Sai Baba.* New Delhi: APH Publishing Corporation, 2015.

Steel, Brian. *The Powers of Sathya Sai Baba.* Delhi: BR Publishing Corporation, 1999.

———. *The Sathya Sai Baba Compendium: A Guide to the First Seventy Years.* York Beach, ME: Samuel Weiser, 1997.

Stewart, Tony K. *Perceptions of the Divine: The Biographies of Chaitanya.* Chicago: The University of Chicago Press, 1985.

Strauss, Sarah. "Locating Yoga: Ethnography and Transnational Practice." In *Constructing the Field: Ethnographic Fieldwork in the Contemporary World*, edited by V. Amit, 162–94. New York: Routledge, 2000.

———. *Positioning Yoga*. Oxford/New York: Berg, 2005.

———. "Sivananda and the Divine Life Society." In *Brill's Encyclopedia of Hinduism*, edited by K. A. Jacobsen, H. Basu, A. Malinar, and V. Narayanan. Brill Online, 2012.

Subba Rao, G. V. "Esoteric Significance of the Veda Purusha Jnana Yajna." *Sanathana Sarathi* 40, no. 12 (December 1997): 335–36.

Swallow, Deborah A. "Ashes and Powers: Myth, Rite, and Miracle in an Indian God-man's Cult." *Modern Asian Studies* 16, no. 1 (1982): 123–58.

Syman, Stefanie. *The Subtle Body: The Story of Yoga in America*. New York: Farrar, Straus, and Giroux, 2010.

Tagliapietra, Andrea. *Esperienza. Filosofia e storia di un'idea*. Milano: Raffaello Cortina, 2017.

Taleyarkhan, Feroza. *Sages, Saints, and Arunachala Ramana*. Foreword by Dr. Sarvepalli Radhakrishnan. Introduction by Shri Sri Prakasa. Madras: Orient Longmans, 1970.

Taraporevala, Zarine. *A Humble Tribute of Praise to Shri Sainath. Marathi Text* of Shri Sainath Stavanamanjari *by Das Ganu*. English Translation and International Phonetics. Bombay: Sai Dhun Enterprises, 1987.

The Divinity Within. Based on Spiritual Museum at Sri Sathya Sai Arts, Science, and Commerce College, Whitefield, Bangalore. Under the Auspices of Sri Sathya Sai Central Trust, India. Bombay: India Book House Education Trust, 1978.

The Path Divine. For Sri Sathya Sai Bal Vikas, Group III. Education in Human Values Series. Prasanthi Nilayam: Sri Sathya Sai Bal Vikas Education Trust, 1983.

Thirumalacharlu, D. *Sri Sathya Sai Bala Ramayanam*. Venkatagiri, 1957.

Thomas, George M. "Religions in Global Civil Society." *Sociology of Religion* 62, no. 4 (2001): 515–33.

Thurston, Edgar, and K. Rangachari. *Castes and Tribes of Southern India*. 7 Vols. Madras: Government Press, 1909.

Tilliette, Jean-Yves. "Introduction," in *Les fonctions des saints dans le monde occidental (IIIe–XIIIe siècle). Actes du colloque organisé par l'École française de Rome avec le concours de l'Université de Rome "La Sapienza," Rome 27–29 octobre 1988*, 1–11. Rome: École française de Rome, Palais Farnèse, 1991.

Timalsina, Sthaneshwar. "Mantra." In *Brill's Encyclopedia of Hinduism*, edited by K. A. Jacobsen, H. Basu, A. Malinar, and V. Narayanan. Brill Online, 2012.

Tulpule, Shankar Gopal. *Classical Marāṭhī Literature: From the Beginning to A.D. 1818*. Wiesbaden: Otto Harrassowitz, 1979.

Tyagananda, Swami, and Pravrajika Vrajaprana. *Interpreting Ramakrishna: Kālī's Child Revisited*. Delhi: Motilal Banarsidass, 2010.

Urban, Hugh B. "Avatar for Our Age: Sathya Sai Baba and the Cultural Contradictions of Late Capitalism." In *Religion* 33 (2003): 73–93.

Valpey, Kenneth. "*Pūjā* and *darśana*." In *Brill's Encyclopedia of Hinduism*. Vol. II. *Sacred Texts and Languages, Ritual Traditions, Arts, Concepts*, edited by K. A. Jacobsen, H. Basu, A. Malinar, and V. Narayanan, 380–94. Leiden: Brill, 2010.

van der Veer, Peter. *Imperial Encounters: Religion and Modernity in India and Britain*. Delhi: Permanent Black, 2006.

Vasudevan, C. S. *Temples of Andhra Pradesh*. Delhi: Bharatiya Kala Prakashan, 2000.

Vaudeville, Charlotte. *A Weaver Named Kabir: Selected Verses, with a Detailed Biographical and Historical Introduction*. Delhi: Oxford University Press, 1993.

Vijayakumari. *Anyathā Saranam Nasthi: Other Than You Refuge There Is None*. Ekrattuthangal, Chennai: Sai Shri Ram Printers, 2000.

Virmani, Arundhati. *Atlas historique de l'Inde. Du VIe siècle av. J.-C. au XXIe siècle*. Préface de Sanjay Subrahmanyam. Paris: Éditions Autrement, 2012.

Viswanathan, Gauri. "Theosophical Society." In *Brill's Encyclopedia of Hinduism*, edited by K. A. Jacobsen, H. Basu, A. Malinar, and V. Narayanan. Brill Online, 2012.

Vivekananda, Swami. *My Master*. With an Appended Extract from the Theistic Quarterly Review. New York: Baker and Taylor, 1901^3.

———. *The Complete Works of Swami Vivekananda*. 8 Vols. Calcutta: Advaita Ashrama, 1970–73.

Waghorne, Joanne Punzo. *Diaspora of the Gods: Modern Hindu Temples in an Urban Middle-Class World*. New York: Oxford University Press, 2004.

———. "Global Gurus and the Third Stream of American Religiosity: Between Hindu Nationalism and Liberal Pluralism." In *Political Hinduism: The Religious Imagination in Public Spheres*, edited by V. Lal, 122–49. New Delhi: Oxford University Press, 2009.

Waghorne, Joanne Punzo, and Norman Cutler, eds. *Gods of Flesh, Gods of Stone: The Embodiment of Divinity in India*. New York: Columbia University Press, 1985.

Warren, Marianne. *Unravelling the Enigma: Shirdi Sai Baba in the Light of Sufism*. New Delhi: Sterling, 1999 (Rev. ed. 2004).

Warrier, Maya. "*Guru* Choice and Spiritual Seeking in Contemporary India." *International Journal of Hindu Studies* 7, no. 1–3 (2003): 31–54.

Weiss, Richard S. "The Global Guru: Sai Baba and the Miracle of the Modern." *New Zealand Journal of Asian Studies* 7, no. 2 (2005): 5–19.

White, Charles S. J. "Swāmi Muktānanda and the Enlightenment Through Śakti-Pāt." *History of Religions* 13, no. 4 (May 1974): 306–22.

———. "The Sai Baba Movement: Approaches to the Study of Indian Saints." *Journal of Asian Studies* 31, no. 4 (1972): 863–78.

Williamson, Lola. *Transcendent in America: Hindu-Inspired Meditation Movements as New Religion*. New York/London: New York University Press, 2010.

Witz, Klaus G. *The Supreme Wisdom of the Upaniṣads: An Introduction*. Delhi: Motilal Banarsidass, 1998.

Yeolekar, Mugdha. Gurucaritra Pārāyaṇ*: Social Praxis of Religious Reading*. PhD Diss., Arizona State University, 2014.

Yocum, Glenn. "The Coronation of a Guru: Charisma, Politics, and Philosophy in Contemporary India." In *A Sacred Thread: Modern Transmission of Hindu Traditions in India and Abroad*, edited by R. B. Williams, 68–91. Chambersburg, PA: Anima Publications, 1992.

Yogananda, Paramhansa. *Autobiography of a Yogi*. With a Preface by W. Y. Evans-Wentz. New York: The Philosophical Library, 1946.

Youngs, H. S. *Translations by Baba*. Tustin, CA: Sathya Sai Book Center of America, 1975.

Zoller, Claus Peter. "Kabir and Ritualized Language." *Acta Orientalia* 65 (2004): 33–68.

Documentaries

Bock, Richard, and Janet Bock. *Aura of Divinity*. Prasanthi Nilayam: Sri Sathya Sai Books & Publication Trust, n.d. (Video-CD of a film taken in the 1970s).

———. *The Message I Bring*. Prasanthi Nilayam: Sri Sathya Sai Books & Publication Trust, n.d. (Video-CD of a film taken in 1968).

———. *Truth Is My Name*. Prasanthi Nilayam: Sri Sathya Sai Books & Publication Trust, n.d. (Video-CD of films taken in the 1970s and 1980s).

Internet Sites

http://appmithistories.blogspot.it/2013/02/sri-venka-avadhoota.html

http://en.wikipedia.org/wiki/Sathya_Sai_Baba

http://home.hetnet.nl/~ex_baba/engels/shortnews/Mumbai%20Mirror.htm

http://hubpages.com/entertainment/Chitravati-The-painful-story-of-pollution-of-a-sathya-sai-baba-holy-river

http://media.radiosai.org/journals/Vol_04/01SEP06/CoverStory_Army.htm

http://saivrinda.org

http://sathyasaiwithstudents.blogspot.it/2013/08/a-north-indian-tour-with-sri-sathya-sai.html#.WMOfhtP2bwo

http://vasukir.blogspot.it/2012/10/anartha-kosha.html

http://www.eaisai.com/baba/docs/pv960617.html

http://www.exbaba.com/findings.html
http://www.gandhistudycentre.org/pdf/truth.pdf
http://www.geocities.com/Athens/Olympus/9158/d15101999.html
http://www.historiatrivandrum.com/docs/downloads/history.pdf
http://www.kamat.com/indica/faiths/gods/13040.jpg
http://www.labri.org/england/resources/05052008/AF02_Goodness_Beauty_3E64FE.pdf
http://www.lordmeher.org/rev/index.jsp?pageBase=page.jsp&nextPage=4926
http://www.ourkarnataka.com/Articles/starofmysore/venka009.htm
http://www.radiosai.org/program/listen.php?f=DD_1987_07_11_GURU_POORNIMA.mp3
http://www.saibaba.ws/avatar/naadiinscriptions.htm
http://www.saiprakashana.online
http://www.sssbpt.info/english/showers.html
http://www.sssbpt.info/ssspeaks/volume20/sss20-15.pdf
http://www.sssbpt.info/ssspeaks/volume33/sss33-08.pdf
http://www.vedanta-nl.org/GOSPEL.pdf
https://robertpriddy.wordpress.com
https://robertpriddy.wordpress.com/tag/divya-weed
https://robertpriddy.wordpress.com/2015/01/10/souljourns-narasimha-murthys-secret-of-prema-sai
https://saivrinda.org/?s=Prema+Sai
https://vimeo.com/97850716
https://vimeo.com/139318585
https://www.saiprakashana.online/web/en
https://www.youtube.com/watch?v=aatcu88uKNE
https://www.youtube.com/watch?v=ahMI9pzjPj8
https://www.youtube.com/watch?v=c7mk0SwKOyA&feature=youtube_gdata_player
https://www.youtube.com/watch?v=Gmm4I_Al0CE
https://www.youtube.com/watch?v=hL_bB7PeEAg
https://www.youtube.com/watch?v=HpV8fhK0QFg
https://www.youtube.com/watch?v=kR5NPvBsZQY
https://www.youtube.com/watch?v=kVzxmUv9ZJU
https://www.youtube.com/watch?v=pux1v6U6z-Y
https://www.youtube.com/watch?v=qw1WB6Kj88Y
https://www.youtube.com/watch?v=RAZb76__EeE
https://www.youtube.com/watch?v=rDLJAe5HBfA ("Souljourns—Part 2, Vijaya Kumari")
https://www.youtube.com/watch?v=TfySaF0Dyjg
https://www.youtube.com/watch?v=UnRYvBd9ac4

https://www.youtube.com/watch?v=wFMJ_H0jdNY
https://www.youtube.com/watch?v=WZoM_zzQHuE
https://www.youtube.com/watch?v=YpGME3Iv7Yg
https://www.youtube.com/watch?v=2BX4z26kJSQ
https://www.youtube.com/watch?v=5JxCPB-ti-c
https://www.youtube.com/watch?v=6Nr8g96VrpI
https://www.youtube.com/watch?v=7eQ5VHmB-JE

Works by Narayan Kasturi

1. Prior to Becoming a Follower of Sathya Sai Baba

A. Poems and Songs in Kannada

Anaku minaku. Mysore: Sahitya Mandir, 1947.
Jagada Jeevanagalalva.

B. Plays in Kannada

Bank divali.
Citra-vicitra. Bellary: Timma Sahityamala, 1951.
Ekacakra. Mysore: Samsthanada Akshara Prachara Samiti, 1943.
Gaggayyana gadibidi. Bangalore: Sharada Prakatanalaya, 1961.
Gundurayana gulige.
Mankasura vadhe.
Nandanar.
Ramakrishnaiahna darbaru.
Shambhu.
Tapatraya tappitu.
Tiruppanalvar.
Vara pareekshe.

C. Plays in English

Headmaster's Daughter.

D. Plays in Malayalam

Shahajahan.

E. Satirical Essays in Kannada

Allola. Shivamogga: Shivamogga Printing and Publishing Co., 1950.
Donku bala. Dharwad: Lalita Sahityamale, 1944.
Hasya-kasturi. Edited by K. B. Prabhuprasad and H. C. Kesavamurti. Bangalore: Kannada Pustaka Pradhikara, 1997.
Kallola. Shivamogga: Shivamogga Printing and Publishing Co., 1950.
Navaratri-kempa maisurige hodaddu. Mysore: Samsthanada Vayaskare Sikshana Samithi, 1965.
Samagra Haasya Sahitya. Bangalore: Sapna Book House, 2012.
Upāya-vedānta. Dharwad: Lalita Sahityamale, 1951.
Yadwa-tadwa.

F. Novels in Kannada

Chakradristi. Dharwad: Manohara Grantha Prakashana Samiti, 1944 (Bangalore: Sapna Book House, 2013; Bangalore: Directorate of Kannada and Culture, 1990).
Chenguli cheluva. Malladihalli: Anatha Sevasrama, 1953 (Bangalore: Sapna Book House, 2012).
Gaaligopuram. Dharwad: Manohara Grantha Prakashana Samiti, 1940 (Bangalore: Sapna Book House, 2013).
Grihadaaranyaka. Dharwad: Manohara Granthamala Prakashan, 1953 (Bangalore: Sapna Book House, 2013).
Nandigrama. Mysore: Grama Sevanilaya; Bangalore: Okkaligara Sangha Press, 1939.
Ranganayaki. Dharwad: Manohara Grantha Mala, 1961 (Gadag: Manohara Grantha Mala, 1999; Bangalore: Sapna Book House, n.d.).
Shankha vadya. Mysore: Usha Sahitya Male, 1948 (Bangalore: Sapna Book House, 2013).

G. Dictionaries

Anarthakosha. Mysore: Talukina Venkannayyanavara Smaraka Granthamale, 1952 (Bangalore: Ankita Pustaka, 1999, 2012).

H. Koravanji

Koravanji–CD Rom. Bangalore: Koravanji-Aparanji Trust, Bharatiya Vidya Bhavan and Department of Kannada and Culture, 2011.
Koravanji Kasturi. Bangalore: Aparanji Prakashan, 1996.

I. Monographs and Research Articles in English and Kannada

Ashoka. Edited by K. V. Puttappa. *Mysore University Kannada Granthamale*, 25. Mysore: Wesley Press, 1952.

Factory Laws in India.

History of the British Occupation of India. Being a Summary of Rise of the Christian Power in India *by Major B. D. Basu, Vols. I to V*. Calcutta: R. Chatterjee, n.d. [192?]

Kerala in Karnataka.

Maduve. Mysore: Mysore University, 1940.

The Dutch Merchants at Cochin.

"The Huttari Festival of Coorg." *Proceedings and Transactions of the 8th All-India Conference*, 655–66. Mysore, 1935.

"The Last Rajas of Coorg." *The Half-Yearly Journal of the Mysore University: Section B-Science* 1, 1 (1940): 75–79.

"Tipu Sultan's Projected Confederacy Against the British, 1790." In *Confronting Colonialism: Resistance and Modernization Under Haidar Ali & Tipu Sultan*, edited by I. Habib, 87–92. London: Anthem Press, 2002 [1935].

"Two Folk Festivals of Coorg." *Proceedings and Transactions of the 10th All-India Conference*, 516–21. Mysore, 1940.

J. Translations in Kannada

Babur (Zahir-ud-Din Muhammad). *Memoirs of Babur*: *Dilliswarana dinachari*. Bangalore: Sapna Book House, 2013 (Bangalore, 1930).

China Japan kathegalu. Tiptur: Sudarshan Prakashan, 1962.

Dodgson, Charles Lutwidge, alias Carroll, Lewis. *Alice in Wonderland*: *Pataladalli papacci*. Bangalore: Sapna Book House, 2013 (Shivamogga: Karnataka Sangha, 1935).

Hugo, Victor. *Les Misérables*: *Nonda jivi*. Bangalore: P.T.I. Book Depot, 1956.

Krishna Menon. *Chairman Perumal*.

Pillai, Thakazhi Sivasankara. *Chemmeen*: *Kempu meenu*. New Delhi: Sahitya Akademi, 1990.

Williams, James Howard. *Elephant Bill*: *Gajendra loka*. Bangalore: N. S. Vasan, 1958.

Wodehouse, Sir Pelham Grenville. *Kadane*.

Kasturi, Narayan, Shankara Bhatta. Pillai, Thakazhi Sivasankara. *Randidangazhi*: *Eradu balla*. New Delhi: Sahitya Akademi, 1996 (Reprint).

Kasturi, Narayan et al. Carlyle, Thomas. *On History*.

Kasturi, Narayan et al. Russell, Bertrand. *A Free Man's Worship*.

Kasturi, Narayan et al. Shelley, Percy Bysshe. *Defense of Poetry*.

2. After Becoming a Follower of Sathya Sai Baba

A. In English

"Baba–As Speaker." In *Sai Chandana: Book of Homage*, edited by V. K. Gokak, 282–86. Prasanthi Nilayam: Sri Sathya Sai Institute of Higher Learning, 1985.

Easwaramma: The Chosen Mother. Prasanthi Nilayam: Sri Sathya Sai Books and Publications Trust, 1984.

Garland of 108 Precious Gems: Ashtothara Sathanama Rathnamala. Prasanthi Nilayam: Sri Sathya Sai Education and Publication Foundation, 1979.

Gurudev. Prasanthi Nilayam: Sri Sathya Sai Books and Publications, 2005[3].

"In the Altar of Your Heart." In *Sai Baba and His Message: A Challenge to Behavioural Sciences*, edited by S. P. Ruhela and D. Robinson, 246–50. Delhi: Vikas Publishing House, 1982.

Loving God. Eighty Five Years Under the Watchful Eye of the Lord. Prasanthi Nilayam: Sri Sathya Sai Books and Publications, 1982.

Prasanthi: Pathway to Peace. As Learnt at the Lotus Feet of Bhagavan. Prasanthi Nilayam: Sri Sathya Sai Books and Publications, 1985.

"Rain Rain Go Away." In *Sai Humour*, edited by P. Mason, S. Lévy, and M. Veeravahu, 61–63. Prasanthi Nilayam: Sri Sathya Sai Towers Hotels, 1996.

Sathya Sai Baba Announces His Mission and Why the Avatar Has Come, November 23, 1968. Prasanthi Nilayam: Sri Sathya Sai Books and Publications, 1968.

Sathyam Sivam Sundaram, Part I (1926–1960). Bhagavan Sri Sathya Sai Baba. Prasanthi Nilayam: Sri Sathya Sai Books and Publications, 1980 (1961; Reprint with additional photos, 1983).

Sathyam Sivam Sundaram, Part II. The Life of Bhagavan Sri Sathya Sai Baba. Prasanthi Nilayam: Sri Sathya Sai Books and Publications, 1981 (1968).

Sathyam Sivam Sundaram, Part III. Prasanthi Nilayam: Sri Sathya Sai Books and Publications, 1981.

Sathyam Sivam Sundaram, Part IV. Prasanthi Nilayam: Sri Sathya Sai Books and Publications, 1981[2].

Sathyam Sivam Sundaram: The Life of Bhagavan Sri Sathya Sai Baba. Editorially revised in collaboration with N. Kasturi by Charles Penn et al. Tustin, CA: Sathya Sai Book Center of America, 1988[2].

"Singular and Plural." In *Golden Age 1980*, 133–37. Prasanthi Nilayam: Sri Sathya Sai Books and Publications Trust, 1980.

Siva Sakthi Swarupa. Prasanthi Nilayam: Sri Sathya Sai Sadhana Trust, 2012 (Bombay: Parijat Prakashan, 1963 [With a foreword by Dinesh N. Desai]).

"The Divine Photographer." In *Sai Humour*, edited by P. Mason, S. Lévy, and M. Veeravahu, 75–77. Prasanthi Nilayam: Sri Sathya Sai Towers Hotels, 1996.

"The Interview He Grants." In *Garland of Golden Rose*, 50–53. Prasanthi Nilayam: Sri Sathya Sai Trust, 1975.

The Light of Love: An Account of Bhagawan Sri Sathya Sai Baba's Visit to East Africa and His Divine Discourses. Prasanthi Nilayam: Sri Sathya Sai Sadhana Trust, 2014 (Bombay: Sri Sathya Sai Press; London: Sai Publications, 1968).

"The Teacher of Truth." In *Garland of Golden Rose*, 19–25. Prasanthi Nilayam: Sri Sathya Sai Central Trust, 1975.

"What Is Truth." http://media.radiosai.org/journals/Vol_03/05MAY01/truth.htm (originally published in 1987 in *Sanathana Sarathi*).

Shivaram, H. M., ed. *Sathya Sai Baba: God in Action. Talks by Prof. N. Kasturi*. Prasanthi Nilayam: Sri Sathya Sai Sadhana Trust, 2015.

B. In Kannada

Sai Bhagavatham.

Shri Krishnarajendra Odeyaravaru. Mysore: Samsthanada Vayaskara Shikshanasamiti, n.d.

C. Translations of His Own Works on Sathya Sai Baba in English and Other Indian Languages

C1. English Translations from Kannada

The Annunciation Song. Prasanthi Nilayam: Sri Sathya Sai Books and Publications, n.d.

C2. Kannada Translations from English

Sathyam Sivam Sundaram, Parts I–IV.

Shivashakti svarupa divya pavada. Shivamogga: Prashanta Prakashan, 1964.

C3. Malayalam Translations from Kannada

Sai Bhagavatham.

C4. Tamil Translations from Kannada

Sai Bhagavatham.

C5. *Telugu Translations from Kannada*

Sai Bhagavatham.

D. Editor of Sanathana Sarathi

Sanathana Sarathi (1958–1987).

E. Editor of Kannada Texts

Shriranga and Kasturi, Narayan, eds. *Cheppudu Matalu and Other Kannada Plays in Telugu.* Translated by T. Ramachandra. Vijayawada: Adarsa Grantha Mandali, 1960.

———. *Ekanka Natakagalu.* Bangalore: Sharat Agency, 1957.

F. Editor and Translator from Telugu into English of Sathya Sai Baba's Works

Sathya Sai Speaks Series (11 Vols.):

Sathya Sai Baba, *Sathya Sai Speaks, Vol. 1. Discourses of Bhagawan Sri Sathya Sai Baba (Delivered during 1953–1960).* Prasanthi Nilayam: Sri Sathya Sai Sadhana Trust, 2015.

———. *Sathya Sai Speaks, Vol. 2.* Discourses of Bhagawan Sri Sathya Sai Baba Delivered During 1961–62. Prasanthi Nilayam: Sri Sathya Sai Books and Publications, 2008.

———. *Sathya Sai Speaks, Vol. 3. Discourses of Bhagawan Sri Sathya Sai Baba (Delivered During 1963).* Prasanthi Nilayam: Sri Sathya Sai Books and Publications, 2008.

———. *Sathya Sai Speaks, Vol. 4. Discourses of Bhagawan Sri Sathya Sai Baba (Delivered During 1964).* Prasanthi Nilayam: Sri Sathya Sai Sadhana Trust, 2012.

———. *Sathya Sai Speaks, Vol. 5. Discourses of Bhagawan Sri Sathya Sai Baba (Delivered During 1965).* Prasanthi Nilayam: Sri Sathya Sai Sadhana Trust, 2009.

———. *Sathya Sai Speaks, Vol. 6. Discourses of Bhagawan Sri Sathya Sai Baba (Delivered During 1966).* Prasanthi Nilayam: Sri Sathya Sai Sadhana Trust, 2012.

———. *Sathya Sai Speaks, Vol. 7. Discourses of Bhagavan Sri Sathya Sai Baba (Delivered During 1967).* Prasanthi Nilayam: Sri Sathya Sai Sadhana Trust, 2012.

———. *Sathya Sai Speaks, Vol. 8. Discourses of Bhagawan Sri Sathya Sai Baba Delivered in 1968 (Including Six Discourses Given During Dasara).* Prasanthi Nilayam: Sri Sathya Sai Sadhana Trust, 2010.

———. *Sathya Sai Speaks, Vol. 9. Discourses of Bhagawan Sri Sathya Sai Baba (Delivered during 1969, including Dasara Discourses).* Prasanthi Nilayam: Sri Sathya Sai Sadhana Trust, 2011.

———. *Sathya Sai Speaks, Vol. 10. Discourses of Bhagavan Sri Sathya Sai Baba (Delivered During 1970).* Revised and Enlarged Edition. Prasanthi Nilayam: Sri Sathya Sai Sadhana Trust, 2011.

———. *Sathya Sai Speaks, Vol. 11. Discourses of Bhagavan Sri Sathya Sai Baba (Delivered During 1971–1972).* Revised and Enlarged Edition. Prasanthi Nilayam: Sri Sathya Sai Sadhana Trust, 2011.

Vahini Series (15 Vols.):

Sathya Sai Baba, *Bhagavatha Vahini.* Bangalore: Sri Sathya Sai Education and Publication Foundation, 1979.

———. *Dharma Vahini.* Discourses by Bhagavan Sri Sathya Sai Baba. Prasanthi Nilayam: Sri Sathya Sai Books and Publications, 1985.

———. *Dhyana Vahini.* Discourses by Bhagavan Sri Sathya Sai Baba. Prasanthi Nilayam: Sri Sathya Sai Books and Publications, 1980.

———. *Geetha Vahini.* Discourses by Bhagavan Sri Sathya Sai Baba. Prasanthi Nilayam: Sri Sathya Sai Books and Publications, 1983 (Reprint).

———. *Jnana Vahini.* Discourses by Bhagavan Sri Sathya Sai Baba. Prasanthi Nilayam: Sri Sathya Sai Books and Publications, 1982.

———. *Leela Kaivalya Vahini.* Discourses by Bhagavan Sri Sathya Sai Baba. Prasanthi Nilayam: Sri Sathya Sai Books and Publications, 1990.

———. *Prasanthi Vahini.* Discourses by Bhagavan Sri Sathya Sai Baba. Prasanthi Nilayam: Sri Sathya Sai Books and Publications, 1982.

———. *Prasnothara Vahini: Answers to Spiritual Questions.* Prasanthi Nilayam: Sri Sathya Sai Sadhana Trust, 2010.

———. *Prema Vahini.* Discourses by Bhagavan Sri Sathya Sai Baba. Prasanthi Nilayam: Sri Sathya Sai Books and Publications, 1982.

———. *Ram Katha Rasavahini: The Rama Story: Stream of Sacred Sweetness.* Part 1 & 2. Prasanthi Nilayam: Sri Sathya Sai Books and Publications, 1981–82.

———. *Sandeha Nivarini (Dissolving Doubts). Dialogues with Bhagavan Sri Sathya Sai Baba.* Prasanthi Nilayam: Sri Sathya Sai Books and Publications, 1985 (Rev. ed.).

———. *Sathya Sai Vahini.* Discourses by Bhagavan Sri Sathya Sai Baba. Prasanthi Nilayam: Sri Sathya Sai Books and Publications, 1981.

———. *Sutra Vahini: Stream of Aphorisms on Brahman.* Prasanthi Nilayam: Sri Sathya Sai Sadhana Trust, 2014.

———. *Upanishad Vahini*. Bangalore: Sri Sathya Sai Education and Publication Foundation, 1975.

———. *Vidya Vahini*. Discourses by Bhagavan Sri Sathya Sai Baba (Translated from the Original Telugu). Prasanthi Nilayam: Sri Sathya Sai Books and Publications, 1984.

Other Texts

Sathya Sai Baba. *Chinna Katha: Stories and Parables*. Prasanthi Nilayam: Sri Sathya Sai Books and Publications, 1975.

———. *Sadhana: The Inward Path. Quotations from the Divine Discourses of Bhagavan Sri Sathya Sai Baba*. Bangalore: Sri Sathya Sai Education and Publication Foundation, 1976 (Rev. ed. 1978).

———. *Teachings of Sri Satya Sai Baba*. Lakemont, GA: CSA Press, 1974.

Internet Sites on Narayan Kasturi

http://media.radiosai.org/journals/Vol_03/05MAY01/truth.htm

http://media.radiosai.org/journals/Vol_05/01MAY07/14-h2h_special.htm ("He Is My Swami")

http://media.radiosai.org/journals/Vol_06/01JAN08/03-coverstory.htm

http://media.radiosai.org/journals/vol_10/01DEC12/living-the-divine-presence-Prof-N-Kasturi-biographer-translator-of-sathya-sai-baba.htm

http://www.saibaba-x.org.uk/27/kasturi.html

http://www.saibaba.ws/articles/srikasturi.htm

http://www.saibabaofindia.com/he_is_my_swami.htm

http://www.saibabaofindia.com/he_is_my_swami_2.htm

http://www.saibabaofindia.com/he_is_my_swami_3.htm

http://www.saibabaofindia.com/he_is_my_swami_4.htm

http://www.saibabaofindia.com/he_is_my_swami_5.htm

http://www.saibabaofindia.com/sais_kasturi_heart2heart.htm ("Sai's kasturi . . . A Phantasmagoric Fragrance Forever")

http://www.saicast.org/1968/kasturi681123.pdf

http://www.thehindu.com/news/national/karnataka/spotted-by-koravanji-as-a-student/article6826047.ece

http://www.theprasanthireporter.org/category/from-kasturis-pen

http://www.theprasanthireporter.org/2013/04/baba-and-the-animal-world ("From Kasturi's Pen; November 1958 issue of *Sanathana Sarathi*")

http://www.vahini.org/Discourses/d3-kasturispoem.html#poem
https://en.wikipedia.org/wiki/Narayana_Kasturi
https://m.yourstory.com/2016/01/republic-day-early-works-cartoonist-r-k-laxman
https://soundcloud.com/kg-sreeganeshan/interview-padma-kasturi
https://www.youtube.com/watch?v=O-_aFlHf-7M
https://www.youtube.com/watch?v=sndiadTPH1c

Works on Narayan Kasturi

IN CHRONOLOGICAL ORDER:

Ranganath, H. K. *The Karnatak Theatre*. With a Foreword by Wrangler D. C. Pavate. Dharwar: Karnatak University, 1960, 210 (1982).

Who's Who of Indian Writers: Compiled by Sahitya Akademi. New Delhi: Sahitya Akademi, 1961, 159.

Umapathi, K. S. "Children's Literature in Kannada." *International Library Review* 13, no. 4 (1981): 435–43.

Murthy, M. Venkata Narayana. *The Greatest Adventure: Essays on the Sai Avatar and His Message*. Prasanthi Nilayam: Sri Sathya Sai Books and Publications, 1983, 1–7.

Garg, G. R. *International Encyclopaedia of Indian Literature. Vol. IV: Kannada*. Delhi: Mittal Publications, 1987, 71.

"Kasturi Dead." *The Indian Express*. Bangalore, August 17, 1987.

"Litterateur Who Worked for Adult Education." *The Indian Express*. Bangalore, August 18, 1987.

Narasimhan, V. K. "Unto Sai a Witness." *Sanatana Sarathi* (September 1987): 260.

Wontner, Julian. "Letter to Peggy Mason" (April 18, 1988).

Seshagiri Rao, L. S. "Kasturi N." In *Encyclopaedia of Indian Literature*, edited by A. Datta. Vol. 3, 2004. Reprint, New Delhi: Sahitya Akademi, 2010 (1989).

Venugopala Rao, A. S. *Nā. Kastūri: Nārāyaṇa Raṅganātha Kastūri-baduku-baraha. Amṛtotsava male* 29. Bangalore: Kannada Sahitya Parishat, 1990.

Chandra Mohan, N. B., and K. Subba Rao, eds., *Kastūri śatakam*. Bangalore: B. S. Rajaram, Canvas Creatives Pvt. Ltd., 1996.

Nanjunda Swamy, H. K. *Where the Angels Roamed*. English Adaptation of *Nenapina Nandana* (Kannada) of Dr. H. K. Ranganath. Bangalore: Alex Price Publication, 2002.

Gundu Rao, Y. V., ed. *Best of Kasturi*. Bangalore: Ankita Book House, 2005.

Padmamma. *Twameva Matha*. Bangalore: Sadguru Screens, 2009.

Gries, David, and Phil Gosselin. "The Sources of a Historic Discourse" (July 2009; Updated July 2010). http://www.saicast.org/1968/kasturi681123.pdf

Baliga, Padma. "Translating for Children: Changing Notions of Autonomy and Gender" (*Katha Yatra: The Story Festival*, November 2014. *Translations and Migrations*). http://www.bhaashaa.org/download/Full%20Papers%20for%20Our%20First%20issue.pdf (70–73)

Boratti, Vijayakumar M. "*Paapachchi* (*Alice*) in the Kannada Netherworld." In *Alice. In a World of Wonderlands: The Translations of Lewis Carroll's Masterpiece*, edited by Jon A. Lindseth, Vol. 1, 324–25; Vol. 2, 316–17; Vol. 3, 560–61. New Castle, DE: Oak Knoll Press, 2015.

Index

Page numbers in *italic* refer to figures.

Abhedananda, Swami, interview with Sathya Sai Baba in Prasanthi Nilayam, 123–124
Advaita Vedānta:
  and the practice of Vedic rituals according to Śaṅkara, 74
  and the Ramakrishna Mission, 15, 108–109
  Sathya Sai Baba's recapitulation of its religious pluralism and ultimate truth, 63
  triad theorized by Śaṅkara, 262
  and Vivekananda, 69, 108–109, 133
Aitken, Bill, 151, 319n29, 324n128, 343n128, 404n87
  on Kasturi's *Carita,* 41, 332n17, 333n23
  on Sathya Sai Baba's egalitarian outlook, 68
  on Sathya Sai Baba's visit to Swami Sivananda, 62
Akkaḷkoṭ Mahārāj (d.1878), 187, 210, 344n147
Allāh, and Kasturi on Sathya Sai Baba as the multi-faceted *Avatar,* 97
Anandamayi Ma, 259
Andhra Pradesh:
  Dattātreya gurus in, 398n10
  Sathya Sai Baba's tour of the Godavari Districts of, 98
  Shirdi Sai Baba temples concentrated in, 426n32
  See also Prasanthi Nilayam (Puttaparthi)
antyeṣṭi, 421–422n83
Arjuna, 152, 252, 315n6
  America identified as, 86
  epithet Kuru-nandana or "Son of the Kuru [clan]," 123
  and Kṛṣṇa in *Bhagavadgītā* 3.20, 3.25, 361n48
  and Kṛṣṇa in *Bhagavadgītā* 4.7–8, 344n148
  and Kṛṣṇa in *Bhagavadgītā* 15.15, 252
Arjuna Kārtavīrya, 398n4
  worship of Dattātreya, 217, 219
ash:
  and cremation, 421n82
  from Kasturi's cremation immersed in the sea, 282
—sacred ash (*vibhūti*), 270, 277, 408n136, 408n144

ash *(continued)*
Dattātreya associated with, 239–242
as an emblem of asceticism, 324n75
on Kasturi's forehead, 178, 263
materialized by Sathya Sai Baba, 50, 56, 60, 77, 100, 269, 278, 284, 298, 300, 318n21, 341n104
materialized by Sathya Sai Baba daily, 97
materialized by Sathya Sai Baba during private interviews, 122
materialized by Sathya Sai Baba for Jagadanandaji Maharaj, 138–139
materialized by Sathya Sai Baba for Murthy (M. V. N.), xix
materialized by Sathya Sai Baba for Swami Sivananda, 53–54
packet given to Kasturi by Sathya Sai Baba, 26
therapeutic efficacy of, 100
Aśoka (r. c. 272–231 BCE), 22, 320–321n48
Aśvaghoṣa, 9
ātman (self):
and *Brahman* (the ultimate divine principle), xix, 18
and the *divyātma svarūpulara* ("incarnations of the divine *ātman*"), 95
and Kasturi, xix, 274–277, 419n48
Kṛṣṇa's hymn to the *ātman* in *Bhagavadgītā* 2.19–10, 419n48
realization of one's ātmic identity, 174–175
and the triad theorized in Śaṅkara's Vedānta, 262
true self described by Sathya Sai Baba, 121–122
See also true identity and true identity realization
Aurobindo Ghose, Sri (1872–1950), 104, 136, 259, 372–373n193
Sathya Sai Baba's advent prophesized by, 98, 360–361n39
Avadhūtagītā ("The Song of the Free"), 224, 387n2, 388n19
attribution to Dattātreya, 401n37
*avadhūta*s:
Akkaḷkoṭ Mahārāj revered as, 187, 210
bālāvadhūta identified as Dattātreya in the *Bhāgavata Purāṇa,* 218, 398n7
and Dattātreya and his incarnations, 180, 187, 210, 218, 222, 226, 238, 387n7, 412n195
definition of, 387n2
Gajānan Mahārāj revered as, 187, 210–211
Kabīr revered as, 187, 210
Māṇikprabhu revered as, 187, 210
as the model of *mokṣa,* 291
Shirdi Sai Baba revered as, 180, 187, 387n8
Śrī Pant Mahārāj of Bāḷekundrī revered as, 232
Veṅkāvadhūta revered as, 189, 194
See also Sathya Sai Baba, Shri—as Dattātreya
*avatāra*s:
and *Bhagavadgītā* 4.7–8, 344n148
Sathya Sai Baba as a, 63, 97, 207–208
spiritual oneness of Shirdi Sai Baba and Sathya Sai Baba, 212–213
See also Dattātreya and the Dattātreya tradition
Ayodhya, 59, 65, 70, 105, 362n64

Babb, Lawrence A., 45, 66, 123
on Kasturi's "hierarchical intimacy" with the guru, 283
on Sathya Sai Baba as a social deity par excellence, 238

on Sathya Sai Baba's ad hoc etymologies, 123
on Sathya Sai Baba's ideal social order, 68
on the symbolism deployed in Bal Vikas programs, 112
Badrinath, 60, 65, 71, 146, 156, 427n40
Bahadur, Sri Jaya Chamarajendra Wadiyar (1919–1974), 178, 245, 386n4
Bailey, David and Faye, 369n152
Balachandran, T. P.:
death of, 264
grandfather Potti Iyer, 27
and Kasturi, 27, 325n82
marriage to Padma, 28–29, 33, *34*f1.5, 325n82, 327n105
Bal Vikas and Seva Dal:
educational mission prioritized by, 101, 118
and Kasturi, 94–95, 305, 307
service to society emphasized in programs of, 112
Balse, Mayah, 407n111
Bangalore, 17, 24–27, 29, 31–32, 36, 48, 51, 61, 85, 88–89, 97, 99, 115, 117, 146, 149–150, 157, 168, 187, 198, 248, 265, 275, 279, 321n48, 321n53, 325n83, 326n100, 327n105, 328n114, 329n125, 337–338n80, 360n34, 373n204, 378n69, 379n75, 383n142, 390n37, 416n11, 423n102,
Baranowski, Frank G., 117
Barz, Richard, 9
Baskin, Diana (d. 2014), 84, 235, 289, 358n25
on Sathya Sai Baba's strictness, 160–161
Beatles, 50, 351–352n245
Benares, xviii, 59–60, 65, 77, 178, 187, 236, 278, 314n24, 420n54, 425n10
Bhagavadgītā, 148, 166, 422n88
2.19–25 (Kṛṣṇa's hymn to the *ātman*), 419n48
4.34 (explanation by Shirdi Sai Baba), 388n24, 389n31
4.7–8 (*avatāra* theory), 344n148, 389n31
8.5, 8.9–13, 422n88
15.15, 252
17.15b (on true speech [*satya*]), 43
18.62c (and the meaning of *praśānti*), 173–174, 338n85
and *karman, bhakti,* and *jñana* as one indivisible whole, 249
and Kasturi's biography of Sathya Sai Baba, 45
Kasturi's Vivekanandian interpretation of, 17–18, 43
Kṛṣṇa's epithet Madhu-sūdana ("Destroyer of [the demon] Madhu") in, 122–123
Sathya Sai Baba's *Geetha Vahini* (commentary to the *Bhagavadgītā*), 121, 127
Bhagavan, Manu, 104–105
Bhagavantham, S., 79, 103, 149, 351n239, 389n27
Bhagwan Shree Rajneesh/Osho movement, 417n17, 428n45
Bharatiya Janata Party (BJP), 70, 215
Bharatiya Vidya Bhavan, 91, 99, 104–105, 322n59
Bible:
and the "Jesus model" as found in the Gospels, 126
and Sathya Sai Baba's inclusivist strategy, 371–372n186
three schools of Vedānta detected in Jesus's sayings by Vivekananda, 108–109

Bible—books of:
Matthew 6.9, 109
Matthew 16.25, 254
Matthew 19.14, 423n104
Matthew 25.31–46, 430–431n91
Mark 2.17, 126
Luke 2.34, 129
Luke 18.16, 423n104
Luke 23.34, 129
John 4.24, 297
John 10.30, 109
John 14.6, 129
John 15.5, 109
Revelation 19.11–16, 364n94
Bilimoria, Purushottama, 68
Blavatsky, Helena Petrovna, Theosophical Society founded by, 351n240, 425n10
Bock, Richard and Janet, 126, 299, 370n170
Bombay, xviii, 78, 81, 88, 91, 94, 99, 104, 117, 119, 125, 148, 156, 183, 188, 212, 248, 313n21, 345n162, 362n65
Bozzani, Robert A., 126, 370n169
Brahmā:
and the Hindu *trimūrti,* 102, 221, 222f6.1, 229–231, 242, 244–245, 248, 400n23
and the *Purāṇas,* 1
and Sathya Sai Baba as Dattātreya, 103, 184–185
and Shirdi Sai Baba as Dattātreya, 184–185
See also trimūrti
Brooke, Tal, 259, 364n94
Buddha:
Buddhacarita ("The Deeds of the Buddha"), 9
and Kasturi on Sathya Sai Baba as the multi-faceted *Avatar,* 97
portrait for the Sathya Sai Baba's Prayer Hall (*mandir*), 51
Sathya Sai Baba identified with, 165
Buddhism and Buddhists:
and Sathya Sai Baba, 64, 107, 119, 358n26, 365n97
wheel of Buddhism incorporated on the *sarvadharma* emblem, 79

Caritas ("Biographies"):
as *exempla* for subsequent hagiographies, 5, 7
Kasturi's *Sathyam Sivam Sundaram* viewed as, 2–3, 5, 9, 12, 41–45, 152, 332n17
Purāṇas and *Kathās* distinguished from, 1–2
See also Gurucaritra ("Life of the Master")
Charlton, Hilda (1906–1988), 333n25, 358n26
first attraction to Sathya Sai Baba, 96
Christianity and Christians:
and the Sai religion, 63, 425n11
and Sathya Sai Baba, 119, 307, 365n97
and the seven corporal works of mercy, 430–431n91
transcendentalism of Christian Scholasticism, 42–43
See also Bible; Jesus (Isa/Issa)
—symbol of the cross:
and elimination of self, 254
incorporated on the *sarvadharma* emblem, 79
Chitravathi River, 8, 26, 32, 281, 285, 324n73, 422n84
Cohen, Allan Y., 212
Copeman, Jacob, 234, 260
Cowan, Elsie, first attraction to Sathya Sai Baba, 95–96

Cowan, Walter:
and claims of his resurrection by Sathya Sai Baba, 114, 358n24
first attraction to Sathya Sai Baba, 95–96
Craxi, Antonio (1936–2017), 270, 357n13, 417n30
Craxi, Bettino (1934–2000), 270, 417n30

Dabholkar, Govind Raghunath (Hemadpant, 1859–1929)—*Śrī Sāī Saccarita*:
Kasturi's comparison of himself with, 39–40
as the modern *Gurucaritra,* 226
Shirdi Sai Baba identified with Dattātreya by, 226
Shirdi Sai Baba's nicknaming him after Hemadpant, 313n21
and Shirdi Sai Baba's methodological advice, 7
darśan given by Sathya Sai Baba:
filmed by Jack Lenchiner of Sathya Sai Baba giving it, 422n84
and gender separation, 160
granted by Sathya Sai Baba to dying devotees, 33, 122
Kasturi's experience of, 27, 123, 191–192, 263, 269, 273, 278
and the materializations of Sathya Sai Baba, 298, 300
and the Sathya Sai Baba movement, 288
Sathya Sai Baba's illness preventing his giving it, 271
and Sathya Sai Baba's overseas devotees, 163
Sathya Sai Baba's silent *darśans*, 127
and Sathya Sai Baba's travels in India, 140
and Sathya Sai Baba's utilization of old and new media, xx, 297–305, 417n20
and witnessing the transcendent principle (*brahmatattva*), 260
Das Ganu (1868–1962), 56, 193, 195, 223–224, 389–390n32, 391n53, 391n69
Dattātreya and the Dattātreya tradition, 178–192, 201–208, 217–262*passim*
Anasūyā as his mother, 217, 229
as *avadhūta,* 180, 187, 210, 222, 226, 238, 387n7
celebration of his birthday, 402n51
as the "chosen deity" (*iṣṭadevatā*) of many Hindus, 387n12
and dogs, 180, 202, 221, 242
and the *Gurucaritra,* 7, 220–221
and *kevalavidyānidhi* ("He is the treasure-house of all facets of knowledge"), 185
manifestation of *avatāras* of, 185, 209–211, 410n36
mantras beginning with *daṃ/draṃ,* 218
and Mount Girnār, 220, 245, 398n10
one-headed (*ekmukhī*) iconography of, 221
portrayal in the *Upaniṣads*, 218
and Purāṇic sources, 217–218
and Śaṅkara, 218
self-giving nature as an *avadhūta,* 412n7
and the three *da*-s of the *Bṛhadāraṇyaka Upaniṣad,* 403n62, 412n202
trimūrti incorporated by, xvii–xix, 102, 111, 181, 217, 221, *222*f6.1, 226, 250, *258*f6.5, 400n23, 400n25, 406n105

Dattātreya and the Dattātreya tradition *(continued)*
  and *vibhūti* (sacred ash), 239–242
  and Viṣṇu, 217
  See also Sathya Sai Baba, Shri—as Dattātreya
Davis, Richard H., 17–18
Delhi/New Delhi: xxiii, 24, 31, 54, 115, 117, 119, 141, 156, 323n69, 345n169, 358n26, 419n53, 426n32
demons:
  and beliefs in village India, 369n153
  and compassion cultivated by the "thunder's voice," 255
  Durgā's defeat of the buffalo-demon Mahiṣāsura, 327n106
  Hiranyakashipu, 323n71
  Rāvaṇa, 302, 317n17, 327n106
Devi, Indra (1899–2002), first attraction to Sathya Sai Baba, 80, 92, 95, 353n248
devotees and devotion:
  devotees' fear of being in Sathya Sai Baba's presence, 161
  and feelings of being tested or forsaken by Sathya Sai Baba, 266, 416–417n17
  See also *darśan*; Sathya Sai Baba, Shri—and his devotees; Western devotees
Divine Life Society (DLS):
  All-India Conference (1957), 53, 62, 339n95, 339–340n96
  charitable and educational activities of, 343n132
  Sathya Sai Baba perceived negatively by, 61
  and Swami Sivananda, 339n95, 340n101
  and Swami Satchidananda, 53
Diwakar, Sri R. R., 99
Drucker, Al (1927–2016), 126, 370n167
Dwyer, Rachel, 251

Easwaramma (1890–1972):
  concerns for the well-being of her son, 158
  death in Whitefield, 116
  Easwaramma Day (anniversary of her death), 171
  and Kasturi's writing of his *Carita,* 40
  original name Namagiryamma, 171
  parents of, 336n66
  Sathya Sai Baba's power of "materialization" transferred to, 340–341n104
Eknāth (1533–1599):
  and Dabholkar, 7
  and Dattātreya, 222–223
  gurubhakti described in the *Pratiṣṭhāncaritra,* 401n39
Eliot, T. S., *The Waste Land–What the Thunder Said,* 412n202

Gajānan Mahārāj (d. 1910), 187, 210–211
Gandhi, M. K. (1869–1948), 43, 91, 102, 115, 136, 319n30, 350n229, 362n65, 416n8,
  assassination of, 345–346n169
  reinterpretation of caste by, 68
Ganapati Sastri, Sri, 72–73
Gaṇeśa, 211, 278, 389n29, 421n71
Gauranga, and Kasturi on Sathya Sai Baba as the multi-faceted *Avatar,* 97
Geetha Vahini, Sathya Sai Baba's commentary to the *Bhagavadgītā,* 422n88
gender:
  and ashram bodily practices, 90

Hindu traditional views of the position of women, 65–66
and male progeny, 388n23
Padma and Balachandran's wedding, 33, 327–328n107
Sathya Sai Baba's views of women's roles, 65, 345n163
See also sexuality
genealogies, and the *Purāṇas,* 1
Giri, Sri V. V., president of India, 103
Godavari River, 98, 193, 220, 226, 353n253, 361n40
Goddess, the, and the *Purāṇas,* 1
Gokak, Vinayak Krishna (1909–1992), 79, 389n27
and the miniature replica of a portrait materialized by Sathya Sai Baba, 232
on Sathya Sai Baba's mission, 346n178
and the Summer Course on Indian Culture and Spirituality in Whitefield, 116
Gorakhnāth, 220, 242
and Sathya Sai Baba, 207
guṇas, sattva, rajas, tamas, 400n25, 404n74
Gurucaritra ("Life of the Master"):
in contemporary Maharashtra, 399n21
Dabholkar's *Śrī Sāī Saccarita* as the modern *Gurucaritra,* 226
and the Dattātreya tradition, 7, 220–221
Gurugītā ("Song of the Master") incorporated in, 401n39, 406n105
Sarasvatī Gaṅgādhar's composition of, 7, 220
Gurugītā ("Song of the Master"):
and Dattātreya's incorporation of the *trimūrti,* 406n105
incorporation into the *Gurucaritra* ("Life of the Master"), 401n39, 406n105
guru of Puttaparthi. *See* Sathya Sai Baba, Shri (Ratnākaram Sathyanārāyaṇa Rāju)

Hacker, Paul (1913–1979), 318n28, 344n153, 363n84, 373n194
hagiographical writing, 1–12, 311n1
genres of. *See Caritas* ("Biographies"); *Kathās* ("Stories"); *Purāṇas* ("Legends")
and *The Incredible Sai Baba* by Osborne (Arthur), 92, 195
See also Dabholkar, Govind Raghunath—*Śrī Sāī Saccarita;* Narasimhaswami, B. V.—*Life of Sai Baba*
Halbfass, Wilhelm, 136
Hanuman, 283
Haraldsson, Erlendur (b. 1931), 89–90, 130, 239, 369n157, 423n90
Hare Krishna movement, 96, 426n30, 428n45
magazine "Back to Godhead," 413n220
Hawkins, Sophie, 70, 296–297, 303, 304, 307
Heidegger, Martin, 255
Hinduism and Hindus:
Hindu students in Sathya Sai Baba's schools, 119
as the mother of all religions, 67
om symbol incorporated on the *sarvadharma* emblem, 79
Sathya Sai Baba's ad hoc etymology of *Hindu,* 123
Sathya Sai Baba's appeal to the Hindu middle and upper class, 107, 261

Hinduism and Hindus *(continued)*
  Sathya Sai Baba's entry into mainstream Hindu culture, 62–70
  and Shirdi Sai Baba, 251
  traditional views of women, 65–66
  See also Arjuna; Brahmā; Dattātreya; Gaṇeśa; Hare Krishna movement; Rāma; Shirdi Sai Baba; Śiva-Śakti; *trimūrti*; Vedāntic schools
Hislop, John S. (1904–1995), 370n166, 370n169
  the essence of Sathya Sai Baba's teaching explained to, 128
  first attraction to Sathya Sai Baba of, 96, 122
  ring bearing the guru "materialized" for him, 142
  and Sathya Sai Baba on his materializations, 55
  and Sathya Sai Baba on Ramakrishna and Vivekananda, 329n123
  and the Sathya Sai Baba Organization of America, 106, 358n25
  on Sathya Sai Baba's correspondence with devotees, 154
  Sathya Sai Baba's revelation of his "true self" to him, 296
  wooden cross bearing the figure of Jesus "materialized" by Sathya Sai Baba for him, 116–117, 165

Ikegame, Aye, 234, 260
Islām:
  crescent and star symbol incorporated on the *sarvadharma* emblem, 79
  and Dattātreya, xviii, 226, 402n45
  disputes between Hindus and Muslims over Shirdi Sai Baba's body, 196
  Muslim devotees and their presence in Shirdi, 426n30
  Muslim devotees of Sathya Sai Baba, 107, 365n97, 414n224
  Muslim students in Sathya Sai Baba's schools, 119
  and the Sai religion, 425n11
  and Shirdi Sai Baba, 251
Iyer, Potti, 26–30

Jains:
  and Dattātreya, 226
  and Sathya Sai Baba, 365n97
Janābāī (d. 1350), 311n3
Janakamma, N. (b. 1882), *34*f1.4, *36*f1.6, 328n113
  background of, 13
  death of her grandson Venkatadri (1929–1947), 25
  and Kasturi's English education, 13–14
Jānakīrām Rāju (1931–2005), 336n65
Jatti, Sri B. D., president of India, 114
Jehovah, Sathya Sai Baba identified with, 165
Jesus (Isa/Issa):
  Jesus's apostles as hagiographers, 283
  Kashmir and Tibetan monastery visited by, 109, 363n77
  portrait for the Sathya Sai Baba's Prayer Hall (*mandir*), 51
  Sathya Sai Baba identified with, 116, 165
  Sathya Sai Baba's materialization of pictures of his future incarnation with a Christ-like countenance, 108

three schools of Vedānta detected in Jesus's sayings by Vivekananda, 108–109
and the Virgin Mary, 172
and Western devotees of Sathya Sai Baba, 107, 111, 365n97
wooden cross bearing the figure of Jesus "materialized" by Sathya Sai Baba for Hislop (John S.), 116–117, 165
Jñāndev (d. 1296), *Amṛtānubhava,* 389–390n32
Judaism and Jews:
and the Sai religion, 425n11
and Sathya Sai Baba, 365n97

Kabīr (fifteenth century):
and the Dattātreya tradition, 187, 207–208, 210
and Nāthism, 207
and Shirdi Sai Baba, xviii, 195–197, 420n54
Kamaraju, Anil Kumar, 89
on Kasturi's role as Sathya Sai Baba's hagiographer, 154–155, 161, 163–164, 166–167, 282–283
Kanu, Victor (d. 2011), 384n156
Kapferer, Bruce, 299
Kapoor, Raj (1924–1988), 43
Karanjia, Rustom Khurshedji:
interview with Sathya Sai Baba, xviii, 125, 212–215, 251, 252
reinterpretation of caste discussed with Sathya Sai Baba, 68
solutions to conflict between wealth and power discussed with Sathya Sai Baba, 130–131
"spiritual socialism" of Sathya Sai Baba, 70
Kashmir:
Dattātreya's presence in, 218
and Jesus, 109
Kasturi's travels with Sathya Sai Baba to, 54, *54*f2.3, 156
Kasturi, Narayan (1897–1987), *104*f3.1
Akash Vani ("sky voice") for his Kannada broadcasting, 24
Aśoka as the name of his house in Bangalore, 321n48
and astrology, 275–276
birth of, 13
death and cremation of his son Murthy (M. V. Narayana), xix, 263–266, 416n11
death of, xix, 269–274, 279–285, 417n26, 423nn102–103
and the death of his wife Rajamma, xix, 267–226
as editor of *Sanathana Sarathi,* 376n36
English education of, 13–14
grandson Ramesh (b. 1951), xix, 74, 163, 269–270, 274, 277–278, 414n1, 417n25, 418n43, 420n67
on his name, 13, 315n1
on *jnana* as a goal, 284, 423n101
as lecturer at Maharaja's College of Arts, 19–21, *20*f1.1
lectures to foreign devotees, 136–137, 423n98
mother of. *See* Janakamma, N.
as Principal of the Intermediate D.R.M College of Davangere, 33, 35
and Sathya Sai Baba's statements about his rebirth, 84–85
service (*sevā*) activities, 15–21, 35, 40
visit to the Kashmir Valley with Sathya Sai Baba, 54, *54*f2.3, 156
wife. *See* Rajamma

Kasturi, Narayan *(continued)*
—and Sathya Sai Baba, *300*f8.1
and his conversion from Ramakrishna to belief in Sathya Sai Baba, 25–38*passim*, 120
and his translations of Sathya Sai Baba's discourses, xvii, 144–149, 326n101
and the imagery of the deep dive, 369n155
Kasturi addressed as Nannaya Bhaṭṭa by Sathya Sai Baba, 40, 163
Kasturi as exemplary *bhakta,* xxi, 282–283, 309–310
Kasturi as a mediator between Sathya Sai Baba and his devotees, xvii, xxii, 12, 159–160
and Sathya Sai Baba as Śiva-Śakti, 76, 84–85, 84–85, 93, 98–99, 110, 165, 168, 182, 231, 245–246, 257, 349n218, 354n257, 383n146, 405n92
Sathya Sai Baba's appointing of Kasturi to write his biography, 30–31, 39–40
and Telugu, 35
—as theologian:
and his skill with the *saguṇa* and *nirguṇa* aspects of divinity, 123–124, 167
and the 108 Sanskrit names of Sathya Sai Baba, 94, 106, 110, 167–168, 203, 206, 248, 301, 367n141, 368n150, 383n145, 389n27, 390n35, 395n110, 407n113
—writing:
Anarthakosha, 22–23, 321n56
Ashoka, 22, 320–321n48
Easwaramma: The Chosen Mother, 171–173, 263, 285
English utilized as his medium, xvi, 2
humor and satire by, 22–24, 299, 321n50
and the impact of translating Sathya Sai Baba's discourses, 325n101
plays by, 22, 321n51
Prasanthi: Pathway to Peace, 173, 212, 250, 263, 285, 296, 309–310
Shri Krishnarajendra Odeyaravaru (biography of Krishnaraja Wadiyar IV), 329n117
translation of English literature into Kannada, 21
See also Sathyam Sivam Sundaram [Truth Goodness Beauty]
—writing—autobiography *Loving God,* xvii, 62, 158, 165, 170–171, 202, *265*f7.1
on his role as postmaster of Prasanthi Nilayam, 154
—writing—*Sai Bhagavatham*:
composition of, 164–165
and "Jay Sathya Sanathana Sarathi," 165
and the overall purpose of Sathya Sai Baba's universal mission and movement, 167
and Sathya Sai Baba's true identity, 167, 283, 309–310
and the spiritual values and lifestyle cultivated by Sathya Sai Baba's followers, 167
Kasturi, Padma (b. 1934), *156*f4.2
on the death of her brother M. V. N. Murthy, 264–266
on the death of her brother Venkatadri, 323n71
on the death of her father, 282
on her father's conversion to complete belief in Sathya Sai Baba, 33

on Kasturi's composure in the face of hardships, 263
on Kasturi's devotion to his teaching in the Harijan community, 35
on Kasturi's English education, 14
on Kasturi's realization of being *ātman,* 277
marriage to Balachandran, 28–29, 33, *34*f1.4, *34*f1.5, 327n105, 327–328n107
and Sathya Sai Baba's materialization of an image of Dattātreya, 231
on the sickness and death of her mother Rajamma, 267–268
Kathās ("Stories"), as a genre of hagiographical writing, 1
Kenya, Sathya Sai Baba's travels to, 92, 169
Keune, Jon, 401n39
Kher, Indira, on the name "Sai" of the Shirdi *faqīr,* 196
Kher, V. B., 192, 195
on Dattātreya as Shah Faqir, 402n45
Knipe, David M., 61, 353n253, 361n40
Kondappa, V. C.:
on the Rājus as a "scholarly race," 49
Sri Sayeeshuni Charitra by Kondappa, 8, 25, 47, 192, 253, 332n20
Koran, and Sathya Sai Baba's inclusivist strategy, 371–372n186, 389n27
Kovoor, Abraham (1898–1978), 368–369n152
Krishna, M.:
on Kasturi's impact on Sathya Sai Baba's lectures, 146
on people who left the guru, 161
on Sathya Sai Baba's political skills, 307–308
Kṛṣṇa, 2, 8–9, 45–46, 50, 73, 85, 95, 98, 110, 118, 149, 152, 185, 188, 213, 219, 239, 244, 274, 315n6, 334n34, 337n77, 355n272, 361n48, 367n129, 391n53, 419n48
and Arjuna in *Bhagavadgītā* 4.7–8, 344n148
and Arjuna in *Bhagavadgītā* 15.15, 252
epithet Madhu-sūdana ("Destroyer of [the demon] Madhu"), 122–123
flute (*muralī*) of, 53
and Sathya Sai Baba as a multi-faceted *Avatar,* 97
Sathya Sai Baba identified with, 45, 123, 165
and Sathya Sai Baba's identification with Viṣṇu-Kṛṣṇa, 251
Krystal, Phyllis, 126, 132–133, 369–370n166
Kuvempu (K. V. Puttappa, 1904–1994), 19, 320n37

Laing, Ron, 126, 370–371n171
Laxman, R. K. (1921–2015), 23
Lenchiner, Jack, 417n20, 422n84
Levin, Howard, 61, 155, 209, 254, 259, 276, 374n3, 413n220, 413n221, 416–417n17
private interview with Sathya Sai Baba described by, 122, 368n146
Llewellyn, J. E., 426n30

Madhva (thirteenth century), 95
Madras, 14–16, 48, 56, 59, 71, 79–80, 88–89, 98, 114, 146, 148–149, 158, 197, 248, 279, 282, 289,

Madras *(continued)*
292, 328n112, 351n240, 394n96, 405n100, 410n169
Mahābhārata, and Kasturi's biography of Sathya Sai Baba, 45
Mahajan, Sri Sai Kumar, 403n66
Maharashtra:
and Dattātreya's incorporation of the *trimūrti,* 226
the *Gurucaritra* in contemporary Maharashtra, 399n21
Shirdi Sai Baba temples concentrated in, 426n32
Maharishi Mahesh Yogi (1917–2008), 80, 351–352n245, 413n218
and Sathya Sai Baba's disregarding of, 259
Mahendra (circa 580–630), and *trimūrti* worship in India, 387n11
Mahīpati (1715–1790), 222–223, 312n15
Bhaktavijaya of, 196
Mallinson, James, 219, 401n37
Mallison, Françoise, 3
Māṇikprabhu (1817–1865), 187, 210
Mason, Peggy, 126, 269, 370–371n171
materializations of Sathya Sai Baba:
for *bhakta*s during private interviews, 122
and *darśan,* 300
rejection by rationalists and skeptics, 119–120, 130
and Sathya Sai Baba's identification of himself as a manifestation of Dattātreya, 231–232
and Sathya Sai Baba's inherent Divine Power, 55, 97
Sathya Sai Baba's power transferred to others, 340–341n104
significance and multiple functions of, xviii, 396n128
materializations of Sathya Sai Baba—cases of:
fruits extracted from a wish-fulfilling tree, 50
gems and rings, xviii, 50, 208–209
marriage threads (*maṅgalasūtra*) materialized by, 72, 157–158
miniature replica of a portrait for Gokak (V. K.), 232
multiple items materialized at the temple of Badrinath, 60
photo of Dattātreya showing Sathya Sai Baba's countenance as his central face, 201–202, *201*f5.2, 232–234
picture of Dattātreya, xviii
picture of Shirdi Sai Baba for his sister Venkamma, 199
picture of Shirdi Sai Baba surrounded by Kṛṣṇa, Rāma, Śiva, and Hanumān, *44f2.1*
pictures of his future incarnation with a Christ-like countenance, 108
ring bearing the guru for Hislop (J. S.), 142
ring materialized for Munshi (K. M.), 91
sacred ash (*vibhūti*), 50, 60, 77, 122, 318n21
sacred ash (*vibhūti*) for Swami Sivananda, 53–54
sacred ash (*vibhūti*) materialized for Jagadanandaji Maharaj, 138–139
silver coins with images of Shirdi Sai Baba and himself, 381n111
Someśvaraliṅga materialized for the Somnath Temple, 99

wooden cross bearing the figure of Jesus for Hislop (J. S.), 116–117, 165
McKean, Lise, 291
Meher Baba (Merwan Sheriar Irani, 1894–1969), xviii, 187, 397n144
and Sathya Sai Baba, 211–212, 259
and the symbolism of the *sarvadharma* emblem of Sathya Sai Baba, 351n237
Modi, Narendra (b. 1950), 141
Mother Kali, and Ramakrishna, 330n130
Muktananda, Swami (1908–1982), 344n147, 413n218
and Sathya Sai Baba's disregarding of, 259
Müller, Friedrich Max (1823–1971), 70
and Vivekananda's neo-Hinduism, 347–348n192
Munshi, Kanaiyalal Maneklal (1887–1971), 94, 275–276, 308, 357n17
as a Congress politician, 104–105
Sathya Sai Baba's miracles performed for, 91
Murphet, Howard (1906–2004):
first attraction to Sathya Sai Baba, 95
his account of materialization by Sathya Sai Baba for V. K. Gokak, 232
on Shirdi Sai Baba's statue in Guindy, 360n36
and Western devotees of Sathya Sai Baba, 90, 95, 106
and C. S. J. White, 207–208
Murthy, M. Venkata Narayana (1923–1983), *36*f1.6
childhood of, 16
children of, *36*f1.6, 281
cremation in Bangalore, 416n11
death of, xix, 265–266, 416n9
devotion to Sathya Sai Baba, 166
geology as his specialization, 415–416n6
recital of the *Sai Bhagavatham* by, 165, *165*f4.4

Nadig, S. K. (1928–2008), 23
Naidu, Madhusudhan Rao, 140–141, 253, 373n206, 374n208, 411n191
Nannaya Bhaṭṭa, Kasturi addressed as by Sathya Sai Baba, 40, 163
Narasimha Murthy, A. V., 194, 391n56
Narasimha Murthy, B. N.:
Muddenahalli-based faction led by, 139–141
Sathyam Sivam Sundaram Parts 5–7 prepared by, 137–138, 233–234
on Sathya Sai Baba's materialization of a photograph of Dattātreya, 233
Narasimhan, V. K. (1912–2000):
as editor of *Sanathana Sarathi,* 376n36, 385n162, 417n32
on Kasturi's death, 284–285, 385n162
on Kasturi's life and works, 170, 423n104
Narasimhaswami, B. V. (1874–1956), and devotion to Shirdi Sai Baba, 193
—*Life of Sai Baba*:
on the Guru in Sufism, 225
on Puttaparthi visited by, 199, 394n96
on Shirdi Sai Baba's "crushing out lower impulses," 241
on Shirdi Sai Baba's not posing himself as a guru, 227

Narayana Sastri, Sri Gunjuru, 274–276, 398n7
Nārāyaṇ Mahārāj (1885–1945), as *avadhūta,* 210
Nāths and the Nāth tradition:
and the *Avadhūtagītā,* 401n37
and Dattātreya, 219–220
and Haṭha Yoga, 224
and Kabīr, 207
Mount Girnār in the sacred geography of, 220
Nepāl (Bhaktapur):
Dattātreya's presence in, 218
Saivite Gurus in, 96
Sanathana Sarathi published in Nepali, 153
Nikhilananda, Swami (1895–1973), 16, 317n20
Nisargadatta Maharaj (1897–1981), 325n79
Nṛsiṃha Sarasvatī (c. 1378–1458), 7, 210, 220–221, 399n18

Old Mandir (Puttaparthi):
inner shrine of, *32*f1.3
Kasturi's visit to the guru at, 32–33
Padma and Balachandran's wedding in, *34*f1.5
Sathya Sai Baba's temple and headquarters in, 51, 242
Osborne, Arthur (1906–1970):
on meeting Sathya Sai Baba, 389n27
The Incredible Sai Baba, 92, 195
Osis, Karlis, 125, 371n179

Padmanaban, Ranganathan, 194, 326n95, 327n105, 332n16
Palmer, Norris W., 292, 301, 306, 308, 344n151, 426n28
Pant Mahārāj of Bāḷekundrī, Śrī (1855–1905), 232
Parvathamma (1920–1996), 336n65
Patel, Rajeshwari:
on Kasturi's lecturing, 136–137
Padma Kasturi interviews, 416n11
Peḍḍaboṭṭu (Gali Sharada Devi or Shirdi Mā, 1888–1986), 190–191, 390–391n45, 391n46
Pedda Veṅkama Rāju (1885–1963), 40, 49, 194, 335n56
Penn, Charles, first attraction to Sathya Sai Baba, 80, 92, 95, 352n246
Prasanthi Nilayam (Puttaparthi):
guru of Puttaparthi. *See* Sathya Sai Baba
Kasturi's roles in, 153–155
Sathya Sai Baba's ashram in, 298, 303
Swami Abhedananda's interview with Sathya Sai Baba in, 123–124
"Western invasion" of, 105–106
Prasanthi Vidwan Mahasabha:
inauguration of the Sanatana Bhagavata Bhakta Samaj, 77
and Sathya Sai Baba's visit to Tiruchirappalli, 79
praśānti/prasanthi (highest peace), 51, 173–174, 338n85
Kasturi's *Prasanthi: Pathway to Peace,* 173–174, 212, 250, 263, 296, 309–310
Prema Sai Baba, xviii, 6, 76, 84, 108, 132, 140, 142, 158, 168, 178, 188, 212, 237, 250, 252–254, 285, 294, 297, 310, 349n219, 350n220, 374n213, 379n91, 390n37, 411n191
Premanand, Basava (1930–2009), 130, 371n177

Priddy, Robert:
on Kasturi acting as 'spin doctor'/'ghost writer' for Sathya Sai Baba, 146
on Kasturi as interpreter of Sathya Sai Baba's Telugu discourses, 144
on Kasturi's biography of Sathya Sai Baba, 45, 332n18
on Sathya Sai Baba's statements about his rebirth, 84–85
Purāṇas ("Legends"):
as a genre of hagiographical writing, 1
and Kasturi's biography of Sathya Sai Baba, 45
reference to a visionary in the *Padma Purāṇa*, 347n192
—*Bhāgavata Purāṇa,* 2, 8, 95, 121, 127, 166, 196, 228, 314n24, 328n113
1.3.11 (Dattātreya as an *avatāra* of Viṣṇu in), 217
11.7.24–11.9.3 (Dattātreya featured in), 218, 398n7
and Kasturi's *Sai Bhagavatham,* 164
—*Mārkaṇḍeya Purāṇa,* 217–219
Puttaparthi (Telugu: Puṭṭaparti):
B. N. Narasimha Murthy's first meeting of Sathya Sai Baba in, 138–139
Super Specialty Hospital in, 87
visits by high-ranking politicians paying homage to Sathya Sai Baba, 308, 431n107
See also Old Mandir; Prasanthi Nilayam

Radhakrishna, Sri N., 403n66
Radhakrishna, V., 350n236
Radhakrishnan, S. (1888–1975), 136, 350n236, 372n193
Rajagopalacharya, Desikacharya (1900–1993), 354n262
Rajamma, *36*f1.6, *268*f7.2, 323n71, 328n113
death of, xix, 267–269
marriage thread and golden pendant materialized for her and Kasturi, 157–158
Ram Tirtha, Swami (1873–1906), 4
Rāma, Sathya Sai Baba identified with, 45, 165
Ramakrishna (Guru Maharaj, 1836–1886):
on emotions felt by divine incarnations, 239
and the imagery of the deep dive, 369n155
and Kasturi's conversion to belief in Sathya Sai Baba, 25–26, 31, 33, 37–38, 120
mention in Sathya Sai Baba's public discourses, 330n131, 350n222
and Sathya Sai Baba as a multi-faceted *Avatar,* 43, 97
Sathya Sai Baba distinguished from, 64
Sathya Sai Baba on his spiritual development, 330n130
Sathya Sai Baba on his views of miracles, 78
Sathya Sai Baba's high esteem for, 259, 329n125
and Vivekananda (according to Sathya Sai Baba), 329n123
Ramakrishna Mission, xvi, xxi
apolitical stance of, 105
Jagadanandaji Maharaj, 138–139, 380n97

Ramakrishna Mission *(continued)*
and Kasturi, xvi, xxi, 15–18, 25, 26, 37–38, 77, 112
Sathya Sai Baba perceived negatively by, 61, 78, 120
Ramakrishna Rao, B., 59, 74, 79, 80, 88, 138, 308, 342n127
Ramakrishna Rao, K. V., 138
Ramana Maharshi (1879–1950), 16, 64, 123, 259, 313n21, 317n18, 317–318n21, 389n27, 412n210
disciple Swami Abhedananda on Sathya Sai Baba's divinity, 123
Rāmānuja (d. 1137):
portrait for Sathya Sai Baba's Prayer Hall (*mandir*), 51
qualified nondualism of, 95
teacher Yādava Prakāśa, 399n19
Rāmāyaṇa, and Kasturi's biography of Sathya Sai Baba, 45
Rangacharya, Adya (pen name Shriranga, 1904–1984), 329
Ranganath, H. K. (b. 1923):
on his relations with Kasturi and his family, 320n41
on Kasturi as a College lecturer, 20–21
on Kasturi's Kannada broadcasting, 24, 25
on Kasturi's reaching *Sthitaprajna,* 265
on Kasturi's writing process, 321n49
Rao, Kutumba, 271
Rao, Lakshmīnārāyaṇa, 49, 62
Rao, M. N.:
on Kasturi's sense of humor, 177
on Kasturi's University years, 21
on Sathya Sai Baba's materialization of an image of Dattātreya, 233
Ratnākaram Kondama Rāju (1840–1952):
Sathyanārāyaṇa's divine nature recognized by, 50, 238
Sathya Sai Baba's mother called Easwaramma by, 171, 336n66
and Veṅkāvadhūta, 189–190, 193–194, 251, 390n40
wife Lakshmamma (1852–1931), 194
Ratnākaram Sathyanārāyaṇa Rāju. *See* Sathya Sai Baba, Shri
Raymer, Bob (1921–2008), first attraction to Sathya Sai Baba, 93, 95
Reddy, B. V. Raja, as editor of *Sanathana Sarathi,* 376n36
Rinehart, Robin, 4
Roumanoff, Daniel, 75, 89, 344n149, 350n232, 383n140, 412n192, 424n3
royal dynasties, and the *Purāṇas,* 1
Rudert, Angela, 291, 307
Ruhela, Satya Pal, 309, 379n91

śakti, three aspects linked to the three *guṇa*s, 404n74
Sanathana Sarathi:
global audience of, 153
images in, 152–153
Kasturi as editor of, 120, 149–153
and Sathya Sai Baba's *Upanishad Vahini,* 121, 127, 150–152
Sandweiss, Samuel H., 85, 125–126, 240–241, 351n239, 369n159
Śaṅkara/Śaṅkarācārya (eighth century), 69, 74, 95, 167, 182, 237, 262
and Dattātreya, 218, 387–388n13
five *liṅga*s brought to the temple of Badrinath, 60
portrait for the Sathya Sai Baba's Prayer Hall (*mandir*), 51

and Sathya Sai Baba as the multi-faceted *Avatar,* 97
and Sathya Sai Baba's early discourses, 349n208, 406–407n110
See also Advaita Vedānta
sarvadharma emblem of Sathya Sai Baba:
symbolism of, 79, 351n237
and Vivekanandian ideology, 86, 288
Sathyam Sivam Sundaram [Truth Goodness Beauty]:
and animals—especially dogs, 102
as a *camatkāramālā* ("string of miracles" demonstrating Sathya Sai Baba's divine spontaneity), 125–126
as *Carita,* 2–3, 9, 41–45, 152, 332n17
popularity of, 39–40
programmatic title and Trinitarian import of, 42–43, 246–262
Sathya Sai Baba's appointing of Kasturi to write it, 39
on Sathya Sai Baba's omniscience, 389n27
subsequent volumes by B. N. Narasimha Murthy, 137–138, 233–234
—Part 1, 46–60
critical evaluation of, 60–70
photo of Sathya Sai Baba with Swami Sivananda in 1983 reprint of, 62–63
Sathya Sai Baba presented as an *avatāra* of Dattātreya in, 207–208
Sathya Sai Baba's conception and miraculous early days, 48–50
Telugu translation of, 39
universalism emphasized in, 46–47
Chapter 1, *In Human Form,* 48–49
Chapter 2, *Balagopala,* 48–49
Chapter 3, *Natanamanohara,* 48–49
Chapter 4, *Gana-Lola,* 48–49
Chapter 5, *The Serpent Hill,* 48–49
Chapter 6, *Bala Sai,* 51
Chapter 7, *Prasanthi Nilayam* ("Abode of Highest Peace"), 51–53
Chapter 8, *From Cape to Kilanmarg,* 53–54
Chapter 9, *The Wave of the Hand,* 54–55
Chapter 10, *The Same Baba,* 55–56
Chapter 11, *The Rain Cloud,* 56
Chapter 12, *Sai Sadguru,* 56
Chapter 13, *"I am Here,"* 54–55
Chapter 14, *The Sarathi,* 56–57, 101–102
Chapter 15, *The Mission Begun,* 59–60
epilogue, *For You and Me,* 46
—Part 2, 70–81
critical evaluation of, 81–90
Chapter 1, *Resume (1926–1961),* 71
Chapter 2, *The Sugar and the Ants,* 71
Chapter 3, *The Task,* 72–75
Chapter 4, *The Call,* 75
Chapter 5, *This Siva-Sakthi,* 75–76
Chapter 6, *The Constant Presence,* 76
Chapter 7, *With Wounded Wings,* 76
Chapter 8, *Incredible–Still,* 76–77
Chapter 9, *Holy Joy,* 77
Chapter 10, *Gifts of Grace,* 77
Chapter 11, *Cities Aflame,* 77–79
Chapter 12, *Sings and Wonders,* 79
Chapter 13, *Facets of Truth,* 79–81
Chapter 14, *The Call–The Response,* epilogue, 71
—Part 3, 91–103
critical evaluation of, 104–112
Chapter 1, 87–88

Sathyam Sivam Sundaram (continued)
Chapter 2, *Attention, World at Prayer,* 91–92
Chapter 3, *Awakening Continent,* 92–94
Chapter 4, *Example and Precept,* 94–95
Chapter 5, *Signs and Signature,* 95
Chapter 6, *The Festival of Lights,* 95
Chapter 7, *The White Man's Burden,* 95–97
Chapter 8, *The Shirdi Feet,* 97–98
Chapter 9, *The Delta of Delight,* 98
Chapter 10, *The All in All,* 99
Chapter 11, *Unearthing the Light,* 99
Chapter 12, *Filling the Emptiness,* 100
Chapter 13, *So Kind! So Kind!,* 100–101
Chapter 14, *The Miraculous Appendix,* 101–102
Chapter 15, *Live in Love,* 102
Chapter 16, *Beacon of Bliss,* 102
Chapter 17, *The Names We Know,* 103
—Part 4, 76, 112–126
critical evaluation of, 126–137
Chapter 1, *In Confidence,* 113
Chapter 2, *Love on the March,* 113–119
Chapter 3, *Call and the Echo,* 119–120
Chapter 4, *Words with Wings,* 120–122
Chapter 5, *Moves in His Game,* 122
Chapter 6, *Closer and Closer,* 122–124
Chapter 7, *Dabbling and Diving,* 124–126
Sathya Sai Baba, Shri (Ratnākaram Sathyanārāyaṇa Rāju, 1926–2011; Telugu: Satya Sāyibābā)—biographical details:
appendicitis attack miraculously recovered from, 101–102, 107, 233
Bhatrāju caste of, 49–50
brothers. *See* Jānakīrām Rāju; Seshama Rāju
cerebral thrombosis suffered by, 349–350n220
criticism of, 334n37
death of, 285–286
father. *See* Pedda Veṅkama Rāju
funeral of, 430n77
and M. K. Gandhi, 345–346n169
grandfather. *See* Ratnākaram Kondama Rāju
his future incarnation prophesized by, 142, 349n219
and Kasturi's family, *36*f1.6, 265–269, *268*f7.2
sisters. *See* Parvathamma; Veṅkamma
travel abroad to Kenya and Uganda, 92–94, 169, 357n17
views about traveling abroad of, 413n219, 413n220
—claims to divinity:
and a reference to a visionary in the *Padma Purāṇa* cited by H. H. Wilson, 347–348n192
as being both *saguṇa* and *nirguṇa,* 123–124, 261, 368n150
"extracorporeal journeys" by, 33, 326n102
his declaration as being the *avatāra* of Śiva-Śakti, 93, 133–135, 168–169, 185
his miracles regarded as lessons in spiritual discipline, 100
Kasturi on him as the multi-faceted *Avatar,* 96–97

marriage thread (*maṅgalasūtra*) and golden pendant materialized for Kasturi and his wife, 157–158
marriage thread (*maṅgalasūtra*) materialized at the Viṭṭhal temple in Pandharpur, 72
108 Sanskrit names of, 167–168, 390n33
and similarities with Jesus, 96–97, 108–110, 129
See also materializations of Sathya Sai Baba
—as Dattātreya, xvii–xix, 102, 111, 178–192passim, 201–207, 228–245
and *avadhūta* typology, xx, 238, 291, 398n7
and the Christian Trinity, 111, 129
and his countenance as his central face, 201–202, *201*f5.2, 232–234
and his materializations of images of Dattātreya and his incarnations, 231–232
Kasturi's assertion in an interview, 178–191
and Kasturi's quoting of his master's teachings, 103
—denouncers of, 368–369n152
and accusations of his partiality to the rich, 126, 130–131, 369n164, 369n165
and demonstrations at the All-India Divine Life Society Conference at Venkatagiri, 339–340n96
and E. Haraldsson investigations, 369n157
and opinions about Kasturi's impact on him, 146
rejection of his divine powers by rationalists and skeptics, 119–120, 130
—and his devotees:
and gender separation, 94
Kasturi viewed as a mediator by his devotees, xxii, 159–160
and rules of conduct and discipline, 86–87, 102, 127, 132–133, 160–163
See also *darśan* given by Sathya Sai Baba; Gokak, Vinayak Krishna; Kasturi, Narayan; Krishna, M.; Peḍḍaboṭṭu (Gali Sharada Devi or Shirdi Mā); Shah, Indulal H.; Western devotees
—teaching by:
and the building of schools and colleges, 111–112
on death and dying, 415n4
educational mission and charitable service of, 113, 118, 238, 431n98
and his egalitarian outlook, 68, 346n176
and his inclusivist strategy, 291, 296–297, 371–372n186, 389n27
his mission to transform the individual as well as society, 346n178
and his promotion of spiritual values in education, 35, 97–98, 133
and hypocrisy as the worst sin, 113, 365n105
on *mantras* translated into any language, 367n131
on Ramakrishna and Vivekananda, 329n123
and service (*sevā*), xxi, 5, 10, 66, 70, 76–77, 81, 83, 87, 93–95, 100,

Sathya Sai Baba, Shri *(continued)*
105, 112, 117, 121, 127, 132, 139, 173–174, 206, 254, 260, 282, 284–285, 288, 304–310
and so-called untouchables, 346n172
and Swami Shraddhananda's challenges, 367n138
and the transnational character of the Sathya Sai Baba movement, 116, 118, 426n30
and universalism, xix–xx, 5, 46, 51, 56, 63, 66–68, 80–81, 85–86, 88, 92, 110, 115, 133, 153, 197, 260, 288–297
"Work is Worship" motto of, 100–101, 102, 215, 353n249
—writing:
diving imagery in *Sathya Sai Speaks,* 369n155
Telugu poems, 363n103
Vahinis published in the *Sanathana Sarathi,* 120–121, 127, 300
Sathya Sai Organization:
center set up by S. H. Sandweiss in his home, 369n159
centers in East Africa, 93
education and service of, 139, 141–142, 305–306
establishment in America of, 106, 369–370n166, 370n169
films and videos by, 428n64
growth of, 126, 283
Kasturi as president of, xvii, 155, 298
and Kasturi's discussions with Sathya Sai Baba, 155
Muddenahalli-based faction condemned by, 139–141
Sathya Sai Baba Center in Tustin, CA, 358n24
and Indulal H. Shah, 362n65
texts utilized by, 372n187
and the transnational character of the Sathya Sai Baba movement, 116, 118, 152–153, 263, 426n30
See also Bal Vikas and Seva Dal; *sarvadharma* emblem of Sathya Sai Baba; Sathya Sai Seva Organization
Sathya Sai Seva Organization:
All India Conference of, 100, 114, 149
and Indulal H. Shah, 105
Sathya Sai Shree Lakshmi, *Sweeya Charithra* by Shirdi Mā translated by, 391n46
Sathya Sai Speaks, on *karman*, *bhakti*, and *jñana* as one indivisible whole, 249, 410–411n171
Sati Godavari Mata (1914–1990), 59, 234
Satpathy, C. B., 426n32
Savant, P. K., 78
Schulman, Arnold (b. 1925), 84, 130, 209, 343n140, 359n27, 362n67, 374n1
book about Sathya Sai Baba, 41, 106
on devotees' fears of being in the guru's presence, 161
first attraction to Sathya Sai Baba, 96
on Sathya Sai Baba's building an ashram, 338n85
Seeman, Reiner, 356n7
self. *See ātman* (self); true identity and true identity realization
Seshagiri Rao, L. S., 21, 23, 167, 323n69, 337n80, 383n142
Seshama Rāju (1911–1985), 40, 47, 71, 148–149, 199, 303, 335n56, 336n65

sexuality:
  and ashram bodily practices, 90
  and Sathya Sai Baba's treatments to control sexual urges, 424n3
  and Sathya Sai Baba's views of Western-style sexual freedom, 66, 413n220
Shankar Pillai, K. (1902–1989), 24
Shah, Indulal H., 105, 140, 362n65, 423n92
Shirdi Sai Baba (d. 1918), 7–8, 38, 40, 51, 55–56, 59, 71–72, 75–77, 84, 89, 107, 132, 152, 167–168, 173, 178, 180, 182–183, 187–194
  as *avadhūta,* 180, 387n8
  and Banne Miyan of Aurangabad, 403n57
  as Brahmā, 250–251
  as Dattātreya, 184–186, 224–228
  death of, 196
  and dogs, 388n15, 409n149
  evening procession from the mosque to the *cāvaḍī,* 388n21
  and figures claiming to be his reincarnation, 341n110
  and Gajānan Mahārāj, 187, 210–211
  granting of offspring to childless couples by, 184, 388n23
  and the Indian film industry, 428n64
  and Kabīr, xviii, 195–197, 420n54
  refusal to give *mantropadeśa* to Radhabai Deshmukh, 236, 405n104
  sacred ash (*vibhūti, udī*), materialized by, 56
  as *sarvajña,* 389n27
  Sathya Sai Baba as his reincarnation, xviii, 6, 8, 26, 76, 197–201, 213, 381n111
  and *Sri Sayeeshuni Charitra* by V. C. Kondappa, 8, 47, 192, 253, 332n20
  statue at the Shirdi Sai Baba temple in Guindy, 98, 360n36
  See also Narasimhaswami, B. V.—*Life of Sai Baba*
Shivananda, Swami (Tarak Nath Ghosal, 1854–1934), 17
Shivaram, M. (pen name Rashi, 1905–1984), and *Koravanji* magazine, 23, 322n59
Siddheshwarananda, Swami (1987–1957), 16, 37, 317n18
Siegel, Lee, 55
Sikhs, and Sathya Sai Baba, 107, 119, 365n97
Sivananda, Swami (Kuppuswami Iyer, 1887–1963), xxi, 215, 259
  and the Divine Life Society, 339n95, 340n101, 344n147
  and Sathya Sai Baba, 53–54, 62–63
  universalist message of, 343n132
Śiva-Śakti:
  and the future incarnation of Prema Sai Baba, 252–253
  and the Hindu *trimūrti,* 102, 221, *222f6.1,* 229–231, 242, 244–245, 248, 400n23
  and the *Purāṇas,* 1
  and Śaiva Siddhānta circles, 253
  and Sathya Sai Baba as Dattātreya, 103, 165
  Sathya Sai Baba identified with, 76–78, 84–85, 93, 98–99, 110, 133–135, 168–169, 182, 185, 231, 244–246, 251, 257, 349n218, 354n257, 383n146, 405n92
  See also trimūrti
Spurr, Michael James, 133–135
Srikantayah, B. M. (1884–1946), 19

Srinivas, Smriti, 81, 131, 152, 289–291, 299, 306, 430n85
Srinivas, Tulasi, 41, 57, 86, 86–87, 107, 137, 260, 334n32, 414n224, 427n39
Śrīpād Śrīvallabh (c. 1323–1353), 7, 210, 220–221, 339n18
Sufism:
contemplation of the Guru in, 225
and Sathya Sai Baba's inclusivist strategy, 371–372n186, 389n27

Thirumalacharlu, Dhupati, 39, 339n91
Tibet, Jesus's visit to a monastery in, 109, 363n77
Tigrett, Isaac, 126, 140, 370n168
Tilliette, Jean-Yves, 10
Tirupati, 25, 51, 53, 60, 65, 71, 146, 156, 194, 323n70, 338n81, 338n82, 361n46, 391n53
trimūrti:
and Anasūyā, 217
and the Christian Trinity, 111, 129, 229
Dattātreya's incorporation of, xvii–xix, 102, 111, 181, 183–185, 217, 221, *222*f6.1, 226, 250, *258*f6.5, 389n28, 400n23, 400n25, 406n105
and divine fullness and completeness, 400n24
and the emblems of Brahmā, Viṣṇu, and Śiva, 102, 221, 229–231, 242, 244–245, 248, 400n23
and the triad of the sacred syllable *oṃ*, 229
and the triad of waking, dreaming, and deep-sleep states, 229
worship in India of, 387n11
true identity and true identity realization:
and the *avatāra*'s total giving of himself to his creatures, 189, 253–254
and the charisma of the guru, 423n95
and Dattātreya's theology, 254
and the *divyātma svarūpulara* ("incarnations of the divine *ātman*"), 95
and Kasturi's relationship to Sathya Sai Baba, 167, 283
Sathya Sai Baba's revelation of his "true self" to J. S. Hislop, 296
Tukārām (1598–1649), poetic portrayal of Dattātreya, 223
Tulsīdās (1532–1623), 2, 314–315n33

Uddhavagītā, 167, 398n6, 398n7
Uganda, 169, 342n113
Idi Amin Dada, 93, 357n16
Sathya Sai Baba's travels to, 92–94, 342n113
Upaniṣads, 148, 166, 422n88
Dattātreya portrayed in the minor *Upaniṣads*, 218
neti neti ("not this, not this") theology of, 102–103
nondual Vedānta (identity of *ātman* and *Brahman*), 18, 75, 218
Sathya Sai Baba's *Upanishad Vahini,* 121, 127, 150–151
and the three *da*-s (*dāmyata datta dayadhvam*), 255–256
and the title *Sathyam Sivam Sundaram* [Truth Goodness Beauty], 42
Upaniṣadic self-inquiry, 174
—*Bṛhadāraṇyaka Upaniṣad*:
1.3.28 (*asato mā* prayer), 416n11
5.2, 255, 412n202
—*Chāndogya Upaniṣad,* 8.6.6, 422n88

—*Dattātreya Upaniṣad,* Dattātreya glorified in, 218
—*Īśa Upaniṣad,* 389–390n32
—*Kaṭha Upaniṣad,* 412n198
6.15–17, 281–282
6.16, 422n88
—*Māṇḍūkya Upaniṣad,* 229
—*Nāradaparivrājaka Upaniṣad,* Dattātreya portrayed in, 218
—*Saṃnyāsa Upaniṣads*, Dattātreya glorified in, 218
—*Yoga Upaniṣads,* Dattātreya glorified in, 218
Upasani Baba (1870–1941), 234
Urban, Hugh B., 65, 261–262

Vājasaneyī Saṃhita (*White Yajurveda* recension), *Rudrādhyāya* (or *Śatarudrīya* ["Hundred names of Rudra"]), 167
Vajpayee, Atal Bihar (b. 1924), 70, 308
Vālmīki, 40, 143
Vāsudevānanda Sarasvatī (1854–1914):
as *avadhūta,* 210
as a Dattātreya *avatāra,* 223–224
Vaudeville, Charlotte, 207
Vedāntic schools:
Sathya Sai Baba's coordinating of, 95
See also Advaita Vedānta; Madhva; Rāmānuja; Śaṅkara
Vedas:
Ṛgveda 1.164.46, 364–365n96
role of Vedic *yajñas* and rituals in the Sathya Sai Baba movement, 106–107
and Sanathana Dharma, 425n20
Sathya Sai Baba's mission to propagate Vedic *dharma,* 63, 75, 98, 260–262, 427n40
—and Kasturi's *Sathyam Sivam Sundaram,* 45, 87–88
and *The Task* (Chapter 3 of *Sathyam Sivam Sundaram,* Part 2), 72–75
Veṅkamma (1918–1993), 336n65, 390n43
picture of Shirdi Sai Baba materialized by Sathya Sai Baba for, 199
Venkatadri (1929–1947), 320n41
death of, 25–26, 33, 323n70, 323n71
Venkatagiri, All-India Divine Life Society Conference at, 339–340n96
—*rāja* of:
Sathya Sai Baba's Telugu poems collected and published by, 363n103
Sathya Sai Baba's visits to, 53, 61–62, 74, 78, 88, 97, 146, 299, 308, 339n91, 343n138
Veṅkaṭeśvara, 25, 51, 110, 194, 323n70, 324n72, 338n81, 361n45, 391n53
Veṅkāvadhūta:
as *avadhūta,* 18, 194
death of, 194
and Kondama Rāju (Ratnākaram), 189–190, 390n40
local hagiography of, 194
temple in Hussainpur, 194, 392n61
and Veṅkūśā/ Veṅku Shāh, 189–190, 193–194, 235, 390n39
Veṅkūśā/ Veṅku Shāh:
Das Ganu on, 193, 195, 391n53, 392n69
as Kabīr's guru, 195
vibhūti (sacred ash). *See* ash

Vijayādaśamī:
death of Shirdi Sai Baba, 326n102
Sathya Sai Baba's public speeches during, 57–59, 144
Sathya Sai Baba's trances during, 33, 326n102
and the wedding of Padma and Balachandran (1948), 33, 327n105, 327n106
Vijayakumari, Mrs.:
on the All-India Divine Life Society Conference at Venkatagiri, 339–340n96
on Kasturi's devotion to Sathya Sai Baba, 32–33, 326n101
Vishwa Hindu Parishad (VHP), 70, 386n4, 424n2
Viṣṇu:
and the Hindu *trimūrti,* 102, 221, *222*f6.1, 229–231, 242, 244–245, 248, 400n23
and the *Purāṇas,* 1
and Sathya Sai Baba as Dattātreya, 103
Sathya Sai Baba identified with, 45, 96
and Sathya Sai Baba's identification with Viṣṇu-Kṛṣṇa, 251
See also trimūrti
Viṭṭhal, marriage thread (*maṅgalasūtra*) materialized by Sathya Sai Baba at temple in Pandharpur, 72
Vivekananda, Swami (1863–1902), 5, 10, 14–18, 26, 38, 43, 51, 63–70, 77, 114–115, 127, 136, 215, 259, 315n8, 315n9, 316n10, 318n26, 318–319n28, 319n31, 319n32, 343n132, 347n191, 354–355n272, 363n83, 363n84, 373n194
and Advaita Vedānta, 69, 108–109, 133
appropriation by right wing political movements, 347n190
on the guru as avatar, 133–135
on Hinduism as the mother of all religions, 67
inclusivism of and Sathya Sai Baba's appropriation, 10, 63, 66–67, 69, 257–259, 288, 344–345n153
mention in Sathya Sai Baba's public discourses, 345n164, 350n222
and F. Max Müller, 347n192
neo-Hinduism and "practical Vedānta" of, 5, 10, 18, 136
and Ramakrishna (according to Sathya Sai Baba), 329n123
reinterpretation of caste by, 68
relevance of education and service grounded in the ideology of, 112
and the *sarvadharma* emblem of Sathya Sai Baba, 86, 288
three schools of Vedānta detected in Jesus's sayings by, 108–109
Vyāsa, 40, 143, 283

Waghorne, Joanne Punzo, 70
Weed, Eileen, on Kasturi's reaction to the loss of his son, 265–266
Western devotees:
Kasturi on their first contacts with Sathya Sai Baba, 95–96
Kasturi's networks of relations with, 166
Kasturi's promotion of Sathya Sai Baba to, 261, 300
W. Messing's meeting of Sathya Sai Baba during his school days, 351n241
Sathya Sai Baba's conversations in English with them, 342n120

and Sathya Sai Baba's warnings about Western fads and attractions, 86–87
and the transnational character of the Sathya Sai Baba movement, 90–91, 426n30
See also Bailey, David and Faye; Baskin, Diana; Bock, Richard and Janet; Bozzani, Robert A.; Charlton, Hilda; Cowan, Walter; Craxi, Antonio; Devi, Indra; Haraldsson, Erlendur; Hislop, John S.; Laing, Ron; Lenchiner, Jack; Levin, Howard; Mason, Peggy; Murphet, Howard; Penn, Charles; Priddy, Robert; Raymer, Bob; Roumanoff, Daniel; Sandweiss, Samuel; Sathya Sai Organization; Schulman, Arnold; Tigrett, Isaac

White, Charles Sidney John (b. 1929):
on Dattātreya and Kabīr, 207–208
on Dattātreya and Sathya Sai Baba, 234
film of Sathya Sai Baba's activities, 395n124

Whitefield:
Easwaramma's death at, 116
Sathya Sai Baba's residence in, 88, 89, 263, 270–271, 274
Sathya Sai Brindavan College for boys, 115
and Sri Sathya Sai Arts and Science College, 94, 97, 133, 378n69
and Sri Sathya Sai University, 152, 378n69
Summer Course on Indian Culture and Spirituality held at Sathya Sai Baba's ashram in, 115–116
Super Specialty Hospital in, 87

Williamson, Lola, 413n218

Wilson, Horace Hayman (1786–1860), reference to a visionary in the *Padma Purāṇa*, 347–348n192

Wontner, Julian, 269–270, 417n31

Yādava Prakāśa (twelfth century), 399n19

Yama, 365n96, 412n198, 415n3, 423n91

Yeolekar, Mugdha, on the *Gurucaritra* in contemporary Maharashtra, 220, 399n21

Yogananda, Paramahamsa (1893–1952), 93, 357n14, 363n70, 413n218

Zoroaster (Zarathustra) and Zoroastrians:
fire symbol incorporated on the *sarvadharma* emblem, 79
and Kasturi on Sathya Sai Baba as the multi-faceted *Avatar,* 97
portrait for Sathya Sai Baba's Prayer Hall (*mandir*), 51
as students in Sathya Sai Baba's schools, 119

www.ingramcontent.com/pod-product-compliance
Lightning Source LLC
Chambersburg PA
CBHW051842300426
44117CB00006B/244
* 9 7 8 1 4 3 8 4 8 2 2 8 6 *